The Origins of the British Welfare State

Also by Bernard Harris:

The health of the schoolchild: a history of the school medical service in England and Wales

Race, science and medicine, 1700–1960 (co-edited with Waltraud Ernst)

The Origins of the British Welfare State

Society, State and Social Welfare in England and Wales, 1800–1945

Bernard Harris

First published 2004 by
PALGRAVE MACMILLAN
Houndmills, Basingstoke, Hampshire RG21 6XS and
175 Fifth Avenue, New York, N.Y. 10010
Companies and representatives throughout the world

PALGRAVE MACMILLAN is the global academic imprint of the Palgrave
Macmillan division of St. Martin's Press, LLC and of Palgrave Macmillan Ltd.
Macmillan® is a registered trademark in the United States, United Kingdom
and other countries. Palgrave is a registered trademark in the European
Union and other countries.

ISBN 0–333–64997–4 hardback
ISBN 0–333–64998–2 paperback

This book is printed on paper suitable for recycling and made from fully
managed and sustained forest sources.

A catalogue record for this book is available from the British Library.

Library of Congress Cataloging-in-Publication Data
Harris, Bernard, 1961–
    The origins of the British welfare state : society, state, and social welfare in England
and Wales, 1800–1945 / Bernard Harris.
        p. cm.
    Includes bibliographical references and index.
    ISBN 0–333–64997–4 (cloth)–ISBN 0–333–64998–2 (pbk.)
        1. Public welfare – Great Britain – History. 2. Welfare state – Great Britain – History.
    3. Great Britain – Social policy. I. Title.
HV245H346 2004
362.942'09'034—dc22   2003070659

10 9 8 7 6 5 4 3 2 1
13 12 11 10 09 08 07 06 05 04

Printed in China

For Deborah and Ben

Contents

Tables

Figures

Preface

The last twenty years have witnessed the publication of a growing number of books on the history of British social policy. This reflects the importance of the field in relation not only to the understanding of present-day social policy concerns, but also to the central concerns of British social history more generally. However, given the profusion of new studies, it is important to explain why it might seem desirable to add to what some readers might consider is already a sufficiently well-crowded field.

As the first chapter shows, the last thirty years have witnessed a profound change in attitudes towards the 'inevitability' of state welfare, and a growing interest in the role played by the voluntary and informal sectors in meeting welfare needs. This book aims to summarise much of this literature and to provide a much more rounded picture of the development of social welfare provision in Britain in the nineteenth and early-twentieth centuries. However, it is important to recognise the fact that the years between 1800 and 1945 also witnessed a profound increase in the extent of state welfare intervention. It is for this reason that the main title of the book is '*The origins of the British welfare state*', despite the faintly teleological overtones which such a phrase must inevitably convey.

During the last twenty years, historians of social policy have devoted particular attention to the late-nineteenth and twentieth centuries, and the significance of developments in the earlier part of the nineteenth century has sometimes tended to be neglected as a result. Pat Thane's account of the foundations of the welfare state began in 1870 because 'it was around that time that important demands began to arise for the state in Britain to take a permanent, as distinct from a temporary and residual, responsibility for the social and economic conditions experienced by its citizens.'[1] However, as Derek Fraser pointed out, this approach was not without its limitations. Even though it enabled Thane to pay much more attention to the role of women in the making of social policy and the importance of international comparisons, it also meant that she was unable to devote much attention at all to some of the most important innovations in state welfare intervention in the middle years of the nineteenth century, including the establishment of a central Poor Law authority, the emergence of the concept of 'less eligibility', the growth of state intervention in education, and the introduction of national legislation in the fields of public health and housing.[2]

The choice of starting-point is also important in relation to much of the theoretical literature on the origins and growth of state welfare provision more generally. As Fraser has also argued, the history of British social policy since 1800 is, to a significant extent, the history of 'the response of government and people to the practical individual and community problems of an industrialised society', and this perspective has been reinforced by a large number of theoretical and comparative studies which have traced the origins of modern welfare states to the economic and social problems generated by the process of industrialisation.[3] As a result, the empirical sections of this book begin with an account of the economic, social and political history of Britain in the late-eighteenth and early-nineteenth centuries, since this is clearly an essential foundation for much of what followed.

There are also at least two other features of the book which may require explanation. In the first place, it is important to recognise that it is primarily a history of social welfare in England and Wales, and not the United Kingdom as a whole. This point is worth emphasising because, even though developments in England and Wales were often influenced by evidence drawn from throughout the United Kingdom, there were (and still are) major differences in the organisation of welfare services in each of the country's constituent parts. It is also important to acknowledge that this book does not attempt to provide more than a very general account of the history of social welfare in England and Wales after 1945. This decision was made partly for reasons of space, but it also reflects the fact that the years around 1945 do mark a significant staging-post in the history of British social policy, and that the period after 1945 has already been well served by writers such as Michael Hill, Howard Glennerster, Rodney Lowe and Nicholas Timmins.[4]

In recent years, historians and social scientists have paid an increasing amount of attention to the comparative study of social policy, and this has thrown up some important new questions for historians of British social welfare. In 1990, Gøsta Esping-Andersen appeared to suggest that the British welfare state was most closely aligned with the 'liberal, residualist welfare states' of Australia, Canada and the United States of America but, as José Harris has pointed out, it also forms 'one of the most uniform, centralised, bureaucratic and "public" welfare systems in Europe', and it boasts, or has boasted, extremely high levels of direct state intervention in the areas of health, education and housing.[5] One of the main aims of this book is therefore to show how this distinctive pattern of welfare provision emerged in Britain before 1945, and to try to shed some light on the ways in which it might develop in the future.

One of the many pleasures associated with the completion of this book is the opportunity to thank all those who have contributed to its making. I am particularly grateful to those friends and colleagues who read different chapters of the book and provided generous help with readings and comments, including Thomas Adams, Paul Bridgen, Susan Burt, Graham Crow, Martin Gorsky, Andrew Hinde, Roger Lawson, Rodney Lowe, Viv Mackay, Brenda Phillips, Tony Rees and Daniel Weinbren. I should also like to thank two anonymous readers for their helpful suggestions, and Catherine Gray, who commissioned the book on behalf of Palgrave Macmillan, and showed great patience and forbearance throughout its gestation. I am also grateful to Beverley Tarquini, for overseeing the final stages of the preparation of the manuscript, and to Brian Morrison, for copy-editing. Although the book is based on both primary and secondary research, it does make copious use of the work carried out by other authors, and I hope that each will feel that I have represented their work fairly. Finally, and most importantly, I should like to express my greatest thanks to Deborah and Ben Harris, who have lived with the book, if not the subject matter, from the very beginning.

1 Introduction

During the Second World War, the British government published a series of reports on the need for changes in welfare provision which helped to fuel a widespread desire for social reconstruction in the postwar period. Although there were undoubtedly many important disagreements over different aspects of social policy, the 1950s and 1960s witnessed what many people regarded as an unprecedented degree of inter-party agreement on the broad principles of welfare provision. This led the American political scientist, Hugh Heclo, to argue that during this period 'the welfare state acquired an ideological life of its own', in which 'Britain's welfare state became infused with a series of vague but deeply and widely held beliefs: as part of a common society, we *do* have shared needs; people – all people – *are* entitled to a decent life; privilege and greed *must not* be allowed to emasculate citizens' social rights; government *can* be a force for good in securing these ends'.[1] However, during the 1970s this 'welfare state consensus' was assailed by critics on both the left and the right, and this contributed to the election of a new Conservative government in 1979 which was much more overtly hostile to the principles of state welfare provision than any of its postwar predecessors. The Conservatives remained in power for the next 18 years, and when Labour returned to office in 1997 it seemed determined to rid itself of its historical reputation as the party of 'tax and spend'. Since the government was reelected in 2001, it has shown a rather greater willingness to take the political risk of drawing a direct link between increased levels of personal taxation and the improvement of public welfare provision, but it has also sought to distance itself from the '1945 "big state" that wrongly believed it could solve every social problem', and it has promoted the concept of 'an enabling state founded on the liberation of individual potential', in which 'a bigger role for the voluntary sector in framing and delivering local services is central to our vision'.[2]

Although this brief and rather over-simplified account is mainly designed to summarise the history of welfare provision in Britain since 1945, it also provides a rough guide to the historiography of welfare provision over the same period. For much of the twentieth century, the history of British social policy appeared to be largely synonymous with the 'coming' of the welfare state and the 'rise' of state welfare provision, but during the 1970s and 1980s historians began to develop a much more critical view of the role of the state in the provision of welfare services and, consequently, to devote rather more attention to the history of alternative forms of welfare provision. As a result of this work, we now possess a much more

1

nuanced view of the 'mixed economy of welfare', in which 'the state, the voluntary sector, the family and the market have played different parts at different points in time',[3] and the demand for welfare services as a whole has grown considerably over the course of the period. However, in spite of this, it is difficult to deny that the part played by the state in the expansion of this 'mixed economy' also increased substantially between 1800 and 1945. The main task of this book is therefore to provide an account of the reasons for the growth of state welfare intervention within the context of this broader world of welfare provision.

1.1   The historiography of the welfare state

Sidney and Beatrice Webb's famous study of *English Poor Law history* provides a valuable starting point for an examination of the historiography of the British social policy. Beatrice Webb began her career in social research when she accepted an invitation to take part in Charles Booth's survey of poverty in London in 1886, whilst Sidney had been elected as a Labour member of the London County Council in 1892, and they continued to play a major role in the development of Labour party ideas for much of the next 50 years.[4] They were both strongly critical of the traditional Poor Law policy of deterrence, and one of the main aims of their *History* was to demonstrate the need for the state to play a more active role in the prevention and treatment of poverty by offering minimum standards of wages, a maximum working day, access to medical services, the right to a healthy environment, and educational opportunities to all citizens.[5] Their belief in the moral superiority of state intervention was echoed by Gilbert Slater in his book, *Poverty and the state*, which appeared in 1930. Slater regarded the existence of poverty as a symptom of the state's failure 'to achieve "the good life" for the community which it serves'. He said that the aim of his study was 'to give in broad outline the story of the social struggle of the community against the more glaring evils of poverty, and against poverty itself in its extremer forms'.[6]

The association of the history of social policy with the extension of public responsibility was reinforced by the formal 'creation' of the welfare state after 1945. During the late 1940s and 1950s there was a growing tendency to regard the establishment of the welfare state as the inevitable consequence of long-term growth of state intervention, and as the institutional expression of public benevolence. T. H. Marshall argued that 'the modern drive towards social equality is ... the latest phase of an evolution of citizenship which has been in continuous progress for some 250 years', and Maurice Bruce observed that 'the widening of both the area of responsibility and the range of services has been an essentially practical response to the problems and conditions of English society as it developed and became more self-conscious.'[7] These sentiments were also reflected in Derek Fraser's assertion that 'the history of social policy is to a large extent the history of individual and collective response to the practical problems thrown up by an industrialised society.'[8]

We can therefore see that much of the historiography which was produced during what Rodney Lowe has described as the 'classic' welfare state[9] was dominated by two basic considerations: first, that the establishment of the welfare state was part of a pragmatic response to the existence of 'social problems'; and, second, that the consequences of this process had been broadly beneficial. However, this assumption has increasingly been called into question by a new generation of historians, who have used oral and other records to try to reconstruct the reality of welfare services from the point of view of those who depend most closely upon them. Stephen Humphries showed how the expansion of state education could be seen as little more than an attempt to discipline and control working-class children, and Joanna Bornat and Dorothy Atkinson have used the recollections of one individual, 'Margaret', to 'challenge ... the rather benign picture painted by [Kathleen] Jones ... and ... others who have charted the histories of large residential institutions for people with learning difficulties'.[10] However, it would be wrong to assume that the evidence produced by oral historians has always been critical of state welfare initiatives. Elizabeth Roberts has shown how people growing up in Barrow in the early years of the twentieth century welcomed the introduction of national health insurance in 1911 as 'an extension of the previously limited insurance schemes', and Diana Gittins has claimed that 'a great many people from all walks of life' found that the county psychiatric hospital at Severalls in Essex provided 'a vibrant and thriving – if not always trouble-free or entirely benign – community which, over time, offered valuable employment, refuge, asylum and a sense of cooperation and belonging'.[11]

Although much of this work might be regarded as the natural outcome of the introduction of new methods of historical enquiry, it also reflects the impact of a range of ideological influences which have all raised powerful questions about our attitudes to welfare provision. One of the most important challenges came from a number of Marxist writers who recognised that the expansion of state welfare was not only a means of redressing the imbalances created by a free market capitalist society, but also a means of reinforcing the inequalities associated with that society.[12] John Saville argued that even though 'the pace and tempo of social reform have been determined by the struggle of working class groups and organisations', it would be wrong to ignore the fact that state welfare was also a means of improving the quality of the workforce and preserving political stability.[13] This analysis was echoed by Norman Ginsburg:

> The welfare state has been formed around the contradictions and conflicts of capitalist development in specific historical contexts. From the working class point of view it is a response to their continual struggle to improve and secure their conditions of existence or standard of living. From the capitalist point of view state welfare has contributed to the continual struggle to accumulate capital by materially assisting in bringing labour and capital together profitably and containing the inevitable resistance and revolutionary potential of the working class ... Thus the possibility of securing a fundamental shift in the structure of class inequality in favour of the working class through administrative and policy reform or working-class political struggle within the state apparatus is severely constrained by the essential form and functions of the capitalist state, which boil down to the reproduction of the relationship between capital and labour.[14]

Marxist accounts of the history of state welfare have also been influenced by the work of Antonio Gramsci. Gramsci argued that the ruling class maintained its power in capitalist societies partly by its control of the state apparatus, and partly by its ability to maintain 'hegemony' over civil society.[15] The concept of hegemony, and the distinction between the state and 'civil society', have played an important part in historical and contemporary debates over the nature of welfare provision. Hall and Schwarz argued that at the end of the nineteenth century, the traditional liberal state was facing a growing crisis of legitimation, and that the expansion of state welfare provision represented a deliberate attempt to respond to this crisis and to restore the authority of the ruling elite, and John Keane urged present-day socialists to abandon their conventional commitment to state-led initiatives in favour of a new strategy based on 'innovation from below through radical social initiatives which expand and equalise civil liberties'.[16]

The emergence of new attitudes to the role of state welfare has also been influenced by the work of the post-structuralist philosopher, Michel Foucault. Foucault refused to accept the centrality of economic interests and rejected the Marxist view that the 'end result' of all human history was the emergence of a classless society.[17] He was particularly interested in the ways in which different interest groups (and particularly professional groups) constructed 'discourses', or bodies of knowledge, which shaped the ways in which other people thought about the basic features of their existence.[18] Foucault's ideas have played a major part in recent attempts to reevaluate the history of such central institutions as the hospital, the asylum, the prison, the factory and the workhouse. One of the key characteristics of this reevaluation has been the way in which the history of 'social reform' has been recast as a history of class repression and 'social control'.[19]

The recent historiography of social welfare provision has also been strongly influenced by feminism. Feminist writers have shown that women's movements have played an important part in the development of state welfare provision, but they have also argued that the welfare state has played its own part in the reinforcement of patriarchal structures. The feminist critique of state welfare provision has had four major strands. In the first place, it has been argued that state welfare reforms have brought only limited benefits to women because they have been predicated on the persistence of traditional assumptions about the primacy of the male breadwinner.[20] Second, it has also been claimed that a number of welfare services have been designed with the explicit intention of limiting women's opportunities.[21] Third, a number of authors have argued that particular 'welfare' measures, such as the Contagious Diseases Acts of the 1860s, were intended to control women's behaviour and to impose a particular notion of female 'respectability'.[22] Finally, it has been claimed that state welfare measures penalised women by invading their sphere of responsibility and by imposing new burdens on them, such as the obligation to seek medical treatment for their children in the early part of the twentieth century.[23]

The fourth strand which has contributed to the reevaluation of the history of state welfare has come from the anti-collectivist New Right. The New Right's approach to state welfare is predicated on the view that the free market is the best available means of generating and distributing economic resources. It is opposed to the growth of state welfare because it believes that this has diverted resources from the productive sectors of the economy and made the market less efficient. It also believes that the growth of the welfare state has undermined individual freedom and encouraged welfare dependency.[24] As a result of this, New Right and anti-collectivist historians have made a major contribution to the reevaluation of the history of state welfare and have reinvigorated the study of alternative forms of welfare provision. This is reflected in a number of recent works on the (alleged) failings of the welfare state, the history of self-help and mutual aid, and the history of philanthropy.[25]

1.2   The new history of social welfare

The previous section has sought to demonstrate how some of the main intellectual currents of the last 20–30 years have transformed attitudes to the history of welfare provision. Historians of social welfare are no longer content to view the history of state welfare provision as a straightforward record of enlightenment and progress, and they have begun to show much greater interest in the provision of welfare services 'outside the state' by individuals, families, mutual-aid associations and private charities. This trend has been reflected in a number of recent works which have all made a major contribution to debates in the history of welfare provision. The present section summarises some of the most important examples of this work in relation to the history of poverty, state welfare, charity, mutual aid and the family.

The history of poverty and anti-poverty policy has been a particularly important field of study for revisionist historians over the last two decades. In an important and challenging study, David Vincent argued that the expansion of statutory forms of welfare provision at the start of the twentieth century 'was built at the expense of older forms of mutual support', and that whilst this increased the amount of security available to poor people, it also meant that 'they were exposed to a form of bureaucratic welfare which denied them the dignity and status essential to their social citizenship.'[26] This argument reinforced the views of those historians, such as Karel Williams and Mitchell Dean, who believed that there was a fundamental continuity between the repressive and deterrent policies of the New Poor Law and the system of social security which developed in Britain after 1945.[27] As Tony Novak has observed, 'the maintenance of poverty and inequality as the primary incentive to work has throughout history overshadowed all other considerations in the state's dealings with poverty ... [The social security system has played a central part in] the creation of a range of ideas and beliefs – about poverty, or wealth, or responsibility for unemployment, or the proper role of women – which legitimate and sanction the prevailing patterns of social inequality.'[28]

The history of state welfare policy has also been examined, from a very different ideological perspective, by Martin Wiener and Correlli Barnett. Wiener argued that the values of a landed élite and the persistence of an 'anti-industrial' culture had laid the foundations of Britain's relative economic decline.[29] Although Wiener was not directly concerned with the evolution of the welfare state, his book provided a foundation for Correlli Barnett's sweeping denunciation of postwar social developments in *The audit of war*. Barnett argued that the 'commanding heights' of public policy-making had been captured by an 'enlightened establishment' of high-minded Christian social reformers who pursued the goal of a 'New Jerusalem' with breathtaking disregard for the need for economic reconstruction. He was particularly critical of the reformers' failure to recognise the need for economic reform as a precondition for successful social reform, but he also argued that the large scale provision of state welfare services was a drain on the economy and a debilitating source of welfare dependency.[30]

The reaction against state-centred histories of welfare provision has also been reflected in recent work in the history of philanthropy. Both Geoffrey Finlayson and Frank Prochaska have published studies which set out to challenge the traditional emphasis on the rise of collectivism. Finlayson's study was explicitly designed to challenge the notion of a 'welfare state escalator', even though the author was forced to conclude that 'the result of the growth of the welfare state is that the voluntary sector is increasingly influenced by the state, and often functions within or as an agent of the statutory sector, although not always willingly.'[31] Prochaska's work offered an even more overt challenge to state-centred history partly because it sought to demonstrate the moral relevance of earlier philanthropy, and partly because it sought to assert its continuing vitality:

> Both philanthropy and the state have made immense contributions to reducing human misery, but neither has lived up to expectations if only because expectations have been too high. Now that centralised state welfare is losing its plausibility as a panacea for all of the nation's ills (just as philanthropy once did), perhaps we can take a more balanced view of the contribution philanthropy has made to British life and more fully appreciate its character.[32]

Recent years have also witnessed the revival of interest in friendly societies and mutual aid associations. This revival was prefigured by the work of Peter Gosden in 1961 and 1973, and by Norman McCord and C. G. Hanson in their contributions to *The long debate on poverty* in 1972. The most outspoken accounts of the role of friendly societies have been provided by Stephen Yeo and David Green. Yeo wrote that 'the friendly societies ... were enormous, but not universal, mutual associations of working men, the theory of whose practice was collective self-help ... Their "failure" to become universal ... must not be attributed to their intentions, or lack of intentions, [but] rather to the material constraints of majority working class life ... the absolute deprivation of space, time, money and cultural resources for all but a minority stratum of workers.'[33] Green argued that these organisations provided a highly responsive healthcare system which was much more attuned to patient needs than the state systems which were introduced in 1913 and 1948. He claimed that 'the unhappy outcome of legislation intended to extend to all citizens the benefits of Friendly Society membership ... was a victory for the political muscle of the Combine [that is, the commercial insurance companies] and the British Medical Association. They achieved a very considerable transfer of wealth and power from the relatively poor working class to the professional class.'[34]

In addition to studies of the role played by working class organisations in the provision of welfare services, historians have also examined the attitude of these organisations to the development of state welfare itself. Pelling argued that many working-class organisations were actively hostile to the introduction of new forms of state welfare at the beginning of the twentieth century, and this insight has also received considerable attention from such writers as Peter Gosden, Stephen Yeo and Pat Thane.[35] Much of the early work on this theme concentrated on the attitude of predominantly male organisations, such as the friendly societies, but recent years have also seen a rise in interest in the attitude of working-class women. Jane Lewis has argued that the introduction of compulsory education, school meals and school medical inspection 'tended to exacerbate ... [the] financial problems [of the working class wife] and weaken her domestic authority, while ... at the same time remind[ing her] of her pivotal position in the working class family.'[36]

One of the most important contributions to the history of social welfare in recent years was Ellen Ross's *Love and toil*, a study of motherhood in 'outcast London' between 1870 and 1918. Although the book examined the impact of poverty on many different aspects of motherhood and working-class life in this period, it also provided a detailed account of the way in which wives and mothers used their resources to maximise their families' welfare, and of the complicated nature of their interactions with both the state and voluntary agencies. One of Ross's most significant achievements was to demonstrate the significance of the neighbourhood and the family as providers of welfare services. In the poorest areas of London, neighbours provided advice, aid, solidarity, childcare, nursing and midwifery services, and they played a vital role in helping mothers to discharge their own responsibilities. Mothers themselves were central to the maintenance of family life. They managed the family budget, earned their own incomes, fed and clothed their children, and maintained the domestic environment, together with a host of other activities.[37]

So far, this brief review of recent writing on the history of social welfare has concentrated on the provision of welfare services, either by the state, or by charities, or by self-help associations, or by families, but the history of social welfare must also take account of other ways in which the poor in particular sought to maximise their standard of living. Such an approach could easily stretch the boundaries of the subject to breaking-point, especially if we were to include the history of work, which has probably been the primary determinant of welfare for the vast majority of the population throughout recorded history, or crime, which has often been seen as a way of compensating for material disadvantages.[38] However, whilst accepting the need to impose some boundaries, it is important to recognise the importance of a number of recent studies which have extended our knowledge of the strategies deployed by poor people to 'make ends meet'. Three of the most useful examples of this kind of work are Gosden's account of voluntary associations in the nineteenth century, Johnson's study of the working-class economy between 1870 and 1939, and Tebbutt's discussion of pawnbroking and working-class credit.[39]

Gosden, Johnson and Tebbutt demonstrated the need to look beyond the institutions of welfare provision in order to gain a fuller understanding of the ways in which working-class people sought to cope with the hazards and uncertainties of daily life. Gosden's book was concerned with the full range of voluntary associations which provided working-class people with protection against sickness, unemployment, old age and death during the course of the nineteenth century. In addition to his earlier work on the history of friendly societies, he also examined the growth of burial and savings banks, building societies, cooperative societies and collecting societies. Johnson's book covered much of the same ground as Gosden's, but it provided a much more integrated account of the working-class economy, and also discussed the role of commercial arrangements, such as the provision of credit by local shopkeepers, 'tallymen', hire-purchase retailers, money-lenders and pawnbrokers. Tebbutt's book was specifically concerned with the last of these. Her study was expressly designed to challenge the conventional image of the rapacious pawnbroker, and to demonstrate the importance of pawnbroking to working-class life.

1.3   Bringing the state back in?

The previous section has shown how a new generation of historians has challenged some of the conventional images of the 'rise of the welfare state', and provided a much more rounded picture of the history of social welfare provision. However, in spite of this, historians and other social scientists have continued to devote considerable attention to the increasing role of the state in providing welfare services. This is particularly apparent in the field of comparative analysis, where various scholars have devoted considerable energy to understanding the long-term growth of state welfare services in a wide range of countries, and to elucidating the different ways in which those services have developed in those countries.[40]

There is no necessary contradiction between the argument that the 'rise of the welfare state' remains an important focus of study, and many of the arguments which have been reviewed in the first two sections of this chapter. Many of those who have questioned the traditional emphasis on the more teleological aspects of the history of the welfare state have done so on the basis that it is important to know more about the ways in which individuals and communities provided welfare services in periods when the role of the state was much more limited than it is today.[41] It is also worth noting that many of those who are most hostile to state-centred approaches to welfare history have framed their own accounts of the development of non-state welfare against the background of increasing state intervention. This is particularly, though not exclusively, true of those authors on the right of the political spectrum who believe that the history of non-state welfare has been obliterated by the onward march of welfare collectivism.[42]

The significance of the enhanced role of the state in providing welfare services can be demonstrated in a variety of ways. At the beginning of the nineteenth century, the primary functions of the state were limited to the servicing of the national debt, the maintenance of the army and navy, and the administration of the Poor Laws.[43] However, by the mid-century, the state was already intervening in a growing number of ways to protect and improve the welfare of its citizens, and by the end of the century it was already playing a major role in the provision of both health and education services. In 1906 the Liberal government embarked on a series of measures (including free school meals, old age pensions and national insurance) which gradually undermined the traditional Poor Law, and in 1919 the postwar coalition government embarked on the first concerted attempt to make the provision of subsidised housing one of the central features of state welfare provision. By 1950, the state had become the majority provider of health and education services, more than 15 per cent of all households lived in state-owned accommodation, and the benefits of a comprehensive national insurance scheme had been extended to the vast majority of the population.

As Martin Daunton has recently pointed out, 'the capacity of the state to act and realise its policy goals depends, more than anything else, on its financial resources',[44] and this is as true at the level of local government as it is at the level of central government. During the nineteenth and twentieth centuries, local authorities derived the bulk of their revenue from rates, loans and central government grants. The rate was a narrowly-based property tax (subsequently replaced by the community charge and the council tax), which was theoretically capable of being levied on movable or personal property, but which came to be confined in practice to immovable or 'real' property – in other words, to houses or business premises. In 1835, Parliament attempted to improve the accountability of local authorities by passing the Municipal Corporations Act, but this tended to strengthen the political power of those responsible for paying the rates, and in the short term it tended to encourage the forces of retrenchment at the expense of municipal growth. However, from the 1860s onwards, local authorities began to play an increasingly active role in the provision of welfare services. Many of these developments were financed with the aid of central government loans and, subsequently, the provision of government grants.[45]

The increasing reliance of local government on central government support reflects the fact that central government has always tended to have access to a wider range of revenue-raising devices, and this is particularly true in the field of taxation. As we can see from Figure 1.1, throughout the period between 1700 and 1950, central government derived at least 70 per cent of its total income from tax revenues, and in the vast majority of years the figure was much higher than this, but the balance between different sources of tax revenue changed over time. During the eighteenth century, the government derived the bulk of its income from indirect taxes in the form of customs and excise duties, but it also derived a smaller proportion of its income from direct taxes on land and other forms of assessable wealth and from stamp duties (including taxes on probate valuations and legacies), and in 1799 William Pitt the Younger introduced the first income tax. This was originally designed as a temporary measure to help pay for the costs of the Napoleonic War, and it was abandoned during the short-lived peace of 1802–3 and again in 1816, before being reintroduced by Robert Peel in 1842. Peel had originally intended that the income tax should be seen as an alternative to more traditional forms of taxation rather than as a means of raising extra revenue, but in 1909 the Liberals saw increases in the level and scope of income tax as an essential part of their strategy for raising public expenditure more generally. This was one of the main reasons why the

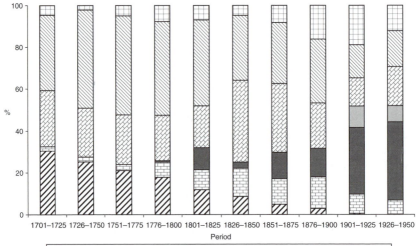

Note: Data for the period 1701–1801 represent net public income for Great Britain; data for 1802–1950 represent gross public income for the United Kingdom as a whole. From 1871 onwards, all assessed taxes except land tax and house duty were replaced by excise licences, and their revenue has been transferred accordingly.

Sources: B. R. Mitchell, *British historical statistics*, Cambridge: Cambridge University Press, 1988, pp. 575–7, 581–6. See also M. Daunton, *Trusting Leviathan: the politics of taxation in Britain 1799–1914*, Cambridge: Cambridge University Press, 2001, p. 34; *ibid.*, 'Trusting Leviathan: the politics of taxation, 1815–1914', in D. Winch and P. K. O'Brien (eds), *The political economy of British historical experience, 1688–1914*, Oxford: Oxford University Press, 2002, pp. 319–50, at p. 322; *ibid.*, *Just taxes: the politics of taxation in Britain, 1914–79*, Cambridge: Cambridge University Press, 2002, p. 16.

Figure 1.1 Sources of government finance, 1701/25–1926/50

percentage of total revenue derived from income taxation rose substantially between 1900 and 1950.[46]

The methods which governments use to generate income have an important bearing on the ways in which the tax system redistributes income and resources among different sections of the population. As we can see from Figure 1.1, even after the reintroduction of income tax in 1842, the government still derived well over half its total revenue from taxes on expenditure and, as the Liberals recognised in 1913, these taxes tended to weigh most heavily on those who had least.[47] By contrast, direct taxes such as income tax are generally perceived as being more equitable because they tend to claim a higher proportion of the incomes of the better off, and this tendency will be reinforced if those who enjoy higher incomes are also liable to higher rates of tax on the upper portions of those incomes. As a result, the gradual shift from taxes on expenditure towards taxes on income, combined with the introduction of higher tax rates for those on higher incomes in the 1909 budget, helped to ensure that the tax system became significantly more redistributive over the course of the period.[48] It is perhaps a noticeable paradox of social welfare history that this tendency only began to be thrown into reverse after 1945, when a growing proportion of households on lower incomes became liable to income tax for the first time, and the establishment of universal welfare services meant that these services became increasingly attractive to middle-class consumers.[49]

The different tax-raising capacities of the central and local authorities are also reflected in the changing balance between central government and local authority expenditure. At the end of the eighteenth century, central government was largely content to leave the provision of welfare services in the hands of local authorities, and the major form of public welfare provision was the Poor Law. During the middle decades of the nineteenth century, Parliament introduced new legislation which extended the powers of local authorities and, subsequently, began to impose new duties upon them, but it only offered them a limited amount of support in their efforts to discharge these responsibilities. However, during the late-nineteenth and early-twentieth centuries it became increasingly apparent that local authorities would only be able to honour their obligations if they were either given the opportunity to find new sources of local revenue or if they were granted additional support by the central authority, and this led to a substantial increase in the use of government grants to finance local services. The Liberal government of 1906–11 also introduced a number of centrally financed and administered welfare services, such as old-age pensions, unemployment insurance and health insurance, which gradually eroded many of the traditional welfare functions of local authorities. This generated two very different patterns of change in the balance between central and local expenditure in the nineteenth and twentieth centuries, as shown in Table 1.1. In the nineteenth century, public expenditure by local authorities increased more rapidly than central government expenditure, but this trend was first halted, and then reversed, between 1890 and 1950.[50]

At the end of the eighteenth century, more than 80 per cent of central and local government expenditure was devoted to administrative costs, defence and repayment of national debt, and only 18 per cent was devoted to social, economic or environmental services. However, during the course of the nineteenth century, the proportion of funds devoted to debt repayment declined, whilst the proportion devoted to social, economic and environmental services

Table 1.1 Expenditure by central and local government, as a percentage of total government expenditure, in the United Kingdom, 1790–1951

Year	Central government	Local government		Total
		Including central government grants	Excluding central government grants	
	(1)	(2)	(3)	(1) + (2)
1790	82.61	17.39	17.39	100.00
1840	78.13	21.88	21.88	100.00
1890	59.35	40.65	32.52	100.00
1910	49.61	50.39	37.98	100.00
1932	64.67	35.33	22.85	100.00
1951	77.02	22.98	15.26	100.00

Source: J. Veverka, 'The growth of government expenditure in the United Kingdom since 1790', *Scottish Journal of Political Economy*, 10 (1963), 111–27, at 119.

increased substantially. During the first half of the twentieth century, the proportion of funds devoted to administrative costs also declined (partly as a result of more efficient accounting procedures), whilst the proportions allocated to defence and debt repayment fluctuated in the wake of the two world wars, but the proportion allocated to social, economic and environmental services continued to increase. By 1950, more than two-fifths of total public expenditure was devoted to social services, and by the start of the twenty-first century this figure had increased to more than 60 per cent, as shown in Table 1.2.[51]

These changes in the distribution of public expenditure have had an important bearing on the growth of public expenditure as a whole. As we can see from Figure 1.2, public expenditure increased as a proportion of gross national product during the early years of the nineteenth century as a result of the Napoleonic War, but it declined during the 1820s and 1830s, and remained at a comparatively low level for the remainder of the century. However, the apparent stability of public expenditure as a whole in this period conceals the fact that the proportion of expenditure, and therefore the proportion of gross national product, devoted to debt repayment was declining, whilst the proportion

Table 1.2 General government expenditure by function as percentage of total expenditure, 1890–2000

Year	Administrative & other	Law & order	Overseas services	National debt	Military defence	Social services	Economic & environmental services	Total
1790	17.4	n/a	n/a	39.1	26.1	8.7	8.7	100.0
1840	15.6	n/a	n/a	42.2	23.4	9.4	9.4	100.0
1890A	22.0	n/a	n/a	15.4	28.5	19.5	14.6	100.0
1890B	12.1	6.9	0.3	18.2	26.7	20.9	14.8	100.0
1900	5.9	3.5	0.4	7.0	48.0	18.0	17.3	100.0
1910	8.1	4.7	0.4	7.4	27.3	32.8	19.2	100.0
1920	4.5	2.1	0.2	20.4	32.6	25.9	14.4	100.0
1930	4.1	2.8	0.1	25.4	10.4	42.3	14.9	100.0
1938	3.8	2.4	0.2	13.4	29.8	37.6	12.7	100.0
1950[a]	5.9	1.7	3.9	12.0	18.8	41.9	15.7	100.0
1960	3.4	2.1	1.4	12.4	19.5	46.1	15.1	100.0
1970	2.6	2.0	1.6	9.8	11.4	47.1	25.5	100.0
1980[b]	2.6	2.5	2.0	11.1	11.2	54.3	16.2	100.0
1990	5.0	5.0	1.0	11.8	9.5	55.0	12.5	100.0
2000	4.9	5.6	1.0	12.1	6.4	60.3	9.8	100.0

Notes: For definitions of expenditure categories, see A. Peacock and J. Wiseman, *The growth of public expenditure in the United Kingdom*, Princeton, NJ: Princeton University Press, 1961, pp. 182–4. [a] These figures differ slightly from the equivalent estimates in Peacock and Wiseman *op. cit.*, Table A–15. They have been preferred to Peacock and Wiseman's estimates because they are more directly comparable with the later figures. [b] Non-trading capital consumption is excluded from the estimate of total expenditure.

Sources: 1790–1891A: J. Veverka, 'The growth of government expenditure in the United Kingdom since 1790', *Scottish Journal of Political Economy*, 10 (1963), 111–27, at 119; 1890B–1938: A. Peacock and J. Wiseman, *The growth of public expenditure in the United Kingdom*, Princeton, NJ: Princeton University Press, 1961, Table A-15; 1950 and 1960: Central Statistical Office, *National income and expenditure 1961*, London: HMSO, 1961, Table 43; 1970: Central Statistical Office, *National income and expenditure 1971*, London: HMSO, 1971, Table 50; 1980: Central Statistical Office, *National income and expenditure 1981*, London: HMSO, 1981, Table 9.4; 1990 and 2000: HM Treasury, *Public expenditure: statistical analyses 2001–2*, London: HMSO (Cm. 5101), 2001, Table 3.4.

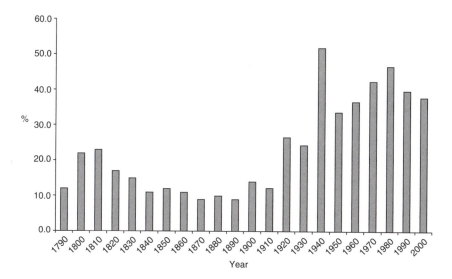

Notes: 1790–1900: Public expenditure as % of Gross National Product (GNP); 1910–50: General government expenditure as % of Gross Domestic Product (GDP); 1960–2000: Total managed expenditure as
% of GDP.

Sources: 1790–1840: J. Veverka, 'The growth of government expenditure in the United Kingdom since
1790', *Scottish Journal of Political Economy*, 10 (1963), 111–27, at 114; 1850–1900: A. Peacock and
J. Wiseman, *The growth of public expenditure in the United Kingdom*, Princeton, NJ: Princeton University
Press, 1961, Tables 1, A-5; 1910–50: Office for National Statistics, *General government expenditure as a
percentage of gross domestic product, 1901 to 1998. Social Trends dataset ST30531*. www.statistics.gov.
uk/statbase/xsdataset.asp?More;=Y&vlnk=295&All=Y&B2.x=65&B2.y=6 (2000); 1960–2000: Office for
National Statistics, *Total managed expenditure as a percentage of gross domestic product: Social Trends
32*. www.statistics.gov.uk/statbase/ssdataset.asp?vlnk=4978&B4.x=16&B4.y=9 (2002).

Figure 1.2   Public expenditure as % of GNP/GDP, 1790–2000

devoted to social expenditure was increasing.[52] During the first half of the
twentieth century, the proportion of government expenditure which was
devoted to debt repayment fluctuated between 7.0 per cent in 1900 and 25.4
per cent in 1930, whilst the proportion which was devoted to social services
continued to increase, and this was the main reason for the increase in the level
of public expenditure as a whole over the course of the period.

We can also examine the growth of the welfare state through the statistics of
public employment. In the middle of the nineteenth century, public employment accounted for less than 2.5 per cent of total employment, and it still represented less than 7 per cent of total employment in 1911. However, the scale
of public employment rose rapidly between 1938 and 1951, and by 1981 more
than 28 per cent of all employees were employed in some form of public service.
The increase in the overall level of public employment disguises the fact that
there has in fact been a disproportionate increase in the number of workers who
are employed in the social services. These workers accounted for 21 per cent of
the total volume of public employment in 1951, and for 45 per cent of all
public employees at the beginning of the 1980s.[53]

1.4   Conclusions

This chapter has tried to provide an introduction to the historical debates over the nature and course of social welfare provision over the last 200 years, and to demonstrate the importance, within this framework, of the growth of state intervention. During the last three decades, historians have become increasingly critical of the origins, nature and consequences of state welfare provision, and they have also begun to pay increasing attention to the provision of welfare services outside the state. This has been reflected in the publication of a number of studies which have sought to demonstrate the inadequacies of state welfare provision, and the importance of philanthropy, self-help and family and community support.

However, although there has been a considerable reaction against state-centred approaches to the history of social welfare, the growth of state intervention is still the most important single feature of the history of welfare provision between 1800 and 1945, and one of the main aims of this study is to understand and explain the reasons for this. Although we are primarily concerned with the history of welfare provision and the growth of state intervention in Britain, it is important to recognise that this has also been a central feature of the experience of the vast majority of advanced industrial countries, and in Chapter 2 we shall examine some of the different ways in which social scientists have sought to explain this. We shall then move on in the following chapters to provide a much more detailed account of the history of British social welfare from the late-eighteenth century to the end of the Second World War.

2 The growth of state intervention

Although the growth of state intervention in the provision of welfare services is intimately connected with the concept of the 'welfare state', the definition of what constitutes a 'welfare state' can sometimes appear to be fraught with difficulty. Slack suggested that Britain (or, at any rate, England) already possessed a local welfare state by the end of the eighteenth century, whereas Roberts argued that the foundations of the welfare state were only truly laid between 1833 and 1854, when the reformed House of Commons oversaw the introduction of central administration in the areas of factory reform, the poor law, penal policy, education and public health.[1] However, most commentators have tended to argue that it is more appropriate to confine the use of the term 'welfare state' to the range of welfare services which have been provided by the majority of western governments since 1945.[2] According to Asa Briggs:

> A welfare state is a state in which organised power is deliberately used (through politics and administration) in an effort to modify the play of market forces in at least three directions – first, by guaranteeing individuals and families a minimum income irrespective of the market value of their work or their property; second, by narrowing the extent of insecurity by enabling individuals and families to meet certain 'social contingencies' (for example, sickness, old age and unemployment), which lead otherwise to individual and family crises; and third, by ensuring that all citizens without distinction of status or class are offered the best standards available in relation to a certain agreed range of social services.[3]

Some commentators have complained that too many accounts of the growth of welfare states concentrate disproportionately on the British experience. These complaints are undoubtedly justified, insofar as Britain's actual experience of welfare state development deviates in a number of respects from that of other countries.[4] Nevertheless, it remains the case that the long-term growth of public expenditure on social provision, which was noted at the end of Chapter 1, has been a central feature of virtually all advanced industrial societies. It is for this reason that historians and other social scientists have sought to explain the growth of the British welfare state, not just in terms of Britain's historical experience, but also in terms of the growth of state welfare provision in the rest of the industrialised world as well.[5]

2.1 The welfare state and 'collectivisation'

Abram De Swaan argued that the welfare states have grown as a result of people's need to protect themselves against the 'external effects' of other people's misfortune. He utilised Norbert Elias's concept of the 'civilising process' to explain how the growth of nation states and the increasing complexity of modern societies transformed local and voluntary relief schemes into the centralised state welfare systems which we know today.[6] He also examined the extent to which globalisation and the development of an increasingly interdependent international world will see the development of global welfare agencies but, somewhat surprisingly perhaps, he concluded that 'even though the dynamics of interdependency between rich and poor and the dilemmas of collective action among the established repeat themselves on a world scale, there is no historical necessity for the collectivising process to proceed at a global level.'[7]

We can provide a brief illustration of De Swaan's argument by looking more closely at his account of the evolution of collective provision for social security. According to De Swaan, collective welfare provision begins when rich people recognise an obligation to make some form of provision for their less advantaged neighbours. In the earliest instances, such provision begins with particular individuals, but each individual benefactor also needs to protect themself against exploitation by other well-off individuals, and this leads to the development of some form of collective effort to provide welfare services for the local poor. However, just as the charitable individual needs to enter into collective agreements with other individuals, so individual communities need to enter into collective arrangements with other communities in order to ensure that their burdens are shared equally, and that they do not become a magnet for all the disadvantaged people of a wider area. These arrangements may need to be enforced by national authorities and, ultimately, it may become necessary for these authorities to assume direct responsibility for the provision of welfare services.[8]

De Swaan's account has attracted considerable interest among sociologists and social policy specialists, but it has been less warmly received by historians.[9] Its main strength lies in its attempt to incorporate the previously unconnected theoretical traditions of welfare economics and historical sociology into a theory of welfare state development.[10] However, the author's reluctance to delve more deeply into the primary literature of the countries he studies also raises a number of questions. In the first place, as Claus Offe has observed, De Swaan is much better at explaining why élite groups *should* introduce measures of social protection than he is at demonstrating that they actually did make the kinds of calculations he attributes to them. The second major criticism is that De Swaan fails to attach sufficient weight to the particular circumstances under which different social problems emerge and are brought to the attention of those in a position to deal with them. In order to address these issues, it is necessary to look beyond the logic of collectivisation, and to look more closely at the problem of industrialisation.[11]

2.2   Industrialisation and the growth of welfare states

As José Harris has observed, 'writers on social questions often refer to "social policy" as though it were a peculiarity of modern or advanced industrialised societies, but this view is misplaced. All political régimes have social policies of some kind, even if such policies consist simply in leaving the pursuit of welfare to the family or the local community or the corporation or the market.'[12] Nevertheless, it is clear that the propensity of societies to provide such services through the state has increased dramatically since the early-nineteenth century, and this has led many historians and social scientists to argue that the growth of state welfare is, above all, a consequence of industrialisation. 'The evolution of the welfare state', wrote Derek Fraser, 'is seen as an erratic and pragmatic response ... to the practical individual and community problems of an industrialised society.'[13] Ursula Henriques observed that 'social administration grew in the last years of the eighteenth century and the first half of the nineteenth century in response to the challenge of the Industrial Revolution.'[14]

Although writers such as Fraser and Henriques have emphasised the extent to which the development of welfare provision was a response to the problems associated with the growth of *industrial* societies, it is important to remember that many of the most important social policy debates of the late-eighteenth and early-nineteenth centuries took place in a society which was still overwhelmingly agricultural. This was particularly true of the campaign to reform the Old Poor Law, which had been placed under increasing stress by changes in the organisation of agriculture and the growth of rural poverty. However, the process of industrialisation also generated new problems of its own, including not only the problem of urbanisation, but also the need for a partially skilled and more literate workforce, the recognition of involuntary unemployment, the growth of white-collar employment, and the creation of unprecedented levels of personal and public wealth. The dramatic population increases which accompanied industrialisation led to major changes in family and community life, a growing division between home and work, increased life expectancy, and the emergence of publicly-sanctioned non-participation in the labour force. The growth of nation-states led to the centralisation of government power, the development of a 'professional' civil service, and the introduction of new techniques of surveillance and communication. Finally, and more controversially, the growth of industrial societies led to the rise of more democratic political systems, and these in turn generated new demands for social reform.[15]

Wilensky and Lebeaux argued that the growth of state welfare schemes in the United States occurred as a direct result of the demands generated by the growth of industrial society.[16] In 1975, Wilensky published a wide-ranging account of the origins and growth of welfare state expenditures around the globe. He concluded that the level of economic growth was the major cause of variations in welfare state expenditure, and that the main reason for this was the pressure of demographic trends, and the momentum generated by existing welfare state programmes. He explicitly rejected the view that political ideology made a major difference to the level of welfare state spending, although he conceded that 'political arrangements' played a significant role in explaining variations in 'welfare effort'.[17]

Although much of the work which has been devoted to explaining the links between industrialisation and social policy has focused on the problems generated by industrialisation, it also generated the resources needed to address these problems. The nineteenth-century German economist, Adolph Wagner, suggested that 'citizens' demands for services and willingness to pay taxes are income-elastic, and therefore bound to increase with the increase in economic affluence.'[18] The British historian and political scientist, Samuel Finer, argued that industrialisation 'vastly enhanced' the information-gathering capacity of the modern state, and led to a dramatic growth in the size of public bureaucracies, but it also generated the wealth needed to overcome the problems which bureaucratic investigation unearthed: 'Industrialisation first enabled wealth to keep pace with the rapidly-rising population; then it overtook population growth and threw up an ever-increasing social surplus. Living standards improved and then – but not without popular pressure – the state began increasingly to make up for certain material difficulties which the citizen might be suffering.'[19]

The argument that welfare states have developed in response to the needs generated by industrial society and in proportion to the resources created by industrial society has been widely accepted, but there are doubts as to the extent of its applicability. In the first place, several observers have noted that, whilst economic performance may be broadly correlated with welfare spending, there are still substantial variations in the level of expenditure among countries at comparable stages of economic development.[20] Second, it is also clear that the extent of the correlation between welfare state spending and economic performance is heavily dependent on the definition of welfare expenditure.[21] Third, and perhaps most importantly, the 'industrialisation' thesis fails to explain the precise mechanisms by which concerns about social conditions are translated into political action. Even if we were to accept that welfare states developed in response to the needs generated by industrial society, it would still be necessary to explain the particular ways in which the identification of these needs led to the introduction of welfare reforms.

2.3　Modernisation and the growth of state welfare

The concept of 'modernisation' has much in common with the concept of 'industrialisation' in its capacity to explain the growth of welfare states. Its supporters tend to share the belief that the welfare state is a feature of 'modern' societies, and that the emergence of these societies is linked inextricably to the process of industrialisation. However the theory of modernisation differs from that of industrialisation in that it gives far more weight to the social and political changes which have been associated with industrialisation. As Flora and Heidenheimer explained in 1981:

> The theory of modernisation or structural differentiation ... leads us to understand the welfare state as an answer to the growing needs and demands for socioeconomic security in the context of an increasing division of labour, the expansion of markets, and the loss of 'security functions' by families and other communities. In this sense, the

basic goals and legitimising principles of socioeconomic security and equality are interpreted as the core of the welfare state.[22]

The view that welfare states are a quintessential feature of *modern* societies has often been associated with the work of the British sociologist, T. H. Marshall. Marshall outlined a model of economic and social development in which ordinary members of the population acquired (or reacquired) civil rights, such as freedom of speech, during the eighteenth century, political rights during the nineteenth century, and social rights during the twentieth century. However, although Marshall has often been cited as a key figure in debates about modernisation, his account of the causal relationship between the acquisition of political rights and the acquisition of social rights is not entirely clear. It is certainly true that Marshall described the gradual process of acquiring citizenship rights as one of 'evolution', but he also likened the different types of citizenship to three 'runners' who had only recently 'come abreast of one another'.[23]

The concept of modernisation has been developed more fully in Flora and Alber's account of the development of welfare states in Western Europe. Flora and Alber argued that the development of welfare states was a response to the objective pressures exerted by the industrialisation and urbanisation, on the one hand, and by working-class political mobilisation on the other. In their analysis of the development of social insurance programmes in Finland, Sweden, Italy, Switzerland, the United Kingdom, Belgium and the Netherlands, they concluded that 'the introduction of social insurance [was] ... a function of the combined effects of growing social problems (socioeconomic development) and an increasing political pressure (mobilisation of the working class).' They also argued that the form of welfare state development could be influenced by a variety of constitutional and religious factors. Thus, constitutional-dualistic monarchies tended to introduce social insurance schemes earlier than parliamentary democracies, and Protestant countries tended to introduce state welfare measures earlier than Catholic countries.[24]

The theory of modernisation offers a more nuanced view of the development of welfare states than the theory of industrialisation *per se*, and, unlike the first theory, it provides a basis for explaining the differences between welfare states as well as their similarities. However, it also suffers from a number of weaknesses. In the first place, it assumes, to a rather greater extent than some more recent explanations, that the rise of welfare states is ultimately a rational and even inevitable process. Second, insofar as it associates the rise of welfare states with some implicit notion of social justice, it neglects the extent to which they have also been associated with such factors as professional self-interest and the pursuit of 'national efficiency'. Third, the theory tends to assume that the primary beneficiaries of welfare state development have been the working classes, and this interpretation has been questioned by those observers who associate the growth of welfare states after 1945 with the pursuit of middle-class self-interest.[25]

2.4 Capitalism and the growth of welfare states

The growth of welfare states in capitalist societies has also been a key concern for Marxist writers from the 1850s onwards. Marxists share the concern shown by other writers to relate the growth of the welfare state to the development of industrial societies and the pressures of modernisation, but they also argue that the growth of welfare states needs to be tied more closely to the role played by class conflict in the development of capitalist societies. In their most famous publication, *The Communist Manifesto*, Marx and Engels argued that the process of industrialisation had led to the emergence of two social classes, the bourgeoisie – who owned the means of production – and the proletariat, who owned nothing but the value of their own labour power. They argued that the interests of these two groups were diametrically opposed, and that the conflict between them was the main driving force in human history.[26]

Marx argued that the state was always likely to pursue policies which were determined by the interests of the dominant social group, and, since this usually meant the bourgeoisie, it meant that the state could usually be expected to pursue policies which would promote the interests of the bourgeoisie and help to ensure the survival of capitalist societies.[27] Miliband argued that the bourgeoisie was able to maintain control of the state as a result of the occupancy of key state positions, including not only the legislative arm of government (Parliament), but also its executive and bureaucratic arms (the civil service, police, judiciary and armed forces); the political power of business interests; and the constraints imposed by the capitalist system, but others have argued that this view places too much emphasis on the importance of individual actors.[28] Poulantzas believed that the class identities of particular individuals were less important than the underlying characteristics of the 'system' within which they operated. Since the essential features of this system were already determined by the nature of capitalist society, the policies pursued by the state would ultimately serve to reinforce that society.[29]

In *Das Kapital*, Marx argued the introduction of the English Factory Acts was directly attributable to the conflict 'between collective capital, i.e. the class of capitalists, and collective labour, i.e. the working-class', and to the capitalists' need to invest in the social structure in order to ensure the reproduction of a new generation of workers or, in other words, 'the same necessity as forced the manuring of English fields with guano'.[30] This account of the origins of welfare reform has exercised a profound influence on many subsequent accounts of welfare state development. Saville argued that the welfare state had come about as a result of '(1) the struggle of the working class against their exploitation; (2) the requirements of industrial capitalism … [and] (3) recognition by the property owners of the price that has to be paid for political security'.[31] Gough attributed the growth of the welfare state to 'the degree of class conflict, and, especially, the strength and form of working class struggle; and the ability of the capitalist state to formulate and implement policies to secure the long-term reproduction of capitalist social relations.[32]

Although this chapter is mainly concerned with the *growth* of welfare states, it is also important to consider the extent to which this process might sometimes be thrown into reverse. James O'Connor argued that the welfare state was in crisis because it was unable to reconcile the conflicting demands of *social capital* (that is, the investment required to stimulate production and reduce labour costs) and *social expenses* (the projects and services required to maintain social peace).[33] O'Connor's emphasis on the 'contradictions of the welfare state' was echoed by Claus Offe, in a lecture first delivered in 1980. Offe argued that the welfare state had owed its earlier popularity to its ability 'to serve many conflicting ends and strategies simultaneously', but 'the very diversity of the forces that inaugurated and supported the welfare state could not be accommodated forever within [its] institutional framework' and 'the machinery of class compromise' found itself the object of attack.[34]

In an earlier essay, coauthored with Gero Lenhardt, Offe suggested that one of the main attractions of the Marxist account of the growth of the welfare state was its ability to explain the rationale behind the introduction of social welfare measures as well as the functional necessity for such measures.[35] Marxist accounts have also highlighted the ways in which social policy can be used to bolster an established social order, and warned against any easy association of 'social policy' with 'social reform'. However, many writers believe that the Marxists have over-simplified the nature of the modern state, and paid insufficient attention to the conflicts which undoubtedly exist between different sections of the 'capitalist class'.[36] Critics have also argued that there is an 'inherent contradiction' between the Marxists' support for welfare reform as a means of improving working-class living standards, and their opposition to such reform as a means of reinforcing 'social control'.[37] However, it is arguable that the greatest weakness of Marxist approaches is their tendency to present an over-simplified view of the class interests which support welfare state measures. It is certainly true that, for much of the period covered by this book, such measures have been primarily concerned with the provision of services to members of the working class, but there have also been many instances where the ability of political groups to foster support for the extension of state welfare measures has depended at least as much on their ability to construct alliances across social classes as on 'the strength and form of working-class struggle'.[38]

2.5 Professionalisation and the middle-class origins of the welfare state

Many of the preceding analyses of the growth of welfare states have tended to assume, or imply, that the welfare state is primarily a means by which resources are transferred, for whatever reasons, from wealthy to less wealthy groups. However, the welfare state has also been a major source of benefit to the middle classes, both as a source of status and employment, and as a source of welfare provision. A number of recent commentators have sought to examine the impact of these factors on the development of the welfare state, first by looking at the role played by professionals in the development of welfare state services, and second by examining the increased involvement of the middle classes in the welfare state as welfare consumers.

One of the most important contributions to the study of the impact of professionalisation on the growth of welfare states is the work of Michel Foucault. In works such as *Madness and civilisation* and *The birth of the clinic*, Foucault argued that the medical profession had made itself indispensable to the management of illness in contemporary society.[39] This insight also played an important, if secondary, role in Abram De Swaan's account of the impact of the 'collectivising process' on the development of state welfare provision.[40] The British historian, Harold Perkin, has argued that 'the professional ideal' played a key role in the development of British welfare provision from the late-nineteenth century onwards.[41] Finally, as we shall see in section 2.9, the theoreticians of the New Right have also argued that bureaucratic self-interest has played a key role in the expansion of state welfare programmes.[42]

Writers such as Foucault, De Swaan and Perkin have focused attention on the role played by the middle classes as *providers* of state welfare services, but the middle classes have also played an important role as welfare state *consumers*. According to Peter Baldwin, the middle classes were the single most important group in determining the evolution and shape of the different kinds of social insurance scheme which emerged in Britain, France, Germany, Sweden and Denmark in the nineteenth and twentieth centuries.[43] The middle classes also played a central role in Dryzek and Goodin's account of the reasons for the growth of state welfare provision in Britain after 1945. They argued that the Second World War created a shared sense of *risk* in Britain, and that this persuaded the middle classes that they had as much to gain from the establishment of a universal welfare state as the working classes.[44]

We can therefore see that there is a powerful body of research which demonstrates that the middle classes have played an important role in the development of the welfare state, both as providers and consumers. It is unlikely that such explanations will be able to provide a complete explanation for the expansion of the whole range of state welfare programmes, but they demonstrate the need for welfare state historians to take a more rounded view of the development of state welfare provision. Many of the more traditional accounts of welfare state history have tended to assume that the welfare state represents a series of concessions which have needed to be wrung from the hands of a reluctant bourgeoisie.[45] Whilst this has often been the case, there is also a powerful body of research which shows that the continued survival of the welfare state will depend as much on its ability to satisfy middle-class interests as on its ability to satisfy the needs of the working classes.[46]

2.6 Maternalism and the origins of the welfare state

Recent years have also seen a pronounced upsurge in feminist approaches to the history of the welfare state. A considerable part of this work has focused on the role played by state welfare in reinforcing the patriarchal nature of modern society, but a growing number of historians have also focused attention on the role played by women's organisations in the growth of the welfare state.[47] Much of the debate about the role played by women in welfare state development has revolved around the concept of 'maternalism'. In 1990, Koven and Michel defined this concept in the following terms:

> We apply the term [maternalism] to ideologies that exalted women's capacity to mother and extended to society as a whole the values of care, nurturance and morality.[48]

Koven and Michel identified three main ways in which 'women's reform efforts and welfare states not only coincided in time, place and sometimes personnel, but also reinforced and transformed one another in significant and enduring ways.' They argued that the growth of welfare bureaucracies led to the expansion of care-taking professions dominated by women; that 'maternalist' discourses lay at the heart of debates about the nature of state intervention; and that women played a leading role in the development of private-sector philanthropy.[49] The role played by women in the development of welfare states has also been examined by Skocpol and Ritter. They argue, rather more cautiously, that the nature of women's participation in the political process had a significant effect on the shape of welfare measures in Britain and America.[50]

The attempt to place women at the forefront of debates about the origins of the welfare state deserves considerable respect, but it is not entirely convincing. Koven and Michel are undoubtedly correct to focus attention on the part played by women in the development of welfare policies and on the part played by the welfare state in the expansion of women's employment opportunities, but it is difficult to argue that the development of the welfare state was a direct result of women's enhanced role in society.[51] The most powerful objection concerns the fact that many of the most important welfare services were initiated before women had secured the right to effective participation in the political process.[52] However, this is not to deny the fact that, as women became more powerful politically, they also began to play an increasingly important part in welfare debates.[53]

2.7   War and social policy

A number of writers have also focused attention on the role played by war in accelerating, or even distorting, the path of social development. According to Andrzejewski, the impact of war on social policy was directly related to the 'military participation ratio', which he defined as either 'the proportion of militarily-utilised individuals in the total population' or as 'the ratio of militarily-utilised individuals to the total able-bodied population'.[54] He argued that societies which experienced a high military participation ratio were more likely to witness the pursuit of egalitarian social policies and a reduction in the scale of social inequalities, and that

> success in war, more than any other human activity, depends on coordination of individual actions, and the larger the group the more necessary is the coordination, and the larger the hierarchy required ... [but] the intensification of warfare may make it necessary to enlist the support of the masses by granting them various privileges, in which case a substantial levelling may take place. The necessity of such a course will depend mainly on whether mass armies are, in view of the state of tactics and armament, more or less efficient than professional armies.[55]

Although Andrzejewski recognised that there were a number of important respects in which Britain's experience departed from this model,[56] his work has exercised a powerful influence on British studies of the effects of war on social policy. However, whereas Andrzejewski focused his attention on the proportion of the population which was called upon to fight, his successors have argued that this was rather less important than the extent to which the conduct of war required the active participation of the population as a whole. Titmuss argued that 'the aims and content of social policy, both in peace and in war, are ... determined – at least to a substantial extent – by how far the cooperation of the masses is essential to the successful prosecution of war. If this cooperation is thought to be essential, then inequalities must be reduced, and the pyramid of social stratification must be flattened', and Reid has claimed that 'the larger the proportion of the population which is involved in the national war effort, the more likely it is to be accompanied by major social reforms or, to restate it in other terms, the further down the social hierarchy this involvement goes, the more egalitarian the social consequences are likely to be.'[57] Arthur Marwick concluded:

> My view ... has always been that men participating under strict conditions of military discipline are likely to make far fewer gains from their participation than those participating in the much more permissive atmosphere of the home front. However, this should not invalidate the general thesis [that] conditions for the under-privileged may well, nonetheless, improve. The precise processes ... have to be scrutinised very closely ... but on a broad appraisal across Europe it would seem that in the First World War the participation effect did have benefits for women, sections of the working class, and various national minorities.[58]

The relationship between war and social policy has also been examined by two economists, Alan Peacock and Jack Wiseman. In the first place, war exerted a 'displacement effect', whereby 'people will accept ... methods of raising revenue previously thought intolerable, and the acceptance of new tax levels remains when the disturbance has disappeared'. Second, war imposed new obligations on government, such as the payment of war pensions, debt interest and reparations, which led to a permanent increase in the scale of government spending. Finally, war also 'force[d] the attention of governments and people to problems of which they were formerly less conscious – there is an "inspection effect" which should not be underestimated'.[59]

We can therefore see that there is a substantial body of literature which focuses on the long-term consequences of war and the part played by war in long-term development, but this 'positive' or 'transformative' view of the effects of war has also been challenged, especially in relation to Britain, from a number of different perspectives. Although most historians would probably agree that the Boer War of 1899–1902 played an important part in the debates about the question of 'national efficiency',[60] both Philip Abrams and Rodney Lowe have drawn attention to the 'failure of social reform' and the 'erosion of state intervention' after 1918, and a number of writers have questioned whether the Second World War really did produce a new 'consensus' on the need for social reform in the way that Titmuss and his supporters imagined.[61] However, Middleton concludes that 'there is some evidence for an acceleration in the rate of growth of expenditure on goods and services after the First World War, but not after the Second', and that 'the force of war is reaffirmed, as

Peacock and Wiseman meant it' by the historically high rate of growth in public expenditure as a whole between 1924 and 1937.[62]

2.8   International influences on social policy

Although many of the approaches which have been examined in this chapter have been designed to address the emergence of similar types of social policy in a range of different countries, it is nevertheless the case that they still seek to explain these developments in terms of the internal logic of social development within these countries, without necessarily paying a great deal of attention to the processes by which policies which may have developed in one country might then be adopted by another. However, during the last two decades, a growing number of political scientists have become interested in what Dolowitz and Marsh have called 'policy transfer' or '[the] process ... [by] which knowledge about policies, administrative arrangements, institutions etc. in one time or place is used in the development of policies, administrative arrangements and institutions in another time or place'.[63] Even though these ideas have not exercised a great influence on historical research, it is interesting to explore the extent to which such processes may have contributed to the development of social policies in different parts of the world over the last 150–200 years.[64]

During the second half of the nineteenth century, improvements in international trade and the expansion of higher education led to the emergence of an increasingly multinational or transnational scientific and policy community, and this was reflected in the organisation of a large number of international gatherings and congresses devoted to social, educational and medical questions.[65] These gatherings provided a valuable opportunity for scientists and practitioners to exchange ideas and lobby for changes in social policy within their own countries, as indicated by the role played by such gatherings in the campaign for improvements in school hygiene in Britain from the 1870s onwards.[66] Professional groupings also used their knowledge of developments in other countries to reinforce the case for the introduction of similar measures at home. For example, during the early years of the twentieth century, when the British Medical Association was campaigning for the introduction of a national system of school medical inspection in the United Kingdom, it drew repeated attention to the successes achieved by similar schemes in such countries as Poland, Sweden, France, Belgium, Finland, Norway, Russia, Germany, Austria, Romania, Czechoslovakia, Serbia, Portugal, Spain, Argentina, Chile, the United States and Japan.[67]

Although much of the initial stimulus for cross-country investigation came from individuals and pressure groups, it would be wrong to ignore the extent to which governments also sought to learn from each other, and this tendency was particularly apparent in Britain, as Geoffrey Searle has pointed out, at the end of the nineteenth and the beginning of the twentieth centuries.[68] During the 1890s, the Department of Education published the results of a series of official investigations into the development of educational provisions in eleven other countries, and in 1906 the Board of Education dispatched one of its senior civil servants to investigate the practice of school medicine in Germany.[69] However, the most famous examples of policy transfer in the Edwardian period concerned the role played by German developments in the introduction of old-age pensions and national health insurance. In the case of old-age pensions, although British ministers were aware of the existence of the German scheme, they preferred to introduce a non-contributory scheme which was financed out of general taxation, whereas their proposals for the creation of a national system of health insurance were much more directly linked to German precedents.[70]

It is also worth considering the role played by international and supranational organisations after the First World War. During the interwar period, international voluntary organisations such as the Save the Children Fund and supranational organisations like the League of Nations and the International Labour Office drew attention to problems of child and adult poverty and helped to establish new minimum standards against which all governments could be held to account. In 1932, the Save the Children Fund published a major report on the social consequences of unemployment, and in 1937 the Technical Committee of the League of Nations established new dietary standards which made a significant contribution to British debates about the need for improvements in the provision of school meals.[71] Thus, even though national governments continued to make policies, they did so against a background of increasing international surveillance.

2.9 The New Right and the growth of the welfare state

The majority of social theorists tend to assume that the development of state welfare provision is, in some sense, a functional response to the needs generated by industrial, or modern, or capitalist societies, and even those who are opposed to state provision have based their opposition on the belief that state welfare provision reinforces the established social order. It is in this sense that the theoreticians of the New Right represent a sharp contrast to older, more established schools of thought. The New Right is not only opposed to many of the moral arguments which are put forward in favour of state welfare provision; it also believes that the growth of state welfare is a dysfunctional development which threatens the long-term survival of capitalist societies.[72]

One of the most important ways in which New Right thinkers have contributed to the understanding of welfare policies is by their analysis of the processes of collective decision-making. They argue that the mechanisms which are normally used to determine voter preferences are highly inefficient, and that many voters are forced to support the introduction of policies which they might not necessarily favour. The position of these individuals can be contrasted with that of politicians and civil servants. In modern democracies, politicians compete with each other by assembling packages of policies which are likely to appeal to a broad range of voters, but this can lead to the introduction of unnecessary or inappropriate policies which undermine each other and increase public expenditure. In the meantime, the interests of public officials are best served by expanding the range of services for which they are responsible, even if these services fail to meet the needs of the people who depend upon them.[73]

The New Right's analysis of the inefficient nature of collective decision-making and the inability of ordinary voters to control the actions of either politicians or civil servants is directly associated with its analysis of the reasons for welfare state growth. The New Right argues that the welfare state has grown, in part, because the advent of mass democracy has encouraged politicians to promise an ever-expanding range of public services to prospective voters, and partly because these politicians have failed to find ways of controlling the natural tendency of public officials to maximise their own budgets.[74] In addition, the New Right has also focused attention on the ways in which external events, and in particular wars, have distorted the 'natural' pattern of socio-economic development and persuaded voters to agree to the payment of higher taxes in return for welfare services.[75]

The majority of observers have tended to regard New Right explanations of the growth of welfare states with some suspicion. The principal weakness of these explanations is the New Right's reluctance to recognise the extent to which the origins of the welfare state are rooted in the historical failures of *laissez-faire* economics. However, even the opponents of the New Right are willing to concede its ability to shed some light on the ways in which welfare states have developed over the last 100 years.[76] This is reflected in the increasing popularity of such ideas as 'market socialism', and in the appropriation of a range of public-choice theories by left-wing theorists.[77]

2.10   Conclusions

This chapter has summarised some of the main intellectual theories and schools of thought which have sought to account for the growth of welfare states in modern societies. The chapter has emphasised the way in which these theories differ from each other, but it is also important to recognise the extent to which they complement one another. Some of the discrepancies are attributable to differences of politics and ideology, but the theories also differ because they offer different levels of explanation and focus on different aspects of welfare state development. These differences highlight the fact that the history of the welfare state is multifaceted, and that different factors come into play at different points in time. Although no single theory will ever be able to provide a full explanation for all aspects of the history of the welfare state, the theories and perspectives which have been examined in this chapter can help us to understand a large part of it.

3 Britain in the age of industrial growth

In *Prices, food and wages in Scotland 1550–1780*, Gibson and Smout quoted from two hitherto unpublished recollections of eighteenth-century life. Alexander Maxwell recalled the difficulties faced by his grandfather and great-uncle in the spring of 1740, a time 'of people wandering from Dundee through the country in search of food, and bodies being found in dens and moors with wild herbs in their mouths'. John Mackinnon described how his father, a Glasgow handloom weaver, had been 'unable to get wages owing to him from his employer in the dearth of 1799–1800':

> There was nothing in the house to eat, and they had little coals except what was on the fire. They went to bed supperless, and as they had nothing to eat, they thought it better to remain in bed instead of rising on Sunday morning as it was warmer than sitting in a house with neither food nor fire. A rap came to the door on the Sunday morning, and your grandmother rose to see who it was; it turned out to be an acquaintance who was a maidservant in a gentleman's family, and who wanted a letter written to an acquaintance who had enlisted sometime before … [she] brought with her a few pounds weight of good oatmeal, and some other odds and ends of provisions; she had not money to get paper or pay the postage of the letter, and she brought these articles of provisions instead; she gave your grandmother an idea of what she wanted written, and left her to pile up the letter according to her own taste. Thus the provisions brought so unexpectedly by this woman kept them in a sufficiency of food, till the manufacturer obtained money.[1]

Although these extracts refer to Scotland rather than England and Wales, they nevertheless provide a salutary warning against any attempt to romanticise the reality of ordinary life before the beginning of the nineteenth century. As Alexander Maxwell observed in 1843, 'we have no cause to regret that our lot was not cast in those "good old times"'.[2] However, even though the basic standard of living of the majority of the population may have improved during the first half of the nineteenth century, the context of social policy also changed. In addition to the ongoing problems of personal hardship and poverty, policymakers also had to grapple with the consequences of rapid economic and social change, population growth, urbanisation, social and political unrest, and the changing needs of an increasingly industrial economy. This chapter examines the background to these issues, and looks at the nature of society's response to the problems they created during the first half of the nineteenth century.

3.1 The pattern of industrial growth

According to the great Victorian historian, Arnold Toynbee, Britain experienced a rapid and fundamental transformation in the structure of its economy during the late-eighteenth and early-nineteenth centuries. However, many historians have questioned whether such a revolution, 'tied directly to radical changes in methods of production, having their decisive consequences over a relatively short period of time', actually occurred. The 'new economic historians' have argued that the roots of British industrialisation must be sought in the seventeenth and early-eighteenth centuries, and that their impact was slower and more patchy than previously thought.[3]

Although the growing tendency to 'backdate' the onset of the industrial revolution has led some historians to reject the concept altogether, it is clear that the British economy did undergo a series of fundamental changes between 1700 and 1850. However, some of the most important changes occurred not in industry but in agriculture. During the eighteenth and early-nineteenth centuries, British agriculture experienced a series of developments in both organisation and methods which enabled total agricultural output to rise by a factor of between 3.37 and 3.56 between 1700 and 1850, but this increase was not achieved without considerable social cost. Snell argued that it led to a reduction in the demand for agricultural labour and an increase in rural unemployment, but Allen has suggested that even though the demand for female and child labour may have declined, the demand for adult male labour increased. However, many agricultural workers and their families still experienced increasing hardship towards the end of the eighteenth century, resulting in the introduction of such measures as the Speenhamland system of poor relief in the 1790s in order to relieve the distress caused by rising prices and falling real wages.[4]

Although changing methods of organisation may have contributed to an upsurge in rural poverty, they also have to be set against the background of a dramatic increase in the size of the British population. According to Wrigley and Schofield, the English population increased from 2.77 million to 5.58 million between 1541 and 1741, and from 5.58 million to 16.74 million between 1741 and 1851. The rate of population growth was not only unprecedented within Britain; it was also unparalleled elsewhere. Thus, while the populations of Denmark, Iceland, Italy, Norway, Portugal, Spain and Sweden barely doubled between the mid-eighteenth and mid-nineteenth centuries, the population of the United Kingdom more than trebled.[5]

The industrial revolution also witnessed a fundamental change in the population's occupational structure. At the end of the eighteenth century, 35.9 per cent of the employed population was employed in agriculture, forestry and fishing, but by 1851 this figure had fallen to 21.7 per cent. At the same time, the proportion of the population engaged in manufacturing, mining and industry increased from 29.7 per cent to 42.9 per cent. Both the agricultural and the industrial populations were increasing in terms of absolute numbers, and the distinctions between the two sectors may sometimes be misleading.

Nevertheless, the figures still show that there was a fundamental change in the way in which the majority of the population earned its living.[6]

The third major change was the urbanisation of the population. The proportion of the population which resided in towns containing more than 2,500 inhabitants increased from 18 per cent in 1700 to 34 per cent in 1801 and to 54 per cent in 1851. During the eighteenth century, the bulk of this increase was concentrated in towns containing between 2,500 and 10,000 inhabitants, but the nineteenth century also witnessed a dramatic increase in the number and proportion of people in towns with more than 100,000 inhabitants. At the beginning of the nineteenth century, the typical town-dweller lived in a small market town containing around 10,000 people, but the tendency of the future was to larger and larger conurbations. In 1801 only London contained more than 100,000 people; by 1851 there were ten such towns, and by 1901 there were nearly thirty.[7]

Much of the heat that has been generated in discussions about the industrial revolution has been concerned with the nature and organisation of work. Landes argued that the industrial revolution was characterised by the replacement of human skill by machines, the substitution of inanimate for animate sources of power, and the introduction of new and more abundant raw materials, but Berg claimed that too much weight had been attached to the factory and the cotton industry and that more attention should be paid to developments elsewhere in the economy. She argued that 'innovation was not necessarily mechanisation[; i]t was also the development of hand and intermediate techniques, and the wider use ... and division of cheap labour', and she urged historians to acknowledge that 'the Industrial Revolution [w]as a more complex, many-sided and long-term phenomenon' than they had previously recognised.[8]

The process of industrialisation was also associated with profound changes in the social structure of the population. In the early years of the eighteenth century, British society was still structured along largely 'traditional' lines. According to Royle, 'most writers assumed that people were bound together according to broad occupational interests which were vertically structured, and within which people had a recognised status.' However, by the early years of the nineteenth century there was a growing feeling that the vertical ties which bound people of different social status were gradually being replaced by the horizontal ties of social class, and the traditional certainties of the older society began to give way. Fraser summarised the impact of these changes in the following terms:

> Urban industrial society placed the individual in a new relationship with his fellow-man [sic] and the symbols of social authority. In place of the security of a cohesive vertical social structure in which every individual had a formal or informal connection with those above and below, there was the uncertainty of a mass society in which a horizontal class structure gradually emerged. It was during the process of change, when the first-generation migrant had forsaken his niche in the old world yet was without the security of a stable position in the evolving new one, that alienation and anomie permeated English society.[9]

3.2 Years of unrest

Between 1801 and 1852, the House of Commons established more than seventy Select Committees dealing with such subjects as the threat of insurrection, the reform of the police, and the condition of the country's penal establishments.[10] The sense of unease was exacerbated by a series of political challenges which rocked the country's establishment between 1789 and 1848. These included the various 'Jacobin' movements of the 1790s; the naval mutinies of 1797; the petitions of the weavers, hosiers, framework-knitters, lace-makers and stockingers (1809, 1812, 1818, 1819); the Luddite disturbances (1812); the formation of the Hampden Clubs (1812–16); the meetings at Spa Fields (1816); the march of the Blanketeers (1817); the Pentrich Rebellion (1817); the Peterloo Massacre (1819); the Cato Street Conspiracy (1820); 'Captain Swing' (1830); the campaign for Parliamentary Reform (1830–2); the formation of the National Union of the Working Classes (1831); the rise of Chartism (1838–48); and even the Anti-Corn Law League (1839–46).[11]

The overthrow of the French aristocracy in 1789 sparked a wave of repression against the English 'Jacobins', which was intensified by the outbreak of war with France in 1793. The fear of unrest was also reinforced by the wave of revolutions which swept through Europe after 1815. In the early 1820s, the 'good cousins' or *Carbonari* launched a successful revolution in Greece, and abortive risings took place in Spain and Italy. In the early-1830s, the overthrow of the Bourbon Kings of France was followed by the achievement of Belgian independence, the suppression of Polish nationalism, and outbreaks of discord and unrest in Italy, Germany, Switzerland, Spain and Portugal. In 1848, successful revolutions took place in France, Germany, Italy and Austria-Hungary, and the established order faced serious challenges in Spain, Denmark and Romania.[12]

The most important examples of domestic unrest were the Swing riots of 1830 and the Chartist movement of 1838–48. 'Captain Swing' was a revolt of agricultural labourers who objected to the introduction of new methods of production (particularly, the introduction of threshing machines) and the increased level of poverty in rural districts. The movement was launched in Lower Hardres, near Canterbury, in East Kent, in August 1830, and during the course of the next three months it spread to more than twenty English counties. However, the bulk of the disturbances, which usually took the form of rick-burning and machine-breaking, were concentrated in Berkshire, Hampshire, Kent, Norfolk, Sussex and Wiltshire. These counties were responsible for almost two-thirds of all the disturbances recorded in England between 1 January 1830 and 3 September 1832.[13]

In contrast to the Swing riots, which were overwhelmingly rural and agricultural in their orientation, the Chartist movement was much more clearly a movement of the urban centres. In May 1838 the Chartist leaders drew up the first of three national petitions, calling for universal adult male suffrage, secret ballots, the abolition of property qualifications for Members of Parliament, the payment of Members of Parliament, equal electoral districts, and annual elections. The petition was presented to Parliament in July 1839, and in November a Newport draper, John Frost, led an abortive attempt at armed rebellion in South Wales. The Chartists made two further attempts to present their petition to Parliament, in 1842 and 1848. On the last occasion, the Duke of Wellington was summoned from retirement to organise the defence of London, and the presentation of the petition was preceded by a mass demonstration of approximately 20,000 people on the site of what is now Kennington Oval.[14]

Both Captain Swing and the rise of Chartism had a major influence on the social and political debates of the period. The Swing riots caused considerable alarm about the breakdown of social order in rural areas, and played an important part in the establishment and deliberations of the Royal Commission on the Poor Laws.[15] The growth of Chartism forced the reformed House of Commons to demonstrate its ability to legislate in the interests of the country as a whole, and not just those of those sections of the population who were directly represented. Chartism thus played a part in the introduction of such measures as the Mines Act of 1842, the Factory Act of 1844, the Ten Hours Act of 1847, and the Public Health Act of 1848.[16]

3.3   The politics of reform

In a famous article, Oliver MacDonagh argued that the growth of social intervention in the nineteenth century could usually be traced to some form of 'intolerable evil'. The initial exposure of this evil was followed, first by the introduction of permissive legislation, and then by the development of a growing number of administrative controls which were designed to make the legislation more effective. During the 1960s, MacDonagh's critics argued that he had paid insufficient attention to the role of ideas in highlighting the existence of 'intolerable evils', and shaping the public's response to them.[17] At the time, most attention was paid to the ideological impact of Jeremy Bentham and his followers, but, since then, much more attention has been paid to the broader context of eighteenth- and nineteenth-century intellectual thought and to the ideological and practical significance of Adamite and Ricardian economics, Malthusianism, 'moderate' and 'extreme' Evangelicalism, Whiggism and Liberal Toryism.

Adam Smith (1723–90) was one of the founding figures of modern economics. His most famous book, *An inquiry into the nature and causes of the wealth of nations* (1776), was intended 'to explain in what has consisted the revenue of the great body of the people, or what has been the nature of those funds which, in different ages and nations, have supplied their annual consumption', and to establish, first, the necessary expenses of government; second, the methods by which each section of society might be made to contribute to the expenses of the whole; and, third, the causes and consequences of government debt. One of his main aims was to attack the system of controls and regulations, known as mercantilism, which had dominated British economic policy over the preceding 200 years. He argued that the role of government should be limited to the performance of three central duties:

> First, the duty of protecting the society from the violence and invasion of other independent societies; secondly, the duty of protecting … every member of the society from the injustice and oppression of every other member of it … and, thirdly, the duty of erecting and maintaining certain public works and … institutions which it can never be for the interest of any individual, or small number of individuals, to erect and maintain.[18]

Although Smith was firmly convinced of the need to limit the functions of government, it is important to note that he does not appear to have called for the abandonment of the Elizabethan Poor Law, which charged each parish with the responsibility for the maintenance of its own poor. However, whilst he appears to have recognised the need to make some form of communal provision for the relief of poverty, he was strongly opposed to the Settlement Acts, which had been introduced in the mid-seventeenth century in order to protect the rate-payers of one parish from the need to support migrants from neighbouring parishes (see Chapter 4 below). He argued that the difficulty of obtaining a set-tlement, or of proving a right to relief in a particular area, was instrumental in dissuading unemployed workers from moving from one area to another in search of work, and he claimed that this was one of the main causes of the 'very unequal price of labour which we frequently find in England in places at no great distance from one another.' He alleged that 'there is scarce a poor man in England of forty years of age ... who has not in some part of his life felt himself most cruelly opposed by this ill-contrived law of settlements.'[19]

Smith's most immediate successor was the Reverend Thomas Malthus (1766–1834). Although Malthus shared many of Smith's misgivings about the evils of state intervention, he was a supporter of agricultural protectionism, because he believed that this provided the best means of increasing the food supply. However his most famous contribution to the development of eco-nomic thought was derived from his theory of population. He argued that there was a natural tendency for the growth of population to outstrip any increase in the resources available to feed it, and that the unrestricted growth of population would lead inevitably to war, famine or disease. This led him to become a fierce opponent of the existing system of poor relief. He believed that if people could rely on the Poor Law to provide them with a subsistence income, regardless of the size of their families, then one of the principal incentives to the exercise of voluntary restraint would be lost.[20]

Both Smith and Malthus exercised a profound influence on the work of David Ricardo (1772–1823), a City stockbroker who made a fortune speculat-ing on the value of government securities at the end of the Napoleonic Wars before entering Parliament in 1819. Ricardo believed that wages, like other contracts, 'should be left to the fair and free competition of the market and should never be controlled by the interference of the legislature'. He claimed that the Poor Laws diverted resources from the productive sections of the economy, removed the incentives for people to work harder, and encouraged them to have more children than they could afford.[21] In one of many critical passages, he wrote:

> No scheme for the amendment of the poor laws merits the least attention, which has not their abolition for its ultimate object; and he is the best friend to the poor, and to the cause of humanity, who can point out how this end can be attained with the most secu-rity, and ... the least violence ... The principle of gravitation is not more certain than the tendency of such laws to change wealth and power into misery and weakness; to call away the exertions of labour from every object, except that of providing mere subsis-tence; to confound all intellectual distinction; to busy the mind continually in supplying the body's wants; until at last all classes should be infected with the plague of universal poverty.[22]

These ideas also made a significant contribution to the development of Evangelical thought in the early part of the nineteenth century. Although the term 'Evangelicals' has sometimes been used to describe the pre-millenarian or 'extreme' Evangelicals who believed that, just as God intervened in human affairs, so governments had a duty to intervene in society's affairs, the supporters of this view formed only one section of the Evangelical community. In the early-nineteenth century, the majority of Evangelicals (the 'moderates') believed that hardship and misfortune were the predictable consequences of human error. They believed that governments should intervene as little as possible, in order to give people the opportunity to take responsibility for their own lives, and to harmonise their behaviour with the laws of both God and nature.[23]

The divisions between the two branches of Evangelical thought were also reflected in divisions within the Tory party. Mandler argued that many Tories responded to the crisis of aristocratic paternalism in the late-eighteenth and early-nineteenth centuries by attempting to restore traditional patterns of social regulation – 'a strategy exemplified by the proliferation of "poor man's justices" in the southern counties and by Robert Southey's extraordinary paeans ... to the lost gold ages of rural society'.[24] Many of these ideas found a sympathetic echo in the writings of 'radical Tories' such as Thomas Carlyle, and in the ideas and works of Tory philanthropists such as the seventh Earl of Shaftesbury, as well as in the social policies of 'one-nation' Conservatives such as Benjamin Disraeli.[25] However, in the years immediately after 1815, the voices of these more paternalistic Tories were drowned out by the more sceptical tones of such 'Liberal Tories' as George Canning, William Huskisson and Robert Peel. The Liberal Tories combined a more repressive attitude towards social unrest with a much more restrictive approach to the question of social intervention and, in particular, poor relief.[26]

Although a large part of what we might call the 'political nation' in the first third of the nineteenth century was opposed to the expansion of state intervention, there was also a growing body of opinion which believed that the evils associated with poverty, ignorance and ill-health could only be addressed by some form of government activity. In 1784, a Manchester physician, Dr Thomas Percival, persuaded the local magistrates to refuse to allow pauper children to be apprenticed to the owners of cotton mills and other works in which children were obliged to work at night or for more than ten hours during the day, and in 1795 Percival extended his campaign to include the regulation of working hours and conditions for all factory children. In 1802, Parliament passed the Health and Morals of Apprentices Act, which limited the working hours of apprentices to 12 hours during the day, and abolished night work for apprentices from June 1804 onwards. It also insisted that factories employing more than 20 people (regardless of whether they included apprentices) should be whitewashed twice a year, and ventilated at all times. However, even though the Act possessed considerable symbolic importance, it was largely ineffective. This was partly because of its concentration on apprentices (and its failure to distinguish between different categories of apprentice), and partly because it relied too heavily on the ability and willingness of local magistrates to enforce its conditions.[27]

Much of the early concern for factory children was focused on the employment of apprentices, but during the early years of the nineteenth century attention began to shift towards the problem of child labour as a whole. In

1813, the Utopian factory-owner and founder of New Lanark, Robert Owen, launched a campaign to limit working hours and improve factory conditions, and in 1816 Robert Peel established a House of Commons Select Committee to investigate the matter further. In 1819, Parliament agreed to prohibit the employment of children under the age of nine in cotton mills, and said that children between the ages of nine and 16 should not be required to work for more than 12 hours a day, exclusive of mealtimes. In 1820, the opponents of factory reform succeeded in watering down some of the requirements of the 1819 Act, but in 1825 Parliament agreed to limit the maximum amount of time which could be allocated to mealtimes to one and a half hours (thereby limiting the total length of the working day, including meal times, to thirteen and a half hours), and in 1831 these limitations were extended to all persons under the age of 18, with nightwork being prohibited for all those under the age of 21. However, the most important of all the early Factory Acts was the Act of 1833. Although this Act was in some ways rather less generous than its predecessors (it only prohibited nightwork for those under the age of 18), it covered all types of textile mill (rather than just cotton mills), and it established the first independent factory inspectorate. Even though there were only four inspectors, the Act represented a major step forward in terms of the state's acceptance of its responsibility to provide some means of effective protection for the most vulnerable members of the working population.[28]

As Fraser has argued, the early Factory Acts represented an important extension of the state's role in protecting the interests of children, but they also tended to reinforce the view that adults were independent individuals who should continue to be held responsible for their own working conditions.[29] However, there was also a growing body of opinion which believed that some form of additional intervention was necessary in the areas of education and public health, if only to preserve order and stability. In 1832, the Benthamite reformer, James Phillips Kay (later Kay-Shuttleworth) argued that it would soon become necessary to establish 'permanent organised centres of medical police, where municipal powers will be directed by scientific men to the removal of those agencies which most powerfully depress the physical condition of the inhabitants', and in 1833 J. A. Roebuck persuaded Parliament to award an annual grant of £20,000 to the Church of England National Society for the Education of the Children of the Poor and the British and Foreign Schools Society to enable them to build schools for working-class children in the north of England.[30] This small measure provided a launching pad for the introduction of a long series of reforms which significantly extended the role of government in social affairs, including the establishment of the Metropolitan Police force and the creation of the Privy Council Committee on Education in 1839, the introduction of government grants for the purchase of school equipment and teacher training in 1843 and 1846, and the formation of the General Board of Health in 1848.[31]

Roberts argued that even though many people conceded the need for reform, 'few English thinkers … had a comprehensive theory of government and fewer systematic awareness of the problems of public administration,' but this interpretation has been challenged, or at least qualified, by Peter Mandler's account of the role played by the Whigs in promoting the growth of state intervention between 1830 and 1852. Mandler argued that during the second half of the eighteenth century the Whigs had defined themselves primarily by their attitude to the role of the monarchy, but during the first half of the nineteenth century they became increasingly interested in social questions. During the early-1830s, they played a leading role in the campaign to reform the Poor Laws, on the grounds that these were undermining the fabric of rural society by encouraging poverty, but they also recognised the need for much more interventionist approaches to such issues as education, factory reform, the establishment of municipal corporations, and public health. Mandler also suggested that Roberts may have underestimated the Whigs' enthusiasm for centralisation. Even though they often claimed that they had no 'abstract love for centralisation', they also oversaw many of the most important developments in the construction of what Roberts described as 'that most rambling of structures, the Victorian administrative state'. This was reflected in their support for the establishment of a long list of central government agencies, including the creation of the factory and prison inspectorates, the Poor Law Commission, the Privy Council Committee on Education, and the General Board of Health.[32]

One of the most important disagreements between Roberts and Mandler concerns their account of the relationship between the Whigs and the Benthamites. Roberts believed that because the Whigs did not have a 'theory of government' of their own, they relied on the Benthamites to provide a consistent and thoroughgoing model of how an interventionist state might work, whereas Mandler argued that this underestimated the extent to which the Whigs were capable of developing their own independent rationale for government growth. One of the main differences between the two groups concerned their attitude to the relationship between the government and the people. The Whigs believed that it was not only appropriate but also necessary for the government to take on the mantle of social reform in order to demonstrate that the governing élite was responsive to popular needs, whereas the Benthamites deplored what Mandler calls 'the Whigs' pandering to agitation', whilst insisting that the case for government growth should only be made on the basis of scientific investigation and rational enquiry.[33]

Dicey suggested that the apparent popularity of Benthamite ideas could be explained on the grounds that Benthamism, or 'legislative Utilitarianism' was 'nothing less than systematised individualism, and individualism has always found its natural home in England', but this interpretation has often been criticised as an oversimplification of Bentham's ideas.[34] As Halévy showed, Bentham and his followers were strongly influenced by the teachings of the political economists and they shared many of the concerns of the Liberal Tories, but they also believed that government could play a positive role in framing laws and institutions which would mould human behaviour and, perhaps most importantly, promote what Bentham himself called 'the greatest happiness of the greatest number'.[35] In recent years, historians have tended to play down the significance of the Benthamites in their understandable desire to shed more light on the social and political attitudes of the politicians who actually held the reins of power. However, the Benthamites in general, and the indefatigable

Edwin Chadwick in particular, played a major role in the development and implementation of a wide range of new policies, including not only the introduction of the New Poor Law, but also the establishment of both the Metropolitan and county police forces, the development of a national education system, the reform of working conditions and, of course, the introduction of the Public Health Act.[36]

3.4 The standard of living

The economic and social changes associated with the Industrial Revolution have led to a long-lasting and highly polarised debate about the impact of industrialisation on the standard of living. Clapham claimed that 'after the price fall of 1820–1, the purchasing power of wages in general – not, of course, everyone's wages – was definitely greater than it had been just before the Revolutionary and Napoleonic Wars,' but J. L. Hammond argued that, even if it could be proved that the purchasing power of wages in general had improved, this would still form only part of the story. He concluded:

> There were thousands of men and women for whom life was easier and more comfortable because the industrial revolution had given them stockings and cotton clothes without making them pay the price that the mill-worker paid, or thought he paid, for these improvements. But the ugliness of the new life, with its growing slums, its lack of beautiful buildings, its destruction of nature and its disregard of man's deeper needs, affected not this or that class of worker only, but the entire working-class population.[37]

Despite their obvious limitations, the most obvious starting point for any discussion of the impact of industrialisation on the standard of living is the question of real wages. Lindert concluded that the average level of real wages showed no clear signs of progress between *circa* 1750 and 1820, and then rose substantially between 1820 and 1850. He claimed that these trends were still apparent, even after making allowances for fluctuations in unemployment, and the value of the wages paid to women and children.[38] However, Feinstein has recently presented new data, based not only on information about wages and prices, but also about levels of labour force participation and changes in the ratio of workers to dependants, which suggest that the extent of any improvement was much more limited. He argued that the average level of real wages may have begun to increase as early as the 1770s, but in spite of this, the average working-class family was still only 10–15 per cent better off at the beginning of the 1850s.[39]

In view of the problems associated with the analysis of real wage data, it is not surprising that historians should have also looked at other forms of evidence, and, in particular, at statistics of health and mortality. Wrigley *et al.*'s investigations into the history of mortality suggest that even though average life expectancy rose between the mid-eighteenth century and the end of the 1820s, there was little progress between *circa* 1830 and 1870.[40] Although the authors made little attempt to explain the reasons for this stagnation, the most obvious explanation is that it was linked to the pattern of urbanisation. It is well known that urban conditions were more damaging to health than rural conditions, and it is not unreasonable to conclude that the disproportionate increase in the size of the urban population acted as a brake on the improvements in aggregate mortality rates which might otherwise have occurred.[41]

In addition to looking at real wages and mortality rates, historians have also focused attention on the questions of education and literacy. The majority of educational historians believe that educational opportunities expanded during the first two-thirds of the eighteenth century, before declining, in the face of rising population growth and an increased demand for child labour, between about 1780 and 1830. This view is broadly consistent with the results obtained from various investigations into the level of adult literacy. These investigations, which are usually based on the numbers of marriage partners signing their names in the parish registers, suggest that even though literacy levels rose during the first half of the eighteenth century, they changed very little between the middle of the eighteenth century and the middle of the nineteenth century.[42]

In recent years, economists and demographers have sought to develop a composite index of human welfare, known as the Human Development Index, to measure changes in the standard of living of men and women living in different parts of the world today. The index utilises available information on Gross Domestic Product *per capita*, life expectancy at birth and basic literacy. Floud and Harris used a modified form of the Human Development Index to measure changes in the standard of living of the British population between 1756 and 1981. They found that there was very little change, either in the individual components of the Human Development Index or in its overall value, before the end of the eighteenth century. There was rather more evidence of an improvement in average living standards between *circa* 1800 and 1830, but this was followed by a further period of stagnation between 1830 and 1850, and it was only after 1850 that average living standards began to show a sustained pattern of improvement up to the present day.[43]

The results of this analysis are broadly consistent with the conclusions obtained by Floud, Wachter and Gregory in their study of soldiers' heights in the United Kingdom between 1750 and 1914. It is well known that the average value of children's heights and rates of growth is highly sensitive to fluctuations in the quantity and quality of their diet, and to changes in environmental conditions, and this has led some historians to argue that height provides a good summary measure of those aspects of life which are generally understood by the term 'standard of living'.[44] Floud, Wachter and Gregory argued that the average heights of successive birth cohorts rose between the 1740s and 1760s, fell between the 1760s and the 1780s, rose once more between the 1780s and the 1820s, and fell sharply between the 1820s and the 1850s. They concluded that:

> The early part of the Industrial Revolution led to an absolute as well as relative increase in the welfare and nutritional status of the working class, but…the impact of urban growth eroded this increase and even led to decreases in average height as larger proportions of the working-class community were subjected to town life. This erosion and decrease took place despite well-attested rises in real wages for the bulk of town-dwellers. This finding is the main contribution of this book to the lengthy debate about the standard of living of the British working class.[45]

3.5   Conclusions

This chapter has highlighted some of the most important aspects of social, economic and political life in early-nineteenth-century Britain. In addition to being a period of profound economic change, these years also witnessed growing evidence of civil and political unrest, and the emergence of new ways of thinking about economic and social problems. These new ways of thinking led to major changes in the relationship between central and local government, and the role of the state in relation to social policy. The impact of these changes on the growth of state intervention, and the relationship between public and private forms of welfare provision, will form the subject of the following chapters.

The New Poor Law and the relief of poverty, 1834–1914

Although the agricultural writer, Arthur Young, believed that 'everyone but an idiot knows that the lower classes must be kept poor, or they will never be industrious', other writers regarded the equation of the 'labouring classes' and 'the poor' as counterproductive. In 1797, the Conservative philosopher, Edmund Burke, argued that 'when we affect to pity, as poor, those who must labour or the world cannot exist, we are trifling with the condition of mankind.' In Burke's eyes, 'this affected pity only tends to dissatisfy them with their condition, and to teach them to seek resources where no resources are to be found, in something else than their own industry, and frugality, and sobriety.'[1]

Social commentators continued to use the term 'poor' in a variety of ways, but Burke's arguments about the need to distinguish between those who were able to work and those who were not are central to understanding the changes which affected the administration of the English Poor Law during the first half of the nineteenth century. In 1834, Parliament passed the Poor Law Amendment Act, which created the central Poor Law Commission and introduced far-reaching changes in the conduct of Poor Law policy. The aim of this chapter is to examine the background to this legislation, and to understand its impact on the system of poor relief in England and Wales during the remainder of the century.

4.1 The Old Poor Law, 1597–1834

The foundations of the Poor Law in England and Wales were laid by a series of Acts passed in the late-fifteenth and sixteenth centuries, and owed as much to concerns about the preservation of public order as they did to the relief of poverty. In 1495, local magistrates were empowered to punish vagrants and return them to their original homes, and in 1531, they were allowed to issue licences to 'deserving paupers' in order to allow them to beg. In the autumn of 1535, an anonymous author drafted a Bill which recognised that many people were unable to work for a living despite being willing to do so, recommended the establishment of a national (though temporary) programme of public works (in return for 'reasonable wages'), outlined plans for an annual levy or graduated income tax, and advocated the provision of free medical care for the poor, but these proposals were never implemented. However, in 1536, magistrates were given the power to outlaw 'indiscriminate almsgiving' and set vagabonds to work, whilst also allowing poor children to be set to service and authorising the establishment of weekly collections for the relief of the 'impotent poor'.[2]

Although the Poor Law of 1536 had little practical effect, it did lay down the main lines along which English Poor Law policy was to develop over the next 60 years. In 1547, the government introduced an ineffective measure to impose two years of slavery on convicted vagabonds, but it also introduced new policies regarding the employment of poor children and the collection of funds for the 'impotent', and in 1563 it agreed that those who refused to contribute to the upkeep of the poor might be bound over to appear before the local magistrates. The Poor Law of 1572 instructed the magistrates to establish the number of poor people in their area and to tax and assess the inhabitants of each area to pay for them, and in 1576 magistrates were given the power to establish Houses of Correction and to maintain stocks of materials which would enable the able-bodied poor to be 'set on work'. These Acts culminated in the famous Elizabethan Poor Laws of 1597 (39 Elizabeth I C. 43) and 1601 (43 Elizabeth I C. 2). These Acts relieved the magistrates of any responsibility for the day-to-day administration of the Poor Law by giving the churchwardens and overseers of each parish the right to levy a tax, or poor rate, on every inhabitant, and every occupier of land, and by making them responsible for 'setting the poor on work', maintaining those who were unable to work, and boarding out pauper children to become apprentices, and they defined the basic features of the English system of poor relief for the next 230 years.[3]

The establishment of what later became known as the 'Old' Poor Law was a unique achievement in the context of early-modern social policy. Despite its geographical proximity, Scotland only possessed a much more rudimentary system of poor relief, and Ireland lacked any poor law at all before 1838.[4] The English Poor Law was also without parallel elsewhere in Europe. In most parts of Protestant Europe, welfare provision was coordinated by the state through a mixture of local, municipal and parochial agencies, whilst in Catholic Europe provision was much more dependent (though by no means exclusively so) on the support of the Church, but the English system was unique because of its extensive reliance on a system of compulsory taxation.[5] As Alexis de Tocqueville observed in 1835, 'the only country in Europe which has systematised and applied the theories of public charity on a grand scale is England.' He also claimed, rather more controversially, that this was one of the main reasons why the level of indigence in England was much greater than that found elsewhere.[6]

Although Slack has argued that the Poor Law was 'in all essentials... complete' in 1601, this does not mean that no further changes were introduced over the course of the next two centuries.[7] The Elizabethan Acts failed to establish the machinery needed to ensure that every parish honoured its obligations consistently, and this encouraged many poor people to migrate to the more generous areas. In 1662 the government attempted to address this difficulty by introducing what subsequently became known as the Act of Settlement (3 & 4 Charles II C. 12), under which the overseers of each parish were given the power to remove any strangers who were likely to become a charge on the parish, provided that they did so within 40 days of the newcomers' arrival. During the eighteenth century, this Act became the subject of particular controversy amongst the advocates of free trade. Adam Smith declared that whilst 'the obstruction which the Corporation Laws give to the free circulation of labour is common … to every part of Europe[, t]hat which is given to it by the poor laws is … peculiar to England. It consists in the difficulty which a poor man finds in obtaining a settlement, or even in being allowed to exercise his industry, in any parish but that to which he belongs.'[8]

Adam Smith regarded the Settlement Act as 'the greatest [disorder] perhaps of any in the police of England', but others were more concerned with controlling the cost of poor relief and making appropriate arrangements for 'setting the poor on work'.[9] In 1691 Parliament instructed the parish overseers to submit a list of the names of all those who received relief to an annual meeting of the parish ratepayers, or 'vestry'. The Act (3 William & Mary C. 12) stated that nobody should be entitled to receive relief unless their name had been approved by the vestry, or with the approval of the nearest magistrate. The Poor Law Act of 1722 (9 George II C. 7) gave overseers the power to build special houses 'to keep, maintain and employ all such poor in their respective parishes … as shall desire to receive relief or collection from the same parish', and to deny relief to anyone who 'shall refuse to be lodged, kept or maintained in such houses'. However, by the 1760s many overseers believed that it would be cheaper to relieve the able-bodied poor in their own homes.[10] This change was reflected in the passage of Gilbert's Act in 1782 (22 George III C. 83), which stated that 'no person shall be sent to such poor house or houses, except such as are become indigent by old age, sickness or infirmities; and except such orphan children as shall be sent thither by Order of the Guardians … and such children as shall necessarily go with their mothers … for sustenance.'

The outbreak of the Napoleonic Wars led to considerable economic and social dislocation, and the Poor Law itself came under increasing pressure. In 1795 magistrates in a number of areas, including the Berkshire parish of Speenhamland, near Newbury, decided to introduce a system of wage subsidies, under which poorly paid labourers could apply to the magistrates to have their wages 'made up' by allowances from the poor rates. In December 1795, the Whig MP, Samuel Whitbread, made an unsuccessful attempt to give magistrates the power to regulate agricultural wages, and in the following year, the Tory Prime Minister, William Pitt the Younger, introduced his own consolidated proposals for Poor Law reform, including the provision of relief to large families, the introduction of 'Schools of Industry', a compulsory friendly society scheme, the use of loans, and the provision of relief to the owners of small properties.[11] However, although both Bills were generally regarded as being well intentioned, they also provoked a storm of criticism. The legal philosopher, Jeremy Bentham, complained that Pitt's Bill placed 'the *idle* and *negligent* exactly upon a footing in point of prosperity and reward with the *diligent* and *industrious*'.[12]

During the late-eighteenth and early-nineteenth centuries, a number of different strands of opinion began to converge in favour of a harsher and more restrictive attitude to the provision of poor relief. In 1795, Edmund Burke argued that it was necessary to draw a clear distinction between those who were 'poor' because they were obliged to work, and those who were, in his view, genuinely poor because they were unable to work. He argued that it was wrong in any case to expect the state to assume responsibility for the relief of poverty, and that such responsibility ought to be left in the hands of private charity. However, he denied that charitable individuals had any obligation to relieve the wants of those who were capable of supporting themselves.[13]

Burke's efforts to limit the use of the word 'poor' to those who were unable to work were only partially successful, but his efforts to distinguish between the different types of poverty were much more influential.[14] In 1796, Jeremy Bentham redrafted Burke's original distinction in terms of a distinction between 'poverty' and 'indigence'. He argued that 'poverty is the state of everyone who, in order to obtain *subsistence*, is forced to have recourse to *labour*. Indigence is the state of him who, being destitute of property ... is at the same time *unable to labour* or unable, even *for* labour, to procure the supply of which he happens thus to be in want.'[15] This distinction was developed by Patrick Colquhoun in 1799 and again in 1806, and it exercised a major impact on the authors of the Poor Law Report in 1834.[16]

Even though writers such as Bentham and Colquhoun thought that the scope of poor relief ought to be restricted, they did not argue that the Poor Law ought to be abolished altogether; such arguments were advanced, however, by Thomas Malthus and David Ricardo. Malthus argued that the poor laws diverted resources from 'the ... more industrious and more worthy members' of the population, and encouraged people to marry and have children before they were able to support them, thereby exacerbating the tendency 'to increase population without increasing the food for its support'. Ricardo claimed that 'the clear and direct tendency of the poor laws ... is not, as the legislature benevolently intended, to amend the condition of the poor, but to deteriorate the condition of both poor and rich ... and, whilst the present laws are in force, it is quite in the natural order of things that the fund for maintenance of the poor should progressively increase until it has absorbed all the net revenue of the country, or at least so much of it as the state shall leave to us, after satisfying its own never-failing demands for the public expenditure.'[17]

The argument in favour of abolition gained further support from the statistics of Poor Law expenditure. During the period between 1783–5 and 1802–3, the annual cost of poor relief rose from just under £2,000,000 to £4,000,000, and it doubled again between 1802–3 and 1818.[18] This increase could only partly be explained by the increase in the size of the population. As we can see from Figure 4.1, the average annual cost of poor relief per head in England and Wales rose from just over two shillings in the middle of the eighteenth century to four shillings in 1776, more than nine shillings in 1802–3, and 13 shillings in 1818.

In 1816, the maverick Whig MP and 'self-styled spokesman for the landed interest', J. C. Curwen, persuaded Parliament to appoint a Select Committee on the Poor Laws.[19] This Committee, which was chaired by the Radical Tory, William Sturges-Bourne, was unable to complete its deliberations in 1816, and was reappointed in the following year. Although it stopped short of recommending outright abolition, its Report showed clear evidence of abolitionist sympathies. Under the heading 'Evils of Present System', it observed that 'by diminishing the natural impulse by which men are instigated to industry and

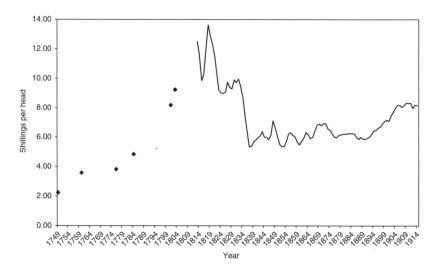

Sources: S. Webb and B. Webb, *English Poor Law History. Part II. The last hundred years* (first edition 1929), London: Frank Cass, 1963, pp. 1037–40; B. R. Mitchell, *British historical statistics*, Cambridge: Cambridge University Press, 1988, pp. 11–13, 605; A. Kidd, *State, society and the poor in nineteenth-century England*, Basingstoke: Macmillan (now Palgrave Macmillan), 1999, p. 168.

Figure 4.1 Poor law expenditure per head of population in England and Wales, 1749–1914

good conduct, by superseding the necessity of providing in the season of health and vigour for the wants of sickness and old age, [and] by making poverty and misery the conditions in which relief is to be obtained, your Committee cannot but fear… that this system is perpetually encouraging and increasing the amount of misery it was designed to alleviate.'[20] Its principal practical recommendations were for the reform of the local system of Poor Law administration in order to give greater authority to larger land-owners. These recommendations were reflected in the Select Vestries Acts of 1818 and 1819, which gave large land-owners greater power over the appointment of vestry members, and enabled resident clergymen to sit as *ex officio* members.[21]

The Select Vestries Acts (also known as the Sturges-Bourne Acts) contributed to the reduction of Poor Law expenditure during the first half of the 1820s, and prompted the Royal Commission on the Poor Laws to argue that 'the Acts under which the ratepayers are empowered to elect a Committee for the management of their parochial concerns have proved highly beneficial.'[22] However, during the second half of the 1820s the number of select vestries began to decline, and, perhaps coincidentally, the cost of poor relief began to rise, prompting renewed calls for reform. In 1828, a group of magistrates, meeting in Cambridgeshire, called for the system of select vestries to be made mandatory across the whole country, and the House of Commons appointed a Select Committee to investigate 'that part of the poor laws relating to the employment or relief of able-bodied persons from the poor rate'. In 1830, the Commons' Select Committee on Select and Other Vestries echoed the call made by the Cambridge magistrates two years earlier.[23]

Although a number of attempts were made to introduce further changes into the system of poor law administration towards the end of the 1820s, the most important event prior to the passage of the Poor Law Amendment Act in 1834 was the outbreak of a series of riots and arson attacks in the southern counties of England during 1830 and 1831. Historians have offered different interpretations of these outbreaks – some regard them as sporadic outbreaks of disorder, whilst others believe that they constituted a serious challenge to the existing social order – but there is little doubt over the extent to which they alarmed the landed élite.[24] The Swing riots appeared to be most prevalent in areas where the allowance system – the system of subsidising wages out of the poor rate – was most highly developed, and this reinforced claims that the existing system of poor relief was not only a potent cause of poverty, but also a serious threat to social peace.[25] The apparent association between the breakdown of law and order and high levels of poor relief was one of the most important factors behind the decision to appoint the Royal Commission on the Poor Laws in 1832.

4.2 The Poor Law Report of 1834

The Royal Commission which was appointed in February 1832 was responsible for what was arguably the most important single document (or set of documents) in the history of British social policy, certainly in the nineteenth century. Although appointed by the Whigs, it was chaired by the Tory Bishop of London, Charles Blomfeld, and included eight other members, together with a further 26 Assistant Commissioners. Its most influential members were the economist, Nassau Senior (Professor of Political Economy at the University of Oxford), and the Benthamite reformer, Edwin Chadwick, who became a full member of the Commission in 1833. Senior has been credited with responsibility for directing the investigation and negotiating with members of the Cabinet; Chadwick was responsible for drafting some of the most important sections of the Report, and for helping to ensure that at least some of its recommendations were subsequently translated into action.[26]

Although the Report is best known for its criticisms of the existing methods of poor relief, it also devoted a great deal of attention to questions of administration. The Commissioners condemned the appointment of unpaid overseers to administer the Poor Law because 'neither diligence nor zeal are to be expected from persons on whom a disagreeable and unpaid office has been forced, and whose functions cease by the time that they have begun to acquire a knowledge of them.' They questioned the representativeness of the ratepayers' meetings, or vestries, which had been set up to control the power of the overseers, because they excluded large land-owners who were not actually resident in the area, and claimed that they were 'the most irresponsible bodies that ever were entrusted with the performance of public duties, or the distribution of public money'. They believed that the involvement of magistrates in the administration of poor relief had also been counter-productive, because too many magistrates lived outside the areas for which they were responsible, and this led them to support applications for relief without consulting the parish officers.[27]

However, although the Report called for major changes in the administrative structure of the Poor Law, it reserved its most sweeping criticisms for the basis upon which relief was administered. It argued that the allowance system – the system of subsidising wages out of the poor rate – destroyed work incentives, because it encouraged workers to believe that their incomes no longer depended upon their own efforts, and that it depressed wages, because employers could no longer afford to pay the full cost of their own wages, together with the costs of an inflated poor rate, and because they could not compete with low-wage competitors. It also argued that the Poor Law demoralised 'independent labourers', because they could see that other people were being supported even though they were not working, and because the existence of such a large number of paupers made their own situation more precarious. However, the Commissioners believed that the group who suffered the greatest disadvantage under the existing system were the paupers themselves. These individuals became 'callous to their own degradation', and their reliance on poor relief drove a barrier between themselves and their families, and weakened, if not destroyed, 'all ... ties of affection'.[28]

The Commission's description of the Old Poor Law has often been questioned. The Webbs argued that 'the investigation was far from being impartially or judicially directed and carried out', and that the absence of any attempt to estimate the extent of either pauperism or poverty 'led ... to disastrous errors in proportion; and made the suggested remedial measures lopsided and seriously imperfect'.[29] Blaug published two highly influential articles which showed that the allowance system was less widespread than the Commissioners alleged, and that it was far more likely to have developed in response to rural poverty than to have been a cause of it.[30] Huzel showed that there were no grounds for supporting the view, advanced by Thomas Malthus and reiterated by the Commission, that the allowance system either encouraged population growth or discouraged labour mobility.[31] Boyer concluded that the system of outdoor relief as a whole 'was an endogenous response to changes in the economic environment of the rural south and east ... [which] substituted outdoor relief and, in particular, unemployment insurance, for allotments and employment in cottage industry'.[32]

Although the Commission almost certainly exaggerated the perceived evils of the Old Poor Law, it did not claim that the community's obligation to provide a statutory system of poor relief could be abandoned altogether. It argued that 'to refuse relief, and at the same time to punish mendicity when it cannot be proved that the offender could have obtained subsistence by labour, is repugnant to the common sentiments of mankind,' and that as a result of this, 'in all extensive civilised communities ... the occurrence of extreme necessity is prevented by alms-giving, by public institutions supported by endowments or voluntary contributions, or by a provision partly voluntary and partly compulsory, or by a provision entirely compulsory, which may exclude the pretext of mendicancy.' However, it then went on, in terms sharply reminiscent of Jeremy Bentham, to attempt to circumscribe the sphere of public generosity by drawing a clear distinction between indigence and poverty. It argued that 'in no part of Europe except England has it been thought fit that the provision, whether compulsory of voluntary, should be applied to more than the relief of *indigence*, the state of a person unable to labour, or unable to obtain, in return for his labour, the means of subsistence. It has never been deemed expedient that the provision should extend to the relief of *poverty*, that is, to the state of one who, in order to obtain a mere subsistence, is forced to have recourse to labour.'[33] This distinction provides the key to understanding its subsequent recommendations.

The Poor Law Report was designed to devise a system of public relief which would be capable of distinguishing the indigent from the merely poor. In order to achieve this, the Commissioners argued that 'the first and most essential of all conditions, a principle, which we find universally admitted, even by those whose practice is at variance with it, is that [the] situation [of the pauper] shall not be made really or apparently so eligible as the situation of the independent labourer of the lowest class.' It believed that the best way to put this principle into practice was by abolishing the distribution of outdoor relief to able-bodied persons and their families, and by ensuring that such individuals only qualified for relief if they agreed to enter a 'well regulated workhouse'. The Commissioners claimed that such a system would provide an infallible test of genuine destitution: 'if the claimant does not comply with the terms on which relief is given to the destitute, he gets nothing; and if he does comply, the com-pliance proves the truth of the claim – namely his destitution.' There would therefore be no need for any further regulations, or appeals procedures, to decide whether an individual's claim was genuine or not.[34]

The Commission also put forward a number of far-reaching proposals for reforming the administrative structure of the Poor Law. Prior to 1834, one of the defining characteristics of the English Poor Law had been its 'intensely localised' character.[35] Under the Acts of 1597 and 1601, Parliament imposed a basic duty on all parishes to make provision for the relief of destitution, but no central body was created to oversee its administration, and each parish retained control of its own arrangements. The Royal Commission on the Poor Laws chal-lenged this in two ways. In the first place, it called for the appointment of 'a central Board to control the administration of the Poor Laws, with … [the power] to frame and enforce regulations for the government of workhouses' and to impose these, in the most uniform possible manner, across the entire country. Second, in order to improve the efficiency of local administration, it recommended that 'the central Board be empowered to cause any number of parishes which they think convenient to be incorporated for the purpose of workhouse management, and for providing new workhouses where necessary'.[36] These two recommendations – the establishment of a central coordinating authority and the creation of Poor Law Unions – were among the most important legacies of the Royal Commission on the Poor Laws, and they represented a major change in the history of central–local relations in the nineteenth century.

4.3 The New Poor Law, 1834–70

Following the publication of the Poor Law Report, two of the original Commissioners, Nassau Senior and William Sturges-Bourne, were given the responsibility for drafting a new Poor Law Bill, but they did not work alone. They were required to consult frequently with members of the Cabinet, and they also worked closely with the indefatigable Edwin Chadwick, who had started to circulate his own legislative proposals even before the Report was completed, and was bitterly disappointed not to have been asked to take formal responsibility for the Bill himself. The new Bill was introduced by the Chancellor of the Exchequer, Viscount Althorp, on 17 April, and passed through the House of Commons with relatively little difficulty, but it encountered much more opposition outside the House of Commons, and the government was forced to make a number of significant concessions before the Bill became law.[37]

As we have already seen, the Poor Law Report devoted particular attention to the 'evils' of the allowance system, and this was reflected in the government's original proposals. When Althorp introduced the Poor Law Amendment Bill, he argued that it was 'essentially necessary' to fix a day 'when the allowance system, as it was called, should entirely and altogether cease', and the Bill itself proposed that 'no overseer, guardian or other person having the distribution of the poor rates shall give any relief…to able-bodied persons or their families, who at the time of applying for such relief shall be wholly or partially in the employment of any person or persons' after 1 June 1835.[38] However, even though this clause passed through the Commons with comparatively little difficulty, Chadwick failed to convince the influential Conservative peer, the Marquis of Salisbury, to support its passage through the Lords, and the government was forced to substitute a new proposal which gave the members of the new Poor Law Commission the power to issue 'rules, orders or regulations… declar[ing] to what extent and for what period the relief to be given to able-bodied persons or…their families…may be administered'.[39] When Althorp presented this amendment to the House of Commons, he argued that the changes were not particularly important because the overseers or guardians would still have to justify the special circumstances 'which, in their opinion, might render such relief expedient in any particular case' but it also meant that the Commissioners would now have to negotiate changes in relief policy with local guardians, rather than imposing their will upon them by legislative fiat.[40]

Ministers were also forced to accept modifications to their original proposals for changes in the arrangements governing plural voting, the role of magistrates in authorising the payment of outdoor relief, the age at which children were deemed to be responsible for their own welfare, the opportunity to provide relief in the form of loans, the administration of the settlement laws, the maintenance of children born out of wedlock, and the right of Dissenting Ministers to enter workhouses.[41] The government regarded the majority of these changes as being relatively unimportant, but the disagreements over the question of bastardy were particularly heated. When the Bill was first introduced, the government had tried to place the whole of the responsibility for maintaining illegitimate children on the mother, but the Commons had baulked at the apparent unfairness of this and Ministers accepted a proposal by the MP for East Somerset, William Gore-Langton, to give parish overseers the right, under certain circumstances, to recover the costs of any additional poor relief from the child's father.[42] However, when the Bill was debated by the House of Lords, a new clause was inserted which made it virtually impossible for parishes to issue orders against errant fathers by insisting that such orders could only be issued at the Quarter Sessions and that additional evidence, beyond that provided by the mother, would be required to prove paternity.[43]

Although the government had been forced to accept a number of modifications to its original Bill, the passage of the new Poor Law Amendment Act was nevertheless an extremely important moment in the history of British social policy. Its most important innovation was the establishment of a new central body, known as the Poor Law Commission, 'to make and issue … rules, orders and regulations for the management of the poor' throughout England and Wales. The Commissioners were given the power to appoint up to nine Assistant Commissioners (although the number could be increased with the support of the Treasury), and to create Unions of parishes 'for the administration of the laws for the relief of the poor'. However, although the Act conferred unprecedented powers on the central authority, it also fell some way short of the plans and recommendations of the Poor Law Report. It failed to abolish outdoor relief, and the Commissioners were only permitted to order the construction of workhouses 'by and with the consent in writing of a majority of the Guardians of any Union, or with the consent of a majority of the ratepayers and owners of property entitled to vote' in Guardians' elections.[44]

When the Poor Law Amendment Act was passed, there was widespread support for the principles of the New Poor Law among the rural élite, and the Commissioners' efforts to implement the new legislation in rural areas passed off largely without incident. However, the Commissioners encountered much fiercer resistance when they attempted to implement the New Poor Law in many northern areas. The opposition was led by the existing local authorities, who regarded the construction of workhouses as an inappropriate and expensive solution to the problem of urban unemployment, and who resented the threat posed by the Poor Law Commission to local autonomy. It was reinforced by working-class organisations who wanted to defend traditional relief rights, and to prevent the incarceration of the poor in inhuman 'bastiles'. The combined weight of the opposition led to a number of delays in the creation of Poor Law Unions. The Commissioners were forced to give assurances that control over the administration of poor relief would remain in the hands of local Guardians, and no new workhouses were constructed in the West Riding of Yorkshire throughout the 1840s.[45]

Although the Royal Commission had recommended the establishment of workhouses as an essential part of its strategy for deterring claimants of outdoor relief, many Boards of Guardians believed that they represented an expensive and impractical solution to the problem of able-bodied pauperism and both the Poor Law Commission and its successor, the Poor Law Board, were forced to pursue alternative strategies for achieving their objectives. During the 1830s and 1840s, the Commission issued a stream of regulations, some of which limited the distribution of outdoor relief to all destitute persons other than able-bodied males, whilst others said that outdoor relief should only be granted to able-bodied males under exceptional circumstances, but they were also forced to recognise that this policy might still prove impractical in northern manufacturing districts. As a result, the Commissioners decided to introduce the 'outdoor labour test', which allowed Boards of Guardians to distribute outdoor relief to able-bodied men in return for a task of work.[46] The outdoor labour test was clearly much cheaper than the 'workhouse test', but it performed a similar deterrent function. As Anthony Brundage has recently observed, the test 'was to be as unpleasant and monotonous as possible, stone-breaking and oakum-picking being the leading examples of such drudgery. Thus, it was thought, the "less eligibility" principle could be honoured without compelling a worker and his family to enter the workhouse.'[47]

Whilst the introduction of the Outdoor Labour Test Order enabled many Boards of Guardians to offer relief to able-bodied men without requiring them to enter a workhouse, there were still many other categories of pauper – children, women, the sick and the elderly – who were compelled by circumstances to enter its doors.[48] When Chadwick and Senior were writing the Poor Law Report, they had outlined plans for the creation of a number of different workhouse institutions, each of which would cater for a different type of need, but the Poor Law Commission abandoned this idea in favour of the 'general mixed workhouse', which would not only be cheaper than the creation of several more specialised institutions, but also act as a much more potent symbol of the Guardians' authority.[49] Finer suggested that if it had been possible to realise Chadwick's vision, the results would have been considerably more humane than the 'promiscuous barracks' which actually resulted but, as Crowther has argued, there is little evidence to show that Chadwick actually resisted the Commissioners' decision at the time it was being reached. Nevertheless, it seems clear that the new workhouses did indeed become 'places of dread' to many of those who might be forced to enter them.[50]

During the 1830s and 1840s, the editor of *The Times* published more than a hundred accounts of workhouse cruelty, including 16 allegations of children being separated from their parents and elderly husbands from their wives; 32 accounts of cruel punishments, including dowsings with cold water and floggings; 14 accounts of overcrowding; 24 allegations of inadequate diet; ten accounts of diseased conditions; and seven 'workhouse murders'. Roberts examined the results of official enquiries into 21 of these allegations and concluded that 12 were largely false, five were largely correct, and four 'went uninvestigated'. His overall conclusion was that many of the worst abuses were encountered in those parts of the country where the local authorities had been most reluctant to implement the New Poor Law in the first place, and that when cruelty did occur, it usually occurred in spite of the efforts of the Poor Law Commissioners rather than as a direct result of the new regime. However, other historians have argued that Roberts was too ready to accept the conclusions reached by official investigators, and that he tended to ignore the extent to which the New Poor Law itself created a climate of opinion in which abuses were more likely to occur.[51]

Even though the workhouse was designed, at least in part, to deter able-bodied men from seeking relief, it was also intended to provide institutional accommodation to those sections of the population who were unable to manage by themselves either in their own homes or 'in the community', but its ability to do this humanely was severely compromised by the principle of 'less eligibility'. As both Brundage and Crowther have shown, the physical appearance of the workhouse, with its 'grim, prison-like exterior', was explicitly designed to intimidate the surrounding population, and this impression was reinforced by the conditions within. When paupers entered the workhouse, they were required to surrender their own clothes in return for a drab workhouse uniform, family members were separated and assigned to separate wards, and all those who were deemed capable of work were expected to do so. Meals were monotonous and unappetising, and were expected to be eaten in silence, whilst sleeping accommodation was provided in dormitories which offered little opportunity for personal privacy. In 1834, Chadwick and Senior had argued that the work which was carried on inside the workhouse ought to be 'useful employment', but in practice the work was usually of a deliberately irksome and unpleasant character. Prior to 1845, able-bodied men were often set to work pulverising bones for fertiliser, and even after that date the most common forms of employment involved stone-breaking, oakum-picking and flour-grinding, whilst women were more likely to be assigned long hours of domestic work, including cleaning, scrubbing, laundrywork, preparing food and tending infants. Even children could be set to work as seamstresses and laundresses, gardeners, and even factory-workers.[52]

Although people might enter a workhouse at any age, workhouse officers did make some effort to establish a slightly more humane regime for elderly inmates. Paupers who were over the age of 60 were entitled to small additional allowances of tea and sugar, elderly married couples were provided with their own sleeping accommodation (after 1840), and those who were too old to work were not required to do so, but many inmates continued to experience a particular dread of what might happen to them after their deaths. During the late-eighteenth and nineteenth centuries there was a rapid growth in the demand for corpses which could be used by medical schools in the teaching of anatomy, and in 1832 Parliament passed the Anatomy Act (2 & 3 William IV C. 75), which enabled 'any executor or other party having lawful possession of the body of any deceased person', including workhouse managers, 'to permit the body of such ... person to undergo anatomical examination', providing that no objections had been raised either by the deceased person themselves (either in writing, or in front of two witnesses), or by their surviving relatives. Even with these safeguards, many workhouse inmates appear to have dreaded the prospect of post-mortem dissection, not only because it seemed to underline the connection between criminality and poverty (previously, medical schools had only been able to conduct legal dissections on the corpses of condemned criminals), but also because they believed that it threatened their chances of resurrection in the after-life. As one contemporary writer observed, the aged pauper faced 'a worse than felon's doom! For when his life / Returns to God! Then, then, the bloody knife / Must do its work – the body that was starved / By puppy doctors must be cut and carved.'[53]

Even though most historians would accept the fact that the Poor Law Amendment Act was designed to discourage applications for poor relief, it is important not to exaggerate its effect. As Fraser has argued, the overwhelming majority of paupers continued to receive outdoor relief, and when one looks at the implementation of the New Poor Law in local areas there is a considerable amount of evidence to support the view that 'there was a good deal more continuity between pre-1834 and post-1834 than the national story would suggest.'[54] In Sunderland, 'there was no sign that the new régime was more cruel than its predecessor and indeed, the overwhelming impression is of continuity with the best of the former system and of slow improvement upon this foundation.' In Shropshire, 'the year 1836 may have introduced the New Poor Law into this region, but the terms Old and New Poor Law in themselves tell us little about the character of Shropshire's Poor Laws in the nineteenth century.' In the eastern counties of England, many Boards of Guardians continued to pay outdoor relief to unemployed workers, even though they attempted to conceal this by entering the recipients under other headings. In Lancashire, a high proportion of able-bodied paupers continued to receive relief-in-aid-of-wages, even though this practice had been condemned by the members of the Royal Commission.[55]

However, the fact that the central Poor Law authorities were often forced to work with the grain of local opinion does not mean that the 1834 Act had no effect. Possibly the most striking evidence in support of the view that it did make a difference is provided by the statistics on Poor Law expenditure. As was shown in Figure 4.1, the amount of money devoted to poor relief fell from approximately ten shillings per head on the eve of the reform to less than six shillings just two years later. Fraser suggested that this change could be attributed, at least in part, to the reduced demand for poor relief caused by a succession of good harvests and the economic stimulus provided by the railways, but this explanation fails to account for the continuation of low levels of expenditure when economic conditions deteriorated.[56] At the end of the 1840s, following a decade of severe hardship and marked political unrest, per capita expenditure on poor relief was still well below the levels experienced before 1834, and only slightly higher than it had been a decade earlier.

There is in fact a good deal of evidence, both qualitative and quantitative, to support the view that 1834 was indeed one of the great watersheds of British social policy history. In one of the most important recent contributions to this debate, Harling argued that the Assistant Poor Law Commissioners, working on behalf of the central Poor Law Commission, were able to exert significant influence on the appointment of Poor Law officers, and were able to remind both Guardians and officials 'that a central agency was monitoring their activities and assessing them against a rigorous standard'.[57] It would also be a mistake to assume that the members of local élites were necessarily hostile to the new legislation in any case. As Apfel and Dunkley observed: 'since the legislation ... largely sprang from a transformation of attitudes towards the poor on the part of those engaged in making law, it should not be surprising if other men of property, in positions of local influence but far from the centre of power, also felt the need to readjust their relations with the poor.'[58]

These arguments are also supported by a great deal of local evidence. Snell has argued that 'the New Poor Law ... had surely the most harmful and socially damaging effect on rural class relations in the south [of England] of any nineteenth-century legislation,' whilst Apfel and Dunkley have shown that the introduction of the New Poor Law in Bedfordshire was quickly followed by reductions in poor law expenditure and in the numbers of able-bodied men in receipt of outdoor relief.[59] The history of the New Poor Law on Tyneside 'demonstrates that the new system could be introduced and set to work reasonably smoothly even in one of the developing areas of the north of England', and the length of time which elapsed between the onset of unemployment and the receipt of relief in Manchester between 1845 and 1850 'attests to the depth of private and communal resources which ... [the unemployed] could resort to in times of distress, their hostility to the Poor Law, and the depth of poverty reached before they obtained relief from the poor law authorities'.[60] In Coventry, the Poor Law Commission gained control of Poor Law policy in 1844, and within months the regulations regarding outdoor relief had been tightened up, and the standard of discipline within the workhouse reinforced. In Carlisle, 'the Guardians were the prisoners of the limited discretion allowed by the Poor Law Commission', and in Durham the introduction of the New Poor Law created 'a considerable body of poor wholly divorced from the relief mechanism'.[61] In Shrewsbury, 'the emergence of new local figures and other circumstantial developments' meant that 'by 1850 the Incorporation had voluntarily adopted the Poor Law Commission's workhouse standards, while each parish slowly assimilated the New Poor Law's spirit of rigid opposition to any outdoor relief to the able-bodied'.[62]

The strongest advocate of the view that the 1834 Act was indeed a watershed in the history of the English Poor Law has been Karel Williams. In 1981, Williams argued that previous authors, such as Digby and Rose, had underestimated the significance of the Poor Law Amendment Act because they had failed to notice that the main aim of the Act was not to abolish all forms of outdoor relief, but rather to abolish the provision of outdoor relief to able-bodied *men*. Judged by this standard, there can be little doubt that the advent of the New Poor Law did lead to a significant abrogation of the welfare rights of male workers, whether this occurred as a result of the introduction of the workhouse test, or as the result of alternative forms of deterrence.[63] By the end of the 1850s, the *total* number of able-bodied men in receipt of outdoor relief was only 26,286. The vast majority of these men (24,505) were being relieved on account of sickness, accident or infirmity; only 1,687 were relieved on account of work or other causes, and only 94 were relieved on the basis of sudden and urgent necessity.[64] However, this did not alter the fact that a much larger number of non-able-bodied men, women and children were receiving relief outside the workhouse, and that their numbers continued to dwarf those receiving indoor relief. The apparent intractability of this side of the problem provided one of the key launching-pads for the 'crusade against outdoor relief' at the beginning of the 1870s.

4.4 The 'crusade against outdoor relief' and the development of the New Poor Law, 1870–1914

By the end of the 1850s, the supporters of the New Poor Law could afford to look back on the first 25 years of their creation with some satisfaction.

The number of able-bodied male paupers had declined substantially, the cost of the poor rates (after allowing for the increase in the size of the population) had remained largely unchanged since the middle of the 1830s, and the institutions of the New Poor Law had been firmly established throughout the country. However, there were still a number of reasons for disquiet. During the first half of the 1860s, the outbreak of the American Civil War severely disrupted the supply of raw cotton to the Lancashire textile towns and local Boards of Guardians were forced to distribute large amounts of outdoor relief in order to cope with the exceptional volume of distress. There was also growing evidence to suggest that poor rates were beginning to rise more consistently in London, and it remained the case that outdoor relief continued to be distributed to large numbers of women and children throughout the country.[65] The combined effect of all these factors was to spark a new campaign for a return to the 'principles of 1834' and the curtailment of outdoor relief. This campaign was led by organisations such as the Society for the Relief of Distress and the Charity Organisation Society, which called for an end to the 'indiscriminate' distribution of outdoor relief and for a closer relationship between the poor law authorities and local charities, and it was reinforced by changes in the system of local finance, which strengthened the influence of those ratepayers who were most strongly opposed to the distribution of outdoor relief.[66] At the same time, these changes also improved the financial base of many Poor Law Unions, and enabled them to invest more heavily in institutional solutions to the problem of poverty.[67]

In view of what has already been said about the impact of the 1834 Act on the welfare rights of able-bodied men, it is tempting to regard the crusade against outdoor relief as being largely, though not exclusively, a crusade against the distribution of outdoor relief to aged and infirm adults, able-bodied women, and children.[68] In December 1871, the Local Government Board issued a Circular (no. 20) prohibiting the distribution of outdoor relief to single able-bodied men and women, to women whose husbands had deserted them for less than 12 months, and to able-bodied widows with only one dependent child. It also suggested that where an able-bodied widow had been left with more than one child, 'it may be desirable to take one or more of the children into the workhouse in preference to giving outdoor relief.' The Board also called for 'improvements' in the administration of the Poor Law generally. It said that outdoor relief should only be granted to applicants after they had been visited by a Relieving Officer, and that such relief should only be granted for a limited period of not more than three months. The Relieving Officers were instructed to visit the homes of all people in receipt of outdoor relief at regular intervals, and Boards of Guardians were encouraged to renew their efforts to ensure 'that the provisions with respect to the compulsory maintenance of paupers by relations legally liable to contribute to their support be more generally acted upon.'[69]

The impact of these rules and exhortations was reflected in the official statistics produced by the Local Government Board at the end of each year. During the six years from 1 January 1871 to 1 January 1877, there were significant reductions in every major category of individuals receiving outdoor relief, and the total number of outdoor paupers fell by more than 340,000 from 917,890 to 571,892 (see Table 4.1). However, as we can see from Figure 4.2, these

Table 4.1 Number of paupers relieved outside the workhouse on 1 January in each year between 1871 and 1880

Year	Able-bodied			Not able-bodied			Lunatics, insane persons and idiots			Vagrants	Total
	Males	Females	Children	Males	Females	Children	Males	Females	Children		
1871	44,112	116,407	282,087	117,681	265,638	54,784	15,952	19,772	506	951	917,890
1872	29,793	98,925	238,683	111,098	257,535	51,385	15,895	19,936	534	816	824,600
1873	22,044	83,600	204,683	100,662	242,605	45,523	16,068	20,338	461	462	736,446
1874	18,245	75,486	187,798	92,241	228,557	40,290	16,426	20,656	422	368	680,489
1875	20,166	73,847	182,055	88,949	221,010	37,318	17,122	21,370	429	291	662,557
1876	14,940	64,070	161,942	80,686	206,099	33,610	17,424	22,017	336	295	601,419
1877	13,680	60,133	153,798	75,607	195,979	31,726	17,874	22,482	360	343	571,982
1878	14,971	61,549	160,162	73,856	191,275	31,841	18,483	23,509	375	562	576,583
1879	24,480	71,803	185,895	75,470	190,847	33,197	18,969	24,135	437	458	625,691
1880	24,734	74,503	197,636	78,168	193,456	35,422	19,514	24,981	406	567	649,387
1871–80	−19,378	−41,904	−84,451	−39,513	−72,182	−19,362	3,562	5,209	−100	−384	−268,503

Note: According to the *First Annual Report of the Local Government Board*, the total number of people in receipt of outdoor relief in 1874 was 680,483, but this is probably a calculation error.

Source: PP 1881 C. 2982 xlvi, 1, *Tenth Annual Report of the Local Government Board 1880–1*, p. 353.

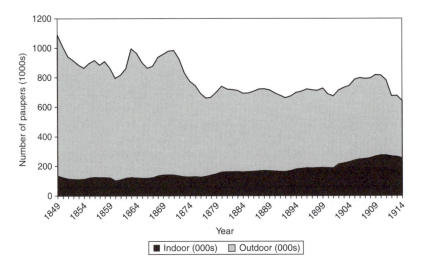

Notes: The Central Poor Law Authority began to keep records of the number of indoor and outdoor paupers at the end of the 1830s. Between 1840 and 1848 figures were published showing the total number of people claiming relief during the first three months of each year. From 1849 onwards, figures were produced showing the average of the numbers claiming relief on 1 July of the previous year and 1 January of the current year. The figures for the years 1849–59 show the total number of paupers, including both the insane and casual paupers. These groups are not included in the figures from 1860 onwards. The figures for the period 1902–14 only exclude those 'insane' who were institutionalised in county and county borough asylums, registered hospitals and licensed houses.

Source: K. Williams, *From pauperism to poverty*, London: Routledge & Kegan Paul, 1981, pp. 156–66.

Figure 4.2   Numbers receiving indoor or outdoor relief in England and Wales, 1849–1914

year-on-year reductions in the number of outdoor paupers were comparatively short-lived. The decline in the total number of people in receipt of outdoor relief began to level off during the 1880s and 1890s, and the numbers of both indoor and outdoor paupers rose during the early years of the twentieth century. In 1909, the total number of paupers was higher than at any time since the late-1880s.

The failure of both the Local Government Board and the local Poor Law authorities to make further inroads into the number of outdoor paupers was underlined by a number of changes which began to take place during the 1880s and 1890s. The Medical Relief (Disqualifications Removal) Act of 1885 enabled sick people to obtain medical treatment from a Poor Law dispensary without incurring the status of paupers, and the Chamberlain Circular of 1886 invited Boards of Guardians and other local authorities to consider ways in which public works could be used to provide temporary relief to 'artisans and others who have hitherto avoided Poor Law assistance'.[70] Even though the Circular had only limited practical effect, it represented an important break with traditional Poor Law orthodoxy, and signalled the first official acknowledgement of the inability of traditional Poor Law practices to cope with the problem of unemployment.[71] The development of a new approach to the treatment of poverty was also foreshadowed by the Local Government Act of 1894, which removed the property qualification for members of Boards of Guardians, allowed women to stand as candidates, and extended voting rights to all county-council and parliamentary electors. Even though the Act failed to lead to any dramatic changes in poor law policy, it created an opportunity for working-class voters to begin to exercise a rather more profound influence on local relief policies.[72]

These were not the only changes which hinted at the development of a new approach to the problem of poverty as a whole. One of the most interesting changes took place in the context of the development of a national system of state education after 1870. Under the terms of the Forster Education Act, school boards were given the power to make education compulsory for all children between the ages of five and ten, and this power was gradually extended to the whole of the country between 1870 and 1880. However, the 1870 Act failed to abolish school fees in elementary schools (these remained in force until 1891), and this meant that the new school boards were forced to construct income scales in order to identify those children whose fees could be remitted. Even though many parents were reluctant to apply for this remission, the introduction of the new scales highlighted the fact that there was a class of people, outside the poor law, who now became eligible for a new form of public subsidy.[73]

The introduction of income scales by school boards has tended to attract rather less attention from historians than the emergence of a growing national debate on the causes of poverty in old age. As Macnicol has shown, many of the earliest proposals were originally designed to inculcate habits of thrift and sobriety among younger workers, but they also focused attention on the problems being experienced by those who had already reached the end of their working lives. In 1895, the Royal Commission on the Aged Poor concluded that, in addition to the 20 or 30 per cent of elderly people who were already receiving poor relief, there were also many others who, whilst undeniably poor, were reluctant to apply for relief because of the stigma which the Poor Law imposed.[74] Both Charles Booth and Seebohm Rowntree also highlighted the problem of old-age poverty in their studies of London and York respectively. Booth claimed that many older workers were being forced out of the labour market by the demands of modern industry (although the evidence for this has been questioned), and Rowntree suggested that as much as ten per cent of the household poverty in York was attributable to the illness or old age of the chief wage-earner.[75]

These studies helped to ensure that the problem of poverty and the development of Poor Law policy became the focus of renewed controversy during the early years of the twentieth century. In 1905 the Conservative government appointed a Royal Commission to enquire 'into the working of the laws relating to the relief of poor persons ... [and] the means which have been adopted outside ... the Poor Laws for meeting distress arising from want of employment.'[76] The majority of the Commission's members called for the abolition of the Poor Law Unions and the Boards of Guardians, and their replacement by Public Assistance Committees whose members would work closely with local voluntary agencies. The authors of the Minority Report agreed with many of the Majority's findings, but they argued that the Poor Law should be broken up altogether, and that its responsibility for the relief of unemployment should be transferred to a national body which would be responsible for the prevention of unemployment as well as the relief of distress. However, despite the attention which has been paid to the Commission's findings, neither the Majority Report nor the Minority Report had any immediate influence on anti-poverty policy. This was partly because of the extent to which the two Reports cancelled each other out, but it was mainly because of the fact that the Liberal government of 1906–11 had already embarked on a series of policies which were designed not so much to break up the Poor Law, as to bypass it altogether.[77]

4.5 Conclusions

This chapter has examined the background to the introduction of the Poor Law Amendment Act and its impact on the development and implementation of anti-poverty policy after 1834. The Act set out to establish a clear distinction between indigence and poverty, and to deter able-bodied men, in particular, from seeking poor relief. During the 1830s and 1840s, the central poor law authorities (the Poor Law Commission and the Poor Law Board) succeeded in sharply reducing the number of able-bodied men in receipt of poor relief, and even though they failed to abolish the distribution of outdoor relief to other sections of the population, they were able to ensure that the cost of poor relief remained at extremely low levels, even after allowing for the increase in the overall population. During the 1860s, organisations such as the Society for the Relief of Distress and the Charity Organisation Society encouraged the Poor Law Board (and its successor, the Local Government Board) to impose new limitations on the provision of outdoor relief to women and children, but by the end of the nineteenth century it was becoming increasingly apparent that even though the New Poor Law had almost certainly succeeded in reducing pauperism, it had failed to address the problem of poverty. It was for this reason that a growing body of opinion was coming to recognise the need for alternative forms of welfare provision.

In view of the obvious limitations of the New Poor Law as a mechanism for addressing problems of human need, it is important to ask what other resources were made available to poor people to help them survive. Throughout the nineteenth century, advocates of poor law reform drew attention to the importance of private charity, and to the efforts which individuals could make on their own account, together with their friends and families, to support themselves. These two sets of issues – charity and philanthropy, on the one hand, and self-help and mutual aid, on the other – form the basis of the following two chapters.

5

Charity and philanthropy in the nineteenth century

Historians of social policy have recently begun to pay much more attention to the history of charity and philanthropy. This reflects a growing recognition of the part which philanthropy must have played in the past, and an increasing disenchantment with the claims made on behalf of state welfare in the present. However, there is still considerable disagreement over the evaluation of Victorian philanthropic activity. During the 1970s and 1980s, many historians criticised Victorian charities for being 'élitist rather than egalitarian, patchy and moralising, ameliorative rather than curative, amateur rather than professional, overlapping and wasteful rather than properly-planned, [and] dependent on suspect goodwill or objectionable ability to pay rather than [being] centred on needs and entitlements' and yet, as Finlayson has argued, such accounts may also obscure the extent to which philanthropy provided both individuals and groups with opportunities for active participation in the meeting of needs whilst neglecting 'its role in drawing public attention to social issues, in exerting pressure – and, more generally, in promoting choice'. In the end, as Finlayson himself suggests, our attitudes to the nature and role of Victorian philanthropy may reveal as much about ourselves as they do about the period we are investigating.[1]

5.1   The charitable impulse

According to Gorsky, 'philanthropy' is derived from a Greek word denoting the gods' love for humanity, but it subsequently came to mean the love which people might hold for their fellow human beings, and Samuel Johnson defined the word as 'love of man' and 'good nature'. By contrast, 'charity' is derived from the Latin word 'carus', meaning 'dear', and has often been used to denote the practice of giving aid or succour to those less fortunate than oneself. Checkland drew an important distinction between the two concepts when she suggested that nineteenth-century Christian charity 'was often a social observance, designed rather for the reassurance of the giver than for the good of the receiver', whereas philanthropy 'is a broader concept, based on humanitarian considerations ... [which] should not be involved with making moral judgements of the recipients'. However, even though this distinction helps to draw attention to the complex web of motives associated with Victorian philanthropy, other historians have argued it is not one which would have made a great deal of sense to the Victorians themselves and many contemporary definitions still imply that the two terms should be used interchangeably.[2]

We can obtain some valuable insights into the motives behind Victorian philanthropy from the biographical details of individual philanthropists. In a number of cases, including that of the Jewish philanthropist, Ferdinand Mocatta, philanthropy provided compensation for the lack of any children and took the place of a family, whilst other philanthropists argued that involvement in charitable and philanthropic activity provided an outlet for intense feelings of sadness and loss. Both Josephine Butler, who campaigned against the Contagious Diseases Acts, and Olive Malvery, a campaigner for the establishment of women's refuges, attributed their concern with social issues to the loss of a loved one.[3] Several philanthropists were drawn to philanthropy by feelings and both personal and collective guilt, whilst others looked to philanthropy as a means of resolving internal conflicts and tensions. Finlayson suggested that the most famous of all Victorian philanthropists, the seventh Earl of Shaftesbury, derived his inspiration not merely from his deep religious convictions and his desire to improve the social standing of the aristocracy, but also from his need to escape from 'inner conflicts of personality'.[4]

However, whilst it is important to recognise the particular factors which have influenced individual philanthropists, it is also necessary to acknowledge the broader role which philanthropy played in Victorian society. Engagement in philanthropic activities was often a useful way of establishing social contacts and cementing relationships, and participants might also derive a certain amount of kudos from the belief that they were in some way associating with their social superiors.[5] Other writers have argued that philanthropy played a particularly important role in the lives of middle-class women. Harrison argued that philanthropy provided women with 'all the excitements and dangers of penetrating or observing the unknown whilst at the same time securing that change of scene and activity which is the essence of recreation', but it also played a much more important role in the process of female emancipation. As Prochaska observed: 'In an age in which women found so many doors closed, they discovered a crack in the doors of the charitable societies. With a quickness of perception for which they were supposed to be noted, they spotted their opportunity and made the most of it.'[6]

Although historians have often drawn attention to the 'strange mixture of idealism, humanity and *arrière pensée*' which lay behind so much Victorian philanthropy, it is important to ask not only why the Victorian middle classes lavished so much money on 'good works', but also why they thought it appropriate that social needs should be met through voluntary rather than statutory provision.[7] Fraser argued that the vast outpouring of philanthropic activity in the middle years of the nineteenth century exposed the limitations of an ideology based on self-help, because there would have been little need for such an 'over-liberal dose of charity' if the recipients had been able to help themselves, but even some of the most progressive Victorian thinkers continued to be wary of the growth of state welfare provision.[8] Leslie Stephen claimed that 'after all we may say about the social development, the essential condition of all social improvement is not that we should have this or that system of regulations, but that the individual should be manly, self-respecting, doing his duty as well as getting his pay, and deeply convinced that nothing will do any permanent good which does not imply the elevation of the individual in his standards of honesty, independence and good conduct.'[9]

One way of addressing this paradox is by considering the importance which many early-nineteenth-century thinkers attached to the role played by charity in the performance of religious duty. Many early-nineteenth-century thinkers believed that individuals should be forced to take greater responsibility for their own welfare, but they also recognised the importance of charity as a fundamental religious duty, and this was why many Evangelical leaders, such as John Wesley and Thomas Chalmers, promoted the importance of charitable giving. However, they also argued that charity could only be regarded as a truly moral activity if it was based on individual free-will, and this led them to reject the notion of statutory welfare as a form of compulsory charity which did not depend on the moral sentiments of the individual concerned. It was for this reason that the authors of the Sturges-Bourne Report argued that 'every system of relief founded on compulsory enactment must be divested of the character of benevolence', and it also explains why the Scottish Evangelical, Thomas Chalmers, insisted that each act of charity ought to be a genuine 'free-will offering'.[10] The chronicler of London's Metropolitan charities, Sampson Low Jr, echoed this view when he complained that those 'who look upon charity merely as an economical resource, and who conceive that it ought to be dispensed with in favour of rates of shillings and pence in the pound' were 'forgetting that this would destroy all opportunity for generous impulse and active faith, without ensuring the exercise of one whit more judgement.'[11]

Early-nineteenth-century theorists also argued that private charity was more likely to improve the moral health of the recipient and maintain social harmony. Stedman Jones noted that 'to give, from whatever motives, generally imposes an obligation upon the receiver', but many of the supporters of voluntary philanthropy argued that the development of an automatic set of welfare entitlements under a statutory welfare system would weaken the bonds which existed between members of different social classes and eliminate the need for the recipients of welfare services to modify their behaviour in accordance with the wishes of the giver. As the Sturges-Bourne Committee complained in 1817, the extension of welfare provision under the Old Poor Law 'creates no feelings of gratitude and not infrequently engenders dispositions and habits calculated to separate rather than unite the interests of the higher and lower orders of the community', whilst Thomas Chalmers argued that 'all the tenderness of charity on the one hand, and all its delicacy on the other, have been put to flight by this metamorphosis of a matter of love into a matter of angry litigation.'[12] The Benthamite reformer, James Phillips Kay, claimed that 'the artificial structure of society, in providing security against existing evils, has too frequently neglected the remote moral influence of its arrangements on the community' and that the 'invisible chain of sympathy' which charity once extended between the higher and lower ranks of society had been destroyed by 'the luckless pseudo-philanthropy of the law'.[13]

The growth of philanthropy has often been regarded as part of a general strategy of 'social control', but such views have become increasingly controversial.

The pro-voluntarist writer, Frank Prochaska, has argued that even though 'the ruling classes...openly expressed a desire to subordinate the lower classes through charitable agencies', the concept of social control is 'rather murky and reductionist, for the wish to make another conform to the same values and speak the same language is important in social relations generally, from family life to national politics.'[14] Nevertheless, many Victorian philanthropists did believe that one of the chief virtues of philanthropy was the way in which it could be used to maintain social harmony and create mutually advantageous links between members of different social groups in an unequal society. In 1844, the Newcastle Ragged School Committee thanked 'the Worshipful the Mayor and the other gentlemen...[for] providing the children with a handsome dinner...on Easter Monday' because 'the social mingling of the rich and poor on such occasions, and the personal interest thus exhibited in the enjoyments of the humbler classes, are well adapted to strengthen and consolidate the bonds of civil society.'[15] The Charity Organisation Society defended the introduction of home visiting on the grounds that 'the rich, in seeing something of the distress of the poor...will have forced upon their minds the responsibility attaching to wealth and leisure...the poor will...have the comfortable assurance that, if the day of exceptional adversity should come, they will not be left to encounter it without a friend.'[16]

Even though philanthropy performed a number of very important secular functions, it is essential to recognise the extent to which religious feeling not only provided a general foundation for philanthropic activity, but also helped to influence both its character and orientation. Early-nineteenth-century Evangelicalism emphasised the importance of strict religious observance and the responsibility of the poor for their own misfortune, and this was reflected in the firmly religious character of many early-Victorian charities. Low found that more than 40 per cent of the money donated to London's charities was intended for missionary work at home or overseas, and Hicks suggested that a large proportion of the funds devoted to education was directly associated with the dissemination of religious literature.[17] However, the second half of the nineteenth century witnessed a reorientation of religious belief and a growing emphasis on the need for social initiatives, and this was also reflected in the changing nature of charitable activity. As Harrison suggested, 'the thirst for souls had been a most powerful influence on early-Victorian charity...[but] by the late-Victorian period...Toynbee and other social reformers were making their confessions not to God but to the working classes, and Stewart Headlam was pleading with Anglicans to show more profundity in their social concern.'[18]

The Evangelicals did not have a monopoly on philanthropic sentiment, and many other religious communities were also active in charitable endeavours. Throughout the nineteenth century, and particularly after 1850, both Roman Catholics and Jews provided educational, health and welfare services for members of their own communities, and their responsibilities increased following the influxes of Irish and eastern European immigrants from the 1840s onwards. MacRaild has argued that 'by the late-1830s there were Catholic benevolent societies throughout all the centres of Irish Catholic settlement, especially in the north of England. These networks became stronger and more important in the second half of the century, when the scale of migration made the experience more impersonal.'[19] The Jewish community also took steps to provide communal welfare services for both established members and new immigrants. The first Hebrew Philanthropic Society was established in Liverpool in 1808 and a second society was established in Manchester seventeen years later, and this was followed by the establishment of the Manchester Jews' School in 1842, a Jewish Board of Guardians in 1867, and a Jewish Sanitary Association, modelled on the Manchester and Salford Ladies' Health Visiting Society, in 1884.[20] There was no 'systematic' form of communal welfare provision in London during the first half of the nineteenth century, but the paid officials of the Great Synagogue were allowed to dispense charity 'either according to the established list of monthly allowances' or to 'the casual poor applying for relief', and the president was allowed to authorise grants of between five shillings and two guineas.[21] The honorary officers of three synagogues – the Great Synagogue, the Hambro' Synagogue and the New Synagogue – came together to form the London Jewish Board of Guardians in 1859, and a separate organisation – the Poor Jews' Temporary Shelter – was established for the benefit of homeless immigrants in 1885.[22]

Although Fraser criticised the 'sectarian' nature of many Victorian charities (including the 'significantly-named Jewish Board of Guardians'), this needs to be set in context.[23] Many of the main Evangelical societies were explicitly designed to promote the religious values of their sponsors, and it is hardly surprising that the members of other religious communities should have thought it necessary to establish their own organisations to combat the threat of missionary activity.[24] The existence of separate welfare agencies for members of minority groups can also be an index of their isolation from the mainstream of British society. In the particular case of the Jewish Board of Guardians, one of the main concerns of its founders was the need to protect the established Jewish community against the charge that the new immigrants were imposing a burden on the rest of society, and it was for much the same reason that many of the leading figures of Anglo-Jewry sought to discourage prospective immigrants from settling in the United Kingdom at the end of the nineteenth century.[25]

Whilst many historians have acknowledged the importance of the role played by religion in the development of philanthropic activities, the upsurge in philanthropy in the second half of the nineteenth century was also influenced by the loss of religious faith and the search for a new secular morality in a post-Darwinian world. Webb argued that it was 'during the middle decades of the nineteenth century that … the impulse of self-subordinating service was transferred, consciously and overtly, from God to man', and this sense was reflected in the writings of many Victorian atheists and freethinkers.[26] Fraser used this quotation to illustrate the changes which took place *within* religious belief, but Webb herself argued that this transition formed part of a 'stream of tendencies [which] culminated in Auguste Comte's vision of a "religion of humanity", with a glorification of science, in opposition to both theology and metaphysics, as the final stage in the development of the human intellect.'[27] The Victorian 'public moralist', Leslie Stephen, who had abandoned his own religious beliefs at the start of the 1860s, argued that 'the man who is occupied with his own interest makes grief an excuse for effeminate indulgence in self-pity .... The man who has learnt habitually to think of himself as part of a greater whole, whose conduct has been habitually directed to noble ends, is purified and strengthened by the spiritual convulsion.'[28]

5.2 The scale and range of charitable activity

It is a commonplace that, even though philanthropy played such an important role in Victorian society, we know relatively little about the precise dimensions of charitable activity. Best believed that 'only the vaguest answers can be given' to the question of 'just how much charity was actually dispensed' and Checkland claimed that 'the resources of particular charities can sometimes be discovered but philanthropy as a totality cannot, at least as yet, be measured.'[29] Finlayson believed that the problems of aggregative quantification were 'virtually intractable'; all one could say was that 'the nineteenth century saw the charitable organisation "come to a full, indeed, almost rankly luxuriant, bloom".'[30]

One of the main difficulties involved in attempting to measure the extent to which philanthropy was directly involved in the relief of poverty is that so much assistance was provided on an informal basis. At the beginning of the 1860s, an anonymous contributor to *Macmillan's Magazine* recalled how, as a child, he had been sent first to a local farmer to beg a few turnips, and then to the church parson, who gave him a shilling to purchase half a bushel of bread, and another anonymous working-class autobiographer, Jack Lanigan, recalled how he and his brother used to beg food from departing factory workers outside the gates of Mather and Platt's in Salford in the 1890s and early-1900s. Lanigan also related how 'we kids every school day at lunch time paid a visit to the Police Station, Berley Square, Salford, for a bowl of soup and a chunk of bread, which was issued free', and Alice Foley described how the local parish priest, Canon Burke, 'stuffed some food tickets' into her sister's hands 'to help tide the family over a cruel Christmas'. Such incidents must have played an important part in much working-class life, but they are unlikely to have found their way into the tables of official charity statistics.[31]

However, even if it is impossible to provide a complete calculation of the scale of Victorian philanthropy, it is possible to offer some tentative conclusions about the rate at which charitable organisations were formed and the purposes for which they developed. Barry argued that the roots of Victorian philanthropy needed to be traced back to the seventeenth and eighteenth centuries, but others believe that there was 'a cyclical upsurge of voluntary effort with quite distinctive features' in the late-eighteenth and early-nineteenth centuries. Gorsky argued that it was possible to divide the history of philanthropic activity in Bristol into three separate but overlapping phases. During the first phase, which lasted from *circa* 1790 to *circa* 1820, the city's leading citizens set aside their political and sectarian differences in order to establish a number of high-profile societies concerned with such issues as moral reform, non-denominational missionary work, health, education and the relief of poverty. This was followed by a second phase (between *circa* 1820 and *circa* 1860), during which older differences reasserted themselves, and a number of previously established charities lost their broad appeal. Even though this period witnessed the foundation of approximately 40 new societies in each decade, these societies tended to be smaller and more specialised than the charities which preceded them. This tendency continued into the third phase, which lasted from *circa* 1850 [*sic*] to the start of the 1880s. The most important change in this period was the decline in the number of educational charities from the 1870s onwards. This reflected the rise of state education following the introduction of the Forster Education Act, and heralded the emergence of a new relationship between the state and the voluntary sector.[32]

We can obtain a clearer picture of the quantitative dimensions of Bristol's charitable history from Table 5.1. Most of the societies which came into existence at the start of the period were largely concerned with health, education, poverty and religious activities, but the following decades witnessed the emergence of a new range of more specialised societies concerned with such issues as the rescue of prostitutes, the reform and rehabilitation of prisoners, the 'civilisation' of the poor, temperance reform, and the establishment of institutional residences for the improvement of morals. The table also shows the number of new societies formed in each decade. It appears that there was a definite increase in the number of new societies in the late-eighteenth and early-nineteenth centuries, followed by a levelling-off in the middle decades of the nineteenth century, a further upsurge in the 1870s, and a sharp decline in the 1880s which was only partially reversed during the 1890s. This was largely associated with the decline in the number of new educational charities, but there was also a reduction in the number of newly formed charities concerned with health care and institutional provision.

Although Gorsky's figures provide a good account of the rate at which new societies were being formed in Bristol in the late-eighteenth and nineteenth centuries, they do not tell us how long these societies lasted, and it is important to bear this in mind when comparing them with the statistics for other centres. Low found that 103 of the 640 charities which existed in London at the beginning of the 1860s had been founded before 1700, 114 had been established between 1700 and 1800, 279 were founded between 1800 and 1850, and a further 144 were established between 1850 and 1861. He also found that there were only two categories (out of 21) in which the number of charities founded before 1800 exceeded the number established after 1800 (see Table 5.2). In 1863, when Low published his fourth report, he calculated that the total number had risen to 770, and his last two reports, published in 1870 and 1872 respectively, each contained details of more than 900 charities. Thomas Hawksley claimed that there were 989 registered charities in London at the end of the 1860s.[33]

Low also provided information about the amounts of money expended under different headings. While these figures must inevitably be viewed with considerable caution, they do provide some indication of the main priorities of London's registered charities. Of the total amount of money collected by these charities in 1860/1, 14.98 per cent was devoted to general and special medical

Table 5.1 Numbers and types of voluntary societies and institutions formed by decade, Bristol 1780–1899

Category	Definition	1780s	1790s	1800s	1810s	1820s	1830s	1840s	1850s	1860s	1870s	1880s	1890s	Total
Poverty	Visiting charities, mendicity, emigration, providence societies	1	–	1	5	5	3	8	2	3	7	4	3	42
Education	Adult, infant, day, Sunday schools	1	1	3	12	17	19	16	24	16	20	3	1	133
Health	Hospitals, dispensaries, Dorcas societies, institutions for deafness, blindness	–	3	3	5	3	8	3	5	5	4	2	4	45
Church	Evangelising organisations, home and foreign missions	–	2	1	8	13	3	6	2	5	8	2	4	54
Temperance	Abstention from drink	–	–	–	–	–	3	–	1	1	1	2	2	10
Reform	Rescue of prostitutes, prisoners, 'civilising' the poor	–	–	–	–	–	2	1	4	4	1	1	7	20
Housing	Institutional residence for moral reform	–	–	2	1	–	–	1	3	3	7	2	3	22
Campaign	Philanthropic/political groups, i.e. anti-slavery, peace, animal welfare	–	–	–	–	2	–	7	–	2	2	3	1	17
Total		2	6	10	31	40	38	42	41	39	50	19	25	343

Note: The totals given at the end of each column and each row have been recalculated using the data in Gorsky's original table. Although the societies have been grouped into categories using Gorsky's original classification, they often combined a variety of different purposes. For example, although Gorsky included Dorcas societies under the general heading of 'Health', they could also be concerned with the relief of poverty, and they often had a strong religious motivation (see F. Prochaska, *The voluntary impulse: philanthropy in modern Britain*, London: Faber, 1988, p. 23; *ibid*, 'Philanthropy', in F. M. L. Thompson (ed.), *The Cambridge social history of Britain 1750–1950, Volume 3*, Cambridge: Cambridge University Press, 1990, pp. 357–94, at pp. 380–1; R. Liedtke, *Jewish welfare in Hamburg and Manchester c. 1850–1914*, Oxford: Clarendon Press, 1998, p. 166).

Source: M. Gorsky, *Patterns of philanthropy: charity and society in nineteenth-century Bristol*, Woodbridge: Royal Historical Society/Boydell Press, 1999, p. 138.

Table 5.2 The charities of London in 1861

Type of institution	Number of institutions in 1861					Income			
	Founded pre-1700	Founded 1701–1800	Founded 1801–1850	Founded 1851–61	Total	From voluntary contributions £	From dividends £	Total £	As % of total charitable income
General medical hospitals	2	5	5	2	14	58,049	126,809	184,858	7.57
Hospitals, infirmaries etc.	1	11	39	15	66	73,950	81,075	155,025	6.35
Dispensaries	0	10	21	8	39	23,377	2,500	25,877	1.06
For preservation of life, health and public morals	0	2	8	2	12	34,674	11,815	46,489	1.90
Institution for foundlings; hospitals and penitentiary institutions for females; relief to prisoners, reformatory and refuge institutions	1	4	16	18	39	42,387	51,594	93,981	3.85
Institutions for the relief of street destitution	1	3	20	5	29	54,551	10,213	64,764	2.65
Homes for needlewomen and servants etc., and otherwise aiding the industrious	0	0	7	14	21	6,250	2,005	8,255	0.34
Benevolent pension or annuity funds	1	0	0	8	9	15,314	4,300	19,614	0.80
Societies and funds for the benefit of poor clergy of the Church, and for Protestant and Dissenting Ministers	2	6	8	4	20	18,873	30,735	49,608	2.03
Professional and trade provident and benevolent funds	0	15	43	14	72	55,513	117,058	172,571	7.07
Abstract summary of funds arising from City Company and Parochial Trusts	24	0	0	0	24	0	38,000	38,000	1.56
Special National Fund (Indian famine)	0	0	0	1	1	114,807	0	114,807	4.70
Ditto, now closed, but producing income	1	0	0	3	4	0	53,000	53,000	2.17
Colleges, hospitals, almshouses and other asylums for the aged	64	27	29	4	124	9,734	85,587	95,321	3.90
Charities for the blind, deaf and dumb, and for poor cripples	2	4	5	5	16	14,274	29,247	43,521	1.78
Societies and funds promoting and aiding schools, including nine associations for adult instruction, partly self-supporting	1	5	17	8	31	73,443	14,934	88,377	3.62
Asylums entirely maintaining and educating 1986 orphan children	0	4	9	1	14	48,017	16,930	64,947	2.66
Asylums wholly maintaining and educating 2894 children	2	9	4	5	20	48,747	63,791	112,538	4.61
Bible and Home Missionary Societies	1	4	31	20	56	332,679	35,780	368,459	15.09
Foreign missionary funds and societies	0	5	13	7	25	570,440	66,000	636,440	26.06
Miscellaneous societies	0	0	4	0	4	5,515	0	5,515	0.23
Total	103	114	279	144	640	1,600,594	841,373	2,441,967	100.00

Source: S. Low, *The charities of London in 1861, comprising an account of the operations, resources and general condition of the charitable, educational and religious institutions of London*, London: Sampson Low, Son and Co., 1862, pp. vii–xi.

hospitals and dispensaries; 1.9 per cent was expended on the 'preservation of life, health and public morals'; 3.85 per cent was used for what Low had previously described as 'reclaiming the fallen'; 2.65 per cent was spent on the relief of street destitution, and specific claims; and 0.34 per cent on the provision of homes for needlewomen and servants, and for otherwise aiding the industrious. Of the remaining money, 9.91 per cent was spent on benevolent pension funds, on the relief of distressed clergy, and on the support of professional and benevolent funds; 1.56 per cent was devoted to City and parochial charities; 6.87 per cent was used to support victims of the Indian famine; 3.9 per cent was expended on colleges, hospitals, almshouses and asylums for the aged; 1.78 per cent on the support of people with disabilities; and 10.89 per cent on the education and support of children. The most striking figures are those for missionary charities: 15.09 per cent of all the money listed in Low's publication was used for domestic missionary work, and 26.06 per cent was expended on missionary work overseas.[34]

The impression which is conveyed by these figures is supported by figures collected by G. Hicks in his synopsis of the reports of 364 London charities in 1869. Hicks' figures excluded money raised by the City of London, the City Companies, and any 'strictly parochial' funds, but the distribution of funds across categories is broadly consistent with the picture Low painted. Hicks found that the major categories of expenditure were sickness (24.84 per cent of total expenditure); education (22.14 per cent) and the support of professional groups such as members of the Church of England, the armed forces, gentlewomen and widows, and members of other faiths (20.26 per cent). The devotion of such a large proportion of charitable funds to 'education' may appear to contradict Low's figures, but only a small fraction of this money was used to support children. The vast majority of the funds devoted to education were spent on adults, and the main categories of expenditure were 'Church of England', 'Book societies', and 'Missionary' (Table 5.3).[35]

While these figures appear to provide a reasonable guide to the main priorities of London's organised charities, they almost certainly underestimate the total amount of money which was actually contributed. In 1869 Thomas Hawksley calculated that there was a total of 989 registered charities in London, with an estimated income of approximately £5.3 million. After subtracting the incomes of those charities which spent either the whole or part of their income elsewhere, he concluded that the total amount expended in London was just over £4,000,000, including £630,000 on the relief of disease, £1.7 million on 'the ordinary necessaries of life', and £1.7 million on 'educational, moral and religious purposes'. However, he also argued that these figures failed to take account of 'the benefactions of the charitable and the religious'; the donations made by 'the compassionate, the weak-minded and the thoughtless' to private appeals and street-beggars; the funds distributed by the Mendicity Society; the amounts authorised by magistrates' courts; and those distributed by local and parochial funds. When these figures were added to the equation, Hawksley estimated that the total value of London's charitable expenditure was at least £5.6 million.[36]

Table 5.3 A synopsis of reports of some of the Metropolitan charities, 1868

Category and age group	Expenditure (£)	Expenditure as % of total expenditure
Sickness		
Infancy	770	0.04
Childhood	4,679	0.23
Manhood	501,516	24.57
Total	506,595	24.84
Convalescence		
Infancy	958	0.05
Childhood	3,427	0.17
Manhood	24,097	1.18
Total	28,482	1.40
Homes and refuges		
Infancy	1,599	0.08
Childhood	114,085	5.59
Manhood	82,012	4.02
Total	197,696	9.69
Orphanages		
Infancy	49,114	2.41
Childhood	79,205	3.88
Total	128,319	6.29
Education		
Childhood	25,991	1.27
Manhood	425,781	20.86
Total	451,772	22.14
Self-improvement	9,871	0.48
Denominational	24,301	1.19
Provident	102,395	5.02
Professional	413,428	20.26
Afflicted	70,597	3.46
Old age	25,95	1.27
General assistance	81,086	3.97
Grand total	2,040,897	100.00

Source: Adapted from G. Hicks, 'A synopsis of reports of some of the Metropolitan charities', *The Times*, 11 February 1869, pp. 3–5.

5.3   Charity and social provision

In the late-eighteenth century, it was generally assumed that the main burden of responsibility for dealing with the needs of the indigent poor rested with the statutory authorities, and 'only if poverty were complicated by other factors – a bad winter, crop failure, or an epidemic – was it thought to lie within the proper sphere of associated philanthropy.' However, the advent of the New Poor Law meant that charity was obliged to bear a much larger share of responsibility during the second half of the nineteenth century. 'Conceiving of poor relief in punitive and deterrent terms', wrote Owen, 'the framers of the new law were prepared to offer only the barest minimum, assuming that more constructive assistance would be provided by voluntary charity. It was … taken for granted [that charity] would carry the main burden of working-class welfare, insofar as this was not handled by workers' self-help organisations. Those whose needs could not be met through self-help, mutual aid or charity must be prepared to face the rigours of the workhouse.'[37]

The difficulties involved in calculating the extent of charitable provision have prompted a number of conflicting claims about the role played by charity in relieving poverty. Fraser argued that 'the Poor Law was catering for only a minor part of the demonstrable need in Victorian England. The relief of poverty was channelled more through unofficial than official agencies', and McCord claimed that even though 'it is not possible to estimate with any accuracy the total sums of money expended on voluntary relief measures, still less possible to estimate the amount of time and energy so employed ... it is very clear that unofficial far outweighed official exertion.'[38] However, Humphreys has claimed that if 'reference to the charitable generosity of the Victorians includes the vast amount of capital used to build the public edifices that mushroomed in nineteenth-century Britain, this would have little bearing on the provision of direct financial relief to the poor in the sense of providing an alternative to Poor Law outdoor doles.'[39]

Although the statistics presented in Tables 5.1–5.3 need to be treated with considerable care, they do lend some support to Humphreys' view. According to Low, less than 3 per cent of the charitable funds collected in London in 1861 were used for the relief of street destitution and specific distress, and Hicks found that only 3.65 per cent of the money raised by the charities in his study was used for 'general assistance'. However, it is important to recognise that a large amount of 'unofficial' charity was not recorded in the charity statistics, and that a significant proportion of the money which was recorded was used, if not to deal with the direct consequences of poverty, then at least to address its indirect consequences. As we have already seen, there are significant problems with the attempt to assign individual charities to any particular category (see the note to Table 5.1), and Hicks noted that a substantial proportion of the money recorded in his study was used to support not just hospitals and infirmaries, but also homes, orphanages and refuges. He argued that 'surely a Poor Law ought to be so administered as to make unnecessary such as these: the special character of one being the gift of a bed only, with a dry crust for supper, as a test of true destitution. That outside the Poor Law there always will be large scope for individual charity is of course admitted, but at present the public, instead of supplementing the relief by the Poor Law, is, and has been doing for some years past, the work of the Poor Law itself.'[40]

Charity also worked alongside the Poor Law to relieve distress in other areas. More than 40 'anti-poverty' societies were founded in Bristol between 1780 and 1899, and in Carlisle a special mendicancy society was formed in 1841 to bypass the restrictions imposed by the New Poor Law.[41] The long-established charity trusts played an important role in relieving poverty in many agricultural districts, such as the Warwickshire village of Tysoe and the town of Colyton in Devon.[42] However, formal charity was most likely to be used in its traditional role as a way of generating extra revenue during periods of particular distress. The citizens of Coventry organised seven separate emergency appeals between January 1837 and April 1860, and a national appeal was launched on behalf of the town's ribbon-weavers in November 1860.[43] The inhabitants of Lancashire raised more than £1.5 million during the cotton famine of the early-1860s, and the Lord Mayor of Manchester launched a national appeal in April 1862.[44] The Lord Mayor of London launched two separate Mansion House appeals for the relief of distress in London in 1866 and 1886 respectively.[45]

Although charity played an important part in the relief of distress, it made a much larger contribution to the development of the country's health services. Pinker calculated that in 1861 more than a quarter of the country's hospitals, and more than a fifth of all hospital beds, were administered by voluntary agencies.[46] Low's survey of London charities identified 14 general medical hospitals, 66 'institutions for special medical purposes', 39 dispensaries, 12 organisations for the preservation of life, health and public morals, one foundlings' hospital, 22 hospitals and penitentiary institutions for females, 124 colleges, hospitals, almshouses and asylums for the aged, 16 charities for the blind, deaf and dumb, and one charity for 'poor cripples', with a combined annual income of £645,072.[47] Hicks listed 98 charities concerned with the treatment and support of sick children and adults, and Hawksley calculated that there were 173 charities in London for the relief of bodily and mental disease, with an estimated income of £630,875.[48] During the second half of the nineteenth century, female volunteers pioneered the development of professional health visiting. The Ladies' National Association for the Diffusion of Sanitary Knowledge distributed information on the laws of health to cottagers and artisans from 1857 onwards, and the Manchester and Salford Ladies' Health Visiting Society organised regular visits to the homes of the poor from the mid-1870s.[49]

The voluntary sector also played an important role in the development of elementary education. Although Bible-reading and the development of basic literacy skills were an established part of many eighteenth-century Puritan and Evangelical congregations, there is little doubt that the development of 'Sunday schools' accelerated rapidly at the end of the eighteenth century, and Laqueur has estimated that they were being attended by more than one million children by the early-1830s.[50] The British and Foreign Schools Society established its first weekday school in 1808, and the Church of England launched its own organisation – the National Society for the Education of the Children of the Poor in the Principles of the Established Church – in 1811. The state began to supplement the incomes of these organisations from 1833 onwards, but it did not assume direct responsibility for the provision of elementary education until 1870. Even then, voluntary-aided schools continued to be responsible for the education of the majority of the country's children throughout the whole of the nineteenth century.[51]

During the second half of the nineteenth century, the voluntary sector became increasingly interested in the nation's housing problems. In 1864, Octavia Hill bought up the first of a series of properties in order to let them to 'model' tenants, but other philanthropists went further than this, by devoting resources to the construction of new buildings.[52] The Society for Improving the Condition of the Labouring Classes was a commercial organisation which sought to combine financial profitability with the provision of good quality housing, but the low rates of return meant 'support was limited in reality to those disposed to philanthropy'. The Metropolitan Association for Improving the Dwellings of the Working Classes constructed its first building in 1847, and by 1854 provincial associations had been founded in a number of centres, including Brighton, Newcastle, Dudley, Ramsgate, Southampton, Torquay, Liverpool and Bristol. The Peabody Trust concentrated on housing because 'the long pent-up invasion of Metropolitan railroads ... [was] overthrowing whole streets inhabited by humble and industrious labourers and artisans', and oversaw the construction of estates in Spitalfields, Islington, Shadwell, Westminster and Chelsea between 1864 and 1870.[53]

5.4 The organisation of charity

Although philanthropy made a substantial contribution to the improvement of social conditions in the nineteenth century, it would be wrong to ignore its limitations. As we have already seen, charity was an important part of working-class life and many people depended on it in times of need, but they often viewed the whole notion of 'charity' with considerable ambivalence. As Mabel Ashby's grandmother told the Vicar of Tysoe's wife in the 1860s, 'if it is charity, I cannot take the money. I have no need. If it is Town Lands money, I can.' The significance of this episode was underlined a day or two later, when one of the women of the village was asked why she had decided to wash a piece of scarlet flannel which she had just been given by the Charity Trustees: ' "Why, I bin washin' the charity out on it", she said. And there it hung, a long scarlet banner, pure of charity, and the three towns laughed.'[54]

One of the most important questions raised by the role of charity was the question of entitlement. Many of the leading 'ideologists' of private charity, such as Thomas Chalmers and the members of the Sturges-Bourne Committee, believed that one of the principal virtues of charity was the fact that it was conditional on the goodwill of the giver, but many people believed that welfare provision was a right rather than a gift. In March 1928, the leader of the Parliamentary Labour Party, James Ramsay MacDonald, told the House of Commons that it was 'most distasteful to the individual to beg of his friends for their cast-off clothing' and that 'the only thing that can redeem private charity is the personal touch', and in December, when the government responded to the growing crisis in south Wales and north-east England by offering to extend the scope of the Lord Mayors' Fund, he said that 'it is a repulsive thing for the great mass of our people to receive charity. Charity which is given with personal affection ... may be regarded ... as pleasing both [to] him who gives, and [to] him who receives, but charity given in the mass ... is not the sort of charity that our mothers would have received with whole-hearted gratitude as they would the charity of a personal friend.' The MP for Rhondda West, William John, put the matter even more forcefully when he asked 'why should the government not utilise the services of the local authorities .... After all ... this is not a question of charity, but a question of the rights of the people as citizens who have done their duty to the government and the country, and they ought to receive something far higher and nobler than charity from the hands of the government.'[55]

Although many working-class people resented their dependence on charity and did all they could to avoid it, it is clear that many other people were prepared to take a more pragmatic, and even instrumental, view of the uses to which charity could be put. Gorsky recounted an episode in which 'a poor woman ... having become very straitened in her circumstances, one day observed that she must go to "some place" ... and see what she could get.' She was then advised to go to a particular chapel but declined the advice on the grounds that 'I must go round and see where I can get most.'[56] Episodes of this nature fed a growing anxiety within philanthropic and middle-class circles about the effects of charity on the character and morals of those it sought to assist. In the early-1860s, the Vicar of Stepney, J. R. Green, complained that 'it is not so much poverty that is increasing in the East [End of London], as pauperism, the want of industry, of thrift or self-reliance – qualities which [the Poor Law] legislation of thirty years ago has ever since ... been with difficulty producing among the poor, but which melt away before the certainty of money from the West [End] ... Some half a million people in the East End of London have been flung into the crucible of public benevolence and ... come out ... simple paupers.'[57]

Whilst many observers agreed that the primary responsibility for this situation rested with the poor themselves, others blamed the charitable world itself for its want of organisation and discipline. The locally-born editor and translator of Faucher's *Manchester in 1844* (J. P. Culverwell) complained that 'the number and extent of our charitable institutions, and the large amount of indiscriminate relief afforded' represented 'a growing evil', and that 'any public institutions which lead [the working classes] ... to depend upon the bounty of others ... are not public charities, but public evils', and in 1850 a contributor to the *Westminster Review* claimed that 'under the specious mask of mercy to the criminal and benevolence to the wretched, we spare our own feelings at the cost of the most obvious principles of morality, the plainest dictates of prudence, the dearest interests of our country. We are kind to everyone except society.'[58] Hicks believed that 'undirected charity is twin sister to ill-directed charity. It overflows in one place to the impoverishment of several others. How much would be gained by self-organised and sustained effort ... let those who can speak from experience testify. Everyone wishes to create a little circle round his own particular hobby, and resists rather than invites cooperation from those around him.'[59]

Although many contemporaries devoted particular attention to the indiscriminate nature of charity and its demoralising effects on the character of the poor, other commentators have drawn attention to the resources which some charities lavished on themselves. As Harrison has noted, part of the problem lay in the development of charity frauds and the emergence of a new kind of criminal 'who devoted years to acquiring Episcopal smiles while quietly misappropriating the charity's funds', but it was also – at least in some respects – a function of the organisation of the charitable world itself. 'The numerous charity balls, philanthropic dinners and *conversaziones*, the pretentious central offices, the pages of print devoted to lists of subscribers, the elegant membership cards – the very organisation of the philanthropic world itself (not to speak of the causes on which its resources were spent) all ensured that such redistribution of the national income as did take place in the nineteenth century gave pleasure to and even profited many of the not-so-poor before it finally filtered down to those in real need.' Whilst such observations may be unfair to many of the smaller local societies which sought to provide education and health care to the poor, as well as food, clothing and money, they certainly seem applicable to some of the leading philanthropic societies, such as the British and Foreign Bible Society, whose expensive London headquarters revealed 'an architectural splendour worthy of the Medici in their most palmy days'.[60]

Many of the concerns expressed in previous decades about the organisation of charity and its impact on the character of the recipients culminated in the establishment of the Charity Organisation Society at the end of the 1860s. The Society was particularly concerned with the effects of what it saw as the indiscriminate distribution of charity on the character and independence of the recipients. It argued that special committees should be set up in each district, and that these should be charged with the responsibility of investigating all applications for charitable relief before any assistance was given.[61] The Society also called for a much greater degree of cooperation between the voluntary sector and the Poor Law. It argued that charity should only be given to the 'deserving' poor, and that the undeserving should be left to the mercies of the Poor Law. This would not only limit the numbers dependent on statutory relief; it would also enable the Poor Law authorities to deal more firmly with those who did come before them, and to apply the 'principles of 1834' more rigorously.[62]

The Charity Organisation Society has been the subject of a variety of historical opinions. Stedman Jones argued that the methods adopted by the Society grew out of what C. L. Mowat called its 'sternly individualist philosophy' and that they were 'designed to reintroduce the element of obligation into the gift in districts where a small number of mainly non-resident rich were confronted with a vast and anonymous mass of poor applicants', but other writers have taken a more magnanimous view of the Society's work.[63] Fido and Lewis have argued that the Society's founders were also motivated by a genuine belief in the obligations of the rich and the need to develop a more organic sense of 'community', and Vincent has shown that the Society was by no means universally opposed to all forms of social reform.[64] It was even prepared to countenance the development of public works schemes as a remedy for unemployment, providing these were placed under its own control.[65]

The Charity Organisation Society enjoyed its period of greatest influence during the first half of the 1870s. It was directly involved in the 'crusade against outdoor relief' which was launched by the President of the Poor Law Board in November 1869, and local Charity Organisation Societies were formed in several towns and cities during the 1870s and 1880s.[66] It also played a major role in many important official enquiries, including the Royal Commission on the Aged Poor in 1894 and the Royal Commission on the Poor Laws between 1905 and 1909.[67] However, it is becoming increasingly apparent that, for much of this period, the Society was swimming against, rather than with, the tide of public and charitable opinion. It failed to secure control over the distribution of charitable funds, and many of the provincial organisations were ostracised by local Boards of Guardians and charities.[68] The Society was also powerless to prevent the introduction of such important state welfare measures as free school meals, old-age pensions, and national insurance.[69]

One of the main reasons for the failure of the Charity Organisation Society was its inability to reconcile the basic principles of charity with its own apparently hard-faced philosophy. During the early years of the twentieth century, the Society lost many of its erstwhile supporters to new philanthropic movements such as the Guilds of Help and the Councils of Social Welfare. These organisations shared the Charity Organisation Society's belief in the need for 'personal service' and the importance of 'community', but they believed that its desire to form links between the rich and the poor had been undermined by its emphasis on 'investigation', and they took a much more sanguine view of the development of state welfare. In the long run, they looked forward to a new form of partnership between the state and the voluntary sector, in which the voluntary sector would no longer act as the gate-keeper to state services, but would help the state to administer those services which it now felt compelled to provide.[70]

5.5 Conclusions

Attitudes to Victorian philanthropy have undergone something of a sea-change during the last 20 years. Many earlier historians argued that the very nature of Victorian philanthropy was rooted in the characteristics of a deeply unequal society, and that it was designed primarily to salve the consciences of the rich and to reinforce their control over the poor. In contrast, more recent writers have tended to emphasise the moral imperatives which lay behind Victorian philanthropy, and the extent to which it provided support and services to people who were in considerable need.

This chapter has tried to show that it is possible to hold both points of view. Many Victorians were deeply convinced of the importance of philanthropy, both as a moral duty, and as a way of improving the lot of others. At the same time, a great deal of nineteenth-century philanthropy reflected the attitudes and prejudices of an unequal society and many philanthropists regarded philanthropy as a way of maintaining order and preserving deference, and this caused many of the potential recipients of Victorian charity to regard their efforts with considerable ambivalence. Towards the end of the nineteenth century, many of those involved in philanthropy became increasingly aware of the limitations of private philanthropy as a means of meeting social needs, and this was why they became convinced of the need for more extensive forms of state action.

Although this chapter has tried to illustrate the full range of philanthropic activities, it is obviously impossible to provide more than the briefest sketch within the confines of a single chapter. One of the most important omissions has been any reference to what Prochaska has called working-class philanthropy, and what others might regard as neighbourhood provision, self-help or mutual aid.[71] The history of voluntary social provision among the poor will be discussed in more detail in Chapter 6.

6 Welfare from below: self-help and mutual aid

Historians of nineteenth-century social policy have often drawn attention to the inadequacy of societal arrangements for meeting social needs. State welfare provision was grudging and limited, and charity was inefficient, unpredictable and indeterminate. However, much less attention has been paid to the ways in which working-class people sought to protect themselves and their families in the face of these deficiencies. This chapter builds on recent work in the social history of welfare by looking first at the role played by informal arrangements within working-class communities themselves; second at the role of working-class credit; third at the development of institutional forms of mutual aid such as friendly societies and trade-union welfare schemes; and finally at the role of more individualistic or commercially-oriented organisations such as building societies, savings banks and industrial assurance companies.

6.1 Families, neighbourhoods and communities

Although the aid provided by friends, relatives and neighbours was often unrecorded, its existence was acknowledged by many contemporaries. The Canon of Manchester, Dr Richard Parkinson, claimed that 'the poor give one another more than the rich give the poor', and Dr Bardsley, a local physician, declared that 'the total sum which the poor yearly bestow upon one another surpasses that which the rich contribute in the same time.' This was the kind of philanthropy which persuaded Friedrich Engels that 'the workman is far more humane in ordinary life than the bourgeois', and which led the working-class autobiographer, Joseph Terry, to claim that 'the poor have much warmer sympathies than the rich, and are more ready to help each other.'[1] However, even though the Edwardian cleric, William Conybeare, placed the 'kindness of the poor to the poor ... between our civilisation and revolution', it would be wrong to exaggerate its impact. As Treble noted, 'mutual assistance ... although an integral part of working class social life ... was usually on too small a scale to raise its recipients above the primary poverty line.'[2]

Although working-class people were able to draw on a variety of sources in times of particular need, many of the most important forms of mutual support came from members of an individual's own family.[3] In rural areas and small towns, individuals and families were more likely to have access to more formal kinds of provision, such as those provided by the poor law and charities, but these sources might be less well developed in the more rapidly growing urban areas. Dupree argued that 'the co-residence patterns of the elderly in northern, urban industrial areas such as the Potteries and Preston, in contrast to rural areas and small towns and to the twentieth century, suggest that family and kin were important sources of assistance.'[4] According to Anderson, when an individual migrated to a town 'it was advisable, or even well-nigh essential, to make every effort to keep in contact with, or to enter into reciprocal assistance with, kinsmen, if life-chances were not to be seriously imperilled.'[5]

Some modern commentators have complained that the growth of state welfare provision has undermined the role of the family as a provider of welfare services. Milton and Rose Friedman claimed that in the past, 'children helped their parents out of love or duty. They now contribute to the support of someone else's parents out of compulsion and fear. The earlier transfers strengthened the bonds of the family; the compulsory transfers weaken them.'[6] However, other writers have argued that the ties which bound family members owed as much to mutual self-interest as familial affection. Anderson argued that family members 'deliberately organised their relationships to ensure that the maximum of mutual advantage ensued in the short-run.'[7] On the other hand, Dupree found that in the Potteries, 'there is evidence of reciprocity negotiated between family members over the long-term and even asymmetrical relationships with little prospect of reciprocity.'[8]

Many people also looked to their neighbours for assistance. Anderson found that neighbours were often prepared to help in cases of sickness and death and with the care of orphans, but they were more likely to provide assistance to individuals who were well known and who lived in neighbourhoods which were long-standing.[9] Dupree has described how the local beerhouse 'could also serve as a focus for the provision of general assistance for neighbours and for transferring neighbourliness into friendship.' John Finney recalled how the landlord of the Commercial Inn in Stoke would regularly open 'a subscription list ... for cases of urgent necessity. Sam Swann, James Robinson ... and others followed on, for we knew all calls for assistance were deserving ones.'[10] James Winter has estimated that between one-third and two-thirds of a widowed mother's income in the Scottish fishing village of Kirkcudbright was likely to come from 'informal aid'. In North Uist, Tobermory and Rosemarkie, members of the local community raised subscription funds for women whose husbands had died in fishing accidents or after prolonged illness. In other cases, it was customary for poor women to call on their neighbours, who might then assist them with gifts of money, food or clothing.[11]

Neighbourhood support networks also played an important role in providing help to disadvantaged individuals in late-Victorian and Edwardian London. According to Ross, poor women frequently helped one another with minor household expenses, such as heating and lighting, linens, washtubs and clothing. They also raised collections to cover the cost of funerals, looked after children, provided assistance during childbirth, offered homes to battered wives, and took in evicted families. If a man fell ill or died, his fellow-workers might organise a collection to pay for his medical expenses, or to provide support for his widow and children. There was therefore a great deal of truth in Margaret

Loane's contemporary assertion that many old people would have been unable to maintain themselves without 'valid and recognised claims on the services of neighbours or relatives earned by former kindnesses and exertion'.[12]

6.2 The role of credit

In addition to relying on many different kinds of informal help from friends, family and neighbours, working-class people also depended to a considerable degree on a variety of formal and informal credit arrangements to see them through periods of particular need. In an important essay, Paul Johnson suggested that these arrangements could either be spontaneous or premeditated. He used the term 'spontaneous' to describe the kind of credit provided by local shops in times of particular need. Such arrangements appear to have been a normal part of working-class life during the nineteenth century, and they served the interests of both shopkeeper and client. Shopkeepers who provided their customers with credit during times of need were more likely to retain their custom during periods of plenty, and the customers were able to obtain essential items even when they could not afford to pay for them. As Frank Bullen explained in 1908:

> Many hundreds of families would come to the workhouse long before they do, especially in hard winters, but for these small tradesmen giving them credit for the bare necessities of life, and thus tiding them over the pinching time. This system of first aid can hardly be called philanthropy, since those who extend it do it for a living, and yet in the multitudinous life of poor London it is a huge and most important factor.[13]

Whilst a great deal of working-class credit was of this 'spontaneous' type, much credit was also entered into on a more premeditated basis. At the beginning of the twentieth century, several investigators commented on the importance of various kinds of clothing clubs in working-class communities. In 1902, the Women's Cooperative Guild reported that 'drapery and hardware clubs at drapers' and other shops abound ... practically every poor person we spoke to bought boots, drapery and furniture through these clubs.' Florence Bell explained that 'the difficulty of paying for anything for which more than a very small sum in ready money is needed explains the eagerness with which the housewives of [Middlesborough] embraced any system by which they are enabled to buy in small instalments.' More than 30 years later, the authors of a report on the provision of social services in North Lambeth and Kennington reported that 'nearly every shop in Lambeth runs a club of some kind. In the case of some this is a real help to mothers and families; they can choose the goods they want and are not forced to pay more than the ordinary cash price; in others there is no choice and the goods are very expensive.'[14]

The other great institution of working-class credit, as Johnson puts it, was the pawnshop. Every week, thousands of working class families would leave households items with a pawnbroker (or 'pledge' them) in return for cash. Helen Bosanquet observed that 'to many thousands, the pawnshop is their one financial recourse, their one escape from charity or the Poor Law ... to raise money on the home is not among the lower class the last expedient of despairing misfortune, but the ordinary resource of the average man.'[15] The significance of pawnshops in working-class communities was reflected in their numbers. According to Johnson, the total number of licences issued to pawnbrokers throughout Great Britain rose from 3390 in 1870 to a peak of 5087 on the eve of the First World War. In 1870, the House of Commons Select Committee on Pawnbrokers calculated that the annual number of pledges taken by each outlet varied from 40,000 in the provinces to 60,000 in London. As Cuthbert Keeson pointed out in 1902, these figures were equivalent to each Londoner pledging six items in any one year, or to one pledge per household every two to three weeks.[16]

The proliferation of pawnbrokers meant that most working class people only needed to resort to moneylenders when they had nothing left to pawn, since the interest charged on a secured loan was always likely to be lower than the interest charged by a moneylender on an unsecured loan. Robert Roberts, who grew up in a poor part of Salford before the First World War, recalled that 'only those in dire straits, and with a certainty of cash to come, patronised the local bloodsucker; he charged threepence in the shilling per week. To be known to be in his clutches was to lose caste altogether. Women would pawn to the limit, leaving the home literally comfortless, rather than fall to that level.'[17] However, as Johnson has pointed out, there were opportunities for the financially astute to combine borrowing with other forms of credit in order to obtain 'maximum purchasing power at minimum cost'. Just after the end of the First World War, Rose Gamble's mother borrowed one shilling from her local moneylender, at one penny a day interest, in order to make a down payment on a pair of sheets at fifteen shillings the pair. She then pawned the sheets for 7/6, paid off the loan and the interest, and still had 5d left after spending six shillings on rent. As Johnson suggests, such examples provide a good illustration, not only of the financial ingenuity displayed by poor people in straitened circumstances, but also of the lengths to which they would go to maintain appearances and avoid the need to apply either to charities or the poor law.[18]

6.3 Mutual aid organisations

During the course of the nineteenth century, working-class people formed a growing number of organisations which were designed for the collective provision of individual need. The most important of these organisations were the friendly societies, the trade unions, and the cooperative societies.

As their name suggests, friendly societies were designed to perform both an economic and a social function. Although some societies, such as the Antediluvian Order of Buffaloes, claimed great antiquity, the movement appears to have really 'taken off' from the mid-eighteenth century onwards. Hopkins suggested that 'the greater risks of ill-health and injury' associated with industrial occupations 'supplied compelling reasons for joining a friendly society', but Gorsky has argued that their development was more closely related to the need felt by young migrants to urban centres 'to recreate the ties and dependencies of the agrarian community'.[19] The vast majority of friendly societies were exclusively male (although there were also a growing number of female societies), and, in return for a small weekly sum, they provided an important opportunity for social contact and recreation. They also conferred entitlements to sickness benefits and death benefits, and, in a growing number of cases, they provided their members with rudimentary medical attendance.[20]

The earliest friendly societies were small, local societies which drew their members from the surrounding area, but from the 1830s onwards these began to lose ground in comparison with the 'affiliated orders', such as the Ancient Order of Foresters and the Manchester Unity of Oddfellows. These were large national or regional organisations with several local branches or courts. During the middle years of the nineteenth century, the growth of these organisations was hampered by legislative developments which required each branch to register as a separate society. However, the Friendly Societies Act of 1875 removed this obstacle, and this enabled the affiliated orders to operate much more efficiently. In 1890, the outgoing Chief Registrar of Friendly Societies, J. M. Ludlow, wrote:

> It is among the affiliated bodies especially that the benefits of the legislation of 1875 are apparent. The conditions required by the act for the registration of branches, the contribution to a central fund, and control of a central body, have given to the organisation of most of them a cohesion and vitality which they did not possess before; whilst the obligation of periodical valuation has awakened, or is awakening, one after the other to the necessity of setting their house in order by providing for a fair balancing of contributions and liabilities.[21]

Although the majority of upper- and middle-class observers welcomed the creation of friendly societies, they also aroused some hostility. During the Napoleonic Wars, many societies were suspected of being 'fronts' for illegal trade union activity, and in 1849, the author of an official report to Birmingham's Board of Health complained that 'vast sums of money' were being wasted on 'unmeaning, gaudy and childish show'. However, whilst many observers criticised friendly societies for being either subversive, or inefficient, or both, they also represented a useful way of encouraging values of self-help and independence, and a possible alternative to the Poor Law. During the 1810s and 1820s, the government attempted to resolve this dilemma by encouraging members of the local gentry to establish county or 'patronised' friendly societies, which could be operated under aristocratic or gentry management, but the new societies found it difficult to make much headway outside a small number of largely agricultural areas. In 1825, the House of Commons Select Committee on Friendly Societies reported that even though 'county societies undoubtedly possess many advantages ... the people themselves are disinclined to substitute a subscription to these general institutions for their contributions to clubs managed by themselves', and in 1871, when the total number of friendly society members was already past two million, the four largest county societies could only muster a combined membership of 22,921 between them.[22]

The Chief Registrar also recorded information about a large number of other organisations, also registered under the Friendly Societies Acts, which shared some of the characteristics of traditional friendly societies, whilst rejecting others. The most important of these were the deposit societies, dividing societies, local burial societies, and collecting burial societies. The deposit society was really more of a savings bank than a true friendly society. Each member paid in a certain amount to their own fund, and their entitlement to benefit ceased when this was exhausted. The dividing society was a special kind of friendly society which used the unallocated share of its funds to issue a dividend to its members at the end of each year (or sometimes a longer period). Local burial societies were friendly societies which only provided benefits at the time of a member's death in order to help defray the costs of the funeral. Collecting societies were large, impersonal organisations which were also largely concerned with the provision of funeral benefits. As the Royal Commission on Friendly Societies observed in 1874: 'the great bulk of collecting societies are burial societies; the great bulk of burial societies are collecting societies.'[23]

During the last 30 years, there has been considerable debate over the question of how many people belonged to friendly societies at different times. Hanson and Green have argued that the Chief Registrar of Friendly Societies consistently underestimated the total number of people belonging to ordinary friendly societies, or, in Hanson's words, 'friendly societies proper', during the last quarter of the nineteenth century because he failed to take account of the number of people belonging to unregistered societies. However, the Chief Registrar himself addressed this problem during the 1870s, when he claimed that most of the increase in recorded membership during this period was attributable to improvements in recording procedures. In his *Annual Report* for 1876, he wrote that 'a comparison of these figures with those in the report for last year will show that although the number of societies is less (owing in great measure to more careful weeding of the registers), an increase appears in every other column.... Such increase, however...is, in the main, statistical only, and represents...chiefly more accurate figures, not advancing prosperity.'[24] Consequently, although it is always advisable to treat official statistics with a reasonable degree of care, it is likely that the official figures do offer a reasonable guide to the main changes in friendly society membership from the 1880s onwards.

We can now turn to the official estimates of friendly society membership in Table 6.1. In 1803, the overseers of the poor estimated that there were nearly 10,000 individual societies, with a combined membership of 704,350 members. The number of members rose to more than 800,000 in 1813 and 1814, and to 925,000 in 1815.[25] Nearly 60 years later, in 1872, the Royal Commission on Friendly Societies reported that there were at least 1,857,896 known members of friendly societies in England and Wales, and a further 396,985 members in Scotland and Ireland, but only about half of the societies to which it had sent out enquiries had responded to them, and many of the societies that submitted returns did so unsatisfactorily.[26] However, the Chief Registrar devoted a great deal of effort to improving the quality and quantity of the returns submitted during the second half of the 1870s, and this led to a substantial increase in recorded membership during this period.[27] In 1912, the last year before the introduction of the statutory system of national insurance, the Chief Registrar estimated that there were approximately 7.2 million members of 'ordinary' friendly societies (that is, affiliated orders and branchless societies), 730,000 members of other friendly societies (other than collecting societies), and around

Table 6.1 Membership of friendly societies in the United Kingdom, 1801–1914

Year	Branches									Members/policies								
	Orders with branches	Branchless societies providing sickness benefit	Other branchless societies	All branchless societies	Other societies registered under the Friendly Societies Act, 1875	All societies other than affiliated orders and collecting societies	All societies (including affiliated orders) other than collecting societies	Collecting societies	Total	Orders with branches	Branchless societies providing sickness benefit	Other branchless societies	All branchless societies	Other societies registered under the Friendly Societies Act, 1875	All societies other than affiliated orders and collecting societies	All societies (including affiliated orders) other than collecting societies	Collecting societies	Total
1801[a]	—	—	—	—	—	—	—	—	7,200	—	—	—	—	—	—	—	—	648,000
1803[a]	—	—	—	—	—	—	—	—	9,672	—	—	—	—	—	—	—	—	704,350
1813	—	—	—	—	—	—	—	—	—	—	—	—	—	—	—	—	—	821,319
1814	—	—	—	—	—	—	—	—	—	—	—	—	—	—	—	—	—	838,728
1815	—	—	—	—	—	—	—	—	—	—	—	—	—	—	—	—	—	925,429
1872[b]	—	—	—	—	—	—	—	—	22,923	—	—	—	—	—	—	—	—	2,254,881
1875[c]	—	—	—	—	—	—	—	—	26,087	—	—	—	—	—	—	—	—	3,404,187
1876[d]	—	—	—	—	—	—	25,207	27	25,234	—	—	—	—	—	—	2,936,009	1,428,763	4,364,772
1889–91[e]	16,400	—	—	10,426	1,022	11,448	27,848	39	27,887	1,727,809	—	—	2,133,710	235,510	2,369,220	4,097,029	3,318,942	7,415,971
1899	19,341	—	—	7,090	1,308	8,398	27,739	46	27,785	2,409,438	—	—	2,807,823	610,254	3,418,077	5,827,515	5,922,615	11,750,130
1902	20,555	—	—	6,897	1,644	8,541	29,096	45	29,141	2,614,322	—	—	2,994,480	728,295	3,722,775	6,337,097	7,007,397	13,344,494
1905	20,144	—	—	6,773	1,999	8,772	28,916	45	28,961	2,673,246	—	—	3,226,672	822,744	4,049,416	6,722,662	7,884,307	14,606,969
1910	20,660	3,151	3,213	6,364	2,335	8,699	29,359	66	29,425	2,803,429	1,289,271	2,617,683	3,906,854	629,488	4,536,442	7,339,871	7,168,092	14,507,963
1911	20,638	2,957	3,232	6,189	2,449	8,638	29,276	64	29,340	2,795,000	1,258,904	2,720,113	3,979,017	661,813	4,640,830	7,435,830	7,504,273	14,940,103
1912	21,042	2,381	3,208	5,589	2,632	8,221	29,263	54	29,317	3,006,043	1,339,034	2,852,482	4,191,516	730,184	4,921,700	7,927,743	7,753,270	15,681,013
1913	20,521	1,966	3,156	5,142	2,762	7,763	28,284	57	28,341	2,969,875	1,313,346	2,699,501	4,012,847	786,336	4,799,183	7,769,058	7,629,624	15,398,682
1914	21,161	1,845	2,937	4,782	2,942	7,724	28,885	55	28,940	2,935,272	1,220,397	2,668,567	3,888,964	811,458	4,700,422	7,635,694	7,554,266	15,189,960

Notes: [a] These figures refer to England and Wales only. [b] In 1872, the Royal Commission on Friendly Societies sent out returns to 22,923 societies, and received replies from 12,928 societies. The figures quoted here differ from those quoted by other authorities because they also include figures for Scotland and Ireland. [c] In 1875, the Chief Registrar of Friendly Societies issued returns to 26,087 societies, and received replies from 11,282 societies. [d] In 1876 the Chief Registrar issued returns to 25,234 societies, and received replies from 12,338 societies. [e] In 1889, the Chief Registrar issued returns to 10,465 independent societies (including collecting societies) and 16,400 societies with branches. In the return which he published in 1890–91, he reported that returns had been received from 5,144 independent societies and 12,442 societies with branches. In his Annual Report for 1891, he reported that he had received replies from 22,313 friendly societies (not including collecting societies) and societies with branches (out of a total of 26,826); 35 replies from collecting societies (out of 39); and 494 other societies recognised as friendly societies under the Friendly Societies Act (out of 1,022). It is difficult to reconcile these figures, since the membership figures quoted in the Annual Report for 1891 for societies with branches, independent societies, and collecting societies were the same as those reported in the earlier return. The figures for 1899 onwards are based on the number of returns received, rather than the number of societies to which returns were issued.

Sources: 1801: F. M. Eden, *Observations on friendly societies for the maintenance of the industrious classes during sickness, infirmity, old age and other exigencies*, London: J. White & J. Wright, 1801, p. 7; 1803: PP 1803–4 (175) xiii, 1, *Abstract of the answers and returns made pursuant to an Act, passed in the 43rd year of His Majesty King George V, titled 'An Act for procuring returns relative to the expence and maintenance of the poor in England'*, p. 714; 1813–15: PP 1818 (107) v, 1, *Report from the Select Committee on the Poor Laws* (1818), with Appendix, p. 11; 1872: PP 1874 C. 961 xxiii, 1, *Fourth Report of the Royal Commission on Friendly and Benefit Building Societies*, p. 21; 1875: PP 1877 lxxviii, 103, *Reports of the Chief Registrar of Friendly Societies for the year ending 31 December 1875*, p. 54; 1876: PP 1878 (388) lxix, 3, *Reports of the Chief Registrar of Friendly Societies for the year ending 31 December 1876*, pp. 6, 46, 65–71; 1889–91: PP 1890–91 (332) lxix, 685, *Return showing the total number of ordinary friendly societies on the register at 31 December 1889, etc.*, p. 2; PP 1892 (137-I) lxxiii, 233, *Reports of the Chief Registrar of Friendly Societies for the year ending 31 December 1891*, p. 45; 1899: PP 1902 (109) xcvi, 1, *Reports of the Chief Registrar of Friendly Societies for the year ending 31 December 1901*, p. 29; 1902: PP 1904 (55) lxxix, 1, *Reports of the Chief Registrar of Friendly Societies for the year ending 31 December 1903*, p. 28; 1905: PP 1907 (49-XI) lxxix, 343, *Reports of the Chief Registrar of Friendly Societies for the year ending 31 December 1906*, Appendix A, Section XI, p. 234; 1910: PP 1912–13 (123-I) lxxxi, 193, *Reports of the Chief Registrar of Friendly Societies for the year ending 31 December 1911*, Appendix N, p. 7; 1911: PP 1913 (89) lvii, 173, *Reports of the Chief Registrar of Friendly Societies for the year ending 31 December 1912*, p. 60; 1912: PP 1914 (121) lxxvi, 1, *Reports of the Chief Registrar of Friendly Societies for the year ending 31 December 1913*, p. 80; 1913: PP 1914–16 (139) lix, 1, *Reports of the Chief Registrar of Friendly Societies for the year ending 31 December 1914*, p. 74; 1914: PP 1916 (30) xxiv, 1, *Reports of the Chief Registrar of Friendly Societies for the year ending 31 December 1915*, p. 82.

7.75 million members of collecting societies, throughout the whole of the United Kingdom. Taking all these classes of membership into account, and without making any allowance for double-counting, the total membership of all the societies recognised under the Friendly Society Acts was nearly 16 million.[28]

Although the extent of the coverage provided by the friendly-society movement has been the subject of considerable controversy, it would be wrong to exaggerate the significance of their growth. If one concentrates solely on those individuals who belonged to ordinary friendly societies (that is, societies providing sickness benefit) and members of affiliated orders, then it is probably true to say that the majority of the societies' members continued to be drawn from the better-off sections of the working class, even though there was a substantial increase in the number of agricultural workers who belonged to friendly societies in the second half of the nineteenth century, but if one extends the definition of a 'friendly society' to include the collecting societies, then, clearly, total membership extended much further down the social hierarchy.[29] However, one should not exaggerate the extent of the benefits which these workers were able to enjoy. There was a world of difference between an affiliated order, such as the Manchester Unity of Oddfellows, which paid its members ten shillings a week in sickness benefit during the middle years of the nineteenth century, and a friendly collecting society, making a one-off payment to cover the funeral expenses of an insured member or, in some cases, his wife and family.[30] It would also be wrong to assume that all of the individuals who belonged to a particular society were eligible for the full range of benefits. As Gosden and others have shown, one of the main ways in which the affiliated orders managed to expand their membership during the second half of the nineteenth century was by offering lower rates of benefit in return for smaller contributions, and Edwards, Gorsky, Harris and Hinde found that many of the individuals who joined the Hampshire Friendly Society at the end of the nineteenth century and the beginning of the twentieth century were only eligible for death benefits.[31] These findings suggest that even though there was a substantial increase in the number of people who joined friendly societies at the end of the nineteenth century, it would be wrong to assume that the growth of these organisations represented a viable alternative to the development of statutory welfare provision.[32]

Although the friendly societies were undoubtedly the most important (and, collectively speaking, the largest) of the organisations providing mutual assistance during the nineteenth century, they were not the only ones. As Hopkins has pointed out, many early trade unions chose to depict themselves as friendly societies in order to evade the impact of restrictive legislation, but the provision of friendly society and other benefits provided their members with an additional reason for belonging to the union, and enabled them to protect their position in the labour market. In 1824, the Liverpool Shipwrights' Society, with nearly 900 members, drew up plans for the development of an ambitious superannuation scheme, including the purchase of land for housing, a pension of five shillings a week, coal, a burial grant of £7, and a payment of £4 to each deceased member's widow. Hanson estimated that fourteen trade unions spent more than £3.5 million on the provision of funeral, sickness, superannuation and accident benefits between 1830 and 1889, and a further £4 million on unemployment and strike pay. During the 1880s and 1890s, many of the 'new' trade unionists criticised the leaders of the 'old' unions for devoting too much of their efforts to the provision of welfare benefits, but, as Hopkins has also shown, many of these new unions also provided welfare benefits in the late-nineteenth and early-twentieth centuries.[33]

We can obtain a more detailed picture of the range and extent of the benefits provided by trade unions in the early years of the twentieth century by examining the data in Tables 6.2 and 6.3. Table 6.2 shows the number of trade union members who were eligible to receive unemployment benefit, sickness and accident benefits, and accident benefits alone, in 1908. The figures suggest that more than 60 per cent of trade unionists belonged to unions which offered unemployment benefit, and that nearly 40 per cent belonged to unions which provided either accident benefits, or both accident benefits and sickness benefits. Table 6.3 shows the proportion of total union expenditure devoted to different purposes between 1907 and 1914. In the final year, trade unions devoted more than 60 per cent of their total expenditure to the provision of unemployment benefit, strike pay, sickness and accident benefits, funeral benefits and superannuation payments. They spent nearly £716,000 on unemployment

Table 6.2   Trade union members eligible to receive welfare-related benefits, 1908

Maximum weekly rate of benefit receivable	Membership eligible to receive		
	Unemployed benefit	Sick and accident benefits	Industrial accident benefit only
15/3 and over	26,469	11,518	–
12/3 to 15/-	142,090	66,537	2,257
11/3 to 12/-	109,851	90,146	15,907
10/3 to 11/-	17,774	17,193	524
9/3 to 10/-	606,456	307,112	66,786
8/3 to 9/-	200,460	98,356	12,902
5/3 to 8/-	158,796	88,061	78,956
5/- and under	149,506	42,481	34,581
Exact rate not ascertainable[a]	62,191	7,189	10,021
Total	1,473,593	728,593	221,934
Total membership of unions submitting returns	2,364,489	2,364,489	2,364,489
Total membership of all unions	2,383,244	2,383,244	2,383,244
Members entitled to receive benefits as percentage of total membership of unions submitting returns	62.32	30.81	9.39
Members entitled to receive benefits as percentage of total membership of all unions	61.83	30.57	9.31

Note: [a] The figure for unemployed benefit includes 17,955 members who did not receive unemployed benefit except in cases of infectious disease at home.

Source: PP 1912–13 Cd. 6109 xlvii, 655, *Report on trade unions for 1908–10, with comparative statistics for 1901–10*, pp. lxiv–lxv.

Table 6.3 Expenditure on welfare-related benefits by trade unions, 1907–14

Item	1907	1908	1909	1910	1911	1912	1913	1914
Number of trade unions on register	n/a	n/a	n/a	n/a	680	683	696	690
Number of trade unions making returns[a]	554	546	551	553	648	644	655	643
Number of members[a]	1,897,270	1,899,298	1,884,281	1,941,775	2,378,957	2,597,772	3,264,669	3,261,050
Unemployed, travel and emigration benefit (£)[b]	459,340	1,046,258	904,104	663,928	482,972	632,389	407,394	715,560
Dispute benefit (£)	146,969	580,263	242,411	525,939	609,859	1,658,913	457,927	667,370
Sickness and accident benefit (£)	475,100	517,348	518,648	473,782	511,413	515,363	708,366	679,874
Funeral benefit (£)	110,615	114,315	121,683	112,147	130,867	139,041	152,318	164,825
Other benefits (including superannuation and grants to members) (£)	403,654	537,259	448,013	469,004	510,630	525,940	523,640	540,556
Total expenditure on benefits (£)	1,595,678	2,795,443	2,234,859	2,244,800	2,245,741	3,471,646	2,249,645	2,768,185
Total expenditure (£)	2,273,789	3,567,124	3,027,522	3,030,501	3,241,603	4,571,238	3,614,780	4,193,789
Benefits expenditure as % of total expenditure	70.18	78.37	73.82	74.07	69.28	75.95	62.23	66.01

Notes: [a] Membership figures for 1913 and 1914 are end-of-year figures. [b] Unemployment expenditure for 1913 and 1914 is net expenditure – that is, total expenditure less contribution from Board of Trade.

Sources: 1907 and 1908: PP 1910 (171) lxxxiii, 189. Report of the Chief Registrar of Friendly Societies for the year ending 31 December 1909. Part A, pp. 100–1; 1909 and 1910: PP 1912–13 (123) lxxxi, 1, Reports of the Chief Registrar of Friendly Societies for the year ending 31 December 1911, Part A, pp. 100–1; 1911: PP 1913 (89) lvii, 173, Reports of the Chief Registrar of Friendly Societies for the year ending 31 December 1912, pp. 54–5; 1912–14: PP 1916 (30) xxiv, 1, Reports of the Chief Registrar of Friendly Societies for the year ending 31 December 1915, pp. 76–7.

benefit, and just under £1.4 million on sickness and accident benefit, funeral benefit, superannuation benefit, and other grants to members.

The third form of mutual aid to be considered in this section is the retail cooperative movement. The earliest cooperative stores can be traced back to the seventeenth and eighteenth centuries, and some authorities have claimed that more than 250 cooperative societies were formed between 1826 and 1835, but the modern cooperative movement really took off following the establishment of the Rochdale Equitable Pioneers Society in 1844. As is well known, the Rochdale Cooperative Society was established by 28 'Pioneers' who agreed to purchase shares of £1 each in order to raise sufficient capital to purchase the store. Their original aims were to protect themselves against the adulteration and overpricing of food by local shopkeepers, and to raise enough money 'to establish a self-supporting colony of united interests or to assist other societies in establishing such colonies'. However, their most important innovation was the decision to issue a dividend to all their members based on the value of the goods which they themselves had purchased. This apparently simple idea provided the basis for the establishment of more than 1500 cooperative societies by the end of the nineteenth century, with a total membership of around 1.5 million. The number of societies continued to increase during the early years of the twentieth century, and by 1914 the number of 'cooperators' stood at more than three million.[34]

In recent years, the question of how far the cooperative movement succeeded in improving the living conditions of people in working-class communities has become more controversial. Floud argued that 'the Coop captured, for the poor, the economies of bulk purchasing which they could not, individually, secure. It provided an alternative to the corner shop which, however well-located and friendly, could often lead the poor housewife into debt by the provision of credit. Once in debt, she was unable to complain about poor quality.' However, the provision of credit could itself be an important aid to the survival strategies of many poor families, and, in any case, the cooperative movement was itself convulsed by a series of debates over the provision of credit during the late-nineteenth and early-twentieth centuries. An even more important factor which tended to compromise some of the ideals behind the cooperative movement was the importance which cooperative-society members attached to the generation of profit and the issuing of dividends. According to Johnson, this factor meant that the price of goods in cooperative stores was often higher than that charged elsewhere, so that the shops themselves were less likely to be situated in the poorest areas.[35]

6.4 Commercial welfare

The final section of this chapter focuses on a number of organisations which were either aimed more consciously at more affluent members of the working class (or even the middle class), or organised on a more overtly commercial basis, or both. These organisations include the building societies, savings banks, and industrial assurance companies.

According to the Royal Commission on Friendly Societies in 1872, 'building societies ... are ... investment associations, mainly confining themselves to real securities.' The earliest societies, dating from the late-eighteenth and early-nineteenth centuries, were designed to raise sufficient funds to enable their members, or subscribers, to build their own houses, but during the nineteenth century, the societies began to operate more and more like savings banks, borrowing money from investors in order to lend it to borrowers who used the resulting loans to purchase their own property. It is extremely difficult to form an accurate estimate of the number of people who were enabled to buy their own homes with the aid of building society loans. In 1896, the Chief Registrar of Friendly Societies, E. W. Brabrook, estimated that there were approximately 115,000 mortgages currently in existence, and that over the previous 60 years, more than 250,000 householders had become the 'proprietors of their own houses' as a result of the societies' activities. However, one should also note that this figure accounts for less than one-third of the total number of owner-occupied households in England and Wales on the eve of the First World War, and for less than one-thirtieth of the total number of households overall.[36]

Like many organisations, savings banks were welcomed by the government as engines of thrift, but they differed from organisations such as friendly societies and building societies in that 'the user-members of the banks, the depositors, had no legal right whatever to any say in the management of the institutions to which they might entrust their savings.' The earliest savings banks were established at the end of the eighteenth century, but the movement grew rapidly following the introduction of the Savings Bank Act in 1817. However, it was still beset with difficulties, including irregular opening hours, an apparent failure to appeal to members of the ordinary working class in towns, and the embezzlement (or defalcation) of funds by bank officials. These failings played an important part in the government's decision to establish its own savings bank, the Post Office Savings Bank, in 1861.[37]

Some historians have questioned the extent to which either the trustee savings banks or the Post Office Savings Bank were genuinely working-class institutions. In 1888 the Select Committee on Trustee Savings Banks concluded that the Post Office Savings Bank was 'carrying provident habits into a lower stratum of society than that reached by the ordinary savings banks.' This opinion was justified on the grounds that the average amount of money deposited in the Post Office Savings Bank by each investor was smaller than the average amount of money deposited by investors in the trustee savings banks. However, Johnson has argued that the Committee exaggerated the differences between the two types of bank, and that even the better-off members of the working class found it difficult to set aside even small amounts of money on a regular basis. Johnson concluded that even though 'the bulk of account-holders were wage-labourers or their dependants ... the bulk of the funds in these savings institutions were the property of people who were not working class.'[38]

One of the most important forms of working-class saving was life assurance or, more accurately, burial insurance. The provision of burial insurance, or death benefit, was one of the most important functions of the friendly-society movement, and death benefits were also provided by trade unions, but these organisations were dwarfed by the industrial-assurance companies, of which the most notable was the Prudential Assurance Company. These companies grew

Table 6.4   Industrial-assurance policies, 1871–1914

Year	Paid-up policies (000,000)	Free policies (000,000)	Premium income (£m)	Total funds (£m)
1871	0.81[a]	–	–	–
1876	2.64[a]	–	–	–
1881	4.82[a]	–	2.25	1.91
1886	9.14	0.06[a]	3.74	5.36
1891	12.83	0.25[a]	5.46	9.59
1896	15.86	0.50[a]	7.15	14.40
1901	21.21	0.77[a]	9.61	22.10
1906	26.85	1.19[a]	12.44	34.40
1911	35.47	1.95	16.27	49.30
1914	36.37[b]	2.29[b]	17.98	58.70

Notes: [a]These figures relate only to the Prudential Assurance Company. In 1886, the Prudential had 7.11 million policies outstanding, 78 per cent of the total. [b] These figures have been estimated from the Prudential figures. Between 1913 and 1922 the Prudential share of policies fell from 56 per cent to 49 per cent of the total; its share of free policies fell from 86 per cent to 79 per cent.

Source: P. Johnson, *Saving and spending: the working-class economy in Britain 1870–1939*, Oxford: Oxford University Press, 1985, pp. 16–19.

very rapidly during the second half of the nineteenth century as people tried to ensure that their families would have access to sufficient funds to spare them the indignity of a pauper's funeral. The companies were generally far more successful than the friendly collecting societies because they were more efficiently run, kept more exact records, and only paid commissions to their salesmen on the *net* increase in policies (that is, they penalised their salesmen if policies were not maintained). As a result, as can be seen in Table 6.4, by 1914 more than 30 million industrial-assurance policies were currently in operation, and the industry as a whole was worth more than £58 million.[39]

6.5   Conclusions

If statutory provision, in the form of the Poor Law, and voluntary provision, in the form of private charity, represented two 'arms' of nineteenth-century welfare provision, then it is legitimate to regard self-help and mutual aid as the third 'arm' of what might be called the Victorian 'welfare state'. During the course of the nineteenth century, public officials and other opinion-formers were quite open in their belief that one of the main aims of social policy should be to encourage individuals and families to intensify their efforts to provide for themselves, either by joining voluntary organisations, or by accumulating individual savings. As John Stuart Mill observed in 1848:

A good government will give all its aid in such a shape, as to encourage and nurture any rudiments it may find of a spirit of individual exertion. It will be assiduous in removing obstacles and discouragements to voluntary enterprise, and in giving whatever direction and guidance may be necessary: its pecuniary means will be applied, when practicable, in aid of private efforts rather than in supersession of them, and it will call into play its machinery of rewards and honours to elicit such efforts. Government aid, when given merely in default of private enterprise, should be so given as to be as far as possible a course of education for the people in the art of accomplishing great objects by individual energy and voluntary cooperation.[40]

A number of more recent writers have also drawn attention to the nineteenth-century tradition of working class self-help and mutual aid, often for polemical purposes. While those on the left have regarded the growth of organisations such as friendly societies as manifestations of working-class resilience and collective endeavour,[41] those on the right have argued that they represented a genuine and viable alternative to the modern welfare state. Hanson claimed that:

The growth of friendly societies at the turn of the century and occupational pension schemes in recent years both illustrate the same principle: that the instinct of groups of people to provide independently for their welfare where a need exists and the means are available is amazingly strong ... The state can encourage [this instinct] by granting tax concessions for independent welfare schemes and in other ways; or it can discourage and suppress it, deliberately or inadvertently, by expanding state welfare and increasing taxation still further.[42]

This chapter has certainly demonstrated the importance of the part played by self-help and mutual aid in working-class communities. This took the form of both family and neighbourhood support, and more formal methods of mutual aid such as friendly societies and trade unions, as well as the expansion of individual attempts at saving, whether through building societies, savings banks, or even industrial assurance companies. However, very many people continued to suffer the consequences of poverty despite their own efforts and the support of their communities. Although the number of people belonging to organisations such as friendly societies and trade unions increased rapidly during the second half of the nineteenth century, the majority of these organisations confined their membership to those who were, relatively speaking, better off. The only organisations which could truly claim to have penetrated all sections of the working class were the collecting societies and the industrial-assurance companies, and even though the benefits provided by these organisations were not unimportant, they were of only indirect benefit to those still living.

7 Medicine and health care in the nineteenth century

During the last 30 years, medical historians have made great efforts to place the history of medicine in its social context, and to emphasise the full range of factors affecting the health of individual people. They are now less inclined to assume that the intentions of health-care providers were necessarily benevolent, and more sceptical of their claims to have made a significant contribution to the improvement of public well-being.[1]

This chapter seeks to reflect the impact of this new work on the history of health care during the nineteenth century. It begins by examining the ways in which ordinary people obtained health care, and the impact of legislative developments on the 'rise' of the medical profession. Section 7.2 examines the history of hospital provision, and, especially, the factors which lay behind the emergence of the hospital as the major 'locus' of medical care. Section 7.3 considers a specialised form of hospital provision, namely the development of institutional care for people who were considered to be mentally ill. This has been a particularly controversial area in recent years: some historians believe that the development of the asylum system was a benevolent or pragmatic response to the problems caused by mental illness in an industrialising society, whilst others argue that the emergence of large county asylums was part of an oppressive strategy of 'social control'.

7.1 Medicine and health care

Early-modern historians have shown that people living in the seventeenth and eighteenth centuries were not only affected by a wide range of unpleasant and often debilitating illnesses, but they also consumed a vast range of medical and herbal treatments in the hope of combating them. According to Dobson, 'there were drugs and pills of all kinds, for all diseases and for many occasions[, including] … tinctures, drops, balsams, syrups, draughts, potions, linctuses, poultices, gargles, cordials, evacuations, waters, blisters, decoctions, vomits, unguents, oils, liniments, emetics, laxatives, purges, powders, elixirs, lozenges, dressings, possets, leeches, electuaries, papers, mixtures, infusions, plasters, fermentations, salves, galenicals, pectorals, enemas, boluses, essences, tablets, ointments, salts, berries, juices, roots, herbs, seeds and scores of herbal, chemical and medicinal compounds and concoctions.' These treatments (and, no doubt, many more) were prescribed and dispensed by a surprisingly large number of medical practitioners. In 1783, Samuel Foart Simmons identified a total of 3,266 medical practitioners in provincial England (that is, outside London), including 89 surgeons, 363 physicians, 2,607 surgeon-apothecaries, 105 apothecaries and two man-midwives, but there were many other practitioners, not listed by Simmons, who were also practising medicine and treating the sick. One of the most notable features of this period is the extent to which 'regular' practitioners and 'irregular' practitioners worked alongside one another in a spirit of what might be called 'medical pluralism'. However, during the second half of the eighteenth century and the early part of the nineteenth century, the boundaries between 'regular' and 'irregular' medicine became increasingly rigid, and the status of the irregular practitioners increasingly controversial.[2]

One of the most important reasons for the growing hostility towards unqualified practitioners was the gradual increase in the provision of formal medical training. The first formally designated medical school was founded at the University of Edinburgh in 1726, and a series of private 'medical schools' developed in London from the 1740s onwards. The growth of these medical schools reflected the increasing demand for a set of skills and qualifications which might help to differentiate the 'qualified' practitioners from their unqualified competitors.[3] The growing number of voluntary hospitals after *circa* 1740 also provided an environment in which more formal training could be provided. However, the main reason for the growing tension between the 'regular' practitioners and the 'irregular' practitioners was the emergence, towards the end of the eighteenth century, of a species of practitioner known as the 'dispensing druggists'. As one contemporary observed in 1820:

> The apothecary, who was formerly only a druggist, had become a physician; and, as the apothecary was still more than ever required, the druggist took possession of his vacant stool and thus excited the same jealousy in the new physicians as the encroachment of the apothecary had done in the mind of the old physician... The apothecaries were certainly wrong for becoming grand, and shutting up their own shops, because they hastened the said catastrophe; but we believe that nothing could have prevented it.[4]

The campaign for a more exclusive and 'professional' form of medicine was also affected by developments within orthodox medicine itself. Medicine had traditionally been organised into three great 'branches', namely physic, surgery and pharmacy (four if one includes midwifery). Each of these branches was represented by its own collective organisation – the Royal College of Physicians, in the case of those who practised 'physic'; the Company of Surgeons, for those who practised surgery; and the Worshipful Society of Apothecaries, for those who dispensed drugs, or practised pharmacy. However, these distinctions became increasingly anachronistic, as more and more practitioners began to style themselves as 'general practitioners', capable not only of prescribing and dispensing drugs, but also of performing operations. The emergence of these new practitioners (the term 'general practitioner' was first used, according to Irvine Loudon, in 1809) fuelled demands for the reorganisation of the medical profession and the elimination of traditional hierarchies.[5]

The first attempt to reform the organisation of the medical profession and distinguish between licensed and unlicensed practitioners was the Apothecaries

Act of 1815. This Act has sometimes been described as the 'zenith of the apothecary in history' and as 'the great landmark in the history of the general practitioner' but its major aims were fatally compromised by the interventions of the Royal College of Physicians.[6] By insisting that the powers conferred by the Act should be exercised by the Society of Apothecaries, and that the words of the original Charter which established the Society should be incorporated into the Act, the Royal College ensured that general practitioners would continue to occupy a subordinate position in the ranks of the medical profession and that the dispensing druggists would be able to continue to practise their trade with relative impunity. In Holloway's words:

> The 1815 Act sought to perpetuate the obsolete hierarchical structure of the medical profession; it placed the general practitioner under the supervision of a London mercantile company and tied him to a system of education more suited to a trade than to a liberal profession; it failed to protect him from the competition of the unqualified and did nothing to change the degrading system by which he was remunerated; above all, it deterred many of the more highly-qualified members of the profession from acting as general practitioners.[7]

Although the medical profession had already acquired most of the structural characteristics associated with the modern medical profession by the middle years of the nineteenth century, it was not until the passage of the Medical Act of 1858 that these began to be recognised in law. This Act created the General Medical Council and said that all persons who had obtained a recognised qualification in either medicine or surgery or both should be entitled to have their names entered on the medical register. However, it failed to establish a uniform body of qualifications for all registered practitioners; unregistered practitioners continued to be allowed to practise; and the rules governing the constitution of the General Medical Council failed to guarantee any representation for general practitioners. On the other hand, the Act did prevent unregistered practitioners from holding any public appointments, such as that of Poor Law Medical Officer or Medical Officer of Health, or from holding any appointments with mutual aid societies, such as friendly societies, and the establishment of the medical register gave registered practitioners a definite advantage in the market for medical care.[8]

The third major piece of legislation was the Medical Act of 1886. This Act sought to address the reformers' principal criticisms in two main ways. In the first place, it set out to establish a common set of qualifications for the medical profession by insisting that all registered practitioners should be qualified in all three branches of medicine, namely general medicine, surgery and midwifery. Secondly, it said that the General Medical Council should contain five representatives elected by the registered medical practitioners of 'the several parts of the United Kingdom'. This clause meant that the directly elected representatives of the general practitioners remained in a minority on the Council, but it did succeed in breaking the monopoly hitherto exercised by Royal Colleges of Physicians and of Surgeons, the Society of Apothecaries, and the university medical schools.[9]

While historians have tended to devote particular attention to the main legislative developments associated with the 'professionalisation' of medicine, other factors also contributed to the growing dominance of the qualified practitioner. One of the most important of these was the increase in the number of medical charities and voluntary hospitals. These were not only an important source of medical training, but also a means of providing qualified medical care for both out-patients and home-patients. In 1860–1, the Huddersfield and Wakefield Infirmaries treated a total of 367 in-patients and 7,168 out-patients, between 20 and 50 per cent of whom received qualified medical attention in their own homes. There was also a substantial increase in the number of publicly funded medical appointments. By 1844 there were over 2,800 Poor Law Medical Officers throughout England and Wales, and the number of Medical Officers of Health rose from 825 in 1876 to more than 1,700 by the end of the century. The third important factor was the increase in the number of friendly societies, and the growing importance attached by these societies to the provision of medical attendance. Marland has argued that 'the friendly societ[ies] … gave their members a degree of choice in selecting their medical attendants and some control over their own health, and led to a decreased reliance upon charity and poor relief.' Riley has reinforced this view, arguing that 'the friendly societies … played some role in training working people in how to be patients' and 'brought working-class males as a group into contact with formal medicine'. [10]

These changes contributed to a substantial increase in the number of qualified medical practitioners during the second half of the nineteenth century, even though the number of registered doctors appears to have increased more slowly than the population as a whole. According to Cherry, the number of registered practitioners in England and Wales rose by more than 50 per cent between 1861 and 1911, but the population as a whole increased by nearly 80 per cent.[11] It is also difficult to gauge the impact of changes in access to medical care on the health of the population. Most of the conditions which might have encouraged people to consult a doctor were themselves non-fatal, but historians have tended to devote most of their attention to the impact of medical attendance on those conditions which were life-threatening.[12] James Riley has argued that changes in medical attendance may have contributed to the decline of mortality by enabling people who were suffering from fatal diseases to manage their conditions more effectively, but the evidence for this is still rather thin, and most historians continue to believe that medical attendance made very little contribution to the decline of mortality before the first half of the twentieth century.[13]

7.2 The hospital system

At the end of eighteenth century, it was still comparatively unusual for sick people to seek treatment in hospitals. As Granshaw pointed out, 'home was where the sick should be treated; hospitals were associated with pauperism and death'.[14] However, during the course of the nineteenth century, this attitude gradually changed, and by the beginning of the twentieth century hospitals had come much closer to occupying the central position in the provision of medical care which they occupy today. This transformation was related, at least in part, to developments which took place within the hospitals themselves. At the end of the eighteenth century, and during the early years of the nineteenth century, doctors began to play a much more positive role in identifying their patients' symptoms, rather than relying on the patients' own accounts, and this was followed by the introduction of a range of new techniques, such as the use of anaesthesia and the introduction of antiseptic and aseptic operating theatres, which enabled surgeons to offer a much wider range of hospital services.[15]

At the beginning of the nineteenth century, the majority of those who received any form of hospital care were likely to obtain it through a charitable dispensary. Loudon described the typical form of dispensary as 'a charitable institution where medicines are dispensed and medical advice given gratis or for a small charge'. The classic form of dispensary was established by a London Quaker, John Coakley Lettsom, in 1770, but the movement grew rapidly during the next 30 years, and by 1800 there were 16 general dispensaries in London alone, and a further 22 elsewhere. The dispensaries offered services to a number of different types of patient whom the more prestigious voluntary hospitals tended to exclude, including children, those suffering from chronic conditions, and the indigent poor, and patients could obtain treatment on most days of the week without needing to obtain a letter of recommendation from a hospital subscriber. By the end of the eighteenth century, it has been calculated that the voluntary hospitals of London were 'admitting' between 20,000 and 30,000 cases per year; the equivalent figure for the London dispensaries was approximately 50,000, and the total number of new sickness episodes treated by dispensary physicians in the country as a whole was 'at least 100,000, and probably more'.[16]

The dispensaries also played an important role in the development of specialist hospitals during the first half of the nineteenth century. A small number of specialist hospitals had been established during the eighteenth century, including some for the treatment of pregnant women, such as the British Lying-in Hospital at Woolwich, and others for the treatment of particular kinds of infectious or contagious disease, such as the London Smallpox Hospital and the Lock Hospital for the treatment of venereal disease. However, during the nineteenth century, a growing number of hospitals were established for the treatment of particular parts of the body, such as Moorfields Eye Hospital, or particular types of medical condition, such as the Royal National Orthopaedic Hospital, or for particular population groups, such as the Great Ormond Street Hospital for Sick Children. These institutions were bitterly resented by the general medical profession, who believed that they were undermining the principles of general medicine and designed solely to promote the interests of their founders, but they succeeded in attracting a growing number of new patients, and, as a result, made a vital contribution to the expansion of hospital medicine during the course of the nineteenth century.[17]

Despite the growth of the specialist hospitals, the most prestigious institutions continued to be the voluntary general hospitals. Although some of these institutions were able to trace their origins back to the twelfth and thirteenth centuries, the majority were of much more recent origin.[18] Most of these hospitals were founded and maintained by individual subscribers, but some of them also derived a growing proportion of their income from institutional subscribers, such as employers or Poor Law parishes, which purchased health-care rights for their employees or sick paupers.[19] Despite the threat which was allegedly posed to the voluntary hospitals by the specialist hospitals, the number of voluntary hospitals continued to rise during the first half of the nineteenth century, and they also began to play an increasingly important part in the provision of medical training. However, although the hospitals treated an ever-growing number of patients in this period, they continued to concentrate on the care and treatment of the 'deserving poor'. In 1861, out of 10,414 individuals identified as hospital inmates at the time of the national census, only 157 were classified as 'professional people', and only 14 were described as 'persons of rank or property not returned under any office or occupation'. The vast majority were wage-earners employed in industry, domestic service, or agriculture.[20]

Although the voluntary hospitals continued to expand in both size and numbers during the second half of the nineteenth century, they also experienced a number of fundamental changes which radically altered their role in the provision of health care. These changes were brought about partly as a result of the enhanced role played by the medical staff in the administration of the hospital, and partly by the increased financial difficulties which the hospitals now faced.[21] One of the most important changes was the decision to focus on the treatment of people suffering from acute conditions at the expense of those suffering from chronic conditions; the latter group were now much more likely to be consigned to the care of the Poor Law. Second, as hospitals began to select their patients more on the basis of medical need rather than social need, and as the population as a whole began to perceive more benefit in the use of hospital services, so the hospitals began to introduce charges for those who could afford to pay. This innovation was highly controversial (the *Lancet* complained that 'once the commercial principle comes in, the charitable principle begins to walk out') but it also enabled them to raise much-needed revenue, and helped to illustrate the growing importance of the hospital, and of professional medicine, in the provision of health care. Third, the hospitals also began to focus much more energy on the development of out-patient clinics. These provided the medical staff with a much greater opportunity to identify prospective patients, and also enabled the hospital authorities to bolster their claims to be providing a service to the whole community.[22]

In recent years, historians have begun to devote rather more attention to the development of Poor Law medical services before 1834, and it is now recognised that there was a substantial growth in the provision of institutional and domiciliary services during the late-eighteenth century and the early-nineteenth century, but this was much more apparent in the midlands, and in the south and east of the country, than it was in the north or west. In those areas where medical services were already well established, the advent of the New Poor Law led to very little improvement, and may have even have caused a deterioration in the level of service, as Boards of Guardians strove to enforce the principle of less eligibility. However, in the expanding industrial towns of northern England, there is at least some evidence to suggest that the Act did provide the institutional basis for the development of services which had scarcely existed previously.[23]

Although the years between 1834 and 1860 witnessed some important changes in the provision of Poor Law medical services and, especially, in the development of institutional facilities, these changes were much less significant than those which occurred after 1860. A series of reports and enquiries highlighted the appalling condition of many workhouse infirmaries, particularly in London, and these paved the way for a series of reforms which led to the gradual separation of the Poor Law's medical functions from its poor-relief functions and, as a result of this, to something resembling the establishment of a state medical service for the population as a whole.[24] The first major reform was the Metropolitan Poor Act of 1867, which led to the creation of a separate administrative authority – the Metropolitan Asylums Board – for the provision of medical services to the sick poor in London. Although this measure was confined to the capital, it foreshadowed developments on the ground in a range of other cities during the last 30 years of the century. In 1871, the Board took a further step towards the creation of a *public* medical service, as opposed to a Poor Law medical service, when it started to allow non-pauper patients to use the hospitals under its control, and in 1885 Parliament itself decided that individuals who took advantage of the Poor Law's medical services should no longer be subject to the same legal penalties which prevented the 'ordinary' poor from voting in Parliamentary elections.[25]

During the nineteenth century, public authorities began to take a much closer interest in the provision of specialist facilities for people suffering from infectious diseases. During the first half of the century, the majority of these patients were housed either in a small number of voluntary hospitals, such as the London Fever Hospital or the London Smallpox Hospital, or the House of Recovery in Manchester, or in the sick wards of Poor Law infirmaries. However, during the 1860s and 1870s, public health doctors began to pay much more attention to the role played by infected individuals in the transmission of disease, and this led to the establishment of a large number of specialist institutions for the isolation and treatment of infected individuals. In London, the Metropolitan Asylums Board took the lead in establishing a network of infectious disease hospitals from 1870 onwards, whilst elsewhere the initiative was taken by the local sanitary authorities. By 1891, more than 400 sanitary authorities (out of a total of 1,600) had established some form of specialist institution, and their number continued to rise following the introduction of the Infectious Diseases Notification Act of 1889, and the Isolation Hospitals Act of 1893 (which empowered county councils, though not county boroughs, to provide hospitals for the isolation of people with infectious diseases). By 1911, there were more than 700 infectious disease hospitals throughout England and Wales, and the total number of beds was just under 32,000.[26]

As the previous paragraphs have shown, the expansion of hospital provision in the eighteenth and nineteenth centuries represented a major change in the organisation and provision of medical care, but a number of writers have questioned whether this was really in the best interests of the population. McKeown and Brown argued that 'there is little difficulty in coming to a conclusion about the nature of eighteenth-century surgery' and that even during the nineteenth century, 'results of the common operations were, by any standards, appalling'. They also claimed that many patients placed themselves at greater risk simply by entering a hospital because of the likelihood of infection, and that it was not until the end of the nineteenth century (or even the twentieth century) 'that hospital patients could be reasonably certain of dying from the disease with which they were admitted'. However, they did not believe that hospital developments were invariably bad. They agreed with John Coakley Lettsom that the development of out-patient dispensaries performed a useful role in disseminating information about hygiene and ventilation, and thought that their impact was comparable to that of obstetricians 'who added nothing to the safety of the act of delivery, but justified their presence in the labour ward by recommending improved standards of hygiene'.[27]

Although many historians would agree that hospitals played a useful role in disseminating information about health care, McKeown and Brown may have underestimated the value of surgical operations and overstated the hazards of hospital admission. As Cherry has demonstrated, the majority of voluntary hospitals took concerted steps to exclude those sections of the population, such as children, who were most likely to be carrying infection, and, as a result, it seems likely that the number of people who died in hospital after contracting an infection from a fellow patient was much lower than McKeown and Brown appeared to believe.[28] McKeown and Brown also appear to have exaggerated the proportion of patients who died following surgical treatment. In 1874, the senior surgeon at London's University College Hospital claimed that the mortality rate following all forms of amputation was between 35 and 50 per cent, and that in certain cases the figure was as high as 90 per cent, but these figures have not been borne out by investigations elsewhere. Sigsworth found that only three patients (out of a total of 110) who underwent surgical operations at York County Hospital in 1868 died before leaving the hospital, and in Leeds, post-operative mortality rates varied between 7 per cent and 11 per cent between 1861 and 1874. Cherry examined post-operative mortality rates at hospitals in Bristol, Cambridge, Leeds, Leicester, Manchester, Norwich and Worcester, and concluded that 'deaths after operations were not uncommon, but mortality rates were usually of the order of 10–15 per cent'. There are some indications that mortality rates may have risen towards the end of the nineteenth century, as surgeons attempted to carry out more ambitious forms of treatment, but this may also have been the result of an increase in hospital overcrowding, which meant either that patients had to wait longer before being admitted to hospital, or that hospitals only chose to admit more serious patients, or that there was pressure to discharge patients before they had made a complete recovery.[29]

The debate over the impact of hospitals has tended to focus on the role of voluntary hospitals, but it is also worth considering the impact of developments in Poor Law hospitals and hospitals for the isolation and treatment of infectious diseases. Poor Law infirmaries were much more likely to admit patients suffering from chronic conditions and, as a result, they also admitted a much higher proportion of elderly patients who were unable to care for themselves and who were unable to receive appropriate assistance from members of their families.

During the 1860s, the Poor Law Board and the *Lancet* organised separate enquiries into conditions in workhouse infirmaries and uncovered a litany of complaints, including overcrowding, inadequate ventilation, a failure to segregate infectious and non-infectious cases, poor standards of hygiene, lack of comfort or opportunities for recreation, adequate but unappetising food and insufficient nursing provision, and even though many of these conditions improved during the second half of the nineteenth century, they continued to lag behind the standards provided in most voluntary hospitals. This may help to explain why death rates in some workhouse infirmaries were higher than voluntary hospital death rates. Edwards found that age-specific death rates at the Shoreditch Poor Law Infirmary were consistently higher than in Bristol's Royal Infirmary, but she also pointed out that these differences could be the result of differences in patient intake rather than the quality of care.[30]

It is also worth considering the potential impact of hospitals for infectious diseases. Hardy showed that many families were, at least initially, reluctant to enter isolation hospitals and that isolation itself was unlikely to have had much effect on the spread of such diseases as measles, whooping cough, smallpox, scarlet fever or diphtheria, but it may have contributed to the decline of mortality from both typhoid and typhus.[31] However, other authors have been more critical of the benefits of isolation policies. Macfarlane suggested that the increased provision of sanatorium accommodation for the isolation and treatment of tuberculosis patients in Glasgow in the early decades of the twentieth century may have had a negative effect, because it diverted attention away from the potentially greater need to improve standards of housing.[32]

7.3 The problem of lunacy

The previous sections have concentrated primarily on the development of more formal and institutional types of medical care for predominantly physical ailments, but this period also witnessed similar developments in the organisation of treatment for those regarded as mentally ill. However, whilst most observers have tended to regard the development of a more professionalised system of medical practice and the emergence of a modern hospital system as broadly (though not entirely) desirable changes, there is much less certainty surrounding the history of mental-health provision. It is clear that many Victorians had already become disillusioned with the results of mental-health 'reform' by the end of the nineteenth century, but the most dramatic changes in the historical understanding of these developments occurred in the third quarter of the twentieth century.[33]

Although Bartlett and Wright have recently drawn attention to the importance of family and community provision in the nineteenth century, the most important development in this period was the rise of the asylum. As Scull has shown, the total number of county and county borough asylums in England and Wales rose from nine in 1827 to 66 on 1 January 1890, and the total number of patients admitted to all types of asylum rose from under 7,000 in 1855 to more than 16,000 some 35 years later. According to Bartlett and Wright's own figures, it is likely that at least 40 per cent of all those regarded as 'idiots, imbeciles and lunatics' were housed in licensed asylums at the time of the 1871 census. When one considers that 'approximately 40–50 per cent of patients admitted to public (lunatic) asylums in the nineteenth century stayed twelve months or fewer', it seems reasonable to conclude that a much larger number of people passed through the doors of the asylum at some point in their lives.[34]

In 1955, Kathleen Jones argued that 'lunacy reform ... sprang from a conception of the community's responsibility for the well-being of its members, and revealed a new spirit of humanity in public life', but this confidence was about to be shattered by the work of a new generation of writers, including Thomas Szasz and Erving Goffman, who argued that the labelling of people as 'mad' represented an arbitrary act of social power, and that asylums, together with other 'total institutions', were 'forcing houses for changing persons; each is a natural experiment on what can done to the self'.[35] Although these writers were primarily concerned with the treatment of mental illness in their own times, their work inspired a number of others, including Michel Foucault and Andrew Scull, to adopt a much more critical approach not only to the history of insanity itself, but also to the history of society's attempts to deal with the problems associated with the 'insane'. However, in the more recent past, there have been some indications that the pendulum of historical opinion may have begun to swing once more. As historians and other commentators have become increasingly aware of the social costs of the large-scale deinstitutionalisation of mental-health services in the 1980s and 1990s, even the strongest critics of the asylum system have come to accept 'that for some substantial fraction of the psychotic, asylum care in its original sense is a virtual necessity'.[36]

The first steps towards the development of a national asylum 'system' were taken by a number of private entrepreneurs during the latter stages of the eighteenth century.[37] Although a small number of public asylums, such as St Luke's Hospital in London and the Manchester Lunatic Hospital, were set up during the second half of the eighteenth century, it was only during the first half of the nineteenth century that the state began to get involved in a significant way. The first major piece of legislation was the County Asylums Act of 1808, which gave the Justices of the Peace in each county the power to establish county asylums. This Act was followed by a second County Lunatic Asylums Act, passed in 1828, and the Madhouse Act, passed in the same year. However, the most important pieces of legislation were the Lunacy Acts of 1845 and 1890. The first of the 1845 Acts (8 & 9 Vict. C. 100) established a permanent national Lunacy Commission, with the power to make detailed and frequent inspections of all types of asylum, both public and private. The second (8 & 9 Vict. C. 126) instructed every county council and county borough to provide adequate asylum accommodation for pauper lunatics. The 1890 Act was primarily a consolidating measure, but it also introduced a number of important legal safeguards which were designed to protect asylum patients from unlawful confinement.[38]

In order to account for the growth of the asylum as a solution to the problems of mental illness, it is helpful to identify at least three distinct issues. In the first place, it is clear that there was a significant demand for asylum care from the families of those suffering from mental illness. This seems have been particularly important in terms of the rise of the private madhouses at the end of the eighteenth century, but it is also clear from nineteenth-century records which show that many ordinary families regarded the growth of the asylum as a way of relieving them of some of the burdens which the presence of a mentally-ill family member might impose. Second, one also needs to recognise the importance of the state's growing preference for institutional solutions to social problems, reflected not only in the construction of lunatic asylums, but also in the construction of prisons and workhouses. The third factor is the interest of the medical profession itself and, in particular, of that section of the medical profession which had most to gain from the expansion of the asylum system. Scull has argued powerfully that one of the most important questions concerning the rise of asylum growth is the question of 'how and why ... insanity [came] to be differentiated from the previously inchoate mass of deviant behaviours, so that it was seen as a distinct problem requiring specialised treatment in an institution of its own, the asylum'. In seeking to answer this question, Scull has focused particular attention on the role played by asylum managers in 'captur[ing] and organis[ing] the market' for the care and treatment of the insane, but other historians have challenged this emphasis, and Scull himself has acknowledged that 'the professional status of asylum doctors remained distinctly questionable' throughout the nineteenth century.[39]

One of the most contentious issues in the history of asylum provision is the question of treatment. During the eighteenth century, 'mad-doctors' attached particular importance to the use of physical restraints and fear to control their patients and help them to recover their reason, but at the end of the century, and during the early part of the nineteenth century, reformers such as Philippe Pinel in France and Samuel Tuke at York sought to replace the use of physical restraint with that of 'moral restraint'. They argued that patients were more likely to be cured with the aid of moral persuasion than physical fear. As Kathleen Jones and others have argued, these arguments played a large part in the campaign to improve the treatment of 'lunatics' generally. However, it is also clear that many of the more optimistic claims made by the reformers were not fulfilled. As the nineteenth century progressed, the number of people in asylums continued to rise, but the reformers' hopes of being able to cure their patients receded, the use of physical restraints was not abandoned, and the asylums came to be seen more and more as a dumping-ground for the irretrievably afflicted.[40]

One of the main difficulties in approaching the history of madness and mental health services generally is the problem of terminology. Despite the enormous amount of research which has been devoted to the history of insanity in the nineteenth century, we still know relatively little either about the actual experience of those who passed through the asylum, or about the real nature of the conditions from which they may or may not have been suffering.[41] For much of the nineteenth century, medical reformers and other observers used the term 'lunacy' to describe all those who were suffering from some form of mental illness or debility, and this can lead to confusion when we use the same terminology today.[42] The interpretation of the statistics on lunacy is also complicated by the fact that condition was often conflated with various forms of mental disability. Although it is possible to argue that 'idiocy was recognised in law as distinct from lunacy as early as the thirteenth century', this distinction was not recognised in the lunacy legislation of the nineteenth century. The Lunacy Acts of 1845 applied the term 'lunatic' to 'every insane person, and every person being an idiot or lunatic or of unsound mind', and the Lunacy Act of 1890 decreed that ' "lunatic" means an idiot or person of unsound mind'. Consequently, it was only during the course of the twentieth century that the state began to make a clear distinction between those adjudged to be lunatics, and those judged to be 'feeble-minded', 'idiots', 'imbeciles', 'mentally sub-normal' and 'mentally impaired'.[43]

7.4 Conclusions

By the end of the nineteenth century, the average individual was more likely to consult a qualified medical practitioner, or to attend a hospital, than at any time previously. However, despite these changes, there were also a number of limitations in the services provided. Although the number of qualified medical practitioners had increased, they were much more likely to be located in more affluent areas, and even though a substantial proportion of working-class men had obtained rights to medical care through their friendly societies, these organisations rarely conferred similar benefits on their wives or children. The development of hospital services also left room for improvement. There were substantial variations in both the quality and quantity of the hospital services provided in different areas, and the division between the voluntary hospitals and the Poor Law hospitals militated against any efforts to build a more unified service. Even though significant progress had been made in removing some of the stigma of the Poor Law from the Poor Law hospitals, these continued to be viewed with a certain amount of suspicion by many members of the population, and they continued to suffer from significant levels of under-funding and under-provision.[44]

One of the most important questions concerns the impact of these changes on the population at large. It seems unlikely that either the medical profession or the hospitals were able to exercise a decisive influence on mortality rates during the nineteenth century, but their impact may have been rather less negative that some commentators have been inclined to suggest. Recent work on the history of hospital provision has suggested that only a small proportion of patients in voluntary hospitals contracted new infections before they were discharged and that post-operative mortality rates may have been rather lower than some writers have been inclined to allege, and even though conditions in many Poor Law hospitals left a great deal to be desired, the establishment of isolation hospitals at the end of the nineteenth century may have led to reductions in the incidence of some infectious diseases. Hospital staffs and general practitioners may have also played a valuable role in disseminating advice and providing palliative care.

Although this chapter has paid particular attention to the treatment of physical complaints, it is also important to examine the history of the state's response to the problems of mental illness. The rise of the asylum has often been portrayed as part of a general, though by no means straightforward, process of reform, but this interpretation has been challenged by writers, such as Scull and Foucault, who have questioned both the motives and the outcomes of the reformers' efforts. However, as a number of writers have pointed out, it is important to try to judge the Victorian lunatic asylums by the standards of the time as well as by more modern standards of what constitutes acceptable care. Judged from this standpoint, it is at least arguable that the standard of care provided in the asylum was no worse and possibly somewhat better than the alternatives which may have been available at any one point in time.[45]

This chapter has concentrated primarily – though not exclusively – on the development of therapeutic medicine and the treatment of illness, but this was probably less important, in the context of the nineteenth century, than the history of the state's efforts to improve the environment and protect the population against the initial onset of disease. This history – the history of the public health movement – forms the subject of Chapter 8.

8

Public health in the nineteenth century

Although the nineteenth century witnessed many improvements in therapeutic medicine, most medical historians have tended to accept the view that these improvements made only a small contribution to the decline of mortality. McKeown argued that approximately one-third of the overall decline in mortality during the second half of the nineteenth century was caused by a decline in the incidence of water- and food-borne diseases, which he attributed to the impact of Victorian sanitary intervention, and that approximately 44 per cent of mortality decline was associated with a reduction in the death rate from airborne diseases, which he attributed to improvements in diet and nutrition.[1] This chapter explores the history of this debate, and examines the development of the campaign to improve public health from the late-eighteenth century onwards.

8.1 The origins of sanitary reform

As Dorothy Porter has recently demonstrated, there can be few societies, if any, which have not attempted to make some provision to protect themselves against the threat of disease. In the ancient world, both the Greeks and the Romans prescribed detailed and highly ritualised codes of individual behaviour to maintain health, and doctors working within the Hippocratic tradition used the medicine of 'airs, waters and places' to draw up detailed recommendations for the location of new settlements. During the Middle Ages, municipal authorities attempted to identify and isolate lepers, prohibited the dumping of animal carcases and other refuse in local rivers, and introduced quarantine measures to ward off the threat of plague. In sixteenth- and seventeenth-century England, straw was placed over the windows of houses containing plague victims, and household members were required to carry a white stick if they ventured outside. This period also witnessed new efforts to control sexual morality, as populations sought to protect themselves against the spread of syphilis.[2]

Although plague continued to be a major threat in England until well into the seventeenth century (the last major outbreak occurred in London in 1665), the most feared disease in the eighteenth century was smallpox. It is not entirely clear why smallpox should have become so important at this time, but it seems likely that the disease became increasingly virulent between the late-sixteenth and the end of the nineteenth centuries. One of the reasons why this disease was so feared was because there appeared to be no obvious way of combating it before the introduction of inoculation in the second decade of the eighteenth century. In 1721, Lady Mary Wortley Montagu showed that it was possible to limit the severity of an attack by inoculating children with blood taken from an existing sufferer, but the practice of inoculation only began to spread more rapidly (and even then only in rural areas) from the 1750s onwards. In 1798, a Gloucestershire physician, Edward Jenner, showed that it was also possible to protect children against smallpox by injecting them with cowpox, and this method, known as vaccination, became the preferred method of smallpox prevention from the early-nineteenth century onwards.[3]

Whilst historians have long been aware of the importance of inoculation and vaccination, more attention has begun to be paid in recent years to the somewhat broader range of environmental measures taken by cities, towns and villages in different parts of Britain (and elsewhere in Europe) to avoid disease during the seventeenth and eighteenth centuries. Dobson has provided a vivid account of the efforts taken to drain the marshland areas of Essex, Kent and Sussex between the 1670s and early-1800s. These efforts played a major role in the campaign to eradicate malaria and they appear to have played a pivotal role in reducing the general mortality rate in marshland areas (see Table 8.1). Between the 1670s and the early-1800s, marshland mortality fell from 60 deaths per 1,000 living in rural areas and 67 deaths per 1,000 living in urban areas to 28 deaths per 1,000 living in rural areas and 29 deaths per 1,000 living in urban areas, whilst mortality rates in non-marshland areas fell from 30 deaths per 1,000 living in rural areas and 37 deaths per 1,000 living in urban areas to 21 deaths per 1,000 living in rural areas and 23 deaths per 1,000 living in urban areas.[4]

Although the draining of marshland areas provides what is probably the best example of the 'environmental medicine' of the seventeenth and eighteenth centuries, it was not the only example.[5] Individual litigants used the manorial courts to bring complaints against the perpetrators of 'nuisances', such as 'the emission of smoke, heaping refuse on unoccupied land, [and] permitting privies and cesspools to drain into the newly-made sewers', and, from 1748 onwards, more than 300 towns and cities established Improvement Commissions, whose responsibilities included street-paving, gas-lighting, waste-removal and the

Table 8.1 Mortality rates in marshland and non-marshland areas in the south-east of England, 1670s–1800s (deaths per 1000 living)

Type	Rural		Urban	
	1670s	1800s	1670s	1800s
Non-marsh	30	21	37	23
Marsh	60	28	67	29

Note: Dobson's figures were based on returns from 403 rural parishes and 83 urban parishes in the 1670s, and from 488 rural parishes and 93 urban parishes in the early-1800s.

Source: M. Dobson, *Contours of death and disease in early-modern England*, Cambridge: Cambridge University Press, 1997, pp. 141, 153.

regulation of new buildings.[6] However, although significant improvements may have been made to the urban environment in London and many southern market towns, the pace of reform in the industrial towns of northern England was much slower.[7] Sidney and Beatrice Webb argued that 'the powers of municipal government which [the Improvement Commissioners] sought from Parliament were inadequate to the task that lay before them; and they usually came to the end of their borrowing powers, and found themselves levying their maximum rate, before they had done more than begin the "paving, cleansing, lighting, sewering, watching and generally improving" of their town, which was assumed to be their task'.[8] Hennock concluded that the Improvement Commissioners 'were primarily concerned with the comfort of the wealthier citizens ... As measures of sanitary reform, their value was marginal. For the same reason, they are not conclusive evidence that there existed an effective local public opinion in favour of sanitary reform.'[9]

Although it is difficult to find much evidence of a concerted national campaign for public health reform before the end of the eighteenth century, a number of writers had begun to focus attention on sanitary issues. In 1774 the pioneering epidemiologist, John Haygarth, showed that the incidence of disease in Chester appeared to be significantly lower than in the country as a whole, and in 1782 John Heysham examined the links between insanitary conditions and the spread of disease in Carlisle and other manufacturing districts, but very little action had been taken to improve sanitary conditions in many parts of the country before the outbreak of the first great cholera epidemic in 1831/2. As Flinn observed, 'cholera struck swiftly and sharply, raising local death rates dramatically if ephemerally. Cholera frightened people ... It was the clearest warning of the lethal propensities of the swollen towns of the new industrial era.'[10]

Cholera was undoubtedly a 'shock disease',[11] but the disease which probably had the greatest impact on discussions about public health in the first half of the nineteenth century was typhus. Although contemporaries often confused it with typhoid, typhus is a louse-borne infection which causes high temperatures, headaches, and either drowsiness or delirium. It also causes rashes to develop on the abdomen, arms, chest, back and trunk, and can lead to death from septicaemia, heart failure, kidney failure or pneumonia.[12] It appears to have been endemic in British towns and cities from the late-eighteenth century onwards, and frequently reached epidemic proportions during the first half of the nineteenth century. It appeared to be closely associated with poverty, and occurred most commonly in the insanitary and overcrowded districts of large towns. It therefore provided one of the main points of focus for a range of concerns regarding the habits and living conditions of the poor, and the consequences of urban growth.[13]

The growing importance of public health reform was reflected in a spate of publications in the 1830s and early-1840s. In 1833, Richard Millar drew attention to the links between poverty and typhus, and in 1839 Richard Howard showed that there was a close correlation between periods of scarcity and high mortality, but the majority of writers preferred to focus attention on the role played by the urban environment itself in the generation of disease. In 1838 and 1839, James Phillips Kay, Neil Arnott and Thomas Southwood Smith examined the relationship between insanitary conditions and the spread of disease in London, and their reports paved the way for the publication of Edwin Chadwick's *Report on the sanitary condition of the labouring population of Great Britain* in 1842. Although Chadwick recognised that many of the worst living conditions were to be found in rural areas, the most powerful sections of his report were those which demonstrated the stark differences in life chances between people from different social backgrounds growing up in different parts of the country. In the heavily agricultural county of Rutland, the average age at death of individuals belonging to labouring families was 38, and the average age at death among professional persons and their families was 52. By contrast, in the rapidly expanding manufacturing town of Manchester, the average age at which labourers and their families succumbed was just seventeen, and even among professional families, the average age at death was just 38.[14]

Hamlin has pointed out that many of the medical writers who campaigned for improvements in public health conditions drew a distinction between the 'predisposing factors' which caused some people to succumb to the effects of disease, and the 'exciting causes' which led them to become exposed to disease in the first place. Doctors such as William Pulteney Alison, Professor of Medicine at Edinburgh University, believed that it was necessary to tackle both the predisposing factors and the exciting causes, and this led them to advocate measures which would reduce the incidence of poverty and inadequate nutrition, as well as improving the quality of the urban environment. However, figures such as Edwin Chadwick and Thomas Southwood Smith rejected these arguments. They believed that 'no government can prevent the existence of poverty [and] no benevolence can reach the evils of extreme poverty under the circumstances which at present accompany it', but that it would be possible to address these circumstances by means of sanitary reform.[15]

Although Chadwick and his allies have been sharply criticised in recent years, some of this criticism may be misplaced. Even though many of the medical writers cited by Hamlin believed that poverty was one of the chief causes of disease (or of susceptibility to disease), they did not necessarily have a coherent programme of anti-poverty reform, and it is worth remembering that William Pulteney Alison's main aim was not to undermine the operation of the New Poor Law in England, but to campaign for its extension to Scotland, where the existing level of provision was even more rudimentary.[16] It is also important to remember that even though Chadwick may have been concerned to distract attention from the question of poverty, he still had to overcome a great deal of concerted opposition from a variety of vested interests in order to make the case for the sanitary alternative.[17] It would also be wrong to underestimate the extent to which sanitary reform appeared to offer a solution not only to problems of ill-health, but also to the whole range of social and moral problems associated with urban growth. As Wohl has argued, 'public health ... became a kind of *fundamental* reform, an underpinning and *sine qua non* for other reforms. Chadwick was simply voicing a common attitude of mind when he commented "how much of rebellion, of moral depravity and of crime has its root in physical disorder and depravity ... The fever nests and seats of physical depravity are also the seats of moral depravity, disorder and crime".'[18]

Although the *Sanitary report* provided a devastating critique of existing sanitary arrangements, there were still a large number of technical questions which needed to be addressed before legislation could be introduced, and in 1843 the Home Secretary, Sir James Graham, appointed a Royal Commission to investigate these issues as part of its enquiry into the state of large towns and populous districts.[19] During the next two years, the Commission surveyed the existing state of sanitary legislation and interviewed 65 expert witnesses, including Thomas Hawksley, the Engineer for the Trent Waterworks Company in Nottingham, on such issues as the supply of pure water to all houses, the disposal of urban refuse, the reduction of overcrowding, and the regulation of common lodging houses. The Commission endorsed Chadwick's calls for the creation of some kind of central body to supervise the activities of local authorities, and said that the powers of these authorities should be expanded, and their boundaries extended so that they would correspond with the natural areas for drainage. It also recommended that the responsibility for all matters relating to public health, namely drainage, paving, cleansing and the provision of an ample water supply, should be vested in a single local authority body, and that Parliament should frame national regulations for the construction of new buildings, the width of streets, and the inspection and control of common lodging houses.[20]

By the time the Commissioners had completed their second report, there was widespread support for the principle of sanitary reform but there were also a considerable number of additional obstacles which still needed to be overcome. Both the private water companies and many factory-owners were concerned about proposals to control municipal water supplies and place curbs on atmospheric emissions, and there was a predictable outcry from ratepayers' groups about the potential cost of any additional municipal responsibilities. However, the strongest objections concerned the threat of increased central control and the consequent loss of local autonomy. These fears were reinforced by persistent allegations that Chadwick himself was more concerned with the improvement of his own position than with the improvement of the urban environment.[21]

During the period between 1845 and 1848, Chadwick and his allies made a series of attempts to win Parliamentary support for a national programme of public health reform. In July 1845, Lord Lincoln (the Commissioner for Woods and Forests), introduced a limited Public Health Bill which was then withdrawn almost immediately for further consideration and amendment, and even though the Bill was reintroduced in the following year, it was quickly overtaken by the crisis over the repeal of the Corn Laws and the fall of Peel's Conservative government. In 1847, Lincoln's successor, Lord Morpeth, introduced a further Bill which was then talked out by the Conservative opposition, and had to be reintroduced, in a revised form, in February 1848. Even then, the Bill still had to endure a further six months of often heated debate before it passed into law.[22]

One of the most controversial issues concerned the government's efforts to establish a mechanism under which further action might be taken. When Morpeth reintroduced the Public Health Bill in February 1848, he suggested that a public enquiry should be carried out 'upon the petition of not less than fifty inhabitant householders of any city, town, borough or place to which the Act may be applied', but this clause was subsequently amended, so that an enquiry could only be undertaken if the petition had the support of one-tenth of the resident ratepayers.[23] If this amendment had been accepted without any further change, the Act would have become almost entirely inoperable because, as Chadwick pointed out, 'all the butchers, all the fishmongers, all the poulterers who are to be subjected to inspection, all the lodging-house keepers, all the owners of ... houses having cellar tenements, and persons carrying on trades which are nuisances ... all these are ratepayers ... and yet we are to expect unheard-of combinations amongst them for the introduction of measures which benefit chiefly the working classes'.[24] In July, the Bishop of London proposed that an enquiry might also be undertaken if the death rate 'from typhus fever, diarrhoea, scarlatina, and other febrile epidemic, endemic and contagious diseases' exceeded 20 per cent of the total number of deaths or the average death rate from such diseases in other parts of the country, but the Registrar-General objected that the incidence of these diseases 'would not always afford a fair criterion of the sanitary condition of the district'.[25] However, in August Morpeth proposed an alternative formulation, authorising enquiries in districts where the average death rate exceeded 23 deaths per 1000 living over a seven-year period, and even though Chadwick believed that 'the infantile mortality rate would really have been the best test', he still wrote to Morpeth to congratulate him on 'a very decided improvement ... in every way'.[26]

Although Chadwick believed that the introduction of the new clause would help to ensure that the new Act could be applied to a larger number of areas, it was still largely dependent on the goodwill of local ratepayers. Its most important innovation was the establishment of a General Board of Health, with the power to appoint a Secretary and as many superintending inspectors as were deemed necessary to implement it, but in practice its powers were quite limited. As we have just seen, it was given the power to institute an enquiry into the sanitary condition of any area if more than ten per cent of the ratepayers requested such an enquiry, or if the local death rate had exceeded an average of 23 deaths per 1000 living over the previous seven years, and it was also given the power to appoint a local Board of Health if, as a result of such an enquiry, it felt that it was necessary to impose the provisions of the Act on that area. However, the General Board was only appointed for a limited period of 'five years ... [from] the day after the passing of [the] Act, and thenceforth until the end of the then next session of Parliament, and no longer', and the largest local authority, London, remained under the control of the Metropolitan Commission of Sewers. The key to the successful implementation of the Act was the appointment of local Boards of Health, but even in those areas where such Boards were established, the General Board lacked the power to ensure that they did their jobs either carefully or conscientiously.[27]

8.2 Public health in Britain, 1848–1914

Although the Public Health Act marked the culmination of almost 20 years' worth of campaigning, its significance can easily be exaggerated. James Hanley has recently argued that 'the strength of public support for national sanitary legislation ... is evidenced by the speed with which localities tried to adopt the permissive Public Health Act after it received Royal Assent in August 1848', but it is also important to look at the size of the populations covered by the areas in which the new legislation took effect.[28] Between 31 August 1848 and 5 March 1850, 192 towns and districts applied for sanitary inspection, but only 50 of these areas contained more than 10,000 inhabitants, and only five contained more than 50,000 inhabitants.[29] Of the 50 'large towns and populous districts' whose sanitary condition had been investigated by the Royal Commission in 1843 and 1844, only 29 had applied for inspection under the Public Health Act by 9 March 1853.[30] Between 31 August 1848 and 31 December 1853, local Boards of Health were established in 14 areas where the local death rate had exceeded 23 deaths per 1000 over the previous seven years, and in 168 areas where an enquiry had been requested by more than ten per cent of the local rate-payers, but the average population of the areas which acquired a local Board of Health was only 11,538, and their combined population was only 2.1 million.[31] The total population of England and Wales at the time of the 1851 census was 16.9 million.[32]

In 1852, the Secretary of the General Board of Health, Edwin Chadwick, complained that the Board's efforts had been undermined by an unfair campaign of 'foul dealing ... which no more required to be calculated upon than the revival of the practices of the dark ages of poisoning and assassination'. Although he acknowledged that 'the science of prevention is a new one', he also bemoaned the fact that 'vast sums are spent in the charity of alleviation [whilst] the sanitary association can with difficulty obtain subscriptions of a few hundreds'.[33] However, even the most sympathetic of Chadwick's biographers cannot conceal the fact that he could sometimes be his own worst enemy. Finer described him as 'an ardent crusader in other people's causes, moving ruthlessly and fanatically to his own preconception of what he thought was good for them', and Lewis commented that 'there never was a man more suspicious of his antagonists' motives than Chadwick, more convinced that their objections sprang from a materialist root, a trading profit, a family connection or some snug little place'.[34] Even though many of Chadwick's contemporaries were ultimately prepared to concede that he might have done some good for them, it is not altogether surprising that he should have experienced so much difficulty in finding others who were prepared to work with him.[35]

In 1854, Parliament decided to replace the first General Board of Health with a new Board, under the direct control of Sir Benjamin Hall, the Member of Parliament for St Marylebone and St Pancras, and in 1855 John Simon was invited to become the new Board's first Medical Officer. This was an appointment of considerable importance in the history of public health. Simon was a medical man, who had worked as a surgeon as St Thomas's Hospital before becoming Medical Officer to the City of London in October 1848. He was much more attuned to the individual causes of disease than Chadwick, with his all-embracing view of the importance of sanitation, and as an individual, he was much more receptive to new ideas and alternative remedies. Although his own reputation has also been attacked, his 'open-mindedness' was reflected in the large number of enquiries which he authorised during the course of his career, first as Medical Officer to the Board of Health (1855–8), then as Medical Officer to the Privy Council (1858–71), and finally as Medical Officer to the Local Government Board (1871–6). These included enquiries into such subjects as occupational health, infant mortality, dietary standards, food adulteration, poisons, the location of hospitals and the improvement of housing conditions.[36]

The years after 1854 also witnessed some important changes in the understanding of the causes of disease. As we have already seen, many late-eighteenth and early-nineteenth century medical writers had a multi-factorial view of the origins of disease, involving an understanding not only of the 'predisposing factors' which caused some people to become sick, but also of the 'exciting causes' which exposed them to disease in the first place. During the 1830s and 1840s, Chadwick and his allies had succeeded in minimising the importance of the first set of causes, and reinterpreting the second set of causes in terms of an overwhelming emphasis on the idea that diseases were 'caused' by exposure to the 'miasma', or bad air, emanating from the decomposing bodies of dead animals and other organic matter, such as rotting fruit and vegetables and human faeces.[37] However, during the 1850s and 1860s, this theory began to give way to a range of new ideas, centring on the view that many diseases were actually spread by different microscopic organisms in the air which people breathed, and in the food and water which they ate and drank. These ideas laid the foundations for a much more wide-ranging approach to public health policy than that envisaged by Chadwick. They meant that the government would have to introduce a much broader range of measures to combat different sources of infection, and that sanitary engineering by itself could not be relied upon to produce all the necessary improvements in public health standards.[38]

Simon's open-mindedness, combined with the extra legitimacy conferred by the new understandings of the causes of disease, helped to bring about a number of highly significant changes in the nature and scope of public health legislation, and in the relationships between central and local government. One of the most important illustrations of this new mood was the growing willingness to introduce, and accept, compulsory public health legislation. The first 'compulsory' Act was the Sanitary Act of 1866, which not only extended the scope of public health legislation, by expanding the legal definition of 'nuisances' prejudicial to health, but also extended the power of central government and the obligations of local authorities by compelling local authorities to inspect their districts and exercise their basic powers. This Act was followed by the Public Health Act of 1872, which sought to simplify the pattern of sanitary administration in England and Wales by creating a single sanitary authority for each area, and obliged every sanitary authority to appoint its own Medical Officer of Health. The process of reform was continued by the Public Health Act of 1875. This enormous Act – it ran to 343 separate sections and five schedules – consolidated the public health legislation of the previous 27 years, and established the basic legal framework for the development of public health policy for the next 60 years.[39]

The changing relationship between central and local government was also reflected in the increase in the value of the loans made by central government to local authorities to enable them to finance public health works. The

Government first acquired the power to issue such loans under section 108 of the 1848 Public Health Act, and a special Act to provide loans to manufacturing districts was passed in 1863, but the value of these loans increased sharply following the establishment of the Local Government Board in 1871. During the 1850s and 1860s, the average value of the loans contracted by local authorities for public works varied between £300,000 per year and £700,000 per year, but the average value of the loans contracted during the 1870s and 1880s was over £2,000,000. During the 1890s, the value of the loans contracted by local authorities ranged from £2.8 million (in 1890) to £7.3 million (in 1893).[40]

The period after 1848 also witnessed some important developments in the relationship between the state and the individual. In 1840, Parliament established a voluntary vaccination service for infants against smallpox. The scheme was administered by the Poor Law medical service, and parents could choose whether or not to take advantage of it. However, in 1853 a further Act was passed, under which all parents were compelled to have their children vaccinated, regardless of their personal beliefs.[41] In 1864 Parliament authorised what some writers regarded as an even more blatant infringement of individual liberty, when it passed the first of three Contagious Diseases Acts, under which women living in selected areas could be subjected to a compulsory medical examination if they were believed to be prostitutes.[42] Both sets of measures were fiercely contested, and there are good reasons to doubt whether they were ever fully implemented, but they provide a salutary illustration of the lengths to which a supposedly liberal and individualistic society was prepared to go in limiting the exercise of personal freedom when it felt that the circumstances warranted it.[43]

The second half of the nineteenth century also witnessed a number of important changes in the scope of public health legislation. The Government took action to improve standards of food and drug quality under the Food and Drug Act of 1860, and the Sale of Food and Drug Acts of 1875 and 1879. In 1863 Parliament passed the Alkali Act, which was designed to reduce levels of atmospheric pollution by controlling emission levels from alkali factories, and in 1876 legislation was passed to prevent the dumping of industrial waste products and other refuse into local rivers. A series of Acts were passed to improve the health of people at work: the Factory Act of 1864 introduced new regulations regarding the ventilation of factories; the Factory and Workshops Act of 1878 prohibited the employment of women and young children in lead factories; and the Prevention of Lead Poisoning Act of 1883 established minimum standards of hygiene for all lead-workers. In 1868 Parliament gave local authorities the power to demolish insanitary dwellings, and in 1878 they acquired the power to purchase private water companies, in order to ensure the provision of a clean water supply. During the 1870s a number of local authorities began to build specialist hospitals for people suffering from infectious diseases, and in 1893 Parliament gave county councils the power to build isolation hospitals. The Infectious Diseases Notification Act of 1889 gave local authorities the power to compel local medical practitioners to inform the local public health department if any of their patients was suffering from one of a range of notifiable infectious diseases. The number of infectious disease hospitals rose from none to 353 between 1861 and 1891, and from 353 to 703 between 1891 and 1911.[44]

Despite the tremendous expansion in the scope of public health activity, the vast majority of these measures were really concerned with the protection of the community as a whole, rather than the individuals who comprised it. However, during the late-nineteenth and early-twentieth centuries, public health officials became increasingly concerned with what they regarded as the 'personal factors' associated with the spread of disease. This emphasis on the role of personal factors led in the first instance to a growing concentration on the need for health education, particularly in the areas of infant management, food preparation and personal hygiene, but it soon spilled over into a more general campaign for the provision of health services which were aimed directly at particular groups of individuals. In 1899 the first milk depot was established in St Helens in Lancashire, to provide cheap milk for infants at affordable prices, and the first 'School for Mothers' was established in the London borough of St Pancras in 1907. This year also witnessed the passage of the Notification of Births Act, which gave local authorities the right to be informed of any new births, and the Education (Administrative Provisions) Act, which led directly to the establishment of a national system of school medical inspection, and, subsequently, the creation of local authority school clinics. In 1911 Parliament passed the National Insurance Act. This Act was concerned primarily with the provision of cash benefits to workers who were either sick or unemployed, but it also contained a national health-insurance scheme which gave insured workers unprecedented rights to medical treatment. These included the offer of free accommodation in a sanatorium for workers who were suffering from tuberculosis, leading to the establishment of a national system of local authority tuberculosis services under the administrative control of the Medical Officer of Health.[45]

8.3 Public health and the decline of mortality

McKeown argued that 33 per cent of the net reduction in mortality between 1848/54 and 1901 was associated with a decline in mortality from water-borne diseases, and that 44 per cent of the net reduction in mortality was associated with a decline in mortality from air-borne diseases, and this led him to conclude that the *main* cause of mortality decline during the second half of the nineteenth century was an improvement in the standard of nutrition, which meant that more people were able to resist the effects of an infectious disease at the time it struck them.[46] However, other writers have argued that the principal reason for mortality decline was an improvement in the quality of the public health environment. Hardy claimed that:

> The problems of nineteenth-century cities called for a systematic and professional administrative response, which was provided with the establishments of sanitary authorities and, more especially, of Medical Officers of Health in London in 1855 and elsewhere in 1872. The Medical Officers of Health played a central part in the transformation of England's disease experience during the last decades of the nineteenth century. It was they who spearheaded the Victorian struggle against infectious diseases,

and it was their initiative and their labours which led to the eventual eradication of the epidemic streets.[47]

In order to examine this issue more closely, it may be helpful to take a more long-term view of the changing level of mortality in England and Wales between 1700 and 1914. At the beginning of this period, England experienced a high rate of underlying mortality, coupled with frequent episodes of extremely high 'crisis' mortality. As the century progressed, outbreaks of crisis mortality became less marked, and the average level of life expectation at birth began to rise consistently from the mid-eighteenth century onwards. However, average life expectancy fell between the 1810s and 1840s, and there was little further improvement before the end of the 1860s. By the time of the First World War, the average rate of mortality in the whole of England and Wales had fallen to exactly 14 deaths per 1,000 living,[48] and babies born during the first decade of the twentieth century could expect to live for at least fifty years (see Figure 8.1).

Although there is a still great uncertainty surrounding the reasons for the decline in mortality in England and Wales before 1800, it seems clear that one of the main contributory factors was the gradual spread of inoculation and vaccination against smallpox. As both Razzell and Mercer have demonstrated, smallpox was a major cause of infant and child mortality in the first half of the eighteenth century, and there is a substantial body of evidence to show that the introduction of prophylactic measures was associated with a substantial reduction in smallpox mortality in those areas where such measures were introduced.[49] However, it seems unlikely that the introduction of inoculation and vaccination can account for the whole of the decline in mortality, especially in

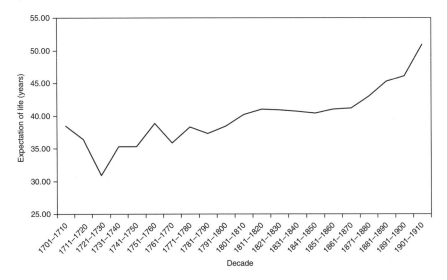

Sources: E. A. Wrigley, R. Davies, J. Oeppen and R. S. Schofield, *English population history from family reconstitution 1580–1837*, Cambridge: Cambridge University Press, 1997, pp. 614–15; R. Woods, *The demography of Victorian England and Wales*, Cambridge: Cambridge University Press, 2000, p. 365.

Figure 8.1   Expectation of life at birth, 1701–1910

those areas where the practice of inoculation spread more slowly, and this has led many historians to look at other factors which might have contributed to mortality decline, including improvements in both nutrition and the urban environment.

As we have already seen, the eighteenth century witnessed a number of significant improvements in the quality of both the urban and rural environments. During the period between 1650 and 1800, a concerted attempt was made to drain the marshlands of south-eastern England, and this appears to have led to a substantial reduction in both urban and rural mortality rates in the marshy areas of Essex, Kent and Sussex.[50] This period also witnessed significant improvements in the quality of the built environment in London and in many of the small market towns of southern England, although such efforts appear to have been much less well advanced in the industrial towns of northern England which were to bear the main brunt of population growth in the nineteenth century.[51] However, in spite of this, many historians have continued to express doubts about the extent to which these developments can explain the whole of the decline in mortality before *circa* 1800. Schofield and Reher concluded that, in the absence of further information about the extent and impact of early environmental measures, 'it is very difficult to argue in favour of the importance of public health measures in Europe before the second half of the nineteenth century'.[52]

Although some historians have claimed that environmental improvements were responsible for the decline in mortality before 1800, others have continued to claim an important role for improvements in nutrition. Livi-Bacci suggested that the link between nutrition and mortality was unproven, but Fogel concluded that even though 'there can be little doubt that the high disease rates prevalent during the early-modern era would have caused malnutrition even with diets otherwise adequate in calories, proteins and other critical nutrients ... recent research indicates that, for many European nations before the middle of the nineteenth century, the national production of food was at such low levels that the poorer classes were bound to have been malnourished under any conceivable circumstances, and that the high disease rates of the period were not merely a cause of malnutrition but undoubtedly, to a considerable degree, a consequence of exceedingly poor diets.'[53]

One of the major obstacles to acceptance of the nutritional view is the apparent contradiction between the evidence of declining mortality and falling real wages. Wrigley and Schofield concluded that it was extremely unlikely that dietary standards could have improved during the second half of the eighteenth century since real wages were falling, and Livi-Bacci has argued that 'if real wage trends are tied to trends in nutritional level, and this is certainly true for the wage-earning population, there appears to be no perceptible direct link, at least in the aggregate, with mortality. If anything, the exact opposite is true'. However, more recent research has cast doubt on the assumption that real wages were indeed falling. Feinstein showed that the average value of real earnings (after allowing for variations in unemployment) rose in England, Scotland and Wales by 12.5 per cent between 1770/2 and 1818/22, and Fogel has argued that the proportion of meat in the average British diet increased during the course of the eighteenth century, whilst the calorific value of the food consumed by the average member of the population increased by 3.2 per cent between 1750 and 1800.[54]

These findings suggest that nutrition may after all have played an important role in the decline of mortality in Britain before 1800, but it is rather more difficult to see how changes in nutrition may have been related to the apparent cessation of mortality decline between 1820 and 1870. Komlos argued that the quality of the average diet may have deteriorated because increases in the relative price of meat may have encouraged consumers to transfer expenditure from meat and dairy products to nutritionally inferior grains, and Haines has recently suggested that changes in the ratio of agricultural prices to industrial prices may have led to a reduction in food expenditure altogether, but the evidence for these claims is not convincing.[55] Horrell showed that British consumers devoted an *increasing* proportion of their food budgets to expenditure on meat and dairy products between 1801 and 1841, and Feinstein's figures suggest that even though there was a reduction in the proportion of expenditure devoted to all types of food between 1828/32 and 1858/62, the extent of this change was more than outweighed by the increase in working-class earnings as a whole.[56] These findings are reinforced by the evidence from contemporary dietary surveys. Fogel has argued that the proportion of meat in the average diet fell from 25–30 per cent during the second half of the eighteenth century to approximately 20 per cent in 1850, but he also claims that the average daily consumption of calories rose by 5.6 per cent between 1800 and 1850, and both Clark, Huberman and Lindert and Oddy have suggested that there were improvements in both the quality and the quantity of the diets consumed by labouring families between the end of the eighteenth century and the beginning of the 1840s.[57]

In view of these findings, it seems unlikely that the cessation of mortality decline after 1820 can be attributed, to any significant degree, to a deterioration in the level of nutrition, but it may be attributable to a change in the nature of the disease environment in which a growing proportion of the population lived. During the first half of the nineteenth century, several contemporaries drew attention to the appalling health associated with urban areas, and these fears were compounded by the very fast pace at which the size of the urban population was increasing. As Wohl has pointed out, the number of towns and cities containing more than 100,000 inhabitants increased from one to eight between 1801 and 1851, and by the end of the period the population of London had risen to more than one million. During the period as a whole, the proportion of the population residing in towns containing more than 10,000 inhabitants rose from 24 per cent to 44 per cent, and the proportion of the population residing in towns with more than 100,000 inhabitants rose from 11 per cent to 25 per cent. Many of the most rapid rates of urban growth were experienced by the growing industrial towns of northern England. Between 1801 and 1851, the population of Manchester increased from 75,000 people to 303,000, whilst the population of Liverpool rose from 82,000 to 376,000. The population of Bradford rose from 13,000 to 104,000.[58]

A number of recent authors have suggested that urban conditions were not only less healthy than rural conditions, but that conditions within towns may have grown worse. Huck showed that there was a significant increase in the level of infant mortality in nine urban parishes in central and northern England between 1813/18 and 1831/6, and evidence from four of these parishes (Walsall, West Bromwich, Wigan and Ashton) suggested that this deterioration was unlikely to have been reversed, and may even have continued, into the 1840s.[59] Floud, Wachter and Gregory found that there was a substantial deterioration in the average heights of men born in London and other urban centres, and that this was at least partly responsible for the decline in the average height of the male population as a whole during this period.[60]

Although there is strong evidence of a deterioration in infant mortality and in stature, it has proved rather more difficult to establish whether or not there was any deterioration in mortality rates as a whole within urban areas. In 1985 Woods suggested that the average level of life expectancy at birth rose in all parts of Britain during the first half of the nineteenth century, including rural areas, small towns, large provincial towns and the capital, and that the absence of any clear improvement in national mortality rates was a direct result of changes in the proportions of the population inhabiting different types of district, but Szreter and Mooney argued that average life expectancy at birth declined sharply in the largest provincial cities during the 1830s, and only began to improve consistently from the 1870s (even though their figures also showed that the average level of life expectancy at birth in these towns increased by four years during the 1850s). Woods has since revised his earlier estimates, and he now believes that average life expectancy may have declined after all in both large and small towns between the 1830s and the 1850s.[61]

In view of these conflicting claims, it is difficult to reach any categorical conclusions regarding the detailed pattern of mortality change in different types of settlement before the latter part of the nineteenth century, but a number of important points have emerged. As we can see from Table 8.2, both Woods and Szreter and Mooney suggest that mortality rates were improving in some parts of the country between 1820 and 1870, even if they were deteriorating elsewhere. Second, even though Szreter and Mooney believe that the average level of life expectancy in Britain's largest provincial towns declined during the 1830s, both they and Woods suggest that the average level of life expectancy in these areas rose during the 1850s, even if they disagree about the course of mortality in the 1860s. Third, even though the average level of mortality remained relatively unchanged during the middle decades of the nineteenth century, children's mortality rates began to fall during the 1850s, and men who were born in the 1850s were taller than men who had been born in the 1830s and 1840s.[62] When these changes are taken together, they suggest that even though it would be wrong to underestimate the importance of sanitary intervention after 1870, other factors also need to taken into account when seeking an explanation for the overall pattern of mortality decline. However, in order to investigate these issues further, it is necessary to take a closer look at the main changes in cause-specific mortality during the second half of the nineteenth century. This question formed a major part of McKeown's original analysis, and has been the focus of a great deal of investigation and debate in recent years.

As we have already seen, McKeown attached a great deal of importance to the cause-specific pattern of mortality decline after 1850. Although he recognised

Table 8.2 Average life expectancy at birth in different parts of England and Wales, 1801–1900

Source/category	Year(s)									
Woods (1985)	*1801*	*1811*	*1821*	*1831*	*1841*	*1851*	*1861*	*1871*	*1881*	*1891*
London	–	30	31	32	33	35	37	39	41	44
Over 100,000	–	30	30	31	32	34	35	37	39	41
10–100,000	–	32	33	35	36	38	40	42	44	46
Rural	–	41	42	43	43	45	45	46	47	49
England and Wales	–	38	39	40	40	41	41	42	44	46
Woods (2000)	*1801–10*	*1811–20*	*1821–30*	*1831–40*	*1841–50*	*1851–60*	*1861–70*	*1871–80*	*1881–90*	*1891–1900*
London	35.0	36.0	36.9	36.9	36.7	38.0	37.7	40.4	42.6	43.7
Over 100,000	32.0	32.5	32.7	32.6	32.0	32.3	33.0	36.6	39.0	39.6
10–100,000	34.2	35.3	36.2	36.3	36.0	37.2	38.0	41.4	44.0	44.8
Rural	42.2	43.3	43.5	43.5	44.0	45.5	46.5	47.7	51.0	53.5
England and Wales	40.3	41.1	41.1	40.7	40.4	41.1	41.2	43.0	45.3	46.1
Woods (1985)	*1801*	*1811*	*1821*	*1831*	*1841*	*1851*	*1861*	*1871*	*1881*	*1891*
Large provincial towns	–	30	30	31	32	34	35	37	39	41
Other centres	–	39	39	40	40	42	43	44	45	47
England and Wales	40	41	39	40	40	41	41	42	44	46
Szreter & Mooney (1998)	*1800s*	*1810s*	*1820s*	*1830s*	*1840s*	*1850s*	*1860s*	*1870s*	*1880s*	*1890s*
Large provincial towns	–	n/a	35	29	30	34	34	38	40	42
Other centres	–	n/a	41	42	42	42	42	44	47	47
England and Wales	40	41	41	41	41	41	41	43	45	46
Woods (2000)	*1801–10*	*1811–20*	*1821–30*	*1831–40*	*1841–50*	*1851–60*	*1861–70*	*1871–80*	*1881–90*	*1891–1900*
Large provincial towns	32.0	32.5	32.7	32.6	32.0	32.3	33.0	36.6	39.0	39.6
Other centres	40.4	41.4	41.6	41.4	41.3	42.4	42.9	44.6	47.2	48.6
England and Wales	40.3	41.1	41.1	40.7	40.4	41.1	41.2	43.0	45.3	46.1

Sources: R. Woods, 'The effects of population redistribution on the level of mortality in nineteenth-century England and Wales', *Journal of Economic History*, 45 (1985), 645–51, at 648, 650; S. Szreter and G. Mooney, 'Urbanisation, mortality and the standard of living debate: new estimates of the expectation of life at birth in nineteenth-century British cities', *Economic History Review*, 51 (1998), 84–112, at 104; R. Woods, *The demography of Victorian England and Wales*, Cambridge: Cambridge University Press, 2000, pp. 362, 369.

that a substantial proportion of the decline in the incidence of deaths from water- and food-borne diseases was caused by improvements in hygiene, he thought that there was little evidence to show that environmental improvements had any substantial effect on exposure to air-borne diseases before the start of the twentieth century. He therefore concluded that the decline in the death rate associated with these conditions (respiratory tuberculosis; bronchitis, pneumonia and influenza; whooping cough; measles; scarlet fever and diphtheria; smallpox; and infections of the ear, pharynx and larynx) was most likely to have been caused by an improvement in the population's capacity to resist infection, which was itself the result of improvements in nutrition.[63]

During the last two decades, several historians have attempted to cast doubt on the form of McKeown's argument and on the conclusions he drew from it. One of the most intriguing features of the argument concerns the treatment of the decline in the number of deaths attributable to scarlet fever. In 1962, McKeown and Record argued that 'scarlet fever was responsible for about nineteen per cent of the reduction of mortality during the second half of the nineteenth century' and that 'there is no reason to differ from the general opinion that [the decline in the number of deaths attributed to scarlet fever] … resulted from a change in the nature of the disease', but in 1976 McKeown included scarlet fever and diphtheria in the category of air-borne diseases whose decline he attributed to an improvement in nutrition.[64] If the decline in the number of deaths attributed to scarlet fever and diphtheria had been excluded from this category, then the overall contribution of the remaining air-borne diseases to the overall decline in mortality would have fallen from 43.63 per cent to 31.20 per cent – i.e. less than the figure associated with the decline in the incidence of mortality from water- and food-borne diseases (see Table 8.3 below).

Despite the obvious importance of scarlet fever to the construction of McKeown's argument, his critics have often tended to focus rather more attention on the question of tuberculosis. Szreter argued that McKeown had exaggerated the extent of the contribution made by pulmonary tuberculosis to the overall decline in mortality, and that this had led him to underestimate the significance of improvements in the incidence of mortality from water- and food-borne diseases, but he subsequently conceded that 'the recorded fall in respiratory tuberculosis was probably genuine, [even though] it also confirms the full extent of the contradictory rise in bronchitis/pneumonia/'flu'.[65] This conclusion has since been reinforced by Robert Woods' analysis of the cause-of-death data in the Registrar-General's Decennial Supplements for the period 1861/70 to 1891/1900. Although Woods' figures cover a slightly different period to those employed by McKeown, they are broadly consistent with his original interpretation (see Table 8.3).

One of the most interesting attempts to account for the decline of mortality in the latter part of the nineteenth century has come from attempts to relate the history of mortality to that of morbidity. Riley argued that one of the reasons for the decline of mortality was that improvements in medical attendance had enabled sick people to manage their diseases (and, especially, respiratory and organ diseases) in such a way as to enable them to survive for longer and postpone death. However, much of the increase in the duration of sickness episodes

Table 8.3 The contribution made by different diseases to the decline of mortality in England and Wales during the second half of the nineteenth century

Disease	McKeown & Record (1962)			McKeown (1976)			Woods (2000)		
	1851/60 Deaths per million	1891/1900 Deaths per million	Contribution to change %	1848/54 Deaths per million	1901 Deaths per million	Contribution to change %	1861–70 Standardised deaths	1891–1900 Deaths	Contribution to change %
Phthisis/Respiratory tuberculosis	2,772	1,418	43.89	2,901	1,268	33.34	777,350	426,224	35.19
Bronchitis, pneumonia and influenza	–	–	–	2,239	2,747	-10.37	–	–	–
Diseases of the lung/respiratory system	–	–	–	–	–	–	971,696	1,044,719	-7.32
Whooping cough	433	363	2.27	423	312	2.27	140,748	115,670	2.51
Measles	357	398	-1.33	342	278	1.31	119,471	126,841	-0.74
Scarlet fever	779	152	20.32	–	–	–	272,437	48,290	22.46
Diphtheria	99	254	-5.02	–	–	–	52,319	80,671	-2.84
Scarlet fever & diphtheria	–	–	–	1,016	407	12.43	–	–	–
Smallpox	202	13	6.13	263	10	5.17	46,713	4,058	4.27
Infections of the ear, pharynx and larynx	–	–	–	75	100	-0.51	–	–	–
Cholera, diarrhoea, dysentery	990	715	8.91	1,819	1,232	11.98	294,643	226,143	6.86
Non-respiratory tuberculosis	–	–	–	753	544	4.27	–	–	–
Tabes mesenterica and other tuberculous and scrofulous diseases	706	603	3.34	–	–	–	121,864	189,782	-6.81
Typhus	891	184	22.92	–	–	–	–	–	–
Typhoid and typhus	–	–	–	990	155	17.05	268,467	55,996	21.29
Cancer	–	–	–	307	844	-10.96	119,413	232,178	-11.30
Violence	–	–	–	761	640	2.47	283,484	202,363	8.13
Others (McKeown & Record)	13,890	14,024	-4.34	–	–	–	–	–	–
Others (McKeown)	–	–	–	9,967	8,421	31.56	–	–	–
Others (Woods)	–	–	–	–	–	–	4,076,386	2,895,523	28.30
Total	21,209	18,124	100.00	21,856	16,958	100.00	6,573,295	5,575,435	100.00

Note: According to Woods (2000, p. 351), the total number of deaths in 1891–1900 was 5,575,375. However, the figures in his column sum to 5,575,435, and this figure has been used to calculate the figures shown in this table.

Sources: T. McKeown and R. G. Record, 'Reasons for the decline of mortality in England and Wales during the nineteenth century', *Population Studies*, 16 (1962), 94–122, at 104; T. McKeown, *The modern rise of population*, London: Edward Arnold, 1976, pp. 54–62; R. Woods, *The demography of Victorian England and Wales*, Cambridge: Cambridge University Press, 2000, pp. 350–1.

on which Riley based his case may have been caused by increases in the average age, and changes in the age distribution, of the population who submitted sickness claims. It is difficult to know how far this may have been true of the friendly-society members whose health Riley investigated, but it certainly appears to provide the most likely explanation for changes in the pattern of morbidity experienced by members of the Hampshire Friendly Society, in the south of England, over the same period.[66]

Although Riley has raised important new questions about the effects of medical attendance and the relationship between mortality and morbidity, his work offered a much less sustained critique of the McKeown thesis than Robert Woods' recent publications. Woods' most striking finding was that even though the decline in the death rate from pulmonary tuberculosis accounted for more than one-third of the total decline in mortality during this period, it appeared to decline at much the same rate in all parts of the country. He therefore concluded that this decline was unlikely to have been caused by changes in either diet or environmental conditions, and that, consequently, it was most likely to have been caused by a change in virulence of the infective organism. However, Landers thought that it was 'rather unlikely' that 'tuberculosis underwent a spontaneous reduction in virulence', and Szreter noted that Woods' discussion of the main trends in tuberculosis was 'uncharacteristically lacking' in references to the most recent medical research. Livi-Bacci has argued that the frequency and severity of tuberculosis depend on many factors, including the virulence of infection, and 'these factors ... evolve over long periods of time and so cannot explain how the disease changed over the course of the nineteenth century.'[67]

Although we may not be able to exclude the possibility of biological change altogether, the decline of tuberculosis is more likely to have been caused by a combination of better housing and improvements in nutritional status, even though it may not always be possible to demonstrate this statistically. Pooley and Pooley found that housing density accounted for only 17 per cent of the variance in crude mortality rates in Manchester between 1871 and 1875, and Vögele argued that there was surprisingly little relationship between housing and population density and either all-cause mortality or tuberculosis mortality in the country as a whole. Moreover, both Vögele and McKeown believed that there was comparatively little evidence of any substantial improvement in housing conditions before the start of the twentieth century. However, other historians have challenged this view. As Daunton has argued, there was a substantial increase in the average value of real wages after 1850, and this enabled a significant proportion of the population to pay higher rents in return for better and more spacious accommodation, and this was reinforced by the introduction of more rigorous bye-laws governing the construction of new housing from the 1870s onwards. Consequently, even though it may be difficult to establish a precise relationship between housing improvement and mortality decline, there are strong circumstantial grounds for believing that these improvements did make an important contribution to the decline of tuberculosis (and, possibly, other diseases) after 1850.[68]

Although many historians might be prepared to accept the view that housing conditions did play a part in the decline of tuberculosis mortality, the relationship between diet and mortality has proved even more contentious. Hardy claimed that 'recent research ... reinforces the conclusion that, for a significant propor-tion of Britain's population, rising real incomes had little direct impact on improving nutritional standards', but the foundations of this statement are unclear.[69] Burnett wrote that the period between 1873 and 1896 'brought increased purchasing power ... and a bigger margin which could go towards providing a better and more varied diet' and that 'improvements are observable in the general standard of the working-class diet' during the last quarter of the nineteenth century, and Oddy argued that even though the energy value of the food consumed by the average working-class consumer fell by 360 calories (on a daily basis) between the 1860s and the 1890s, the quality of the average diet improved, mainly as a result of a reduction in the daily consumption of bread and an increase in the consumption of meat and sugar. Dewey concluded that 'well before 1914, consumption had begun to shift away from "inferior" foods (cereals, potatoes) towards "superior" ones (mainly meat and dairy produce). This process reflected mainly the rise in average real income which became apparent from about 1850, but it was also related to the greater availability of certain foods and, in some, but not all, cases, a lowering of the price of individual commodities.'[70]

These findings suggest that the decline of tuberculosis was related, at least in part, to improvements in the quality of working-class housing and in diet and nutrition, but this does not mean that the impact of sanitary intervention can therefore be excluded. As Preston and van de Walle showed in their analysis of French mortality rates, insanitary living conditions can have a decisive effect on the body's capacity to absorb essential nutrients and ward off disease.[71] Dasgupta and Ray showed that individuals who are subjected to repeated bouts of diar-rhoeal infection and whose diets contain large proportions of dietary fibre are only able to digest approximately 80 per cent of the nutrients they consume, whilst conventional estimates of food adequacy tend to assume that around 95 per cent of nutrients will be digested under normal hygienic conditions. Consequently, even though sanitary reform may not have been directly responsi-ble for the decline of tuberculosis, it is likely to have exerted a strong indirect effect as a result of its ability to lead to improvements in nutritional status.[72]

In addition to considering the indirect effects of sanitary reform on mortality, it is also necessary to examine its direct effects. Both McKeown and Record and McKeown believed that a substantial proportion of the decline in mortality dur-ing the second half of the nineteenth century was linked to a decline in the death rate from water- and food-borne diseases, and this argument has been reinforced by Woods' exhaustive analysis of the Registrar-General's *Decennial Supplements* for the period between 1861/70 and 1891/1900. However, Woods' disaggregated analysis of the decline of mortality in each of Britain's 614 registration districts also showed that there were significant variations in the rate at which mortality from these diseases declined in different areas. He calculated that just 14 registration districts, containing 13 per cent of the total population, accounted for 25 per cent of the overall decline in mortality from diarrhoea and typhus, whilst 53 districts, containing 35 per cent of the popula-tion, contributed 50 per cent of the decline in mortality. However, he also emphasised the point that progress in mortality decline did not necessarily depend on the progress of sanitary reform in a small number of 'high-performing' areas (that is, areas whose contribution to the overall decline in mortality exceeded their share of the national population). In London, all but three of the 25 Metropolitan registration districts made substantial contributions to the overall decline in mortality, but only six made contributions which exceeded their share of the national population. These figures demonstrated that even small improvements in sanitary provision could lead to a significant reduction in national mortality rates if they affected a sufficiently populous area.[73]

Although Woods' analysis of the decline of mortality from these diseases provides an impressive indication of the importance of sanitary intervention, it also helps to underline the limitations of the improvements which did occur. Even though there were many 'high-performing' areas whose contribution to mortality decline exceeded their share of the population, there were also many other areas, particularly in Lincolnshire, Cumbria, north Lancashire, south-west Wales and the West Country, whose contribution to mortality decline failed to match their population share, and even though the aggregate rate of mortality from diarrhoeal diseases fell by 23.25 per cent between 1861/70 and 1891/1900, the rate of diarrhoeal mortality among infants only began to decline after the turn of the century.[74] Third, as Bell and Millward argued, most of the initial increase in sanitary expenditure was concerned with the provision of better water supplies, but such measures were often counterproductive because the authorities failed to make any equivalent investment in sewerage facilities. They argued that many local authorities only began to make significant investments in the full range of sanitary measures during the 1890s and that, consequently, it was only after this date that the 'sanitary revolution' really began to take hold. As a result, even though many local authorities began to invest more heavily in their sanitary infrastructure from the 1870s onwards, it was not until the first decade of the twentieth century that these efforts began to exercise a decisive effect on the decline of mortality in the country as a whole.[75]

8.4   Conclusions

This chapter has examined the background to the history of public health reform in the nineteenth century, and assessed the extent to which the measures associated with public health reform may have contributed to the decline of mortality after 1870. As we have just seen, the onset of the 'modern' decline of mortality can be traced back to the second half of the eighteenth century, and was probably initiated by a combination of factors, including the spread of inoculation and subsequently vaccination against smallpox, a limited degree of environmental improvement, and improvements in nutrition. However, the beneficial effect of these changes was interrupted, and in some cases may even have been reversed, by the increasing pace of urbanisation during the first half of the nineteenth century, and the aggregate rate of mortality remained stubbornly high between *circa* 1830 and 1870. The resumption of mortality decline was caused, in part, by the growing realisation of the need for urban sanitary reform, but it also reflected the beneficial effect of parallel improvements in the quality of the nation's housing and the standard of nutrition.

Although this chapter has been primarily concerned with the evolution of public health policy, it has also demonstrated the extent to which the implementation of public health reforms was closely bound up with other social questions, of which the most important – in the eyes of many contemporaries – was the question of housing. In 1842, when Edwin Chadwick published his *Report on the sanitary condition of the labouring population*, he tended to play down the importance of housing in order to emphasise the overriding importance, from his point of view, of atmospheric impurities, but the significance of bad housing was underlined by the Royal Commission on the State of Large Towns and Populous Districts in 1844 and 1845, and Wohl has argued that 'healthy housing was one of the cornerstones of the sanitary reformers' philosophy and programme. It was to so many of them the very heart of the matter, the reform without which all other reforms would be weakened.'[76] At the beginning of the 1840s, the Medical Officers for the Poor Law Union of Bishops Stortford, Messrs Smith and Moore, said that 'we have always found the smallest and most slightly-built houses the seats of the lowest forms of disease', and the Medical Officer of Health for the London borough of St Giles thought that overcrowding was the single condition which was most likely to produce 'an excess of zymotic diseases ... of consumption and lung diseases, and a larger infantile mortality'.[77] This question, which exerted such a vital effect on the standard of public health, forms the subject of the following chapter.

9 Housing policy and housing conditions, 1800–1914

Housing is both a personal and a public issue. Throughout the period covered by this book, the majority of people obtained their housing through the private market, either by renting from private landlords, or by borrowing large sums of money from banks or building societies, or (more rarely) by purchasing their property outright. At the same time, housing is also a public issue. The state accepts that it is in the public interest to ensure that all housing meets certain basic standards, if only to guarantee basic standards of public health, and it also accepts a more specific responsibility to ensure that all individuals are guaranteed access to shelter. The aim of this chapter is to examine the different ways in which the private and public aspects of housing interacted to shape the history of working-class housing in Britain in the nineteenth century.

The chapter itself is divided into five sections. The first two sections describe the basic features of working-class housing in agricultural and urban areas respectively. Section 9.3 discusses the different ways in which the state attempted to intervene in the housing market in order to ensure that basic standards were met. Section 9.4 examines the efforts made by various philanthropic individuals and organisations to meet particular housing needs. The final section will provide a brief summary of the main reasons for change in the housing market, and the strengths and weaknesses of efforts at housing reform.

9.1 Rural housing and the agricultural labourer

In 1797, the poverty researcher F. M. Eden presented examples of the household budgets of 53 agricultural labourers and their families. Five families were not listed as paying any rent at all, and three families had their rent paid for them by the parish. Of the remaining families, one was reported as paying two shillings a year in rent, and one was listed as paying £7 5s, but most paid between 20 shillings and 66 shillings. Among those families paying rent, the mean cost was just over £2.00 (40.13 shillings). Although this did not necessarily represent a high proportion of a family's total income (the average annual income of the 45 rent-paying families was just over £30 9s 9d), it was nevertheless one of the most inflexible aspects of working-class expenditure. Eden himself observed that 'the article of expenditure of a poor working family which, though not the heaviest in amount is, in effect, their heaviest disbursement, is their rent. It is an article of expense that has all the inconvenience of a direct tax, and is often called for when it is most inconvenient to pay it.'[1]

Between 1750 and 1850, the housing problems faced by agricultural labourers and their families were exacerbated by three different factors. The rapid increase in the size of the rural population placed increasing stress on existing housing stock, and the low wages received by rural workers provided prospective landlords with little incentive to build new accommodation. Second, many landlords started to pull down existing accommodation as part of the process of consolidating their estates and enclosing the common land, and this put even more pressure on the existing housing stock in unenclosed areas. Third, the decline of living-in farm service meant that children who would previously have left the family home in their early teens remained with their parents for much longer, thus increasing the level of overcrowding, and also tended to marry earlier, thus increasing the rate of population growth.[2]

The failure of the rural housing market to keep pace with rising demand led to a sharp increase in agricultural rents. In 1770, Arthur Young calculated that the average level of wages among agricultural labourers in 15 English counties was £19 6s 3d, whilst the average rent of an agricultural cottage in the same counties was £1 16s 6d. In 1850/1, when the *The Times* Commissioner, James Caird, revisited the same areas, he found that average wages had increased to £24 15s 10d, whilst rents had risen to £3 14s 2d, an overall increase of more than 100 per cent. As Burnett has argued, the bulk of the rent increase occurred before 1820. In 1824, Henry Drummond told the Parliamentary Select Committee on Labourers' Wages that 'before the [Napoleonic] war, the average rent of cottages, with good gardens, was 30 shillings a year; it is now in our own neighbourhood [of Guildford] commonly as high as five, seven or even ten pounds per annum; and where cottages are in the hands of farmers, they always prohibit the labourers from keeping a pig, and claim the produce of the apple trees and of the vine which normally covers the house.'[3]

The failure to build new houses, the reluctance to make necessary repairs, and the sharp increase in the cost of rent, led to a significant deterioration in the overall standard of rural housing. The Assistant Poor Law Commissioner, W. J. Gilbert, told Edwin Chadwick that many of the cottages in Tiverton, in Devon, were 'built on the ground without flooring, or against a damp hill. Some have neither windows nor doors sufficient to keep out the weather, or to let in the rays of the sun, or supply the means of ventilation; and in others the roof is so constructed or so worn as not to be weathertight.' The Medical Officers for Bishops Stortford Union said that despite the absence of epidemic or infectious diseases, 'it is but just to state that, generally speaking, the cottages of labourers in this district are small, badly-protected from both extremes of weather, badly-drained, and low in the ground'.[4] Burnett has rightly pointed out that many agricultural labourers were housed in conditions which were considerably better than these, but there is little evidence to suggest that the examples quoted by Chadwick were that unusual. In 1843, the Assistant Poor Law Commissioner, Alfred Austin, compiled the following report on housing conditions in Wiltshire, Dorset, Devon and Somerset:

It is impossible not to be struck, in visiting the dwelling of the agricultural labourers, with the general want of new cottages, notwithstanding the universal increase of population.

Everywhere the cottages are old, and frequently in a state of decay, and are consequently ill-adapted for their increased number of inmates of late years. The floor of the room in which the family live during the day is always of stone in these counties, and wet or damp through the winter months, being frequently lower than the soil outside. The situation of the cottage is often extremely bad, no attention having been paid at the time of its building to facilities for draining. Cottages are frequently erected on a dead level, so that the water cannot escape; and sometimes on spots lower than the surrounding ground.[5]

In 1864, Julian Hunter examined the condition of more than 5,000 homes in every county in England. He found that 2,195 houses contained only one bedroom, 2,930 contained two bedrooms, and only 250 contained three bedrooms or more. The average number of people per house was 4.61, and the average number of people per bedroom was 2.81. The average number of people living in a house with only one bedroom was 4.02. The average amount of space in each bedroom was equal to 156 cubic feet per individual. This was approximately 60 per cent of the legally-prescribed figure for common lodging houses; just over 50 per cent of the figure for army barracks; slightly less than half the figure in 'model dwellings'; and less than 20 per cent of the amount regarded as necessary by public health officers.[6] Conditions undoubtedly improved during the second half of the nineteenth century, aided partly by an increase in real wages and partly by rural depopulation, but many families continued to live in considerable squalor. In 1885 the Royal Commission on the Housing of the Working Classes concluded that 'the particular difficulty that attaches to an investigation of the housing of the working classes in rural districts is to avoid being drawn into an examination of cognate subjects which, though of the highest importance, are beyond the scope of the present enquiry. It is not easy to elicit evidence on the condition of agricultural labourers' cottages without obtaining information and opinions upon the causes which determine the rate of wages, or the relations of the labourer to the land, but … such considerations are only incidental to the present enquiry, and the temptation to discuss them at length must be avoided.'[7]

9.2   The impact of urbanisation

During the course of the nineteenth century, social investigators frequently drew attention to rural housing conditions which were every bit as appalling as those found in urban areas, but these problems rarely excited the same degree of public concern as the problems encountered in Britain's cities. Gauldie suggested that this was because 'the decay of the towns caught the attention of the reformers if only because of the smell',[8] but this was only part of the story. The two factors which made the problems of urban housing particularly distinctive were, firstly, the sheer scale of housing problems in urban areas, and, secondly, the impact of rapid population growth on the urban environment as a whole.

Before moving on to a more detailed examination of urban housing problems, it is important to recognise that the term 'urban' covers a wide range of settings. As Rule has emphasised, not all the inhabitants of 'rural' Britain were employed in agricultural activities; there were also many industrial workers, including – most notably – coalminers, who lived in small towns and villages which had much more in common with agricultural villages than major urban centres.[9] Secondly, the term 'urban centre' itself covers towns of many different sizes, and it would be wrong to suppose that the housing problems of a small town such as Stourbridge, with a population of just over 20,000 in 1851, were necessarily the same as those of a large city.[10] Nevertheless, many medium-sized and large towns did encounter enormous problems, and it was these which tended to dominate the national debates and, subsequently, to exert the greatest influence on both philanthropic and legislative developments.[11]

One of the greatest problems caused by the pace of Britain's urban development was the problem of spatial overcrowding. Between 1801 and 1851, the number of people living in towns with more than 10,000 inhabitants increased by more than 270 per cent.[12] Urban landlords responded to this growth by subdividing existing properties and by cramming new buildings into every available space. Daunton has described the resulting chaos as 'a promiscuous sharing of facilities in the private domain of the house, a cellular quality of space in the public domain, and a threshold between public and private which was ambiguous and permeable'. Engels summed this up more pithily when he wrote:

> Of the irregular cramming together in ways which defy all natural plan, of the tangle in which they are crowded literally one upon the other, it is impossible to convey an idea. And it is not the buildings surviving from the old times of Manchester which are to blame for this; the confusion has only recently reached its height when every scrap of space left by the old way of building has been filled up and patched over until not a foot of land is left to be further occupied.[13]

The most notorious examples of nineteenth-century housing were the common lodging-houses. These dwellings had originally been designed to provide temporary accommodation for young men seeking one or two nights' accommodation whilst they searched for work, but '[they] all too often ... became permanent homes for the near-destitute and near-criminal classes and almost indistinguishable from a normal tenement house except by their gross overcrowding and promiscuity.'[14] James Phillips Kay described them as 'fertile sources of disease and demoralisation', whilst Peter Gaskell thought they were 'deplorable in the extreme'.[15] Henry Mayhew complained that 'the sanitary state of [the cheapest] houses is very bad. Not only do the lodgers generally swarm with vermin, but there is little or no ventilation in the sleeping rooms, in which sixty persons, of the foulest habits, usually sleep every night.' He estimated that there were 221 lodging houses in London of this type, with accommodation for between 10,000 and 12,000 inhabitants.[16] In 1854, an official survey suggested that the total number of lodging houses in the capital was 10,824, with a combined population of more than 82,000.[17]

If the common lodging-houses were the worst kind of Victorian housing, the cellar-dwellings were not much better. During the late-eighteenth and early-nineteenth centuries, many landlords sub-let the basement areas of their properties as separate units of accommodation, and their number increased during the first half of the nineteenth century. In 1840 Dr William Rayner described the cellar dwellings in Heaton Norris as 'dark, damp and very low', whilst the Medical Officer for West Derby reported that the cellars in his area were almost invariably 'small and damp, and often crowded with inhabitants to excess'. In the same year, Dr William Duncan reported that in Liverpool '[out] of 6571 cellars whose condition is reported on, 2988 are … either wet or damp, and nearly one third of the whole number are from five to six feet below the level of the street.'[18] In Manchester, between five and ten per cent of the population lived 'below ground' during the second quarter of the nineteenth century. In Liverpool, where more consistent estimates are available, it seems likely that as many as 13 per cent of the total population, and 22 per cent of the working-class population, lived in cellar-dwellings at the beginning of the 1840s.[19]

The next rung on the housing ladder was occupied by the inhabitants of subdivided properties, or tenement dwellings. As Burnett has argued, 'it was always cheaper and quicker to subdivide than to build, especially in central areas which were usually already heavily built-up, and where land prices were forced up by commercial competition.'[20] At the same time, the constant pressure to maximise the number of people in existing properties led to predictable problems of poor sanitation and overcrowding. In 1832, James Phillips Kay reported that in Manchester, out of 6,951 houses under investigation, 960 were in need of repair, 1,435 were damp and 2,221 were in need of privies.[21] In 1851, Lord Ashley pointed out that the number of people living in a row of 27 houses in Church Lane, Westminster, had increased from 655 inhabitants in 1841 to 1,095 just six years later.[22] Gauldie suggested that there were cultural as well as economic reasons for the widespread tolerance of overcrowding in Victorian society, but the underlying cause was undoubtedly economic insecurity. As she herself pointed out, many working class people were forced to accept the cheapest possible accommodation because 'their chances of earning a regular wage made it difficult to pay the kind of rents demanded for good house property'.[23]

The majority of these houses were not built originally for working-class use; in many cases they consisted of much older properties which had simply been adapted to satisfy the interests of their owners and the needs of new tenants. However, during the first half of the nineteenth century a substantial number of new houses were built for rent by working-class tenants, and the best known of these were the back-to-back houses which became particularly widespread in the midlands and northern England. During the 1830s and 1840s, these houses were roundly condemned by the majority of sanitary reformers, not only because they were badly built, but also because the mode of construction made it impossible for air to circulate properly.[24] However, other observers defended back-to-backs on the grounds that they were at least better than many of the alternatives. In 1843 the London builder, Thomas Cubitt, told the Royal Commission on the State of Large Towns and Populous Districts that 'building them back-to-back is a much cheaper mode, and … if we were to prevent their being built back-to-back, we might in many cases prevent houses being built which would be a great accommodation for poor people.'[25]

Despite its limitations, the back-to-back house represented the highest form of housing for many working-class families during the first half of the nineteenth century, but during the second half of the century it was gradually supplanted by the 'through-terrace'. The earliest through-terraces were simple two-up-two-down affairs, but during the second half of the century, they were gradually extended to include two or three upstairs bedrooms, two downstairs living rooms, a separate kitchen or scullery, a coal-house, and a WC. The through-terrace was much preferred by sanitary reformers, partly because it provided much better opportunities for ventilation, and partly because it was expected to lead to higher standards of domestic hygiene and family life, and it is not unreasonable to suppose that most working-class families would also have favoured it for much the same reasons.[26] Daunton has argued that the increasing proliferation of through-terraces towards the end of the nineteenth century was largely attributable to the introduction of new bye-laws, but it also owed a great deal to the general improvement in the standard of living. As Daunton himself has observed: 'Prices fell between 1873 and 1896, and it was possible for tenants to pay higher rents in return for a better house. When prices rose between 1896 and 1914, real wages came under pressure and the level of effective demand from the tenants was less buoyant.'[27]

9.3 Housing reform

During the late-eighteenth and early-nineteenth centuries, more than 300 towns acquired Improvement Commissions, and more than 400 Local Improvement Acts were passed between 1800 and 1840. In addition to their primary responsibilities for paving and cleansing the main thoroughfares, the Improvement Commissions also acquired the power to enforce building regulations, but these were often ineffective. Rodger attributes this to a wide range of deficiencies, including 'lax drafting, unenforceable clauses, ineffectual monitoring, jurisdictional limitations, regulatory exclusion of existing housing, and administrative responsibility fragmented among several vestries, parishes and town councils within the urban area'. He also points out that even if local authorities had been more successful in their efforts to establish minimum standards, the result would simply have been to force up the cost of housing for those living in sub-standard accommodation.[28]

During the 1830s and 1840s, Parliament passed a series of Acts which, in many ways, marked the beginnings of a more serious attempt to address housing difficulties. The Municipal Corporations Act of 1835 sought to cut through the tangle of competing urban authorities by establishing a single unitary authority for the larger towns and cities, and this paved the way for a series of more effective Local Improvement Acts in the later-1830s and 1840s. In 1846 Parliament gave local authorities the power to prosecute the owners of any property which was found to be in a 'filthy and unwholesome condition', and in 1847 local authorities acquired the power to demolish 'ruinous or dangerous buildings'. In 1848 the Public Health Act was passed. This Act (11 & 12 Vict. C. 63) gave local Boards of Health the power to prohibit cellar-dwellings (section 67), regulate common lodging-houses (section 66), ensure that all new buildings were connected to sewers (section 49), and make arrangements for the removal of nuisances (section 58).[29]

The first explicit attempt to address housing problems in their own right came with the Common Lodging Houses Acts of 1851 and 1853. The first of these Acts (14 & 15 Vict. C. 28) instructed local authorities to maintain a register of licensed lodging-houses, and gave them the power to issue regulations, not only regarding the sanitation of common lodging-houses, but also 'for the well-ordering of such houses, and … the separation of the sexes'. The second Act (16 & 17 Vict. C. 41) gave local authorities the duty of taking action against any common lodging-house which was found to constitute a nuisance under the Nuisance Removal Act of 1848. These two Acts have often been bracketed with a third Act – the Labouring Classes Lodging Houses Act – which was also introduced by Lord Ashley (the future seventh Earl of Shaftesbury) in 1851. This Act (14 & 15 Vict. C. 34) gave local authorities the power to acquire land and build their own lodging-houses for the 'labouring classes', but it was rarely invoked, and only one local authority – Huddersfield – ever sought to implement it in the way Shaftesbury intended.[30]

In 1884, Shaftesbury told the Royal Commission on the Housing of the Working Classes that the Labouring Classes Lodging Houses Act had failed because 'when that Act was passed, there was no feeling in the country on the matter at all', and that as a result it 'passed unnoticed',[31] but others have offered a variety of different explanations for its lack of success. J. L. and Barbara Hammond considered that the Act was an inadequate response to the problems it sought to address, but Hodder and Gauldie have argued that Shaftesbury's original plans were mutilated in the House of Commons.[32] Wohl claimed that the Act was hampered by a number of factors, including the cumbersome nature of the procedures required to implement its proposals, and the failure to incorporate a clear definition of the kind of accommodation it was designed to provide.[33] Nevertheless, for all its limitations, the Labouring Classes Lodging Houses Act showed that Parliament was willing to give some support to the principle of public housing provision, and it provided the basis of Lord Salisbury's proposals for the development of municipal housing under the Housing of the Working Classes Acts in 1885 and 1890.

Although the Common Lodging Houses Acts led to a substantial improvement in the condition of this particular type of accommodation,[34] they made little difference to the great mass of working-class housing. However, during the 1850s and 1860s a series of Acts were passed which made further efforts to establish minimum standards for both old and new housing. In 1855 a new Nuisance Removal Act was passed, amending and extending the Acts of 1848 and 1849, and creating a new legal offence of overcrowding, although the definition of overcrowding was left to the vagaries of local medical practitioners. This Act was followed by the Local Government Act of 1858, which replaced the Public Health Act of 1848, and provided an extended set of building bye-laws which were adopted by 568 towns over the next ten years.[35] However, the most important single piece of legislation in this area was the Public Health Act of 1875. This Act consolidated all the public health legislation of the previous 27 years, and set out to establish a basic sanitary code for the entire country.

Daunton argued strongly that 'the Public Health Act of 1875 was the turning point in the regulation of house-building in British cities. Although there had been building bye-laws in some towns at an earlier date, the Act of 1875 permitted sanitary authorities throughout the provinces to make bye-laws to control building standards and lay-out. The bye-laws specified in detail the minimum standards of construction of houses, and also laid down street widths and the amount of open space to be provided on each plot.'[36] However, whilst this Act, and the regulations associated with it, undoubtedly contributed to the improvement of housing standards before the First World War, their significance should probably not be exaggerated. In the first place, it is important to remember that it would have been impossible to raise housing standards if there had not also been a concomitant increase in working-class purchasing power, which enabled more people to afford better-quality housing; and, second, the improvement in the quality of new housing in itself could do little to improve the situation of those who were still too poor to escape from the grip of the slums.

The earliest attacks on this problem were made by individual local authorities. In 1860 Glasgow Corporation acquired the power to buy up and clear old houses, and similar powers were acquired by the Corporations of Liverpool and Edinburgh in 1864 and 1867 respectively. The first attempts to deal with the problem on a national scale were made by the Torrens and Cross Acts in 1868 and 1875. The first Act (the Artizans' and Labourers' Dwellings Act) gave local authorities the power to demolish properties which were found to be 'in a condition or state dangerous to health so as to be unfit for human habitation', and the second (the Artizans' and Labourers' Dwellings Improvement Act) gave them the power to draw up improvement schemes and to 'provide for the accommodation of at least as many persons of the working classes as may be displaced in the area with respect to which the scheme is proposed'. However, neither of these Acts was particularly effective. One of the greatest problems was that it was extremely difficult to build replacement properties for tenants of slum accommodation at rents which they could be expected to afford.[37]

The question of working-class housing standards returned to the fore at the beginning of the 1880s. In 1883 the Secretary of the London Congregational Union, Andrew Mearns, published *The bitter cry of outcast London*, and this, together with a series of newspaper and journal articles, led to the establishment of the Royal Commission on the Housing of the Working Classes in March 1884.[38] One of the Commission's principal recommendations was that local authorities should be allowed to build additional housing as a way of reducing the amount of pressure on the housing market and easing overcrowding.[39] In 1885 Lord Salisbury pushed through the first of several Housing of the Working Classes Acts, in which he sought to revive the house-building clauses of the Labouring Classes Lodging Houses Act of 1851 by extending the definition of 'lodging-house' to include 'separate houses or cottages for the labouring classes, whether containing one or several tenements'.[40] This Act was followed by the Housing of the Working Classes Act of 1890, which relaxed some of the conditions surrounding the preparation of improvement schemes, and offered further encouragement to local authorities to develop their own housing programmes.

Although the 1890 Act was primarily concerned with the problems of insanitary and overcrowded housing, it also paved the way for a major new development in housing provision. As Swenarton has noted, the Artizans' and Labourers' Dwellings Improvement Act of 1875 (the Cross Act) gave local authorities the power to provide replacement housing for those who had been evicted from slum properties, but the 1890 Act gave them the opportunity to build new houses for more affluent workers in the hope that this would 'free up' properties for those at the bottom of the housing market.[41] This trend received further encouragement from the Housing of the Working Classes Acts of 1900 and 1903, and the Housing and Town Planning Act of 1909.[42] However, despite these inducements, none of these Acts led in themselves to the development of municipal housing on a large scale. Local authorities were responsible for less than five per cent of all new houses built in England and Wales between 1890 and 1914, and only 0.3 per cent of all households were living in local authority accommodation on the eve of the First World War.[43]

9.4 Housing and philanthropy

It is important to recognise too that a considerable amount of effort was also devoted to various philanthropic housing schemes, including the work of Octavia Hill and a variety of different philanthropic and commercial housing schemes. Whelan has suggested that this philanthropic housing movement might have offered a viable alternative to the development of state-subsidised municipal housing in the twentieth century, although this suggestion has not won universal approval. It is at least arguable that Whelan has himself succumbed to the fault he attributes to others, namely, the tendency '[to project] backwards into the past the intellectual fads and political prejudices of the present'.[44]

Octavia Hill was a founder member of the Charity Organisation Society, and she shared the Society's fervent belief in the promotion of individual responsibility. In contrast to the majority of housing reformers, she believed that the root of Britain's housing problems did not lie in the shortage of affordable housing, but in the attitudes of the slum tenants themselves, and instead of seeking to build new properties, she preferred to buy up old properties in the hope of 'improving' the tenants who lived in them. By the end of the nineteenth century, it has been estimated that she was responsible for between 1800 and 1900 separate properties, together with an unknown number of individual rooms, but her overall achievement is unclear. She herself claimed that the essence of her work was to 'reclaim the tenants that nobody else will touch', but Wohl has argued that even though she catered for a poorer class of tenant than the model dwelling companies, she failed to reach 'the very poor who remained the hard core of the slum problem right into the twentieth century'.[45]

Although Octavia Hill has been the focus of particular interest in recent years, her efforts were far less important numerically than those of the various model-dwelling companies. As Dennis has pointed out, these organisations represented a curious combination of commercial and philanthropic principles.[46] They set out to demonstrate that it was possible to construct good quality housing for rent by working-class tenants at rates which could be guaranteed to produce an economic return, but the fact that the anticipated rates of return were lower than those demanded in the commercial sector meant that the majority of those who invested in the companies were more likely to do so for philanthropic than strictly commercial reasons.[47] The most famous of the strictly philanthropic organisations involved in the construction of model dwellings was the Peabody Donation Fund, which was founded by the American philanthropist, George Peabody, in 1862. By 1882, the Fund had helped to finance the construction of more than 3,500 individual dwellings, with accommodation for more than 14,600 people, and by 1887 the number of dwellings had risen to 5,014.[48]

Morris has attempted to rescue the model-dwelling companies from the obscurity into which much historical research has appeared to cast them. She argues that the companies 'fulfilled their aim of providing a higher standard of accommodation at an equivalent or lower price than the working classes paid for insanitary properties in central London', but in spite of this they only succeeded in recruiting a relatively small proportion of their tenants from the ranks of those whom Charles Booth described as either poor or very poor.[49] One of their principal limitations was that they needed to be able to recruit a higher class of tenant – one who was reasonably well-paid and in regular employment – in order to ensure that rents were paid and financial targets were met. This meant that even though their efforts represented an important addition to existing housing stock, they failed to reach even the 'ordinary' poor, and because they tended to focus their activities on slightly more affluent areas, they had a relatively limited impact on the alleviation of housing problems in those areas where the problems of poor sanitation and overcrowding were at their greatest.[50]

Historians of housing policy have also examined the role of employer-provided housing. In some areas, this appears to have been a survival from more traditional forms of employment practice, where employee-housing was provided as part of the job, and in others it was conceived as a way of enticing particular groups of workers to new industries, but some employers were also concerned to establish model housing schemes for more philanthropic purposes.[51] In 1853, the Bradford alpaca manufacturer, Titus Salt, founded the village of Saltaire. In addition to meeting the immediate needs of his workforce, he was also concerned to ensure that 'the dwellings of the operatives' should be 'a pattern to the country'.[52] The housing schemes which were developed later in the century by philanthropically-minded employers such as William Hesketh Lever (at Port Sunlight), George Cadbury (at Bournville) and Joseph Rowntree (at New Earswick) were also conceived with didactic purposes in mind. In addition to providing a relatively high standard of accommodation for the employer's workforce, they also acted as flagships for the nascent town-planning movement. This was reflected in the very close links between employers such as Lever, Cadbury and Rowntree and architects such as Raymond Unwin, who not only designed Rowntree's village of New Earswick, but also designed Hampstead Garden Suburb, and sat with the other three on the National Housing Reform Council.[53]

9.5 Conclusions

By the end of the nineteenth century, the state intervened in the housing market to a degree which would have seemed almost unimaginable in 1840.

During the intervening 60 years, legislation was passed to regulate common lodging-houses, prohibit cellar-dwellings, establish minimum standards for new housing, permit the demolition of insanitary accommodation, and license the development of municipal housing schemes. However, despite these changes, a large number of people continued to live in insanitary and overcrowded accommodation. In 1891, the Registrar-General for England and Wales calculated that more than 11 per cent of the total population was living in overcrowded conditions (a household was considered to be overcrowded if it contained more than two adults to each room, with each child under ten counting as half an adult, and children under the age of one not counting at all). Even though the incidence of overcrowding fell during the late-nineteenth and early-twentieth centuries, more than two million people were still living in overcrowded conditions according to this definition at the time of the 1911 census.[54]

In recent years, historians of housing policy have devoted particular attention to the question of council housing. Some writers, such as Avner Offer, David Englander and Richard Rodger have argued that the private housing market entered a period of protracted decline in the late-nineteenth century, and that this made the subsequent rise of municipal housing all but inevitable.[55] Others, such as Michael Thompson and Martin Daunton, have claimed that even though the private housing market did enter a period of decline, this was not irreversible, and that the market might have improved had it not been for the outbreak of the First World War and the introduction of rent controls in 1915.[56] However, the most important point is that even though there was a sharp increase in the level of municipal provision after 1919, the main emphasis continued to be placed on the provision of additional housing for better-off workers, in the hope that this would lead to a 'levelling-up' of conditions at the bottom of the housing market. It was not until the start of the 1930s that the abolition of slum housing and the provision of replacement housing for the former tenants of slum accommodation became the major focus of housing policy.

10 Education and schooling, 1800–1914

According to Rees, 'there is one … major service which has every right to be classed as "social", namely *education*, but convention does not usually admit it into the fold, perhaps because it is too large a subject, or because it raises too many issues peculiar to itself', but historians of social policy have usually regarded the history of educational provision as an essential part of their canvas. This is reflected in both Derek Fraser's and Pat Thane's accounts of the origins and development of the welfare state, as well as in more recent accounts of twentieth-century social policy, including those by David Gladstone, Howard Glennerster and Rodney Lowe.[1]

In reality, there are very strong reasons for giving the same weight to education as to other aspects of social welfare provision. The history of public education is, first and foremost, the history of *children's* education, and the history of childhood 'is inescapably inseparable from the history of social policy'.[2] Second, as T. H. Marshall argued, the right to be educated (or, alternatively, the right to have been educated) was just as much a right of citizenship as the right to health, housing or social security.[3] Third, the development of publicly-subsidised education after 1833, followed by the development of state-provided education after 1870, was one of the most remarkable applications of the principle of state intervention prior to the outbreak of the First World War. Finally, the nature of welfare policy in the early part of the twentieth century meant that the development of public education and the expansion of other welfare services were in any case very closely, if not inextricably, intertwined.

It is important to recognise that education can serve a number of different ends. It can be a means of acquiring the knowledge and skills which are necessary to improve one's position in society and participate in public life and a means of transmitting the values of the dominant groups in society and preserving the status quo. It can also be seen as a necessary form of investment in the country's economic future. As the Liberal politician, W. E. Forster, observed in 1870: 'Civilised communities throughout the world are massing themselves together, each mass being measured by its force; and if we are to hold our position among men of our own race or among the nations of the world, we must make up the smallness of our number by increasing the intellectual force of the individual.'[4]

10.1   Elementary education in the late-eighteenth and early-nineteenth centuries

Educational historians have often been tempted to look at evidence of adult literacy rates in order to gauge the extent and adequacy of educational provision. Stone suggested that the proportion of marriage partners who were able to sign their names in the marriage registers rose consistently during the second half of the eighteenth century, and continued to rise in most parts of the country during the first 40 years of the nineteenth century, but Michael Sanderson has argued that literacy rates declined in industrial areas from the 1770s onwards.[5] Schofield found that literacy rates rose in non-industrial areas whilst declining elsewhere, so that the overall effect was that literacy rates remained largely unchanged during the second half of the eighteenth century, and only rose slowly during the first half of the nineteenth century. He also highlighted some intriguing differences in the trends for male and female marriage partners. The percentage of wives who signed the registers increased consistently throughout the period, whereas the percentage of husbands who signed the registers only began to increase after *circa* 1815.[6]

Although these figures provide some indication of the extent to which ordinary people were able to acquire basic literacy skills, they can only provide a very limited indication of the demand for education in the late-eighteenth and early-nineteenth centuries. As Kiesling has argued, the majority of the population existed on very low incomes which only left a very small margin for educational expenditure, and this meant that even those who were able to pay for their education were often only able to do so for very limited periods.[7] The Northamptonshire poet, John Clare, recalled how 'my mother's hopeful ambition ... of being able to make me a good scholar ... was often cross'd with difficulty ... [and] till I was eleven or twelve but three months or more at the worst of times was luckily spared for my improvement.'[8] However, it seems clear that many working-class parents were prepared to sacrifice a great deal so that their children could learn to read and write. In 1813, the *Edinburgh Review* claimed that 'even around London, in a circle of fifty miles ... there is hardly a village that has not something of a school; and not many children of either sex who are not taught, more or less, reading and writing,' and in 1818 the Brougham Committee (on the Education of the Lower Orders) concluded that 'there is the most unquestionable evidence that the anxiety of the poor for education continues not only unabated but daily increasing.' Nevertheless, the Committee went on to suggest that this anxiety was often frustrated because 'no means of gratifying it are provided by the charitable efforts of the richer classes'.[9]

During the late-eighteenth and early-nineteenth centuries, upper- and middle-class observers expressed divergent opinions on the education of working-class children. In 1807, when Samuel Whitbread introduced a Bill to promote the education of pauper children, the MP for Bodmin, Davies Giddy, claimed that 'the bill ... would teach [the labouring classes] to despise their lot in life ... render them factious and refractory... [and] insolent to their superiors,'[10] but other observers believed that education provided the best opportunity to ensure stability. In 1819, the Reverend Daniel Wilson told an Evangelical congregation in Spitalfields that 'religious education … is the spring of tranquillity,' and John Arthur Roebuck believed that 'one of the first … results from a proper education of the people would be a thorough understanding … of the circumstances on which their happiness depended, of the powers by which these circumstances were controlled…. It should be remembered that no system of police or of punishment, and no system for the regulation of the poor, can be complete without embracing education as a part of the means to be employed.'[11] In 1837, the factory inspector, Leonard Horner, argued:

> Independently of all higher considerations, and to put the necessity of educating the children of the working classes on its lowest footing, it is loudly called for as a matter of police, to prevent a multitude of immoral and vicious beings, the offspring of ignorance, from growing up around us, to be a pest and a nuisance to society; it is necessary to render the great body of the working class governable by reason.[12]

During the eighteenth century, the majority of those children who attended school probably attended a local 'dame school' or 'private venture' (or adventure) school. 'Dame schools' were usually run by women, and were primarily concerned with the teaching of reading, and possibly writing, to children under the age of seven. The private venture schools catered for older children and sought to offer a more varied curriculum, including reading, writing and arithmetic, together with sewing and knitting for girls, and possibly some instruction in such subjects as geography and grammar. However, as Stephens points out, the boundaries between the different types of school were often blurred, and later commentators often used the different terms interchangeably.[13]

These private educational initiatives were supplemented by charity schools and, subsequently, by Sunday schools. The earliest charity schools were set up towards the end of the seventeenth century, and were mostly concentrated in towns. They taught reading, writing, arithmetic and religion to children from the age of seven onwards. The majority also sought to provide their pupils with some form of occupational or vocational training, but some concentrated on more advanced forms of academic training. Such schools tended to be more attractive to the better-off or more skilled members of the working class, and were believed to provide greater opportunities for social advancement.[14]

Although many of the charity schools had serious educational objectives, they were much less important, in numerical terms, than the Sunday schools. Laqueur argued that these institutions should be seen as manifestations of an autonomous working-class educational culture, but Dick claimed that they were dominated by middle-class interests.[15] It is also arguable that some commentators may have tended to overestimate the contribution made by Sunday schools to the improvement of literacy, since they became increasingly hostile to the teaching of writing, as opposed to reading, on the Sabbath Day.[16] However, it is difficult to deny the numerical importance of the movement. According to Laqueur, the total number of Sunday-school members in England rose from 59,980 in 1788 to just under 2.1 million in 1851.[17] In 1861, the Royal Commission on Popular Education (the Newcastle Commission) estimated that the total number of people (including adults) who attended Sunday schools in the whole of England and Wales was 2,411,554.[18]

The most important new development in the early part of the nineteenth century was the establishment of voluntary day schools. The vast majority of these schools were administered by religious societies, of which the most important were the Royal Lancasterian Society, which was founded in 1808 and became the British and Foreign Schools Society in 1814, and the National Society for Promoting the Education of the Poor in the Principles of the Established Church, founded in 1811. The schools were financed by contributions from members of the clergy and religious congregations, and by the fees which they were able to charge to the parents of the children who attended them. Although the schools were particularly concerned to promote the spread of religion, and used the Bible to reinforce respect for the existing social order, they also provided a basic instruction in reading, writing and arithmetic, and, in some cases at least, provided exposure to such subjects as science, geography and singing.[19] The British and Foreign Schools Society set out to be a non-denominational venture, but the avowedly Anglican nature of the National Society meant that the British schools tended to derive most of their support from members of the Non-Conformist Churches.[20]

We can gain some impression of the numbers of children attending day schools, and the types of school they attended, from the Report of the Newcastle Commission in 1861. The Commission estimated that the total number of children 'on the books' of the 'public' schools (that is, schools which were in receipt of either philanthropic funds or Government grants) was 1,675,158. This figure included 1,549,312 children on the books of schools supported by religious denominations, 43,098 pupils at schools not specially connected with religious denominations, 47,748 children at schools largely or entirely dependent on taxation, and 35,000 children at 'collegiate and superior or richer endowed schools'. The Commission also despatched Assistant Commissioners to ten 'specimen districts' to ascertain the number of children attending 'private' schools (that is, schools which were not in receipt of either Government or philanthropic funds). On the basis of their findings, they estimated that 573,536 children were on the books of working-class private schools (dame schools and private venture schools), and 286,768 were on the books of middle- or upper-class schools.[21]

The Commissioners also obtained information about the regularity of school attendance, the length of time for which children remained 'on the books', and the ages of the children attending different types of school in ten 'specimen' areas (see Table 10.1). Unfortunately, they failed to distinguish between the number attending working-class schools and those attending schools for the middle and upper classes, and this makes the figures for private schools particularly difficult to interpret, but the findings are nevertheless instructive. The Commission estimated that the average length of school attendance was 5.7 years (although this figure has been challenged by modern authorities), and that the number of children in average daily attendance ranged from 76.1 per cent of the total number of registered pupils in the public schools to 84.8 per cent of registered pupils in the private schools. It also showed that the private schools recruited relatively high proportions of children under the age of seven and over the age of 14. More than three-quarters of the children who were attending school between these ages were on the books of the grant-aided 'public' schools.[22]

Table 10.1 Numbers of children attending public and private schools at different ages in ten specimen areas, 1861

Age	Public schools		Private schools		Total on school books (%)		
	Number	%	Number	%	Public (%)	Private (%)	Total (%)
< 3	5,422	3.0	4,645	5.4	53.86	46.14	100.00
3–6	35,787	19.8	29,848	34.7	54.52	45.48	100.00
6–7	20,424	11.3	11,526	13.4	63.92	36.08	100.00
7–8	22,231	12.3	9,462	11.0	70.14	29.86	100.00
8–9	22,412	12.4	7,742	9.0	74.33	25.67	100.00
9–10	20,966	11.6	6,365	7.4	76.71	23.29	100.00
10–11	18,616	10.3	4,989	5.8	78.86	21.14	100.00
11–12	14,278	7.9	4,129	4.8	77.57	22.43	100.00
12–13	10,844	6.0	3,355	3.9	76.37	23.63	100.00
13–14	5,603	3.1	1,978	2.3	73.90	26.10	100.00
14–15	2,350	1.3	1,118	1.3	67.75	32.25	100.00
> 15	1,807	1.0	860	1.0	67.75	32.25	100.00
Total	180,740	100.0	86,018	100.0	67.75	32.25	100.00

Source: PP 1861 (2794) xxi (Part I), 1, *Report of the Commissioners appointed to enquire into the state of popular education in England*, pp. 648–9, 653, 655.

10.2 The growth of state intervention

Although religion was undoubtedly one of the major spurs to the growth of educational provision in the early part of the nineteenth century, it was also one of the major obstacles to the growth of state educational provision. This was partly because the majority of educational reformers were convinced of the centrality of religion to education, and partly because neither the Church of England nor the Non-Conformist Churches could agree on the role which the state should play in the provision of education. The Church of England was opposed to any scheme which threatened to place it on an equal footing with the Non-Conformists, and the Non-Conformists were opposed to any scheme which gave priority to the interests of the Church of England.[23] However, in spite of these difficulties, the state nevertheless became increasingly involved in the provision of public education from the 1830s onwards.

The first major breakthrough in the provision of government funds for the development of mass education came with the introduction of the government grant for public education in 1833. Mindful of the sensibilities of the religious societies, the government agreed to make a grant of £20,000 to support the construction of new buildings. All applications for aid had to be submitted either through the National Society or through the British and Foreign Schools Society, and at least half the total cost had to be met through private subscription. As Murphy has noted, both the scale and scope of the government's support were closely circumscribed, but once the government had agreed to bear some of the cost of educational development, it was probably inevitable that demands would follow for the establishment of some form of government machinery to ensure that the money provided by Parliament was being used in the ways Parliament intended.[24] In 1839, the government established the Privy

Table 10.2 Government expenditure on public education in Great Britain, 1839/40–1869/70

Year	£	Year	£	Year	£
1840	10,642	1851	164,346	1862	774,743
1841	31,370	1852	188,856	1863	721,392
1842	31,904	1853	250,659	1864	655,042
1843	29,356	1854	326,036	1865	636,810
1844	38,702	1855	369,062	1866	675,535
1845	54,327	1856	423,633	1867	679,157
1846	58,282	1857	559,974	1868	750,486
1847	62,122	1858	668,874	1869	822,713
1848	83,407	1859	723,116	1870	894,561
1849	109,949	1860	724,403		
1850	193,026	1861	813,442		

Notes: The figure for 1861 is taken from the *Report of the Committee of Council on Education 1861–2.* The figure recorded by Sadler and Edwards in their summary of education statistics in 1898 was £833,534.

Sources: PP 1862 (3007) xlii, 1, *Report of the Committee on Council on Education, with Appendix, 1861–2,* p. xlviii; PP 1898 C. 8943 xxiv, 1, *Special Reports on subjects relating to education in England and Wales, Ireland, and foreign countries, Volume 2,* p. 527.

Council Committee on Education, and over the next 20 years, both the scale and scope of government support increased significantly (Table 10.2). Grants became available for school equipment in 1843, teacher-training in 1846, and for individual pupils (capitation grants) in 1853. The total cost of Government support rose from its original figure of £20,000 in 1833 to more than £700,000 at the end of the 1850s.[25]

As the scale of the Government's financial commitment to education increased, both the supporters and opponents of increased state intervention became increasingly concerned about the value of the service which the state was supporting. In 1855 and 1857, the Conservative MP for Droitwich, Sir John Pakington, introduced Bills which would have enabled borough councils to provide their own schools, and in 1856 the Liberal peer (and former Prime Minister) Lord John Russell issued a similar proposal of his own, but their efforts were rebuffed. In 1858, Pakington proposed the establishment of a Royal Commission to investigate the state of educational provision. After a long debate, during which the Vice-President of the Education Committee persuaded Pakington to modify the proposed Commission's terms of reference, the Government agreed to endorse his wishes.[26]

Although the terms of reference of the Royal Commission emphasised the need for an enquiry into 'the extension of sound and cheap elementary instruction to all classes of the people', the Commissioners' recommendations showed that they were just as concerned to promote the extension of elementary education as they were to ensure that such education should be – in their own terms – sound and cheap.[27] The Commission argued that the overwhelming majority of children between the ages of six and 12 already attended some form of school, but it also insisted that more money was needed in order to ensure that they attended more regularly, and that they left school with a proper command of reading, writing and arithmetic. In order to achieve these objectives, it argued that the existing arrangements governing the terms of the government grant should be simplified, and that this should be supplemented by a county rate based on the children's actual educational performance.[28]

The Commission's Report received considerable attention, both in Parliament and in the press.[29] The government rejected the Commission's proposals for the introduction of a local authority or county rate, but it agreed that too many children were leaving school without having acquired the most basic educational qualifications. It therefore decided to use the method recommended by the Commission for the calculation of the county rate to provide a new basis for calculating the government grant. In February 1862 the new Vice-President of the Education Committee, Robert Lowe, told the House of Commons that this method – payment by results – would either be cheap or efficient: 'if the schools do not give instruction, the public money will not be demanded, but if instruction is given, the public money will be demanded'.[30]

Although many commentators have argued that 'payment by results' led to a significant reduction in the state's contribution to educational spending during the first half of the 1860s, it is important to note that the initial fall in expenditure (between 1861 and 1862) occurred before payment by results had been properly introduced.[31] The Department of Education attributed the fall to a change in the regulations regarding the payment of building grants, and Lowe himself argued that the purpose of payment by results was not to reduce educational expenditure, but to ensure that whatever money the government did spend on education should achieve the results intended for it. He claimed that he did not know whether this would lead to a reduction in expenditure, since schoolteachers would soon come to realise the changes that they needed to make to their methods of teaching in order to maintain, or even increase, their school's income.[32] The figures presented in Table 10.2 suggest that Lowe's expectations were not entirely unfounded, because even though educational expenditure fell during the first half of the 1860s, it began to rise once more from the end of 1865 onwards, and had reached its highest level so far by the end of the 1860s.[33]

10.3   From state support to state provision

As the previous section has suggested, the period between 1833 and 1870 undoubtedly witnessed some major changes and improvements in educational provision. The number of children attending school increased, the quality of educational provision improved, and literacy rates, as indicated by the numbers of people signing their own names in marriage registers, also increased.[34] However, in spite (or possibly because) of this, the government came under increasing pressure to respond to calls for increased state provision. These calls culminated in the successful passage of William Forster's Education Bill in 1870.[35]

Fraser argued that, whilst 'it is by no means clear why [the 1870 Education Act] should have been passed at [this] time … the most obvious [reason] was the connection between the Second Reform Act of 1867, with its enfranchisement of the urban working class, and the need to educate the new electorate', but this interpretation has not gone unchallenged.[36] Marcham described the connection between educational reform and the Parliamentary Reform Act of 1867 as 'the centrepiece of one of the curious but persistent legends of educational history'.[37] Hurt argued that the majority of Parliamentarians regarded Parliamentary reform as a long overdue recognition of the rights of a class of men who had already been educated, and that the Education Act itself was the product of a long process of educational reform, and not a short-term response to political change.[38]

It is interesting to compare these interpretations with the reasons given by W. E. Forster for the introduction of the Education Bill in 1870. He argued that the introduction of statutory education would remove 'that ignorance which we are all aware is pregnant with crime and misery, with misfortune to individuals and danger to the community', and that the speedy provision of elementary education was also essential to the maintenance of industrial prosperity and the preservation of national power. However, he also claimed that 'I am one of those who would not wait until the people were educated before I would trust them with political power. If we had thus waited we might have waited long for education; but now that we have given them political power, we must not wait any longer to give them education.'[39] This statement clearly suggests that, even if the advent of Parliamentary reform was not the main reason for the introduction of educational reform, the architects of educational reform were well aware of the extent to which they could use the fears raised by Parliamentary reform to reinforce the case for educational change.[40]

It is also important to consider the more direct ways in which the advent of Parliamentary reform strengthened the hand of Forster and his supporters. Marcham argued that earlier attempts to introduce educational reform, such as those by Pakington and Russell in the 1850s, had foundered because the governments of the time lacked the numerical strength to embark on controversial legislation which might imperil their own existence. The advent of Parliamentary reform changed this because it led to the election of a new government with a large enough majority to embark on substantial legislative programmes and the enfranchisement of a large number of new voters who, 'like many middle-class radicals and dissenters, disliked the Anglican domination of voluntary schooling', and, in the longer term, it forced both Liberal and Conservative politicians to give much greater consideration to the ways in which changes in educational policy could be used to win the support of working-class voters.[41]

When Forster introduced the Education Bill, he emphasised that the purpose of reform was not to supplant the existing voluntary system, but to use the power of the state to 'fill up the gaps' which had been left by the state's dependence on it. Even though he acknowledged the importance of the improvements which had already taken place, he nevertheless concluded that 'the result of the State leaving the initiative to volunteers is, that where State help has been most wanted, [it] has been least given, and where it was desirable that State power should be most felt, it was not felt at all'. In order to rectify this situation, he argued that the Department of Education should investigate the level of educational provision in each area, and that school boards should be set up in those areas where the existing level of state-supported education was deemed inadequate. The boards would be elected by local town councils in urban areas and by select vestries and vestries in rural areas; they would have the power to establish their own rate-aided schools; and they would have the power (though not the duty) to make education compulsory for children between the ages of five and 12 in their own areas.[42]

Although many of the more economically and politically orientated arguments in favour of state education appeared to be aimed more directly at the needs of boys than girls, there was no attempt, at least in Parliament, to suggest that the new educational arrangements should be limited to boys.[43] However, educational policy-makers continued to emphasise the need for different kinds of training for girls and boys – girls were expected to spend much more of their time in needlework and, from 1875 onwards, in 'domestic economy' – and much of the reading material supplied to elementary schoolchildren tended to emphasise the importance of gender-specific codes of behaviour.[44] The boards' own attitudes also revealed a continuing ambivalence towards the whole question of girls' education. According to Davin, many schoolbooks encouraged girls to value their domestic roles above their scholastic achievements, and, following the introduction of compulsory education, many school-attendance officers were willing to turn a blind eye to the non-attendance of girls if it could be shown that they were helping their mothers at home.[45]

Although feminist historians have been rightly critical of the limitations of public education in the latter part of the nineteenth century, their criticisms have tended to be directed at the education system as a whole, rather than the Forster Education Act in particular. However, the Act has been attacked, both on the left and on the right, for its alleged failure to recognise the importance of the different forms of privately-funded education which were already on offer. West argued that the government deliberately ignored the success of the voluntary and private institutions, and that the advent of direct state intervention led to a reduction, and not an enhancement, in the rate of educational progress.[46] On the other hand, left-wing historians have argued that one of the main purposes of educational reform was to undermine the existing tradition of autonomous working-class schools, and to replace it with a statutory system of public education, in which the state could exercise a much greater degree of control over what children were actually taught.[47]

Although the application of the concept of 'social control' to educational history has been particularly influential in recent decades, there are now clear indications of a return to more traditional reformist interpretations of the role played by the state in educational reform.[48] As Stephens has argued, the number of parents sending their children to government-supported schools increased as soon as the grants themselves became available, because they enabled the schools themselves to offer a higher standard of education than the majority of unaided schools were able to offer. However, in spite of this, many children continued to live in areas where the rate of school attendance was comparatively low, and the standard of provision was still inadequate. It was largely because of this that so many Parliamentarians were prepared to accept the need for new forms of state intervention by the end of the 1860s.[49]

Although the Forster Act did not make state education universal, compulsory or free, it made a substantial contribution towards the development of all three. As we have already seen, when Forster introduced the Elementary Education

Bill in February 1870, he went to considerable lengths to emphasise that the purpose of the proposed legislation was not to supplant the existing voluntary system, but to build upon it by 'procuring as much as we can the assistance of the parents, and welcoming as much as we rightly can the cooperation and aid of those benevolent men who desire to assist their neighbours'.[50] However, even though Forster had no desire to supplant the voluntary schools, he did place them at an important disadvantage, because the new board schools were able to supplement their income from fees and grants with money raised by local rates, whereas the voluntary schools derived the whole of their additional income from subscriptions, the occasional endowment and donations.[51] The funding imbalance was reflected in the statistics of school attendance: by 1900, almost half (46.95 per cent) of all the children attending public elementary schools in England and Wales were attending a type of school which had not even existed at the beginning of the 1870s (Table 10.3).

The 1870 Act also made an important contribution to the development of both compulsory and free education. When Forster introduced the Bill, he recognised that many ratepayers would be reluctant to contribute to the development of schools which might not be fully used, and he therefore decided to grant school boards the power to make education compulsory for all children between the ages of five and 12 in their own areas.[52] In 1876, the Conservative government introduced a further Act, known as Sandon's Act (39 & 40 Vict. C. 79), which imposed a duty on the parent of every child 'to cause such child to receive efficient elementary instruction in reading, writing and arithmetic', and prohibited employers either from offering employment to children under the age of ten, or from offering employment to children over the age of ten unless they had either attended a recognised school, or obtained a certificate of proficiency in reading, writing and arithmetic (sections 4–5). The same Act also said that either the Board of Guardians or the local borough council should have the power 'to make bye-laws respecting the attendance of children at school under section 74 of the Elementary Education Act, 1870, as if such councils and guardians respectively were a School Board' (section 21). However, it was not until 1880 that Parliament finally agreed to make education compulsory across the whole country. The Elementary Education Act of that year (43 & 44 Vict. C. 23) imposed a duty on all local authorities to pass bye-laws making education compulsory in their districts, and gave the Department of Education the power to frame its own bye-laws if the local authority failed to do so (section 2).

One of the most controversial issues concerning education was the question of school fees. In 1870, Forster had argued that even though it would be wrong to exempt all children from the payment of school fees, nevertheless school boards should be empowered to remit fees in cases of exceptional hardship, and to establish free schools in areas of particular poverty.[53] In 1876, Sandon attempted to extend the principle of free education to areas which were not covered by school boards by transferring the power to remit school fees to Boards of Guardians, but many parents refused to apply to the Guardians because of their association with the Poor Law, and the measure was largely ineffective. During the 1880s a series of attempts were made to overcome this deficiency, either by transferring the power of remission to a School Fees Committee, or by enabling

Table 10.3 Numbers of children attending voluntary and board schools in England and Wales, 1870–1902

Year ending 31 August	Voluntary schools		Board schools		Total public elementary day schools	
	Schools	Average attendance	Schools	Average attendance	Schools	Average attendance
1871	8,798	1,231,434	0	0	8,798	1,231,434
1872	9,772	1,327,432	82	8,726	9,854	1,336,158
1873	10,574	1,412,497	520	69,983	11,094	1,482,480
1874	11,408	1,540,466	838	138,293	12,246	1,678,759
1875	12,081	1,609,895	1,136	227,285	13,217	1,837,180
1876	12,677	1,656,502	1,596	328,071	14,273	1,984,573
1877	13,105	1,723,150	2,082	427,533	15,187	2,150,683
1878	13,611	1,846,119	2,682	559,078	16,293	2,405,197
1879	14,027	1,925,254	3,139	669,741	17,166	2,594,995
1880	14,181	1,981,664	3,433	769,252	17,614	2,750,916
1881	14,370	2,007,184	3,692	856,351	18,062	2,863,535
1882	14,421	2,069,920	3,868	945,231	18,289	3,015,151
1883	14,491	2,098,310	4,049	1,028,904	18,540	3,127,214
1884	14,580	2,157,292	4,181	1,115,832	18,761	3,273,124
1885	14,600	2,183,870	4,295	1,187,455	18,895	3,371,325
1886	14,620	2,187,118	4,402	1,251,307	19,022	3,438,425
1887	14,662	2,211,920	4,492	1,315,461	19,154	3,527,381
1888	14,659	2,236,961	4,552	1,378,006	19,211	3,614,967
1889	14,686	2,257,790	4,624	1,424,835	19,310	3,682,625
1890	14,743	2,260,559	4,676	1,457,358	19,419	3,717,917
1891	14,761	2,258,885	4,747	1,491,571	19,508	3,750,456
1892	14,681	2,300,377	4,831	1,570,397	19,512	3,870,774
1893	14,673	2,411,362	4,904	1,688,668	19,577	4,100,030
1894	14,628	2,448,037	5,081	1,777,797	19,709	4,225,834
1895	14,479	2,445,812	5,260	1,879,218	19,739	4,325,030
1896	14,416	2,465,919	5,432	1,871,653	19,848	4,337,572
1897	14,418	2,465,193	5,539	2,023,850	19,957	4,489,043
1898	14,427	2,484,717	5,595	2,087,519	20,022	4,572,236
1899	14,412	2,525,968	5,622	2,132,201	20,034	4,658,169
1900	14,359	2,486,597	5,758	2,201,049	20,117	4,687,646
1901	14,294	2,482,372	5,857	2,259,259	20,151	4,741,631
1902	14,275	2,546,217	5,878	2,344,020	20,153	4,890,237

Sources: 1871–1896: PP 1897 C. 8447 xxv, 1, *Special Reports on Educational Subjects 1896–7*, pp. 6–7, 16, 22, 49; 1897: PP 1898 C. 8862 lxxx, 101, *Return showing (1) expenditure from the grant for public education in England and Wales in 1897, upon annual grants to elementary schools; and (2) actual number of elementary schools on the annual grant list on 31 August 1897; the accommodation and number of scholars in those schools; and the results of the inspection and examination of elementary schools during the year 1896–97*, pp. 10–11;1898: PP 1899 C. 9210 lxxv, 85, *Return showing (1) expenditure from the grant for public education in England and Wales in 1898, upon annual grants to elementary schools; and (2) actual number of elementary schools on the annual grant list on 31 August 1898; the accommodation and number of scholars in those schools; and the results of the inspection and examination of elementary schools during the year 1897–98*, pp. 10–11; 1899: PP 1900 Cd. 315 lxv (Part II), 1, *Return showing, under county boroughs and administrative counties, for each public elementary school inspected in England and Wales, the name and denomination of school; the number of scholars for whom accommodation was provided; the average number of scholars in attendance; the annual grant paid; and particulars of school income and expenditure; for the year ended 31 August 1899 (with summaries)*, p. 1100; 1900: PP 1901 Cd. 568 lvi, 1, *Statistics of public elementary schools, evening continuation schools, pupil-teacher centres, training colleges and certified efficient schools for the year ended 31 August 1900*, p. 10; 1901: PP 1902 Cd. 1139 lxxviii, 659, *Statistics of public elementary schools, evening continuation schools, pupil-teacher centres, training colleges and certified efficient schools for the year ended 31 August 1901*, p. 8; 1902: PP 1903 Cd. 1476 li, 361, *Statistics of public elementary schools, evening continuation schools, pupil-teacher centres, training colleges and certified efficient schools for the year ended 31 August 1902*, p. 16.

the children to 'earn' exemption by good attendance, but these attempts were defeated.[54] Consequently, it was not until 1891 that legislation was finally passed which resulted in the vast majority of elementary-school children being exempted from school fees. One of the supporters of the new Act, T. Ellis, the MP for Merionethshire, argued that the measure could be justified 'on the ground of social justice ... Relatively to their income, the working classes contribute more to the Imperial Revenue than any other class, and it [is] only fair in the matter of education that they should as soon as possible receive a grant from the Imperial Exchequer. The parents will also be relieved of a heavy burden which presses upon them at the time when it is most difficult to be borne.'[55]

10.4   Unification and control

Although the 1870 Act was undoubtedly the major turning point in the history of nineteenth-century education, it did have a number of important limitations. In the first place, the Act was avowedly concerned with the question of *elementary* education, and it did not attempt to offer the vast majority of children anything other than elementary education. However, a growing number of children began to stay on at school beyond the minimum school-leaving age, and, many school boards began to establish 'higher-grade' schools to cater for these pupils. This brought the school boards into conflict, both with the Department and, subsequently, the Board of Education, who felt that the school boards were exceeding their powers by providing education other than elementary, and with the existing providers of post-elementary education, who felt that the school boards were encroaching on their territory. In 1899, the Camden School of Art petitioned the District Auditor to declare expenditure by the London School Board on the provision of Science and Art classes illegal, and the Permanent Secretary of the Board of Education, Sir Robert Morant, began drafting regulations which were specifically designed to prevent school boards from offering any form of education to children over the age of 15.[56]

The second major issue concerned the relationship between the school boards and the voluntary sector. Under the terms of the 1870 Act, school boards were only supposed to be set up in areas where the existing level of voluntary provision was deemed inadequate, but once the boards had been set up, they were thrust into direct competition with the existing voluntary providers. During the 1890s, the voluntary schools became increasingly concerned both by what they saw as the increasing secularisation of the board schools, and by the imbalance between their own financial resources and those of the state sector. In 1897, the Church of England persuaded the government to introduce the Voluntary Schools Act, which sought to redress the disadvantages of the voluntary sector by providing additional state subsidies, but the benefit was short-lived. Consequently, the government came under increasing pressure from the Church for a much more thorough-going reform of the education system.[57]

The campaign for further changes in the organisation of public education received further support from the 'campaign for national efficiency'. During the 1890s, many commentators became concerned about what they saw as the haphazard nature of British education, and the need for a more coherent administrative structure. They were particularly critical of the way in which school boards had been set up independently of the established machinery of local government, and they believed that this was hampering efforts to unify the different elements of the elementary-school system, and to connect them 'rationally or organically' to the secondary system.[58] They therefore advocated the abolition of the school boards, and the transfer of their responsibilities to what became known as 'local education authorities'.[59]

The campaign waged by members of the 'Efficiency Group', combined with the continuing anxieties over the place of secondary education and the problems faced by the voluntary sector, formed the background to the emergence of the Balfour Education Act of 1902. This Act (2 Edw. VII C. 42) abolished the school boards and transferred their existing responsibilities for the provision of elementary education to the local county, county borough, borough and urban district councils. Part II of the Act gave the larger authorities – the county and county borough councils – the power 'to consider the educational needs of their areas and to take such steps as seem to them desirable, after consultation with the Board of Education, to supply or aid the supply of education other than elementary'. The third part of the Act sought to create a more unified framework for the development of elementary education by bringing the voluntary schools under the overall control of the local education authorities. Section six of the Act gave the authorities the power to nominate up to one-third of the managers, or governors, of the voluntary schools in their area. In return for this, the authorities acquired the responsibility for maintaining the schools, and 'keeping them efficient'.

Simon argued that the 1902 Act was anti-progressive, because it prevented the growth of alternative forms of post-elementary or secondary education of the kind represented by the higher-grade schools, and anti-democratic because it replaced the elected school boards with the appointed members of local education authorities.[60] However, whilst the 1902 Act was, at least in part, a struggle for control, it would be wrong to ignore its positive significance. Stephens argued that the retention of the higher-grade schools would have increased the degree of social segregation in post-elementary education by channelling 'all intellectually-endowed working- and lower-middle-class children' into secondary schools with a very different curriculum to the one followed by middle-class children.[61] Sanderson has also claimed that the suppression of the higher-grade schools, and the consequent expansion of the secondary schools, increased educational opportunities. In 1897, boys from skilled manual and unskilled backgrounds constituted only nine per cent of all grammar school pupils, and 40 per cent of higher-grade school pupils. By 1910, more than 20 per cent of all grammar school pupils were from working-class backgrounds.[62]

10.5 Conclusions

At the beginning of the nineteenth century, it is most likely that the majority of children had some experience of formal schooling, but they attended irregularly and for a comparatively short period. By the end of the century, it was compulsory for all children to undergo a recognised form of education between the ages of five and 12, and a growing number of children stayed on to the ages of 14 or 15. These developments were underpinned by a massive expansion in the extent of state intervention in the provision of public education. By the end of the nineteenth century, the state was well on the way to being the dominant provider, as well as the principal purchaser, of educational services for children of school age.

Although this chapter has concentrated, necessarily, on the those aspects of educational history which are most directly related to the organisation of schooling, the development of statutory educational provision also represented a dramatic change in the relationships between the state, the individual and the family. At the beginning of the nineteenth century, it would have seemed almost inconceivable that the state should not only pay for educational services, but also compel parents to force their children to attend the schools the state provided. The history of public education is therefore directly related to the history of the family, and, as a result, to the development of social policy in its broadest context.[63]

11 The Liberal welfare reforms, 1906–14

Dicey argued that nineteenth-century Britain experienced a transition from 'Benthamite individualism' to 'collectivism'. He highlighted the existence of a number of Acts, including the Elementary Education Acts, which pointed to a new relationship between the state and the individual. However, even Dicey was unprepared for the extension of public welfare provision in the years immediately following the first edition of his lectures. In 1914, he suggested that 'the main current of legislative opinion from the beginning of the twentieth century has run vehemently towards collectivism. When the last century came to an end, belief in *laissez faire* had lost much of its hold on the people of England. The problem now before us is to ascertain what are the new causes or conditions which have since the beginning of the present century given additional force to the influence of more-or-less socialistic ideas.'[1]

This chapter examines the background to the introduction of what have come to be known as 'the Liberal welfare reforms', and assesses their relationship to the long-term development of British social policy. It begins by looking at some of the main changes which affected British society between *circa* 1870 and 1914, and examines the range of factors which contributed to the growth of state intervention in this period. It then goes on to take a more detailed look at some of the major legislative reforms passed between 1906 and 1911, including the introduction of free school meals (1906), school medical inspection (1907), the Children Act (1908), old-age pensions (1908), the Labour Exchanges Act (1909), the Trade Boards Act (1909), the Development and Road Improvement Funds Act (1909), the Housing and Town Planning Act (1909), the Finance Act of 1910, and the introduction of unemployment and health insurance in 1911. Even though the immediate results of many of these measures were somewhat limited, there can be little doubt that they did indeed mark the opening of a new chapter in the history of British social policy.

11.1 The origins of the Liberal welfare reforms

The last three decades of the nineteenth century witnessed a number of profound changes in the demographic structure of the British population. The crude birth rate fell from 36.3 births per 1000 living in 1876 to 23.8 in 1914, and the average number of children per family fell from approximately six children per married woman in the middle years of the nineteenth century to just two children at the end of the 1920s. The crude death rate fell from 22.9 deaths per 1,000 living in 1870 to 14 deaths on the eve of the First World War, and average life expectancy rose from just over 40 years at the beginning of the 1860s to more than 50 between 1910 and 1912. These changes had a substantial effect on the population's age structure. Between 1881 and 1911, the proportion of people aged 65 and over changed very little, but the proportion of children (that is, people under the age of 15) fell from just under 36 per cent to less than 31 per cent, whilst the proportion of the population which was of working age (that is, aged 15–64) rose from 59.72 per cent to more than 64 per cent. One of the consequences of these changes was that the dependency ratio, which compares the number of children and elderly people with the population of working age, fell from 0.67 to 0.56.[2]

The late-nineteenth century also witnessed a significant change in the occupational and geographical distribution of the population. The proportion of the working population which was employed in agriculture had already begun to decline between 1800 and 1850, but this trend accelerated after 1850, and the numbers employed in both manufacturing and, especially, service industries increased substantially.[3] The decline of the agricultural sector was reinforced by the agricultural depression of 1873–96, which led to a sharp reduction in the price of many agricultural goods, and encouraged a further movement of population away from rural areas.[4] By 1901, it was estimated that approximately 78 per cent of the population of England and Wales resided in towns containing more than 5,000 inhabitants, 69 per cent of the population lived in towns with more than 10,000 inhabitants, and 44 per cent lived in towns with more than 100,000 inhabitants.[5] In 1851, there were only eight towns and cities, including London, whose populations exceeded 100,000. By 1901, 28 towns and cities contained more than 100,000 inhabitants, and 14 towns and cities contained more than 200,000 inhabitants.[6]

Although the decline in agricultural prices caused a great deal of hardship in many rural areas, it also contributed to a substantial improvement in the living standards of many urban wage-earners.[7] According to Feinstein, the cost of living fell by more than 23 per cent between 1873 and 1896, and even though prices rose again after 1896, they continued to increase more slowly than earnings. The different movements of wages and prices meant that the real value of average earnings rose by 39 per cent between 1873 and 1896, and by 7.1 per cent between 1896 and 1913.[8] However, even though the average standard of living (as measured by real earnings) was undoubtedly improving, there was still a substantial proportion of the population which lived in conditions of considerable poverty. As we have already seen, the introduction of compulsory education between 1870 and 1880 forced many school boards to introduce poverty scales in order to identify those children whose fees should be paid for them, and in 1895 the Royal Commission on the Aged Poor discovered that, in addition to the 25–30 per cent of elderly people who were already claiming poor relief, there were also many others who were living in conditions of considerable hardship.[9] The 1870s and 1880s also witnessed the emergence of a 'new' problem of mass unemployment. The average annual rate of unemployment rose above ten per cent in both 1879 and 1886, and in February 1886 the Lord Mayor of London was sufficiently alarmed to launch a special Mansion House Fund for the relief of distress.[10] The problem of unemployment also led to changes in government policy. In March 1886, the President of the Local Government Board, Joseph Chamberlain, issued his famous Circular, authorising the establishment of local authority public works programmes, and the Circular was reissued (though not to any great effect) on four separate occasions between 1886 and 1893.[11]

Although the average standard of living improved during the latter part of the nineteenth century, this period was also characterised by a growing awareness of the extent of working-class poverty. In 1886, a Liverpool ship-owner, Charles Booth, began his exhaustive investigation into the incomes of families and households containing school-age children in East London, and he subsequently extended this to cover the rest of the city. He found that 8.4 per cent of the population was living 'in want' (although 'only a percentage – and not, I think, a large percentage – would be said, by themselves, or by anyone else, to be "in distress"'), and that a further 22.7 per cent were living 'in poverty', although he went on to insist that 'they are neither ill-nourished nor ill-clad, according to any standard that can reasonably be used'. He also made the first serious attempt to enumerate the different causes of poverty. Out of 4,076 families who were found to be living in either poverty or great poverty in East London, 1.5 per cent were said to be 'loafers', 62.5 per cent were in poverty as a result of questions related to employment (casual work, low pay, irregular earnings or small profits), 13.6 per cent were in poverty as a result of questions of habit (drunkenness or lack of thrift), and 22.5 per cent had been impoverished by circumstances (illness or infirmity, large family, or a combination of illness, infirmity, large family and irregular work). In his earliest writings, he suggested that a high proportion of the poverty which was experienced by the merely poor was caused by 'the competition of the very poor', and that the time may have come for the 'individualist community ... to take charge of the lives of those who, from whatever cause, are incapable of independent existence up to the required standard', but he subsequently abandoned this position, and in the final volume of his study he suggested that the best solutions were likely to come from the coordinated efforts of voluntary organisations and, especially, 'the deepening of the sentiment of Individual Responsibility'.[12]

Although some contemporaries thought that Booth had exaggerated the extent of poverty, he himself did not believe that his findings were particularly alarming.[13] He thought that only a small minority of those who were suffering from poverty were experiencing real distress, and that their problems were most likely to be resolved through the intensification of voluntary effort.[14] However, any complacency which might have been engendered by these conclusions was dealt a much stronger blow by the results of Seebohm Rowntree's investigations into the extent of poverty in York in 1899.[15] Rowntree estimated that 9.91 per cent of the total population was living in a state of what he called 'primary poverty' (in other words, their total earnings were 'insufficient to obtain the minimum necessaries for the maintenance of merely physical efficiency'), and that 17.93 per cent were living in 'secondary poverty' (in other words, their total earnings 'would be sufficient for the maintenance of merely physical efficiency, were it not that some portion of it [*sic*] is absorbed by other expenditure'), and that all those who were living either primary or secondary poverty were living in conditions of 'obvious want and squalor' which made it impossible for them to be 'economically efficient'.[16] Although he was reluctant to get drawn too closely into debates about the appropriate solutions to poverty, he insisted that they were likely to include 'questions dealing with land tenure, with the relative duties and powers of the state and the individual, and with legislation affecting the aggregation and the distribution of wealth', and he emphasised that even though 'the immediate causes of "secondary poverty" call for well-considered and resolute action, its ultimate elimination will only be possible when these causes are dealt with as part of, and in relation to, the wider social problem'.[17]

In recent decades, historians and sociologists have engaged in a vigorous debate concerning the meaning which Rowntree attached to the concept of poverty. Townsend claimed that Rowntree had pioneered an 'absolute' conception of poverty, which left little or no room for personal, social or recreational expenditure, whereas Veit-Wilson argued that Rowntree's method of identifying secondary poverty was much closer to Townsend's own concept of 'relative deprivation', because it was based on the subjective impressions gathered by an 'experienced investigator' who judged the poverty of each household by comparing their standard of living with the standards which were recognised and approved by society at large.[18] However, although Veit-Wilson was right to draw attention to the impressionistic nature of the evidence on which Rowntree based his findings, it is important to remember that he himself believed that the standard of living which he defined as poor was one associated with the minimum level on which the basic requirements for physical health could be achieved, and it was this which made his work so shocking to contemporaries. If Rowntree had been trying to argue that between one-quarter and one-third of the population of York was unable 'to obtain the type of diet, participate in the activities and have the living conditions and amenities which are customary, or at least widely encouraged and approved' within his society, then his work would still have been important, but it would have been much less shocking than the claim that 27.84 per cent of the population was living under conditions which made it impossible for them to make a full contribution to the economic and even military life of their country.[19]

The significance of this debate was underlined by the nature and extent of the political changes which took place in Britain during the latter part of the nineteenth century. The Conservatives introduced a major Parliamentary Reform Act in 1867 which extended voting rights to a large number of working-class householders in urban areas, and in 1884 voting rights were also extended to agricultural workers, whilst the Parliamentary Reform Act of 1885 led to a significant alteration in the balance between urban and rural constituencies. Even though approximately 40 per cent of adult men and the whole of the female population were still unable to vote in Parliamentary elections, these changes enabled the working class to play a much more direct role in both local and national politics, and both the Conservative and Liberal parties were forced to devote much more attention to the need to mobilise their own supporters and broaden their appeal to a wider and less pliable electorate. There was also a growing demand for independent working-class representation. The first

'Lib-Lab' MPs (Labour representatives taking the Liberal whip) were elected during the 1870s, but in 1899 the Trades Union Congress agreed to cooperate with other working-class organisations in the establishment of a separate Labour Representation Committee, and the first Labour MPs (Richard Bell and Keir Hardie) were elected in the following year.[20]

A number of writers have identified a direct connection between the extent of working-class mobilisation and the growth of state welfare provision, and this conviction was shared by many contemporaries. In 1891, the MP for Falkirk, W. P. Sinclair, attributed the Conservative party's support for the abolition of school fees to the fact that 'political power in this country has shifted; the governing power is now handed over to the people', and Dicey thought that this was one of the main reasons for the growth of collectivism.[21] However, some historians have questioned the extent to which many working-class voters were actually in favour of increased state intervention. Pelling argued that 'the extension of the power of the state at the beginning of … [the twentieth] century … was by no means welcomed by members of the working class', and may even have been undertaken 'over the critical hostility of many of them, perhaps of most of them', and that this hostility was rooted in 'working-class attitudes of suspicion or dislike towards existing institutions which were the expression of national social policy'. However, many historians have criticised this view, and in recent years much more attention has been focused on the extent to which working-class organisations actively campaigned for the extension of state welfare provision.[22]

Although it is inevitably difficult to obtain a great deal of information about the attitudes of working-class individuals to the growth of state welfare, it is possible to obtain some information from the testimony of oral historians and from working-class autobiographies, and these accounts can be supplemented with evidence obtained from surveys of the views expressed by the members of working-class organisations, such as trade unions and friendly societies. Thane suggested that 'many poorer people … were grateful for any amelioration of hard lives', and that it was the trade-union leadership which was often most sceptical of reformist promises, believing that these were designed to distract workers from the struggle for better wages, or that they were likely to undermine institutions of working-class solidarity. However, even these who were most hostile to state intervention were forced to concede that some form of state welfare provision might be necessary in order to improve the lot of the very poor, and during the 1890s and early-1900s trade unionists and friendly-society members played an increasingly active role in campaigns for state welfare provision. This was reflected in the growth of working-class campaigns for the introduction of school meals and school medical inspection, old-age pensions, the abolition of the Poor Law, the establishment of trade boards, and measures to combat unemployment.[23]

Although it seems clear that there was growing working-class support for state welfare, it is difficult to argue that the Liberal welfare reforms were a *direct* response to working-class pressure. As Thane has argued, '[the] early Liberal reforms can be attributed to successful Labour pressure to the extent that it is highly unlikely that they would have been implemented at all but for the existence of an increasingly well-organised labour movement ... but [they] cannot simply be interpreted as a direct result of Labour pressure. They were far from being complete victories for Labour; they were granted very much on Liberal terms. They contain controls and limitations which were closer to the demands of politicians like [Joseph] Chamberlain and employers in the Chamber of Commerce [*sic*] than to those of the labour movement.'[24]

In view of this, it is worth looking at some of the other reasons why both Conservative and Liberal politicians became more sympathetic to reformist measures in this period. One of the most potent factors was their fear of the growth of working-class power and their need to legitimise the status quo. In 1892, the Radical politician, Joseph Chamberlain, claimed that 'the foundations of property are made more secure when no real grievance is felt by the poor against the rich', and in 1895, the Conservative leader, A. J. Balfour, told an audience in Manchester that 'socialism will not get possession of the great body of public opinion ... if those who wield the collective force of the community show themselves desirous to ameliorate every legitimate grievance and to put society upon a proper footing.'[25] In 1909, Winston Churchill told a *Daily Mail* reporter that:

> The idea [behind the introduction of unemployment insurance] is to increase the stability of our institutions by giving the mass of industrial workers a direct interest in maintaining them. ... [This] scheme ... will help to remove the dangerous element of uncertainty from the existence of the industrial worker. It will give him an assurance that his home, got together through long years and with affectionate sacrifice, will not be broken up, sent bit by bit to the pawnshop, just because ... he falls out of work. It will make him a better citizen, a more efficient worker, [and] a happier man.[26]

Although the reforms were at least in part a response to working-class pressure, they were also influenced by pressure from employers. Blackburn suggested that the chain-masters of Cradley Heath supported the campaign for the establishment of trade boards (which were set up to establish minimum wage levels) because they believed that this would help them to combat the threat of cut-throat competition, but there were also other reasons for employers to support the expansion of state-sponsored welfare schemes.[27] Hay argued that members of the Birmingham Chamber of Commerce supported the campaign for social reform because they believed that this would help to prevent working-class unrest, promote social harmony, and encourage economic and industrial efficiency.[28] However, it is also important not to exaggerate the extent to which the majority of employers were in favour of Liberal social legislation. Melling pointed out that many employers – including some within the Birmingham Chamber of Commerce itself – were actively hostile to state welfare schemes, and that their failure to develop 'a political strategy to deal with the advent of New Liberalism' had major implications for the development of organised capitalism after 1914.[29]

During the early-twentieth century, concerns for the health of the working-class population became closely identified with the belief that the average standard of public health was deteriorating, or even degenerating, as a result of urbanisation. In the late-nineteenth and early-twentieth centuries, a number of writers, including James Cantlie and J. P. Williams-Freeman claimed that the stresses of urban life were leading to a progressive deterioration in the physical condition of the working-class population, and that if nothing was done to arrest this, then the population would eventually die out as a result of its inability to reproduce itself.[30] These fears came to a head following the outbreak of the Boer War in 1899, when the Inspector-General of Recruiting reported that up to 40 per cent of those who were willing to join the army were unfit to serve, and in 1903 the government appointed an Interdepartmental Committee on Physical Deterioration to investigate claims that the health of the population was indeed deteriorating. The Committee concluded that the spectre of hereditary physical deterioration was unfounded, but it agreed that the health of large sections of the urban population was being undermined by poverty, ignorance and neglect. It therefore proposed a series of 53 separate recommendations, which were designed to counter these tendencies by introducing changes in the system of public health administration, introducing new methods of monitoring health status, improving the standard of public health provision, highlighting the need for improvements in standards of personal hygiene and 'social education', and introducing new forms of welfare provision for schoolchildren, including the introduction of school meals and a limited form of school medical inspection.[31]

The feelings of alarm which were aroused by the spectre of physical deterioration were closely related to growing fears about the threat to Britain's 'national efficiency'. These fears developed steadily throughout the second half of the nineteenth century (and were undoubtedly a major factor in the decision to pass the Elementary Education Act of 1870), but they gathered fresh impetus following the outbreak of the Boer War and the defeats experienced by the British army at Nicholson's Nek, Stormberg, Magersfontein and Colenso, the 'alternate hope and disappointment' of six weeks' fighting on the banks of the Tugela, and the 'long anxiety' for the fate of Ladysmith, Kimberley and Mafeking. As Leo Amery wrote in 1900: 'the war has been the nation's recessional after all the pomp and show of ... [Queen Victoria's Diamond] Jubilee. It has transmuted the complacent arrogance and contempt of other nations begotten of long years of peace and prosperity to a truer consciousness both of our strength and of our defects, and has awakened an earnest desire to make those defects good.'[32]

The campaign for national efficiency influenced arguments about social policy in two main ways. In the first place, it encouraged policy-makers to look more closely at the social and economic policies which were being implemented by Britain's international competitors, and to identify those policies which might enhance the country's economic and military competitiveness. Secondly, it also focused particular attention on the importance of Britain's human resources as the ultimate foundations of national power. 'In the view of the "efficiency group"', wrote Searle, 'men and women formed the basic raw material out of which national greatness was constructed: hence, they argued, the statesman had a duty to see that these priceless resources were not squandered through indifference and slackness.'[33]

The campaign for social reform was also influenced by changes in the nature of Liberalism itself. For much of the second half of the nineteenth century, Liberalism had appeared to be largely synonymous with low taxation, the reduction of public expenditure and the promotion of individual responsibility, but during the 1880s and 1890s these ideas faced a growing challenge from Idealist thinkers such as T. H. Green and D. G. Ritchie, who emphasised the importance of the obligations which existed between individuals and the organic nature of human society.[34] The popularisation of these ideas coincided with the emergence of a new generation of Liberal politicians, such as Winston Churchill and David Lloyd George, who were much more strongly committed to the promotion of state-sponsored collective action for the public good. As Churchill himself suggested in 1906, 'it is not possible to draw a hard-and-fast line between individualism and collectivism ... . No man can be a collectivist alone or an individualist alone. He must be both an individualist and a collectivist. The nature of man is a dual nature. The character of the organisation of human society is dual.'[35]

Although it is tempting to regard the views expressed by men such as Churchill and Lloyd George as the reflections of class or party-political interest, they also reflected a genuine commitment to social justice.[36] In 1908, during a debate on the introduction of old age pensions, Lloyd George told the House of Commons that 'the wealth of this country is enormous ... and I do not think it is too much to expect the more favoured part of the community ... to make a substantial contribution to improve the lot of the poorer members of the ... community to which they belong.'[37] Winston Churchill may not have had the same personal experience of poverty as Lloyd George, but his writings and speeches also demonstrated a genuine understanding of some of the hardships of working-class life and a desire to relieve them. 'I do not want to see impaired the vigour of competition,' he told a Glasgow audience in 1906, 'but we can do much to mitigate the consequences of failure. We want to draw a line below which we will not allow persons to live and labour, yet above which they may compete with all the strength of their manhood. We want to have free competition upwards; we decline to allow free competition downwards. We do not want to pull down the structures of science and civilisation: but to spread a net over the abyss.'[38]

11.2   From school meals to national insurance

Although the Liberals are best known for their contributions to the development of old-age pensions and the introduction of national insurance, the initial stages of Liberal welfare reform were primarily concerned with the welfare of children. On 18 April 1905, the previous Conservative government had given Boards of Guardians the power to make arrangements for the provision of school meals under the Relief (Schoolchildren) Order, but many parents, who might otherwise have been eligible for assistance, refused to apply to the Guardians for fear of being labelled as paupers.[39] On 3 May, the independent Labour MP, Arthur Henderson, introduced a slightly amended version of a Bill which he had first introduced on 29 March, giving local education authorities the power to feed children who were 'unable by reason of lack of food to profit from the education provided for them', but neither this measure, nor a second

Bill, introduced by the Liberal MP, Dr Thomas Macnamara, passed beyond its first reading.[40] However, on 22 February 1906, the newly elected Labour MP for Westhoughton, W. T. Wilson, introduced an almost identical version of Henderson's original Bill, and even though the Liberals were unhappy about certain aspects of the proposal, they agreed to allow it to be considered in the government's own time. They therefore paved the way for the Bill to become law later in the same year.[41]

As a number of commentators have pointed out, there were various important differences between the version of the Education (Provision of Meals) Bill which Wilson originally proposed, and the version which the Liberals ultimately backed.[42] In contrast to the original Bill, the amended version emphasised the importance of cooperation between the local education authorities and voluntary agencies, and said that the parents of children who were fed at school should be subject to a charge, to be determined by the local education authority, unless it was satisfied that they were unable to pay. It also said that a local education authority could only use public funds to provide school meals after applying to the Board of Education, and provided that the total cost of such expenditure came to less than the yield of a half-penny rate.[43] However, in spite of these changes, the Act's opponents continued to believe that it constituted an unwarranted extension of the scope of public responsibility. Dicey claimed that:

> No-one can deny that a starving boy will hardly profit from the attempt to teach him the rules of arithmetic. But it does not necessarily follow that a local authority must therefore provide every hungry child at school with a meal ... [or] that a father who first lets his child starve, and then fails to pay the price legally due from him for a meal ... should, under the Act of 1906, retain the right of voting for a Member of Parliament. Why a man who first neglects his duty as a father and then defrauds the state should retain his full political rights is a question easier to ask than to answer.[44]

The second major reform, following the passage of the Education (Provision of Meals) Act, was the establishment of a national system of school medical inspection. After a long campaign, supported by members of the labour movement and by supporters of the campaign for national efficiency, the Liberals introduced a proposal to allow local education authorities 'to make such arrangements as may be sanctioned by the Board of Education for attending to the health and physical condition of children attending public elementary schools', and they subsequently added a further clause, giving local education authorities the duty 'to provide for the medical inspection of children before or at the time of admission to a public elementary school, and on such other occasions as the Board of Education direct'. These proposals formed part of the Education (England and Wales) Bill, which was primarily concerned with the status of religion in grant-aided schools, and when this measure was withdrawn at the end of 1906, the government came under strong pressure to reintroduce the clauses relating to medical inspection in the following year. In February 1907, these clauses were reintroduced in a Private Member's Bill, introduced by the Liberal backbench MP, Walter Russell Rea, and in the government's own Education (Administrative Provisions) Bill. This Bill was passed on 28 August 1907, and the school medical service was formally established on 1 January 1908.[45]

The third major piece of legislation to affect children was the Children Act of 1908. Although some historians have argued that this Act was primarily a consolidating measure, it also embodied a radically new conception of the relationship between children, adults and the state, and it reflected concerns about national efficiency and social discipline, as well as a growing sense of humanitarian social concern.[46] Although much of the Act was designed to reinforce existing legislation in relation to the protection of infant life, the prevention of cruelty to children, and the law relating to industrial and reformatory schools, it also contained a large number of new clauses, covering such matters as the overlaying of infants (section 13), the failure to protect children from the hazards of open fires (section 15), allowing children between the ages of four and 16 to reside in brothels (section 16), the inspection of homes for destitute children (section 25), the prohibition of juvenile smoking (sections 39–43), the placing of 'wandering children' in industrial schools (section 58), and the reform of the juvenile criminal justice system (sections 94–133).

Whilst most historians would probably agree that the early Liberal welfare reforms represented a major change in the development of British social policy, they were probably rather less significant, in terms of their long-term implications, than the introduction of old-age pensions. One of the key arguments in favour of the initial measures was that even if they did mark a significant extension in the scope of state intervention, this could be justified on the grounds that children were the future of the nation and should not be punished, directly or indirectly, for the failings of their parents.[47] The same could not be said of old-age pensioners. These were individuals who had failed to make sufficient provision for their own old age, and whose working lives lay behind, rather than ahead, of them.[48]

As Macnicol has shown, the earliest proposals for the establishment of old-age pensions were designed not so much to make provision for those who were already old, as to facilitate the development of more sober and thrifty habits on the part of those who were still comparatively young, but it soon became apparent that a large proportion of those over the age of 65 were living in conditions of considerable deprivation.[49] However, there was still considerable disagreement as to the best way of remedying this. Many Conservatives were in favour of a contributory scheme, but the government believed that the majority of workers would be unable to afford the contributions needed to sustain a healthy retirement, and that such a scheme would provide little help either to women or to those who had already left the workforce. It therefore recommended the introduction of a means-tested, tax-funded scheme which could be targeted on those in greatest need, subject to a small number of limitations based on tests of previous character and behaviour. It also recommended that pensions should be denied to those who had recently been in receipt of poor relief. This clause was designed not so much to draw a line beneath the point at which pensions would become payable, as to prevent Boards of Guardians from transferring their responsibilities for *existing* pensioners to the national Treasury.[50]

Although the Old Age Pensions Act has sometimes been criticised for providing 'a pension for the very poor, the very respectable and the very old', it also marked the beginning of a fundamental and decisive shift in the funding of welfare provision away from local authorities and bodies such as the Boards of Guardians, towards the central state.[51] When Lloyd George introduced the debate on the second reading of the Old Age Pensions Bill in the House of Commons on 15 June 1908, he acknowledged that many MPs would have preferred to see pensions paid from the age of 65, rather than the government's recommended age of 70, but he insisted that this could only be done with the aid of local authorities and that 'the charges for the local rates' were already 'much too high'. Secondly, even though the Act was designed to exclude existing paupers, the government was adamant that its long-term effect would be to lift the bulk of old-age pensioners off their dependence on the Poor Law, and even though the pension continued to be subject to a means test, the majority of the other tests imposed by the Act proved to be much more symbolic than practical in their effects. Thirdly, even though the Act itself only applied (in the first instance) to less than 500,000 individuals, the government also insisted that it was only the starting point for a much more far-reaching plan of reform. The Secretary of State for War, Richard Haldane, said that it was 'the first step in a journey ... which it is our bounden duty to enter upon', and the Prime Minister, Herbert Asquith, claimed that it was a 'new departure' on an 'unmeasured road of future social progress', and not a final destination.[52]

Following the passage of the Old Age Pensions Bill, the government was able to turn its attention more closely to the operation of the labour market. During the latter part of the nineteenth century, a number of local philanthropists had established bureaux where employers could exchange information about the availability of jobs with prospective employees, and in 1905, the Unemployed Workmen Act gave local Boards of Guardians the power to established similar exchanges as part of their general relief policy. However, in 1909 the Liberals established a national network of labour exchanges, and placed them under the overall control of the Board of Trade rather than the Local Government Board. As a result, the operation of the exchanges came to be seen very much as a matter of employment policy rather than relief policy.[53]

The same years also marked the passage of the Development and Road Improvement Funds Act. Part 1 of the Act was designed to give financial assistance to agriculture and rural industries, and to encourage the development of fisheries and the construction and improvement of harbours and inland navigations. Part 2 established a Road Board, with responsibility for the construction and maintenance of new roads and the provision of financial assistance to local highway authorities. However, the real significance of these measures lay in the way in which they sought to use public funds to generate employment. As José Harris has commented, the most remarkable feature of the Act was that when the establishment of the Development Fund was put to a vote, 'only six MPs opposed the abandonment of a theoretical principle that had governed orthodox financial policy for nearly a hundred years.'[54]

The Trade Boards Act of 1909 also broke new ground in relation to labour-market regulation by establishing the principle of a minimum wage. For much of the second half of the nineteenth century, public opinion had been considerably agitated by the practice of 'sweating', under which small groups of employees, working either at home or in small factories and workshops, received very low wages, usually in the form of piece-rates.[55] The Act empowered the Board of Trade to establish individual trade boards for different trades, and to fix minimum rates of pay for either time-work or piece-work. When the Act was first introduced, its application was limited to four specific trades – tailoring, box-making, lace-making and chain-making – but it was subsequently extended to cover sugar-confectionery, shirt-making, hollow-ware, and the embroidery of cotton and linen in Ireland.[56]

The government also introduced a major piece of legislation affecting housing and town planning. The first part of the Act extended Part III of the Housing of the Working Classes Act, 1890 to all urban and rural districts, and therefore continued the trend in favour of giving local authorities more power to build additional houses for more affluent workers which had begun in the final years of the nineteenth century. However, the most significant sections of the Act were those relating to the provision of town planning. During the late-nineteenth and early-twentieth centuries, a growing number of writers and thinkers had begun to focus attention on the problems of urban development and the need for a more planned approach to urban growth, and in 1904 the Interdepartmental Committee on Physical Deterioration had offered strong encouragement to the establishment of garden cities.[57] The new Act sought to build on this by giving local authorities the power to develop town-planning schemes, subject to the approval of the Local Government Board. It also sought to strengthen the administration of local authority public health services by preventing newly-appointed Medical Officers of Health from engaging in private practice, and granting them greater security of tenure.[58]

Although all of these measures represented an important part of the Liberals' overall social policy strategy, it is arguable that none was quite as important as the Finance Bill which the Chancellor, David Lloyd George, presented to Parliament in the same year. During the nineteenth century, the government had derived the bulk of its revenue from a relatively low rate of income tax, and from a range of taxes and duties on such items as tea, tobacco, and beers and spirits, but the increase in the burden placed on the public finances by the growth of public expenditure forced politicians of all parties to consider new ways in which the volume of tax revenues could be increased. In 1901, the senior Treasury official, Edward Hamilton, suggested that the most important need was to preserve the balance between direct and indirect taxation, but others believed that this balance could no longer be maintained. In 1903, Joseph Chamberlain, who had abandoned the Liberals for the Conservatives over the question of Home Rule for Ireland in 1886, persuaded his new party that the best way to increase government revenue and protect the interests of British producers was by abandoning the historic policy of free trade in favour of tariff reform, but the Conservatives suffered a heavy defeat in the 1906 general election, and this enabled the Liberals to focus their attention on the question of raising direct taxes.[59]

Although the Liberal party had traditionally been seen as the party of low taxation and low public expenditure, its attitude to these questions underwent a profound change during the 1890s and early-1900s. In 1894, the Liberal Chancellor, William Harcourt, had made an unsuccessful attempt to change the basis of taxation by introducing a graduated form of income tax and increasing death duties, and these proposals formed the basis of the Bill which Lloyd George introduced 15 years later. The new Bill proposed to change the balance between direct taxation and indirect taxation by increasing the standard rate of income tax, and it proposed to make the burden of income tax itself more progressive by introducing a new 'super-tax' on all incomes in excess of £500. Lloyd George also proposed to introduce a new tax on any income derived from increases in land values. These changes were explicitly designed to lay the foundations of a more redistributive tax system, and as such they had major long-term implications for the financing of the British state in the twentieth century.[60]

The new proposals also had major constitutional ramifications. When the government presented its Bill to Parliament in April 1909, the House of Lords rejected it, thereby provoking a General Election in January 1910. As a result of this election, the Liberals lost their overall majority, and became dependent on the support of the Labour Party and the Irish Nationalists. After considerable internal debate, the Liberals decided to reintroduce the Finance Bill, and the measure was finally given the Royal Assent on 29 April. In December 1910, the Liberals called a second General Election, in which the relationship between the Houses of Parliament became the major issue. In the election, the Liberal and Conservative parties each obtained 272 seats, and the Liberals retained power with the support, once again, of Labour (42 seats) and the Irish Nationalists (84 seats). In 1911, the government introduced a new Bill, the Parliament Bill, which was designed to impose strict limits on the extent to which the House of Lords could veto legislation supported by the Commons, and threatened to create a large number of new peers if the Lords refused to endorse it. Faced with this threat, the Lords acceded to the government's demands, and the Bill became law on 18 August.[61]

The long-drawn-out passage of the 'People's Budget' enabled the government to continue with its plans for the introduction of national insurance. During the nineteenth century a growing number of workers had sought to insure themselves against the risks of unemployment and ill-health by subscribing to friendly societies and trade-union benefit schemes, and the government believed that a similar scheme might provide the basis of an alternative approach to the relief of poverty. In 1907, a young civil servant, William Beveridge, had told the Royal Commission on the Poor Laws that a system of unemployment insurance could be 'one of the great general methods of dealing with the problem', and in August 1908, immediately after the passage of the Old Age Pensions Bill, Lloyd George had made a five-day trip to Germany to investigate the possibility of a scheme of health insurance. These two ideas formed the basis of the National Insurance Bill which Lloyd George presented to the House of Commons on 4 May 1911.[62]

The basic features of the National Insurance Act are well known. Part I of the Act introduced a general scheme of insurance against ill-health and its consequences. Unlike the Old Age Pensions Act, which was financed entirely out of general taxation, the health insurance scheme depended on the payment of contributions by employed men (four pence per week), employed women (three pence), employers (three pence) and the state (two pence), and it applied to all manual labourers, and to all those over the age of 16 earning less than £160 per year.[63] The scheme enabled insured workers to obtain free medical treatment from a designated general practitioner, and provided workers and their dependants with access to free sanatorium treatment if they were suffering from tuberculosis, but it did not entitle them to any other forms of hospital treatment. However, insured workers were offered a range of financial benefits to compensate them for the loss of income caused by ill-health. Benefit rates were set at ten shillings a week for insured men, and seven shillings and sixpence a week for insured women, for the first 26 weeks of any work-preventing illness, and members could apply for a disablement benefit of five shillings a week if they were unable to work after 26 weeks. Insured women, and the wives of insured men, also qualified for a maternity allowance of 30 shillings when they gave birth to a baby.[64]

The second part of the Act dealt with the question of unemployment insurance. Like the health insurance scheme, this was also financed by contributions from employers, employees and the state, albeit at lower levels (employers and employees each contributed 2.5 pence, and the state contributed the equivalent of 1.67 pence).[65] It was also a more limited scheme, at least in the first instance. It only applied to approximately 2.25 million workers in a small number of selected trades, and it provided lower rates of benefit – five shillings a week (after the first week), for 15 weeks in any one 52-week period.[66] However, despite its limitations, the scheme did provide a clear indication of one of the ways in which the problem of involuntary unemployment might be dealt with outside the Poor Law, and it provided the basic foundation for the development of a much more widespread system of unemployment insurance after the end of the First World War.

Although national insurance has long been regarded as one of the cornerstones of Liberal welfare reform, it has not passed without criticism. Johnson contrasted the 'individualistic' nature of national insurance with the 'solidaristic' approach represented by the Poor Law, but the Poor Law was only able to maintain its 'solidaristic' nature by imposing a highly deterrent framework on its administration and stigmatising those who accepted relief. Consequently, although many workers may have resented the compulsory nature of their insurance contributions, they also appear to have welcomed the automatic entitlement to benefit which the Poor Law clearly lacked.[67]

In May 1911, when the National Insurance Bill received its second reading in the House of Commons, the Labour leader, Ramsay MacDonald, applauded the fact that 'for the first time … a government has come before the country and has said that the repair of these breaches in the way of life [that is, sickness and unemployment] is a responsibility imposed upon the government,' but it is important not to exaggerate its redistributive effects.[68] In 1913, a Treasury official pointed out that, despite the introduction of a sliding scale of contributions for workers on very low incomes, the flat-rate nature of the employees' contributions still imposed a disproportionate burden on the poorest households (see Table 11.1). It is also worth noting that neither the employer's contribution nor the state's contribution was necessarily as redistributive as it seemed. Even though the majority of working-class people were not liable to income tax, they

Table 11.1 The relationship between contributions and income in working-class families, 1912

Total family income per week	Percentage of income paid in taxes on food, tobacco and alcohol	Percentage of income paid in contributions under Part 1 of the National Insurance Act	Percentage of income paid under Part 2 of the National Insurance Act	Percentage of income paid in indirect taxation and Insurance contributions by families covered by Parts 1 and 2 of the National Insurance Act
	(1)	(2)	(3)	(1) + (2) + (3)
18 shillings	7.10	2.00	1.15	10.25
21 shillings	6.10	1.72	0.99	8.81
25 shillings	5.12	1.40	0.83	7.35[a]
30 shillings	4.27	1.20	0.69	6.16
35 shillings	3.65	1.03	0.59	5.27

Note: [a] Harris gives this figure as 7.39, but the figures in the other three columns sum to 7.35.

Source: J. Harris, *Unemployment and politics: a study in English social policy 1886–1914*, Oxford: Clarendon Press, 1972, p. 380.

still made a substantial contribution to government funds as a result of indirect taxation, and even though many labour representatives may have welcomed the introduction of the employer's contribution, there was still an understandable and widespread fear that many employers would seek to limit their own liability either by subtracting the cost of their contribution from the workers' wages, or by passing it on in the form of higher prices to the consumer.[69]

Whilst many historians have criticised both the motives and the content of many of the Liberal welfare reforms, they have also accepted them as a necessary part of the development of the welfare state. However, it is rather more difficult to see the government's proposals for dealing with the problem of 'mental deficiency' in quite the same light.[70] The campaign to address the problem of mental deficiency grew out of an increasing concern over the 'borderland' between lunacy and normality, and reflected a growing sense of panic over the impact of 'mental deficiency' on the future of the British 'race'.[71] In 1912, the Home Secretary, Reginald McKenna, introduced a Bill which promised to establish a separate Commission for the Care of the Mentally Defective, and aimed to give the Home Secretary a potentially unlimited power to authorise the detention of any individual who was deemed to be 'mentally defective'.[72] This Bill was withdrawn at the end of 1912, and a new Bill was introduced in the following year. However, even though McKenna insisted that the new Bill had been stripped of any reference to 'what might be regarded as the eugenic idea', and that it was now solely concerned with 'the protection of individual sufferers', it still imposed sweeping restrictions on the liberty of those identified as 'mentally defective', often for social rather than medical reasons.[73] The Act (3 & 4 Geo. V C. 28) allowed individuals to be detained in an institution if, in addition to being defective, they had either been neglected or cruelly treated, found guilty of a criminal offence, convicted of habitual drunkenness, or sent to a special school by the local education authority. It also provided for the compulsory detention of mentally defective women if they were found to be carrying, or giving birth to, an illegitimate child whilst dependent on poor relief. These conditions suggested that even though the Bill's authors claimed to be acting in the interests of 'defective' individuals, they were also prepared to sacrifice the rights of these individuals when this was thought to be in the interests of the wider community.[74]

11.3 Conclusions

Briggs drew an important distinction between what he called a 'social service state' and a 'welfare state'. The former was a state 'in which communal resources are employed to abate poverty and … assist those in distress', whereas the latter 'is concerned not merely with the abatement of class differences or the needs of scheduled groups but with equality of treatment and the aspirations of citizens as voters with equal shares of electoral power'. Judged by these standards, the Liberal 'welfare state' was much closer to the model of a social service state than to the kind of welfare state which developed in Britain after 1945. It provided very limited levels of financial assistance to selected groups of the population and, in a number of important respects, it failed to meet the needs of the poorest sections at all.[75]

However, despite these limitations, the Liberal reforms were also a major watershed in the history of social policy development. Even though some observers have criticised the use of the insurance principle as a form of regressive taxation, the introduction of free school meals, the establishment of old-age pensions and the creation of the unemployment and health insurance schemes marked the beginning of a new approach to the development of welfare policy which offered a genuine alternative to the deterrent and stigmatising policies of the Poor Law. As a result, the reforms undoubtedly played a major role in laying the foundations for the development of the welfare state in the twentieth century.

12

The First World War and social policy

When the First World War broke out, many people believed that it would all be over fairly quickly, but the war lasted far longer, and its effects were much more far-reaching, than the great majority of observers seem to have anticipated. By the end of 1918, more than 1.6 million extra women had been drafted into the civilian workforce, more than six million men had either volunteered or been conscripted for military service, approximately 163,000 men had been taken prisoner, 1.7 million had been wounded, and 723,000 had either died or been killed.[1] When one considers that Britain was only one of the countries directly affected by the war, it is not surprising that many historians should regard the period between 1914 and 1918 as the true beginning of what Eric Hobsbawm has called 'the short twentieth century'.[2]

Although most historians would probably agree that the First World War had a major impact on British society, there is rather more uncertainty about its impact on British social policy. Marwick argued that even though society had changed, the state had not, and both Abrams and Lowe have claimed that the promises of social reform which were made during the war were less important than the 'failure of social reform' and the 'erosion of state intervention' in the years which followed it. However, other historians have taken a rather more positive line. Crowther thought that 'the effects of war on policy should ... be sought less in the period 1914–22, which is too short to demonstrate them, than in the interwar period as a whole', and Runciman argued that the conventional historical assumptions about the significance of the periods 1914–18 and 1939–45 should be reversed: 'The policies initiated by Lloyd George's government in the fields of health, housing, education and unemployment relief were progressively, if sometimes haltingly, expanded by its successors. Those initiated by Attlee's government were progressively eroded by its successors – or, where not eroded deliberately, tacitly permitted to diminish in their effect.'[3]

This chapter examines these debates in the light of the changes which did take place, in both the short and the long term. The opening section provides a brief introduction to the impact of war on working-class living standards and the relationship between government and society, and section 12.2 takes a more detailed look at the problems caused by the outbreak of war and the measures taken to combat them. Section 12.3 examines the plans which were developed during the war for postwar reconstruction, and section 12.4 looks at the factors which affected the implementation of these plans, and the reasons for the so-called 'frustration' of social reform after 1918. The chapter will conclude with an overall assessment of the extent to which the war really did exercise a major impact on the long-term development of British social policy.

12.1   The impact of war

In his autobiographical account of working-class life in Salford in the first quarter of the twentieth century, Roberts argued that even though the first months of the war were marked by rising unemployment and food shortages, it also led, over a longer period, to a dramatic increase in the demand for labour and this enabled men who had previously been regarded as 'unemployable' to take up part-time and casual work, whilst former 'casuals' found regular jobs. These changes removed one of the most important single causes of prewar poverty and enabled 'some of the poorest in the land … to prosper as never before'. However, although the war almost certainly resulted in a reduction in the incidence of extreme poverty, it did not lead to improvements across the board. As Roberts himself explained, the war may have meant that the number of prosecutions for child-neglect began to fall, that many children were better fed, and that their mothers were better-dressed, but it also caused increasing resentment as many skilled workers, on fixed time-rates, found themselves being overtaken by the 'machine-minding tiros' who were prospering under their training, and this became a source of growing unrest as the war continued.[4]

It is possible to gain a clearer picture of the overall trends in real wage rates from the data in Table 12.1. Although these statistics have sometimes been used to support the view that the war led to an improvement in the living standards of the working class as a whole, the extent of this should not be exaggerated. Both Winter's figures for real wages and Feinstein's estimates of average real earnings suggest that the majority of workers suffered a reduction in the real value of both wages and earnings during the first two years of the war, and that wages only began to rise more rapidly than prices in 1917 and 1918.[5] It is also important to remember that those sections of the population who depended on fixed incomes, including many elderly people, suffered considerable hardship as a result of increases in the cost of living. The standard rate of old-age pension remained fixed at five shillings a week until August 1916, and was raised to 7/6 a week for all pensioners in August 1917, but there were no further increases in the value of the state pension before the end of the war.[6]

During the war, many School Medical Officers continued to compile statistics showing the impact of war on the health and nutrition of schoolchildren, and these provide further evidence of the different ways in which the changes associated with the war affected the working-class population. The incidence of malnutrition among children attending public elementary schools in Doncaster fell from 31 per cent in 1913 to just five per cent in 1915, and there was also a steady and continuous decline in the incidence of malnutrition among schoolchildren in London, but the proportion of children whose nutrition was described as 'excellent' also declined. In 1923, the Board of Education's Senior Medical Inspector, Alfred Eichholz, invited more than 20 Medical Officers to say whether 'the regular wages received during the war resulted in a marked

Table 12.1 Fluctuations in the cost of living and in average weekly money wages or earnings among some groups of workers during the 1914–18 war

Group of workers	Weekly earnings and wage rates					Index numbers (1914 = 100)				
	1914	1915	1916	1917	1918	1914	1915	1916	1917	1918
Bricklayers (8 towns) summer rates	42/10	43/9	46/2	52/2	67/5	100.00	102.14	107.78	121.79	157.39
Bricklayers' labourers (7 towns) summer rates	29/1	30/2	33/7	39/0	53/7	100.00	103.72	115.47	134.10	184.24
Engineering fitters and turners	38/11	42/10	43/2	52/2	67/4	100.00	110.06	110.92	134.05	173.02
Engineering labourers	22/10	–	–	35/2	48/8	100.00	–	–	154.01	213.14
Shipbuilding platers	40/4	–	–	68/2	77/10	100.00	–	–	169.01	192.98
Dock labourers	33/8	37/6	43/9	50/3	64/11	100.00	111.39	129.95	149.26	192.82
Coalminers (N. Yorks and Durham) (earnings)	32/0	35/9	42/7	50/5	60/5	100.00	111.72	133.07	157.55	188.80
Compositors (8 towns)	36/9	36/10	38/8	44/0	54/4	100.00	100.23	105.22	119.73	147.85
Railwaymen	26/6	29/2	31/10	41/1	51/8	100.00	110.06	120.13	155.03	194.97
Agricultural workers	16/10	18/10	23/6	31/9	38/0	100.00	111.88	139.60	188.61	225.74
Cotton workers (earnings)	20/0	20/7	22/0	25/7	28/7	100.00	102.92	110.00	127.92	142.92
Trade board rates (men)	25/4	25/4	25/4	31/6	34/1	100.00	100.00	100.00	124.34	134.54
Trade board rates (women)	13/4	13/4	13/4	17/6	20/11	100.00	100.00	100.00	131.25	156.88
Iron & steel (South Wales)	–	–	–	–	–	100.00	102.00	133.00	148.00	159.00
All workers (wages) (Winter)	–	–	–	–	–	100.00	111.00	121.00	155.00	195.00
All workers (earnings) (Feinstein)	–	–	–	–	–	100.00	115.84	131.68	168.32	208.91
Cost of living (Winter)	–	–	–	–	–	100.00	123.00	146.00	176.00	203.00
Cost of living (Feinstein)	–	–	–	–	–	100.00	119.80	141.56	171.32	197.07
Real wages (Winter)	–	–	–	–	–	100.00	90.24	82.88	88.07	96.06
Real earnings (Feinstein)	–	–	–	–	–	100.00	96.69	93.02	98.25	106.01

Note: The figures in columns 7–11 have been recalculated using the data for earnings and wages in columns 2–6.

Sources: J. Winter, *The Great War and the British people*, Basingstoke: Macmillan (now Palgrave Macmillan), 1986, pp. 233–4; C. H. Feinstein, 'Changes in nominal wages, the cost of living and real wages in the United Kingdom over two centuries, 1780–1990', in P. Scholliers and V. Zamagni (eds), *Labour's reward: real wages and economic change in 19th- and 20th-century Europe*, Aldershot: Edward Elgar, 1995, pp. 3–36, 258–66, at p. 265.

improvement in the physique of schoolchildren' and whether their general health was now 'better or worse' than it had been before 1914. Fifteen Medical Officers said that conditions had improved during the war, but six thought that no clear pattern had emerged and three thought that conditions had deteriorated. The School Medical Officer for North Yorkshire said that there had been a definite increase in the incidence of both slight and grave degrees of malnutrition, and that this had been particularly marked in urban areas.[7]

These impressions are broadly consistent with the results obtained from an analysis of the main changes in the average heights of children attending public elementary schools in a range of local authority areas. These figures suggest that the average heights of children increased in Aberdeenshire, Accrington, Banffshire, Batley, Bootle, Bradford, Cardiff, Croydon, Dumbartonshire, Edinburgh, Govan, Leeds, Mountain Ash, Rhondda and Warrington, and declined in Aberdeen, Abertillery, Carlisle, Cambridge, Darwen, Lincoln, Nottingham, Sheffield and Torquay, but neither the increases nor the decreases were particularly great. The war may have been responsible for improvements in the health and nutritional status of many of the poorest children, but it failed to have a dramatic effect on the majority of the school population and the average standard of child health was largely, though not entirely, unchanged.[8]

The war may have led to more significant improvements in other health indicators. Winter argued that men who were too old for active service 'had a greater chance of surviving than they would have done, had there been no war', whilst women experienced 'unanticipated gains in survival chances', but both of these claims are open to dispute. According to Harris, the death rates of males over the age of 45 were generally *higher* than they would have been if prewar rates of decline had been maintained, and even though there was a reduction in the overall rate of female mortality (after discounting the effects of the 1918 influenza epidemic), this decline was largely associated with a small number of specific conditions (cirrhosis of the liver, diabetes and deaths associated with childbirth), and the death rates among women between the ages of ten and 29 rose consistently between 1914 and 1918. Harris has also questioned the extent of the improvement in infant mortality rates. Winter argued that the war years 'witnessed the most striking gains in infant survival chances [in most parts of the country]... in the first thirty years of the [twentieth] century', but infant mortality had actually been declining since the start of the century, and although there was a sharp increase in the infant mortality rate following an outbreak of summer diarrhoea in 1911, there is little evidence to suggest that there was any acceleration in the rate of mortality decline once the war had started.[9]

Although most observers would agree that the average standard of health improved during the war, there was a significant increase in the death rate from pulmonary tuberculosis, and the death rates of older people also increased. Winter argued that the increase in tuberculosis death rates was caused by an increase in the number of women who were exposed to unhealthy working conditions and a general increase in the incidence of domestic overcrowding, but Bryder has claimed that it may also have been related to changes in the standard of nutrition (although, as we have seen, other evidence suggests that nutritional standards in most parts of the country continued to rise), and Winter himself has recently argued that tuberculosis may also have risen as a result of wartime migration. The reasons for the increase in old-age mortality also remain open to debate. Pensioners were amongst those who were worst affected by wartime price rises, and this may well have contributed to the increase in old-age mortality during the first two years of the war, but it is unlikely to provide the only explanation. Both Rollet and Hardy have highlighted the impact of war on the psychological health of elderly people, and Thane has drawn attention to the disruption of the normal support networks provided by friends, family and neighbours.[10]

The First World War also had a profound effect on the nature and role of the British government. Andrzejewski thought that Britain was an exception to his general argument about the importance of the 'military participation ratio', but many other authors have argued that the nature and extent of civilian participation in the conduct of the First World War had a significant effect on the subsequent development of British social policy.[11] Peacock and Wiseman have also argued that the war highlighted existing deficiencies in social arrangements and caused a permanent shift in the population's willingness to tolerate higher levels of personal taxation. They therefore concluded that the war played a profound role in the long-term growth of British public expenditure.[12]

The outbreak of war also forced the Treasury to relinquish some of the controls which it had previously exerted over the functions of government (if only temporarily), and it led to significant changes in both personal and corporate taxation. In November 1914, Lloyd George announced the standard rate of income tax for those earning between £160 and £500 a year would be raised from 9d in the pound (3.75 per cent) to 1/6 in the pound (7.5 per cent), and in September 1915, Reginald McKenna reduced the tax threshold from £160 to £130, so that by the end of the war approximately 5.75 million people had been brought within the tax net, of whom 2.2 million were entirely relieved of payment. The government also introduced new indirect taxes on 'luxuries' (including entertainments, motor cars, cycles, watches, clocks, musical instruments and film), and an Excess Profits Duty was introduced to take account of war profiteering. However, the majority of the funds needed to pay for the war were derived not from taxation but from borrowing. Tax revenues only accounted for approximately 28 per cent of total government expenditure between 1914/15 and 1918/19, and at the end of the war the country's total national debt had risen from approximately £560 million to more than £7.8 billion.[13]

The war also led to a major increase in the powers and functions of government, and extended its control over many areas of national life. On 8 August 1914, Parliament passed the Defence of the Realm Act (4 & 5 Geo. V C. 29), which gave the government sweeping powers to take action 'to prevent persons communicating with the enemy or obtaining information for … any purpose calculated to jeopardise the success of the operations of His Majesty's forces', and 'to secure the safety of any means of communication, or of railways, docks or harbours', and on 28 August it passed a further Act (4 & 5 Geo. V C. 63) 'to prevent the spread of reports likely to cause disaffection or alarm'. However, although these Acts represented a major infringement of civil liberties, the government's main priority was to organise the recruitment of men and women to the armed forces, ensure the supply of sufficient labour for essential industries, maintain war production, and facilitate the efficient distribution of goods and services around the country.[14] The war also saw changes in the organisation of government, with the creation of several new Ministries, including the Ministries of Munitions, Labour, Food, National Service and Shipping, from 1915 onwards, and even though many of these Ministries may not have been terribly effective, they undoubtedly helped to fuel expectations of the role which government might play when the war was over.[15] As 'D. P.' observed in a letter to *The Times* in 1916, 'it is not one of the least compensations for this war that it has necessitated experiments upon an otherwise impossible scale in the handling and rationing of the people's food and drink, and upon the conversion of private into quasi-public businesses. There has been haste and no doubt there has been much waste and a considerable variety of incidental inaccuracies and abuses … but on the whole this series of improvised "nationalisations" is full of suggestion and encouragement for the more deliberate and permanent readjustments that must be made after the war.'[16]

The outbreak of war had a profound effect on the position of labour. Although there was a sharp reduction in the number of days 'lost' to strike action during the first few months of the war, the appearance of industrial harmony was short-lived, and the government found that it was having to take an increasingly active role in the management of industrial disputes as the war progressed. In February 1915, 10,000 engineers went on strike in Clydeside, and in May the government decided to ban strikes and restrictive practices in the munitions industry. In July, Lloyd George was forced to intervene personally in order to settle a dispute involving more than 200,000 coalminers in South Wales, and the government's Chief Industrial Commissioner, Sir George Askwith, complained that 'the so-called settlement did more to cause unrest during the succeeding years than almost any other factor, and to lessen hopes of establishing a sane method for the settlement of disputes.'[17] The government also faced growing pressure from working-class tenants. In 1915, an estimated 20,000 tenants went on rent strike in Glasgow, and Ministers became increasingly concerned that the unrest might not only interfere with war production in the Govan shipyards, but also spread to other areas, and in December 1915 the government introduced the Increase of Rent and Mortgage Interest (War Restrictions) Act, which prevented landlords from raising the rents charged for 'working-class' housing above prewar levels.[18]

The introduction of rent controls was indicative of a wider change in the relationship between the government and the labour movement during the war. As we have already seen, the labour movement had already begun to acquire growing political power before 1914, but the outbreak of war meant (in Asquith's words) that 'for the first time in the history of this country since the Black Death, the supply of labour has not been equal to the demand', and the number of trade unionists increased by more than 50 per cent, from 4.15 million to 6.53 million, between 1914 and 1918. In 1915, Asquith invited Arthur Henderson to become President of the Board of Education and two more

Labour MPs were appointed to junior offices, and when Lloyd George replaced Asquith at the end of 1916, he appointed two trade-union leaders, John Hodge and George Barnes, to run the Ministry of Labour and the Ministry of Pensions respectively. However, although these appointments represented a major step forward for the leaders of the labour movement, they also threatened to drive a wedge between the labour and trade-union leadership and ordinary workers, and the number of strikes rose dramatically during the last two years of the war.[19]

Although the government was primarily concerned to win the war, it was also increasingly conscious of the need to address issues of postwar reconstruction, not only as a means of maintaining civilian morale, but also as a mechanism for enhancing national efficiency. In 1914, the Chief Medical Officer of the Board of Education, Sir George Newman, emphasised the fact that 'apart from the grave disadvantage that much of the value of the education of children will be lost unless they are physically fit … it is a matter of grave national concern to secure that physical unfitness and inefficiency in all [their] forms … [are] reduced to the smallest possible dimensions', and this theme became increasingly important as the war progressed.[20] In 1916, Viscount Milner told an audience of public schoolboys that the country faced a stark choice between 'a huge new effort of reconstruction' and 'chaos and ultimate national decay', and in 1917 Lloyd George told labour leaders that the war presented 'an opportunity for reconstruction of industrial and economic conditions of this country such as has never been presented in the life of, probably, the world'.[21] However, although there was widespread support for the principle of reconstruction, there were also many people who resented the extension of state intervention during the war and wished for nothing more than a 'return to normalcy' when hostilities ceased. As Johnson observed, the proponents of postwar reconstruction 'were a part of public opinion, not the whole'.[22]

12.2   Social policy during the war

One of the most obvious starting points for an examination of wartime social policy is the Education (Provision of Meals) Bill of 1914. This Bill was originally introduced by the Labour MP for Bradford, Fred Jowett, on 13 February, but its passage was given added urgency by the outbreak of war on 1 August. The Act permitted local education authorities to feed elementary schoolchildren 'both on days when the school meets and on other days', and it rescinded the limitations which the Education (Provision of Meals) Act 1906 had placed on the amounts of money which local authorities could spend on school feeding. However, by the spring of 1915, many observers had become convinced that the number of children who were in need of school meals had actually declined, and by the end of the war, the number of children receiving meals had fallen below prewar levels.[23]

The outbreak of war meant that the government also needed to ensure a sufficient supply of volunteers for the Army and Navy (the Royal Air Force did not come into being as a separate service until 1 April 1917).[24] The Army had always tended to discourage soldiers from marrying, and only a small proportion of 'Army wives' qualified for separation allowances when their husbands were serving overseas, but it soon became apparent that the government would have to adopt a rather more generous policy if it hoped to encourage large numbers of men, including married men, to join the colours. As a result, on 10 August 1914, the Prime Minister, Herbert Asquith, informed the House of Commons that the government was now prepared to pay separation allowances to all wives, including those who were 'off the strength'. Although there were many problems associated with the payment of these allowances, they made a substantial contribution to the alleviation of poverty among the families of those who were called up. By the end of the war, more than 1.5 million wives and several million children were receiving subsistence-rate benefits, and a further 1.5 million dependent relatives were receiving smaller payments. The total cost of Army separation allowances was approximately £120 million per year, a figure roughly equal to between three-fifths and two-thirds of the total cost of central government expenditure before 1914.[25]

The government was also forced to take special action to safeguard the interests of old-age pensioners. The value of the original state pension was quickly eroded by wartime inflation, and by 1915 a growing proportion of pensioners were facing financial difficulty. However, the government's initial response suggests that it was more concerned with the need to encourage older workers to rejoin the workforce than it was with the problem of pensioner poverty more generally. In April 1915, it agreed to raise the threshold for the receipt of the full old-age pension from £21 a year (just over eight shillings a week) to 20 shillings a week for workers in rural areas and 30 shillings a week for workers in urban areas, but there was no change to the threshold for individuals who derived their income from other sources, and the value of the pension itself also remained unchanged.[26] The government only agreed to raise the pension itself, from five shillings a week to seven shillings and sixpence, for pensioners experiencing hardship as a result of food price rises in August 1916, and it only extended this concession to all pensioners in August 1917, but it failed to take any further action to reform the pension system before the end of the war. Even though the current value of the state pension rose by 50 per cent during the course of the war, prices rose by between 120 and 125 per cent, so that by the end of the war the real value of the pension had fallen by as much as one-third.[27]

Although the war undoubtedly caused many problems for people dependent on old-age pensions and other fixed incomes, these problems were perhaps less serious than the threat of food shortages for the population as a whole. When war broke out, most observers were confident that the country would be able to obtain sufficient food without much difficulty, but by October 1916 food prices had risen dramatically, and the government had become increasingly concerned about the dual threat posed by the prospect of poor harvests in Britain and the USA, combined with a submarine blockade by the German navy. In November, the government introduced a system of price controls, and on 1 January 1917 it announced the creation of a Food Production Department, with the explicit aim of expanding domestic food production. In February 1917 the government announced that it would automatically attack any foreign vessels, including neutral vessels, in British territorial waters, and in January 1918 it introduced a system of food-rationing, with the explicit intention of securing a more equitable distribution of food across all social classes. These policies undoubtedly led to a change in the composition of the average diet, with a switch from animal products to cereals, potatoes and other crops, but they did not lead to any significant deterioration in overall food values. So far as can be ascertained, the average Briton consumed a similar amount of protein, less fat, and more carbohydrates during the war, and average levels of calorie consumption were well maintained.[28]

The outbreak of war also put particular pressure on the provision of existing welfare services. During the early stages of the war, many local authorities, particularly in rural areas, called for the relaxation of the school-attendance laws in order to allow both boys and girls to take advantage of increased employment opportunities, but the most important results of the war were probably the need to release school buildings for military use and, even more significantly, to provide cover for teachers who had volunteered for military service.[29] At the same time, even though the war undoubtedly disrupted the progress of education, many observers felt that it had also contributed to an increased sense of social solidarity and common purpose in the schools, and, perhaps more surprisingly, it also led to an increase both in the number of pupils entering secondary schools and in the number of secondary school pupils staying on past the minimum school leaving age. In its Annual Report for 1914–15, the Board of Education attributed these developments partly to an enhanced appreciation of the benefits of education, and partly to the decline in parental poverty occasioned by the war.[30]

The war also had a major impact on the provision of medical care. Following the outbreak of war, many doctors and nurses volunteered for military service, and by January 1917, more than half the medical profession was serving in uniform. This meant that those doctors who remained in civilian practice were having to treat more patients and work significantly longer hours. The war also placed a considerable amount of stress on the country's hospital services. By the end of the war, approximately one-quarter of all hospital beds had been transferred to military use, with the result that many civilian patients were transferred to workhouses. At the same time, the shortage of private nurses meant that many middle-class patients now chose to go into hospital rather than receiving treatment in their own homes. This had the somewhat paradoxical result of ensuring that even though there was a decline in the number of medical personnel and the number of hospital beds, the number of patients treated in hospital actually rose.[31]

The outbreak of war also led to significant changes in the organisation and staffing of the public health services. During the war, more than one-fifth of all school medical staff joined the armed forces, and many local education authorities abandoned their scheduled programmes of school medical inspection, even though the number of children treated by the school medical service actually rose.[32] This was undoubtedly a more favourable outcome than that experienced by the tuberculosis service. Under the National Insurance Act of 1911, all insured workers and their dependants became eligible for free medical treatment in a tuberculosis sanatorium, but the service had barely got off the ground before war broke out. As a result, little progress was made in the provision of treatment for tuberculosis before the end of the war, and this may also have contributed to the increase in the number of tuberculosis deaths.[33]

The government also introduced a number of measures which had major implications for the development of social policy in the future. In March 1915, Lloyd George had persuaded trade-union leaders to agree to the suspension of normal workplace practices in order to enable untrained workers, and in particular women, to take the places of men who had left for the front, and in July 1915 existing limitations on working hours were also lifted. However, even though the government was anxious to maximise the number of hours worked, it also recognised that excessive working hours could undermine efficiency. This led to a series of wartime innovations in industrial welfare, including the creation of the Health of Munitions Workers' Committee in September 1915, the payment of compensation allowances to munitions workers whose health was adversely affected by toxic substances, a per capita grant to cover hospitalisation costs, the provision of a special diet allowance, the introduction of medical personnel and first-aid units into all metalworking industries, the establishment of factory canteens, special measures to protect the health of women workers, and, in the longer term, the establishment of the Industrial Fatigue Research Board (subsequently the Industrial Health Research Board) under the auspices of the Medical Research Council.[34]

The war also led to major changes in housing policy. During the early stages of the war, there was a large increase in the number of workers and their families moving to areas such as Glasgow where there was a heavy demand for labour in the shipbuilding and iron and steel industries, with the result that house rents rose dramatically. Many tenants refused to pay the new rents, and their example was followed by tenants in a number of other cities, including London and Coventry. Faced with a serious threat of social disorder, the government introduced the Increase of Rent and Mortgage Interest (War Restrictions) Act, which placed statutory controls on rent and mortgage-interest rises. The introduction of rent controls represented an unprecedented degree of interference in the operation of the private housing market, and many historians have argued that it played a major, if not decisive, role in the decline of the private rented sector in Britain and the subsequent expansion of council housing.[35]

There was also a significant expansion in the provision of infant and maternal welfare services. Between 1907 and 1914, a number of voluntary organisations had established their own infant welfare clinics and 'schools for mothers', and in July 1914 both the Local Government Board and the Board of Education acquired the power to make grants to these organisations to enable them to carry out their work more effectively. However, the war itself focused further attention on the importance (and the fragility) of infant life, and this led to a substantial increase in the number of infant welfare clinics and the scale of both central and local government intervention. The war also influenced some important legislative developments in the field of infant and maternal welfare. The Notification of Births Act of 1907, which had given local authorities the power to introduce arrangements for the compulsory notification of all new births in their areas, was extended to cover the whole country in 1916, and the Maternity and Child Welfare Act, which gave local authorities the power to appoint health visitors and establish maternity and child welfare clinics, was passed in August 1918, three months before the cessation of hostilities.[36]

12.3   War and reconstruction

The war fuelled a powerful desire for the creation of a better world, and this was reflected in the government's decision to establish a small Reconstruction Committee in March 1916. However, the pressure for change increased substantially after Lloyd George replaced Asquith at the end of 1916. In February 1917 the new Prime Minister established his own Reconstruction Committee, with a more 'advanced' membership and wider terms of reference, and in July 1917 this Committee was replaced by a new Ministry of Reconstruction, under the control of Dr Christopher Addison. During the next two years, the new Ministry produced over 50 reports on such matters as the acquisition and valuation of land for public purposes, the standardisation of railway equipment, the building industry, currency and foreign exchanges, financial facilities, financial risks, industrial and commercial policy, electricity supply, chemical trades, engineering, relations between employers and employees, the demobilisation of civilian war workers, adult education, agricultural policy, housing, the machinery of government, local government and the reform of health service administration, and it played a major role in helping to shape plans for the development of social policy in the postwar world.[37]

One of the first problems facing policy-makers was the problem of low pay. Booth, Rowntree, and Bowley and Burnett-Hurst had all shown that this was one of the most important causes of prewar poverty, and in 1909 the Liberal government had taken the first steps towards addressing this problem with the establishment of trade boards.[38] During the war, minimum wage rates were established for munitions workers in 1916 and agricultural workers in 1917, and a new Trade Boards Act was passed in 1918, so that by 1921 a total of 63 separate trade boards had been established, covering approximately three million workers in a wide range of mainly non-unionised industries. The government also established more than 50 Joint Industrial Councils (or Whitley Councils), which were designed not only to help set wages, but also to bring employers and employees together to discuss a number of other items of common interest. However, despite these developments, there was also considerable opposition both to the establishment of minimum wages and to the principle of government intervention in the field of industrial relations, and the pace of reform slackened dramatically at the start of the 1920s. The creation of new trade boards was attacked by the Association of British Chambers of Commerce and in the press, and frustrated by the actions of the Treasury, and only six new boards were created after the end of 1921.[39]

A second major cause of prewar poverty was unemployment. Even though both Rowntree and Bowley had claimed that unemployment was not a statistically significant cause of poverty, the Liberals had recognised that it could play a major part in preventing workers from building up the savings necessary to deal with other contingencies.[40] During the war, the government had attempted to extend the original unemployment insurance scheme to all workers engaged in war-related activities, but there was widespread opposition to the scheme on the part of both workers and employers, and even though legislation was passed in 1916, only around 200,000 additional workers had been brought into the scheme by the start of 1918.[41] In the meantime, the government was devoting considerable attention to the Maclean Committee's proposals for the establishment of Prevention of Unemployment and Training Committees, but these proposals were fiercely opposed by the Local Government Board and by individual Boards of Guardians, and even though they were supported by the Cabinet, no further action was taken to implement them.[42]

The problem of poverty was also closely associated with the question of old age. Although the government changed some of the rules on old-age pensions in 1915, and increased the amounts paid to pensioners in 1916 and 1917, it failed to take any further action to reform the pension system before the end of the war. However, in November 1919 the Departmental Committee on Old Age Pensions (the Adkins Committee) suggested that the rules governing the payment of pensions to immigrants should be relaxed, and that restrictions on payments to ex-prisoners and to those who had failed to work 'according to [their] ability, opportunity and need' should be removed altogether. The Committee also recommended that the income limit used to determine entitlement to pensions should be doubled and that the pension itself should be raised from its wartime level of seven shillings and sixpence to ten shillings a week, and in the longer term it called on the government to conduct a much fuller enquiry into the introduction of contributory pensions.[43] All of these proposals, with the exception of those relating to means tests, were accepted by the government and rushed through Parliament, with minimal debate, on 19 December 1919. The minimum income level was raised by approximately two-thirds, well short of the figure which the Adkins Committee had recommended.[44]

One of the most intractable of all the problems facing the advocates of post-war reconstruction was the problem of the Poor Law. The Liberals had already begun the process of breaking up the Poor Law with the welfare reforms of 1906–14, but there were still more than 600,000 individuals in receipt of some form of poor relief on the eve of the war (see Figure 4.2 in Chapter 4). In July 1917, the Ministry of Reconstruction invited the Deputy Speaker of the House of Commons, Sir Donald Maclean, to chair a committee on Poor Law reform. The Committee advocated the creation of 'Prevention of Unemployment and Training Committees' to deal with the problem of unemployment, and suggested that 'recalcitrant persons' could be placed in detention colonies if they refused retraining. It also recommended the creation of 'Home Assistance Committees' to exercise a 'general supervision' over those in receipt of relief and their families. However, the recommendations which aroused the greatest controversy at the time were those dealing with the administrative structure of the Poor Law. The Committee recommended that the existing system of Poor Law Unions and Boards of Guardians should be abolished, and that their powers and duties should be transferred to local authorities, which would establish separate committees to deal with different categories of need. These proposals were bitterly resisted by the Poor Law Division of the Local Government Board and by individual Boards of Guardians, and no further action was taken to reform the Poor Law before 1929.[45]

Although the war failed to bring about major changes in the organisation of the Poor Law, it did lead to important new developments in the provision of health services. As we have already seen, the war years themselves witnessed a significant expansion in the number and scope of infant welfare services, and this paved the way for the passage of the Maternity and Child Welfare Act in 1918. The Act gave local authorities the power to establish Maternity and Child Welfare Committees (with at least two female members), and led to the introduction of government subsidies for a range of services, including the cost of hospital services for children under the age of five, maternity hospitals, home-helps for mothers after childbirth, food for expectant and nursing mothers, homes for the children of widowed, unmarried and deserted mothers, and 'experimental units for the health of expectant and nursing mothers and infants [*sic*] under five years of age'.[46] Somewhat more surprisingly, perhaps, the war also made an important contribution to the development of venereal-disease services. During the war, approximately 400,000 service personnel contracted a venereal disease, and the Army was forced to open its own VD hospitals. In 1917 the government introduced the Venereal Diseases Act, which offered free and confidential treatment to every citizen, and provided generous grants to cooperating local authorities.[47]

However, the government's failure to reform the administrative structure of the Poor Law did have major implications for its efforts to reform the structure of health-service administration. The medical profession had been campaigning for the establishment of a fully fledged Ministry of Health, with sole and exclusive responsibility for the supervision of all health services, for many years, and these demands gathered pace during the early years of the twentieth century as new health services – such as the school medical service and national health insurance – came into being. However, the call for a separate Health Department was resisted by the Local Government Board, which wished to retain responsibility for both health and the Poor Law, and by other government departments, such as the Board of Education, which were anxious to retain their own health-related responsibilities. As a result, even though a new Ministry was created, it failed to satisfy the reformers' demands. Under the terms of the new legislation, the Ministry of Health continued to take responsibility for both the health service and the Poor Law, but it failed to take full control of such services as the school medical service and the factory inspectorate. On the other hand, the Ministry did assume control of the national health insurance scheme, and its establishment provided some indication of the additional importance which was now attached to health issues.[48]

The war also led to a major debate over the future of education. In 1917, the government introduced a comprehensive Education Bill, and although this had to be withdrawn at the end of 1917, it was resubmitted in revised form in 1918 and formed the basis of the Education Act which was passed in August of that year (8 & 9 Geo. V C. 39). The new Act gave local education authorities the power to establish nursery schools for children under the age of five (Section 19), formally abolished fees in elementary schools (Section 26), abolished the exemption clauses which permitted some children to leave school early before the age of 14, and others to attend part-time (Section 8), established a new framework for funding educational expenditure and removed the limits which previous Acts had placed on local authority spending (Sections 7, 44), instructed local education authorities to establish a system of compulsory continuation classes for children between the ages of 14 and 16 (Sections 3, 10), and extended the powers and duties of local education authorities to make arrangements for the medical inspection and treatment of children in elementary and secondary schools (Sections 2, 18). However, although the Act was widely welcomed at the time, it achieved much less than its supporters hoped. In his Annual Report for 1918, the Chief Medical Officer of the Board of Education, Sir George Newman, revealed that the Board had declined to enforce the provision requiring local education authorities to provide medical inspection in secondary schools, and in January 1921 the Board announced that it would be unable to consider any further proposals for the creation of either nursery schools or continuation classes.[49]

Perhaps the most controversial of all areas of postwar reconstruction was the area of housing. During the war, there had been a gradual acceptance of the view that some form of public housing provision was necessary in order to resolve the country's housing difficulties, and a series of reports were produced, which not only estimated the need for new housing, but also provided detailed guidelines for the form which any new houses might take.[50] In 1919, the government passed the Housing and Town Planning etc. Act, which instructed local authorities to survey the housing needs of their areas and offered government subsidies to authorities which built new houses 'for the working classes', and the Housing (Additional Powers) Act, which offered similar subsidies to private builders, but the immediate results were once again disappointing. The government began to scale down its commitment to the council house programme in February 1921, and it was abandoned altogether later in the same year. Between March 1919 and March 1923, local authorities built 171,003 houses with the aid of government subsidies, and private builders constructed 45,857. A further 53,800 'houses for the working classes' were built by private enterprise alone.[51]

12.4   The frustration of social reform

Although the debate over the 'failure' of social reform has tended to concentrate primarily on the years after 1918, it is important to recognise that some of the problems faced by the advocates of reconstruction were already apparent before this. In 1915, the Board of Education and the Local Government Board became embroiled in a dispute over the expansion of maternity and child welfare services, and the Local Government Board was strongly opposed to plans to reform the administration of the Poor Law and transfer control of the Poor

Law and the public health services to different Ministries. The British Medical Association opposed plans to expand the provision of school medical treatment, because it believed that these would jeopardise the interests of family doctors, and in 1920 it launched a successful campaign against the Dawson Report, which proposed sweeping changes in the organisation of medical services and the establishment of health centres.[52] The campaign for social reform was also weakened by the position of the Ministry of Reconstruction itself. Despite the rhetoric which accompanied its formation, it was a weak and inexperienced department, and entirely dependent on the goodwill of other Ministries to implement its proposals.[53]

However, whilst many historians might be prepared to accept many of the criticisms of the Ministry of Reconstruction, they have also argued that it is necessary to look at the performance of other Ministries, and to examine the failure of social reform over a longer period. The war witnessed the creation of a number of new Ministries which might have set the tone for a more interventionist approach to social issues, but they were prevented from achieving these objectives by a combination of bureaucratic timidity, political ambivalence, and, perhaps most importantly, Treasury hostility.[54] These arguments were reinforced by Davidson and Lowe's analysis of the history of the civil service between 1870 and 1945, and Burk's analysis of the impact of the war on the relationship between the Treasury and other civil-service departments. According to Burk, the war served initially to weaken the position of the Treasury, but it was subsequently able to regain control, and it emerged from the war in a stronger position than before.[55]

One of the most controversial issues concerned the problem of taxation. During the war, the government had introduced significant increases in both direct and indirect taxation, and a combination of higher wages and a lowering of the income-tax threshold meant that a growing proportion of working-class voters became liable for income tax for the first time, but there was no consensus over the extent to which these changes should be carried forward into the postwar period. In 1917, the Treasury had ruled out any further increases in indirect taxation, but middle-class campaigners were fiercely opposed to any increases in income tax, and employers' organisations were anxious to avoid any further taxes on profits. These problems were compounded by the need to pay for the war itself. As we have already seen, the government was forced to borrow heavily during the course of the war, and this led to a sharp rise in the cost of interest payments. In 1913/14, interest on the internal debt amounted to £16.7 million or 9.6 per cent of budget receipts, but by 1920/1, interest had risen to £308.7 million or 22.4 per cent of receipts and, as Middleton has shown, debt repayment was responsible for a major part of the increase in public expenditure during the interwar period.[56]

The government's failure to achieve a political consensus over the question of taxation had a profound effect on Lloyd George's efforts to push ahead with his social reform programme.[57] As we have already seen, several writers have questioned the extent to which either Lloyd George or his colleagues were fully committed to the promises made during the war, but this view has been strongly criticised by Kenneth Morgan. Morgan argued that Lloyd George was committed to reform, but that he faced increasing difficulty in achieving his objectives following the election of a large number of Conservative MPs at the 1918 General Election. Even though he was able to push through a significant number of important welfare measures in 1919 and 1920, including the establishment of the Ministry of Health, the reform of old-age pensions, the passage of two major Housing Acts, and the extension of unemployment insurance, his room for manoeuvre was increasingly constrained by the growing demand for 'economy' and by changes within the Conservative party. The most decisive development was the resignation of Andrew Bonar Law and his replacement as leader of the Conservative party by Austen Chamberlain in February 1922. As Christopher Addison noted perceptively in his diary: 'Unless [Chamberlain] becomes less reactionary than at present, it must mean a separation before too long.'[58]

Morgan's account also helps to refocus attention on the importance of economic factors. During the war, the government had introduced a range of controls, including rationing, but these were quickly abandoned, and prices rose sharply during 1919 and 1920. There was overwhelming support for the view that prices had to be brought under control, and most economists agreed that this could only be achieved by raising interest rates and reducing public expenditure. The initial attack on social reform was therefore, at least in part, a response to inflationary pressure. However, as Peden has pointed out, the main cuts in education and housing occurred after the inflationary boom had broken. This was partly because of the political changes which have already been mentioned, but it also reflected the fact that the government was determined to maintain the downward pressure on public expenditure in order to raise the value of sterling so as to facilitate a return to the gold standard – the international exchange rate mechanism of the day – at prewar rates.[59]

The problem of public expenditure was compounded by a sharp rise in the level of unemployment. As we have already seen, the government failed to make any detailed plans for dealing with the problem of unemployment before the war ended, and it was therefore panicked into introducing an 'out-of-work donation' when the soldiers returned home. In the longer term, however, it decided to revive its earlier plans for the expansion of unemployment insurance. However, whereas the original scheme had been carefully designed in order to provide limited amounts of assistance for short periods, by the end of 1921 the government was committed to paying much more generous benefits, including separate allowances to the dependants of unemployed workers, for much longer periods, and although some of the cost of these benefits was borne by the workers' own insurance contributions, a large proportion came from government subsidies. This can only have put further pressure on other social-service budgets.[60]

Finally, one should also consider some of the practical problems involved in the implementation of the reform plans themselves and, especially, the housing programme. When Parliament passed the Housing and Town Planning etc. Act, it instructed local authorities to survey the needs of their areas and to draft plans for the provision of new housing, but many local authorities were slow to carry out these tasks, and many of the plans which were submitted were 'swept aside as mere token gestures'. Second, neither central nor local government demonstrated a proper understanding of the problems of the building industry, and consequently building firms were reluctant to become involved in state ventures. Third, there was an alarming increase in the cost of building materials and transportation, and this contributed to a dramatic rise in the cost of new housing. All of these problems were compounded by a shortage of skilled labourers, and even though the government was aware of this problem, the building unions were reluctant to allow any increase in the supply of new workers for fear of returning unemployment.[61]

While most historians would accept that the housing programme was affected by problems of this nature, some have attempted to explain its demise in more political terms. According to Swenarton, both the wartime government and its successor only endorsed the housing programme as an 'insurance against revolution', and this meant that they were perfectly happy to abandon it once the threat of revolution was seen to have passed.[62] However, this argument fails to take account of the fact that the Cabinet took the initial decision to cut back the housing programme whilst the threat of labour unrest was still very apparent.[63] In the final analysis, the demise of the housing programme owed more to the Conservative party's antipathy to the idea of council housing as a way of meeting general housing needs and to continuing worries over the cost of the housing programme than it did to any specific concerns, or lack of them, about the possibility of revolution.[64]

12.5   Conclusions

As the previous section has shown, there has been a long and vigorous debate over the reasons for the 'failure' of social reform after 1918, but it is also important to recognise the important role which the war did play in the development of British social policy. One of its most important, though sometimes least recognised, consequences was that it created a new set of obligations for the British state in terms of the payment of different types of pension to those who had been injured by the war, and to the dependants of those who had been killed during it. This represented an important contribution to interwar social expenditure. In 1930, the Ministry of Pensions estimated that the average cost of the pensions paid to those who had been injured or bereaved as a result of the war was equal to just under £70,000,000 per year or, in other words, just under £900,000,000 since the Ministry was first established.[65]

The war also made a major contribution to the development of the country's health services (including, most notably, the maternity and child welfare service) and, especially, the development of housing provision. The introduction of rent controls in 1915 represented an unprecedented form of interference in the private housing market, and introduced a system of price regulation which remained in place, despite many changes, for the rest of the century. The Housing and Town Planning etc. Act, which represented the first serious attempt to develop the principle of council housing, was even more significant. Even though the immediate fruits of the Act were disappointing, the principle of public responsibility for housing provision had been firmly established, and the proportion of households inhabiting local-authority accommodation rose steadily for the next 60 years.[66]

The war also had a profound effect on many people's attitudes towards the role of the state in meeting welfare needs. Historians have often commented on the enthusiasm with which so many young men volunteered for military service, but many of those who returned from the trenches did so with a new sense of entitlement to welfare services. This was reflected in the change in public attitudes towards the Poor Law and the support of people in need. In July 1919, the Ministry of Health's Inspector in South Wales, H. R. Williams, complained that 'for some years, especially in industrial centres, there has been an entirely new spirit on the Boards of Guardians ... and the Labour members, who ... predominate on the above Boards ... advocate a policy of more generous if less legal relief. They boldly proclaim for removing the old landmarks and instituting a system of relief more elastic than that based on the legal standard of destitution ... and [they] are too ready to ignore ... the deterrent value of the [work]house as a test.'[67] This new-found reluctance to accept the old ways was to become increasingly apparent during the postwar years.

13

Voluntary action and the 'new philanthropy', 1914–39

In 1913, the Secretary of the Charity Organisation Society, Charles Stewart Loch, wrote that the social legislation enacted since the beginning of the century 'indicates very clearly that the spirit of enterprise in social matters [has] passed from the people to the state', and that the introduction of national health insurance, in particular, was the 'death warrant' of the friendly societies.[1] However, as many historians have pointed out, this was not necessarily the case, and the history of the interwar period demonstrates that the growth of state welfare provision did not necessarily imply the eradication of the voluntary sector. The aim of this chapter is to explain some of the reasons for this, beginning with the history of charitable and philanthropic activity during the First World War.

13.1 Charity and philanthropy during the First World War

As Prochaska suggested, the war may have altered the motivation of many charity workers by undermining their religious faith, but it had also had more immediate, and practical, effects. One of its most important consequences was that it forced many existing charities to compete for donations with organisations which had sprung up as a direct result of the war, thus limiting their ability to maintain existing services. Many voluntary workers joined the armed forces, and this placed additional pressure on the voluntary sector because, as the Charity Organisation Society pointed out in 1915, 'while new workers were introduced, they tended not to be as experienced as those who had gone'. Even this judgement may have been a little sanguine, because a substantial number of female volunteers were forced to seek paid employment as the war continued, thus cutting into one of the major sources of recruitment to the voluntary sector before 1914.[2]

However, even though the war posed a challenge to philanthropists, it also provided a powerful stimulus to voluntary and philanthropic effort.[3] During the early stages of the war, many families experienced particular hardship as a result of the government's failure to provide sufficient support to the families of those who had given up their civilian jobs in order to join the armed forces, and voluntary organisations played a leading role in the organisation of relief work. In December 1914, the Soldiers' and Sailors' Families Association mobilised between three and four thousand volunteers in London alone to provide relief to the families of service personnel, and by 1915, the organisation had a total of 900 separate branches, with approximately 50,000 volunteers, in the country as a whole.[4] The early years of the war also witnessed a large number of appeals for the aid of wartime refugees, with particular attention being paid to the needs of Belgian refugees, for whom at least 93 separate charities had come into being by 1916. It is difficult to deny that the 'philanthropic community' did indeed 'give generously'. By the end of 1915, the Prince of Wales' Fund for the relief of distress at home had raised more than £5,000,000, and between £20,000,000 and £30,000,000 had been raised in the country as a whole.[5]

As the war progressed, it also created numerous other opportunities for voluntary service. Between 1914 and 1918, the number of women who joined Voluntary Aid Detachments in order to provide nursing care in both military and civilian hospitals increased from 80,000 to 120,000.[6] The Salvation Army initiated an emigration scheme for war widows who wished to give their children the opportunity for a new start overseas, and the Children's Aid Society organised children's holidays and found families to care for motherless children whose fathers were on military service. There were also a large number of special appeals for the assistance of those directly involved in the fighting. Vast amounts of effort were devoted to raising funds for the relief of prisoners of war, convalescent soldiers, the Red Cross, soldiers on leave, soldiers at the front and soldiers in base camps.[7] One of the most important areas for concern was the need to raise funds for the care and treatment of those who had been injured or wounded as a result of hostilities. In 1916 and 1917, three new societies were established for the relief of discharged and demobilised soldiers and sailors, and a special hospital was established at Erskine, near Glasgow, for the care and treatment of limbless ex-service personnel. Finlayson has argued that one of the best indications of the increased priority attached to medical charities was the increase in the value of new endowments settled on permanent trusts for investment. In 1919, the Charity Commissioners reported that the value of the sums settled on medical charities rose from £153,851 in 1914 to £426,368 in 1918, an increase of more than 177 per cent.[8]

The war affected the organisation of charities and their relationships with each other and the state. In 1916, a Parliamentary Select Committee investigated allegations that unscrupulous individuals were taking advantage of the general climate of opinion to launch fraudulent appeals, and new legislation was passed to compel all charity organisers to obtain proper registration before appeals could be launched.[9] During the early years of the twentieth century, members of the local Guilds of Help had helped to organise councils of social service to coordinate charitable activity in individual areas, and this trend accelerated during the war as the value of coordination became increasingly apparent.[10] The war also encouraged greater cooperation between voluntary agencies and the state. According to Pedersen, the Soldiers' and Sailors' Families Association 'acted as the administrative agent of the War Office' for the payment of separation allowances to the families of service personnel, and other government departments offered payments to voluntary organisations in order to enable them to continue to provide welfare services. Both the Board of Education and the Local Government Board made grants to voluntary organisations for the provision of maternity and child welfare work, and the Local Government Board worked closely with other organisations to provide relief to servicemen's families. The Board of Agriculture distributed funds to the National Federation of Women's Institutes, although these were eventually given up.[11]

Cooperation was particularly necessary in the area of health care. During the war, many of the doctors who worked in voluntary hospitals transferred to military units and were given service ranks, and many of the hospitals were converted into auxiliary hospital units and used to provide care and treatment to service personnel. However, while this undoubtedly contributed to the success of the war effort, it also led to a deterioration in the quality of care provided for the civilian population. According to Abel-Smith, the government's failure to develop a properly coordinated system of medical care meant that the civilian population 'lost half their supply of doctors and roughly a third of their already inadequate stock of hospital beds'.[12]

In recent years, there has been considerable debate over the impact of the war on the financial position of voluntary hospitals. Abel-Smith argued that many hospitals profited from the war, because they received substantial payments from the government for the treatment of service personnel, and raised large amounts of money from charitable donations because 'wounded soldiers made excellent appeal copy and the "purse-strings" of the charitable public were "unloosened as they perhaps have never been before".'[13] However, as Finlayson has argued, the value of the payments made by the government for the treatment of service personnel was not sufficient to offset the cost, and those hospitals whose work was not directly related to the war effort, such as the Chelsea Hospital for Women, faced substantial financial deficits.[14] Cherry showed that even though some voluntary hospitals may have done relatively well, the sector as a whole did not, partly as a result of poor investment decisions, and partly as a result of wartime inflation.[15] These problems formed the background to the appointment of the Cave Committee on Hospital Finance in 1921 (see Chapter 15).

13.2 Voluntary action between the wars

Prochaska has pointed out that, even though the context of philanthropic work may have changed, many ordinary people continued to devote large amounts of time and money to traditional philanthropic causes. They acted on the basis of traditional motives, and they carried out their work without reference either to national coordinating bodies or the state.[16] However, there were a number of important new developments which affected not only the organisation of charity, but also its focus. These changes will form the main focus for this section.

Although the First World War ended officially on 11 November 1918, its consequences lingered much longer. As we have already seen, the war witnessed the creation of a large number of specialist agencies for the relief of wounded and disabled ex-service personnel and the dependants of those who were killed, and many of these agencies came together after the war to form the British

Legion. One of the main priorities for the Legion during the interwar period was the need to find employment for servicemen and women, especially if they had become disabled. The voluntary sector also devoted enormous efforts to combating the effects of social and economic dislocation in central and eastern Europe. The Save the Children Fund, which was founded in 1919, worked closely with the League of Nations to promote infant and child welfare on an international scale, whilst several other organisations, such as the Women's International League and the League of Nations Union, sought to promote international harmony.[17]

The interwar years also experienced some important changes in the character and scope of voluntary organisations. As Finlayson has noted, many voluntary organisations came under increasing pressure during the second half of the nineteenth century to improve the quality of care and provide a wider range of services, and these pressures continued after 1918. Lipman has described the way in which the Jewish Board of Guardians experienced increasing financial problems as it strove to introduce new convalescent facilities and improve its provisions for the young and the old. The period also witnessed the growth of what might be called a 'salaried bureaucracy' in the voluntary sector. Political and Economic Planning noted that there were already nearly ten thousand people directly employed by voluntary agencies at the time of the 1931 census, and that their number was still growing.[18]

Finlayson suggested that these developments were symptomatic of a broader cultural shift in the ethos of the voluntary sector, and this was also reflected in an increasing emphasis on the coordination of voluntary societies, not only in their relations with each other, but also with the state.[19] A number of organisations had already acknowledged the advantages of cooperation during the First World War, and many of these came together to launch the National Council of Social Service in 1919. This organisation was specifically designed to promote the systematic organisation of voluntary work both locally and nationally, to encourage the development of mutually supportive links between the statutory and voluntary sectors, and to inform voluntary workers of legislative and statutory developments.[20] During the 1930s, the Council became increasingly involved in the coordination of voluntary effort to help unemployed people, particularly in the most depressed areas. It acted as a clearing-house for the distribution of more than £1.5 million in government grants to a variety of organisations concerned with the provision of educational and recreational facilities for unemployed people and their families.[21]

One of the most important challenges was the problem of finance. In 1934, *Whitaker's Almanack* commented that 'the flow of charity still shows so sign of serious abatement' despite 'the shrinkage in values due to the general depression, and very high taxation', but many charities still complained that their funds were no longer adequate to enable them to meet their growing needs.[22] The interwar period also witnessed a substantial increase in the number of charities which received payments, either from the general public or from the statutory authorities, for the services they rendered. Macadam estimated that in Liverpool 'no less than 21 per cent of the total expenditure on maternity and infant welfare is given as subventions to voluntary agencies'. Braithwaite estimated that charities in Liverpool received 13 per cent of their income in form of public grants in 1929, and that charities in Manchester received 17 per cent of their income in the form of public grants in 1938. The amount of money received by London charities in the form of payments, either by individuals or public agencies, rose from 32 per cent of total income in 1919 to 35 per cent in 1927, and 39 per cent in 1938.[23]

These changes had a profound effect on the general philosophy of the voluntary sector. As we have already seen, many nineteenth-century charity workers had been actively hostile to the growth of state welfare, but after 1918 'the old Charity Organisation Society case against outdoor relief simply went by default; and all the voluntary charities had to accommodate themselves...to the changed situation.' In 1945, the socialist writer G. D. H. Cole suggested that whilst 'this meant in part that their function came to be that of supplementing state aid, instead of providing an alternative to it', it also meant 'that the dispensing of money came to be secondary in importance, and the function of acting as advisers and consultants to the poor...leapt into...first place'. One of the consequences of this was that the voluntary sector became less concerned with the provision of cash benefits, and more concerned with what Cole described as 'the spirit of community'. It was no accident, he concluded, 'that the new social service fixed upon the equipment of community centres and the funding of community councils as its most vital activities. It set out to become the point of focus for a new spirit of community accordant with the changing conditions of living.'[24]

Macadam summarised the emergence of this new philosophy in her book *The new philanthropy*. She argued that the voluntary sector's traditional desire to keep the state at arm's length had been replaced by a new sense of partnership between statutory and voluntary workers, and that the role of the voluntary sector within this partnership could be characterised under three broad headings:

1. Social schemes which are experimental and of insufficiently recognised value to have yet acquired a claim on the state.

2. Social activities which call for more flexible, closely-individualised, and highly-specialised work than can be expected from public authorities...

3. Associations of various kinds which act as watchdogs protecting particular classes or interests, and bringing pressure to bear on the state to amend existing and introduce fresh provision for social needs.[25]

During the 1920s and 1930s, organisations such as the National Council of Social Service became increasingly concerned about the growth of working-class leisure, which they associated not only with the impact of mass unemployment, but also with the impact of mechanisation on the amount of time which needed to be devoted to manual labour, and these fears were reflected in their attitude to the emergence of new working-class housing estates in such areas as Watling, in North London, and Becontree and Dagenham, about ten miles east of Charing Cross. In 1928, the NCSS established a New Estates Community Committee, with the specific intention of bringing more opportunities for organised leisure to these areas and helping them to develop the sense of 'community' which they were believed to be lacking.[26] However, although these initiatives attracted a great deal of favourable attention in literary and political circles, their practical impact was rather more limited. According to Olechnowicz, only 92 'community centres' had actually been built by 1939, and less than two per cent of the tenants on large municipal estates between the wars had a community centre.[27]

The issue which posed the greatest challenge to the voluntary sector between the wars was mass unemployment. During the 1920s, the voluntary sector played an important role in the organisation of relief funds for unemployed people and their families, but by the end of the decade it had become increasingly apparent that private charity was unable to keep pace with the demand for assistance. In 1928, the Lord Mayors of London, Newcastle and Cardiff established a general fund for the relief of women and children in distressed mining areas, and many towns and villages in the more prosperous parts of Britain 'adopted' impoverished mining communities, but there was also a clear change in the direction of voluntary effort. Instead of seeking to provide direct assistance to people in order to meet their material needs, the voluntary sector became increasingly concerned with the support of what it regarded as their social and psychological needs.[28]

These concerns were reflected in a wide range of activities undertaken by voluntary organisations in South Wales during the late-1920s and 1930s. Although a large number of organisations, including both the Salvation Army and the Society of Friends, continued to organise general relief work, they also began to focus an increasing amount of attention on the promotion of activities which were designed to maintain the morale of unemployed workers and contribute to the social fabric of their communities. During the late-1920s and 1930s, the Society of Friends established a network of nine 'educational settlements' in the South Wales valleys, and these acted as 'powerhouses' for the creation of nearly 500 unemployed clubs, women's clubs, boys' and girls' clubs and play centres. Voluntary organisations also played an important part in the establishment of a number of social 'experiments' in the depressed areas. In 1929, an ex-member of the Society of Friends, Peter Scott, organised a social survey in the Monmouthshire village of Brynmawr, and during the 1930s he helped to establish a cooperative employment scheme (Brynmawr and Clydach Vale Industries), and an agricultural-production scheme (the Eastern Valley Subsistence Production Society) which sought to enable older men to purchase agricultural goods at cost price.[29]

During the 1930s, some commentators argued that these provisions were simply palliatives, designed to do little more than lull workers into a false state of complacency and prevent unrest. George Orwell claimed that the unemployed clubs, which were in many ways the flagships of voluntary effort in the depressed areas, had 'a nasty YMCA atmosphere' about them, and the leader of the National Unemployed Workers' Movement, Wal Hannington, complained that they were designed 'to deflect [the unemployed]…from the course of struggle, lure them from the influence of militant organisations… and… guide them into a state of complacency'.[30] However, whilst many of the supporters of these voluntary initiatives may have believed that they offered a powerful antidote to revolutionary threats, many others were powered by a genuine sense of idealism. As the Chairman of the National Council of Social Service's Unemployment Committee, A. D. Lindsay, wrote in 1933: 'the movement among the unemployed ... has arisen to meet a national emergency, and is inspired by the conviction that this emergency calls for something more and quite other than what the Government is doing, or could do. The movement embodies a forward-reaching conviction that it is possible not only to arrest the effects on men's minds of long-continued unemployment, but so to counteract these effects as to release and support the energies of the unemployed for constructive and experimental social work of their own.'[31]

13.3 Self-help and mutual aid

Although these forms of organised philanthropy continued to play an important part in the history of welfare provision during the interwar years, it is also necessary to recognise the continuing significance of other forms of non-state welfare. As Johnson has shown, many of the traditional methods used to help people 'get by' continued to make an important contribution of the maintenance of welfare standards during this period. However, the period also witnessed the development of a number of new forms of more commercially-minded welfare provisions which were to have a significant impact on the development of the welfare state after 1945.[32]

As we have already seen, family and community support were an essential part of working-class life in the nineteenth century, and they continued to play a major role in the twentieth century. Elizabeth Roberts argued that 'the extended family ... remained of the greatest importance as a provider of social services, social contacts and to a lesser degree financial assistance' throughout the period. However, the range of help provided by neighbours was also immense: 'children were minded; the sick and dying were fed and nursed; clothes were passed on; funeral teas prepared for the mourners; the dead laid out; shopping done for the elderly; and companionship and friendship provided for all ages'.[33] This pattern was repeated in many other parts of the country. McInnes has commented that even though tensions sometimes existed between neighbours, 'all the people I interviewed [in Stoke-on-Trent] stressed how good neighbours were to one another', and Katharine Nicholas has stressed how 'one of the factors which helped the people of Teesside to withstand ... the depression was the close-knit community strength ... the whole street would rally round to help someone.'[34]

The importance of community ties was also reflected in the proliferation of small, locally-based charitable appeals in the depressed coal-mining areas of South Wales. In 1921, the Miners' Federation of Great Britain organised soup kitchens throughout the region, and local distress committees were established in Pontypridd, Rhondda, Abertridwr, Ferndale and Caerphilly. In 1922, the *Glamorgan Free Press and Rhondda Leader* established a 'shilling fund' 'to provide a Christmas parcel for the children of the poor and needy in Pontypridd, Caerphilly and Aber district, and the Rhondda valleys', and in 1926 appeals were launched in Porth, Pontypridd, Treherbert, Tonypandy, Ynyshir and Wattstown. Distress committees were established in Dowlais, Tredegar, Pontypridd and Rhondda in 1927 and 1928, and appeals for boots and clothing were launched in Pontypridd, Rhondda, Ynyshir, Penygraig and Treherbert during the 1930s. In Pontypridd, a charity appeal was established in 1935 to mark the twenty-fifth anniversary of the accession of George V, and several areas organised Christmas appeals to provide a special dinner for poor children.[35]

Despite the expansion of state welfare services, many working-class families continued to rely on traditional 'coping strategies', such as the use of pawn-broking, to 'make ends meet'. The novelist, Walter Greenwood, drew on his own experience as a pawnbroker's assistant to provide a particularly unflattering fictional account of the weekly routine at Price and Jones's pawnbrokers in 'Hanky Park': 'Next Friday or Saturday ... they would hand over their wages to Mr Price in return for whatever they had pawned today. And next Monday they would pawn again whatever they had pawned today, paying Mr Price interest on interest until they were so deep in the mire of debts that not only did Mr Price own their and their families' clothes, but also the family income as well.'[36] A former Lancaster factory-worker recalled how 'the pawnshops was thriving [*sic*] ... Queues a mile long on a Monday morning pledging. Queues a mile long on a Friday evening redeeming them out again. A watch. Or a wedding ring. Just to buy food.'[37] However, even though more than 2600 pawnbrokers' licenses were being issued annually at the end of the 1930s, the trade as a whole was clearly declining, partly as a result of the expansion of alternative forms of credit, and partly because of broader changes in society and the economy as a whole.[38]

Although pawnbroking was already beginning to encounter difficulties in some areas before 1914, these difficulties increased after the First World War. This was partly related to the impact of interwar unemployment, which meant that in some areas there was nothing left to pawn, but it also reflected changes in social mores and increases in popular expectations. As Tebbutt has argued, 'although pawning had, in the past, been a final gesture before the ignominies of charitable relief, as the movement for statutory welfare grew, its connection with the most degrading aspects of unemployment became increasingly unac-ceptable to some, these attitudes being reinforced by the hostility with which the Labour Party regarded the trade'. At the same time, one of the traditional foundations of pawnbroking – the ability to sell on unredeemed goods – was also being undermined by changes in fashions, and, particularly, women's fashions. 'Constantly-changing fashions, although no new problem, rapidly intensified with the mass fashion revolution which brought smart, cheap cloth-ing within reach of many more women ... The example of Hollywood and a greater involvement in social life generally encouraged women to become... increasingly receptive to the blandishments of the fashion industry.'[39]

The decline of pawnbroking was also abetted by the expansion of alternative credit sources. The second half of the nineteenth century had seen an increase in the numbers of both licensed and unlicensed moneylenders, who were able to compete with more traditional methods of obtaining credit by offering unse-cured loans, albeit at higher rates of interest, and their numbers are unlikely to have fallen much before 1927.[40] In 1932, one of the authors of the Women's Group on Public Welfare study of *Our towns* observed that 'in almost every poor street there is one house with evidences of startling prosperity ... this is a person who has at some time saved or inherited a small sum of money, started a moneylending business, and lived upon it.'[41] The pawnbrokers' problems were also exacerbated by the increase in the number of tallymen and credit drapers (often known as 'Scotch drapers'), which meant that people no longer needed to pawn items in order to finance new purchases, since they could now pay for these by instalments.[42] There was also a substantial increase in the number of more expensive goods being obtained with the aid of hire purchase. In 1938, it was estimated that 50 per cent of furniture, 60 per cent of gramophones, 70 per cent of radios, 85 per cent of sewing machines, and 90 per cent of bicycles were being purchased in this way.[43]

The changing nature of working-class life was also reflected in the role of friendly societies. Gilbert and Finlayson argued that the First World War helped to strengthen the position of friendly societies, not only because of the fall in the number of claims made during the war, but also because 'the immense loss of life among young men ... meant that contributions had been paid by those who would not make any claims in later life, when heavier claims could be expected.'[44] However, the friendly societies appear to have derived comparatively little benefit from the general increase in working-class savings during the last two years of the war and the immediate postwar boom of 1919–20. According to Johnson, the value of the working-class savings held by friendly societies rose by approximately 24 per cent between 1916 and 1921, but the value of the savings held by other institutions rose by more than 90 per cent. The most dramatic increase occurred in the proportion of working-class savings held in the form of either War Savings Certificates or National Savings Certificates. These accounted for only 0.1 per cent of total working-class savings in 1916, and for 19 per cent of working-class savings in 1921.[45]

Although the war was a major watershed in the history of the friendly society movement, the most important changes in this period were more directly related to the introduction of the National Insurance Act in 1911. Under the terms of this Act, the vast majority of existing friendly societies became approved societies with responsibility for the administration of the statutory national health insurance scheme. This undoubtedly helped to ensure the survival of the friendly societies, but it also meant that 'they became more official and less personal, more of insurance agencies and less of social agencies'.[46] This tendency was also reflected in the changing composition of the friendly society movement. As we can see from Table 13.1, the interwar years saw a significant decline, from 1922 onwards, in the number of members belonging to the more socially-oriented affiliated orders, and an increase in the number associated with the less personal, and more centralised, 'branchless societies'. According to Johnson, even the affiliated orders themselves experienced growing problems in maintaining a traditional convivial role. Beveridge and Wells concluded that 'only a very few people appear to have joined a friendly society with the idea of participating in the social functions which it might provide. A small number of people said they had joined because they believed it was compulsory to do so, but this was almost invariably a "younger member" attitude, as, to a large extent, was the assumption that the main object of the friendly society was to administer national health insurance.'[47]

The statistics presented in Table 13.1 also highlight three other important tendencies during this period. The first is the growing concentration of friendly-society members in a smaller number of larger units. During the period between 1915 and 1945, the number of individual branches and societies (excluding collecting societies) fell from just over 29,000 to just over 21,000, whilst the number of members increased from 7.6 million to 10.1 million. The table also reveals the increase in the number of individuals belonging to 'other societies registered under the Friendly Societies Acts', such as workingmen's clubs, over the same period. However, the most dramatic increase is in the number of policies issued by the friendly collecting societies. These organisations were primarily concerned with the provision of life assurance, and the number of policies issued by them rose by more than 250 per cent during the same period.[48]

In view of the fact that life assurance was the main form of traditional friendly-society benefit to be excluded from the national health insurance scheme, it is tempting to attribute the growth of the collecting societies to this omission, but this might also carry the risk of ignoring the growth of other forms of insurance during the interwar period. The collecting societies were still dwarfed by the industrial assurance companies, whose share of total working-class assets increased from 24.2 per cent to 36.6 per cent between 1921 and 1936. Only a small proportion of the policies offered by the industrial assurance companies in the nineteenth century had been designed to mature while their account-holders were still alive, but the number of these policies expanded dramatically after 1918. Johnson has estimated that the number of endowment policies rose by 9.5 million between 1912 and 1931, whilst the income generated by these policies for the industrial assurance companies rose by 350 per cent between 1920 and 1930 alone. This tendency may have been caused partly by the sharp reduction in infant mortality and the increase in overall longevity, and partly by the increase in general prosperity, but, whatever the reason, 'the growth of endowment insurance in the twentieth century may be seen as an indicator of greater long-term financial planning, particularly planning for greater sufficiency in old age'.[49]

The interwar period also witnessed the expansion of a rather different form of health insurance, namely hospital savings schemes. The earliest workmen's contributory schemes originated in areas such as Glasgow and North Staffordshire during the second half of the nineteenth century, but they increased rapidly, both in number and size, after 1918. Although the schemes did not guarantee that subscribers would receive hospital treatment, they did guarantee that any treatment they received would be provided without charge. In 1935, there were 114 separate schemes belonging to the British Hospitals Contributory Schemes Association, with a combined membership of 5.241 million subscribers, and an annual income of £2.722 million, but there was also a large number of smaller schemes which remained outside the Association.[50] In 1943, the Association had 191 members, with about ten million individual subscribers, and an annual

Table 13.1 Friendly societies in Great Britain, 1915–45

Year	Societies							Members/policies						
	Orders with branches	Branchless societies	Friendly societies	Other societies	Total	Collecting societies	Total	Orders with branches	Branchless societies	Friendly societies	Other societies	Total	Collecting societies[a]	Total
	(1)	(2)	(1)+(2) (3)	(4)	(3)+(4) (5)	(6)	(5)+(6) (7)	(8)	(9)	(8)+(9) (10)	(11)	(10)+(11) (12)	(13)	(12)+(13) (14)
1915	21,552	4,531	26,083	3,093	29,176	55	29,231	2,955,424	3,829,477	6,784,901	815,674	7,600,575	8,252,070	15,852,645
1916	20,834	4,381	25,215	3,154	28,369	56	28,425	2,900,159	3,832,832	6,732,991	821,353	7,554,344	8,747,625	16,301,969
1922	18,872	3,753	22,625	2,530	25,155	53	25,208	3,134,222	4,476,965	7,611,187	984,524	8,595,711	13,669,566	22,265,277
1923[b]	—	3,705	—	2,522	—	51	—	—	4,632,308	—	960,778	—	13,709,986	—
1924[c]	18,254	3,521	21,775	2,519	24,294	183	24,477	3,123,333	3,906,894	7,030,227	983,810	8,014,037	14,919,280	22,933,317
1925[b]	—	3,522	—	2,528	—	182	—	—	4,099,792	—	1,003,715	—	15,478,633	—
1926	18,868	3,452	22,320	2,636	24,956	171	25,127	3,190,344	4,260,557	7,450,901	1,014,237	8,465,138	15,870,668	24,335,806
1927[d]	18,734	3,416	22,150	2,673	24,823	164	24,987	—	4,357,441	—	1,027,296	—	16,304,247	—
1928	18,489	3,353	21,842	2,678	24,520	155	24,675	3,048,087	4,442,377	7,490,464	1,032,003	8,522,467	16,786,971	25,309,438
1929[d]	18,241	3,312	21,553	2,690	24,243	151	24,394	—	4,578,053	—	1,035,447	—	17,416,545	—
1930	18,148	3,258	21,406	2,725	24,131	151	24,282	2,982,718	4,689,375	7,672,093	1,075,958	8,748,051	18,199,499	26,947,550
1931	17,780	3,214	20,994	2,760	23,754	153	23,907	2,963,285	4,777,882	7,741,167	1,067,756	8,808,923	18,889,594	27,698,517
1932	17,600	3,195	20,795	2,734	23,529	155	23,684	2,937,213	4,868,129	7,805,342	988,980	8,794,322	19,612,997	28,407,319
1933	17,434	3,123	20,557	2,708	23,265	155	23,420	2,918,571	4,892,990	7,811,561	990,092	8,801,653	20,575,025	29,376,678
1934	17,248	3,074	20,322	2,692	23,014	155	23,169	2,917,778	4,978,817	7,896,595	1,007,174	8,903,769	21,752,114	30,655,883
1935	17,217	3,028	20,245	2,704	22,949	151	23,100	2,903,365	5,297,695	8,201,060	955,513	9,156,573	22,807,064	31,963,637
1936[e]	17,060	2,988	20,048	2,699	22,747	152	22,899	2,892,626	5,334,826	8,227,452	1,075,267	9,302,719	23,816,000	33,118,719
1937	16,921	2,938	19,859	2,705	22,564	151	22,715	2,884,689	5,455,826	8,340,515	1,122,325	9,462,840	24,746,031	34,208,871
1945[e]	16,017	2,518	18,535	2,704	21,239	138	21,377	2,686,836	6,033,136	8,719,972	1,392,875	10,112,847	30,033,000	40,145,847

Notes: [a] The figures for collecting societies refer to the number of policies rather than the number of members. [b] Separate figures for Orders with Branches are not available for these years. [c] The decrease in the number of friendly societies, and the increase in the number of collecting societies, in 1924, was mainly due to the provisions of the Industrial Assurance Act, 1923, which brought 129 friendly societies, with 866,927 members, under the heading of collecting societies. [d] Separate figures showing the number of members belonging to Orders with Branches are not available for these years. [e] The figure for the number of policies held by members of collecting societies has been given to the nearest thousand.

Sources: 1915, 1916: PP 1918 (119) x, 311, *Report of the Chief Registrar of Friendly Societies for the year 1917*, pp. 92–3; 1922, 1923: PP 1924–5 (89) xxi, 831, *Report of the Chief Registrar of Friendly Societies for the year 1924*, pp. 41–2; 1924 and 1925: PP (73) ix, 299, *Report of the Chief Registrar of Friendly Societies for the year 1926*, pp. 29–30; 1926, 1927: PP 1929–30 (3) xiv, 115, *Report of the Chief Registrar of Friendly Societies for the year 1928*, pp. 27–8; 1928, 1929: PP 1930–1 (132) xiii, 705, *Report of the Chief Registrar of Friendly Societies for the year 1930*, pp. 44–5; 1930, 1931: PP 1932–3 (139) xii, 285, *Report of the Chief Registrar of Friendly Societies for the year 1932*, pp. 36–7; 1932, 1933: PP 1934–5 (120) ix, 221, *Report of the Chief Registrar of Friendly Societies for the year 1934*, pp. 33–4; 1934, 1935: PP 1936–7 Cmd. 5556 xxvi, 869, *22nd Abstract of Labour Statistics of the United Kingdom (1922–36)*, pp. 160–1; 1936: PP 1937–8 (150) xi, 175, *Report of the Chief Registrar of Friendly Societies for the year 1937*, pp. 34–5; PP 1938–9 Cmd. 6016 xii, 79, Ministry of Labour, *Annual Report for the year 1938*, p. 2; 1937: PP 1939–40 (12) iv, 241, *Report of the Chief Registrar of Friendly societies for the year 1938*, p. 2; 1945: W. Beveridge, *Voluntary action: a report on methods of social advance*, London: George Allen and Unwin, 1948, pp. 30–1, 88.

income of £6.528 million. Pickstone has estimated that the annual income of the Hospital Saturday Fund in Manchester increased by more than 400 per cent between 1922 and 1938, and accounted for approximately ten per cent of the city's total voluntary hospital income on the eve of the Second World War, but the figure may have been greater elsewhere. According to Cherry, workplace collections and contributory schemes are likely to have been responsible for between 20 and 30 per cent of voluntary hospital income in the country as a whole between 1935 and 1939.[51]

The interwar years also saw two other important developments in the field of what might be called private welfare with profound implications for the future. The first of these was the increase in the number of mortgages taken out with building societies, and the associated increase in the number of owner-occupiers between 1918 and 1939, and the second was the rapid growth in the number of occupational pension schemes.[52] Whilst it is unlikely that either of these schemes had a direct impact on more than a minority of working-class people before 1939, they had a profound impact on patterns of wealth-holding and the distribution of poverty after 1945.[53] It is important to remember that the generation which participated in the initial expansion in the number of endowment policies, owner-occupying households and private-pension holders was also the first generation to experience a significant reduction in the incidence of old-age poverty in the 1970s and beyond.[54]

13.4 Conclusions

As this chapter has shown, the interwar years witnessed significant changes in the nature and scope of voluntary activity. Although many individuals continued to engage in traditional philanthropic and charitable activities, there were important new developments in the organisation of charity and the relationship between charities and the state, and these developments gave rise to a new conception of the role which the voluntary sector might expect to play in the development of welfare services. One of the leading figures in the new philanthropic movement, Elizabeth Macadam, said that the role of the voluntary sector was to act as 'the eyes and fingers of the public authority'; to pioneer the development of new and experimental schemes of social welfare; and to act as a watchdog, protecting the interests of particular groups or classes.[55] Constance Braithwaite reaffirmed this belief in the following terms:

> The function of charity is to demonstrate the desirability and practicability of particular forms of services until such time as the state is willing to finance these services. When public opinion has been converted to approval of such services, the time has come for the pioneers to transfer the financial burden to the whole body of citizens. The charitable resources released can then be used to support types of service which the state is unwilling to finance, and to engage in further pioneer work for the education of future public opinion.[56]

This chapter has also shown that the fears expressed by individuals such as Charles Stewart Loch, that the expansion of state welfare schemes would undermine the drive to self-help, were largely unfounded, and that in many ways it would be more plausible to argue that the expansion of state welfare encouraged the growth of working-class savings by offering the mass of the population greater security.[57] However, the interwar years did witness a significant reorientation of working-class savings behaviour, with a move away from more collectively-orientated forms of saving in favour of more individualistic schemes. This change was reflected, not only in the developments which took place within the friendly society movement during these years, and, especially, in the growth of individual savings accounts of the kind provided by organisations such as the National Deposit Society, but also in the expansion of new forms of savings, such as endowment policies, and the growth of private or occupational pensions and home-ownership. Whilst some of these tendencies made greater inroads into the working class than others, they all had profound implications for the development of social welfare after 1945.

14

Unemployment and poverty between the wars

The interwar period has often been seen as one of strong contrasts. On the one hand, it saw improvements in real wages, an increase in female employment opportunities, the rise of new industries, improvements in health, housing and education and, for those in work, a general improvement in the standard of living. On the other hand, it also experienced the rise of mass unemployment and the persistence of high levels of poverty, even in some of the most prosperous parts of the country.[1] Bowley and Hogg found that 6.5 per cent of the working-class population of Bolton, Northampton, Reading, Stanley and Warrington was living in poverty, and Llewellyn Smith found that 9.8 per cent of the working-class population of London was living in poverty. Rowntree calculated that 6.8 per cent of the working-class population of York was living in 'primary poverty', whilst 31.1 per cent of the working-class population lacked the resources needed for 'human needs'. Tout estimated that 10.7 per cent of the population of Bristol was living in poverty, and that a further 20.8 per cent was living in 'insufficiency'.[2]

Although many different factors were responsible for poverty, it is important to recognise the extent to which the definition of poverty itself changed over the course of the period. In 1899, when Rowntree conducted his first investigation, he defined 'primary poverty' in terms of the number of people whose incomes were below the level needed to purchase minimum standards of food, shelter, fuel and clothing, and this was also the method which his successors used to measure the incidence of poverty between 1918 and 1936. However, he himself argued that the definition of poverty should be broadened to include expenditure on 'sundries' such as national health insurance, trade union subscriptions, newspapers, incidental travelling, recreation, children's presents, beer, tobacco, and other expenses, and this was reflected in the two versions of the 'human needs' standard which he set out in 1918 and 1937. It was the addition of these extra allowances which was largely responsible for the differences between the incidence of 'primary' poverty and the incidence of 'ordinary' poverty in his 1936 survey.[3]

These differences in the definition of poverty had a significant bearing on the ways in which contemporary investigators understood the causes of poverty. In 1925, Bowley and Hogg found that 24.4 per cent of the poverty which they identified was caused by unemployment, and Llewellyn Smith argued that almost half the poverty which he encountered in London between 1928 and 1932 was attributable to the same cause.[4] However, it is unlikely that unemployment would have enjoyed the same prominence in these calculations if the poverty line itself had been defined more generously. In 1936, when Rowntree carried out his research in York, he found that unemployment was responsible for 44.5 per cent of all the primary poverty in the city, but for only 28.6 per cent of the 'ordinary' poverty, and when Herbert Tout conducted his investigations in Bristol, he concluded that the proportion of the population which was living below the level of 'sufficiency' would not have been greatly reduced, even if the whole of the working-class population had been fully-employed. These findings demonstrated that even though unemployment was often responsible for the severest forms of poverty, there was still a large number of people whose circumstances had been reduced by low wages, sickness, old age or the premature death of a major breadwinner.[5]

14.1 The problem of unemployment

As several commentators have pointed out, the characteristic problem of the nineteenth-century labour market was not so much unemployment as underemployment, and the term 'unemployment' itself only began to gain widespread currency during the 1880s and 1890s.[6] However, the problem of unemployment grew very rapidly following the end of the First World War, and by 1921 approximately 1.84 million insured workers, and a further 372,000 uninsured workers, were out of work. During the whole of the period between 1921 and 1938, the average annual number of unemployed insured workers never fell below one million, and it remained above two million in every year throughout the first half of the 1930s. The average annual rate of unemployment among insured workers remained above ten per cent in every year with the exception of 1927, and it reached a peak of 22.1 per cent in 1932. It is therefore hardly surprising that the problem of unemployment should have continued to cast a long shadow over the memory of this period (see Figure 14.1).

Although all sections of the population may have been affected by unemployment, the chances of becoming unemployed were not distributed equally. As Thomas has shown, men were more likely to be unemployed than women, and people between the ages of 18 and 24, and over the age of 55, were more likely to be unemployed than people under the age of 18, or aged between 25 and 54. The incidence of unemployment also varied according to social class, and workers who were employed in the 'new industries', such as chemicals and electrical engineering, experienced much lower unemployment rates than workers in the old staple industries, such as coalmining, shipbuilding, iron and steel work, and textiles, with the result that unemployment rates were also much higher in those areas where these industries tended to predominate, and people who found themselves out of work in these areas tended to remain unemployed for much longer periods.[7] The Pilgrim Trust found that the average unemployment rate among insured men in south-east England, London, the midlands and the south-west was below ten per cent, whereas 18.6 per cent of insured men were unemployed in north-west England, 21.2 per cent were unemployed in north-east England, and 32.2 per cent were unemployed in Wales, where 37 per cent of all unemployed men had been out of work for more than one year.[8]

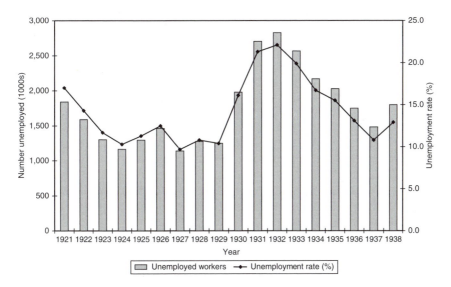

Note: This figure shows the average annual number of unemployed insured workers, and the average annual rate of unemployment among insured workers. It does not include details showing either the incidence or the extent of unemployment among workers who were not covered by the unemployment insurance scheme. For further information regarding this subject, see the sources listed below.

Sources: C. H. Feinstein, *National income, expenditure and output of the United Kingdom, 1855–1965*, Cambridge: Cambridge University Press, 1972, T128; B. Harris, 'Unemployment and the dole in interwar Britain', in P. Johnson (ed.), *Twentieth-century Britain: economic, social and cultural change*, London: Longman, 1994, pp. 203–20, at p. 205.

Figure 14.1   Unemployment in Britain, 1921–38

During the last 80 years, economists and economic historians have devoted enormous effort to the search for an explanation for these figures. Cannan argued that the emergence of mass unemployment was directly related to the expansion of unemployment insurance, and these arguments were revived by two American economists, Daniel Benjamin and Levis Kochin, at the end of the 1970s. They argued that the expansion of the unemployment insurance scheme, and the increase in the real value of unemployment benefits, enabled unemployed workers to prolong their search for new employment and that, consequently, 'the army of the unemployed standing watch in Britain at the publication of [Keynes']... *General Theory* was largely a volunteer army.'[9] However, although this may have affected the incidence of short-term unemployment, it is difficult to see how Benjamin and Kochin's argument can be reconciled with the occupational and geographical distribution of unemployment or with the increase in the proportion of unemployed workers who remained out of work for very long periods. Consequently, it seems likely that the main reasons for the existence of mass unemployment were more closely related to the structural problems of British industry and the impact of the worldwide economic slump at the end of the 1920s.[10]

One of the most important features of Britain's interwar unemployment problem was the increase in the proportion of unemployed workers who had been out of work for more than twelve months, and this prompted a series of enquiries into the impact of 'long unemployment' on the psychological health of those who experienced it. In 1929, Drs James Pearse and Arthur Lowry claimed that 'every thoughtful person with whom we have talked has expressed greater concern at the destructive effect of idleness upon the character and morale of the unemployed than at the hardships involved in the scant supply of the necessaries of life', and when Dr Pearse visited the depressed areas of Sunderland and Durham in the winter of 1934–5, he claimed that many of the unemployed men who described their condition to him reported 'an increase in such psychical manifestations as depression, neurasthenia and various neuroses, especially gastric'.[11] Dr James Halliday surveyed the incidence of 'psychoneurotic disorders' among men who had been unemployed for varying periods. He found that 25.7 per cent of men who had been out of work for less than three months were suffering from some form of psychoneurosis, as compared with 41.5 per cent of men who had been unemployed for between three and 12 months. However, men who had been unemployed for more than 12 months were less likely to be suffering from a neurotic disability, and the incidence of psychoneurotic disabilities among men who had been unemployed for more than three years was 'only' 36.67 per cent.[12]

Whilst it would not be surprising to find that many unemployed workers experienced higher levels of stress as a result of increased poverty, many interwar investigators believed that the most serious effects were directly related to the loss of work itself. One of E. W. Bakke's respondents in Greenwich told him that 'if you can't find any work to do, you have the feeling that you're not human. You're out of place', whilst other writers claimed that unemployed workers became isolated from their communities and experienced a loss of 'the confidence, self-respect and satisfaction that come from having a place in the ranks of the workers'.[13] However, as McKibbin has emphasised, the fact that many unemployed workers were able to recognise these symptoms does not mean that they were therefore incapable of responding to them, and in many ways one of the most striking features of the history of interwar unemployment is not the extent of the despair generated by unemployment, but the resilience shown by unemployed workers in their efforts to deal with it.[14]

Although many contemporary writers believed that unemployment was likely to have some psychological effects, there was much less agreement over its impact on physical health. Pearse and Lowry reported that even though there was no evidence of widespread physical deterioration, there could be no question that in some areas the mothers of young children 'suffered to an unusual extent from languor and anaemia', and the editor of the *Medical Officer* (an independent journal for doctors in the public health service) claimed that even though 'it is just possible that our children can thrive on unemployment diet … most of us believe the malnutrition is there and that we are ignorant of the form it takes and so do not detect it'.[15] However, these claims were vigorously and consistently rejected by the Government's Chief Medical Officer, Sir George Newman. In 1932, he said that there was 'no available medical evidence of any general increase in sickness or mortality which can be traced to the effects of economic depression or unemployment', and in the following year he reiterated his view that there was no evidence of any general physical deterioration or of any increased physical impairment as a result of economic depression, and that the health of the nation compared favourably with previous years.[16]

The polarised nature of this debate has been echoed by a number of historians. Winter argued that 'no direct correlation can be made between economic insecurity and the mortality experience' of either pregnant mothers or young children, and that 'the most important feature of the aggregate data' on infant mortality 'is the persistence of the trend towards better … health … despite the economic crisis' of the early-1930s, but Mitchell claimed that there was a sharp reduction in the pace of infant mortality decline between 1930 and 1940, and that this supported the view 'that a connection between infant mortality and economic crisis is, at the very least, a possibility'.[17] However, this comparison may be misleading, because it fails to take account of the sharp rise in infant mortality at the beginning of the Second World War, and there is little evidence to support the view that there was any marked deceleration in the rate of mortality decline between 1930 and 1939 (see Figure 14.2).

The difficulties involved in using aggregate mortality rates have led a number of historians to consider alternative ways of assessing the relationship between economic change and public health in this period. Webster showed that even if the increase in unemployment was not directly associated with a deterioration in health, there was still plenty of evidence to show that the average standard of health among unemployed people and their families was very low, and Winter himself has argued that unemployment may have affected the reproductive health of women who were born during the depression and that of future generations.[18] Harris examined data on the heights of schoolchildren in 11 different areas between 1923 and 1938. His somewhat tentative conclusion was

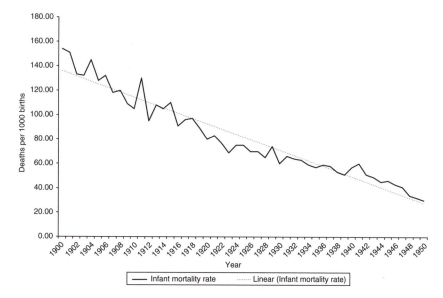

Source: B. Mitchell, *British historical statistics*, Cambridge: Cambridge University Press, 1988, pp. 58–9.

Figure 14.2   Infant mortality in England and Wales, 1900–50

that variations in unemployment may have been associated with variations in the average heights of children in some areas, though not necessarily in others.[19]

Although these statistics provide some support for the view that unemployment did lead to a deterioration in health standards, it is arguable that their real significance lies in the extent to which they help to illustrate the relationship between unemployment and poverty. Harris's data also showed that one the most striking features of the anthropometric history of the interwar period was the growing divide between the heights of children growing up in the more prosperous parts of the country and those of children in the most depressed areas. This suggests that even though there is little evidence of any significant deterioration in the health of children growing up in these areas, unemployment was one of a series of factors, such as poverty and poor housing, which prevented them from enjoying the same improvements in public health standards as those experienced by children in other parts of the country.

14.2 The Poor Law between the wars

During the early years of the twentieth century, a growing number of people became convinced of the need for a new approach to the treatment of poverty, and between 1906 and 1914 the Liberal government introduced a series of reforms which represented a major change in the state's attitude to the relief of sickness, unemployment and old age. Even though the Liberals declined to address the problem of the Poor Law directly, the introduction of these measures constituted a major assault on its traditional functions and mode of operation. The full impact of these changes became increasingly apparent during the interwar period.[20]

In institutional terms, the most important consequences of the First World War, so far as the Poor Law was concerned, were the Representation of the People Act of 1918 and the Ministry of Health Act of 1919. The first of these Acts removed the disqualification clause which prevented those in receipt of poor relief from voting in Parliamentary and other elections, although they continued to be barred from standing as candidates in elections to Boards of Guardians. The Ministry of Health Act transferred central responsibility for the Poor Law from the Local Government Board to the Ministry of Health, but it left the local administration of the Poor Law in the hands of Boards of Guardians.[21] However, even though the war had only a limited impact on the structures of the Poor Law, it undoubtedly exercised a major impact on the minds not only of Poor Law administrators, but also on the minds of those who might become dependent on it. As Crowther has pointed out, 'even Guardians who before 1914 had operated strict policies on outdoor relief knew that the workhouse could not be used against mass unemployment; nor could one send to the workhouse the heroes who had won the war.'[22]

During the 1920s, an increasing number of unemployed workers began to argue that the granting of poor relief was a right rather than a privilege, and many Poor Law Unions responded to this pressure by providing more generous relief payments. Whilst many observers welcomed this development, it also placed increasing financial pressure on the unions concerned, since these were often situated in areas which were least able to bear the cost of the benefits they provided.[23] From the mid-1920s onwards, there was a growing acceptance on the part of all political parties that some form of administrative reform was urgently needed, but it was not until 1929 that this was finally implemented.[24]

Although the majority of observers may have welcomed the 1929 Local Government Act, its passage was not without controversy. The Association of Poor Law Unions continued to protest against the abolition of the Boards of Guardians, and a number of writers have argued that the government's main aim was to undermine the influence of local Labour politicians by transferring responsibility from the elected members of Boards of Guardians to Public Assistance Committees which were appointed by the members of local councils. However, even though the Labour party's attitude to the Poor Law undoubtedly changed during the 1920s, very few MPs made a sustained attempt to defend the existing system, and the Act passed through Parliament with a substantial majority.[25]

The Local Government Act (19 Geo. V C. 17) abolished the Boards of Guardians, and transferred their powers to the county or county borough councils in whose areas they were situated. Each council was required to appoint a special committee, known as the Public Assistance Committee, containing a combination of council and non-council members, at least some of whom should be women. The Public Assistance Committees were also required to establish a number of Guardians' Committees to oversee the administration of poor relief (or, as it now became, public assistance) in each area. In order to establish a degree of continuity with previous policies, the Act encouraged local authorities to 'have regard to the desirability of including persons who are members of poor law authorities … and other persons of experience in the matter' on the membership of these committees.

The history of the Poor Law in the early-1930s was dominated by the shadow of unemployment. Despite the introduction of unemployment insurance, the Poor Law authorities had continued to play a major role in the relief of unemployed people and their families throughout the 1920s, and between 1931 and 1935 the number of individuals who were receiving public assistance as a result of unemployment increased from 155,658 to 452,075.[26] The Public Assistance Committees also became directly involved in the administration of the unemployment insurance system itself when they were given responsibility for the administration of transitional payments in 1931. It was only after the establishment of the Unemployment Assistance Board in 1934 and the extension of unemployment insurance to agricultural workers in 1936 that the Poor Law ceased to play any substantial role in the relief of unemployment in this period.[27]

However, the Poor Law was also affected by the development of a number of other statutory welfare services, including not only the expansion of unemployment insurance (and, to a much lesser extent, health insurance), but also the introduction of contributory pensions for widows and orphans and old-age pensioners. The introduction of these benefits was certainly not sufficient to eliminate the need for poor relief, but it did enable the Public Assistance

Committees to devote more time and resources to other needs. It also meant that, instead of being expected to bear the full cost of providing statutory support to these groups, they were much more likely to be providing additional assistance to those already in receipt of some form of state benefit. On 1 January 1939, Public Assistance Committees granted outdoor or domiciliary relief to more than 101,000 individuals in receipt of widows' and orphans' pensions, and to more than 223,000 individuals in receipt of old-age pensions. As Political and Economic Planning suggested, this represented a major change in the function of the English Poor Law during the interwar period.[28]

14.3 The expansion of unemployment insurance

As early as December 1914, the government had agreed that a non-contributory benefit, or 'out-of-work donation' should be paid to any ex-serviceman who became unemployed at the end of the war, but relatively little thought was given to the problems which faced civilian war-workers. During the war, the government had attempted to extend the principle of unemployment insurance to a number of war-related industries, but these efforts were resisted by both employers and employees, and by 1918 fewer than four million workers, out of a total workforce of nearly 14 million, were covered by unemployment insurance. At the same time, the government was becoming increasingly concerned that any attempt to throw large numbers of civilian workers onto the Poor Law would not only cause severe financial problems for the Poor Law authorities, but would also provoke bitter hostility from the workers themselves. It therefore agreed to extend the principle of the out-of-work donation to all those who had been employed for more than three months during the war, regardless of their civilian status.[29]

Although the Treasury accepted the establishment of the out-of-work donation as a short-term measure, it was increasingly concerned to establish a satisfactory basis for the development of a more comprehensive version of the contributory scheme in the future. In May 1919 an interdepartmental committee, containing representatives of both the Treasury and the Ministry of Labour, was instructed to examine the question more closely, and its recommendations formed the basis of the Unemployment Insurance Act which became law in August 1920. The Act extended the unemployment insurance scheme to all manual workers and to all non-manual workers earning less than £250 a year, except for agricultural workers, domestic servants and those engaged in occupations which were regarded as being free from the risk of periodic unemployment, such as public servants and railway-workers. However, even though benefit rates were raised in order to take account of inflation, the scheme was still primarily concerned with the relief of short-term unemployment, and no effort was made to take account of the needs of dependants.[30]

When the Act came into operation, in November 1920, there was little immediate opposition, and unemployment itself was still relatively low. However, within a month, unemployment had begun to rise sharply, and the limitations of the scheme became increasingly apparent. The government was also becoming increasingly alarmed by mounting evidence of economic distress and reports of social unrest, and this led to the introduction of three more Unemployment Insurance Acts during the first 11 months of 1921. The first Act raised the level of both employers' and employees' contributions, increased the standard level of benefit for an unemployed man from 15 to 20 shillings a week, and introduced a new form of benefit, known as uncovenanted benefit, for those who were 'genuinely seeking whole-time employment', and who had exhausted their entitlement to the standard form of unemployment benefit under the 1911 and 1920 Acts. The second Act reversed the benefit increases which had been introduced by the first Act and raised the level of contributions, but it also relaxed some of the conditions surrounding the payment of uncovenanted benefits. The third Act, the Unemployed Workers' Dependants (Temporary Provisions) Act, introduced separate allowances of five shillings a week for dependent adults and one shilling a week for non-earning children. This meant that by the middle of 1922, an unemployed man with a dependent wife and three non-earning children was receiving eight shillings more than he would have received 18 months earlier.[31]

When Winston Churchill introduced the original unemployment insurance scheme in 1911, he argued that the use of additional 'tests' to determine entitlement to benefit would be unnecessary, since a worker would only qualify for benefit if he was a contributor, but the various changes which were introduced at the start of the 1920s broke the connection between contributions and benefits, and forced successive governments to search for new ways of limiting access to unemployment benefits.[32] In February 1922 the Coalition government introduced a personal means-test for individuals claiming uncovenanted benefit, and in 1924 the new Labour government extended the 'genuinely-seeking-work test' to applicants for the ordinary form of unemployment benefit, whilst requiring applicants for uncovenanted (or, as it now became, extended) benefit to provide further proof that they were 'making a reasonable effort' to find work. When the Conservatives returned to power at the end of 1924, they decided to tighten up the regulations surrounding these tests, and this led to the refusal of a large number of benefit claims. It is difficult to calculate precise figures, but, according to Deacon, the Chief Insurance Officer refused 357,827 claims for ordinary benefit, on the grounds that the applicants were not genuinely seeking work, and the Local Employment Committees refused 427,114 claims for extended benefit, on the grounds that the applicants were not making a reasonable effort to find employment, in the three years between 13 January 1925 and 16 January 1928.[33]

The Conservatives were also anxious to investigate new ways of separating the relief of short- and long-term unemployment, and in November 1925 they invited a retired Lord Justice of Appeal, Lord Blanesburgh, to chair an enquiry into the future of unemployment insurance. The Committee recommended that different rates of contribution and benefit should be introduced for young workers (that is, those aged 18–21), and that the standard rate of benefit should be cut from 18 shillings a week to 17 shillings, although it also said that the payment made in respect of a dependent adult should be raised from five shillings to seven shillings. It also recommended that extended benefit should be abolished, but in order to prevent too many long-unemployed workers from being thrown onto the Poor Law immediately, it suggested that this should be replaced, for a limited period only, by a new form of benefit, known as 'transitional benefit'. These recommendations formed the basis of the 1927 Unemployment Insurance Act, but the transitional benefit scheme remained in operation until August 1931.[34]

When the Labour party returned to office in June 1929, it came under pressure from two different sides. On the one hand, many trade-union members were determined to see the abolition of the genuinely-seeking-work test whilst, on the other hand, the Treasury and the international financial community believed that the cost of the existing scheme was already spiralling out of control. In March 1930, the government acceded to the demands of many of its own supporters by abolishing the genuinely-seeking-work test and placing the onus of responsibility on the labour-exchange officials to prove than an applicant was not seeking work, but in the longer term the demand for economy proved increasingly difficult to resist. On 22 August 1931 the Prime Minister informed his Cabinet colleagues that unless they gave their unanimous support to a ten-per-cent cut in unemployment benefit rates, he would be forced to seek their resignations. Nine members of the Cabinet rejected the Prime Minister's demand, and on 24 August he formed a new National Government, which was largely dependent on Conservative and Liberal support.[35]

The establishment of the National Government was followed by two major changes in unemployment-relief policy. The first change was the decision to introduce the ten-per-cent cut in benefit rates which had led to the Labour Cabinet's resignation. Although this marked a further reduction in the living standards of those who were unemployed, some commentators have argued that its impact was softened by the fact that prices were also falling.[36] The second change was the decision to abolish the transitional-benefit scheme and introduce a new method of dealing with the long-term unemployed. The government said that the standard form of unemployment benefit should be restricted to those who had been unemployed for less than six months, and that those who had been out of work for more than six months would have to apply to the local Public Assistance Committee for a transitional payment. This meant that their entitlement to benefit would now be dependent, not only on their own personal means, but also on those of other household members.[37]

The introduction of the household means-test was probably the most controversial single change in the history of unemployment insurance during the interwar period. Many workers resented the inquisitorial visitations of the 'means-test man', and a large number of applicants found that their claims were rejected altogether, or that their benefits were substantially reduced.[38] However, there is also evidence to suggest that many unemployed workers were able to apply pressure on their local authorities, especially in Labour-controlled areas, to provide benefits which were rather more generous than those which the government might have wished.[39] Burns suggested that even though between 14 and 18 per cent of applicants were denied relief altogether, and between 31 and 35 per cent received less than the full allowance, 'there is evidence that in a great many cases transitional payments were made to families who could not be held to be in need when the resources of the family were taken into account.'[40]

Some of the anomalies associated with the local administration of the transitional payments scheme only became fully apparent when a new Unemployment Act was introduced in 1934. Part I of the Act established a new central body, known as the Unemployment Insurance Statutory Commission, for the relief of all those who had been unemployed for less than six months. Part II established a separate body, the Unemployment Assistance Board, for the relief of those who had been unemployed for a longer period. When the new Board attempted to introduce a uniform set of benefit scales across the whole country, it provoked a storm of protest from unemployed workers who found that the new scales were less generous than those being applied by their own local authority, and the Board agreed to suspend the introduction of the new scales until July 1936. The unemployment insurance scheme underwent a further change in 1936 with the extension of unemployment insurance to agricultural workers, and in 1937 the Unemployment Assistance Board finally assumed responsibility for the relief of those who had been unable to satisfy even the modest contribution requirements of the transitional payments scheme. This represented a major step towards the creation of a truly comprehensive system of unemployment insurance by the eve of the Second World War.[41]

14.4   The economic response to unemployment

During the 1920s, and for much of the 1930s, it was generally agreed that, whilst unemployment insurance was a necessary means of alleviating the distress caused by unemployment, there was little which governments could do, so far as direct intervention was concerned, to reduce the problem of unemployment at its source. During the early-1920s, the government's main priority was to deflate the economy and maintain high interest rates in order to enable sterling to rejoin the gold standard at the prewar rate of exchange, and even though it achieved this aim in April 1925, interest rates remained high until Britain was forced to leave the gold standard in September 1931. This decision enabled the National Government to reduce interest rates and this paved the way for a reduction in unemployment rates between 1932 and 1937, but even the launch of a massive rearmament programme was not sufficient to prevent a further rise in unemployment during the last full year of peace before the outbreak of the Second World War.[42]

Although the government was reluctant to intervene directly in the management of the economy, it recognised that the most depressed areas were experiencing acute structural problems which were unlikely to be solved by conventional means. In 1920, the Coalition government established a special Cabinet Committee on Unemployment, and the Treasury established its own Unemployment Grants Committee (also known as the St Davids Committee), with responsibility for distributing funds to local authorities to enable them to finance public-works schemes, such as the construction of new roads, to help reduce the incidence of unemployment. In December 1925, the Unemployment

Grants Committee agreed that grants should only be made to local authorities in areas where the local unemployment rate exceeded ten per cent of the insured workforce. It has been estimated that approximately £165 million was distributed under schemes approved by these two committees between 1921 and 1929, but the impact of these measures was still very limited. In 1928, a Treasury official estimated that they were responsible for generating no more than 3,928,167 'man-months' of employment, which implied that they provided employment for fewer than 44,000 workers at any one time, which was equivalent to less than 0.3 per cent of the total workforce and only four per cent of the unemployed workforce, and even though these figures do not take account of any additional employment which might have been created in association with the schemes, it is clear that 'special works secured no more than a very modest increase in employment' during the course of the period.'[43]

During the second half of the 1920s, many observers began to argue that the increase in unemployment might be reduced by persuading workers who had previously been employed in areas of high unemployment to migrate to those parts of the country where employment prospects were more buoyant. In 1927, the Blanesburgh Committee observed that 'if the right arrangements can only be devised, useful work can be found for a very large proportion of capable and willing workers ... Some of us have been impressed by the difficulty which certain growing industries experience in meeting their labour requirements even though there are unemployed men in other industries where their services are not likely again to be required, at any rate for a considerable time.'[44] On 1 August 1927, the mine-owners agreed not to recruit any workers over the age of 18 who had not been employed in coalmining before April 1926, and in December the government established a network of Juvenile Unemployment Centres to 'encourage and assist' young workers who wished to move. In January 1928, the government took a more concerted step to promote this policy with the establishment of the Industrial Transference Board. The Board concluded that 'it would be unwise to count upon the recovery by certain areas dependent upon the basic industries, and particularly coal-mining, of the position they occupied before the War', and that consequently 'the first aim of policy should be the dispersal of the heavy concentrations of unemployment by the active encouragement of movement from the depressed areas to other areas, both in this country and overseas.'[45]

Although the Industrial Transference Board played an important role in enabling some workers to migrate to areas with better employment prospects, its benefits can easily be exaggerated. As Hancock pointed out, the scheme had little effect before the end of the 1920s because it was difficult to persuade unemployed workers to move to new areas when the national unemployment rate was also high, but the number of transferees increased substantially during the second half of the 1930s, and over the whole of the period from 1928 to 1938 more than 280,000 individuals moved from areas of high unemployment to areas where prospects were believed to be brighter (see Table 14.1).[46] However, many of those who migrated to new areas failed to settle or to find satisfying employment (nearly 60 per cent of the girls who migrated were placed in domestic service), and the Ministry of Labour itself estimated that

Table 14.1 Individuals transferred under the industrial transference scheme, 1928–38

Category	1928–29	1930	1931	1932	1933	1934	1935	1936	1937 (Jan–Jun)	1937 (Jul–Dec)	1937 (Jan–Dec)	1938	Total
Men	36,843	28,258	17,889	8,359	5,333	6,828	13,379	20,091	10,350	n/a	n/a	n/a	n/a
Women	2,239	1,752	2,631	2,651	4,038	4,420	6,350	8,008	4,285	n/a	n/a	n/a	n/a
All adults	39,082	30,010	20,520	11,010	9,371	11,248	19,729	28,099	14,635	9,365	24,000	18,000	211,069
Boys													
Industrial	4,462	1,313	868	628	1,117	1,661	4,880	8,704	n/a	n/a	6,943	3,526	34,102
Vocational	0	0	0	0	0	0	496	745	n/a	n/a	732	605	2,578
All boys	4,462	1,313	868	628	1,117	1,661	5,376	9,449	4,527	3,148	7,675	4,131	36,680
Girls													
Industrial	64	93	17	171	417	505	1,151	3,585	n/a	n/a	4,933	4,163	15,099
Domestic	1,930	1,615	1,969	2,331	2,638	3,007	3,497	2,373	n/a	n/a	1,517	1,333	22,210
All girls	1,994	1,708	1,986	2,502	3,055	3,512	4,648	5,958	3,681	2,769	6,450	5,496	37,309
Total	45,538	33,031	23,374	14,140	13,543	16,421	29,753	43,506	22,843	15,282	38,125	27,627	285,058

Note: Figures in *italics* are rough figures.

Sources: Figures for juveniles are taken from the Annual Reports of the Ministry of Labour, 1928–38. Figures for adults are taken from A. D. K. Owen, 'The social consequences of industrial transference', *Sociological Review*, 29 (1937), 331–54, at 335 (1928–June 1937), and from PP 1938–9 Cmd. 6016 xii, 79, Ministry of Labour, *Annual Report for the year 1938*, p. 17 (1937 and 1938).

approximately 27 per cent of adult transferees and 35 per cent of juvenile transferees returned to their original areas, whilst D. R. Pitfield has calculated that at least one local job was lost for every five transferees who failed to return. Consequently, it is unlikely that the scheme helped to reduce the total volume of unemployment by more than approximately 160,000 unemployed workers over the whole of the period.[47]

It is also necessary to consider the wider social effects of industrial transference. As Owen pointed out, 'the ebb-and-flow of economic life in different parts of the country has always set up currents of internal migration', but the industrial-transference scheme represented the first significant attempt 'to stimulate or guide internal migration' as an instrument of economic policy, and it had major implications for the areas which 'lost' transferred workers, as well as for the areas which received them. In the case of the distressed areas, the migration of 'surplus labour' helped to reduce the incidence of both unemployment and overcrowding, but it also led to a disproportionate reduction in the number of younger workers, significantly altered the age structure of the remaining population, exacerbated the financial difficulties of many local authorities, and reduced the pool of able and energetic volunteers who were willing to contribute to voluntary organisations. The impact of industrial transference on the receiving areas was in many ways the direct opposite of this. These areas benefited from the introduction of a significant number of young workers who were able to make a substantial contribution to the development of new industries, but the influx of new migrants also placed growing pressure on the supply of schools and houses, and some of the newcomers faced significant hostility from established residents who believed (sometimes rightly, in Owen's view) that their presence was helping to drive down local wage rates.[48]

During the first half of the 1930s, the government came under increasing pressure to offer a more direct response to the problems faced by those who were still living in the depressed areas, and in 1934 it authorised the establishment of four separate enquiries into the effects of unemployment in South Wales, West Cumberland, Durham and Tyneside, and Scotland. These enquiries collected a large amount of useful information on issues such as health and housing, as well as the incidence of unemployment, but they failed to bring forward many substantial recommendations. However, in November 1934 the government introduced proposals for the appointment of two 'Commissioners' for the depressed areas (one for England and Wales, and one for Scotland), and these proposals formed the basis of the Special Areas (Development and Improvement) Act which was passed at the end of the year.[49]

Although the appointment of the Special Areas Commissioners represented an important stage in the development of the government's recognition of the particular nature of the problems being faced by these areas, it did not reflect a fundamental change in the government's underlying policy. When the Act was first passed, the Commissioners' responsibilities were limited to the promotion of small schemes of health and welfare, the provision of smallholdings and the inauguration of measures of environmental improvement, but they were also able to persuade the government to offer some limited financial subsidies to private employers to encourage them to establish new factories and trading-estates in the areas concerned, and they worked closely with voluntary organisations, such as the Society of Friends, to enable them to provide a range of social and recreational facilities, together with 'experiments' in 'sub-economic employment', such as the Eastern Valley Subsistence Production Society. However, although these initiatives may have made an important contribution to the social and cultural life of people living in the Special Areas, they did little to relieve the underlying problem of mass unemployment. As Garside has pointed out, by May 1939, only 273 factories had been established under the Special Areas scheme, and these were only responsible for employing just over 8,500 people. The total number of unemployed people in the Special Areas in July 1939 was 226,193.[50]

14.5   National health insurance

Although historians have devoted considerable attention to the history of unemployment insurance, the provision of financial benefits under the health insurance scheme has sometimes appeared to merit rather less attention. This is in some ways rather surprising because, as a number of authors have pointed out, health insurance could play an important part in helping individuals and their families to survive some of the worst effects of the interwar recession.[51]

When the health insurance scheme was first introduced, it was financed by contributions from employers and employees and subsidised by the state, and it provided cash benefits in the form of a weekly sickness benefit, a disablement benefit, and a maternity allowance (see Chapter 11). The scheme remained substantially unchanged during the First World War, but in 1919 the earnings limit for non-manual workers was raised from £160 a year to £250, where it remained for the whole of the interwar period. In 1920 the level of contributions was raised from four pence to five pence for men, and from three pence to five pence for women, and the standard rate of sickness benefit was raised from ten shillings a week to 15 shillings for men, and from seven shillings and six pence a week to 12 shillings a week for women, but no provision was made for the introduction of dependants' allowances. In 1931 the May Committee on Public Expenditure considered the idea of proposing cuts in the level of health insurance benefits, but was dissuaded from doing so by the Government Actuary. However, in 1933 the government did agree to reduce the benefit paid to married women from 12 shillings a week to ten shillings.[52]

Although the National Health Insurance Acts laid down the minimum amounts which could be paid in cash benefits, the approved societies which administered the scheme were able to offer additional benefits to contributors who insured through them. In 1938–9, the Ministry of Health and the Department of Health for Scotland calculated that approximately 69.2 per cent (14,629,102 insurees out of a total insured population in England, Scotland and Wales of 21,127,400) belonged to societies which made such benefits available.[53] However, the significance of these additional benefits should not be exaggerated. As Political and Economic Planning pointed out, an individual had to belong to the same society for at least four years before qualifying for additional cash benefits, and in 1937 at least three million individuals belonged to societies which only paid additional cash benefits in cases of maternity (that is, they failed to provide additional cash benefits for sickness or disablement). There were also considerable variations in the extent of the benefits provided. The Warehousemen's and Clerks' Association, with 9,317 members (all male), offered nine shillings a week in additional sickness benefit, two shillings a week in disablement benefit, and an extra 40 shillings of maternity benefit, but the majority of societies only paid between one and five additional units of cash benefit (one unit was equivalent to one shilling of sickness benefit, six pence of disablement benefit, and two shillings of maternity benefit), and the average was just under 3.5 units.[54]

It is interesting to compare the value of the benefits provided by the health insurance scheme with those offered by the unemployment insurance and workmen's compensation schemes. When the unemployment insurance scheme was first introduced, it provided a flat-rate benefit of seven shillings a week for a maximum of 15 weeks in any one year, but the scheme expanded rapidly after the end of the war, and by the end of 1921 it offered a substantially more generous set of benefits for a much longer period (see section 14.2 above). This was also true of workmen's compensation. If a worker was forced to stop work as a direct result of a work-related injury, he or she received a cash benefit which was directly related to the previous level of earnings. They received 75 per cent of normal earnings if they earned less than 25 shillings a week; 74 per cent of normal earnings if they earned between 25 and 50 shillings a week; and

Table 14.2 Standard rates of benefit under the national health insurance, unemployment and workmen's compensation schemes in 1934

Category	Weekly benefit
National health insurance	
Adult man	15–20 shillings
Unmarried/widowed woman	12–17 shillings
Married woman	10–15 shillings
Unemployment insurance	
Adult man	17 shillings
Adult woman	15 shillings
Adult man with dependent spouse	24 shillings
Adult man with dependent spouse and three non-earning children	30 shillings
Workmen's compensation	
Adult man earning less than 25 shillings a week prior to injury	75% of normal earnings
Adult man earning 25–50 shillings a week prior to injury	74% of normal earnings
Adult man earning more than 50 shillings a week prior to injury	50% of normal earnings up to a maximum of 30 shillings

Notes: The figures for the standard rates of sickness benefit under the national health insurance scheme include an allowance for additional cash benefits. It should be noted that not all insurees were either eligible for additional benefits or belonged to societies which paid them, and that the rates of additional benefit varied between societies. For further information, see text.

Sources: H. Levy, *National health insurance: a critical study*, Cambridge: Cambridge University Press, 1944, pp. 62–4; W. R. Garside, *British unemployment 1919–39: a study in public policy*, Cambridge: Cambridge University Press, 1990, pp. 86–7.

50 per cent of normal earnings if they earned more than 50 shillings a week, up to a maximum payment of 30 shillings (Table 14.2).[55]

In 1931, a number of the approved societies became concerned that the changes which had recently been made to the unemployment benefit system might encourage some unemployed workers to apply for health insurance rather than submit to the indignities of the household means-test.[56] However, even though some unemployed workers might have been better off if they had been able to obtain health insurance, this benefit was rarely sufficient to meet all their basic needs. In 1933, the British Medical Association calculated that the minimum expenditure needed to sustain a family of five on a basic diet was 23 shillings and two pence a week. When one considers that this figure failed to take account of either rent or the additional costs associated with the treatment of sickness, it is hardly surprising that many of those in receipt of health insurance should have felt compelled to seek additional help from either the Poor Law or the Public Assistance Committees.[57]

Gilbert argued that the main reason for the failure to increase the benefits paid by the health insurance scheme was the opposition of the approved societies. He claimed that these organisations were reluctant to pool their resources, and that the wealthier societies were more concerned to extract large surpluses for the benefit of their 'private' members than with serving the interests of those insured under the state scheme.[58] However, Whiteside has argued that this interpretation ignores the role played by the government itself in determining benefit rates, and that it fails to recognise the responsibility which the societies did feel for protecting the interests of both public and private members. Whiteside may err on the side of generosity in her treatment of the approved societies, but the evidence in favour of her representation of the government's role is certainly compelling.[59]

14.6 Municipal welfare services

In July 1935, when the Children's Minimum Council approached the Prime Minister, Stanley Baldwin, to complain about the inadequacy of unemployment benefit rates, he replied that revision was unnecessary because of the multiplicity of social services which were already provided for those in need. He paid particular attention to the provision of free meals and milk to schoolchildren, and the supply of milk and other forms of nutritional supplementation to expectant and nursing mothers and children of pre-school age. However, as Webster and others have pointed out, it would be easy to exaggerate the benefits which these services provided. In Webster's own words, they were 'too thinly spread and too erratic to serve more than a residual function'.[60]

One of the biggest problems afflicting the municipal welfare services was the fact that even at the end of the 1930s, despite changes in the methods of local-government finance, they were still heavily dependent on the revenue derived from local rates, and this led to significant disparities in the range and quality of the services provided in different areas. Although these disparities were often related to financial circumstances, they also reflected the vagaries of local politics and the ideological preferences of individual Medical Officers of Health.[61] It is also important to recognise that many authorities could only afford to target resources on one area of their activities by making economies elsewhere. In 1935–6, the amount of money spent per head by the Urban District of Rhondda on the provision of school medical inspection and treatment was just over two-thirds of the national average, but the money saved on these items enabled it to spend three times the national average on the provision of free milk and meals.[62]

Some of the most striking examples of local variation in service provision are provided in Webster's account of nutritional supplementation by maternity and child welfare centres in different parts of northern England and South Wales. In the late-1920s and 1930s, the Medical Officer of Health for the Urban District of Mountain Ash in South Wales advocated the distribution of free milk to expectant mothers from the second month of their pregnancy onwards, and the Medical Officer of Health for Rhondda argued that free milk should be provided to all children under the age of three 'whose parents are within the scale of necessity', but other Medical Officers, such as William Frazer in Liverpool, argued that the provision of nutritional supplements would undermine the educational functions of maternity and child welfare centres and turn them into 'relief stations'. There were also wide variations in the sums expended on nutritional supplementation. In 1935, according to Webster, Rhondda spent the equivalent of two shillings and three pence per head on nutritional supplements, whilst the Urban Districts of Mountain Ash and Merthyr spent one shilling and three pence and ten pence respectively, and the County of Monmouthshire spent a miserly 1.2 pence.[63]

Many of the problems associated with the provision of nutritional supplements at maternity and child welfare centres were also evident in the administration of the school meals service. When the Education (Provision of Meals) Act was passed, local education authorities were given the power to supply food to children who were 'unable by reason of lack of food to take full advantage of the education provided them', and after 1908 the Board of Education encouraged local authorities to make full use of the services of local School Medical Officers in identifying children in need of provision. However, during the 1930s this policy was severely criticised by Medical Officers (and others) who pointed out that a truly preventive policy would aim at feeding children before they showed signs of malnutrition instead of waiting until after they had already done so. The Board decided to relax the regulations surrounding the provision of school meals in 1934, and in 1935 it urged local education authorities to carry out periodical nutrition surveys 'at which all children not receiving meals would be passed under review', but in spite of these measures, only 176,767 children, out of a total elementary school population of more than four million, were receiving free school meals (excluding 'milk meals') on the eve of the Second World War.[64]

Whilst the provision of school meals represents one of the more disappointing aspects of interwar welfare provision, there was a significant increase in the number of children receiving either free or subsidised milk, partly on the grounds of health policy, and partly as a way of helping to subsidise the fortunes of the British dairy industry. By the early-1930s, approximately 90,000 elementary-school children were receiving free milk under the Provision of Meals Acts, and around 800,000 were paying a penny a bottle under a scheme initiated by the National Milk Publicity Council in 1923. The number of children receiving milk at school expanded rapidly during the 1930s as a result of the Government's Milk-in-Schools scheme, which was launched by the Milk Marketing Board on 1 October 1934. By the end of the 1930s, 635,000 children were receiving free milk under the Provision of Meals Acts, and approximately 2.7 million were receiving milk, either free or at reduced rates, under the milk-marketing scheme.[65]

14.7   Old-age and contributory pensions

During the years between 1919 and 1924, a number of modifications were made to the law regarding old-age pensions. The Old Age Pensions Act of 1919 (9 & 10 Geo. V C. 102) relaxed the residence requirements imposed by the Acts of 1908 and 1911, and removed the bans on the payment of pensions to ex-convicts and to those who had 'habitually failed to work according to [their] ability'. It also removed the ban on the payment of pensions to those in receipt of outdoor relief, thus enabling the Poor Law authorities to make supplementary payments to existing pensioners, and it raised the income limits used to determine pension entitlements. The basic pension itself was raised from its wartime level of seven shillings and six pence a week to ten shillings. The Old Age Pensions Act of 1924 (14 & 15 Geo V C. 33) allowed pension officials to disregard any unearned income, up to the value of 15 shillings a week or £39 a year, when assessing pension entitlements. However, the most important development in the interwar period was the introduction of contributory pensions for widows, orphans and elderly people between the ages of 65 and 70.

Macnicol has argued that the establishment of the contributory pension scheme represented a major triumph for the Treasury and for the Conservative approach to social policy. During the early-1920s, the Labour party had campaigned strongly for the abolition of means-testing, reductions in the pension age, and the extension of pension rights to widows and orphans, but its leaders were not prepared to support the increases in general taxation which such measures would have required. By contrast, the Conservatives argued that the pension system could only be expanded if those who were currently in work were prepared to contribute towards the cost of their own pension payments. They argued that this would not only provide a more solid financial basis for the pension system, but would also obviate the need for means-testing by giving all insured workers an automatic entitlement to pensions by virtue of their status as contributors.[66]

The Widows', Orphans' and Old Age Contributory Pensions Act extended the existing pension system by grafting a contributory scheme for widows, orphans and elderly people onto the national health insurance scheme. Under the Act (15 & 16 Geo. V C. 70), the employees' health insurance contributions were reduced by one penny a week for men, and by half a penny a week for women, but additional contributions from both employers and employees were levied for the pension scheme. The new scheme provided a basic pension of ten shillings a week for insured workers between the ages of 65 and 70, for the wives of insured men (where the man was over the age of 65 and the woman was aged between 65 and 70), and the widows of insured men, with additional allowances for the widows' children, and for orphans. In 1929, the second Labour government passed an amending Act (20 Geo. V C. 10), which extended pension entitlements to the widows of men who had died before the 1925 Act came into operation, and a further, consolidating, Act was passed in 1936 (26 Geo. V & 1 Edw. VIII C. 33). The only other major legislative change was the Widows', Orphans' and Old Age Contributory Pensions (Voluntary Contributions) Act of 1937 (1 Edw. VIII and 1 Geo. VI C. 39), which enabled women with an annual income of less than £250, and men with an annual income of less than £400, to insure themselves voluntarily.[67]

Although the Acts led to a substantial increase in the extent of state support for widows, orphans and elderly people, many Labour politicians complained both about the method of financing the pensions, and the levels at which they were paid.[68] These criticisms have been echoed both by contemporary analysts and by historians. Political and Economic Planning pointed out that even though the majority of women married men who were older than themselves, the requirement for both parties to be over the age of 65 meant that a large number of women failed to receive any pension at all until some years after their husbands had reached pensionable age. Even more importantly, the value of the pension itself was still very low, with the result that large numbers of pensioners had less than they needed for the basic subsistence, and were obliged to apply for means-tested public assistance. Finally, as Pedersen has argued, the pension regulations made a powerful contribution to the 'engendering' of the British welfare state by making wives' entitlements conditional upon their husbands' insurance status. This tendency was reinforced by the Beveridge proposals for the reform of social insurance after the end of the Second World War.[69]

14.8   Conclusions

Webster claimed that 'the total machinery of welfare was inadequate to compensate the poor and the unemployed for their disadvantages. Welfare services were too thinly-spread and too erratic to serve more than a residual function.'[70] However, other historians have offered a rather more optimistic assessment. Crowther has noted that despite the undoubted limitations of inter-war social policy, 'the working class which entered the Second World War could call upon the resources of the state for material support more comprehensively than their predecessors in 1914', and Thane has concluded that 'the growth of public action and expenditure despite the depression' was one of the central features of the interwar years.[71] Stevenson and Cook commented that 'by 1939 ... Britain had a more comprehensive set of welfare services than almost any other country.'[72]

If one looks at interwar welfare provision as a whole, then it is clear that major changes had occurred. At the beginning of the twentieth century, there was very little statutory provision for the able-bodied unemployed, and the only form of statutory provision for the relief of other forms of need was the Poor Law. However, by the end of the 1930s, the Poor Law had shed much (though certainly not all) of its deterrent framework, and was making a much more successful attempt to cater for a variety of social needs. In 1937, Political and Economic Planning concluded that 'the grim Poor Law of the nineteenth century, with its rigorous insistence on the principle of "less eligibility" and the workhouse test' had been replaced by 'a liberal and constructive service, supplementing the other social services, filling in gaps and dealing with human need in the round in a way in which no specialist service could ever be expected to do.'[73]

These changes were facilitated by the development of alternative forms of statutory provision for different categories of need. Even though the interwar period witnessed few real changes in the organisation of health insurance benefits, or in the size of the pensions provided for the over-70s, it did see a dramatic expansion in the coverage of the unemployment benefit system, and the introduction of a new range of contributory welfare benefits for widows and orphans, in addition to the provision of contributory pensions for those aged between 65 and 70. The introduction of contributory pensions also meant that by the end of the 1930s more than a million pensioners over the age of 70, who might otherwise have had to apply for a means-tested pension, now received their pension automatically.[74]

However, one should not ignore the many defects of interwar welfare provision. Although central government took an increasing share of responsibility for relieving the burdens of both unemployment and old age, local authorities continued to be responsible for the provision of a wide range of social services, including not only the Poor Law itself, but also the welfare provisions of the school meals service and the maternity and child welfare services. These services were subject to a vast range of different means-tests, which varied widely both in terms of the rules applied to different services, and in terms of the rules applied to the same service by different authorities.[75] There was also a wide range of variation in the quality of the services which different local authorities could provide. Thane suggested that during the 1930s Labour-controlled local authorities may have been more willing to invest funds in municipal welfare services, but their ability to do so continued to be hampered by the poverty of their constituents.[76]

From the point of view of many contemporaries, the continuing problems of local government were symptomatic of a broader failure of coordination and planning. During the 1920s, more than 20 different Unemployment Insurance Acts were passed in a vain attempt to grapple with the problems caused by mass unemployment.[77] The lack of coordination also meant that there was a large number of different services catering for different categories of need. This reflected the largely *ad hoc* way in which different services had developed during the early years of the twentieth century, but it also meant that individuals with very similar needs were treated in very different ways, depending, for example, on whether their needs were being assessed by the Unemployment Assistance Board or the Public Assistance Authorities, or whether they were regarded as being eligible for unemployment insurance or health insurance.[78]

One of the most important limitations of the interwar welfare system was the failure to adopt a subsistence basis for the granting of contributory benefits.

It was precisely because of this that so many people, who qualified for insurance benefits, were still required to apply for an additional means-tested benefit, such as poor relief or public assistance. There can be little doubt that the persistence and even the spread of means-testing was one of the most unpopular features of interwar welfare provision, or that it exercised a powerful deterrent function, but, in spite of this, some historians have suggested that the prevalence of means-tests may nevertheless have helped to ensure that state welfare benefits were more accurately targeted than they would otherwise have been. The assessment of interwar welfare services has also been influenced by recent concerns over the redistributive effects of universalist welfare provision after 1945. In 1958, Brian Abel-Smith suggested that 'the main effect of the postwar development of the social services...has been to provide free social services to the middle classes', and Pat Thane has argued that the much more selective benefit system of the 1920s and 1930s may have been more genuinely redistributive, in terms of redistributing resources between classes, than the pattern of welfare provision either before or since.[79]

Despite their obvious limitations, the welfare services of the 1930s undoubtedly whetted the appetite of large numbers of people for a more extensive system of public support in the future. One of the more intriguing aspect of this was the increased demand for middle-class people to be allowed access to state benefits, as reflected in the demand for the extension of the benefits of the health insurance scheme to 'black-coated workers' and the introduction of voluntary insurance under the Contributory Pensions Acts. This was also to be one of the most important forces driving the development of the welfare system after 1945.[80]

15 Health and medical care, 1918–39

As we have already seen, the First World War posed a series of major challenges to the infrastructure of health care. In addition to the physical and psychological stresses inflicted on different sections of the population, the war also led to the call-up of more than half the country's qualified medical personnel, and the redeployment of many civilian medical facilities for military use. However, the war also focused attention on the importance of the nation's health and, as a result, played a major role in the passage of such measures as the Notification of Births (Extension) Act of 1915, the Maternity and Child Welfare Act of 1918, the establishment of the Ministry of Health in 1919, and the conversion of the Medical Research Committee into the Medical Research Council in 1920. It also made an important contribution to the development of medical science, and laid the foundations of a number of major therapeutic developments. Although many of these developments were only slowly absorbed into peacetime practice, the war saw the introduction of blood transfusions, new methods for the treatment of wounds and fractures, improvements in the design of artificial limbs, the development of reconstitutive or plastic surgery, new methods of treating heart disease, the use of oxygen therapy for the treatment of pneumonia, severe bronchitis and heart failure, the development of aviation medicine, and research into wound-shock, shell-shock and gas asphyxia.[1]

This chapter seeks to build on these foundations by examining the history of medicine and health care between 1918 and 1939. Section 15.1 summarises some of the main scientific developments affecting the practice of medicine, and provides a general overview of Britain's health during the interwar period. Section 15.2 examines the impact of the national health insurance scheme on the development of general practice and the provision of primary medical care. The third section discusses the development of the hospital services, and also examines the development of services for the treatment of people with mental illnesses. Section 15.4 looks at the evolution of the local-authority health services, focusing not only on the 'personal health services', but also on the environmental services which had provided the original foundation for local-authority health care in the second half of the nineteenth century. The final section summarises the main developments in health care during the interwar period, and evaluates the adequacy of health service provision on the eve of the Second World War.

15.1   Health, medicine and disease

Although the interwar years witnessed a number of important scientific and therapeutic developments which might have made a significant difference to medicine's capacity to prevent and treat disease, they were often held up by a combination of economic difficulties, bureaucratic inertia, and public scepticism. These obstacles were particularly apparent in the context of the Ministry of Health's efforts to prevent the spread of infectious disease. In 1920, the Hungarian-born paediatrician, Béla Schick, developed a highly effective test for the presence of diphtheria, and this led to the implementation of highly successful immunisation programmes in both Europe and North America, but the Ministry of Health was reluctant to launch a similar campaign in the UK, partly on financial grounds, and partly as a reaction to the long history of public opposition to smallpox vaccination in the nineteenth century.[2] In 1924, two French researchers, Albert Calmette and Jean-Marie Guérin, developed a vaccine for the prevention of tuberculosis, but the Ministry of Health argued that the UK had already developed a widespread network of public health facilities for the prevention and treatment of the disease, and that further measures, which might pose additional risks to the health of the individuals who were subjected to immunisation, were therefore unnecessary.[3]

Although the Ministry of Health was generally reluctant to embrace new approaches to the prevention of disease, the Medical Research Council showed a much greater willingness to promote the introduction of new methods of treatment. In 1922 two Canadian scientists, Fred Banting and Charles Best, demonstrated that it was possible to treat diabetic patients with injections of insulin, and the MRC began to promote its use in Britain from 1923 onwards, although it is difficult to establish how far this contributed to the reduction of mortality from the disease during the interwar period. The MRC also promoted the use of liver extract to treat patients who were suffering from pernicious anaemia, but here too the effects were mixed. The availability of the treatment led to a sharp fall in the death rate among those aged under 65 and who lived in urban areas, but doctors were much more reluctant to offer it to older patients, and to patients in rural areas.[4]

The interwar years also saw several other important therapeutic developments. As we have already seen, the First World War had led to the introduction of new techniques for the treatment of wounds and fractures, and during the interwar period orthopaedists began to play a much more important role in the treatment and rehabilitation of people suffering from industrial injuries.[5] Other developments were rather more controversial. Towards the end of the nineteenth century, a Danish physician, Niels Finsen, had suggested that ultraviolet rays might be used to combat bacterial infections, such as lupus, and during the interwar period the Board of Education played a leading role in encouraging local education authorities to use artificial light to treat a wide range of conditions, including tuberculosis, rickets and other 'bony defects'.[6] The interwar period also witnessed a massive increase in the use of radium to treat patients with cancer, particularly in urban areas. As Hardy has pointed out, 'although both the Medical Research Council and radium specialists were concerned about [the] ... indiscriminate use of [radium therapy] ... it was not until the effects of the atom bomb on the inhabitants of Hiroshima and Nagasaki became known in the later-1940s that the medical uses of radium were more widely called into question.'[7]

Although there were many other important new developments in both the organisation and practice of medicine in these years, few were more important than the discovery of the bactericidal properties of prontosil rubrum by a German researcher, Gerhard Domagk, in 1935. Domagk showed that if mice were injected with live streptococci, then they all died, but if they were treated with prontosil rubrum, then they all survived. Prontosil was the first of the sulphonamides, and its introduction made a major contribution to the decline of puerperal fever, which was one of the major causes of maternal mortality. As Loudon observed: 'those who saw puerperal fever in the 1930s remember the sulphonamides as a "miracle drug", for it must be remembered that previously none of the extremely large number of treatments for puerperal fever had been of any use whatsoever. The sulphonamides provided "one of the rare situations which endorse the identification of an agency of major importance as contributory to a statistical trend".'[8]

The interwar period was also characterised by major changes in the overall profile of ill-health and mortality. As Harris has shown, there were substantial increases in the average heights of children in many parts of the country, and life expectancy at birth increased from 48.5 to 66.4, for males, and from 52.4 to 71.5, for females, over the course of the period.[9] However, although the average standard of public health was improving, the disease profile of the population was also changing, partly as a result of the decline in the incidence of infectious diseases, and partly because of the increase in the proportion of the population in higher age groups.[10] During the third quarter of the nineteenth century, between 1848 and 1872, approximately 32 per cent of all male deaths and 34 per cent of all female deaths had been attributed to infectious diseases, but the major causes of death in the twentieth century were cancer and circulatory diseases.[11] By 1951, these two categories were responsible for more than 61 per cent all male deaths and nearly 68 per cent of all female deaths, whilst the proportion of deaths associated with infectious diseases had declined to less than four per cent for the population as a whole (see Figure 15.1).

Although health standards were undoubtedly rising during the interwar years, health expectations were also changing. By the end of the nineteenth century, it was well known that the dietary constituents of food could be broken down into fats, carbohydrates and proteins, but a number of studies were beginning to point to the existence of other factors which were also vital for health. Many of the earliest studies were specifically concerned with the role played by these 'accessory food factors' or 'vitamines' in the aetiology of specific deficiency diseases, such as scurvy, beri-beri or rickets, but it became increasingly apparent that people who were consuming insufficient quantities of these substances in their diets might also be suffering from sub-optimal nutrition.[12] The nutritionist, F. C. Kelly, described how 'different lines of study began to converge, showing that individuals and communities, while not exhibiting signs of obvious disease, are functioning at levels far below those normally attainable

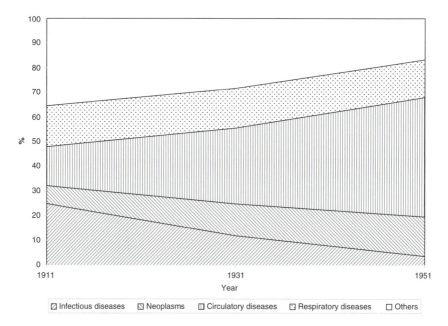

Source: J. Charlton and M. Murphy, 'Trends in all-cause mortality: 1841–1994', in J. Charlton and M. Murphy (eds), *The health of adult Britain 1841–1994, Volume 1, Chapters 1–14*, London: Office for National Statistics, 1997, pp. 30–57, at pp. 43–4.

Figure 15.1 Percentage of all deaths in Britain attributable to different causes, 1911–51

under optimal conditions of feeding', and this had profound implications for the future of health policy.[13] As Political and Economic Planning observed, 'provided that the argument is not pushed too far, it is useful to bear in mind a distinction between the mass of socially and economically incapacitating disabilities usually treated as cases of ill-health and the even larger mass of deficiencies and disabilities which do not incapacitate and are often unrecognised or not thought serious. No contemporary health policy can be considered adequate which does not deal with the second group as well as the first.'[14]

15.2 National health insurance and general practice

As various writers have shown, there was a significant increase in the demand for orthodox medical care during the second half of the nineteenth century. The annual number of outpatient consultations at the London Hospital increased from approximately 25,000 to just over 220,000 between 1860 and 1900, and Riley has claimed that by the end of the nineteenth century between two-thirds and three-quarters of all friendly-society members were covered by health insurance schemes.[15] However, even though the number of qualified practitioners was increasing more slowly than the population as a whole, doctors could only earn what their patients were able or willing to pay, and this contributed to a growing sense of financial and occupational insecurity. In 1909 the Manchester and Salford branch of the British Medical Association complained that 'the chances of being able to save even to the extent of the capital expended in education are in a large proportion of cases slight; while reasonable provision for old age, after family expenses are met, is difficult and too often impossible.' As a result, even though many doctors opposed the introduction of the national health insurance scheme in 1911, it played an essential part in the growth of general practice during the interwar years.[16]

As we have already seen, the national health insurance scheme was designed to offer financial compensation for the loss of income associated with ill-health, together with access to a limited range of health services which might help to preserve the workers' health in normal times and restore them to better health during period of illness. When the scheme was first set up, insured women paid a weekly contribution of three pence, and insured men paid four pence, and in return for this they became entitled to free treatment from a general practitioner, and both they and their dependants became eligible for free treatment in a sanatorium if they were suffering from tuberculosis, but neither they nor their dependants qualified for other forms of hospital or specialist treatment. During the course of the next 13 years, Parliament passed a series of amending Acts, culminating in the National Health Insurance Act of 1924, but the most important change during the interwar period was the introduction of the National Health Insurance (Juvenile Contributors and Young Persons) Act of 1937, which extended rights to medical benefit to young workers between the ages of 14 and 16.[17] By the end of 1938, between two-thirds and three-quarters of general practitioners had joined the scheme, and more than 21 million workers and pensioners derived some form of benefit from it (see Table 15.1).

Although the national health insurance scheme represented a significant improvement in the health-care rights of insured workers, it did not create a universal or comprehensive scheme for the population at large, and there was considerable evidence to suggest that practitioners failed to give insurance patients (or 'panel patients') the same priority they accorded to their private patients. As Digby and Bosanquet observed, 'private patients could more easily obtain a visit in their own homes from the doctor; when coming to the surgery it was common to have an appointment and enter through the front door of the doctor's house. In contrast, panel patients entered through the surgery door and had to wait their turn to see the doctor.' In one Maldon practice, 'private patients were seen by the senior partners; were given more elaborate medications; had minor surgery performed more often; had more frequent visits in their own homes; and might be the subject of laboratory tests, or an occasional referral or consultation. In contrast, the panel and club patients were treated by the most junior doctor in the practice.'[18]

It is also important to remember that the national health insurance scheme did not provide a comprehensive range of benefits. When the scheme was first set up, the range of services was limited to those which fell within the 'competence of an ordinary practitioner', but the approved societies which administered the scheme were able to provide additional services, such as contributions towards the cost of dental and ophthalmic services, and convalescent care, out of the surpluses they generated. By the end of the interwar period, the majority of insured contributors belonged to societies which were able to offer some

Table 15.1   Number of men and women entitled to benefits under the national health insurance scheme in the United Kingdom, 1914–38

Year	Number of persons eligible for health insurance benefits (1000s)		Population (1000s)		Eligible persons as % of population	
	Men	Women	Men	Women	Men	Women
1914[a, b, c]	9,667	4,020	20,187	21,527	47.89	18.67
1915[b, c, d]	9,947	4,146	18,311	21,744	54.32	19.07
1916[b, c, d]	10,316	4,532	17,536	21,901	58.83	20.69
1917[b, c, d]	10,514	4,853	16,977	22,030	61.93	22.03
1918[b, c, d]	10,705	5,183	16,742	22,094	63.94	23.46
1919[b, c, d]	10,308	5,139	18,173	22,074	56.72	23.28
1920[b, c, d]	10,215	5,064	19,920	22,192	51.28	22.82
1921[b, c]	10,245	4,905	20,446	22,369	50.11	21.93
1922[c]	10,429	5,043	21,226	23,146	49.13	21.79
1923	10,687	5,214	21,328	23,269	50.11	22.41
1924	10,946	5,415	21,508	23,407	50.89	23.14
1925	11,110	5,513	21,567	23,492	51.51	23.47
1926	11,427	5,640	21,662	23,570	52.75	23.93
1927	11,607	5,747	21,733	23,656	53.41	24.29
1928[e]	11,901	5,985	21,823	24,024	54.54	24.91
1929	12,064	6,097	21,877	23,796	55.14	25.62
1930	12,326	6,199	21,986	23,880	56.06	25.96
1931	12,469	6,239	22,087	23,987	56.46	26.01
1932	12,566	6,258	22,235	24,100	56.52	25.97
1933	12,463	6,228	22,332	24,189	55.81	25.75
1934	12,522	6,273	22,403	24,263	55.89	25.85
1935	12,705	6,347	22,504	24,364	56.46	26.05
1936	13,246	6,573	22,605	24,476	58.60	26.85
1937	13,546	6,735	22,726	24,563	59.60	27.42
1938[f]	14,303	7,285	22,822	24,672	62.67	29.53

Notes: [a] The figures for 1914 are for the period 12/1/14–31/12/14; all other figures for calendar years. [b] The figures for the years 1914–21 are for Great Britain only (that is, excluding Ireland). [c] The figures for the years 1914–22 include older members (that is, aged 70 and over) who qualified for medical benefit in Scotland, Wales and (in 1922 only) Northern Ireland, but they do not include equivalent individuals in England. The English members are included from 1923 onwards. [d] Population figures for 1915–20 are for civilians only. [e] Individuals aged between 65 and 70 ceased to be eligible for sickness and disablement benefits from 2 January 1928 onwards, but they continued to be eligible for medical benefit. [f] Under the terms of the National Health Insurance (Juvenile Contributors and Young Persons) Act, 1937, boys and girls aged 14–16 became eligible for medical benefits from 4 April 1938.

Sources: Health insurance: 1914–16: PP 1928–9 Cmd. 3253 xxii, 1, *Statistical abstract for the United Kingdom for each of the fifteen years from 1913 to 1927 (72nd number)*, pp. 56–7; 1917–22: PP 1931–2 Cmd. 3991 xxiv, 1, *Statistical abstract for the United Kingdom for each of the fifteen years from 1913 and 1917 to 1930 (75th number)*, pp. 64–5; 1923: PP 1936–7 Cmd. 5353 xxvi, 1, *Statistical abstract for the United Kingdom for each of the fifteen years from 1913 and 1922 to 1935 (80th number)*, pp. 80–1; 1924–38: PP 1939–40 Cmd. 6232 x, 367, *Statistical abstract from the United Kingdom for each of the fifteen years 1924–38 (83rd number)*, pp. 82–3. Population: B. R. Mitchell, *British historical statistics*, Cambridge: Cambridge University Press, 1988, pp. 11–14.

form of additional medical benefit, but they had to belong to the society for at least two years before they became eligible for additional treatment benefits (although the societies were permitted to grant additional treatment benefits after six months in cases of want or distress), and there were considerable disparities between the benefits which different societies were able to offer.[19]

In 1939, the Ministry of Health and the Department of Health for Scotland reported that more than 13 million individuals belonged to approved societies which made some contribution towards the cost of dental treatment, whilst 11.8 million individuals belonged to societies which contributed to the cost of ophthalmic treatment, but only 6.7 million people belonged to societies which contributed to the cost of nursing care, and fewer than two million belonged to societies which contributed to hospital costs (see Table 15.2). One of the main problems with the scheme was that individuals who belonged to societies with a large proportion of relatively healthy workers were able to offer more generous benefits than societies whose members were concentrated in more dangerous occupations. Levy pointed out that 'people living in the same street, even in the same house, may find that they receive entirely different benefits', whilst 'persons suffering from the same sort of illness, or disabled by the same kind of industrial accident or disease, may be given totally different prospects of restoration.'[20]

However, the most important limitation of national health insurance was the failure to provide even rudimentary medical cover to the dependants of insured workers. The Government Actuaries argued that it was not necessary to offer medical benefit to the wives of insured men 'since where the unit is the family, it is the husband's and not the wife's health which it is important to ensure', but this only helped to reinforce existing inequalities in men's and women's access to health care.[21] During the 1930s, a number of general practitioners established public medical services which were explicitly designed for the dependants of their panel patients, but even by 1937 these only catered for approximately 600,000 individuals (out of a total uninsured population of just over 27 million), and the average working-class family devoted less than three per cent of its normal weekly expenditure to medical services.[22] According to Digby and Bosanquet, the wives and children of insured workers were much more likely to obtain medical care from hospital out-patient clinics, maternity and child welfare services, school clinics and local pharmacies, but these services were also limited in their scope, and unable to provide the kind of domiciliary medical care which might normally be expected from a general practitioner.[23]

During the course of the interwar period a number of authors and organisations issued proposals to address the limitations of the health insurance scheme and extend rights to medical care to a broader section of the population. In 1918, the *Lancet* published a series of articles on the need for health-service reform, including a call from two left-wing doctors, Benjamin Moore and Charles Parker, for the creation of a full-time salaried state medical service and the provision of free medical care to the whole population. These proposals were reinforced by the publication of a Labour party report on the health services later in the same year, and they also influenced Bertrand Dawson's proposals for the establishment of a unified health service in 1920. Dawson failed to endorse the Labour party's demand for a free health service, but he echoed the party's call for a closer relationship between preventive and curative medicine, and advocated the creation of a network of primary and secondary health centres in which general practitioners would be brought into a much closer relationship with both hospital services and the public health service.[24]

Table 15.2 Additional benefits provided under the national health insurance scheme, 1939

Category	England and Wales				Scotland			
	Number of schemes	Approximate membership covered	Membership as % of insured population	Membership as % of total population	Number of schemes	Approximate membership covered	Membership as % of insured population	Membership as % of total population
9 Dental	5,019	12,312,465	65.20	29.70	347	1,243,356	55.41	24.83
14 Ophthalmic	5,011	10,522,618	55.73	25.38	349	1,250,580	55.73	24.98
11 Convalescent homes	2,657	11,242,329	59.54	27.12	169	659,238	29.38	13.17
13 Medical and surgical appliances	4,092	11,860,781	62.81	28.61	270	1,089,122	48.53	21.75
10 Hospitals	2,315	1,663,463	8.81	4.01	101	221,426	9.87	4.42
5 Want or distress	749	6,461,761	34.22	15.59	–	–	–	–
16 Approved charitable institutions	394	7,814,039	41.38	18.85	–	–	–	–
15 Nursing	653	6,702,131	35.49	16.17	–	–	–	–
12 Convalescent home premises	21	675,299	3.58	1.63	–	–	–	–
6 Infection	93	4,037,720	21.38	9.74	–	–	–	–
4 Convalescent allowances	53	456,000	2.41	1.10	–	–	–	–
7 Repayment of contributions	–	2,300	0.01	0.01	–	–	–	–
– Others	–	–	–	–	77	–	–	–

Sources: Members eligible for additional benefits: PP 1938–9 Cmd. 6089 xi, 325, Twentieth Annual Report of the Ministry of Health 1938–39, pp. 149, 212; PP 1938–9 Cmd. 5969 xi, 651, Tenth Annual Report of the Department of Health for Scotland 1938, p. 238; Total insured population (1938 figures): PP 1939–40 Cmd. 6232 x, 367, Statistical abstract from the United Kingdom for each of the fifteen years 1924–38 (83rd number), pp. 82–3; Total population (1939 figures): B. R. Mitchell, British historical statistics, Cambridge: Cambridge University Press, 1988, pp. 60–5.

Although the Dawson Report has attracted considerable attention in recent years, the most substantial enquiry into interwar health care was carried out by the Royal Commission on National Health Insurance (the Lawrence Commission) between 1924 and 1926.[25] The majority of the Commission's members believed that the existing arrangements for the provision of additional benefits were inequitable and argued that the approved societies' surpluses should be pooled in order to finance an expanded range of benefits for all insured members. The minority members thought that the range of statutory benefits should be extended to include dental and ophthalmic treatment and maternity care, as well as an expanded range of medical benefits, and that the cost of this should be paid for out of general taxation as well as insurance revenues. They also argued that responsibility for the administration of national health insurance should be transferred from the approved societies to the local authorities, and that entitlements to medical benefit should be extended to the dependants of insured workers, as well as the workers themselves.[26] However, neither of these reports had any immediate effect. In March 1926, one month after the publication of the Commission's reports, the government decided to reduce the value of its own contributions to the health insurance fund from two-ninths of the sum expended in administration and benefits to one-fifth, in the case of female members, and one-seventh in the case of male members, and, having already taken on the approved societies over this issue, it was reluctant to antagonise them any further.[27]

The pressure for health-service reform continued throughout the 1930s. In April 1930 the British Medical Association called for the existing health insurance scheme to be expanded so as to include specialist and nursing services, together with ancillary services such as laboratory reports and X-rays, pharmaceutical services and dental care, and recommended that the benefits of health insurance should be extended to workers' families.[28] However, the most radical proposals came from the Socialist Medical Association and the Labour party. In 1932, Somerville Hastings argued that health services should be financed out of a mixture of central- and local-government taxation, and should be provided free at the point of use to all who wished to take advantage of them. These proposals were formally adopted by the Labour party at its annual conference in 1934, but they had little impact on the government's approach to health policy before the outbreak of the Second World War.[29]

15.3   Hospital provision

Although the advocates of health-service reform devoted considerable attention to the need for improvements in the area of primary medical care, there was also considerable pressure for reform of the hospital system. By 1921, the total number of hospitals (excluding convalescent homes and private nursing-homes) had risen to 2,885, and the number of hospital beds to nearly 230,000 (see also Table 15.3). Of this figure, approximately 56,000 beds were in voluntary hospitals, 74,000 beds were in hospitals maintained by local authorities, and 80,000 were in Poor Law institutions. However, despite these increases, there

Table 15.3 Hospital provision in England and Wales, 1861–1938

Category	1861		1891		1911		1921		1938	
	Institutions	Beds	Institutions	Beds	Institutions	Beds	Institutions	Beds	Institutions	Beds
Voluntary hospitals										
Teaching	23	5,291	24	7,228	24	8,284	25	9,584	25	12,610
General	130	6,658	385	15,184	530	21,651	616	27,443	671	45,397
Infectious diseases	7	238	5	443	1	160	1	178	1	195
Tuberculosis	5	288	14	1,075	53	4,200	113	7,015	108	7,848
Maternity	12	139	16	210	8	311	14	462	235	3,587
Other special	72	2,008	128	4,701	121	6,495	152	9,521	175	15,114
Chronic & unclassified	5	150	12	679	47	2,120	50	2,347	40	2,484
Total	254	14,772	584	29,520	784	43,221	971	56,550	1,255	87,235
Public hospitals										
General	0	0	18	12,138	76	40,927	74	37,840	133	52,974
Infectious diseases	0	0	353	10,314	703	31,786	888	41,415	931	39,256
Tuberculosis	0	0	0	0	n/a	1,300	123	6,531	179	15,609
Maternity	0	0	0	0	0	0	199	2,463	176	6,442
Other special	0	0	0	0	0	0	1	26	18	5,572
Chronic & unclassified	650	50,000	713	60,778	625	80,260	629	83,731	445	56,015
Total	650	50,000	1,084	83,230	1,404	154,273	1,914	172,006	1,882	175,868
Voluntary + public hospitals	904	64,772	1,668	112,750	2,188	197,494	2,885	228,556	3,137	263,103
Related institutions	16	n/a	293	9,528	313	13,000	2,189	40,228	2,663	50,681
Grand total	920	n/a	1,961	122,278	2,501	210,494	5,074	268,784	5,800	313,784

Source: R. Pinker, *English hospital statistics 1861–1938*, London: Heinemann, 1966, pp. 57, 61–2.

were still substantial difficulties affecting not only the financial status of the different types of hospital, but also the relationship between them.

Although the First World War caused considerable problems for all types of health service, it posed particular difficulties for the voluntary hospitals. During the war, there was a sharp reduction in the number of civilian medical practitioners, and this led to a substantial increase in the number of middle-class patients seeking hospital treatment. This not only increased the hospitals' costs, but also raised fundamental questions about their role as charitable institutions for the treatment of the 'sick poor'. The war also distorted the traditional patterns of charitable giving, and this meant that many hospitals, such as the Chelsea Hospital for Women, faced growing financial difficulties, whilst those hospitals whose work was more directly associated with the war effort became increasingly dependent on government payments, and all were affected by the impact of wartime inflation. The sense of crisis was intensified by the outbreak of a serious flu epidemic in the autumn of 1918. This not only led to the deaths of approximately 225,000 people in Britain (and at least 21 million worldwide), but also imposed an unprecedented strain on the country's medical and hospital facilities.[30]

As the First World War drew to an end, the problems of the hospital service attracted growing concern. In 1918, the Labour party had recommended the creation of a unified hospital system, incorporating both the Poor Law hospitals and the voluntary hospitals, and this call was echoed by the Dawson Committee in 1920, but the Committee's report attracted a great deal of hostile criticism and had little practical effect. In the meantime, Dr Christopher Addison, the Minister of Health, made a similarly unsuccessful attempt to address some of the immediate problems by introducing a series of proposals, tagged on to the end of a Housing Bill, to enable county and county borough councils to take over responsibility for Poor Law infirmaries and subscribe to voluntary hospitals. These proposals were criticised by the Labour party because they were insufficiently radical and by the Conservatives because they threatened to undermine the voluntary principle and impose unnecessary burdens on municipal expenditure, and the proposals were dropped when the Bill was reintroduced later in the same year.[31]

Although Addison's efforts failed, they did help to highlight the problems facing the voluntary hospitals in particular, and this led to the appointment of the Cave Committee (the Voluntary Hospitals Committee) in January 1921. The Committee concluded that even though the majority of hospitals had deficits, they could all increase their income by making greater use of workmen's contributory schemes. It advised the government to provide a one-off grant of £1 million to help them through their immediate difficulties, but the Treasury reduced this figure to £500,000, and made it conditional on the hospitals' ability to raise a similar figure through their own efforts.[32] However, despite this setback, the voluntary hospitals were able to restore their financial position with considerable success. In 1924, the Onslow Commission, which had been set up to administer the government grant, concluded that 'there is substantial ground for hope that the voluntary hospitals will, for the most part, be able to balance their budgets. They are actively exploring the possibilities of securing additional income and in general the deficits appear to be decreasing. In some instances the recovery has been astonishingly rapid, and the situation as a whole is decidedly more hopeful than we had any reason to anticipate when we began our work. We believe that the recovery of the voluntary hospitals will continue, and that their financial position is approaching a more stable and satisfactory condition.'[33]

Although the voluntary hospitals increased in number during the interwar period, they also changed in character. During the nineteenth century, voluntary hospitals had developed as charitable institutions for the 'sick poor'; by the mid-1920s they were obtaining an increasing proportion of their income from a variety of contributory schemes and from patients' payments, and they were catering for a much broader section of the population. In 1924, the voluntary hospitals outside London derived 33.5 per cent of their ordinary income from charitable contributions, and 41.6 per cent of their ordinary income from patients' contributions and contributory schemes. In 1934, they derived 24.4 per cent of their ordinary income from charitable contributions, and 53 per cent from payments and contributory schemes. The growth in the scale of charitable income in London was greater than elsewhere, but even here it was outstripped by the increase in income from patients' contributions and contributory schemes. Cherry estimated that charity accounted for 35.6 per cent of the total income of London's voluntary hospitals between 1935 and 1939, whilst income from patients and their societies accounted for 38.2 per cent.[34]

These changes in the financing of voluntary hospitals had a profound impact on their overall role. In 1924, the British Medical Association demonstrated the extent of this change when it rejected a proposal for voluntary hospitals to give 'priority of consideration' to poor patients, and in 1937 Political and Economic Planning concluded that 'voluntary hospitals are becoming an integral part of the public services and ceasing to be merely the domain of charitably-disposed persons.'[35] During the Second World War, some observers claimed that voluntary hospitals were not merely declining to give priority of consideration to poor persons, but were even prepared to turn them away if they could not afford to pay for the treatment they needed. In 1944, Dr H. Joules, of the Central Middlesex County Hospital, accused one London voluntary hospital of refusing to treat an elderly man who had fallen unconscious in the street because he had no money on him, with the result that 'the almoner spent five hours in securing his transfer to a local authority hospital'. Partnership, concluded Dr Joules, 'can only be effected on a basis of equality, and so long as voluntary hospitals demand "power without responsibility", so long will the population fail to get the unified service which it needs and is insistently demanding.'[36]

The increasing importance of the role played by contributory schemes in the financing of voluntary hospitals also raised issues concerning their governance. Before 1914, voluntary hospitals had been run by Boards of Management comprising 'men of proved ability in the professions, industry or commerce, who give their services free to the hospital', but after 1918 these individuals were often joined by representatives of the local authorities, the British Red Cross Society, and the Contributory Schemes Associations, 'partly in recognition of their financial assistance'.[37] However, although the contributory schemes gained some say in the management of the hospitals, this did not necessarily signify a blossoming of 'grassroots associative democracy'. According to Mohan, Gorsky and Powell, representation on hospital boards of management provided workers' representatives with an opportunity to air their views, but they were frequently outvoted by the combined forces of the charitable subscribers and the medical staff.[38]

Although the interwar years saw major changes and improvements in the voluntary hospitals, they also faced a number of challenges and limitations. One of the biggest difficulties was that even though many hospitals enjoyed financial surpluses, others were in deficit, and Political and Economic Planning believed that the constant need to raise money meant that they were often forced to gloss over any deficiencies in order to protect their capacity for fund-raising.[39] The problem of insufficient revenue also had an effect on the location of the hospitals. Abel-Smith famously alleged that 'the pattern of provision depended on the donations of the living and the legacies of the dead', and Powell has shown that the distribution of both hospitals and staff was inversely related to measures of medical need.[40] However, some of the most serious difficulties facing the voluntary hospitals concerned the problem of coordination. Political and Economic Planning showed that a number of efforts had been made to secure greater cooperation not only between the voluntary hospitals themselves, but also between the voluntary hospitals and the public hospitals, but it nevertheless concluded that 'pressure is still rightly being exerted for tightening the bonds which knit together the hospital system of the country.'[41] In order to achieve this, it advocated the creation of regional hospital boards, comprising representatives of the voluntary hospitals, the elected local authorities and, most importantly in its view, the medical profession.[42]

Although the voluntary sector was responsible for most of the net gain in hospital accommodation during the interwar period, there were also important changes not only in the organisation of the public sector, but also in the quality of the services it provided. In 1921, the largest single category of hospitals comprised the unclassified institutions and institutions for the chronic sick which were provided by the Poor Law, but by the end of the period many of these institutions had been transferred to (or appropriated by) the Public Health Committees of the local authorities, and a growing number of public hospitals had been converted to more specialist use. One of the consequences of these changes was that a growing number of local-authority hospitals began to look more like acute voluntary hospitals. Although there was only a very slight increase in the total number of local-authority hospital beds between 1931 and 1938, the total number of admissions increased by 37 per cent, the number of operations by 74 per cent, and the number of out-patient attendances by 192 per cent.[43]

Some of the most important changes in public hospital provision had their origins in developments which occurred before the end of the First World War. During the last 30 years of the nineteenth century, many local authorities had begun the process of developing specialist institutions for the isolation and treatment of patients with infectious diseases, and this trend was reinforced by the National Insurance Act of 1911, which gave insured workers to right to free accommodation in a tuberculosis sanatorium, and led to a further increase in the number of specialist beds after 1918.[44] The Maternity and Child Welfare Act of 1918 also prompted a sharp increase in specialist municipal provision. During the interwar period as a whole, the medical profession became increasingly committed to the promotion of hospital-based births, and this was reflected in the increasing number of women who gave birth under institutional conditions. In 1927, it was estimated that approximately 15 per cent of all live births occurred in hospitals and other institutions; this figure rose to 24 per cent in 1932 and 35 per cent in 1937, and in 1946, 54 per cent of all births occurred in an institutional setting.[45]

The war also had a significant impact on Poor Law hospital provision. As Abel-Smith observed, 'facilities thought adequate for the sick poor had been found to be unsatisfactory for the use of wounded servicemen' and 'the authorities which had "lent" institutions to the armed forces found that ... improvements had been made [to them].' During the 1920s, many Boards of Guardians built on these improvements and tried to develop their facilities further, with the result that more and more patients were being treated in Poor Law institutions, and a growing number were even willing to pay for the privilege. However, these improvements were not universal. In 1925, the Chief Medical Officer of the Ministry of Health noted that 533 of the 699 Poor Law infirmaries in rural areas contained less than 100 beds, and that many of the Medical Officers in the smaller institutions failed to keep clinical records. In 1928, the Ministry complained that there were still 35,684 sick inmates in general mixed workhouses, and that the Poor Law authorities in East Anglia were using buildings which had been constructed before 1834. In 1927, there were still 25 institutions in the West of England with no fully trained nurse in charge of the sick, and ten institutions in which 'there is usually no nurse or attendant on night duty in the sick wards'.[46]

During the 1920s, pressure mounted for more fundamental changes in the organisation of Poor Law hospital services. On the one hand, it was increasingly apparent that the situation in the worst hospitals and institutions was no longer acceptable, and that they were failing to meet the legitimate needs of the populations they served. On the other hand, the development of the better hospitals was being hampered by the stigma of the Poor Law, which meant that prospective patients were failing to make the best use of available hospital facilities. As a result, there was widespread support for the changes introduced by the 1929 Local Government Act, which transferred the responsibilities of the Boards of Guardians to county and county borough councils, and gave them the opportunity to transfer control of Poor Law hospitals from their Public Assistance Committees to their Public Health Committees. However, many local authorities were slow to take advantage of this opportunity. By 1 April 1934, only one county council outside London had transferred its Poor Law hospitals to public health control, and only ten county councils (including London) had transferred their Poor Law hospitals by 31 March 1937.[47]

In a recent article, Powell criticised what he regarded as the 'pessimistic' account of local-authority hospital provision during the interwar period.

He pointed out that local authority expenditure on hospital provision grew substantially between 1932 and 1938, and he questioned the assumption that the appropriation of local-authority hospitals by Public Health Committees was in itself a measure of municipal commitment. He argued that it was not the case that 'appropriation ... necessarily cause[d] better hospitals; rather better hospitals caused appropriation, since they were chosen for transfer'. Nevertheless, even though only a minority of local authorities chose to transfer their hospitals to public health control before 1938, these were the authorities with responsibility for the largest numbers of beds. Consequently, more than 50 per cent of the total number of local-authority beds in England and Wales were under public health control on the eve of the Second World War.[48]

However, even though the 1930s did see significant progress in the development of local-authority hospital services, the extent of these improvements should not be exaggerated. As Abel-Smith showed, even though there were some areas in which the best municipal hospitals were probably better than the surrounding voluntary hospitals, there were also other parts of the country where progress was much slower, and whilst the location of these areas was sometimes determined by economic and social disadvantage, it could also be influenced by the vagaries of different local authorities.[49] In 1944, the Labour MP, Fred Messer, commented that 'in some parts of the country, you will find municipal hospitals of as high a standard as can be found. But in other parts of the country, public hospitals are the last word in a despairing effort to dodge one's obligations.'[50] This was one of the main reasons for the government's decision to take hospital services out of the hands of local authorities after 1945.[51]

The interwar years also saw a number of significant changes in attitudes to the treatment of mental illness. Under the Lunacy Act of 1890, mental illness was regarded primarily as a threat to the community, and individuals could be detained if they were seen to be a threat either to themselves or to society at large. During the interwar years, this attitude began to give way to a different view, which emphasised the close interrelationships between physical and mental illness, and promoted the development of psychiatric out-patient clinics in general hospitals. This period also witnessed the development of a more optimistic and liberal approach to the welfare of those individuals who continued to be confined within asylums or, as they came to be known, mental hospitals. During the 1930s, the Board of Control, which had overall responsibility for the supervision of psychiatric institutions, encouraged these hospitals to provide a better and more varied diet for hospital inmates, together with a wider range of recreational facilities.[52]

These changes were also reflected in attitudes to the treatment of what continued to be known as 'mental deficiency'. The 'problem of mental deficiency' had first been recognised in legal terms by the Mental Deficiency Act of 1913, and the number of individuals who were identified as 'mentally defective' rose substantially between 1913 and 1939. Both the 1913 Act and its successor, the Mental Deficiency Act of 1927, have been seen as promoting institutional approaches to the treatment of mental deficiency but, as we can see from Table 15.4, there was also a substantial increase in the number of people identified

Table 15.4   Total numbers of people provided for under the Mental Deficiency Acts, 1926 and 1939

Category	1 January 1926	1 January 1939
In institutions	20,297	46,054
Under guardianship	785	–
Under statutory supervision	15,733	43,850
Total	36,815	89,904

Source: J. Walmsley, D. Atkinson and S. Rolph, 'Community care and mental deficiency 1913 to 1945', in P. Bartlett and D. Wright (eds), *Outside the walls of the asylum: the history of care in the community 1750–2000*, London: Athlone Press, 1999, pp. 181–203, at p. 186. The summary figure of 36,185 which is quoted by Walmsley, Atkinson and Rolph for 1926 is presumably a misprint.

as 'mentally defective' who were placed under statutory provision in the community.[53] This development has led the historian of 'mental deficiency', Mathew Thomson, to argue that the origins of the present-day policy of 'community care' need to be traced at least as far back as the 1930s, if not beyond.[54]

15.4   Municipal health services

Local authorities were also responsible for a wide range of other health services, including the new 'personal health services' which had developed since the middle years of the nineteenth century. These included the tuberculosis service, which had expanded rapidly following the introduction of the national health insurance scheme, the venereal-disease service, which had been brought into existence by the Venereal Diseases Act of 1917, the maternity and child welfare service and the school medical service.

In many ways, the most important of all the new services was the maternity and child welfare service. The development of infant welfare services had been pioneered by voluntary agencies, with some assistance from local authorities, before the First World War, and central government only began to make a financial contribution to their development just before the outbreak of hostilities. However, after 1914, the scope of infant welfare was expanded to include the welfare of both expectant and nursing mothers and children over the age of one, and the state began to play an increasingly important part in the provision of health services to both mothers and young children.[55] In 1915 the government gave local authorities in Scotland and Ireland the power to 'make such arrangements as they think fit, and as may be sanctioned by the [appropriate] Local Government Board … for attending to the health of expectant … and nursing mothers, and of children under five years of age', and this power was extended to local authorities in England and Wales when the Maternity and Child Welfare Act was passed in August 1918.[56] Section 1 of the new Act gave local authorities the power 'to make such arrangements as they may see fit, and as may be sanctioned by the Local Government Board, for attending to the health of expectant … and nursing mothers, and of children who have not attained the age of five years and are not being educated in schools recognised by the Board of Education', provided that 'nothing in this Act shall authorise the establishment by any local authority of a general domiciliary service by medical practitioners'. Section 2 compelled local authorities to appoint a Maternity and Child Welfare Committee, containing at least two female members, if they wished to exercise these powers.[57]

Although there was a small decline in the extent of the services provided by both local authorities and voluntary agencies during the early part of the 1920s, the interwar period as a whole witnessed an impressive expansion in the scale of maternity and child welfare provision. Between 1918 and 1938, the total number of health visitors in England increased by 72 per cent, and the number of infant welfare centres increased by 131 per cent. The number of antenatal clinics increased by nearly 200 per cent between 1923 and 1938 (see Table 15.5). These figures were reflected in the increase in the amount of work carried out by Maternity and Child Welfare Officers, and the number of people who were able to take advantage of the services they provided. Between 1931 and 1938, the number of visits paid by health visitors to expectant mothers and children between the ages of zero and five rose from more than 7.7 million to nearly 8.2 million, the number of visits by children under the age of five to infant welfare centres increased from 6.7 million to just under 9.9 million, and the number of women attending antenatal clinics rose from just under 200,000 (33.89 per cent of total notified births) to 366,000 (66.2 per cent of total notified births). There was also a small increase in the number of women attending postnatal clinics: this figure rose from 103,000 in 1936 to 140,000 two years later (Table 15.6).

However, there were also substantial disparities in the level and quality of the services provided by different local authorities. During the nineteenth century, local authorities had been largely dependent on the income they could raise from local rates, and this continued to be the case during the early part of the twentieth century. In 1929, the government attempted to transfer more of the responsibility to central government by introducing a system of block grants, but these had little real effect on the balance between central- and local-government expenditure, and, in any case, the formula used to calculate the block grant tended to work against, rather than for, the interests of the poorer local authorities.[58] One of the main consequences was that the services provided by local government, such as the maternity and child welfare service, tended to be least well developed in the areas of greatest need. As Webster observed in 1985, 'distressed areas often developed efficient basic midwifery services, and the occasionally rose to providing certain of the new benefits, but their economic problems and generally low level of expectation inhibited the development of services of the type evolved in more prosperous regions.'[59]

The differences in the quality of the services provided by different local authorities also reflected the impact of political and ideological factors, as well as geographical ones. Marks found that the most important single factor to influence the level of maternity provision in four London boroughs was the political complexion of the local authority, whilst Webster found that attitudes to the provision of nutritional supplements often owed at least as much to the ideological preferences of the Medical Officer of Health as they did to any financial

Table 15.5 Maternity and child welfare services in England, 1918–38

Year	Health visitors (individual officers)			Health visitors (whole-time equivalents)			Infant welfare centres			Antenatal clinics			Postnatal clinics		
	Maintained by local authorities	Maintained by voluntary organisations	Total	Maintained by local authorities	Maintained by voluntary organisations	Total	Maintained by local authorities	Maintained by voluntary organisations	Total	Maintained by local authorities	Maintained by voluntary organisations	Total	Maintained by local authorities	Maintained by voluntary organisations	Total
1918[a]	1,724	1,453	3,177	–	–	1,513	793	619	1,412	–	–	–	–	–	–
1919[b]	1,879	1,480	3,359	–	–	1,607	1,061	693	1,754	–	–	–	–	–	–
1920[b]	2,278	937	3,215	–	–	1,617	1,224	736	1,960	–	–	–	–	–	–
1921[b]	2,328	1,050	3,378	–	–	1,660	1,178	691	1,869	–	–	–	–	–	–
1922[b]	2,017	1,491	3,508	–	–	1,684	1,248	698	1,946	–	–	–	–	–	–
1923[b]	2,017	1,618	3,635	–	–	1689	1,268	707	1,975	346	218	564	–	–	–
1924[b]	2,083	1,643	3,726	–	–	1,738	1,363	759	2,122	390	251	641	–	–	–
1925[b]	2,181	1,697	3,878	–	–	1,800	1,422	773	2,195	418	257	675	–	–	–
1926[b]	2,230	1,733	3,963	–	–	1,836	1,489	835	2,324	474	298	772	–	–	–
1927[b]	2,280	1,761	4,041	–	–	1,869	1,561	870	2,431	520	327	847	–	–	–
1928[b]	2,315	1,816	4,131	–	–	1,897	1,623	899	2,522	521	301	822	–	–	–
1929[b]	2,616	2,279	4,895	–	–	1,920	1,718	902	2,620	658	357	1,015	–	–	–
1930[b]	2,606	2,233	4,839	1,810	521	2,331	1,839	823	2,662	860	189	1,049	–	–	–
1931[c]	2,680	2,267	4,947	1,872	527	2,399	1,914	837	2,751	995	198	1,193	–	–	–
1932[c]	2,708	2,327	5,035	1,900	470	2,370	2,034	749	2,783	1,060	217	1,277	–	–	–
1933[c]	2,737	2,276	5,013	1,911	498	2,409	2,055	765	2,820	1,090	250	1,340	–	–	–
1934[c]	2,809	2,289	5,098	1,935	478	2,413	2,091	793	2,884	1,130	266	1,396	–	–	–
1935[c]	2,901	2,294	5,195	2,020	479	2,499	2,185	808	2,993	1,207	284	1,491	–	–	–
1936[c]	3,115	2,165	5,280	2,088	476	2,564	2,238	813	3,051	1,279	289	1,568	498	91	589
1937[c]	3,320	2,030	5,350	2,267	454	2,721	2,318	827	3,145	1,307	285	1,592	517	90	607
1938[c]	3,451	2,022	5,473	2,452	425	2,877	2,433	828	3,261	1,389	287	1,676	590	100	690

Notes: [a] Figures for infant welfare centres are for the year ending 31 March 1919; figures for health visitors are for the year ending 30 June 1919. [b] Figures for the years 1919–30 are for the years ending 31 March 1920–31. [c] Figures for the years 1931–8 are for the years ending 31 December 1931–8.

Sources: 1918: Annual Report of the Local Government Board for 1918–19; 1919–30: Health visitors: Annual Reports of the Ministry of Health, 1919/20–1930/1; Infant welfare centres and antenatal clinics: Annual Reports of the Ministry of Health (*On the state of the public health*), 1919/20–1930/1; 1931–8: Annual Reports of the Ministry of Health, 1931/2–1938/9.

Table 15.6 Use of maternity and child welfare services in England, 1931–8

Item	1931	1932	1933	1934	1935	1936	1937	1938
Total number of notified live and still births	582,055	571,012	543,623	559,918	563,981	577,394	591,079	602,866
Health visitors employed by local authorities	2,680	2,708	2,737	2,809	2,901	3,115	3,320	3,451
Health visitors employed by voluntary organisations	2,267	2,327	2,276	2,289	2,294	2,165	2,030	2,022
Total officers engaged in health visiting	4,947	5,035	5,013	5,098	5,195	5,280	5,350	5,473
Officers employed by local authorities (WTEs)	1,872	1,900	1,911	1,935	2,020	2,088	2,267	2,452
Officers employed by voluntary organisations (WTEs)	527	470	498	478	479	476	454	425
Total officers engaged in health visiting (WTEs)	2,399	2,370	2,409	2,413	2,499	2,564	2,721	2,877
First visits by health visitors to expectant mothers	159,621	164,145	167,949	172,112	180,815	179,713	203,379	189,916
Total visits by health visitors to expectant mothers	430,538	450,179	470,694	483,565	518,565	543,285	583,552	540,501
First visits by health visitors to children <1 year of age	583,100	566,438	531,985	542,514	546,500	551,463	558,425	567,411
Total visits by health visitors to children <1 year of age	3,073,067	3,161,344	3,097,044	3,044,096	3,075,286	3,033,104	3,088,851	3,095,592
Total visits by health visitors to children aged 1–5 years	3,814,437	4,088,100	4,169,414	4,200,438	4,141,477	4,367,418	4,434,984	4,536,368
Infant welfare centres maintained by local authorities	1,914	2,034	2,055	2,091	2,185	2,238	2,318	2,433
Infant welfare centres maintained by voluntary organisations	837	749	765	793	808	813	827	828
Total number of infant welfare centres	2,751	2,783	2,820	2,884	2,993	3,051	3,145	3,261
Number of children <1 year of age attending for first time	314,220	318,166	305,465	312,004	325,699	336,824	357,121	385,129
Number of children <1 year attending for first time as % of notified live births	56.00	57.80	58.30	57.80	59.90	60.50	62.60	66.20
Total number of attendances of children <5 years	6,745,282	7,223,254	7,476,231	7,561,687	8,123,146	8,333,356	8,904,030	9,874,558
Antenatal clinics provided by local authorities	995	1,060	1,090	1,130	1,207	1,279	1,307	1,389
Antenatal clinics provided by voluntary organisations	198	217	250	266	284	289	285	287
Total number of antenatal clinics	1,193	1,277	1,340	1,396	1,491	1,568	1,592	1,676
Total number of women attending clinics	197,269	222,077	229,549	241,144	273,423	282,035	320,319	365,520
Number of women attending clinics as % of all notified births	33.89	38.89	42.23	43.07	48.48	48.85	54.19	60.63
Total number of attendances	704,722	793,815	842,503	931,978	1,092,400	1,238,967	1,408,315	1,510,445
Postnatal clinics provided by local authorities	–	–	–	–	–	498	517	590
Postnatal clinics provided by voluntary organisations	–	–	–	–	–	91	90	100
Total number of postnatal clinics	–	–	–	–	–	589	607	690
Total number of women attending clinics	–	–	–	–	–	53,337	60,537	71,120
Number of women attending clinics as % of all notified births	–	–	–	–	–	9.24	10.24	11.80
Total number of attendances	–	–	–	–	–	102,532	118,517	139,978

Sources: Annual Reports of the Ministry of Health, 1931/2–1938/9.

difficulties.[60] There were also substantial variations in the cost of providing maternity and child welfare services in different areas. Peretz showed that the London borough of Tottenham was able to provide a high-quality maternity and child welfare service at an annual cost of approximately £6,000, whilst the rural county of Oxfordshire was only able to provide a much more rudimentary service despite accumulating more than twice the level of expenditure. One of the main reasons for this disparity was the high cost of transport and communication in rural areas. In 1936, the County Medical Officer for Oxfordshire estimated that he devoted nearly 25 per cent of his total budget to cars and telephones.[61]

Although geographical factors probably accounted for a large part of the variation in the quality of maternity and child welfare provision, they were not the only source of difficulty. Political and Economic Planning complained that expectant mothers were often reluctant to take full advantage of the services provided by the maternity and child welfare service, that many of the doctors who practised in maternity and child welfare centres were out-of-touch, that the centres themselves were often overcrowded, and that many of the consultations provided by Maternity and Child Welfare Officers were only perfunctory.[62] Lewis argued that the effectiveness of maternity and child welfare centres was often undermined by the staff's reluctance to acknowledge the role played by social and economic factors in the causation of ill-health, and by their inability to provide a comprehensive range of medical treatments.[63] One of the greatest difficulties facing the maternity and child welfare service was the failure to address the needs of the preschool child. As McCleary observed, 'it is generally admitted that much remains to be done for health of [the preschool child] ... As an infant he came under the care of the maternity and child welfare service; after his fifth birthday he will come under the care of the school medical service. Between the two there is a gap ... How to bridge the gap effectively is one of the most urgent problems of the maternity and child welfare movement.'[64]

Although the maternity and child welfare service was formally responsible for children who were below the age of five and not attending a public elementary school, this responsibility passed to the school medical service once these children entered the state education system. The Education (Administrative Provisions) Act of 1907 placed the school medical service in the hands of the Board of Education and the local education authorities, but the Board attached great importance to the coordination of school medical work with other branches of the public health service, and it urged all local education authorities to appoint the local Medical Officer of Health as their School Medical Officer. When the school medical service was first set up, a minority of local education authorities ignored the Board's advice and appointed their own independent School Medical Officers, but the vast majority of these authorities had appointed the local Medical Officer of Health as their School Medical Officer by the end of the 1930s. The Board argued that the separation of school medical work from other branches of the public health service led to unnecessary duplication and waste of resources, but some School Medical Officers felt that the subordination of school medical work to public health work meant that it failed to get the attention it deserved.[65]

Despite these difficulties, the school medical service grew rapidly during the interwar period. When the service was first established, local education authorities were instructed 'to provide for the medical inspection of children immediately before or at the time of or as soon as possible after their admission to a public elementary school, and on such other occasions as the Board of Education direct', but during the interwar period School Medical Officers also conducted a growing number of 'special inspections' outside the normal 'routine' examination periods. There was also a large increase in the amount of treatment offered by local education authorities. Table 15.7 shows that by the end of the 1930s, virtually every local education authority was making arrangements for the treatment of minor ailments, dental and visual conditions, and most authorities also made provision for the treatment of enlarged tonsils and adenoids, ringworm and orthopaedic conditions. There were also 118 local education authorities which made arrangements for the provision of artificial light treatment, which was used to treat a wide range of conditions, including rickets, lupus and various forms of non-pulmonary tuberculosis.[66]

These figures represented an important extension of public welfare provision, but the school medical service, like the maternity and child welfare service, was not without its critics. Throughout the interwar period, a number of School Medical Officers complained that they were required to devote far too much time to the routine examination of healthy children when they could have been devoting more time to the examination and treatment of unhealthy children, and many critics argued that the statistics generated by routine examinations were of little real value because the officers who carried out the examinations worked to different clinical standards. The school medical service also suffered from a similar range of problems to the maternity and child welfare service, because it was prevented from offering a full range of medical treatment services by the opposition of general practitioners, and because there were wide variations in the standard of provision offered by different areas. During the interwar period, the Board of Education's own inspectors showed that the school medical service was often much more fully developed in urban rather than rural areas, and that a great deal could depend on the drive and commitment of individual School Medical Officers and the support they received from their local education authorities. However, the greatest impediments to the development of an effective school medical service were often financial. In 1936, one of the Board's own officials, Cecil Maudslay, reported that 'in the Special Areas, where the health and nutrition of the children ... [are] on the whole below the average of the rest of the country, liberal expenditure on the special services is particularly desirable, but speaking generally the expenditure of the Special Areas on these services falls below that of the rest of the country.'[67]

In 1986, Jane Lewis criticised the interwar public health service for allowing itself to be seduced by the attractions of curative medicine into neglecting its original commitment to preventive medicine and environmental services, but this judgement is perhaps a little harsh.[68] Even before the First World War, Medical Officers of Health had argued that the school medical and maternity and child welfare services represented a logical extension of traditional public health work, because they brought the public health service into closer contact with the individual causes of disease and facilitated the implementation of remedial action which might prevent existing conditions from getting worse in the

Table 15.7 The development of medical treatment services by local education authorities, 1918–38

Year	Number of local education authorities	Number of local education authorities providing treatment							
		Minor ailments	Dental treatment	Defective vision	Supply of spectacles	Adenoids and tonsils	Ringworm (X-rays)	Orthopaedic treatment	Artificial light
1918	318	260	169	242	235	129	92	–	–
1919	318	274	203	264	264	151	101	–	–
1920	316	289	235	280	282	198	129	–	–
1921	317	298	240	290	289	221	141	–	–
1922	317	303	244	293	294	228	145	–	–
1923	317	308	250	303	301	234	153	–	–
1924	317	310	269	309	308	242	161	–	–
1925	317	311	289	313	310	253	167	85	5
1926	317	310	294	315	310	258	170	132	18
1927	317	310	299	315	310	265	171	160	44
1928	317	310	304	315	310	267	176	183	64
1929	317	311	307	316	311	271	182	200	78
1930	317	313	310	316	313	273	188	216	84
1931	317	314	311	316	313	281	188	222	89
1932	316	313	312	315	312	281	193	228	93
1933	316	312	312	315	312	287	196	233	96
1934	316	312	314	315	313	287	198	238	98
1935	316	312	314	315	313	287	203	245	105
1936	316	312	314	315	313	292	204	254	111
1937	315	311	314	314	312	291	206	262	116
1938	315	312	314	314	312	292	200	270	118

Source: B. Harris, The health of the schoolchild: a history of the school medical service in England and Wales, Buckingham: Open University Press, pp. 76, 109.

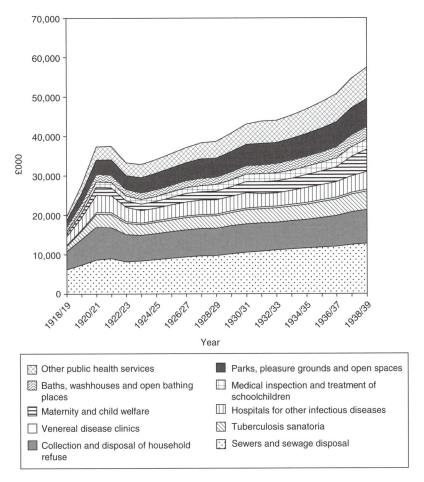

Sources: Medical inspection and treatment of schoolchildren: B. Harris, *The health of the schoolchild: a history of the school medical service in England and Wales*, Buckingham: Open University Press, 1995, pp. 73, 93; All other services: PP 1928 Cmd. 3084 xxiv, 1, *Statistical abstract for the United Kingdom for each of the fifteen years from 1912 to 1926 (71st number)*, pp. 170–1 (1918/19–1924/5); PP 1939–40 Cmd. 6232 x, 367, *Statistical abstract from the United Kingdom for each of the fifteen years 1924–38 (83rd number)*, pp. 236–7 (1925/6–1936/7); Central Statistical Office, *Annual abstract of statistics, Number 84: 1935–46*, London: HMSO, 1948, p. 224 (1937/8–1938/9).

Figure 15.2   Local authority expenditure on public health services, 1918/19–1938/9

future.[69] It is also important to recognise that even though public health departments took on a range of new curative functions during the interwar period (including the administration of municipal general hospitals after 1929), they continued to devote a large proportion of their time and resources to traditional public health activities, including the disposal of sewage, the collection and disposal of household refuse, the provision of baths and washhouses, and the expansion of recreational facilities in the form of parks, pleasure-grounds and open spaces. Whilst these activities may not have represented the most dramatic manifestations of public health activity, they continued to play an important part in the activities of local authority public health departments throughout the interwar years (Figure 15.2).

15.5 Conclusions

In recent years, there has sometimes been a tendency to present a particularly bleak picture of interwar health-service provision, if only to emphasise the importance of the reforms which were introduced after 1945.[70] However, as this chapter has shown, the interwar period did see a number of important advances in health-service provision. There was an increase in the take-up of general medical care, and the number of people covered by the national health-insurance scheme increased by nearly 40 per cent between 1922 and 1938.[71] There were also significant improvements in the quality of hospital provision, and a rapid expansion in the scale and extent of the personal health services administered by the local-authority public health and education departments. These developments all played a part in the ongoing improvement in the general standard of health among the population at large.

However, it would be wrong to deny the obvious limitations of interwar health care. The most fundamental weakness was probably the failure to provide general domiciliary medical care to the dependants of insured workers, and the failure to guarantee the provision of more than a limited range of medical benefits to the workers themselves. These deficiencies were compounded by the division between the voluntary and public hospital sectors, and by the failure to expand the public hospital provision during the interwar years. There were also serious deficiencies in the municipal health services. These had appeared to represent one of the more dynamic aspects of health-service provision at the end of the First World War, but their development was hampered by financial difficulties and a failure of political and ideological will. Consequently, despite the real improvements in health-service provision during the interwar years, there was still considerable scope for further improvement on the eve of the Second World War.

Housing policy between the wars

In 1914, less than one per cent of British households lived in local-authority-owned accommodation, and it is likely that less than 15 per cent owned their own homes. Between 85 and 90 per cent of households are generally assumed to have rented their accommodation from private landlords. By the end of the interwar period, ten per cent of households lived in local-authority accommodation, and between 27 and 35 per cent owned the properties in which they lived. This chapter examines the background to these changes, and assesses their impact on the overall quality of housing provision.

The chapter begins by considering the history of rent controls between 1915 and 1939. It then goes on to look at the development of state-subsidised housing in the 1920s and the beginnings of a more concerted attack on the problems of slum accommodation and overcrowding in the 1930s. The final section will look at the rise of owner-occupation and the expansion of the suburbs.

16.1 The evolution of state rent control

As we have already seen, rent controls were introduced in December 1915, in response to the Glasgow rent strikes which had broken out earlier in the year.[1] The Increase of Rent and Mortgage Interest (War Restrictions) Act (5 & 6 Geo. V C. 97) prevented mortgage-holders from calling in mortgages or raising interest rates, and established maximum rents, based on the rents charged on 3 August 1914, for houses whose rateable value did not exceed £35 in London, £30 in Scotland, and £26 elsewhere. The Act was originally supposed to remain in force 'during the continuance of the present war and for a period of six months thereafter', but the government was forced to extend it in 1919 and 1920. The 1919 Act (9 Geo. V C. 7) permitted mortgage-holders to raise interest rates by 0.5 percentage points, up to a maximum of five per cent per annum, and allowed landlords to raise rents to a level equivalent to 35 per cent above prewar rates on properties whose rateable value did not exceed £70 in London, £60 in Scotland, and £52 elsewhere. The 1920 Act (10 & 11 Geo. V C. 17) permitted mortgage-holders to raise interest rates by one percentage point up to a maximum of 6.5 per cent per annum, and allowed landlords to raise rents to a level equivalent to 40 per cent above the prewar rate on houses with rateable values of less than £105 in London, £90 in Scotland, and £78 elsewhere.[2]

As Daunton has observed, the existence of rent controls presented the immediate postwar government with an apparently intractable dilemma. Although the controls had been introduced in response to a specific wartime emergency, the underlying cause was the inability of the private sector to supply adequate housing at rents which the majority of working-class tenants could afford. This meant that if controls were lifted at the end of the war, rents would automatically rise, but the government's advisers believed that if rents remained fixed, private landlords would have little incentive to add to the existing housing stock. 'Rent controls', in Daunton's words, 'were necessary because the shortage of houses permitted the imposition of scarcity rents; but the existence of rent controls hindered the provision of new houses to end the shortage. "You will not get the houses until the Act is removed, and, therefore, unless the Act is removed, the necessity for the Act remains".'[3]

As we have already seen, the government responded to the problem of housing shortages by offering subsidies to local authorities and private builders to enable them to build good-quality homes at affordable rents, but the Addison Acts were suspended in January 1921, and less than half the projected number of houses were actually built. This meant that the government was forced to retain a modified form of rent control after the 1920 Act had expired. In 1923, the Conservative government introduced 'a cautious element of deregulation' by transferring the controlled rent from the house to the tenancy, with the result that landlords were able to raise rents whenever a change of tenancy occurred, but only six per cent of houses had been decontrolled by the end of 1928, and only 11 per cent of houses had been decontrolled by the middle of 1930.[4] One of the main difficulties caused by this measure was that it tended to encourage tenants to remain in their existing accommodation even when this was no longer suited to their needs, since they were either unable or unwilling to incur the extra costs which a change of tenancy would entail.[5]

At various times during the interwar period, contemporary observers complained that the introduction of rent controls meant that there was no longer any incentive for potential investors to build new houses for rent to working-class tenants, but other commentators have disagreed. Bowley highlighted the fact that rent controls did not apply to properties constructed after 1919, and this point has been echoed by Holmans and Power.[6] Pooley has also suggested that the importance of rent controls should not be overestimated 'as rents could be decontrolled when a property was vacated' under the legislation of 1923.[7] However, prospective landlords may still have been put off if they thought that the rents being charged for existing properties would affect the amounts which they could charge for new properties.[8] They may also have felt that once rent controls had been imposed on existing properties in 1915, they could be extended to new properties in the future, although it is difficult to know how far this actually influenced landlords' thinking.[9]

These arguments suggest that although rent controls may have had some effect on the supply of working-class housing, they were probably not the only factor. The most obvious explanation for the failure of the private investors to supply more rented accommodation for working-class tenants is that it was not sufficiently profitable for them to do so. This was partly the result of rent controls, but it also reflected the sharp increase in building costs in the immediate postwar period, the general improvement in building standards, the increasing availability of local-authority accommodation, and the growing attractiveness of alternative investment opportunities. These factors meant that even when private landlords did choose to invest in rented accommodation, they tended to focus their efforts not so much on the 'ordinary working-class tenant' as on the better-paid manual worker or clerical worker who did not want or could not get a mortgage.[10]

During the 1920s, attitudes to rent control often diverged on party grounds. The Labour party argued that access to good-quality housing was a basic human right, and that rents should therefore be fixed according to moral rather than economic or financial criteria. By contrast, the Conservatives tended to argue that rent controls were a temporary expedient, which could safely be abandoned once 'ordinary economic forces' came back into play. However, during the 1930s, Conservative opinion began to change. In 1931, the Interdepartmental Committee on the Rent Restriction Acts reported that while the private sector was beginning to respond to the demand for the construction of middle-class and upper-working-class accommodation, 'the shortage of the least-expensive houses – i.e. the real working-class houses – is still in many districts acute, and we are unable to say when it will be met.' It therefore concluded that whilst rent controls could either be abandoned, or allowed to lapse, on the more expensive properties, they would need to be retained for the less expensive properties – 'the real working-class houses' – for the foreseeable future.[11] These recommendations formed the basis, not only of the Rent and Mortgage Interest Restrictions (Amendment) Act of 1933, but also the Increase of Rent and Mortgage Interest (Restrictions) Act of 1938.[12]

Although the 1933 Act resulted in the immediate abolition of controls on more than half a million 'middle-class' properties, it also strengthened the controls on a much larger number of 'working-class' houses. In 1937, the Interdepartmental Committee showed that rent controls had been removed on approximately 543,000 'Class A' homes ('the more expensive houses'), and that they had been allowed to lapse on approximately 385,000 'Class B' homes, which had previously been defined as homes which were occupied 'at one end of the scale by the artisan and at the other end by the less well-paid members of the middle classes'.[13] However, the vast majority of those 'working-class' houses which had been subject to rent controls at the beginning of the 1930s were still subject to them in 1937, and these still represented more than 44 per cent of the total number of rented houses in the country as a whole towards the end of the interwar period (see Table 16.1).

16.2   The expansion of state-subsidised working-class housing

The principle of local-authority housing was first introduced by the Labouring Classes Lodging Houses Act of 1851, which was then incorporated into the Housing of the Working Classes Acts of 1885 and 1890. Legislation was also

Table 16.1 Rent controls in England and Wales and Scotland, 1931–7

Class	Status	England and Wales						Scotland					
		April 1931		30 September 1932		1937		April 1931		30 September 1932		1937	
		Number	%	Number	%	Number	%	Number	%	Number	%	Number	%
Class A	Controlled	530,000	44.17	500,000	39.37	0	0.00	45,000	63.38	43,000	59.89	0	0.00
	Decontrolled	320,000	26.67	350,000	27.56	850,000	68.00	21,000	29.58	23,000	32.03	66,000	90.41
	New	350,000	29.17	420,000	33.07	400,000	32.00	5,000	7.04	5,800	8.08	7,000	9.59
	Total	1,200,000	100.00	1,270,000	100.00	1,250,000	100.00	71,000	100.00	71,800	100.00	73,000	100.00
Class B	Controlled	1,350,000	60.00	1,300,000	54.51	950,000	32.20	193,000	74.23	185,000	68.39	150,000	51.19
	Decontrolled	200,000	8.89	250,000	10.48	600,000	20.34	27,000	10.38	35,000	12.94	70,000	23.89
	New	700,000	31.11	835,000	35.01	1,400,000	47.46	40,000	15.38	50,500	18.67	73,000	24.91
	Total	2,250,000	100.00	2,385,000	100.00	2,950,000	100.00	260,000	100.00	270,500	100.00	293,000	100.00
Class C	Controlled	4,375,000	78.13	4,150,000	72.81	3,600,000	57.14	612,000	77.27	583,000	72.54	490,000	59.83
	Decontrolled	625,000	11.16	850,000	14.91	1,200,000	19.05	88,000	11.11	117,000	14.56	140,000	17.09
	New	600,000	10.71	700,000	12.28	1,500,000	23.81	92,000	11.62	103,700	12.90	189,000	23.08
	Total	5,600,000	100.00	5,700,000	100.00	6,300,000	100.00	792,000	100.00	803,700	100.00	819,000	100.00
All classes	Controlled	6,255,000	69.12	5,950,000	63.60	4,550,000	43.33	850,000	75.69	811,000	70.77	640,000	54.01
	Decontrolled	1,145,000	12.65	1,450,000	15.50	2,650,000	25.24	136,000	12.11	175,000	15.27	276,000	23.29
	New	1,650,000	18.23	1,955,000	20.90	3,300,000	31.43	137,000	12.20	160,000	13.96	269,000	22.70
	Total	9,050,000	100.00	9,355,000	100.00	10,500,000	100.00	1,123,000	100.00	1,146,000	100.00	1,185,000	100.00

Sources: PP 1932–3 Cmd. 4208 xxi, 705, *Statistics of Houses: Memorandum by the Minister of Health and the Secretary of State for Scotland*, p. 4; PP 1937–8 Cmd. 5621 xv, 217, *Reports of the Interdepartmental Committee on the Rent Restrictions Acts*, pp. 13–16. The definitions of the different categories of homes were as follows: Class A: rateable value of more than £45 in the Metropolitan Police District; more than £35 in the rest of England and Wales; and more than £45 in Scotland. Class B: between £20 and £45 in the Metropolitan Police District; between £13 and £35 in the rest of England and Wales; and between £26 5s and £45 in Scotland. Class C: less than or equal to £20 in the Metropolitan Police District; less than or equal to £13 in the rest of England and Wales; less than or equal to £26 5s in Scotland.

introduced in 1900 and 1903, and local authorities received further encouragement to build their own accommodation when the Housing and Town
Planning Act was passed in 1909. However, local authorities were responsible
for less than five per cent of all the new houses built in England and Wales
between 1890 and 1914, and only 0.3 per cent of all households were living in
local authority accommodation on the eve of the First World War.[14]

The first of the two Addison Acts (the Housing and Town Planning etc. Act)
was therefore the latest in quite a long line of Acts which gave local authorities
the power to build their own homes for rent to working-class tenants, but it
extended this principle in two important ways. In the first place, it *instructed*
local authorities to carry out surveys of the housing needs of their areas, and to
draw up plans for meeting these needs; and, secondly, it enabled the Treasury to
support their efforts by providing a central government subsidy to cover any
losses in excess of the yield of a penny rate.[15] It is for these reasons that many
historians of public housing have tended to see this Act as the real starting-point
for the development of local authority housing in Great Britain.[16]

Although the Housing and Town Planning etc. Act was designed as a pragmatic response to the problem of housing need, only a small number of new
houses were built in the months immediately following its introduction, and this
prompted the government to introduce a second Act, the Housing (Additional
Powers) Act, in December 1919. This Act (9 & 10 Geo. V C. 99) gave local
authorities the power to issue 'local bonds', in order to raise money for the construction of new houses, and it also empowered them to prohibit the construction of 'luxury' buildings if these were preventing council houses from being
built. However, its most radical innovation was the decision to set aside a sum of
£15 million for the provision of grants to private builders, whether these were
individuals or organisations.[17] The Act enabled grants to be made for the construction of all houses above a certain size, regardless of whether they were to be
constructed for rent or for sale to owner-occupiers. When it first came into operation, the Ministry of Health fixed the value of the grants at £130–£160 per
house, but these figures were subsequently raised to £180–£210, for houses
which began to be constructed before 1 April 1920, and to £230–£260 for
houses whose construction began after that date. The mean value of the subsidies
paid on all the houses constructed under the second Addison Act was £242.[18]

During the last 20 years, housing historians have devoted considerable attention to the political background to the Addison housing programme. Daunton
has argued that the expansion of subsidised housing at the end of the First
World War was primarily a pragmatic response to the problems caused by the
introduction of rent controls for the operation of the private housing market,
but it is also necessary to recognise the importance of the role played by working-class organisations in highlighting the need for housing reform during the
second half of the First World War. It was partly because of this that so many
Conservative and Liberal politicians came to believe that the provision of council housing was essential if the country was to avoid the threat of revolution. As
the Leader of the Opposition, Sir Donald Maclean, observed in 1919, 'one of
the great difficulties of the future will be unrest, and one of the best ways of
mitigating it is to let people see that we are in earnest on this question.'[19]

Although there were many complaints about the number of houses constructed under the Addison Acts, few people complained about their quality. When the first Act was passed, the Ministry of Health produced specimen plans for five different types of houses, which were roughly divided into two categories, 'A' (for non-parlour houses) and 'B' (for houses with parlours). The majority of the houses which were actually constructed were either 'A3' houses (that is, three-bedroomed houses with a living-room and scullery) or 'B3' houses (three-bedroomed houses with living-room, parlour and scullery), and although the Ministry recommended that the average amount of floor-space for a typical three-bedroomed house should be 900 square feet, the 'Addison houses' tended to range in practice from 950 square feet to 1400 square feet. These standards compared extremely favourably, not only with the standard of houses being constructed for sale to middle-class owner-occupiers at the time, but also with the council houses built under the Chamberlain and Wheatley Acts during the remainder of the 1920s and the early-1930s.[20] In the 1980s, when the Thatcher government gave local-authority tenants the opportunity to buy council homes at heavily discounted rates, the houses which had been built under the Addison Acts of 1919 were 'among the most sought-after and attractive sectors of council housing'.[21]

As we have already seen, the Addison Acts were suspended at the beginning of 1921, and abandoned altogether six months later, but this did not mark the end of subsidised housing. In 1923, the Conservative Minister of Health, Neville Chamberlain, introduced an annual subsidy of £6 per house for 20 years for one-storey houses with a floor-space of between 550 and 880 square feet, or two-storey houses with a floor-space of between 620 and 950 square feet. The new Act (13 & 14 Geo. V C. 24) relieved local authorities of the obligation to contribute to the cost of new houses, but they were only allowed to construct the houses themselves if they could demonstrate that the work could not be carried out by private builders, and subsidies were limited to houses completed before 1 October 1925.[22] The new scheme was therefore deliberately designed to favour construction by private builders rather than local authorities, and it was only intended to provide a short-term boost to the housing market.

Although the Chamberlain Act did help to stimulate the construction of new houses during the 1920s, it had a relatively limited impact on the shortage of 'ordinary working-class' houses (that is, houses with a rateable value of less than £20 in London and £13 in the rest of England and Wales). Between 1923 and 1933, local authorities built 75,300 houses with the aid of Chamberlain Act subsidies, but the fixed level of subsidy and the absence of any provision to enable local authorities to subsidise rental payments out of the rates meant that the majority of the new homes were beyond the reach of most working-class tenants.[23] The Act was also used to subsidise the construction of 362,700 homes by private builders, but very few of these were intended for ordinary working-class use, and the majority were sold to owner-occupiers.[24] As Richardson and Aldcroft observed, 'the subsidy policy allowed private enterprise to build houses for a class of people least in need of accommodation and who at the same time could generally afford to pay an economic rent for their accommodation.'[25]

When the Labour party came to power in 1924, it attempted to deal with some of the limitations of the Chamberlain scheme by passing its own Act, the Housing (Financial Provisions) Act, in August of the same year. This Act (the Wheatley Act) extended the original Chamberlain subsidy to 1 October 1939, and removed the restrictions which the previous Act had placed on local-authority building by requiring them to demonstrate that it was more appropriate for them to build their own properties than to rely on the efforts of private builders. The Act also increased the value of the subsidy paid to local authorities which built their own properties from £6 per house for 20 years to £9 per house (in urban areas) and £12 10s per house (in rural areas) for 40 years, and it gave local authorities the power to provide their own subsidies, by insisting that the *average* rent charged on new properties should not exceed the rents charged for similar houses under the Rent and Mortgage Interest (Restrictions) Acts, provided that the cost to the authority was less than the equivalent of £4 10s per house over a 40-year period. In 1927, the Conservatives reduced the value of the Wheatley subsidy to £7 10s per house, and in 1929 they reduced it still further to £5 per house, but this change was reversed by the incoming Labour government later in the same year.[26] However, even though the Wheatley houses tended to attract a wider spectrum of working-class tenants than the Chamberlain houses, they still tended to be beyond the reach of the poorest tenants, and even those who were able to afford the higher rents often faced financial difficulties.[27]

During the 1930s and early-1940s, the new corporation housing estates became a major focus for social investigation. The researchers found that a relatively high proportion of the new tenants tended to be skilled manual workers with young families who enjoyed above-average wages but wished to escape from overcrowded conditions. In general, although there were a number of teething problems, the tenants seem to have welcomed the extra space which their new homes provided, and by the time of the Mass Observation report in 1943, almost half the tenants on the selected estates said that they liked their neighbourhoods, but many tenants also complained of the cost of furnishing larger houses, the additional transport costs, and the higher prices charged by local shopkeepers.[28] These factors meant that when times were hard, 'the costs of living … left practically no margin for bad times'. In 1939, Marion Fitzgerald argued that rents on the Brighton estate of North Moulsecoomb were not exorbitant, 'but with other essential outgoings leave an insufficient margin for food and clothing in the majority of families. The problem seems to be mainly one of inadequate wages to meet family needs on the modern standards of decent housing, reasonable amenities and adequate nourishment'.[29]

The Coalition government argued that the provision of additional housing would help to reduce overcrowding, and thereby remove one of the most important factors which contributed to the development of slum areas, but this did not occur for three main reasons.[30] As we have already seen, the introduction of the Rent and Mortgage Interest (Restrictions) Act of 1923, which allowed rent controls to lapse on a change of tenancy, discouraged the poorest tenants from moving, and therefore tended to trap them in old and insanitary accommodation. Second, even though local authorities and private builders constructed more than 1.6 million new homes in England and Wales between

1919 and 1931, only 36 per cent of these were intended for working-class use, and this figure had only risen to 41.9 per cent by the end of September 1934.[31] The third problem was that even though there was a substantial increase in the overall total of new homes, there was also an even more substantial increase in the number of new households, with the result that there was an even greater shortage of housing in 1930 than there had been ten years earlier.[32]

Although both Conservative and Labour governments devoted most of their efforts to the supply of additional housing during the 1920s, they did make some attempts to address the problem of the slums more directly. The Chamberlain Act gave the Minister of Health the power to contribute up to half the estimated average annual cost of any rehousing schemes which were carried out by local authorities under Section 1 of the Housing of the Working Classes Act of 1890, but the impact of this measure was very limited. During the whole of the period between 1919 and 1930, the government approved 121 slum-clearance schemes, involving the demolition of approximately 15,000 homes and the rehousing of 78,798 people, but these figures compared very unfavourably with the overall size of the slum problem as indicated by the slum-clearance schemes of the 1930s. When the Conservatives returned to power at the end of 1924, Chamberlain attempted to develop an alternative approach to the problem of the slums by promoting the idea of improvement or 'recon-ditioning', but this also had very limited impact. In 1926, Chamberlain managed to pilot through a measure which enabled private landlords to apply for government money to improve or recondition slum properties in rural areas which could then be let out for a limited period at controlled rents, but he was unable to secure support for a similar measure in urban areas.[33] Consequently, the problem of the slums remained largely unaddressed by the time Labour returned to office at the end of the 1920s.

16.3   The attack on the slums

By the end of the 1920s, it was becoming increasingly apparent that the limited attempts at slum clearance and reconditioning had failed to resolve the problem of the slums, and that more radical action was called for. This issue played a major part in the 1929 general election campaign, and it formed the background to the Housing Act which the new Labour Minister of Health, Arthur Greenwood, introduced in 1930. The Greenwood Act (20 & 21 Geo. V C. 39) was the first Housing Act to place the use of public subsidies at the heart of its strategy for dealing with the slums. It gave local authorities the power to demolish properties which were thought to be unfit for human habitation or to pose a danger to the health of the occupants or their neighbours, but the authorities were not allowed to exercise this power unless they also made arrangements to rehouse the people who were displaced. In order to assist them, the government provided an annual subsidy of £2 5s per person in urban areas, and £2 10s per person in rural areas, for a period of 40 years.[34]

Although the Greenwood Act represented a major new development in the state's approach to the problem of the slums, the subsidies were too low to make a significant difference in the short term. Bowley's calculations showed that the value of the Greenwood subsidy for a family of four was only six pence greater than the average Wheatley subsidy, and the difference between the two subsidies only rose by an extra shilling for each additional family member.[35] During the early part of the 1930s, this difference was insufficient to enable local authorities to offer satisfactory accommodation to the sorts of families who were currently living in slum properties, and they therefore chose to continue to build new houses with the aid of Wheatley subsidies rather than seeking to implement the Greenwood Act on a large scale.[36] Between 1 August 1930 and 31 December 1933, local authorities only managed to build 11,796 homes with the aid of Greenwood subsidies, and the 145 largest local authorities in England and Wales only managed to identify a total of 76,524 homes in need of demolition. By contrast, during roughly the same period (1 April 1930 to 31 March 1933), more than 160,000 new homes were built with the aid of Wheatley subsidies.[37]

When the government introduced the Act, it clearly intended that the two Acts should run alongside one another as part of a coordinated approach to the provision of subsidised housing for both general and special needs, but this policy came under increasing attack over the next three years. In November 1932, the Ray Committee on Local Expenditure argued that the government should abandon its policy of providing public subsidies for general needs housing, and that subsidies should only be used to provide housing for those who were unable to obtain adequate housing through the operation of the private market.[38] In 1933, the National Government decided to act on the basis of the Committee's recommendations by abolishing the Wheatley Act and making the Greenwood Act the cornerstone of its housing policy. This decision paved the way for a much more concerted attack on the problem of the slums, but it also marked a radical break with the council-housing policies of the 1920s and converted the role of council housing into that of a form of social service provision for those who were unable to obtain satisfactory housing by other means.[39]

Although the slum-clearance programme began very slowly, the new emphasis did see an increase in the scale of the programmes submitted by local authorities. In 1934, the Ministry of Health reported that the number of houses scheduled for demolition and replacement by the 145 largest local authorities had increased from 76,524 to 172,261, and the number of houses scheduled for replacement in the whole of England and Wales was 266,581, or just over 2.8 per cent of the entire housing stock. However, even though this figure represented a significant increase on the pre-1933 targets, it was still remarkably low, and there were some striking differences in the scale of the programmes submitted by authorities which might have been expected to be experiencing similar problems. Bowley was particularly critical of London and some of the northern conurbations. She pointed out that London only managed to develop plans for the replacement of 33,000 homes out of a total of 749,000 homes at the time of the 1931 census, whilst Manchester scheduled 'a mere 15,000' homes out of a total of 180,000, and Newcastle only managed to identify 2,253 homes out of a total of 61,000.[40]

It is also instructive to compare the number of houses scheduled for demolition and replacement in different parts of the country with those which were actually replaced. Although there was a remarkable similarity between the number of homes targeted for demolition and those actually built, these figures masked the fact that some local authorities were able to exceed their targets whilst others, including some of the country's largest cities, fell some way short of them (Table 16.2). It is therefore clear that concentration on the aggregate figures fails to give a complete picture of the overall impact of the slum clearance campaign.[41]

Although the government was particularly concerned to focus attention on the problem of the slums, it was also concerned with the question of overcrowding, and this led to the second major housing initiative of the 1930s, the Housing Act of 1935. Part I of this Act (25 & 26 Geo. V C. 40) instructed local authorities to conduct an investigation into the level of overcrowding in their areas; to identify overcrowded properties; and to submit plans for the construction of as many new houses or other dwellings as were needed to remove the housing shortage. However, although the attack on overcrowding has often been linked to the campaign for slum clearance, the Act stated that central government would only contribute to the cost of providing new homes if the local authority was building flats on land whose cost, as developed, exceeded £1500 per acre; if it was felt that the cost of building new homes would impose an undue burden on authorities which had already incurred sufficient expenditure under previous Housing Acts; or if they were situated in rural areas where new housing was needed to alleviate overcrowding among agricultural workers. It was not until 1938 that Parliament agreed to establish a uniform subsidy to deal with both slum clearance and overcrowding (1 & 2 Geo. VI C. 16).

Although the 1935 Act has often been singled out as the first measure to offer a legally-enforceable definition of overcrowding, the definition itself was

Table 16.2 Slum clearance in the 1930s: leading cities

City	Houses to be demolished		Persons to be displaced		New houses constructed	
	1930	1933	1930	1933	Houses built by 31/12/38	Houses built by 31/3/40
Birmingham	4,700	4,500	27,500	19,350	5,924	7,540
Bristol	1,500	2,900	9,000	15,212	3,400	3,654
Leeds	2,000	30,000	8,000	111,000	8,588	9,992
London (LCC)	7,779	33,000	49,528	265,000	22,676	27,965
Liverpool	2,000	11,937	11,000	59,685	6,642	7,683
Manchester	5,400	15,000	28,380	63,000	7,888	8,915
Sheffield	2,500	9,000	11,250	40,500	10,012	12,294
Total	25,879	106,337	144,658	573,747	65,130	78,043

Sources: J. L. Marshall, 'The pattern of housebuilding in the interwar period in England and Wales', *Scottish Journal of Political Economy*, 15 (1968), 184–205, at 201–2; J. Yelling, *Slums and redevelopment: policy and practice in England 1918–45, with particular reference to London*, London: UCL Press, 1992, p. 110. The figure for Liverpool in the final column shows the number of houses built before 31/12/38. Richardson and Aldcroft record the number of houses built in Liverpool before 31 December 1938 as 6,742, using figures supplied privately by Marshall prior to the publication of his article (H. Richardson and D. Aldcroft, *Building in the British economy between the wars*, London: George Allen and Unwin, 1968, p. 183).

extremely limited.[42] The Act defined overcrowding by comparing the number of persons in the house with the number of rooms, but it made no allowance for children under the age of one, and children between the ages of one and ten were only counted as halves. It then went on to state that a house should be regarded as overcrowded if the number of rooms was insufficient to enable persons of the opposite sex, who were over the age of ten and not married to each other, to sleep in separate rooms, or if there were more than two 'persons' in a one-roomed dwelling, three 'persons' in a two-roomed dwelling; five 'persons' in a three-roomed dwelling; seven-and-a-half 'persons' in a four-roomed dwelling; or ten 'persons' in a five-roomed dwelling.[43] In 1936, the Registrar-General calculated that 341,554 people were living in overcrowded accommodation according to this definition, of whom 192,797 were regarded as belonging to exceptionally large families (that is, families containing more than five 'units'), and 147,476 were living in exceptionally small accommodation (that is, dwellings containing only one or two rooms). However, he also calculated that if the definition of overcrowding was relaxed only slightly, so as to exclude living-rooms from use for sleeping purposes, then the number of people living in overcrowded conditions would rise immediately to 853,119.[44]

As these comments indicate, neither the slum-clearance campaign nor the campaign against overcrowding can be regarded as an unqualified success, but it is important to acknowledge the changes which did occur. Between 1 April 1934 and 31 March 1939, local authorities succeeded in closing and demolishing 245,272 properties and providing replacement accommodation for just over one million people under the slum-clearance schemes, and building a further 23,651 houses under the overcrowding scheme.[45] Even though these figures still left large numbers of people living in insanitary and overcrowded accommodation, they still represented the most concerted attack on the problems of slum-clearance and overcrowding since these issues were initially identified as matters for public concern during the middle decades of the nineteenth century.[46]

Although this section has been mainly concerned with the evolution of housing policy at a national level, it is important to remember that many of the changes which were introduced as a result of the different Housing Acts still had to be negotiated at local level.[47] This was particularly true of the development of rental policies. During the 1930s, several local authorities introduced differential rent schemes, whereby rebates were offered to poorer tenants to enable them to afford the cost of living in new properties. However, such policies were also highly controversial, since they necessarily involved taking money from better-off council tenants in order to subsidise the housing costs of the very poor. As a result of these conflicts, only 112 local authorities had decided to adopt any form of differential rent scheme by the end of the 1930s. The problem of adjusting council rents to the tenants' ability to pay was therefore one which remained unresolved on the eve of the Second World War.[48]

It is also important to give some consideration to the impact of the slum-clearance and overcrowding campaigns on the architecture of local authority accommodation. As Burnett has argued, although there was no formal decision to reduce the specifications of council properties after 1930, there was a clear tendency to regard former minimum standards as maxima, with the result that the houses which were built under the Greenwood Act tended not only to be smaller than the Addison houses, but also than the less highly-specified Chamberlain and Wheatley houses which followed them. Burnett goes on to suggest that where houses were built under all three schemes, 'three distinct zones of housing, representing Addison, Wheatley and slum-clearance policies, were clearly visible on the ground'.[49]

The second major architectural development of the period was the revival of flat-building. During the nineteenth century, flats, or tenements, had often been associated with some of the least desirable forms of working-class housing, and the number of flats constructed in England and Wales fell after the end of the First World War, before rising once again during the 1930s. However, it would be wrong to assume that the flats which were built during this period were either a return to the tenement blocks of the nineteenth century, or a fore-taste of the high-rise blocks of the post-Second World War era. The majority of the new flats were built in blocks of no more than five storeys, and even the exceptions, such as the much-lauded Quarry Hill estate in Leeds, were only eight storeys high. After 1945, the popular image of local-authority flats declined once more, but in many areas the flats which were built during the 1930s were seen not merely as a solution to the problems of slum-clearance, but also as a clear manifestation of social idealism and faith in the future.[50]

16.4   The growth of owner-occupation, the private building boom and town planning

The second major tenurial change of the interwar period was the growth of owner-occupation, but the precise extent of this remains unclear. It has often been argued that approximately ten per cent of all households lived in owner-occupied accommodation on the eve of the First World War, and that between 27 and 35 per cent of all households in England and Wales lived in owner-occupied accommodation on the eve of the Second World War, but the prove-nance of these figures is open to question. In the most detailed historical examination of the figures, Swenarton and Taylor concluded that 'for the ten per cent figure, it turns out, there is no adequate foundation in data. Of the two supposed bases for the figure, one refers to output, not to the housing stock, and the other depends on a good deal of guesswork, and unfortunately is mis-calculated.' They were also sceptical of the two figures provided for 1938. The lower of the two figures (27 per cent) was derived from a postwar survey of 6,000 households in Great Britain as a whole, and although the higher figure (35 per cent) was derived from a much larger sample, it was also marred by incomplete methods of data collection, and by the deliberate exclusion of a large number of homes which, by their nature, were less likely to include owner-occupied accommodation. They therefore concluded that the true figure was likely to be closer to 27 per cent than it was to 35 per cent.[51]

In view of the uncertainty surrounding the exact number of homes which were under owner-occupation during this period, it is probably not surprising that there should also be a degree of uncertainty over some of the details of this increase. In 1939, the Ministry of Health's Departmental Committee on Valuation for Rates calculated that approximately 27.1 per cent of all the pre-1914 homes which were included in its survey were owned by the people who lived in them, and on this basis a number of writers have concluded that between 1.4 and 1.9 million pre-1914 homes were under owner-occupation on the eve of the Second World War. Whilst it seems reasonable to assume that some of these properties were already under owner-occupation before 1914, it does not seem reasonable to assume that they were all under owner-occupation before 1914, and this means that a substantial number of 'old' houses must have been sold by private landlords to owner-occupiers during the interwar period. This conclusion is supported by Swenarton and Taylor's own research into the history of owner-occupation, which led them to conclude that there was 'a widespread transfer of pre-1914 properties into owner-occupation' during the 1920s'.[52]

Burnett argued that the growth of owner-occupation between the wars was directly related to the growth of the middle classes. During the period between 1911 and 1951, the number of people employed in professional occupations in the whole of Great Britain increased from 744,000 to 1,493,000; the number of managers and administrators rose from 629,000 to 1,246,000; and the numbers of foremen, supervisors and clerical workers rose from 1,068,000 to 2,931,000. Burnett argued that these 'new recruits' were 'keenly anxious to demonstrate their arrival by the adoption of a life-style which separated them from the respectable poverty from which many had risen. To live in a new suburb rather than an old overcrowded town, in a detached or semi-detached villa rather than a terraced or back-to-back house, above all, to be able to buy a house instead of merely renting it ... were the predominant ambitions.'[53]

However, it is also important to consider the political context in which these preferences were formed. Daunton has argued that during the interwar period Conservative politicians abandoned the private landlord and encouraged the growth of owner-occupation as part of a deliberate strategy to maintain political and social stability, and there is considerable evidence to support this view. During the 1920s, the Conservative party in Leeds argued that owner-occupation was 'the best and surest safeguard against the follies of socialism', and their leader, Sir Charles Wilson, told his Labour opponents that 'it is a good thing for the people to buy their houses. They turn Tory directly. We shall go on making Tories and you will be wiped out.'[54] Neville Chamberlain believed that the expansion of owner-occupation 'was a revolution which of necessity enlisted all those who were affected by it on the side of law and order and enrolled them in a great army of good citizens', and the Managing Director of the Abbey Road Society, Sir Harold Bellman, informed his readers that 'the thrifty man is seldom or never an extremist agitator.'[55] In 1935, Bellman claimed that 'home ownership ... increases personal self-respect ... encourages civic pride and adds a wholesome stability to the political institutions of the state by giving people "a stake in the country".'[56]

As we have already seen, one of the most dramatic social changes of the interwar period (or, indeed, of the first 80 years of the twentieth century) was the decline in the importance of private renting, and this affected the position of middle-class tenants just as much as it affected working-class tenants. Merrett argued that one of the main reasons for the decline of the private rented sector was the increase in the availability of cheap mortgages, which made it much more difficult for private landlords to charge rents which were both competitive and profitable. Whilst Merrett was principally concerned with the factors which prevented landlords from building new properties, it is not unreasonable to suppose that this would also have affected their willingness to sell old properties.[57]

However, whilst the increase in the supply of cheap mortgages undoubtedly contributed to the decline of private renting, government policy also discriminated against the interests of the private landlord and in favour of the owner-occupier. After 1925/6, individuals who borrowed money from building societies, for whatever purpose, were able to use the cost of their interest payments to reduce their liability to income tax, and this gave private tenants who were eligible for income tax a powerful incentive to borrow money from a building society in order to become owner-occupiers.[58] However, the importance of this change should not be exaggerated. During the interwar period, a married couple with two children only became liable to tax on the income they derived from employment if they were earning a minimum of £375 a year, and they only became liable to tax at the standard rate if their income exceeded £500 a year. In view of the fact that only around 800,000 individuals came into this category, it seems unlikely that the introduction of mortgage interest tax relief would have played a major part in the expansion of owner-occupation as a whole.[59]

Although the introduction of this particular concession was only likely to have made a small contribution to the growth of owner-occupation, it was not the only way in which the government's fiscal policies helped to tilt the balance between private landlords and owner-occupiers. During the interwar period, both landlords and owner-occupiers were liable to tax on the income they were presumed to derive from renting, but landlords were taxed on the basis of their actual rental income, whereas owner-occupiers were taxed on the basis of a hypothetical figure. Both landlords and owner-occupiers were able to reduce their liability to tax by claiming allowances for the cost of interest payments and repairs, but owner-occupiers often escaped their liability altogether, because the cost of these payments outweighed their hypothetical rent income. Private landlords only qualified for similar treatment if their outgoings exceeded their actual rent income, in which case letting was unlikely to have been an economic option anyway.[60]

The balance between owner-occupation and private renting was also affected by the government's policies on rent control. As we have already seen, rent controls were imposed on all rented properties with a rateable value of less than £30 in Scotland, £35 in London, and £26 in other parts of England and Wales in 1915, and only began to be removed slowly from 1923 onwards. In September 1932, 40.46 per cent of all Class A properties (that is, properties with a rateable value of more than £45 in London and Scotland, and £35 in the rest of England and Wales), and 56 per cent of all Class B properties (properties with a rateable value of between £20 and £45 in London, £13 and £35 in the rest of England and Wales, and £26 5s and £45 in Scotland) were still subject to rent controls, and 34 per cent of Class B properties were still subject to controls in 1937.[61] Consequently, although the main purpose of rent controls was to protect the interests of tenants in 'ordinary working-class' properties, they also affected the value of the rents which landlords could charge for upper-working-class and middle-class properties, and it does not seem unreasonable to suppose that this would also have influenced their willingness to sell unwanted properties to prospective owner-occupiers.[62]

Although the government was strongly committed to the promotion of owner-occupation for most of the interwar period, it played only a small role in promoting the construction of new homes for sale to owner-occupiers. As we have already seen, both the Housing (Additional Powers) Act and the Chamberlain Housing Act enabled private builders to construct subsidised housing for rent or for sale to owner-occupiers, and it seem likely that the majority of these houses were built for owner-occupation, even if the exact numbers remain unclear.[63] However, the Conservative government reduced the value of the Chamberlain subsidies in 1927 and they were abolished altogether in 1929, thus generating an increase in the number of homes built by private enterprise without the benefit of government subsidy.[64] The number of unsubsidised homes increased dramatically during the second quarter of the 1930s, and more than 1.9 million new homes had been added to the total housing stock by the end of the decade (see Figure 16.1).

Economic historians have explained the pattern of private housebuilding during the interwar period in a variety of ways. Most commentators would agree that one of the most important factors was the long-term decline in building costs. As we have already seen, building costs rose sharply in the immediate postwar period, and there was also a small rise between 1923 and 1925, but the

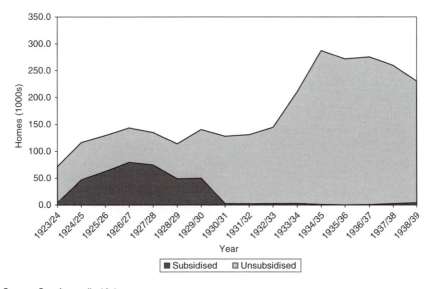

Source: See Appendix 16.1.

Figure 16.1 Construction by private housebuilders, 1923–39

overall trend was downward between 1919 and 1933. According to Richardson and Aldcroft, the combined cost of wages and materials fell by 47.6 per cent between 1920 and 1933, and Merrett has shown that the tender price of a three-bedroomed non-parlour house in the local-authority sector fell from £408 to £308 between 1924 and 1935. Both costs and prices rose during the second half of the 1930s, but house prices were still lower in 1939 than they had been ten years earlier.[65]

For many years, historians have debated the extent to which the demand for new houses was affected by changes in interest rates. During the 1920s, both Labour and Conservative governments had kept interest rates high, initially to facilitate a return to the gold standard, and then to enable the country to remain on the gold standard at the prewar rate of exchange, but the National Government abandoned the gold standard in September 1931, and interest rates began to fall from 1932 onwards.[66] Many historians have argued that the decision to abandon the gold standard and reduce interest rates – the advent of what was called 'cheap money' – was central to the expansion of the private housing market, but Humphries argues that interest-rate policy was less important because the growth of unsubsidised private building preceded the cut in interest rates, and because the building societies themselves only introduced small cuts in their mortgage rates from 1933 onwards.[67]

One of the advantages of Humphries' article is that it helps to focus attention on the role of the building societies themselves. During the First World War, the building societies had managed to negotiate favourable terms for savers in the face of changes in income-tax rates, and these enabled them to attract a growing amount of new investment during the 1920s, which could then be used to finance more flexible arrangements for borrowers, including the introduction of smaller deposit requirements and extended repayment periods. The reduction in the size of the deposits required from mortgage-borrowers was also facilitated by the development of what became known as the 'builders' pool'. Under this arrangement, the building society would advance a loan worth up to 75 per cent of the value of the house against the purchaser's personal security and the security of the house itself, together with a further advance, worth up to 20 per cent of the purchase price, against sums deposited by the builders. This was a powerful device for enabling prospective purchasers to buy their homes for a relatively small deposit, and they then repaid the remainder of the advance, including the value of the money in the builders' pool, in the usual way.[68]

Although the government played only a limited role in the private housing boom, the boom itself raised many questions about government policy, particularly in the area of town planning. During the 1930s, many observers criticised the way in which new estates developed on the outskirts of major cities, and the uniformity of the houses which were constructed within them.[69] However, despite the introduction of the Town Planning Act in 1932, most commentators have concluded that the effort to introduce new principles of town planning into the management of urban and suburban growth was largely unsuccessful. Ashworth concluded that 'by the outbreak of the Second World War, though town planning had been nominally absorbed into the wider function of town and country planning, and though new requirements and

potentialities for it were being perceived, its actual practice had changed little.'
In the end, it was not so much the construction of new housing during the
1930s as the destruction of old houses during the first half of the 1940s which
forced both the government and the local authorities to put the question of
town planning at the top of the housing agenda.[70]

16.5 Conclusions

It is important to recognise the sheer physical significance of the residential
building which took place in Britain during the interwar years. During the
period between 1 January 1919 and 31 March 1939, local authorities constructed more than 1.11 million new dwellings, and private builders constructed
at least 2.89 million, of which just over 430,000 were built with the aid of government subsidies (see Appendix 16.1). These buildings represented a massive
addition to the country's total housing stock. In 1911, there were between 7.6
and 7.7 million homes in England and Wales, and in 1939 there were approximately 11.5 million homes, at least 35 per cent of which had been constructed in
the previous 20 years.[71] The new houses were not merely a quantitative addition
to Britain's housing; they also represented a substantial qualitative improvement
for the majority of the population who lived in them. As Stevenson concluded,
these improvements meant that housing represented one of the major areas of
social advance during the interwar period.[72]

However, it was also clear that some sections of the population had derived
only minimal benefits from housing change, and that much more work needed
to be done on the eve of the Second World War. This was particularly apparent
in the areas of slum-clearance and overcrowding. As we have already seen,
interwar governments were slow to recognise the need for a direct assault on
the problem of the slums, and although the aggregate figures implied that the
efforts they did make were largely successful, these figures need to be read in
the light of the knowledge that many local authorities failed to achieve the very
modest targets which they had set for themselves (see Table 16.2). The authorities also made relatively little progress in attacking the problem of overcrowding. The government's basic definition of overcrowding was particularly
narrow, and the assistance which was provided to local authorities under the
original Overcrowding Act was remarkably ungenerous. The conditions surrounding the government's contribution were relaxed under the Overcrowding
Act of 1938, but only 23,915 houses had been built for the abatement of overcrowding by 31 March 1939, 23,651 of which were built by local authorities,
and 264 by private builders.[73]

The other major issue which concerned both contemporary writers and later
commentators was the relationship between housing policy and social segregation, although they may not always have expressed it in quite these terms.
During the interwar period, many observers were horrified by the development
of what they regarded as uniformly working-class or middle-class estates on
the outskirts of the major cities. In its account of the London County Council
housing estates at areas such as Becontree and Watling, Mass Observation

condemned the emergence of 'these huge new communities, inhabited almost entirely by working-class people', and claimed that 'the growth of these great ill-planned one-class suburbs' typified 'the abject poverty of imagination in social matters that characterised the interwar era'.[74] Mumford used much the same language when he described the new middle-class suburbs as 'a multitude of uniform, unidentifiable houses, lined up inflexibly, at uniform distances, on uniform roads, in a treeless communal waste, inhabited by people of the same class, the same income, the same age-group'.[75] These observations reveal much about the feelings and prejudices of the people who expressed them, but they also hint at a growing social divide with major implications for the postwar era.

Appendix 16.1 Number of houses built by private enterprise and local authorities in England and Wales, 11 November 1918–31 March 1939

Year ending 31 March	Local authorities (1000s)[c]							Private enterprise (1000s)[e]						Grand total (1000s)
	Housing & Town Planning etc. Act, 1919	Housing Act, 1923	Housing (Financial Provisions) Act, 1924	Housing Acts 1930, 1936, 1938 (slum clearance)	Housing Acts 1935, 1936, 1938 (over-crowding)	Housing Acts 1925, 1936, 1938 (general)	Total	Housing (Additional Powers) Act, 1919[d]	Housing Act, 1923	Housing (Financial Provisions) Act, 1924	Housing Acts 1930–8	Unsubsidised private houses	Total	
1920[a]	0.6	—	—	—	—	—	0.6	0.1	—	—	—	—	—	—
1921	15.6	—	—	—	—	—	15.6	13.0	—	—	—	53.8[f]	97.5[f]	252.0[f]
1922	80.0	—	—	—	—	—	80.8	20.3	—	—	—	—	—	—
1923	57.5	—	—	—	—	—	57.5	10.3	—	—	—	—	—	—
1924	10.5	3.8	—	—	—	—	14.3	—	4.3	—	—	67.5	71.8	86.1
1925	2.9	15.3	2.5	—	—	—	20.7	—	47.0	—	—	69.2	116.2	136.9
1926	1.1	16.2	26.9	—	—	—	44.2	—	62.4	0.4	—	66.4	129.2	173.4
1927	0.9	14.1	59.1	—	—	—	74.1	—	78.4	1.2	—	63.9	143.5	217.6
1928	0.2	13.8	90.1	—	—	—	104.1	—	73.1	1.5	—	60.3	134.9	239.0
1929	—	5.1	50.6	—	—	—	55.7	—	48.4	0.7	—	64.7	113.8	169.5
1930	—	5.6	54.6	—	—	1.6	61.8	—	49.1	1.1	—	90.1	140.3	202.1
1931	—	—	52.5	—	—	3.4	55.9	—	—	2.6	—	125.4	128.0	183.9
1932	—	—	65.2	2.4	—	2.5	70.1	—	—	2.3	—	128.4	130.7	200.8
1933	—	1.4[b]	47.1	6.0	—	1.4	55.9	—	—	2.4	0.1	142.0	144.5	200.4
1934	—	—	44.8	9.0	—	2.2	56.0	—	—	2.8	—	207.9	210.7	266.7
1935	—	—	11.1	23.4	—	5.7	40.2	—	—	0.8	0.3	286.4	287.5	327.7
1936	—	—	—	39.1	—	14.4	53.5	—	—	—	0.2	271.7	271.9	325.4
1937	—	—	—	54.7	2.0	15.1	71.8	—	—	—	0.8	274.7	275.2	347.0
1938	—	—	—	56.8	7.3	13.9	78.0	—	—	—	2.6	257.1	259.7	337.7
1939	—	—	—	74.1	14.3	12.5	100.9	—	—	—	4.2	226.4	230.6	331.5
Total	170.1	75.3	504.5	265.5	23.6	72.7	1,111.7	43.7[d]	362.7	15.8	8.2	2,455.6[g]	2,886.0	3,997.7

Notes: [a] Includes houses built 1/1/19–31/3/19. [b] Houses transferred from the Housing Act, 1924. [c] Excluding 15,365 houses built to rehouse people displaced under reconstruction and improvement schemes under the 1890 and 1925 Acts. [d] This column includes 4,500 houses which were not built under the Housing (Additional Powers) Act. [e] Excluding houses with a rateable value exceeding £78 (£105 in the Metropolitan area). [f] Includes an estimated total of 30,000 houses built by unsubsidised private enterprise between 1/1/19 and October 1922. [g] Includes 21,500 houses built by private enterprise with local authority guarantees under the Housing (Financial Provisions) Act, 1933, which are not shown separately for individual years.

Source: M. Bowley, *Housing and the state 1919–44*, London: George Allen and Unwin, 1945, p. 271.

17

Educational provision between the wars

As we have already seen, the status of education within histories of social policy has sometimes been questioned, and Marshall was compelled to omit it altogether from his major textbook on the subject.[1] Gilbert omitted it from his study of interwar social policy on the grounds that 'there is little to write about. When the political leaders of both major parties are unable to redeem a 20-year old promise to increase the school-leaving age beyond 14, a nation can hardly be said to have a deep concern with public education.'[2] However, as Simon pointed out, 'failure on the part of government to implement policies which ... had widespread support is as much a matter of history as achievement of the most forward-looking programme – and such failure shapes later developments just as surely.'[3] The aim of this chapter is to examine the reasons why interwar governments failed to introduce greater changes in public educational provision, but also to examine the extent to which significant changes were introduced, in spite of considerable difficulties.

17.1 The 1918 Education Act

The Balfour Education Act of 1902 (2 Edw. VII C. 42) abolished the school boards and transferred their powers and responsibilities to the education committees of local authorities, and it also endeavoured to introduce a more systematic division between elementary schools, which were designed for the education of the vast majority of children between the ages of five and 14, and secondary schools, which offered a more advanced form of education for a small minority of children between the ages of 11 and 18. In 1907, the Liberal government attempted to increase the proportion of working-class children taking up places in secondary schools by offering a higher grant to secondary schools which made at least 25 per cent of their places available to elementary school children free of charge, and this fuelled a growing demand for enhanced educational opportunities before the outbreak of the First World War.[4] The number of children taking up places in state secondary schools grew rapidly during the early years of the war, and in October 1916 the Workers' Educational Association called for the establishment of a range of different types of secondary school to cater for the interests of different pupils, with similar proposals being put forward by the National Union of Teachers and by the Liberal-dominated Education Reform Council.[5] However, the most radical proposals were those put forward by the Bradford Trades Council in October 1916. These included reductions in the size of classes in public elementary schools, the extension of school meals and medical services, an increase in the number of maintenance grants, and a scheme of physical education for people between the ages of 16 and 20. However, the centrepiece of the Council's proposals was the abolition of half-time education, the introduction of a 'universal, free [and] compulsory' system of secondary education, the raising of the school-leaving-age from 14 to 16, and free access to all forms of higher education, including both technical colleges and universities.[6]

Although there was widespread support for many aspects of the 'Bradford Charter', there were also disagreements. *The Times Educational Supplement* thought that the proposal to place 'all higher forms of education, technical and university, under public control' would undermine their academic independence. However, the most important disagreements concerned the arrangements for the education of older children. Although the government recognised the need for improvements in the existing system of secondary education, it believed that the majority of children should continue to attend elementary schools up to the age of 14, before moving on to attend a system of vocationally-driven, part-time compulsory continuation schools between the ages of 14 and 18.[7] By contrast, the supporters of the Bradford Charter believed that all children should progress from an elementary school to a common form of secondary school, with no differentiation of the curriculum before the age of 15.[8]

When the government introduced its initial Education Bill in August 1917, it emphasised that the measure was designed not only to address the short-term problems caused by the war, but also to establish firm foundations for the development of state education in the future. The President of the Board of Education, H. A. L. Fisher, argued that it had been framed 'to repair the intellectual wastage which had been caused by the War', and to 'provide ... enlarged and enriched opportunities of education to the children of the poor'.[9] However, the Bill also attracted considerable opposition, not only from industrialists who objected to the controls on child labour, but also from some of the smaller local authorities, which feared that they were about to surrender their powers to the county councils.[10] As a result, the government was forced to abandon its original Bill, and introduce a second Bill at the beginning of the following year.

The revised Bill abandoned the proposal to transfer the powers of the so-called 'Part III' authorities to county councils, but most of the other key proposals were retained, and these became law when the Bill was finally passed in August 1918.[11] The new Act gave local authorities the power to establish nursery schools for children under the age of five; abolished fees in public elementary schools; imposed a minimum school leaving age of 14 across the whole country; established a new framework for financing education; instructed local authorities to establish and maintain a network of continuation schools, initially for children between the ages of 14 and 16, but subsequently for children between the ages of 14 and 18; and extended the powers and duties of local education authorities to make arrangements for the medical inspection and treatment of children in both elementary and secondary schools.[12] However, despite the high hopes awakened by the Act, it failed to achieve many of its most important objectives.

The Board of Education declined to enforce the provisions relating to the provision of medical inspection and treatment in secondary schools, and the proposals to establish both nursery schools and continuation classes failed to survive the initial round of public expenditure cuts at the beginning of 1921.[13]

Although the Act failed to bring about many of the changes which Fisher had hoped for, it did have an important effect on the structure of educational finance. During the early years of the twentieth century, the government's own contribution to educational spending, in the form of educational grants, had grown much less rapidly than educational spending as a whole, and local authorities grew increasingly restive in the face of the government's perceived tendency to impose more and more obligations upon them without providing them with the means to pay for them.[14] As President of the Board of Education, Fisher was well aware of this difficulty, and in 1918 he not only removed the restrictions which had been placed upon them by Section 2 of the Balfour Education Act of 1902, but also introduced a system of 'deficiency grants', which were designed to ensure that the government's contribution to educational expenditure should be equal to not less than 50 per cent of the approved net expenditure of each local authority.[15] However, although these reforms were designed to encourage the growth of local authority spending on education, most commentators have concluded that their actual effect was rather different. Following the end of the war, the government came under growing pressure to curtail the growth of educational spending, and, as a result, expenditure on the provision of public education by both central and local government increased quite slowly during most of the interwar period (see Figure 17.1). In 1955 W. B. Rust argued that

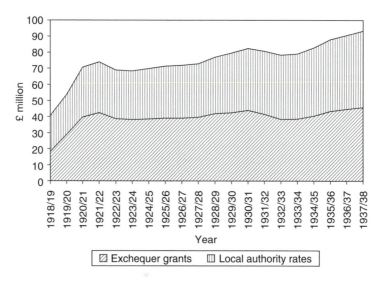

Sources: 1918/19–1922/3: PP 1927 Cmd. 2849 xxiv, 1, *Statistical abstract for the United Kingdom for each of the 15 years from 1911 to 1925 (70th number)*, pp. 44–7; 1923/4–1937/8: PP 1939–40 Cmd. 6232 x, 367, *Statistical abstract from the United Kingdom for each of the 15 years 1924–38 (83rd number)*, pp. 64–5.

Figure 17.1 Net expenditure by central government and local authorities on public education in England and Wales, 1918/19–1937/8 (at current prices)

'it was ... the Treasury which in this century came to exercise control over the whole of education operating through the estimates of the Board of Education', and D. W. Thoms concluded that 'the percentage grant, coupled with such potentially expensive innovations as compulsory continued education, helped to activate the forces which encouraged the Treasury to establish its own authority over Board of Education financial policy and, in turn, to ensure that the Board itself kept a careful watch on local education authority plans.'[16]

In his autobiography, Fisher complained about the failure, as he saw it, of the Labour party to provide appropriate support for the Education Bill as it passed through Parliament. Some Labour members were wary of the impact which the abolition of half-time education was likely to have on the living standards of working-class families, and they were ambivalent about the possible impact of compulsory part-time continuation classes for the same reason, but their main concern was that the proposed reforms did not go far enough. After 1918, the party began to refine its ideas about the meaning of the campaign for 'secondary education for all'. These ideas were to play a significant part in the educational debates of the interwar period.[17]

17.2   The development of nursery education

Although many of the arguments which took place during the interwar period were concerned with the fate of older children and the organisation of secondary education, it is also important to consider the arrangements which were made for children below the age at which school entry became compulsory. During the second half of the nineteenth century, there was a limited growth in the provision of dedicated nursery schools, but these were mainly situated in middle-class areas, and the majority of those children under the age of five who attended formal educational institutions, other than dame schools, were receiving their education in elementary schools. In 1871, the Board of Education calculated that more than 23 per cent of children between the ages of three and five were attending public elementary schools, and that these children accounted for more than 15 per cent of the entire elementary school population, and by 1900 it has been estimated that more than 40 per cent of all the three-to-five-year-olds in England and Wales were attending public elementary schools. However, during the first decade of the twentieth century, the Board began to discourage local authorities from offering places to such children, and the increase in the proportion of older children who were staying on at school past the minimum school-leaving age meant that the proportion of three-to-five-year-olds attending public elementary schools fell from 43.1 per cent in 1900/1 to less than 23 per cent a decade later (Table 17.1).[18]

Despite the fact that only a small proportion of children attended what were formally regarded as 'nursery schools', there was a vigorous debate over the role which such schools ought to play in educational provision. In 1837, the German educationist, Friedrich Froebel, had established a famous kindergarten at Blankenburg near Keilhau in Thuringia, and his ideas spread rapidly in Britain during the second half of the nineteenth century. However, during the

Table 17.1 Public educational provision for 3–5-year-olds in England and Wales, 1870/1–1937/8

Year	Number of 3–5-year-olds being educated in		% of 3–5-year-olds being educated in		3–5-year-olds attending elementary schools as % of all PES children
	Aided and maintained nursery schools	Public elementary schools	Aided and maintained nursery schools	Public elementary schools	
1870–1	0	275,608	0.00	23.37	15.29
1880–1	0	393,056	0.00	29.34	9.72
1890–1	0	458,267	0.00	33.26	9.50
1900–1	0	615,607	0.00	43.09	10.66
1910–11	0	350,591	0.00	22.76	5.78
1920–1	866	175,467	0.08	15.29	2.99
1930–1	2,787	159,335	0.23	13.14	2.86
1937–8	7,141	166,190	0.65	15.20	3.26

Sources: Public elementary schools: 1870/1, 1880/1, 1890/1: PP 1897 C. 8447 xxv, 1, *Special Reports on Educational Subjects 1896–97*, p. 51; 1900/1, 1910/11: PP 1914–16 Cd. 8097 li, 1, *Statistics of public education in England and Wales. Educational statistics 1913–14*, p. 18; 1920/1: PP 1923 Cmd. 1896 x, 731, *Report of the Board of Education for the year 1921/22*, p. 95; 1930/1: PP 1931–2 Cmd. 4068 ix, 39, *Education in 1931, being the Report of the Board of Education and the Statistics of Public Education for England and Wales*, p. 90; 1937/8: PP 1938–9 Cmd. 6013 x, 661, *Education in 1938, being the Report of the Board of Education and the Statistics of Public Education for England and Wales*, p. 91. Nursery schools: 1920/1: PP 1927 Cmd. 2866 viii, 653, *Report of the Board of Education for the year 1925/26*, p. 36; 1930/1: PP 1931–2 Cmd. 4068 ix, 39, *Education in 1931, being the Report of the Board of Education and the Statistics of Public Education for England and Wales*, p. 121; 1937/8: PP 1938–9 Cmd. 6013 x, 661, *Education in 1938, being the Report of the Board of Education and the Statistics of Public Education for England and Wales*, p. 120. The figures for 1920/1 are based on the number of children for whom places were available, rather than the number in average attendance.

late-nineteenth and early-twentieth centuries, some of Froebel's ideas were challenged by the Italian educational theorist, Maria Montessori, who placed much more emphasis on the provision of a specially prepared environment within which the child might develop academic and intellectual skills. In 1933, the Board of Education's Consultative Committee noted that 'the Montessori Method has affected many infant teachers in this country', especially in relation to the development of non-interventionist educational strategies, the provision of appropriately sized equipment, the emphasis on 'sense-training', and 'a growing scientific attitude towards the general care of mind and body, and renewed emphasis on self-education'. However, it also recognised that her methods could sometimes lead to accusations of excessive rigidity: 'much of her apparatus is well adapted to develop capacity for exact observation in number and form; but little provision is made for the development of the young child's free imagination or for his wider interests in the activities of the adult world.'[19]

During the early years of the twentieth century, the Board of Education authorised a number of enquiries into the education of children under the age of five in public elementary schools, and these tended to give increasing support to the campaign for a separate system of nursery schooling. In 1908, the Board's Consultative Committee concluded that at the present time 'nursery schools are in many cases a practical necessity. They believe that great advantage may be secured by their proper use, and that any effort that may be directed to this end will be amply repaid in the improved healthiness, intelligence and happiness of future generations.' However, although the proportion of under-fives attending public elementary schools continued to fall after this date, the government failed to offer any additional financial aid to enable local authorities to establish nursery schools before 1914, and local authorities were not given the power to establish nursery schools by law until the passage of Fisher's Act in 1918.[20]

In view of the importance which Fisher had attached to nursery schools in his speeches on education in 1917 and 1918, one might have expected their number to grow rapidly once the Act came into operation, but these hopes remained unfulfilled.[21] Under the Act, local authorities were given the power 'to make arrangements for supplying or aiding the supply of nursery schools (which expression shall include nursery classes) for children over two and under five years of age, or such later age as may be approved by the Board of Education, whose attendance at such a school is necessary or desirable for their healthy physical and mental development', and the Board was empowered to make grants to local authorities in aid of such schools providing that the schools were subject to inspection by the local authority, and that the authority was adequately represented on their governing bodies.[22] However, in January 1921 the Board announced that 'it cannot for the present entertain proposals for the establishment of nursery schools except in special circumstances and on an experimental basis, where existing buildings are available', and even though the first Labour government removed these restrictions in 1924, it failed to offer much positive encouragement, and the Conservatives imposed new restrictions on the payment of grants to schools providing education to children under the age of five two years later. By 1929, only 28 nursery schools, with a combined average attendance of 1,233 pupils, were receiving grants from the Board of Education, and even though the rate of growth accelerated during the 1930s, there were still only 103 aided or maintained nursery schools, with a combined average attendance of fewer than six thousand pupils, on the eve of the Second World War.[23]

The limited growth of nursery schools during the interwar period meant that the majority of those children who received some form of formal schooling before the age of five were likely to receive it in a public elementary school, even though the number of such children who attended such schools had fallen before the First World War. However, even though there were no major changes in the numbers of such children attending public elementary schools during the interwar period, there was a growing willingness to import some of the ideas associated with nursery schools into the teaching of nursery classes. Since many of these ideas also began to influence the teaching of older children as well, these issues will be considered in more detail in the following section.[24]

17.3 Elementary schools

Although the First World War had helped to stimulate a demand for educational reform, this demand was not shared universally. Even before 1918, many industrialists had expressed strong opposition to the proposals to abolish half-time education, and once the war was over, sections of the Conservative press began to launch a series of bitter attacks on the President of the Board of Education, H. A. L. Fisher, for his ambitious expenditure plans.[25] As a result of this pressure, the Board was forced to issue a series of Circulars which had the effect of undermining many of the key features of the 1918 Act. In December 1920 Fisher announced that the abolition of half-time education was to be delayed by one year, and in January 1921 the Board informed local authorities that even though they should continue to draw up schemes for the implementation of the proposals contained in the 1918 Act, 'it must ... be clearly understood that for the present the Board's approval to any general scheme cannot be given in such a form as would commit them to recognising, for the calculation of substantive or deficiency grant, expenditure incurred under it.'[26] The impact of this second announcement (Circular 1190) was reinforced by the issue of Circulars 1225 and 1228 seven months later. The first of these Circulars required local education authorities to 'confine expenditure within the closest limits consistent with the maintenance of an efficient system of public education', and the second announced that the restrictions imposed by Circular 1190 would remain in force for a further year.[27]

These announcements dealt a severe blow to the hopes of educational reformers, but worse was to follow. In August 1921 the government appointed a special committee, to be chaired by the businessman and former Transport Minister, Sir Eric Geddes, to examine all the public expenditure estimates for the coming year and advise on specific economies. Although the Geddes Committee identified opportunities for spending cuts in all the major areas of public provision (including defence), it dealt particularly harshly with the public education service. It called for reductions in teachers' salaries, an increase in pupil:teacher ratios, the abandonment of any plans to increase the number of free places in secondary schools, increases in the level of secondary-school fees, and the abolition of the system of percentage grants. However, the Committee's most controversial proposal was the suggestion that the age at which children entered school should be raised from five to six. If this proposal had been implemented, the Committee estimated that it would have saved £1.785 million per year, but it would also have excluded up to three-quarters of a million children from school, and deprived all elementary schoolchildren of a full year's worth of compulsory education.[28]

Although the age of school entry remained unchanged, the economy campaign of the early-1920s did have an effect on the school-building programme. During the latter part of the nineteenth century, the Department of Education had been forced to recognise the need for different kinds of accommodation for pupils of different ages, and many Medical Officers of Health had called for improvements to be made to the design of school buildings in order to provide more space for the children who were forced to attend them.[29] In January 1893, the Department had issued its first 'black list' of unsuitable schools, and in 1910 the Board of Education issued new regulations, stipulating that no child ought to be educated in a class containing more than 60 pupils. However, the Board's efforts to implement these recommendations were frustrated, initially by the war, and then by the economy campaign which succeeded it, and in 1925 it was forced to concede that 'upon the whole, the situation in 1924 was much like that of 15 years earlier'.[30] Nevertheless, the next ten years did see a significant amount of progress in the physical fabric of the country's schools. In its Annual Report for 1935, the Board reported that approximately 1.75 million new school places had been provided since the start of the current King's reign in 1910, and that 4,760 schools (out of a total of 20,854) had either been newly built, or extensively refurbished, within the previous 25 years.[31]

The expansion of the school-building programme after 1924 led to a substantial reduction in the number of unsuitable schools and contributed to a further reduction in overall class sizes. During the period between 1925 and 1938, the number of black-listed schools fell from 2,827 to 844, and the proportion of classes containing more than 50 children, which had already begun to decline as a result of changes in the birth-rate, fell from 14.41 per cent to 1.45 per cent, whilst the proportion of classes containing not more than 40 children increased from 56.3 per cent to 69.3 per cent. The school-building programme also played a key role in the reorganisation of the elementary-school system following the publication of Circular 1350 in January 1925. By the end of March 1938, approximately 48.3 per cent of elementary-school pupils between the ages of eight and 12, and a similar proportion of pupils between the ages of 11 and 15, were being educated in schools which had been reorganised into junior and senior departments, whilst a further 120,000 children over the age of 11 were attending schools with 'senior divisions', and 138,473 pupils were waiting to be transferred to senior departments. However, these figures still showed that more than a third of all elementary-school children were continuing to be educated in 'all-age' schools, and such schools were not phased out completely until the beginning of the 1970s.[32]

One of the main aims of the school-building programme was to facilitate the use of more modern methods of teaching in the classroom. As we have already seen, many nursery- and infant-class teachers had become increasingly sympathetic to the ideas of 'child-centred education', and these ideas also had an important influence on the teachers of older children.[33] In 1931, the Board of Education's Consultative Committee commented that 'the question of school buildings and of the size of the classes that may suitably be accommodated in them is inescapably bound up with the problem of the curriculum and methods of study for children at the primary stage', and emphasised the need for primary school buildings to be 'open and sunny, removed as far as possible from the noise and dust of roads, and sufficiently large to provide hard playgrounds', as well as providing, if possible, 'space for games'.[34] Many of these ideas were shared by the Board itself. In 1936, it wrote: 'the modern school is very different from its predecessors. It is no longer regarded, as it were, as a box of class-rooms available for an average attendance of a number of children calculated on a mathematical formula and usable within that limit to capacity, irrespective of the homogeneity of its units. Sufficient class-spaces are now provided to give elasticity of organisation and to enable the children, whether infants, juniors or seniors, to be grouped in accordance with their ages, attainments and abilities. Planned as a rule on one floor with a detached hall and large rooms for practical work and sometimes for dining and gymnastics, the characteristics of the modern school are space, airiness, light, sound sanitation, ample playgrounds and, where possible, its own playing field.'[35]

Although the interwar period has sometimes been characterised as one in which 'progressive ideas in education ... captured the allegiance of the opinion-makers' and became the 'intellectual orthodoxy', the extent of this transition should not be exaggerated.[36] In 1931, the Board of Education's Consultative Committee concluded that the main aim of primary education ought to be 'to supply the pupils with what is essential to their healthy ... physical, intellectual and moral [growth]', and that the curriculum 'is to be thought of in terms of activity and experience, rather than of knowledge to be acquired and facts to be stored', but these principles were easily subordinated to the parallel need to pre-pare the child for the next stage of his or her education.[37] As a result of this, it may be more appropriate to argue that the main theme in interwar education was one of 'differentiation'. It was because of this that educational planners attached so much importance to what they regarded as the 'individuality' of each child and the need to provide separate accommodation for children of dif-ferent ages. However, it also meant that they accepted the view that the educa-tion provided for each child ought to be adapted to a predetermined view of their interests and abilities. It was for this reason that the advocates of selective education favoured the introduction of streaming at an early age. This was also thought to be essential if schools were to succeed in their aim of ensuring that the most talented elementary-school children were able to gain entry to selective secondary schools at the age of 11.[38]

17.4   Educating the adolescent

The question of what kind of education to provide for older children had played a central role in educational debates during the First World War, and at the end of the war the government promised to establish a nationwide system of compulsory day continuation schools, offering part-time education to children between the ages of 14 and 16 (and subsequently to children between the ages of 16 and 18) who were not already in full-time education. However, these ideas were not universally welcomed, and the government's failure to ensure that more than a handful of local authorities established continuation schools enabled a number of alternative proposals to come to the fore.

During the last 80 years, there have been many attempts to account for the demise of the compulsory continuation schools. Allen suggested that the main problem lay in the wording of the 1918 Act, which gave local authorities too much freedom to decide the point at which they would bring the relevant section into operation, but the underlying problem was the absence of any real measure of popular support for the continuation schools idea.[39] Many working-class parents (and their children) were opposed to the establishment of compulsory continuation schools because of their impact on young people's earnings, and the Labour party regarded them as an inadequate substitute for an expanded system of post-primary or secondary education. They were also fiercely opposed by many employers because of their effect on manufacturing industry, and local authorities were reluctant to commit resources to them because they thought that they were a short-term solution which was likely to be superseded in the not-too-distant future by further educational reforms. As a result, it is clear that there was already widespread hostility to the continuation schools movement, even before the deterioration in economic conditions and the resulting pressure for 'national economy'.[40]

Although there was therefore little hard support for the principle of continuation schools, there was nevertheless a great deal of interest in the development of alternative solutions to the problem of what subsequently became known as 'the education of the adolescent', and this was reflected in the publication of the Labour party's statement on education, *Secondary education for all*, in 1922. Its authors argued that even though the continuation schools were 'preferable to the existing neglect of boys and girls who have left the primary school', they were 'not the solution which would have been chosen either by most educationalists or by the labour movement, had their hands been free'. They therefore argued that 'the only policy which is at once educationally sound and suited to a democratic community is one under which primary education and secondary education are organised as two stages in a single and continuous process; secondary education being the education of the adolescent and primary education being education preparatory thereto', and in order to achieve this they called for 'the improvement of primary education and the development of public secondary education to such a point that all normal children, irrespective of their income, class or occupation of their parents, may be transferred at the age of 11 plus from the primary or preparatory school to some type of another of secondary school, and remain in the latter till 16.'[41]

The publication of *Secondary education for all* did not lead to any immediate changes in education policy, but it played a vital role in highlighting the need for further improvements in the education of older children. However, the government and the Board of Education were also anxious to ensure that whatever changes were made to the education system, the existing system of secondary education should remain unaffected by them.[42] This determination was reflected in the Board's decision to refer the whole question of adolescent education to its Consultative Committee in 1923. When the Board invited the Committee to discuss this topic, it deliberately limited the terms of the enquiry to 'the organisation, objective and curriculum of courses of study suitable for children who will remain in full-time attendance at schools, *other than secondary schools*, up to the age of 15', and only incidentally 'to advise as to the arrangements which should be made ... for facilitating in suitable cases the transfer of individual pupils to secondary schools at an age above the normal age of admission.'[43]

Although the Board had decided to refer the whole question of adolescent education to the Consultative Committee, it did not simply sit back and await the Committee's response. In January 1925 it issued a new Circular, Circular 1350, which set out the main lines on which future developments were to be based. The Circular recognised the need for a clear break between what it called 'junior' and 'senior' education, and insisted that 'the age of 11 is increasingly recognised as the most suitable dividing line' between the two stages.[44] In this sense, then, the Board was right to suggest, in 1928, that it was the publication of Circular 1350, and not the publication of the Consultative Committee's report, which marked the real beginning of the process which came to be known, following the report, as 'Hadow reorganisation'.[45]

The Consultative Committee completed its report at the end of 1926. Although it is often regarded as one of the major landmarks in interwar educational history, its principal importance lay in the way in which it helped to consolidate existing trends and give them extra legitimacy by cloaking them in the language of educational advance. It reiterated what was now the Board's official policy by calling for a clear break at the age of 11, but it replaced the terms 'junior' and 'senior' education with the idea of 'primary' and 'secondary' education, and it went beyond official policy by calling for the school-leaving age to be raised from 14 to 15. This would not only make it easier 'for post-primary education ... to be placed on a coherent and progressive course with a character and quality of its own, but would also ... ensure that it continued sufficiently long to act as a permanent influence for good on the lives of those who passed through it.' The addition 'even of a few months to the present school life may not seldom enable [the teacher] to kindle into flame the spark which but for them would have been extinguished.'[46]

In addition to drawing attention to the need for a clear break at the age of 11 and for the school-leaving age to be raised to 15 (though not 16, as advocated in *Secondary education for all*), the Committee also produced a detailed plan for the different forms which 'post-primary' education ought to take. However, as McKibbin has pointed out, the most striking aspect of this was the extent to which it was designed to codify existing practice. The Committee identified three additional types of post-primary or 'secondary' school which were to sit alongside the existing secondary schools within an expanded 'secondary' system. These were described as follows: 'schools of the type of the existing selective central schools ... to be known as modern schools'; 'schools of the type of the present non-selective central schools ... also to be known as modern schools'; and 'departments or classes within public elementary schools ... to be known as senior classes'.[47]

Although the Hadow Report did not initiate the process of 'Hadow reorganisation', it did provide it with an important additional stimulus.[48] In March 1927, three months after the publication of the report, it was estimated that approximately 8.5 per cent of all elementary-school pupils over the age of 11 were being educated in senior departments, and by March 1934 this figure had increased to just under 40 per cent. In addition to this, the Board also argued that there were a large number of children who, despite attending all-age schools, were nevertheless being educated in 'senior divisions' following a separate course of advanced instruction for pupils aged 11 and over, and that there were a further 129,103 pupils attending junior departments of reorganised schools who were waiting to be transferred to senior departments.[49] The pace of reorganisation appears to have slowed during the second half of the 1930s, but by the end of March 1938 more than 48 per cent of all pupils over the age of 11 were being educated in senior departments, and more than 60 per cent of all pupils were attending schools which had benefited from some form of reorganisation (see also Table 17.2).[50]

Table 17.2   Number of pupils attending reorganised public elementary schools, 1925/6–1937/8

Year	Senior departments			Senior divisions in all-age schools			Pupils in junior departments of reorganized schools awaiting transfer to senior departments	
	Departments	Pupils aged 11 and over	Pupils as % of all pupils aged 11 and over	Divisions	Pupils aged 11 and over	Pupils as % of all pupils aged 11 and over	Pupils aged 11 and over	Pupils as % of all pupils aged 11 and over
1925/6	598	86,030	2.25	n/a	n/a	n/a	n/a	n/a
1926/7	649	164,159	8.49	n/a	n/a	n/a	n/a	n/a
1927/8	718	174,574	9.49	n/a	n/a	n/a	n/a	n/a
1928/9	883	209,899	12.59	n/a	n/a	n/a	n/a	n/a
1929/0	1,017	238,681	15.30	1,225	120,440	7.72	n/a	n/a
1930/1	1,352	319,620	19.45	1,483	152,052	9.25	n/a	n/a
1931/2	1,915	519,151	28.12	1,408	162,510	8.80	n/a	n/a
1932/3	2,344	699,077	34.66	1,346	164,450	8.15	120,689	5.98
1933/4	2,612	800,651	39.10	1,322	158,759	7.75	129,103	6.30
1934/5	2,744	792,474	41.29	1,304	*150,000*	*7.81*	129,782	6.76
1935/6	2,864	794,972	43.64	1,341	*144,000*	*7.90*	132,225	7.26
1936/7	2,962	805,335	45.92	1,400	*140,000*	*7.98*	133,025	7.58
1937/8	3,074	818,827	48.27	1,136	*120,000*	*7.07*	138,473	8.16

Notes: Figures in *italics* are estimates.
Sources: Annual Reports of the Board of Education, 1925/6–1938.

Simon criticised the process of 'Hadow reorganisation' because it institutionalised the principle of 'selection by differentiation' and reinforced the position of the selective secondary school at the apex of the post-primary education system, but other writers have highlighted the extent to which the process of reorganisation was in tune with public opinion and left considerable scope for local initiative.[51] In Nottinghamshire, where reorganisation was driven partly by Circular 1350 and partly by the needs of new housing estates, the new senior schools operated alongside the selective secondary schools and delivered a highly 'practical' curriculum, but they were seen as being 'well-organised, well-regarded and well-supported by the community they served'.[52] In Hertfordshire, the community's main priority 'was the provision of a variety of sound schools which would offer a range of courses for pupils of differing abilities'. Parker concludes that there was 'no agitation for universal grammar schooling, or even universal secondary schooling', and that there was 'general approval' for the council's policy of fitting local schools to local needs, and fitting local children as accurately as possible to these schools.[53]

When the Hadow Committee published its report, the President of the Board of Education, Eustace Percy, argued that the immediate priority was to continue with the process of reorganisation, and that this should occur before, rather than at the same time as, any changes in the school-leaving age.[54] However, the Labour party argued that the raising of the school-leaving age was an essential part of the strategy of reorganisation, and when Labour returned to office in 1929, it placed the raising of the school-leaving age at the heart of its educational policy. Nevertheless, despite the strenuous efforts made by Percy's successor at the Board of Education, Charles Trevelyan, the school-leaving age remained at 14 throughout the interwar period.[55]

The Board's failure to secure an increase in the age at which children were permitted to leave school reflected the deep divisions which this issue aroused. The Conservative party believed that it would have made more sense to use any available funds to increase expenditure on higher education, continuation schools and secondary schools, rather than using it to increase the length of time spent by all children in public elementary schools. Secondly, it was widely recognised that many working-class parents would only be prepared to allow their children to remain at school if they were offered maintenance allowances as compensation for the cost of keeping children at school and the loss of their earnings, but this merely added to Treasury fears that any increase in the school-leaving age would lead to a substantial increase in government spending. The government's proposals were also bitterly attacked by representatives of the denominational or voluntary-aided schools, which were likely to face particular financial difficulties if they were forced to provide new accommodation for an increased number of older pupils. The Conservative MP for the Exchange Division of Liverpool, Sir James Reynolds, complained that the Bill would add enormously to the burdens which were already imposed on denominational schools and 'render it almost impossible for us to carry on and live up to the full educational demands of the country'.[56]

Although the government was forced to abandon its efforts to raise the school-leaving age in 1930, the National Government decided to reopen the issue in 1936. However, although the government proposed to raise the school-leaving age to 15, it refused to make any provision for the introduction of maintenance allowances and gave local authorities the power to offer exemptions to any children who were able to show that they could obtain beneficial employment below that age, and many commentators believed that this would have undermined the effect of the increase altogether. *The Times* reported that, in those parts of the country where the school-leaving age had already been raised, with exemptions, under local bye-laws, between 50 and 90 per cent of children left school before the age of 15, and although the government argued that these areas were not entirely representative, the paper's own education correspondent estimated that as many as 85 per cent of children would gain exemptions if the Bill came into effect.[57] In the end, although the Bill was passed, it was overtaken by events, because the day on which it was supposed to come into operation – 1 September 1939 – coincided with the Nazi invasion of Poland, and the question of raising the school-leaving age was postponed until after the Second World War.[58]

It is also important to recognise the extent to which the reorganisation of elementary education ran alongside the existing secondary-school system. As we have already seen, many secondary schools had already become concerned about the 'blurring' of the boundaries between elementary and secondary education before the end of the nineteenth century, and Simon has argued that this was one of the main reasons behind the abolition of the school boards and the introduction of new regulations for both elementary and secondary schools in the early years of the twentieth century. Following the publication of these regulations, the Liberal government had introduced a national free-places scheme in 1907, with the aim of enabling the brightest elementary-school children to pass from the elementary-school system to the secondary-school system at the age of 11, without having to pay secondary-school fees. Nevertheless, despite the increase in the number of children who took up secondary-school places during the First World War, only a small proportion of pupils transferred from elementary schools to secondary schools before 1918.[59]

When H. A. L. Fisher presented his Bill to Parliament, he had devoted most of his attention to the introduction of day continuation schools, but he recognised that there was an unmet demand for places in selective secondary schools, and in October 1919 he appointed a Departmental Committee to look into the whole question of scholarships and free places. This Committee estimated that between 400,000 and 2,000,000 children were being prevented from taking up places at secondary schools for which they were academically qualified, and recommended that the proportion of free places provided under the free places scheme should be raised from a minimum of 25 per cent to a minimum of 40 per cent, but its plans were frustrated by the economy drive of the early-1920s.[60] In 1921, the Geddes Committee urged the government to abandon any plans for increasing the number of free places, and even though the Cabinet rejected this advice, it instructed the Board of Education to prevent any 'undue increase' in the number of free places, and to take a further look at plans to increase the cost of secondary-school fees. The government also decided to reduce the number of new pupils who would be admitted to secondary schools, with the result that this figure fell continuously between 1920 and 1924, and only regained its former level at the beginning of the 1930s. These two factors helped to ensure that there was only a small increase, in absolute terms, in the percentage of public-elementary-school pupils who gained places at selective secondary schools during the interwar period. This figure remained below ten per cent throughout the first half of the 1920s, and only rose to 14.34 per cent towards the end of the 1930s (see also Table 17.3).[61]

Following the end of the Second World War, there was growing interest in the relationship between education and social mobility. Floud argued that one of the reasons for the increase in the proportion of elementary-school children who obtained places at selective secondary schools was the fact that a growing proportion of middle-class parents were sending their children to elementary schools, and that the increase in the proportion of former elementary-school children who attended secondary schools did not necessarily mean that there was an increase in the proportion of poor children attending secondary schools. She herself believed that, if anything, there was a widening of the gap between the educational opportunities offered to children from social classes 1–4 (professional, managerial, supervisory and other non-manual workers) and the opportunities offered to children from social classes 5–7 (skilled, semi-skilled and unskilled manual workers), but this conclusion has been questioned by Heath and Clifford. They have argued that even though the gap between the proportion of children from affluent backgrounds who attended secondary

Table 17.3   Attendance at secondary schools in England and Wales, 1914–38

Year	% of public elementary-school pupils entering secondary schools[a]	% of secondary-school entrants gaining free places	Number of new entrants to secondary schools	Total secondary-school population
1914	6.01	30.29	60,453	187,647
1920	9.50	29.64	96,283	307,862
1921	9.70	34.80	95,561	336,836
1922	9.50	31.82	90,601	354,956
1923	n/a	32.34	80,754	354,165
1924	8.40	33.84	80,340	349,141
1925	9.09	38.03	84,567	352,605
1926	9.39	38.83	86,908	360,503
1927	10.66	41.66	88,946	371,493
1928	11.26	42.68	89,253	377,540
1929	13.20	43.86	84,385	386,993
1930	12.90	45.38	86,119	394,105
1931	10.33	48.86	89,682	411,309
1932	10.52	48.73	96,342	432,061
1933	10.84	47.34	92,652	441,883
1934	11.93	44.44	92,490	448,421
1935	12.63	44.74	94,546	456,783
1936	12.99	45.10	93,850	463,906
1937	13.68	47.32	97,115	466,245
1938	14.34	47.26	98,820	470,003

Note: [a] The percentage of elementary schoolchildren who entered secondary schools has been calculated by dividing the number of new entrants by the number of elementary-school children aged 10–11 in the preceding year. As Sutherland has pointed out, these figures can be misleading, because a large number of children did not enter secondary school until after their twelfth or even thirteenth birthdays. However, the figures do provide a rough indication of the proportion of elementary-school children who were likely to enter secondary school within two to three years, and the annual data do provide a rough indication of the extent to which this figure changed during the course of the inter-war period.

Sources: PP 1914–16 Cd. 7674 I, 355, Statistics of public education in England and Wales, Part I, Educational statistics, 1912–13, pp. 20–1; PP 1914–16 Cd. 8097 Ii, 1, Statistics of public education in England and Wales. Educational statistics 1913–14, pp. 20–1, 104–5; B. Simon, The politics of educational reform 1920/40, London: Lawrence and Wishart, 1974, p. 366; G. Sutherland, Ability, merit and measurement: mental testing and English education 1880–1940, Oxford: Clarendon Press, 1984, pp. 292–3.

schools and the proportion of children from poorer backgrounds who attended secondary schools may have widened in absolute terms, it also narrowed in relative terms, because the proportionate increase in the attendance rates of children from poorer backgrounds was larger. However, even if the gap did narrow, in these terms, it remained the case that only one in ten working-class children attended secondary schools, as compared with more than half of the children from social classes 1–3, and almost a quarter of children from social class 4.[62]

These remarks show that there was still a substantial gap between the educational chances of children from social classes 1–4 and the educational chances of children from social classes 5–7 at the end of the interwar period. During the latter part of the nineteenth century, and for much of the interwar period, the main method which was used to select children for secondary-school places (whether free or otherwise) was the oral interview, which was often conducted in such a way as to favour the child from a middle-class background who was able, in the words of one secondary-school head teacher (the High Master of Manchester Grammar School), 'to resist the infection of the street with its posters and its newspaper placards'.[63] During the interwar period, a growing number of local authorities also began to make use of written tests and, in a number of cases, intelligence tests, but even though these tests were supposed to provide a more objective test of each child's 'intelligence', they also tended to be framed in such a way as to favour children from more affluent backgrounds, and to use language and reference points which would be more familiar to middle-class children.[64] Moreover, even when children from poorer backgrounds were able to surmount these difficulties, they often faced further obstacles which prevented them from taking up secondary-school places. In Bradford, for example, 60 per cent of the children who were offered free places were forced to relinquish them because they could not afford to remain at school beyond the age of 14, and because their parents could not afford the cost of uniforms, books and stationery.[65]

Although the vast majority of children over the age of 11 who attended state schools were being educated in public elementary schools or selective secondary schools, a small proportion of children over the age of 13 were educated in junior technical schools. The main aim of these schools was to prepare boys for work in the engineering or building industries, or in chemicals, mining, fishing or the merchant navy, but a small number of schools were established in the early-1930s without being linked to any specific industry. There were also approximately 10,000 children of both sexes who attended junior technical (trade) schools, which prepared children for entry into non-industrial occupations such as cabinet-making, printing or tailoring, junior housewifery schools and junior commercial schools, all of which came under the general heading of 'junior technical schools'.[66] The overall rate of growth of these schools was extremely slow. In 1938, there were still only 31,516 children attending all types of junior technical schools (including children attending the junior departments of Art Schools and Schools of Nautical Training), as compared with 470,003 children in selective secondary schools, and 5,091,975 children in public elementary schools, of whom 1,726,787 were aged 11 and over.[67]

One of the main obstacles to the growth of junior technical schools was the fact that they were only supposed to take children over the age of 13, by which time the vast majority of children had already been allocated either to a public elementary school or to a selective secondary school (only a very small proportion of children entered junior technical schools before their thirteenth birthday). Second, many local education authorities were reluctant to incur the costs associated with the construction and equipment of junior technical schools, especially when these were likely to exceed the costs involved in running an existing secondary school. Third, although the junior technical schools were designed to prepare children for particular kinds of employment, they received comparatively little support from the employers whose future workforces they were supposed to be training, and they were viewed with suspicion by those on the left, like Albert Mansbridge and R. H. Tawney, who believed that they were a means of funnelling bright working-class children into what were ultimately seen as manual occupations. Many trade unionists were also sceptical of the value of junior technical schools, because they thought that they would lead to an over-supply of skilled labour, and have an adverse effect on the wage-levels of local workers. Finally, the technical schools received very little support from middle-class parents, who were reluctant to send their own children to what were seen as working-class schools, and preferred to see rate-funded expenditure being used to support the schools to which they did send their children, namely the local secondary schools.[68]

Although the slow growth of technical education in the interwar years has recently begun to receive much more attention from historians, mainly because of the relationship between education and economic performance, this issue only really came to the fore in official circles during the second half of the 1930s. In January 1936, the Board of Education's Technical Branch was given the power to develop a new policy initiative for technical education, and in 1938 the Board's Consultative Committee (now known as the Spens Committee) recommended that an unspecified number of junior technical schools (those 'orientated towards the engineering and building industries and any other technical schools which may develop training of such a character as [a] to provide a good intellectual discipline ... and [b] to have a technical value in relation not to one particular occupation but to a group of occupations') should be converted into technical high schools, in order to ensure 'that they should be accorded equality of status with schools of the grammar [that is, selective secondary] school type'. However, although the Committee's proposals for a tripartite system of secondary education, including grammar schools, technical schools and secondary modern schools, exercised a profound influence on plans for the reconstruction of the education system after 1945, they had little effect on the actual provision of technical education before the outbreak of the Second World War.[69]

17.5 Higher education

Although the interwar years saw some improvements in the education of children at school, they have often been seen as years of stagnation rather than progress in the field of higher education.[70] In 1919, the Government attempted to improve the arrangements for financing universities by establishing the University Grants Committee, but the hopes which were raised by this development were not fulfilled. As we can see from Table 17.4, government support for higher education increased by almost 30 per cent between 1919/20 and 1920/1, but it remained almost static between 1920/1 and 1925/6, and the total value of the grants awarded by Parliament to universities in England and Wales was still less than £2,000,000 at the end of the 1930s. These circumstances meant that universities continued to draw the majority of their funds from endowments, local-authority grants, tuition and other fees, and other non-governmental sources, throughout the interwar period (see Table 17.4).

Table 17.4 University education in England and Wales, 1919/20–1937/8[a]

Category	1919/20	1920/1	1921/2	1922/3	1923/4	1924/5	1925/6	1926/7	1927/8	1928/9	1929/30	1930/1	1931/2	1932/3	1933/4	1934/5	1935/6[b]	1936/7[b]	1937/8[b]
No. of students																			
Male (full-time)	16,702	18,170	17,647	24,419	22,892	22,475	22,515	22,824	23,218	24,089	25,110	27,015	28,077	29,578	30,550	30,928	31,175	30,935	30,590
Female (full-time)	6,257	7,080	7,727	9,341	9,538	9,549	9,448	9,432	9,333	9,273	9,301	9,422	9,361	9,602	9,533	9,464	9,290	8,874	8,758
Male (part-time)	8,367	7,703	7,792	7,293	7,732	7,443	8,104	7,926	7,903	7,812	7,571	8,130	7,818	7,701	7,711	7,395	7,148	6,847	6,995
Female (part-time)	3,258	3,880	3,300	3,585	3,158	3,161	3,159	3,215	2,953	2,795	2,780	3,091	2,752	2,814	2,559	2,543	2,409	2,478	2,580
All (full-time)	22,959	25,250	25,374	33,760	32,430	32,024	31,963	32,256	32,551	33,362	34,411	36,437	37,438	39,180	40,083	40,392	40,465	39,809	39,348
All (part-time)	11,625	11,583	11,092	10,878	10,890	10,604	11,263	11,141	10,856	10,607	10,351	11,221	10,570	10,515	10,270	9,938	9,557	9,325	9,575
Full-time students taking courses in[c]																			
Arts	7,424	8,017	8,050	13,883	14,357	14,994	15,563	16,251	16,723	17,135	17,705	18,210	18,416	19,235	19,255	19,039	18,809	18,238	17,804
Pure science	4,462	5,009	5,200	6,722	6,379	6,340	6,314	6,128	6,148	6,325	6,449	6,755	7,022	7,320	7,664	7,667	7,492	7,026	6,636
Medicine	6,325	7,041	7,339	7,932	7,566	6,952	6,427	6,126	5,949	5,975	6,223	7,312	7,677	8,300	8,918	9,440	9,814	10,102	10,159
Technology	4,406	4,775	4,377	4,048	3,433	3,108	3,078	3,122	3,102	3,299	3,403	3,515	3,707	3,746	3,647	3,586	3,634	3,682	3,951
Agriculture	342	408	408	864	615	630	581	629	629	628	631	645	616	579	599	660	716	761	798
Full-time teachers[d]																			
Professors	–	–	–	–	–	–	633	635	648	653	658	687	698	711	715	714	714	729	732
Readers	–	–	–	–	–	–	285	273	280	280	283	288	293	297	310	327	325	321	322
Lecturers	–	–	–	–	–	–	1,482	1,460	1,471	1,511	1,542	1,620	1,667	1,698	1,735	1,788	1,811	1,860	1,878
Others	–	–	–	–	–	–	51	120	167	194	229	259	281	270	247	250	261	258	290
Income (£000)[e]																			
Endowment	–	220	244	271	288	289	497	518	538	573	594	650	648	655	667	691	715	776	823
Parliamentary grants	–	788	1,021	1,042	1,036	1,065	1,556	1,542	1,556	1,565	1,597	1,740	1,743	1,727	1,721	1,730	1,744	1,934	1,988
Local-authority grants	–	240	378	389	392	454	478	481	466	486	515	566	555	542	545	560	492	510	512
Tuition & other fees	–	930	994	958	938	891	1,170	1,237	1,257	1,306	1,351	1,524	1,555	1,622	1,655	1,686	1,682	1,681	1,678
Other sources	–	191	230	231	239	247	376	406	444	449	465	488	508	510	509	554	571	604	609
Total	–	2,369	2,867	2,891	2,893	2,946	4,077	4,184	4,261	4,379	4,522	4,968	5,009	5,056	5,097	5,221	5,204	5,505	5,610

Notes: [a] The figures relate to University institutions in England and Wales in receipt of Treasury grants. Figures for Guy's Medical Hospital and the College of the Pharmaceutical Society were included for the first time in 1930/31; figures for the Courtauld Institute and the Institute of Education were included for the first time in 1932/3. [b] From 1935–6, the figures for Manchester College of Technology under Income were confined to sums applicable to university work only. Had these figures included income for non-university work, as in previous years, then the figure for 1935/6 would have exceeded the figure for the previous year. [c] The figures for 1922/3 and 1923/4 are incomplete. Arts includes Theology, Fine Art, Law, Music, Commerce, Economics and Education. Medicine includes Dentistry. Technology includes Engineering, Applied Chemistry, Mining Metallurgy, Architecture and so on. Agriculture includes Forestry, Horticulture and Dairy Work. [d] The figures for the Universities of Oxford and Cambridge were confined to Professors and Readers only. [e] Income data do not include capital sums received for lands, buildings or endowments. Income earned by the Oxford and Cambridge Colleges is also excluded.

Sources: PP 1921 Cmd. 1263 xxvi. 605, *Returns from Universities and Colleges in receipt of Treasury Grant 1919–20*, pp. 9–10; PP 1932–3 Cmd. 4233 xxv. 1, *Statistical Abstract for the United Kingdom for each of the 15 years 1913 and 1918 to 1931*, pp. 58–9; PP 1939–40 Cmd. 6232 x, 367, *Statistical abstract from the United Kingdom for each of the 15 years 1924–38 (83rd number)*, pp. 62–3.

One of the most contentious aspects of the history of higher education in this period concerns the extent to which the system as a whole became more accessible to students from poorer backgrounds.[71] In 1920, the government introduced a system of state scholarships in order to enable disadvantaged students to take up places which they might not otherwise have been able to afford, but no new scholarships were awarded in 1922 or 1923, and even though the scheme was extended in 1931 and 1936, only 360 scholarships were being awarded annually at the end of the 1930s. In 1939, the Board of Education calculated that 73 per cent of all the awards made between 1928 and 1937 had gone to candidates who began their educational careers in public elementary schools, but less than half the candidates who qualified for awards in 1936 came from families whose annual income was less than £250 (that is, below the income limit for national health insurance), and more than 70 per cent of the students holding awards in 1937/8 attended colleges at Oxford or Cambridge, where the cost of living was higher than elsewhere.[72] During the interwar period as a whole, the proportion of former elementary-school pupils among pupils from grant-aided secondary schools who went to university remained broadly constant, but Jean Floud argued that the gap between the educational prospects of children from state secondary schools and those from private secondary schools expanded. Floud also argued that there was only a small increase in the proportion of children from social classes 5–7 who attended university. When she compared the educational experiences of children born before 1910 with those of children born between 1910 and 1929, she found that the proportion of children from social classes 5–7 who attended university only increased from 0.47 per cent to 0.74 per cent, whilst the proportion of children from social classes 1–4 who attended university rose from 3.05 per cent to 6.26 per cent.[73]

Although there was relatively little change in the social composition of the student body, there was an overall increase in student numbers, with an increasing proportion of students taking full-time degrees. At the end of the first full year of peace, there were 11,625 part-time students, and 22,959 full-time students, attending universities in England and Wales, whereas by 1938 the number of part-time students had fallen to 9,575, and the number of full-time students had risen to 39,348 (see Table 17.4). The number of male students increased by nearly 50 per cent (from 25,069 to 37,585) whilst the number of female students increased by just under 20 per cent (from 9,515 to 11,338). There were also some important changes in the nature of the courses which these students took, although these are not reflected fully in the table. During the period 1919/20 to 1937/8, the number of full-time students taking degrees in technological subjects fell, whilst the numbers studying Pure Science, Medicine (including Dentistry) and Agriculture increased, but the biggest increase was in the number of students taking Arts subjects, which increased from 7,424 to 17,804. However, there were some indications that a growing number of students were beginning to relate their choice of degree programme to the perceived needs of industry. There was a small increase in the number of students taking degrees in such subjects as Commerce, Economics, Modern Languages and Industrial Psychology, although the overall numbers still compared very unfavourably with the numbers pursuing comparable subjects in the United States and Germany.[74]

Although the expansion of student numbers affected all universities, there was little change in the institutional structure of the higher-education system. Between 1918 and 1939, only one new institution acquired full university status (the University of Reading, in 1926), and two new university colleges were formed, at Leicester (1927) and Hull (1928).[75] The period also saw the creation of a central coordinating body for the University of London, and the university's imposing, if controversial, Senate House was built at the end of the 1930s. However, the system as a whole continued to be dominated by the 'ancient' Universities of Oxford and Cambridge. Although these universities were often criticised (the American writer, Abraham Flexner, thought that they amounted to little more than 'advanced secondary schools'), they continued to attract the lion's share of either the wealthiest or the most academically qualified undergraduates, and they provided the model to which the majority of their competitors continued to aspire. The combination of social status and academic prestige associated with Oxford and Cambridge also had an effect on the graduate job market. As the German writer, William Dibelius, observed in 1930: 'from the purely academic point of view, the new universities may beat the old on this or that point. It makes no difference. The average Englishman rates them far below Oxford and Cambridge. If a post is to be filled, the academic qualification of the MA of Liverpool or Leeds will not prevail against the social status of the Oxford BA, which bears no mark of coal dust and the fumes of the brewing vats.'[76]

In 1955, W. H. Armytage commented that 'little wisdom could accrue whilst University teachers were harassed with the plethora of Committees, examination boards and administrative matters which filled the diary and often the life of the average University teacher', but the interwar period did witness some important developments in both the funding and content of academic research.[77] As Sanderson has shown, the First World War played a major role in highlighting the importance of scientific research in particular, and this was reflected in the formation of the Department of Scientific and Industrial Research in 1915, the transformation of the Medical Research Committee into the Medical Research Council in 1920, and the establishment of the Agricultural Research Council in 1931. The interwar period also saw an increasing recognition of the importance of scientific research on the part of private industry, with money being provided not only to support research within individual companies, but also to embark on collaborative work with university departments. Whilst a number of writers have complained about the apparent decline in the proportion of students emerging from their studies with degrees in applied science and technology, private-sector investment played a key role in fostering research into such fields as aeronautics (Cambridge, London, Southampton), building construction (London, Manchester), fuel technology (Leeds, London, Sheffield, Nottingham), industrial relations (Cambridge, Leeds), naval architecture (Durham, Liverpool), oil technology (Birmingham, London), technical optics (London), chemicals (Liverpool, Manchester), and food-processing (Bristol, Liverpool). Such work made an important contribution to the development of the so-called 'new industries' during the interwar period.[78]

17.6 Conclusions

Although Lowndes argued that the inhabitants of England and Wales were transformed 'into a school-taught and substantially literate people' between 1876 and 1935, other writers have questioned the extent to which the task of achieving a 'silent social revolution' had actually been accomplished by the end of the interwar period.[79] Both Gilbert and Simon regarded the interwar years as years of failure in education policy, and Sanderson characterised the period between 1914 and 1944 as one of 'missed opportunities'.[80] Gordon, Aldrich and Dean wrote that 'in spite of [various] innovations ... the overall verdict on this period must be one of stagnation rather than progress ... [T]he 1920s and 1930s, like the 1940s and 1950s, were essentially a period of missed opportunities in education, which left the country with inadequate secondary, further and higher education, particularly in terms of science and technology, inadequacies which were soon to be reflected in her relative economic decline.'[81]

However, although many of these criticisms are undoubtedly justified, it is also important to acknowledge the positive nature of some of the changes which did occur, particularly within the elementary-school system. Although there were no substantial increases in educational spending, the number of 'blacklisted' schools fell by more than 70 per cent between 1925 and 1938, and the proportion of classes containing more than 50 children fell by nearly 90 per cent. The government also introduced a substantial school-building programme, which meant that almost 25 per cent of the schools in existence in 1935 had been built or refurbished within the previous 25 years. These developments paved the way for the introduction of more modern methods of teaching in the classroom and provided an essential foundation for the 'reorganisation' of elementary education after 1925. As a result, between one-half and two-thirds of all elementary-school children were attending 'reorganised' schools by the end of the 1930s.

However, even though substantial improvements did occur within the elementary-school system, these improvements failed to address the fundamental problems associated with the relationship between the elementary-school system and the secondary-school system. Although the government recognised the need for a more advanced form of 'post-primary' education for the majority of the children who continued to attend public elementary schools after the age of 11, less than one-sixth of all elementary-school children passed from the elementary schools into the selective secondary schools, and these continued to provide the only possible route for the vast majority of children from the elementary schools into the universities. The government also failed to promote the growth of technical education, and there was only a small increase in the total number of students entering universities. These deficiencies represented a denial of educational opportunity to a very large number of individuals, particularly from the working class, and a failure to make the most of the country's combined intellectual resources. As Lowndes himself observed, when he looked back at the achievements of the interwar years from the vantage point of the 1960s, 'the country was still largely unprepared for the "third industrial revolution" which would sweep over her after a war from which she would emerge exhausted.'[82]

18 The Second World War and after

Although there were comparatively few major legislative developments in social policy between 1918 and 1939, there were a large number of incremental changes which had a profound effect on the overall pattern of welfare provision. However, even though 'the provision of unemployment benefit, as with other social services, was probably more comprehensive in Britain ... than in any other country which operated a democratic system,'[1] there were still large numbers of people who were living in squalid or overcrowded accommodation, who were unable to obtain adequate medical care, or who continued to depend on means-tested public assistance benefits. It is of course impossible to say how far these issues might have been addressed if the war had not occurred. However, given that it did occur, it is important to try to establish the extent to which it helped to highlight these deficiencies and to generate the political momentum needed to address them.

18.1 The challenge of war

During the last two years of World War One, the German air force launched 18 successful air-raids on the London area, killing 1,413 people and wounding 4,820 others. Although these raids had a negligible impact on the outcome of the war, they had a profound effect on official thinking about the likely course of any future conflict. During the 1920s, concern was focused on the question of how far the effects of such action might disrupt the smooth operation of the country's military, naval and administrative centre, but during the 1930s more attention began to be paid to the logistical aspects of aerial bombardment and its impact on civilian behaviour and morale. In 1934, Winston Churchill, who had served as Secretary of State for War (and Air) in Lloyd George's Coalition government between 1918 and 1921, predicted that if London were to become the target for continuous attack 'at least three million or four million people would be driven out into the open country around the metropolis. This vast mass of human beings, numerically far larger than any armies which have been fed and moved in war ... would confront the government ... with an administrative problem of the first magnitude, and would certainly absorb the energies of our small army and our territorial force.'[2]

One of the most pressing problems posed by the threat of enemy bombing was the need to compensate people for the destruction of homes and property.

During the second half of the 1930s, the government drew up plans for a national scheme to compensate people for the loss of possessions, but the more important question of providing rest centres for people who had been bombed out of their own homes was left in the hands of the public assistance committees of local authorities, and it was not until after the first great wave of air attacks on London, in the autumn of 1940, that this became a national responsibility. In the meantime, the London County Council, acting in concert with a range of voluntary agencies, began to make new arrangements for the provision of communal feeding, and by the end of 1941, 'the bleak inhospitable poor law standards of the centres in September 1940 had given way to good and kindly board and lodging, available without charge to homeless victims of air attack … "They couldn't do too much for me, Miss," said one old lady from Shoreditch who had to spend a night in a centre in December 1941. That comment was typical.'[3]

Although these improvements were clearly necessary, they were not designed to address the long-term need for the repair of damaged properties and the resettlement of those whose homes had been damaged beyond repair. During the period between September 1940 and June 1941, up to 2.25 million people were rendered homeless by enemy bombing, including up to 1.4 million Londoners, but progress in repairing damaged properties and resettling people whose homes had been destroyed was slow.[4] This was partly because the government attached greater priority to the railways, public utilities and essential war-related industries, and partly because different local authorities were reluctant to accept responsibility for people who had been displaced from neighbouring areas. However, by the end of 1940, the government had been forced to recognise that the problem of providing a minimum standard of accommodation for the victims of enemy bombing could no longer be ignored, and the lessons learned from this episode ensured that the country was in a much better position to deal with the threat of aerial bombardment during the flying-bomb attacks of 1944.[5]

One of the most important consequences of the war was to demonstrate that people could be placed in poverty through no fault of their own and that the problems associated with poverty could no longer be addressed on the basis of traditional attitudes to welfare provision, and this led to two major changes in the development of anti-poverty policy. In 1940, the government recognised that wartime inflation had eroded the value of old-age pensions and empowered the Unemployment Assistance Board (now renamed the Assistance Board) to pay supplementary pensions in cases of proven need. In 1941, the government abolished the household means-test for individuals receiving assistance from the Board, and introduced a new test which assumed that household members earning more than 55 shillings a week would contribute no more than seven shillings a week to the total rent. Even though this measure retained some elements of 'family responsibility', it brought additional relief to approximately 240,000 claimants, and paved the way for the National Health Insurance Act of 1941, the Pensions and Determination of Needs Act of 1943, and a substantial increase in the value of assistance benefits in 1944. The abolition of the household means-test and the transformation of the Unemployment Assistance Board were therefore vital steps in the transition from a localised system of poor relief based on the deliberations of Public Assistance Committees to the creation of a national system for the relief of poverty.[6]

The government's efforts to deal with the problems associated with the care and rehousing of people who were unable to remain in their own homes have left a much less durable impression on popular memory than the arrangements made to evacuate mothers and children in the autumn of 1939. The government first began to draw up plans for the evacuation of vulnerable groups from the major centres of population in the early 1930s, but the subject only really began to receive detailed attention following the appointment of a Home Office committee, under Sir John Anderson, in the spring of 1938. The committee identified four groups of people, known as the 'priority classes', who would need to be evacuated from the major population centres in the event of war, and divided the whole country into three separate types of area – evacuation areas (from which evacuation would take place), reception areas, and neutral areas. The priority classes were defined as (1) schoolchildren; (2) younger children, who would be accompanied by their mothers; (3) expectant mothers; and (4) adult blind persons and 'cripples' whose removal was feasible.[7]

The full history of wartime evacuation has been told elsewhere, and does not need to be discussed in great detail here. During the initial wave, which began on 1 September 1939, approximately 1.5 million people, including 826,959 unaccompanied schoolchildren and 523,670 mothers and preschool children, were evacuated from the evacuation areas to the reception areas, and a further two million people moved independently. However, most of the mothers and accompanied children, and approximately 45 per cent of the unaccompanied schoolchildren, had returned home by the beginning of 1940, and this meant that a second 'wave' was required when the bombing campaign began in earnest in the autumn of 1940. The third wave of evacuation occurred as a result of the flying-bomb attacks in the summer of 1944. On this occasion, 307,600 mothers and children were evacuated from London and the southeastern areas in organised parties, and approximately 552,000 mothers and children, old people and homeless people made their own arrangements to leave with the aid of government billeting certificates and travel vouchers. The total number of people who were evacuated with government assistance during this period was therefore not far short of one million.[8]

Titmuss argued that the successive waves of evacuation played a crucial role in reshaping attitudes to welfare provision. Although he recognised that the preparations for the initial wave of evacuation left a great deal to be desired, and that the encounter between hosts and evacuees was often fraught with difficulty, he also argued that it led, during the course of the war, to a reappraisal of traditional attitudes to welfare provision and therefore played a central part in the wartime origins of the welfare state. However, other historians have been more critical. Macnicol argued that, far from stimulating what Titmuss had called 'the war-warmed impulse of people for a more generous society', the experience of evacuation only served to reinforce a traditional, conservative view of what the Archbishop of Canterbury, Cosmo Lang, called 'the heedlessness, the shiftlessness, the carelessness and the ignorance' of working-class mothers.

In Macnicol's words, 'the social debate on evacuation probably served to *reinforce* existing analyses of working-class poverty rather than to change them … [it therefore] shows us that the ideological consensus of wartime, so stressed by Titmuss and some historians, was something of a myth.'[9]

Although Macnicol's conclusions have proved very influential in recent years, they also tend to ignore the extent to which evacuation did act as a catalyst for social change.[10] This was particularly true of its impact on the school medical service. During the 1930s, the school medical service had generated a vast mass of statistical information concerning the nutritional and hygienic standards of the country's schoolchildren. The experience of evacuation showed that, for whatever reasons, these statistics were dangerously misleading, and it prompted a wide-ranging reassessment of the methods which School Medical Officers used to screen child health and the standards which they used to assess it.[11] Although much of this debate focused on the internal practices and procedures of the school medical service, it also had much wider implications for the development of welfare provision as a whole. As the authors of the London County Council's internal survey of evacuation concluded in 1943, 'the experience of evacuation has – in advance of the Beveridge Report – brought home to social workers, and indeed to the nation at large, how real and formidable are the giants of Want, Ignorance and Squalor, and how sadly they are hindering, in town and country alike, the well-being of the rising generation.'[12]

The outbreak of war also led to major changes in the organisation of the country's hospital service. As we have already seen, the government expected that Britain would be subjected to immediate aerial attack, and in 1938 the Ministry of Health conducted the first official review of hospital facilities. This revealed that the standard of hospital accommodation in the country as a whole was low, and that there were 'only 80,000 beds in England and Wales which could be used for the prolonged treatment of casualties'. The government decided to divide the country as a whole into hospital regions, and, within each region, to identify those hospitals which could be used to treat war-related casualties. In the meantime, the Ministry launched an intensive programme to expand and upgrade facilities in these hospitals, and a corps of doctors was recruited into an 'emergency medical service', whose members could be deployed throughout the country. Approximately 10,000 trained nurses were recruited to form a Civilian Nursing Reserve, and a similar number of untrained nurses were appointed as 'nursing auxiliaries'.[13]

These arrangements had serious implications for the maintenance of normal hospital care. One of the most important problems was that the Ministry had agreed to pay many of the leading voluntary hospitals to keep existing beds empty so that they could be kept free for the admission of war-related casualties, but this meant that many 'ordinary' patients were forced to seek admission in the local-authority hospitals which, as a result, became increasingly overcrowded. In June 1940 the Ministry sought to address this problem by converting a large number of houses, schools and other buildings into 'auxiliary hospitals', and in December it advised all hospitals that 'the civilian sick should be admitted freely where waiting lists are accumulating'. However, despite these efforts, the problems faced by the 'ordinary civilian sick' remained formidable.

In 1942, the Ministry conducted a survey of hospital waiting lists which suggested that these had actually declined during the war years, but this was actually a piece of statistical legerdemain to conceal the fact that large numbers of potential patients had been excluded from the waiting lists altogether.[14] Abel-Smith suggested that doctors and hospitals had operated an unofficial system of priorities in which the needs of service personnel, air-raid casualties and war-workers came first, and those of pregnant women, children and elderly people came a somewhat distant second: 'women requiring gynaecological services queued for admission in large numbers and children waited years for orthopaedic and ophthalmic operations. Many elderly patients were left at home with grossly inadequate care and no prospect of admission at all.'[15]

Although the war had a deleterious impact on the availability of care for many sections of the population, it did act as a catalyst for change in other ways. The Ministry of Health's officials had been shocked by the way in which the first hospital surveys had revealed 'the low standard of hospital accommodation in the country as a whole', and Abel-Smith has argued that 'the hospital officers and sector officers [who] were recruited from doctors who had known the best of Britain's hospitals before the war … were grossly dissatisfied with the standards of accommodation in the worst voluntary and council hospitals, and shocked by the standards in the public assistance institutions.'[16] The war forced many hospitals to become more efficient, as they were encouraged to increase the rate at which patients passed through hospital and were returned to the workforce, and they faced growing criticism from middle-class patients who had been forced to seek medical treatment in institutions which they would not have entered before the war. These factors helped to bring about improvements in several aspects of hospital care, including orthopaedic and rehabilitation services, pathology services, blood transfusion services and the quality of hospital catering. They also added to the growing demand for a comprehensive reorganisation of hospital services in the postwar period.[17]

One of the greatest threats posed by the outbreak of war was the threat to the country's food supply, and the government had long recognised the need to ensure that all members of the population were able to gain access to a range of basic foodstuffs. As Zweiniger-Bargielowska has shown, 'civil servants discussed the economic implications of a major war at some length during the interwar years,' and detailed plans 'for the supply, control, distribution and movement of food' began to be drawn up from 1936 onwards. One of the most important considerations was the need to regulate consumer demand by introducing a system of rationing. In its *Annual Report* for 1937, the Board of Trade explained that the first and foremost aim of any rationing policy was to 'remedy an existing shortage, or to prevent an expected shortage'. However, it would also help to 'check a rise in prices … prevent the formation of food queues … economise certain commodities in order to create reserves … [and finally] ensure fair distribution amongst all classes of consumers'.[18]

The government's initial approach to rationing was based on three 'postulates'. Each individual was entitled to the same flat-rate ration (although children under the age of six only received half the meat ration of older people); consumers were only able to obtain rationed foods from a specified retailer (this was known as the consumer-retailer tie-in); and there was to be 'complete control'.[19] These principles were applied to butter, bacon, ham and sugar in January 1940; to meat in March in 1940; to tea, margarine and cooking-fat in July 1940; and to preserves and cheeses in June 1941. In December 1941, the government introduced a points system for canned foods, and this was extended to cover chocolate and sugar confectionery in the summer of 1942. Points-rationing was designed to allow consumers to exercise a degree of choice over the foods they consumed and the outlets from which they obtained them, but its effects were limited. In 1950, a government official concluded that even though the scheme had ensured 'that each consumer ... would be able to spend all points on a reasonable variety of foods', it 'could never succeed in ensuring that he or she would be able to buy any particular food of their preference ... In fact, points never came near to achieving the power of money in drawing particular goods to the point where they were individually in demand.'[20]

One of the main defects of the different rationing schemes was that they were unable to distinguish between the food needs of different individuals, either in terms of age (except in the case of very young children) or occupation, and there were also concerns that food resources might not be distributed in the most efficient or equitable way within the household. These concerns prompted the government to make arrangements for supplementary feeding by expanding the provision of workplace canteens, making arrangements for the provision of communal meals by the establishment of British Restaurants, and dramatically expanding the school-meals service. Zweiniger-Bargielowska has warned against placing too much emphasis on the importance of these measures, since the overwhelming majority of meals (between 24 and 24.5 meals per person per week) were consumed inside the home, but the expansion of the school-meals programme was particularly impressive.[21] In 1939, only 4.4 per cent of children attending public elementary schools in England and Wales received meals at school, and the majority of local education authorities drew a clear (and invidious) distinction between those receiving free meals (who were fed at 'feeding centres') and those whose parents paid for their meals (and were fed in school canteens). This distinction was abolished in December 1940, and by the end of the war more than 34 per cent of elementary schoolchildren (and more than 46 per cent of all secondary schoolchildren) were being fed at school.[22]

Amartya Sen has argued that Britain's experience during the two world wars shows how concerted government action can lead to substantial improvements in health standards, but the argument can be applied much more convincingly to the Second World War than to the First.[23] Rationing was one of the factors which helped to ensure a more egalitarian distribution of foodstuffs in Britain during the Second World War, and this led to a significant reduction in health inequalities and an improvement in the standard of public health as a whole. However, inequalities were not eliminated completely, and public acceptance of rationing declined sharply after the war was over. Popular resentment of the restrictions imposed by rationing played an important part in the defeat of the Labour party at the general election of 1951, and there was considerable relief when rationing was finally abandoned by the Conservative government three years later.[24]

18.2　Proposals for reform

As the previous section has shown, the war had a number of important practical effects which led to important changes in the conduct of social policy even before 1945, but it also helped to stimulate a much broader demand for change across the whole field of welfare provision. Although one should be wary of attaching too much importance to ideas of wartime solidarity and the creation of 'consensus', there can be little doubt that politicians and civil servants expected the war to act as a catalyst for change. As the Deputy Secretary of the Board of Education, R. S. Wood, observed in January 1941:

> While policy will have to command the support of the main elements in all parties, it is clear that the war is moving us in the direction of Labour's ideas and ideals, and the planning for a new 'national order' will be more towards the left than may generally be imagined now ... In these circumstances, it is clear that it will be fatal for officials to formulate their ideas in any spirit of timidity; we must 'dare boldly' in a fair cause ... Planning on bold and generous lines is what is looked for, and it may well be necessary to free our minds from conceptions that from long familiarity seem almost sacred and immutable: in short, to think in new terms for new times.[25]

One of the most contentious issues facing policy-makers during the war was the question of taxation. Although the government had increased personal tax rates during the First World War, it had obtained the bulk of its additional revenue from loans, but this pattern was reversed during World War Two. Between 1939 and 1941, the government imposed an excess profits tax of 60 per cent 'on the amount by which the profits arising in any chargeable accounting period exceed the standard profits', introduced new surtax rates for individuals earning between £2,000 and £30,000 a year, and raised the standard rate of income tax from 27.5 per cent to 50 per cent, but the most important change was the decision to reduce the threshold at which people became liable for income tax at a time when wages and prices were increasing. This meant that a much larger proportion of the population became eligible for income tax, and this had profound implications for the organisation of the tax system and the financing of public expenditure after 1945 (Table 18.1).[26]

During the early stages of the war, the government was mainly concerned with those aspects of social policy which were directly related to the war effort, and the war had little effect on the development of plans for future changes in welfare provision before the fall of the Chamberlain government in May 1940 and its replacement by a more genuinely cross-party Coalition government under the leadership of Winston Churchill. However, in June 1941 Arthur Greenwood, the Minister-without-Portfolio, invited Sir William Beveridge, the architect of the Labour Exchanges Act of 1909, to chair a new committee on the reform of social insurance and allied services. As José Harris has shown, Beveridge initially regarded the appointment as something of a poisoned chalice, but he soon realised that Greenwood's invitation gave him a unique opportunity to draft what has often been regarded as the main blueprint for the creation of the postwar welfare state and his 'scheme' affected the development of British social policy for a generation after 1945.[27]

Table 18.1 Estimated number of individuals with total incomes above the exemption limit, 1936/7–1945/6, Great Britain and Northern Ireland

Year	Number of individuals (1000s)		
	Entirely relieved from tax by the operation of allowances	Chargeable with tax	Total
1936/7	5,750	3,450	9,200
1937/8	6,000	3,700	9,700
1938/9	6,000	3,800	9,800
1939/40	6,200	4,100	10,300
1940/1	6,000	6,000	12,000
1941/2	5,800	10,200	16,000
1942/3	6,300	11,800	18,100
1943/4	5,800	12,500	18,300
1944/5	5,250	13,250	18,500
1945/6	5,000	13,750	18,750

Source: PP 1946–7 Cmd. 7067 xii, 361, *Eighty-ninth report of the Commissioners of His Majesty's Inland Revenue for the year ended 31st March 1946*, p. 53.

Beveridge's report was a complex mixture of traditional Edwardian liberalism and wartime collectivism, and it adopted an essentially gradualist approach to social change.[28] Its main aim was to create a unified system of social insurance which would provide comprehensive cover for workers and their dependants against the hazards of injury and sickness, unemployment, and old age. It continued to emphasise the importance of the contributory principle and Beveridge highlighted the fact that his main aim was not to redistribute income between classes, but 'between times of earning and not earning, and between times of heavy family responsibilities and of light or no family responsibilities'. However, whilst social insurance has often been described as a form of compulsory saving for the working class, it also drew on contributions from employers and the state, and, unlike the previous scheme, it was designed to cover the whole population, and not just manual workers. Beveridge also broke new ground by insisting that the benefits paid out under the scheme should be sufficient to meet subsistence needs. This was perhaps the most revolutionary feature of the insurance proposals, and the one which generated the greatest controversy.[29]

Although Beveridge argued that his scheme would provide a comprehensive system of protection against all forms of need, he recognised that there would still be a significant minority of the population who had already left the workforce and would therefore be unable to make sufficient contributions to qualify for the full range of insurance benefits, and for these people, and for those people who might never be able to work, he recognised that some form of means-tested social-security system would have to remain in place. Second, whilst he argued that the insurance scheme should indeed provide the minimum necessary for the means of subsistence, he also argued that it should not provide any more than the minimum, since this would undermine incentive, opportunity and responsibility. It was for this reason that he continued to attach so much importance to the provision of voluntary insurance by trade unions, friendly societies, occupational pension schemes and life assurance.[30]

Although Beveridge was mainly concerned with the technical details of the insurance scheme, he recognised that these could not be separated from much wider questions of welfare policy. He therefore argued that the scheme would only work if the government introduced a universal scheme of family allowances (to reduce the costs of child-rearing and maintain the differential between income from work and income when out of work); the creation of a comprehensive health and rehabilitation service (to enable every individual to maintain themselves in good health and to seek effective treatment when out of health); and the prevention of mass unemployment (to ensure that all members of the population had the opportunity to work and to minimise the costs of the benefits paid to those who were out of work).[31] He also succeeded in capturing the popular imagination by linking the 'plan for social security' to an all-embracing programme of postwar social reconstruction. The attack on Want, he informed his readers, was only one part of a comprehensive policy of social progress, and it must be accompanied by a parallel assault on the giants of Disease, Ignorance, Squalor and Idleness.[32] Even though Beveridge said relatively little about the ways in which these attacks might be mounted, the rich Bunyanesque imagery with which he identified the main goals of postwar reconstruction ensured that the report would become a powerful symbol of wartime aspirations.

Although the Beveridge Report has often been regarded as one of the prime examples of a supposed wartime consensus on social policy, this was not necessarily how it was seen at the time. After Beveridge had submitted his report, his findings were passed on to a civil service committee, chaired by Sir Thomas Phillips, which questioned the need for family allowances, cast doubt on the feasibility of full employment, and strongly opposed the principle of subsistence benefits. The recommendations were also questioned by the Treasury, which feared that they would inevitably lead to excessive levels of personal taxation, and by powerful sections of the Conservative party, many of whose members were believed to regard Beveridge as 'a sinister old man, who wishes to give away a great deal of other people's money'.[33] However, there was widespread popular support for Beveridge's vision of a world free from Want, and this was reflected in the views expressed by many backbench Labour MPs during a debate on the Beveridge Report in the House of Commons in February 1943. The strength of feeling in favour of Beveridge played a major role in persuading Churchill to authorise the establishment of a further committee (the Sheepshanks Committee) to investigate the best ways of implementing Beveridge's recommendations in April 1943.[34]

Although many historians have argued that the Beveridge Report formed the basis of the main elements of the social-security system which the Caretaker and Labour governments established in Britain between 1945 and 1948, the Sheepshanks Committee did not endorse Beveridge's recommendations uncritically. It accepted the basic assumptions on which the Beveridge Report was based and endorsed the principle of a universal system of social insurance financed by contributions from workers, employers and the state and offering a comprehensive range of flat-rate benefits to protect against sickness, unemployment and old age. However, it continued to reject the idea that these benefits should be linked explicitly to any measure of subsistence needs, and it deliberately avoided any reference to the term 'social security'. As a result, the Committee helped to ensure that means-tested benefits would continue to play a major part in the development of anti-poverty policy throughout the postwar period.[35]

One of the most important assumptions underpinning the Beveridge Report was the commitment to full employment. Beveridge had hoped to be allowed to play a leading role himself in the development of postwar employment policy, but the Treasury was reluctant to allow him to force its hand for a second time, and it went on to draft its own report on the maintenance of full employment in June 1944.[36] The report fell some way short of adopting either the deliberate attempts at demand management which John Maynard Keynes had advocated, or the more self-consciously interventionist approach to economic planning which Beveridge himself had recommended in 1942, but it brought the Treasury much closer to Keynes' ideas than had ever been the case in the 1930s and, most importantly, it marked the first official acknowledgement of the idea that it was a legitimate part of the business of government to seek to ensure a high and stable level of employment under peacetime conditions.[37]

After Idleness and Want, the next major giant on the road to reconstruction was Ignorance. As we have already seen, the interwar years had witnessed a number of important changes in the organisation of public education, but there was still a widespread feeling that many of the promises made at the end of the First World War had still not been redeemed by the start of the Second. Moreover, the war itself had also revealed many glaring defects in the organisation of the public education system, and this helped to fuel a widespread determination, stretching across the political spectrum, to begin the process of educational reform. This commitment was reflected in the publication of the Norwood Report on the Curriculum and Examinations in Secondary Schools on 23 June 1943 and the government's own White Paper on Educational Reconstruction on 16 July, and these reports formed the basis of the Education Act which the Conservative President of the Board of Education, R. A. ('Rab') Butler, and his Labour Deputy, James Chuter Ede, piloted through the Houses of Parliament in the following year.[38]

As many writers have pointed out, the Education Act was the only major piece of reconstruction legislation to be passed before the end of the war in Europe and the collapse of the Coalition government, and this reflected the fact that there was probably less party-political disagreement over this issue than over many others. It is also important to highlight the fact that Butler was able to deflect a good deal of potential criticism by securing agreement over the position of the voluntary-aided or Church-based schools; by appointing a separate committee to investigate the position of the 'public' (that is, private) schools; and by sidestepping the vexed question of the future organisation of secondary education beyond the age of 11. Nevertheless, the Act did represent a major stage of educational advance. It removed one of the major barriers to the coordination of primary and secondary education by abolishing the so-called 'Part III' authorities (that is, authorities empowered to provide elementary education only under the Balfour Education Act of 1902); it instructed all local education authorities to draw up plans for the development of education in their areas; it consolidated the recommendations of Circular 1350 and the Hadow report on *The education of the adolescent* by introducing a clear break between primary and secondary education at the age of 11; and it enhanced the status of education by converting the Board of Education into a fully fledged Ministry. However, its most important provisions were those relating to the schools themselves. It abolished the payment of school fees in secondary schools, which had been a significant barrier to the take-up of secondary school places by working-class pupils before the Second World War, and it raised the minimum school-leaving-age from 14 to 15. It also granted the Minister of Education the power to sanction a further increase in the school-leaving-age, from 15 to 16, as soon as circumstances permitted.[39]

One of the major limitations of education provision before 1939 was the failure to devote more resources to technical education, but this received only limited attention during the war. In 1941, the Board of Education drafted proposals for the expansion of part-time education in day continuation schools and the extension of junior technical schools, but even though the government planned to increase expenditure on technical education after 1945, it was clear that in the years immediately following the war new buildings and equipment for technical education would not be given as much priority as some other educational developments. However, the Board was rather more successful in its efforts to expand the provision of agricultural training. In 1944, the government invited the Vice-Chancellor of Bristol University, Dr Thomas Loveday, to chair an interdepartmental enquiry into agricultural education, and this recommended the expansion of pre-agricultural courses for second-ary school children and the increased provision of agricultural courses in universities. The Committee's recommendations encountered a number of administrative difficulties but they laid the foundations for the development of agricultural education and training after 1945.[40]

Although the Board of Education was primarily concerned with the future of primary and secondary education, it also became increasingly concerned with the future development of further and higher education. This was partly a consequence of the fact that if the government went ahead with its plans to expand the secondary-school system, this would almost certainly result in an increase in the demand for university places. However, the government was also becoming increasingly conscious of the role which the universities might be expected to play in the work of economic and social reconstruction more gen-erally. This was reflected in the appointment of a series of committees covering different aspects of higher education, including the McNair Committee on Teacher Training, the Goodenough Committee on Medical Education, the Teviot Committee on Dentistry (which recommended a threefold increase in the number of dental students), the Percy Committee on Higher Technological Education, and, in December 1945, the Barlow Committee on Scientific Manpower. Both the Percy Committee and the Barlow Committee emphasised the need to increase the number of scientists and expand the provision of scien-tific and technological training, but the extent of progress in the immediate postwar period was mixed. The number of students taking courses in 'pure' science increased from 7,661 to 16,917 between 1938/9 and 1949/50, but the first 'new' university, the University of Keele, only began to admit students in 1950, and the government failed to take any significant action to establish colleges of advanced technology before the publication of the Conservative government's White Paper on Technological Education in 1956.[41]

Although the politics of education reform were not entirely straightforward, they were considerably less fraught than the politics of health service reform. As we have already seen, the interwar period witnessed improvements in many different aspects of health care, but there was also a growing realisation that the existing level of provision fell below the standard required to meet the needs of the whole population. This feeling was reflected in a series of reports produced by a range of different bodies, including the Committee on Medical Insurance and Allied Services (1920), the Royal Commission on National Health Insurance (1926), the Socialist Medical Association (1932), and the British Medical Association (1930 and 1938), and it was reinforced by the experience of many health workers under the Emergency Medical Service from 1939 onwards. During the early years of the war, proposals for health-service reform were put forward by the voluntary hospitals, Political and Economic Planning, the Medical Planning Commission of the British Medical Association, the *Picture Post* and the Labour party, and the Ministry of Health began to draft its own proposals for the creation of a national hospital service during the course of 1941. However, despite all this activity, the government was unable to present any definite proposals for the establishment of a National Health Service before it left office in May 1945.[42]

Webster claimed that the government had originally intended to coordinate the development of its plans for the creation of a national health service with the planned timetable for the introduction of its educational reforms, and that it was only distracted from these plans by a commitment given by the President of the Privy Council, Sir John Anderson, 'that the form of the new service would be worked out in consultation with the parties involved'. However, the political challenges posed by the two issues were very different. As we have already seen, Butler and Ede were able to achieve significant progress in the field of educational reform by postponing discussion on many of the most controversial issues, such as the fate of the public schools and the future shape of secondary education, and by building on a process of reform which had already been underway since the mid-1920s. By contrast, the architects of the proposed national health service wished to make fundamental changes to the organisation of hospital services and the ordinary working conditions of general practitioners. They could not hope to achieve their aims without the support of these groups and it may not be entirely surprising to find that such support was not unequivocally forthcoming.[43]

Although there was widespread support for the principle of health-service reform, there were still profound disagreements over the extent and scope of any reform, and the form which it should take. During the 1920s and 1930s, the British Medical Association argued that the existing national health insurance scheme should be extended to cover a more comprehensive range of treatments, and that its coverage should be extended to the dependants of existing members and to all members of the population with an annual income of less than £250.[44] Although the Association declined to say how many people might be eligible for this scheme, it subsequently estimated that they would account for approximately 90 per cent of the total population.[45] However, when Beveridge presented his report on the future of social insurance and allied services, he assumed that the government would actually provide a comprehensive national health service for the whole population, and this recommendation was accepted by Sir John Anderson on behalf of the government in February 1943.[46] This decision caused consternation in the ranks of the British Medical Association, and even though it was supported by the majority of the Association's members, its leaders continued to oppose any formal agreement on the issue right up until the closing stages of the war.[47]

The BMA's leaders believed that the '100 per cent issue' had profound implications for the status and independence of the medical profession and the future of private medical practice. Although the government tried to reassure the profession that no patients would be forced to register for treatment under the national health scheme, many doctors believed that the scheme would lead to the diminution or even elimination of private practice because relatively few people would choose to remain outside the scheme if they were given the opportunity to belong to it.[48] Many general practitioners were opposed to this, not only because it would remove an important source of medical income, but also because they believed that the medical profession would lose its freedom and independence if it became wholly dependent on income received from government sources.[49] However, some doctors also claimed that it was necessary to protect the future of private practice in order to ensure the quality of medicine in general. In 1943, Dr. G. McFeat told the Association's Council that 'state-provided service and private practice should be continued concurrently, each acting as a spur to the other'.[50]

Although they were formally separate issues, the profession's attitude to the 100 per cent question was closely connected to its attitudes to the development of health centres and the creation of a salaried state medical service. In 1920, the Consultative Committee on Medical Insurance and Allied Services (the Dawson Committee) had advocated the creation of a fully integrated system of health care in which the full range of medical services, including general practitioner services, would be located in health centres, and many observers, including the Permanent Secretary of the Ministry of Health, believed that these proposals could only be put into practice if the new health centres were staffed by doctors employed on a salaried basis.[51] However, this proposal was bitterly resented by both the leadership and the rank and file of the British Medical Association, and it continued to poison relations between the profession and the Ministry of Health right up until the formal establishment of the National Health Service on 5 May 1948.[52] Many doctors also expressed reservations about the government's plans to interfere in the 'market' for medical care by directing newly qualified doctors to work in 'under-provided' areas and by establishing state-funded centres. In 1944, the Secretary of the BMA, Charles Hill, told a meeting of London practitioners that this would have a catastrophic effect on the capital value of existing practices because new doctors would prefer to take up positions in health centres, rather than purchasing their practices from existing practitioners.[53]

The relationship between the government and the British Medical Association was also soured by disagreements over the future of voluntary hospitals. During the interwar period, these hospitals had become increasingly dependent on the income they received from patients themselves, either in the form of direct payments or as a result of contributory insurance schemes, and both the British Medical Association and the hospitals themselves realised that they would lose this income if the government's plans for the creation of a national health scheme included the provision of the full range of hospital services for the whole population.[54] However, it was far from clear how the hospitals would be compensated for this shortfall. When the government published its White Paper on the National Health Service in February 1944, it said that the new joint hospital boards, which would be set up to administer hospital services, would pay the voluntary hospitals for the services they provided, but it also insisted that they would pay them less than the full cost of these services in order to preserve the voluntary principle.[55] This recommendation aroused considerable horror on the part of both the voluntary hospitals and the British Medical Association, which believed that the public was unlikely to make up the shortfall with voluntary donations 'in the atmosphere created by the government "free-for-all" propaganda'.[56]

The Association's misgivings were reinforced by the government's plans for the reform of health-service administration. When the government published its proposals, it said that the joint boards should be based on the local government principle, and that they would normally include representatives of the local county council and the county borough council, but that they would not include representatives of the local voluntary hospitals. It also recommended that the new boards should assume full responsibility for the management and ownership of the existing municipal hospitals, and even though the government recommended that the boards should pay the voluntary hospitals less than the full cost of the services they provided, both the hospitals and the British Medical Association believed that they would inevitably tend to favour their own hospitals at the expense of those which were, in effect, run by private agencies.[57] They therefore proposed the creation of much larger administrative authorities, known as regional councils, which would not necessarily or even usually be coterminous with local authority boundaries, but which would include representatives of both the local authorities and the voluntary hospitals, and which would reimburse the voluntary hospitals for the full cost of the services they provided.[58]

Although historians have often tended to portray the dispute between the government and the British Medical Association as a dispute between the political and administrative élite, on the one side, and the vested interests of the medical profession on the other, there were also significant areas of disagreement between the two main political parties over the nature and scope of health-service reform. As we have already seen, the Labour party had first proposed the establishment of a unified hospital system in 1918, and it had been committed to the creation of a comprehensive national health service, financed out of local and general taxation and available to the whole population, since 1934, but the Conservative party was much more ambivalent.[59] In 1943, following the publication of the Beveridge Report, a group of Conservative backbenchers told Churchill that there was no need to extend the right to free medical care to the entire population, and many Conservatives were also sympathetic to the position of the voluntary hospitals, whose approach to the provision of welfare services was closely attuned to traditional Conservative thinking. As a result, even though both parties had accepted the main recommendations of the Health Service White Paper at the time of its publication, they became increasingly divided over the next 12 months, and the future shape of the proposed national health service became one of the main points of disagreement between the two parties during the 1945 general election.[60]

In view of the differences between the two parties, it is interesting to speculate as to how the health service might have developed if the Conservatives had been returned to power. As we have already seen, the 1944 White Paper had recommended the creation of joint hospital boards, which would take over responsibility for the ownership and management of the existing municipal hospitals and purchase additional services, at less than their full cost, from the voluntary hospitals, and it is likely that the Conservative party would have abandoned these plans in favour of a scheme which was much closer to the one favoured by the British Medical Association and the voluntary hospitals.[61] However, even though the Labour party had been broadly supportive of the White Paper's proposals, it also decided to abandon them in favour of an alternative scheme, under which both the local authority hospitals and the voluntary hospitals were brought under the direct control of the Ministry of Health.[62] This decision enabled the government to meet one of the medical profession's main objections to the White Paper's plans, which was that the voluntary hospitals would be subordinated to the wishes of the local authorities, but it also led to the creation of a much more cumbersome administrative structure, under which local executive councils were made responsible for the provision of general practitioner services, the Ministry of Health assumed responsibility for hospital services, and local authorities retained responsibility for environmental health and the personal health services, such as the school medical service (now renamed the school health service) and the maternity and child welfare service. The new structure soon came to be seen as a barrier to the creation of a more integrated health service, and it was itself replaced following the reorganisation of the National Health Service in 1974.[63]

As we have already seen, the interwar years were characterised by a sustained period of mass unemployment, but this did not affect all parts of the country equally, and large numbers of people migrated from areas of high unemployment in search of work. According to the Ministry of Labour, the number of insured workers who were employed in Wales declined by more than 23 per cent between 1923 and 1938, but the number of insured workers in the midlands rose by 27.9 per cent, and the number of insured workers in London, south-east England and south-west England increased by 46.7 per cent.[64] The redistribution of the British population generated a series of enquiries into the operation of local government and the need for regional planning in the London area, and the government appointed two Special Areas Commissioners (one for Scotland, and one for England and Wales) to try to stimulate the growth of new industries in the most depressed areas, but little attempt was made to deal with the problem on a national basis before the appointment of the Royal Commission on the Distribution of Population (the Barlow Commission) in 1937. The Commission concluded that it was not in the interests of the country as a whole for more than 25 per cent of the population to be concentrated within 25 or 30 miles of the centre of London, and recommended the creation of a new central authority to develop plans for the 'balanced distribution … of the industrial population … throughout the different areas of Great Britain' and for the development of a balanced industrial structure within each of its regions.[65]

Although the Barlow Commission was appointed in 1937, it did not produce its report until the beginning of 1940, and its proposals lay 'inanimate in the iron lung of war' until the publication of the government's White Paper on Employment four years later.[66] However, it would be wrong to ignore the role which the war actually played in stimulating support for its proposals. Although the large-scale evacuation of mothers and children at the start of the war was only a temporary measure, it was also a major experiment 'in the relocation of a significant proportion of the population', and offered important lessons for future action. The war also helped to demonstrate the value of coordinated national planning because it necessitated the construction of a large number of new factories to maintain war production and highlighted the need to make the best possible use of agricultural resources. However, the greatest stimulus to town planning was provided by the bombs which rained down on Britain from the autumn of 1940 and 'transformed "the rebuilding of Britain" from a socially-desirable but somewhat visionary and vague ideal into a matter of practical and defined necessity'. In Ashworth's words, 'the shattering of cities by bombing' ensured that 'the ultimate rebuilding of large urban areas became a necessity for which it was prudent to take thought in advance'.[67]

The depredations of war also accelerated a change in the conception of town and country planning which had been developing since the early-1930s. During the interwar period, both town planners and social investigators had become increasingly alarmed by the proliferation of what they characterised as 'one-class suburbs' with limited social amenities, and this led to the development of a new conception of town planning, in which the planners paid much more attention to social issues, such as the relationship between each district and its region, and the need to secure a broader mix of occupations among the inhabitants of each region. This new-found concern with 'the fundamental problems of social life' was reflected in the various plans which Sir Patrick Abercrombie and his colleagues produced for the rebuilding of shattered communities in places such as Glasgow, Exeter, Hull, Oxford, Coventry and London during the second half of the war. In Ashworth's words, 'comparison of … Abercrombie's *Greater London Plan* of 1944 with the reports of the earlier Greater London Planning Committee would show at once the great widening of scope that had taken place'.[68]

The early years of the war also witnessed a flurry of activity at the level of central government. In October 1940, Churchill appointed the former Chairman of the British Broadcasting Corporation, Lord Reith, as Minister of Works, and the Scott Committee on Land Utilisation in Rural Areas and the Uthwatt Committee on Compensation and Betterment were established at the beginning of 1941. However, although the government finally agreed to establish a separate Ministry of Town and Country Planning in 1943, its practical effects were comparatively limited. Its major achievements were the extension of development controls to all areas where they had not previously been obtained in 1943, and the acquisition of extended powers for the compulsory acquisition of land, principally for reconstruction purposes, in 1944. These were both comparatively minor measures and, as Ashworth has argued, 'there was no fundamental remodelling of town planning law during the Second World War ... the main operative Acts were still the Town and Country Planning Acts of 1932, which had not been a conspicuous success up to 1939.'[69]

Although there was widespread support for the principle of town planning, efforts to secure further progress were frustrated by disagreements over the issue of compensation and betterment. When Lord Reith appointed the Uthwatt Committee in January 1941, he instructed it to carry out 'an objective analysis of the subject of the payment of compensation and recovery of betterment in respect of public control of the use of land' and 'to advise ... what steps should be taken ... to prevent the work of reconstruction ... being prejudiced'. The Committee concluded that the state should acquire all the development rights in land which had either not yet been developed or where redevelopment was necessary, and it recommended the imposition of a betterment levy of 75 per cent on any future increase in the annual site value of land which had already been developed.[70] Although these recommendations fell some way short of the Labour party's original views on the question of compensation and betterment, they were formally adopted by the party's Policy Committee in September 1943, but the Conservative party continued to oppose them on the grounds that they represented an unacceptable level of interference in the rights of existing property-owners.[71] In June 1944 the government rejected the idea that the state should acquire all the development rights in undeveloped land, or on land needing redevelopment, but suggested raising the betterment levy from 75 per cent to 80 per cent. However, the Coalition government was unable to agree to any further action on this basis, and the question was only finally resolved, on the basis of Uthwatt's original proposals, when Labour passed the Town and Country Planning Act in 1947.[72]

These disagreements also prevented any further progress in the development of housing policy. As we have already seen, there was already a significant housing shortage in Britain in 1939, and this was only exacerbated by the war itself. During the period between 1939 and 1945, there was an almost complete cessation of domestic building, 475,000 homes were either destroyed or made uninhabitable, a much greater number suffered serious damage, more than four million people got married, and the birth-rate rose substantially from 1941 onwards.[73] However, although both the major parties recognised the need for housing reform, there was no agreement on the best way of achieving this. In 1944, Churchill announced plans for the immediate construction of 500,000 prefabricated steel houses, and promised 200,000–300,000 permanent homes within two years of the defeat of Germany, but Labour promised to build four to five million new homes, with the leading role being given to local authorities.[74] During the period between 1945 and 1951, the Labour party oversaw the construction of approximately 1,045,000 new permanent homes, and 161,000 temporary homes, in the whole of the United Kingdom, but its efforts to achieve more than this were frustrated by a combination of labour shortages, economic difficulties and high prices. These difficulties ensured that housing continued to be an issue of major political controversy and, even though the postwar Labour government 'managed to achieve the first major impetus in public housing since the days of the Wheatley Act', its failure to build more than just over one million new homes played a major role in its fall from office in the autumn of 1951.[75]

18.3 The road from 1945

Although the war played a vital role in the development of the British welfare state, it is important to recognise the extent to which much of the infrastructure of public welfare provision already existed. The war did not create new welfare services, but it did create the political will to change the basis on which these services were offered. This was reflected in the development of plans to offer a unified system of social insurance to the whole population, the expansion of public housing, the creation of a national health service, and the reform of public educational provision.

As we have already seen, the war witnessed several important changes in both the form and level of personal taxation, including a reduction in the threshold at which individuals became liable for income tax, increases in the standard rate of income tax, and the introduction of a new surtax rate for individuals earning between £2,000 and £30,000 a year, and these changes shaped the broad structure of the personal tax system for much of the postwar period. In 1946, the Chancellor of the Exchequer, Hugh Dalton, took between two and two-and-a-half million individuals out of the tax system by raising tax thresholds and reduced the standard rate of income tax from 50 per cent (ten shillings in the pound) to 45 per cent (nine shillings in the pound), but he retained the surtax for individuals earning more than £10,000 a year and introduced a higher rate for those on larger incomes. However, although these reforms were designed to give the income tax system a more redistributive edge, Dalton's efforts to reduce the number of taxpayers by raising the tax threshold were gradually undermined by the general improvement in average earnings and the effects of price inflation, and this had profound implications for the financing of welfare provision. As Martin Daunton has explained, at the start of the twentieth century, the 'median voter' earned less than the amount needed to qualify for income tax and there was strong support for income taxation, but by the end of the 1970s a married couple with two children became liable for income tax if they earned more than 46.8 per cent of average male full-time earnings, and the payment of income tax was viewed rather differently.[76]

As we have already seen, the Beveridge Report had recommended that national insurance benefits should be sufficient to meet subsistence needs, but both the Phillips Committee and the Sheepshanks Committee had rejected the subsistence principle, and the coalition government was only prepared to state that benefits should be sufficient to provide 'a reasonable insurance against want', bearing in mind 'the maximum contribution which the great body of contributors can properly be asked to bear'. The new government was anxious to restore the link between benefits and subsistence, but it also agreed to credit existing pensioners with contributions which they had never actually paid, so that they could qualify for insurance benefits. However, this meant that the government was unable to increase the national insurance benefits in line with inflation, and even though a large number of pensioners now qualified for national insurance, they also required additional help, in the form of means-tested national assistance benefits, to meet their subsistence needs. This failure to raise the value of national insurance benefits in line with Beveridge's expectations meant that national assistance became an essential part of the social security system from 1948 onwards.[77]

Although the 1950s and 1960s have often been regarded as the high water-mark of the 'classic welfare state', there were nevertheless important areas of disagreement and discontinuity in welfare provision. In 1950, Seebohm Rowntree carried out a third social survey of York, in which he claimed that the kind of poverty experienced in interwar Britain had been largely eliminated by the establishment of the welfare state, but his critics argued that poverty was a relative concept, which could only be defined by reference to the standard of living in society as a whole.[78] In 1965, Abel-Smith and Townsend showed that even a small increase in the definition of the 'poverty line' could lead to a substantial increase in the number of people who were adjudged to be living in poverty and that a high proportion of these people were children, and this led to a long and fiercely contested debate about the best means of tackling child and family poverty. In 1967 and 1968 the Labour government attempted to deal with this issue by reducing the value of the child tax allowance (which tended to offer larger tax concessions to those on higher incomes) and increasing the value of family allowances and in 1971 the Conservatives introduced a new means-tested benefit, known as Family Income Supplement, for families on low incomes. However, neither of these measures was particularly successful, and in 1977 Labour abolished the dual system of child tax allowances and family allowances altogether, and replaced it with a unified system of child benefit, paid directly to the mother, and available to all families with children.[79]

Although the social-security system was, in many ways, the bedrock of the postwar welfare state, it was not the only aspect of Labour's policy to attract controversy. In 1946, the Minister of Health, Aneurin Bevan, had argued that there was vast amount of unmet medical need under the existing system of health care, and the cost of meeting this need led to a substantial increase in health-service expenditure during the early years of the National Health Service.[80] In May 1951 the Labour government introduced charges for dental and ophthalmic services, and in 1952 the Conservatives introduced charges for prescriptions, and these measures helped to ensure that the cost of the National

Health Service rose much more slowly during the first half of the 1950s, but the rate of increase began to accelerate once more during the second half of the 1950s, leading to renewed fears that the nation's appetite for medical care, in Enoch Powell's phrase, '*vient en mangeant*'. During the 1960s, both Labour and Conservative governments became convinced that the cost of funding the National Health Service could only be contained if its administrative structure was substantially reorganised, and this led to the passage of the National Health Service Reorganisation Act in 1973. The new Act abolished the regional hospital boards and established a new two-tier structure of regional health authorities and area health authorities, although these were themselves replaced by district health authorities in 1982.[81]

The postwar period also witnessed some important changes in the orientation of housing policy. As we have already seen, the Labour party believed that local authorities should shoulder the main burden of responsibility for the construction of new houses, but it only succeeded in building just over one million homes by the time it left office in October 1951. The new Conservative government promised to build 300,000 new dwellings, the majority of which were also built by local authorities, but in the longer run, the new government believed that the majority of housing needs should be met by the expansion of private ownership, with local authorities providing a residual service for those unable to obtain a satisfactory standard of housing through other means. Although this marked a fundamental break with Bevan's original policy, the Labour party was forced to recognise that a growing proportion of the electorate had already become home-owners and that many of those who did not already own their own homes had a strong desire to do so, and although it continued to be closely identified with the expansion of public-sector housing, it also became increasingly conscious of the need to appeal to the interests of home-owners. In 1965 it announced that 'the expansion of the public programme now proposed is to meet exceptional needs ... Expansion of owner-occupation, on the other hand, is normal; it effects a long-term social advance which should gradually pervade every region.'[82]

The postwar period also witnessed substantial changes in the development of education policy, particularly in relation to secondary education. As we have seen, the Butler Education Act of 1944 stated that there ought to be a clear break between primary education and secondary education, but it declined to specify the form which the new secondary school system should take. When Labour assumed office, the Ministry of Education argued that all children should have the same opportunity to go to the type of school for which they were most suited, and that there ought to be a range of different types of secondary school – grammar schools, technical schools and secondary modern schools – for children with different types or levels of ability.[83] However, during the 1950s it became increasingly apparent that the mechanisms which were used to select children for different types of school were inefficient and that the schools themselves were reproducing existing social inequalities, and when Labour returned to power in 1964, it pledged itself to the abolition of educational selection and the creation of comprehensive secondary schools catering for children of all levels of ability. The abolition of selective grammar schools and the creation of comprehensive schools was opposed by the Conservative party but widely supported by Conservative voters, and even though the Conservatives sought to obstruct the creation of comprehensive schools between 1970 and 1974, the majority of children were attending schools which were at least nominally comprehensive by the middle of the 1970s.[84]

Although there were many disagreements between the main political parties over the development of social policy after 1945, there was still an underlying consensus concerning the role that the state might justifiably play in meeting social needs. However, during the 1970s, many of the foundations of this consensus began to come apart in the face of rising unemployment and mounting inflation, and in 1976 the Labour Prime Minister, James Callaghan, was forced to tell his party conference that 'we used to think that you could spend your way out of recession and increase employment by cutting taxes and boosting government expenditure. I tell you in all candour: that option no longer exists ... The cosy world which we were told would go on for ever, where full employment would be guaranteed by the stroke of the Chancellor's pen, is gone for ever.'[85] However, even though the government agreed to cut public expenditure in return for a loan from the International Monetary Fund, it did not mount a concerted ideological attack on the principles of state welfare provision, and public expenditure had begun to rise once more when the government left office in 1979. Consequently, although the Callaghan government may have paved the way for the election of Margaret Thatcher, it would be wrong to see her approach as a continuation of that pursued by the government which preceded her.[86]

Although the Conservatives failed to achieve any significant reductions in the proportion of GDP devoted to public expenditure between 1979 and 1987, they made a number of important changes in other aspects of social policy.[87] In 1979, the Chancellor, Geoffrey Howe, reduced the basic rate of income tax from 33 per cent to 30 per cent, lowered the rate at which tax was levied on the highest incomes from 83 per cent to 60 per cent, and increased the rate of value-added tax from eight per cent to 15 per cent, and this set the tone for further reductions in both the standard and higher rates of income tax over the next 18 years.[88] The Conservatives also allowed unemployment to rise as part of their strategy for reducing inflation, and they introduced a number of major changes to the social-security system, including the decision to raise unemployment benefit by less than the rate of inflation in 1981, the abolition of the earnings-related supplement to short-term national insurance benefits and the decision to increase state pensions in line with prices rather than earnings in 1982, the freezing of child-benefit levels in 1981 and 1988, and the withdrawal of death and maternity grants in 1986. However, the most important changes were those which followed the introduction of the 1986 Social Security Act, which introduced a set of common rules for all means-tested benefits, replaced Supplementary Benefit and Family Income Supplement with Income Support and Family Credit, and replaced the existing system of 'exceptional payments' (for the purchase of such items as cookers and replacement furniture) with a system of 'discretionary payments', 70 per cent of which had to be repaid as loans.[89] The government also introduced two major changes in housing policy.

In 1980, they instructed local authorities to offer council houses for sale to existing tenants at heavily discounted rates, and in 1988 they gave private landlords and housing associations the opportunity to assume responsibility for the management of council estates. This policy had relatively little impact, at least in the short term, but the sale of council houses led to a sharp reduction in the proportion of households living in council-owned accommodation, and enabled the proportion of owner-occupying households to increase from 58 per cent in 1981 to 67 per cent 15 years later.[90]

Although the government made some significant changes in health and education policy during its first two terms, these were much less dramatic than the changes made in the areas of housing and social security, but after 1987 the Conservatives pressed ahead with their efforts to expand the role played by market principles in the provision of public services. In 1988, the government introduced a national curriculum in all state schools, with regular national tests (Standard Attainment Tests) at the ages of seven, 11 and 14, supplemented by the publication of 'league tables' which were supposed to provide a clear indication of the way in which different schools were performing. These changes were supposed to give more power to parents and more freedom to schools, but their main effect was probably to transfer more power from local to central government, and even though parents were now able to obtain more information about their local schools, there was no guarantee that they would be able to secure places for their children at the schools of their choice.[91] In 1990, the government made a similar effort to introduce market principles into the provision of public health care. It encouraged family doctors to become independent fundholders, with the opportunity to purchase specialist services on behalf of their patients, the district health authorities were made responsible for purchasing health care, and the services which had previously been under the direct control of these bodies, such as NHS hospitals, became independent NHS trusts, but it is difficult to judge how far these changes made a positive contribution to health care. According to Glennerster, their effects were 'neither as terrible [n]or as positive as the protagonists forecast', but Webster thought that their main impact was to push up administrative costs. During the 1980s, the NHS employed approximately 1,000 senior managers and administrative costs consumed approximately five per cent of the total budget. By the middle of the following decade, the NHS employed 26,000 senior managers, and administrative costs consumed around 12 per cent of the total budget.[92]

When the Labour party regained power in 1997, it committed itself to the pursuit of a 'third way' between the 'extremes' of 'Old Labour' and Thatcherite Conservatism, and this was reflected in many different areas of both economic and social policy.[93] One of the government's most controversial pledges was not to increase either the standard rate of income tax or the higher rate, and to abide by the Conservatives' public-spending plans for the first two years of the new administration.[94] However, although this commitment implied a strong degree of continuity with some aspects of Conservative policy, the government was prepared to make some important innovations in relation to others. In 1998 and 1999, the Chancellor, Gordon Brown, reduced the tax rate on the first £1,500 of taxable income to ten per cent, removed tax allowances on dividends and abolished mortgage-interest tax relief, whilst using the proceeds to finance the introduction of tax credits for families in low-paid employment. The government also honoured its manifesto pledge to introduce a national minimum wage, albeit at a lower rate than had originally been envisaged, and there were substantial increases in government expenditure on both health and education from 1999 onwards.[95]

Although these tax changes resulted in a limited degree of income redistribution, the central plank of Labour's approach to welfare policy was its belief that 'work is the best route out of poverty'.[96] In 1998 and 1999, the government announced the launch of six 'New Deal' programmes – for young people, the long-term unemployed, lone parents, the partners of unemployed people, disabled people and the over-50s – in the hope of 'steer[ing] different unemployed groups through various gateways into the labour market'.[97] However, it is arguable that the most important challenge facing the government concerned the reform of the pension system. When the government came to power, it angered many of its own supporters by deciding to continue with the previous government's policy of only uprating pensions in line with prices rather than earnings, whilst introducing a Minimum Income Guarantee for pensioners on low incomes, and encouraging those who were still in work to make greater provision for their own retirement by taking out stakeholder pensions and offering generous tax incentives to people wishing to invest in Individual Savings Accounts.[98] In December 2002, the government argued that even though the proportion of elderly people in the British population was expected to rise less rapidly than the elderly populations of other European countries, people could not expect the state to provide more than a basic level of support, and 'the amount people should save in addition to the basic State Pension will depend on their own circumstances and preferences'.[99]

The government's desire to promote a more collaborative relationship between the public and private sectors was also reflected in its approach to housing policy. When the government came to power, it continued with the previous government's policy of transferring responsibility for the administration of local authority housing to housing associations and other 'social landlords', and more than 370,000 homes were transferred out of the local authority sector between 1997 and 2002.[100] However, in recent years the most significant areas for debate have occurred in the fields of education and health. The government introduced changes in the national curriculum for primary schools in order to strengthen the emphasis on numeracy and literacy, established national targets for results in the various Standard Attainment Tests, and set out to promote greater 'diversity' in the secondary-school system by encouraging a growing number of schools to apply for 'specialist' status. It also courted growing controversy in relation to higher education by seeking to increase the proportion of 18-year-olds going to university at the same time as it was also trying to make students and their parents shoulder a greater share of the burden of university funding.[101] In the area of health, the government retained the split between the purchasers and providers of health care which the Conservatives had introduced in 1990, and although it was committed to the abolition of fundholding general practices, the arrangements which replaced them were not very different.[102] In 2002, the Secretary of State for Health, Alan Milburn, announced a further new departure in the form of 'foundation trusts'. This change was designed to build on the changes introduced under the Conservatives' National Health Service and Community Care Act of 1990 by 'free[ing] the very best NHS hospitals from direct Whitehall control', and giving them the opportunity to negotiate their own salary and employment contracts. The government defended these proposals on the grounds that they would strengthen the voice of the local community in the development of health services, but its opponents claimed that they would increase the gap between foundation hospitals and other NHS hospitals, and that the newly created foundation hospitals might even seek to opt out of the NHS altogether.[103]

Although there are definite continuities between the market-led policies promoted by the Conservative governments between 1979 and 1997 and the policies pursued by New Labour since 1997, it is also important to try to place these policies in a more long-term context. As both Glennerster and Fraser have argued, there are strong grounds for believing that the 'architect' of the post-war welfare state, William Beveridge, would have been acutely disappointed by the failure to establish a universalist social-security system, based on the principle of national insurance, and by the seemingly irreversible movement in favour of greater means-testing, but he might have drawn rather more encouragement from the government's desire to strengthen the links between social-security policy and employment policy, and he would almost certainly have welcomed the government's efforts to promote the growth of private savings plans, even though he might have been disappointed by the extent to which these were administered by commercial organisations rather than the mutual-aid societies whose history he celebrated in 1948.[104]

Although it seems clear that there are many continuities in social-security provision, there are other respects in which the current government has clearly broken new ground, particularly in relation to public-service provision. As we have already seen, the government is clearly determined to promote greater 'diversity' in the provision of both health and education services, and at the end of 2002 the Prime Minister reiterated his personal belief in the need to '[put] behind us … the 1945 "big state" that wrongly believed it could solve every social problem' and build 'an enabling state founded on the liberation of individual potential'. This is certainly an exciting vision of the future of welfare policy, but there is also a clear danger than the pursuit of 'diversity' in the public services may simply lead to the promotion of greater inequality, with an increasing proportion of the available resources being channelled to the most successful institutions, many of which are likely to be located in the most affluent areas. The Prime Minister has also argued that it is necessary to move beyond 'the narrow, selfish individualism of the 1980s', but he has yet to convince his critics that he has succeeded in developing the new collective ethos which will be needed to carry the welfare state into the twenty-first century.[105]

Notes

Preface

1. P. Thane, *The foundations of the welfare state*, London: Longman, First edition, 1982, p. vii; Second edition, 1996, p. xiii.
2. D. Fraser, 'Review of P. Thane, *The foundations of the welfare state*', *Journal of Social Policy*, 12 (1983), 113–15, at 114.
3. D. Fraser, *The evolution of the British welfare state: a history of social policy since the Industrial Revolution*, London and Basingstoke, Macmillan (now Palgrave Macmillan), First edition, 1973, p. 1; Second edition, 1984, p. 1; Third edition, 2003, p. 1; C. Pierson, *Beyond the welfare state? The new political economy of welfare*, Oxford and Cambridge: Basil Blackwell & Polity Press, 1991, pp. 14–21.
4. M. Hill, *The welfare state in Britain: a political history since 1945*, Aldershot: Edward Elgar, 1993; H. Glennerster, *British social policy since 1945*, Oxford: Basil Blackwell, First edition, 1995; Second edition, 2000; R. Lowe, *The welfare state in Britain since 1945*, London and Basingstoke: Macmillan (now Palgrave Macmillan), First edition, 1993; Second edition, 1999; N. Timmins, *The five giants: a biography of the welfare state*, London: Harper Collins, First edition, 1995; Second edition, 2001.
5. G. Esping-Anderson, *The three worlds of welfare capitalism*, Oxford and Cambridge: Basil Blackwell and Polity Press, 1990, pp. 27, 33; J. Harris, 'Enterprise and the welfare state: a comparative perspective', *Transactions of the Royal Historical Society*, Fifth series, 40 (1990), 175–95, at 194 (reprinted in T. Gourvish and A. O'Day (eds), *Britain since 1945*, Basingstoke: Macmillan (now Palgrave Macmillan), 1991, pp. 39–58, at p. 56); M. Daunton, 'Payment and participation: welfare and state formation in Britain 1900–51', *Past and Present*, 150 (1996), 169–216, at 170–1.

1   Introduction

1. H. Heclo, 'Welfare: progress and stagnation', in W. Gwyn and R. Rose (eds), *Britain: progress and decline*, London and Basingstoke: Macmillan (now Palgrave Macmillan), 1980, pp. 39–56, at p. 39.
2. 'Brown bets all on the NHS', *Guardian*, 18 April 2002, 1. URL: www.guardian.co.uk/guardianpolitics/story/0,3605,686174,00.html; T. Blair, 'My vision for Britain', *Observer*, 10 November 2002, 26. URL: www.observer.co.uk/comment/story/0,6903,837002,00.html.
3. J. Lewis, 'Voluntary and informal welfare', in R. M. Page and R. Silburn (eds), *British social welfare in the twentieth century*, Basingstoke: Palgrave (now Palgrave Macmillan), 1999, pp. 249–70, at p. 249.
4. A. M. McBriar, *An Edwardian mixed doubles: the Bosanquets versus the Webbs. A study in British social policy 1890–1929*, Oxford: Clarendon Press, 1987, pp. 14–33.

5. S. Webb and B. Webb, *English Poor Law History. Part II. The last hundred years* (first edition 1929), London: Frank Cass, 1963, pp. v–xx; see also A. Kidd, 'Historians or polemicists? How the Webbs wrote their history of the English poor laws', *Economic History Review*, 40 (1987), 400–17.

6. G. Slater, *Poverty and the state*, London: Constable & Co., 1930, pp. 1, 4.

7. T. H. Marshall, 'Citizenship and social class', in T. H. Marshall, *Sociology at the crossroads and other essays*, London: Heinemann, 1963, pp. 67–127, at p. 73; M. Bruce, *The coming of the welfare state*, London: B. T. Batsford, 1968, p. 7.

8. D. Fraser, *The evolution of the British welfare state: a history of social policy since the Industrial Revolution*, London & Basingstoke: Macmillan (now Palgrave Macmillan), First edition, 1973, p. 226; Second edition, 1984, p. 223.

9. R. Lowe, *The welfare state in Britain since 1945*, London & Basingstoke: Macmillan (now Palgrave Macmillan), First edition, p. 63; Second edition, p. 63.

10. S. Humphries, *Hooligans or rebels? An oral history of working-class childhood and youth 1889–1939*, Oxford: Basil Blackwell; J. Bornat and D. Atkinson, 'Oral history and the history of learning disability', in J. Bornat, R. Perks, P. Thompson and J. Walmsley (eds), *Oral history, health and welfare*, London: Routledge, 2000, pp. 180–202, at p. 199.

11. E. Roberts, 'The recipients' view of welfare', in J. Bornat, R. Perks, P. Thompson and J. Walmsley (eds), *Oral history, health and welfare*, London: Routledge, 2000, pp. 203–26, at p. 215; D. Gittins, *Madness in its place: narratives of Severalls Hospital, 1913–97*, London: Routledge, 1998, p. 223.

12. K. Marx, *Capital: a critique of political economy. Vol. 1*, Harmondsworth: Penguin, 1976 (First edition, 1867), pp. 340–416.

13. J. Saville, 'The welfare state: an historical approach', *New Reasoner*, 3 (1957), 5–25, at 5–6.

14. N. Ginsburg, *Class, capital and social policy*, London and Basingstoke: Macmillan (now Palgrave Macmillan), 1979, p. 2.

15. A. Gramsci, *Selections from the Prison Notebooks*, London: Lawrence and Wishart, 1973, p. 210.

16. S. Hall and B. Schwarz, 'State and society 1880–1930', in M. Langan and B. Schwarz (eds), *Crises in the British state 1880–1930*, London: Hutchinson, 1985, pp. 7–32; J. Keane, 'The limits of state action', in J. Keane, *Democracy and civil society: on the predicaments of European socialism, the prospects for democracy, and the problem of controlling social and political power*, London: Verso, 1988, pp. 1–30, at p. 27; see also J. Keane (ed.), *Civil society and the state: new European perspectives*, London: Verso, 1988.

17. M. Philp, 'Michel Foucault', in Q. Skinner (ed.), *The return of grand theory in the human sciences*, Cambridge: Cambridge University Press, 1985, pp. 65–81, at p. 76.

18. M. Foucault, *The order of things: an archaeology of the human sciences*, London: Tavistock, 1970.

19. M. Foucault, *Madness and civilisation: a history of insanity in the Age of Reason*, London: Tavistock, 1967; ibid., *The birth of the clinic*, London: Tavistock, 1973; M. Ignatieff, *A just measure of pain: the penitentiary in the industrial revolution 1750–1850*, London: Macmillan (now Palgrave Macmillan), 1978; M. A. Crowther, *The workhouse system 1834–1929: the history of an English social institution*, London: Methuen, 1981; D. Rothman, 'Social control: the uses and abuses of the concept in the history of incarceration', in S. Cohen and A. Scull (eds), *Social control and the state: historical and comparative essays*, Oxford: Basil Blackwell, pp. 106–17.

20. C. Pateman, 'The patriarchal welfare state', in A. Gutmann (ed.), *Democracy and the welfare state*, Princeton, NJ: Princeton University Press, 1986, pp. 231–60.

21. E. Wilson, *Women and the welfare state*, London: Tavistock, 1977, pp. 7–8.

22. J. Walkowitz, *Prostitution and Victorian society: women, class and the state*, Cambridge: Cambridge University Press, 1980.

23. J. Lewis, 'The working class wife and mother and state intervention 1870–1918', in J. Lewis (ed.), *Labour and love: women's experience of home and family 1850–1940*, Oxford: Basil Blackwell, 1984, pp. 99–120, at pp. 110–11; E. Ross, *Love and toil: motherhood in outcast*

London 1870–1918, New York: Oxford University Press, 1993, pp. 209–15; Roberts, 'The recipients' view of welfare', p. 214.

24. D. King, *The New Right: politics, markets and citizenship*, London and Basingstoke: Macmillan (now Palgrave Macmillan), 1987, pp. 17–23, 45–8; V. George and P. Wilding, *Welfare and ideology*, New York and London: Harvester Wheatsheaf, 1994, p. 2035.

25. C. Barnett, *The audit of war: the illusion and reality of Britain as a great nation*, London: Macmillan (now Palgrave Macmillan), 1986; D. Green, *Working class patients and the medical establishment: self-help in Britain from the mid-nineteenth century to 1948*, Aldershot: Gower/Maurice Temple Smith, 1985; Institute of Economic Affairs, *The long debate on poverty: eight essays on industrialisation and the 'condition of England'*, London: Institute of Economic Affairs, 1972; F. Prochaska, *The voluntary impulse: philanthropy in modern Britain*, London: Faber, 1988.; *ibid..*, 'Philanthropy', in F. M. L. Thompson (ed.), *The Cambridge social history of Britain 1750–1950. Volume 3. Social agencies and institutions*, Cambridge: Cambridge University Press, 1990, pp. 357–94; *ibid., Philanthropy and the hospitals of London: the King's Fund 1897–1990*, Oxford: Clarendon Press, 1992.

26. D. Vincent, *Poor citizens: the state and the poor in twentieth-century Britain*, London: Longman, 1991, p. 206.

27. K. Williams, *From pauperism to poverty*, London: Routledge and Kegan Paul, 1981; M. Dean, *The constitution of poverty: towards a genealogy of liberal governance*, London: Routledge, 1990.

28. T. Novak, *Poverty and the state: an historical sociology*, Milton Keynes: Open University Press, 1988, pp. viii–ix.

29. M. Wiener, *English culture and the decline of the industrial spirit 1850–1980*, Cambridge: Cambridge University Press, 1981.

30. Barnett, *The audit of war*, pp. 38–51, 237–64, 304; cf. J. Harris, 'Enterprise and the welfare state: a comparative perspective', *Transactions of the Royal Historical Society*, Fifth series, 40, 175–95 (reprinted in T. Gourvish and A. O'Day (eds), *Britain since 1945*, Basingstoke: Macmillan (now Palgrave Macmillan), 1991, pp. 39–58).

31. G. Finlayson, *Citizen, state and social welfare in Britain 1830–1990*, Oxford: Oxford University Press, 1994, pp. 3, 422.

32. Prochaska, *The voluntary impulse*, p. 88.

33. S. Yeo, 'Working class association, private capital, welfare and the state in the late-nineteenth and twentieth centuries', in N. Parry, M. Rustin and C. Satyamurti (eds), *Social work, welfare and the state*, London: Edward Arnold, pp. 48–71, at p. 50.

34. Green, *Working-class patients*, pp. 1–2; see also *ibid.*, 'Medical care before the NHS', *Economic Affairs*, 14 (1994), 16–21.

35. H. Pelling, 'The working class and the origins of the welfare state', in H. Pelling, *Popular politics and society in late-Victorian Britain*, London and Basingstoke: Macmillan (now Palgrave Macmillan), pp. 1–18; P. Gosden, *Self-help: voluntary associations in nineteenth-century Britain*, London: B. T. Batsford, 1973; Yeo, 'Working class association'; Thane, 'The working class and state "welfare" in Britain 1880–1914', *Historical Journal*, 27 (1984), 877–900.

36. Lewis, 'The working class wife and mother', p. 114.

37. Ross, *Love and toil*; see esp. Chapters 2, 5–7.

38. V. A. C. Gatrell, 'The decline of theft and violence in Victorian and Edwardian England', in V. Gatrell, B. Lenman and G. Parker (eds), *Crime and the law: the social history of crime in western Europe since 1500*, London: Europa, 1980, pp. 238–337.

39. Gosden, *Self-help*; P. Johnson, *Saving and spending: the working-class economy in Britain 1870–1939*, Oxford: Oxford University Press, 1985; M. Tebbutt, *Making ends meet: pawnbroking and working class credit*, London: Methuen, 1983.

40. See for example D. Ashford, *The emergence of the welfare states*, Oxford: Basil Blackwell, 1986; P. Baldwin, *The politics of social solidarity: class bases of the European welfare state*, Cambridge: Cambridge University Press, 1990; A. De Swaan, *In care of the state: health care, education and welfare in Europe and the USA in the modern era*, Oxford and Cambridge: Basil Blackwell

and Polity Press, 1988; G. Esping-Andersen, *The three worlds of welfare capitalism*, Oxford and Cambridge: Basil Blackwell and Polity Press, 1990; P. Flora and A. Heidenheimer, *The development of welfare states in Europe and America*, New Brunswick and London: Transaction Publishers, 1981; C. Pierson, *Beyond the welfare state? The new political economy of welfare*, Oxford and Cambridge: Basil Blackwell and Polity Press, 1991.

41. I. Tait, 'Keeping the jobless occupied: voluntary welfare and unemployment in 1930s Britain', in I. Blanchard (ed.), *New directions in economic and social history*, Avonbridge: Newlees Press, 1995, pp. 57–64; B. Harris, 'Responding to adversity: government–charity relations and the relief of unemployment in interwar Britain', *Contemporary Record*, 9 (1995), 529–61.

42. See for example C. Hanson, 'Welfare before the welfare state', in R. M. Hartwell *et al.*, *The long debate on poverty: eight essays on industrialisation and the 'condition of England'*, London: Institute of Economic Affairs, 1972, pp. 111–39; Green, 'Working-class patients'.

43. J. Veverka, 'The growth of government expenditure in the United Kingdom since 1790', *Scottish Journal of Political Economy*, 10 (1963), 111–27, at 119; J. Brewer, *The sinews of power: war, money and the English state 1688–1783*, London: Unwin Hyman, 1989, p. 40.

44. M. Daunton, *Trusting Leviathan: the politics of taxation in Britain 1799–1914*, Cambridge: Cambridge University Press, 2001, p. 1.

45. Daunton, *Trusting Leviathan*, pp. 41–3, 256–301; S. Szreter, 'Economic growth, disruption, deprivation, disease and death: on the importance of the politics of public health for development', *Population and Development Review*, 23 (1997), 693–728, at 702–7; *ibid.*, 'Health, class, place and politics: social capital and collective provision in Britain', *Contemporary British History*, 16 (2002), 27–58, at 29–32.

46. Daunton, *Trusting Leviathan*, pp. 43–7, 77–9, 225–33, 330–74; see also *ibid.*, 'Trusting Leviathan: the politics of taxation, 1815–1914', in D. Winch and P. K. O'Brien (eds), *The political economy of British historical experience, 1688–1914*, Oxford: Oxford University Press, 2002, pp. 319–50.

47. J. Harris, *Unemployment and politics: a study in English social policy 1886–1914*, Oxford: Clarendon Press, 1972, p. 380; R. Middleton, *Government versus the market: the growth of the public sector, economic management and British economic performance, c. 1890–1979*, Cheltenham: Edward Elgar, 1996, p. 238.

48. This is not to say that all the changes introduced by the Liberals between 1906 and 1914 were redistributive in this way. The introduction of flat-rate contributions for health insurance and unemployment insurance was highly regressive, because the contributions represented a higher proportion of the incomes of poorly paid workers in comparison with better-off workers. See for example Harris, *Unemployment and politics*, p. 380; J. R. Hay, *The origins of the Liberal welfare reforms*, Basingstoke: Macmillan (now Palgrave Macmillan), Second edition, 1983, p. 59.

49. J. Le Grand, *The strategy of equality: redistribution and the social services*, London: Allen and Unwin, 1982; Middleton, *Government versus the market*; P. Thane, *Foundations of the welfare state*, London: Longman, Second edition, 1996, p. 203.

50. Veverka, 'The growth of government expenditure', p. 119; Daunton, *Trusting Leviathan*, pp. 256–301; *ibid.*, 'Trusting Leviathan', pp. 340–8; Szreter, 'Health, class, place and politics', p. 29; see also Table 1.1.

51. G. Peden, 'From cheap government to efficient government: the political economy of public expenditure in the United Kingdom, 1832–1914', in D. Winch and P. K. O'Brien (eds), *The political economy of British historical experience, 1688–1914*, Oxford: Oxford University Press, 2002, pp. 351–78, at pp. 353–61; Veverka, 'The growth of government expenditure', pp. 118–25; see also Table 1.2.

52. R. M. Bird, 'Wagner's "law" of expanding state activity', *Public Finance*, 26 (1971), 1–26, at 7; Middleton, *Government versus the market*, p. 90.

53. R. Parry, 'Britain: stable aggregates, changing composition', in R. Rose *et al.*, *Public employment in western nations*, Cambridge: Cambridge University Press, 1985, pp. 54–96, at pp. 57–63.

2 The growth of state intervention

1. P. Slack, *The English Poor Law 1531–1782*, Cambridge: Cambridge University Press, 1995, pp. 164–5; D. Roberts, *Victorian origins of the British welfare state*, New Haven, CT: Yale University Press, 1960, p. 315.

2. J. R. Hay, *The origins of the Liberal welfare reforms*, Basingstoke: Macmillan (now Palgrave Macmillan), Second edition, 1983, pp. 11–12.

3. A. Briggs, 'The welfare state in historical perspective', *Archives Européenes du Sociologie*, 2 (1961), 221–58, at 228.

4. P. Flora and A. Heidenheimer, 'The historical core and changing boundaries of the welfare state', in P. Flora and A. Heidenheimer (eds), *The development of welfare states in Europe and America*, New Brunswick, NJ and London: Transaction Publishers, 1981, pp. 17–34, at p. 21.

5. I. Gough, *The political economy of the welfare state*, London and Basingstoke: Macmillan (now Palgrave Macmillan), 1979, pp. 1–5; R. Mishra, *Society and social policy: theories and practice of welfare*, London and Basingstoke: Macmillan (now Palgrave Macmillan), 1981.

6. A. De Swaan, *In care of the state: health care, education and welfare in Europe and the USA in the modern era*, Oxford and Cambridge: Basil Blackwell and Polity Press, 1988, p. 2; see also N. Elias, *The civilising process*, Oxford: Basil Blackwell, 1982.

7. De Swaan, *In care of the state*, p. 257; but see also *ibid.*, 'Perspectives for transnational social policy in Europe: social transfers from West to East', in A. De Swaan (ed.), *Social policy beyond borders: the social question in transnational perspective*, Amsterdam: Amsterdam University Press, 1994, pp. 101–15.

8. De Swaan, *In care of the state*, pp. 6–7, 13–51.

9. See for example P. Thane, 'Review of A. De Swaan, *In care of the state: health care, education and welfare in Europe and the USA in the modern era*', *International Review of Social History*, 35, (1990), 454–7.

10. S. Mennell, 'Review of A. De Swaan, *In care of the state*', *Social Policy and Administration*, 23 (1990), 192–6, at 193.

11. C. Offe, 'Review of A. De Swaan, *In care of the state: health, education and welfare in Europe and the USA in the modern era*', *Sociology*, 24 (1990), 153–4.

12. J. Harris, 'The transition to high politics in English social policy, 1880–1914', in M. Bentley and J. Stevenson (eds), *High and low politics in modern Britain: ten studies*, Oxford: Clarendon Press, 1983, 58–79, at p. 58.

13. D. Fraser, *The evolution of the British welfare state: a history of social policy since the Industrial Revolution*, London and Basingstoke: Macmillan (now Palgrave Macmillan), First edition, 1973, p. 1; Second edition, 1984, p. 1; Third edition, 2003, p. 1.

14. U. Henriques, *Before the welfare state: social administration in early industrial Britain*, London: Longman, 1979, p. 1; see also Hay, *Origins of the Liberal welfare reforms*, p. 12.

15. C. Pierson, *Beyond the welfare state? The new political economy of welfare*, Oxford and Cambridge: Basil Blackwell and Polity Press, 1991, pp. 13–14.

16. H. Wilensky and C. Lebeaux, *Industrial society and social welfare: the impact of industrialisation on the supply and organisation of social welfare services in the United States, with a new introduction by Harold L. Wilensky*, New York: The Free Press, 1965.

17. H. Wilensky, *The welfare state and equality: structural and ideological roots of public expenditure*, Berkeley, CA: University of California Press, 1975, pp. 15–49.

18. D. R. Cameron, 'The expansion of the public economy: a comparative analysis', *American Political Science Review*, 72 (1978), 1243–61, at 1245; R. Middleton, *Government versus the market: the growth of the public sector, economic management and British economic performance, c. 1890–1979*, Cheltenham: Edward Elgar, 1996, p. 115.

19. S. Finer, *The history of government. Volume 3. Empires, monarchies and the modern state*, Oxford: Oxford University Press, 1997, pp. 1480–1.

20. H. Uusitalo, 'Comparative research on the determinants of the welfare state: the state of the art', *European Journal of Political Research*, 12 (1984), 403–22.

21. J. O'Connor and R. Brym, 'Public welfare expenditure in OECD countries: towards a reconciliation of inconsistent findings', *British Journal of Sociology*, 39 (1988), 47–68.

22. P. Flora and A. Heidenheimer, 'Introduction', in P. Flora and A. Heidenheimer (eds), *The development of welfare states in Europe and America*, New Brunswick, NJ and London: Transaction Publishers, 1981, pp. 5–14, at pp. 8–9.

23. T. H. Marshall, 'Citizenship and social class', in T. H. Marshall, *Sociology at the crossroads and other essays*, London: Heinemann, 1963, pp. 67–127, at pp. 75–6; cf. Pierson, *Beyond the welfare state?*, pp. 22–4.

24. P. Flora and J. Alber, 'Modernisation, democratisation and the development of welfare states in Europe', in P. Flora and A. Heidenheimer (eds), *The development of welfare states in Europe and America*, New Brunswick, NJ and London: Transaction Publishers, pp. 37–80, at pp. 42–3, 69–70.

25. R. Goodin and J. Le Grand, *Not only the poor: the middle classes and the welfare state*, London: Unwin Hyman.

26. K. Marx and F. Engels, *The Communist manifesto*, Harmondsworth: Penguin, 1967 (first published 1848), pp. 79–94.

27. V. George and P. Wilding, *Ideology and social welfare*, London: Routledge and Kegan Paul, 1985, pp. 95–119; *ibid.*, *Welfare and ideology*, New York and London: Harvester Wheatsheaf, 1994, pp. 102–29.

28. R. Miliband, *The state in capitalist society*, London: Weidenfeld and Nicolson, 1969.

29. N. Poulantzas, *Political power and social classes*, London: New Left Books, 1973; J. Dearlove and P. Saunders, *Introduction to British politics: analysing a capitalist democracy*, Cambridge: Polity Press, Second edition, 1991, pp. 268–83.

30. K. Marx, *Capital: a critique of political economy*. Vol. 1, Harmondsworth: Penguin, 1976 (First edition, 1867), pp. 344–8.

31. J. Saville, 'The welfare state: an historical approach', *New Reasoner*, 3 (1957), 5–25, at 5–6.

32. I. Gough, *The political economy of the welfare state*, London and Basingstoke: Macmillan (now Palgrave Macmillan), 1979, p. 64; N. Ginsburg, *Class, capital and social policy*, London and Basingstoke: Macmillan, 1979, p. 2.

33. J. O'Connor, *The fiscal crisis of the state*, New York: St Martin's Press, 1973, pp. 6–7. It may be worth noting that O'Connor was, of course, using the term 'social capital' in a very different way to that employed by Robert Putnam in more recent years. Putnam's conception of 'social capital' is derived from the work of the early-twentieth-century Progressive reformer, L. J. Hanifan, who defined social capital as 'those tangible substances [that] count most in the daily lives of people: namely goodwill, fellowship, sympathy, and social intercourse among the individuals and families who make up a social unit'. See R. Putnam, *Bowling alone: the collapse and revival of American community*, New York: Touchstone, 2000, p. 19.

34. C. Offe, 'Some contradictions of the modern welfare state', in C. Offe, *Contradictions of the welfare state*, London: Hutchinson, 1984, pp. 147–61.

35. C. Offe, 'Social policy and the theory of the state', in C. Offe, *Contradictions of the welfare state*, London: Hutchinson, 1984, pp. 88–118, at p. 115, note 7.

36. George and Wilding, *Welfare and ideology*, p. 113.

37. R. Lowe, *The welfare state in Britain since 1945*, London and Basingstoke: Macmillan (now Palgrave Macmillan), First edition, 1993, pp. 32–3; Second edition, 1996, p. 33.

38. See P. Baldwin, *The politics of social solidarity: class bases of the European welfare state 1875–1975*, Cambridge: Cambridge University Press, 1990, *passim*.

39. M. Foucault, *Madness and civilisation: a history of insanity in the Age of Reason*, London: Tavistock, 1967; *ibid.*, *The birth of the clinic*, London: Tavistock, 1973.

40. De Swaan, *In care of the state*, pp. 230–46.

41. H. Perkin, *The rise of professional society: England since 1880*, London: Routledge, 1989, pp. 155–70.

42. P. Dunleavy and B. O'Leary, *Theories of the state: the politics of liberal democracy*, Basingstoke: Macmillan (now Palgrave Macmillan), 1987, pp. 114–20.

43. P. Baldwin, *The politics of social solidarity: class bases of the European welfare state*, Cambridge: Cambridge University Press, 1990, pp. 289–90.

44. J. Dryzek and R. Goodin, 'Risk-sharing and social justice: the motivational foundations of the postwar welfare state', in R. Goodin and J. Le Grand (eds), *Not only the poor: the middle classes and the welfare state*, London: Unwin Hyman, 1987, pp. 37–73.

45. Baldwin, *Politics of social solidarity*, pp. 8–9, 289.

46. J. Le Grand, 'Comment on inequality, redistribution and recession', *Journal of Social Policy*, 14 (1985), 309–12; R. Goodin and J. Le Grand, 'Not only the poor', in R. Goodin and J. Le Grand (eds), *Not only the poor: the middle classes and the welfare state*, London: Unwin Hyman, 1987, pp. 203–27.

47. G. Bock and P. Thane (eds), *Maternity and gender policies: women and the rise of the European welfare states 1880s–1950s*, London: Routledge, 1991; S. Koven and S. Michel (eds), *Mothers of a new world: maternalist politics and the origins of welfare states*, London: Routledge, 1993; J. Lewis, 'Gender, the family and women's agency in the building of "welfare states": the British case', Social History, 19 (1994), 37–55; A. Orloff and T. Skocpol, 'Why not equal protection? Explaining the politics of public social spending in Britain, 1900–11, and the United States, 1880s–1920s', *American Sociological Review*, 49 (1984), 726–50; S. Pedersen, 'The failure of feminism in the making of the British welfare state', *Radical History Review*, 43 (1989), 86–110; *ibid.*, 'Gender, welfare and citizenship in Britain during the Great War', *American Historical Review*, 95 (1990), 983–1006; *Family, dependence and the origins of the welfare state: Britain and France 1914–45*, Cambridge: Cambridge University Press, 1993; T. Skocpol, *Protecting soldiers and mothers: the political origins of social policy in the United States*, Cambridge, MA and London: Harvard University Press, 1992; T. Skocpol and G. Ritter, 'Gender and the origins of modern social policies in Britain and the United States', *Studies in American Political Development*, 5 (1991), 36–93.

48. S. Koven and S. Michel, 'Womanly duties: maternalist politics and the origins of welfare states in France, Germany, Great Britain and the United States, 1880–1920', *American Historical Review*, 95 (1990), 1076–1108; see also *ibid.*, 'Introduction: "Mother worlds" ', in S. Koven and S. Michel (eds), *Mothers of a new world: maternalist politics and the origins of welfare states*, London: Routledge, 1993, pp. 1–42, at p. 4.

49. Koven and Michel, 'Womanly duties', 1076–9; 'Introduction', pp. 2–6.

50. Skocpol and Ritter, 'Gender and the origins of modern social policies', 74; see also Lewis, 'Gender, the family and women's agency', 39–40.

51. See also Lewis, 'Gender, the family and women's agency', 39–40.

52. C. Pateman, 'The patriarchal welfare state', in A. Gutmann (ed.), *Democracy and the welfare state*, Princeton, NJ: Princeton University Press, 1988, pp. 231–60, pp. 231–2.

53. See for example P. Thane, 'Women in the British Labour Party and the construction of State welfare, 1906–39', in S. Koven and S. Michel (eds), *Mothers of a new world: maternalist politics and the origins of welfare states*, London: Routledge, 1993, pp. 343–77.

54. S. Andrzejewski, *Military organisation and society*, London: Routledge and Kegan Paul, 1954, pp. 33, 191; see also M. Mann, 'Capitalism and militarism', in M. Mann, *States, war and capitalism: studies in political sociology*, Oxford: Basil Blackwell, 1988, pp. 124–45, at p. 134.

55. Andrzejewski, *Military organisation and society*, pp. 29, 33.

56. *Ibid.*, pp. 71, 124.

57. R. Titmuss, 'War and social policy', in B. Abel-Smith and K. Titmuss (eds), *The philosophy of welfare: selected writings of Richard M. Titmuss*, London: Allen and Unwin, 1987, pp. 102–12, at p. 111; A. Reid, 'World War 1 and the working class in Britain', in A. Marwick (ed.), *Total*

war and social change, Basingstoke: Macmillan (now Palgrave Macmillan), 1988, pp. 16–24, at p. 21.

58. A. Marwick, *The deluge: British society and the First World War*, Basingstoke: Macmillan (now Palgrave Macmillan), Second edition, 1991, p. 20.

59. A. Peacock and J. Wiseman, *The growth of public expenditure in the United Kingdom*, Princeton, NJ: Princeton University Press, 1961, p. xxiv. Strictly speaking, Peacock and Wiseman only identified two effects – the 'displacement effect' and the 'inspection effect'. However, the acceptance of new obligations arising out of the war does not really fall into either of the other two categories.

60. B. Gilbert, *The evolution of national insurance in Great Britain: the origins of the welfare state*, London: Michael Joseph, 1966; G. Searle, *The quest for national efficiency: a study in British politics and political thought, 1899–1914*, Oxford: Basil Blackwell, 1971.

61. P. Abrams, 'The failure of social reform 1918–20', *Past and Present*, 24 (1963), 43–64; R. Lowe, 'The erosion of state intervention in Britain 1917–24', *Economic History Review*, 31 (1978), 270–86; J. Macnicol, 'The effect of the evacuation of schoolchildren on official attitudes to state intervention', in H. L. Smith (ed.), *War and social change: British society in the Second World War*, Manchester: Manchester University Press, 1986, pp. 3–31; H. L. Smith, 'Introduction', in *ibid.*, pp. viii–xi; K. Jefferys, 'British politics and social policy during the Second World War', *Historical Journal*, 30 (1987), 123–44; *ibid., The Churchill Coalition and wartime politics, 1940–45*, Manchester: Manchester University Press, 1991.

62. Middleton, *Government versus the market*, p. 118.

63. D. Dolowitz and D. Marsh, 'Who learns what from whom? A review of the policy transfer literature', *Political Studies*, 44 (1996), 343–57, at 344.

64. For further work on the concept of 'policy transfer', see C. Bennett, 'What is policy convergence and what causes it?', *British Journal of Political Science*, 21 (1991), 215–33.; R. Rose, 'What is lesson drawing?', *Journal of Public Policy*, 11 (1991), 3–30; *ibid., Lesson drawing in public policy: a guide to learning across time and space*, Chatham, NJ: Chatham House, 1993; D. Dolowitz, *Policy transfer and British social policy: Learning from the USA?* Buckingham: Open University Press, 2000; D. Dolowitz and D. Marsh, 'Learning from abroad: the role of policy transfer in contemporary policy-making', *Governance*, 13 (2000), 5–24.

65. See for example P. Weindling, 'Introduction: Constructing international health between the wars', in P. Weindling (ed.), *International health organisations and movements, 1918–39*, Cambridge: Cambridge University Press, 1995, pp. 1–16, pp. 5–7.

66. B. Harris, *The health of the schoolchild: a history of the school medical service in England and Wales*, Buckingham: Open University Press, 1995, pp 27–9.

67. *Ibid.*, pp. 29–32.

68. Searle, *The quest for national efficiency*, pp. 54–60.

69. PP 1897 C. 8447 xxv, 1, *Special Reports on educational subjects 1896–7; PP 1898 C. 8943 xxiv, 1, *Special Reports on subjects relating to education in England and Wales, Ireland, and foreign countries, Volume 2; PP 1898 C. 8988 xxv, 1, *Special reports on educational subjects, Volume 3;* W. H. Dawson, *School doctors in Germany* (Board of Education, Educational Pamphlets, no. 4), London: HMSO, 1906.

70. E. P. Hennock, *British social reform and German precedents: the case of social insurance 1880–1914*, Oxford: Clarendon Press, 1987, pp. 109–215.

71. Save the Children Fund, *Unemployment and the child, being the report on an enquiry ... into the effects of unemployment on the children of the unemployed and on unemployed young workers of Great Britain*, London: Longman's, Green & Co., 1933; League of Nations, *Final report of the Mixed Committee of the League of Nations on the relation of nutrition to health, agriculture and social policy*, Geneva: League of Nations, 1937. See also Harris, *The health of the schoolchild*, p. 129; P. Weindling, 'Social medicine at the League of Nations Health Organisation and the International Labour Office compared', in P. Weindling (ed.), *International health*

organisations and movements, 1918–39, Cambridge: Cambridge University Press, 1995, pp. 134–53; *ibid.*, 'The role of international organisations in setting nutritional standards in the 1920s and '30s', in H. Kamminga and A. Cunningham (eds), *The science and culture of nutrition 1840–1940*, Amsterdam: Rodopi, 1995, pp. 319–32.

72. D. King, *The New Right: politics, markets and citizenship*, London and Basingstoke: Macmillan (now Palgrave Macmillan), 1987, pp. 17–23, 45–8.

73. Dunleavy and O'Leary, *Theories of the state*, pp. 95–108, 114–19; King, *The New Right*, pp. 100–4; D. Green, *The New Right: the counterrevolution in political, economic and social thought*, Brighton: Wheatsheaf, 1987, pp. 92–103; George and Wilding, *Welfare and ideology*, pp. 15–20.

74. G. Tullock, *The vote motive: an essay in the economics of politics, with applications to the British economy*, London: Institute of Economic Affairs, 1976; W. Niskanen, *Bureaucracy: servant or master? Lessons from America*, London: Institute of Economic Affairs, 1973.

75. Peacock and Wiseman, *The growth of public expenditure*.

76. King, *The New Right*, pp. 45–8.

77. For example P. Dunleavy, *Democracy, bureaucracy and public choice: economic explanations in political science*, New York and London: Harvester Wheatsheaf, 1991.

3 Britain in the age of industrial growth

1. A. Gibson and T. C. Smout, *Prices, food and wages in Scotland 1550–1780*, Cambridge: Cambridge University Press, 1995, pp. 12–13.

2. *Ibid.*, p. 13.

3. A. Toynbee, *Lectures on the industrial revolution of the eighteenth century in England*, London: Longman's, Green & Co, 1902, pp. 85–93; C. Lee, *The British economy since 1700: a macro-economic perspective*, Cambridge: Cambridge University Press, 1986, p. 18; N. Crafts, 'The industrial revolution', in R. Floud and D. McCloskey (eds), *The economic history of Britain since 1700, Volume 1*, Cambridge: Cambridge University Press, 1994, pp. 44–59, at p. 47.

4. R. Allen, 'Agriculture during the industrial revolution', in R. Floud and D. McCloskey (eds), *The economic history of Britain since 1700, Volume 1*, Cambridge: Cambridge University Press, 1994, pp. 96–122, at pp. 102, 105–8, 122; K. Snell, *Annals of the labouring poor: social change and agrarian England 1660–1900*, Cambridge: Cambridge University Press, 1985, pp. 138–227.

5. E. A. Wrigley and R. S. Schofield, *The population history of England 1541–1871: a reconstruction*, Cambridge: Cambridge University Press; B. R. Mitchell, *British historical statistics*, Cambridge: Cambridge University Press, 1978, pp. 3–11.

6. N. Tranter, 'The labour supply 1780–1860', in R. Floud and D. McCloskey (eds), *The economic history of Britain since 1700, Volume 1*, 1994, pp. 204–26, at p. 206; N. Crafts, *British economic growth during the industrial revolution*, Oxford: Oxford University Press, 1985, p. 15.

7. P. Waller, *Town, city and nation: England 1850–1914*, Oxford: Oxford University Press, 1983, p. 7; A. S. Wohl, *Endangered lives: public health in Victorian Britain*, London: Methuen, 1984, p. 4; F. M. L. Thompson, 'Town and city', in F. M. L. Thompson (ed.), *The Cambridge Social History of Britain*, Cambridge: Cambridge University Press, Volume 1, 1990, pp. 1–86, at p. 8.

8. D. Landes, *The unbound Prometheus: technological change and industrial development in western Europe from 1750 to the present*, Cambridge: Cambridge University Press, 1969, p. 41; M. Berg, *The age of manufactures*, London: Fontana, 1985, pp. 20, 316–7.

9. E. Royle, *Modern Britain: a social history 1750–1985*, London: Edward Arnold, 1987, p. 83; D. Fraser, *The evolution of the British welfare state: a history of social policy since the Industrial Revolution*, London and Basingstoke: Macmillan (now Palgrave Macmillan), First edition, 1973, p. 5; Second edition, 1984, p. 5; Third edition, 2003, p. 6.

10. This figure is derived from the list of Select Committees and their Reports in the *General Index to the reports of Select Committees, 1801–52* (1853; reprinted in the Irish University Press

Series of British Parliamentary Papers, Shannon: Irish University Press, 1968). For further information, see the items listed under the following headings: Crime and outrage; Gaols; Insolvent debtors – debtors' prisons; London – Police; Convict establishments; Dartmoor Prison; Punishment of offenders; Riots.

11. M. Thomis and P. Holt, *Threats of revolution in Britain 1789–1848*, London and Basingstoke: Macmillan (now Palgrave Macmillan), 1977, *passim*.

12. Thomis and Holt, *Threats of revolution*, pp. 5–28; E. J. Hobsbawm, *The age of revolution: Europe 1789–1848*, London: Cardinal, 1973, pp. 138–41.

13. E. J. Hobsbawm and G Rudé, *Captain Swing*, London: Lawrence and Wishart, 1969, pp. 97–8, 304–5.

14. D. Thompson, *The Chartists: popular politics in the industrial revolution*, Aldershot: Wildwood House, 1984, pp. 57–76, 307–29.

15. Hobsbawm and Rudé, *Captain Swing*, pp. 253–63, 297; A. Brundage, *The making of the New Poor Law: the politics of inquiry, enactment and implementation 1832–39*, London: Hutchinson, 1978, pp. 12, 15.

16. G. Stedman Jones, *Outcast London: a study in the relationship between classes in Victorian London*, Harmondsworth: Penguin, 1984, pp. 173–8; P. Mandler, *Aristocratic government in the age of reform*, Oxford: Clarendon Press, pp. 200–67.

17. O. MacDonagh, 'The nineteenth-century revolution in government', *Historical Journal*, 1 (1958), 52–67, at 58–61; H. Parris, 'The nineteenth-century revolution in government: a re-appraisal', *Historical Journal*, 3 (1960), 17–37; J. Hart, 'Nineteenth-century social reform: a Tory interpretation of history', *Past and Present*, 31 (1965), 39–61; V. Cromwell, 'Interpretations of nineteenth-century administration: an analysis', *Victorian Studies*, 9 (1966), 245–55; W. Aydelotte, 'Conservative and radical interpretations of early-Victorian social legislation', *Victorian Studies*, 11 (1967), 225–36; L. J. Hume, 'Jeremy Bentham and the nineteenth-century revolution in government', *Historical Journal*, 10 (1967), 361–75.

18. A. Smith, *An inquiry into the nature and causes of the wealth of nations*, Indianapolis, IN: Liberty Fund, pp. 11–12, 687–8.

19. *Ibid.*, pp. 156–7, 470.

20. T. Malthus, *An essay on the principle of population* (edited with an Introduction by Anthony Flew), Harmondsworth: Penguin, 1970, pp. 67–103.

21. R. Cowherd, *Political economists and the English Poor Laws: a historical study of the influence of classical economics on the formation of social welfare policy*, Athens, OH: Ohio University Press, 1977, pp. 113–14; J. Garraty, *Unemployment in history: economic thought and public policy*, New York: Harper Colophon, 1978, p. 71.

22. P. Sraffa (ed.), *The works and correspondence of David Ricardo, edited by Piero Sraffa, with the collaboration of M. H. Dobb. Vol. I. On the principles of political economy and taxation*, Cambridge: Cambridge University Press, 1951, pp. 107–8.

23. Cowherd, *Political economists*, pp. 1–26; B. Hilton, *The age of atonement: the influence of Evangelicalism on social and economic thought, 1795–1865*, Oxford: Clarendon, 1988, pp. 3–35; P. Mandler, 'Tories and paupers: Christian political economy and the making of the New Poor Law', *Historical Journal*, 33 (1990), 81–103, at 86–91.

24. Mandler, 'Tories and paupers', 83.

25. M. Levin, *The condition of England question: Carlyle, Mill, Engels*, Basingstoke: Macmillan (now Palgrave Macmillan), 1998, pp. 33–72; R. Pearson and G. Williams, *Political thought and public policy in the nineteenth century: an introduction*, London: Longman, 1984, pp. 71–101.

26. Mandler, 'Tories and paupers', *passim*.

27. B. L. Hutchins and A. Harrison, *A history of factory legislation, with a preface by Sidney Webb*, London: P. S. King & Son, 1926, pp. 7–18.

28. *Ibid.*, pp. 18–42.

29. Fraser, *The evolution of the British welfare state*, First edition, p. 21; Second edition, p. 22; Third edition, p. 23.

30. J. Kay, *The moral and physical condition of the working classes employed in the cotton manufacture in Manchester*, London: Ridgway, 1832, p. 13; Fraser, *The evolution of the British welfare state*, First edition, p. 75; Second edition, p. 81; Third edition, p. 88.

31. Fraser, *The evolution of the British welfare state*, First edition, pp. xiv–xv; Second edition, pp. xvi–xvii; Third edition, pp. xv–xvi; M. Sanderson, *Education, economic change and society in England 1780–1870*, Basingstoke: Macmillan (now Palgrave Macmillan), Second edition, 1991, pp. 21–2.

32. D. Roberts, *Victorian origins of the British welfare state*, New Haven, CT: Yale University Press, 1960, pp. 28, 93–5, 98–9; Mandler, *Aristocratic government*, pp. 6–7, 39, 175–9, 190–1, 256–67; M. Pugh, *Britain since 1789: a concise history*, Basingstoke: Macmillan (now Palgrave Macmillan), 1999, pp. 15–18, 26–7, 50–3.

33. Roberts, *Victorian origins*, p. 99; Mandler, *Aristocratic government*, pp. 175–6.

34. A. V. Dicey, *Lectures on the relation between law and public opinion in England during the nineteenth century*, London: Macmillan (now Palgrave Macmillan), 1962, p. 175; S. Finer, 'The transmission of Benthamite ideas 1820–50', in G. Sutherland (ed.), *Studies in the growth of nineteenth-century government*, London: Routledge and Kegan Paul, 1972, pp. 11–32, at pp. 12–13.

35. J. Bentham, *A fragment on government* (edited by Ross Harrison), Cambridge: Cambridge University Press, 1998, p. 3; E. Halévy, *The growth of philosophic radicalism*, London: Faber & Faber, 1934, *passim*.

36. S. Finer, *The life and times of Sir Edwin Chadwick*, London: Methuen, 1952; A. Brundage, *England's 'Prussian Minister': Edwin Chadwick and the politics of government growth, 1832–1854*, University Park, PA: Pennsylvania State University Press, 1988; Mandler, *Aristocratic government*, pp. 123–274.

37. J. H. Clapham, *An economic history of modern Britain*, Cambridge: Cambridge University Press, 1926, p. 7; J. L. Hammond, 'The industrial revolution and discontent', *Economic History Review*, 2 (1930), 215–28, at 225.

38. P. H. Lindert, 'Unequal living standards', in R. Floud and D. McCloskey (eds), *The economic history of Britain since 1700, Volume 1*, Cambridge: Cambridge University Press, 1994, pp. 357–86, at pp. 369–75.

39. C. H. Feinstein, 'Pessimism perpetuated: real wages and the standard of living in Britain during and after the industrial revolution', *Journal of Economic History*, 58 (1998), 625–58.

40. Wrigley and Schofield, *Population history*, pp. 531–5; E. A. Wrigley, R. Davies, J. Oeppen and R. Schofield, *English population history from family reconstitution 1580–1837*, Cambridge: Cambridge University Press, 1997, pp. 613–5.

41. R. Floud and B. Harris, 'Health, height and welfare: Britain 1700–1980', in R. Steckel and R. Floud (eds), *Health and welfare since industrialisation*, Chicago: Chicago University Press, 1997, pp. 91–126, at pp. 96–9.

42. R. Schofield, 'Dimensions of illiteracy', *Explorations in Economic History*, 10 (1973), 437–54; G. Sutherland, 'Education', in F. M. L. Thompson (ed.), *The Cambridge Social History of Britain, Volume 3*, Cambridge: Cambridge University Press, 1990, pp. 119–70, at pp. 119–32.

43. Floud and Harris, 'Height, health and welfare', pp. 107–8.

44. See B. Harris, 'Health, height and history: an overview of recent developments in anthropometric history', *Social History of Medicine*, 7 (1994), 297–320; R. Steckel, 'Stature and the standard of living', *Journal of Economic Literature*, 33 (1995), 1903–40.

45. R. Floud, K. Wachter and A. Gregory, *Height, health and history: nutritional status in the United Kingdom 1750–1980*, Cambridge: Cambridge University Press, 1990, p. 326; see also Floud and Harris, 'Height, health and welfare', pp. 100–5.

4   The New Poor Law and the relief of poverty, 1834–1914

1. J. R. Poynter, *Society and pauperism: English ideas on poor relief, 1795–1834*, London: Routledge and Kegan Paul, 1969, p. xvi; G. Himmelfarb, *The idea of poverty: England in the early-industrial age*, London: Faber and Faber, 1984, pp. 51–2, 68–9.

2. G. R. Elton, 'An early Tudor poor law?', in G. R. Elton, *Studies in Tudor and Stuart politics and government: Papers and reviews, 1946–72, Volume 2, Parliament/Political thought*, Cambridge: Cambridge University Press, 1974, pp. 137–54; P. Slack, *The English Poor Law 1531–1782*, Cambridge: Cambridge University Press,1995, pp. 9–10.

3. Slack, *The English Poor Law*, pp. 10–11, 39.

4. R. A. Cage, *The Scottish Poor Law 1745–1845*, Edinburgh: Scottish Academic Press, 1981; R. Mitchison, *The Old Poor Law in Scotland: the experience of poverty 1574–1845*, Edinburgh: Edinburgh University Press, 2000; J. Innes, 'The distinctiveness of the English poor laws, 1750–1850', in D. Winch and P. K. O'Brien (eds), *The political economy of British historical experience, 1688–1914*, Oxford: Oxford University Press, 2002, pp. 381–407, at pp. 395–403.

5. J. Innes, 'State, church and voluntarism in European welfare, 1690–1850', in H. Cunningham and J. Innes (eds), *Charity, philanthropy and reform from the 1690s to 1850*, Basingstoke: Macmillan (now Palgrave Macmillan), 1998, pp. 15–65.

6. G. Himmelfarb, *Alexis de Tocqueville's Memoir on Pauperism*, London: Institute of Economic Affairs, 1997, pp. 26, 29; A. De Tocqueville, *Journeys to England and Ireland*, London: Faber and Faber, 1958, p. 72.

7. Slack, *The English Poor Law*, p. 11.

8. A. Smith, *An inquiry into the nature and causes of the wealth of nations*, Indianapolis, IN: Liberty Fund, 1981, p. 152.

9. *Ibid.*; Slack, *The English Poor Law*, pp. 27–36.

10. G. Boyer, *An economic history of the English Poor Law 1750–1850*, Cambridge: Cambridge University Press, 1990, pp. 23–30.

11. J. R. Poynter, *Society and pauperism: English ideas on poor relief, 1795–1834*, London: Routledge and Kegan Paul, 1969, pp. 55–65.

12. *Ibid.*, p. 68; G. Himmelfarb, *The idea of poverty: England in the early-industrial age*, London: Faber and Faber, 1984, p. 75.

13. Poynter, *Society and pauperism*, pp. 52–5; Himmelfarb, *The idea of poverty*, pp. 67–9.

14. Himmelfarb, *The idea of poverty*, p. 77.

15. *Ibid.*, pp. 79–80.

16. Poynter, *Society and pauperism*, pp. 119, 201–2; Himmelfarb, *The idea of poverty*, pp. 77–8; see also section 4.2 below.

17. T. Malthus, *An essay on the principle of population* (edited with an Introduction by Anthony Flew), Harmondsworth: Penguin, 1970, p. 97; P. Sraffa (ed.), *The works and correspondence of David Ricardo, edited by Piero Sraffa, with the collaboration of M. H. Dobb, Volume I, On the principles of political economy and taxation*, Cambridge: Cambridge University Press, 1951, pp. 105–6.

18. S. Webb and B. Webb, *English Poor Law History. Part II. The last hundred years*, London: Frank Cass, 1963, pp. 154, 1040; Himmelfarb, *The idea of poverty*, p. 134.

19. A. Brundage, *The making of the New Poor Law: the politics of inquiry, enactment and implementation 1832–39*, London: Hutchinson, 1978, p. 9.

20. PP 1817 (462) vi, 1, *Report from the Select Committee on the Poor Laws*, p. 4.

21. Brundage, *The making of the New Poor Law*, p. 10.

22. PP 1834 (44) xxvii, 1, *Report from His Majesty's Commissioners for inquiring into the administration and practical operation of the Poor Laws*, pp. 36, 64; S. G. Checkland and E. O. A. Checkland (eds), *The Poor Law Report of 1834*, Harmondsworth: Penguin, 1974, pp. 140, 199.

23. PP 1828 (494) iv, 137, *Report from the Select Committee appointed to consider that part of the Poor Laws relating to the employment or relief of able-bodied persons from the poor's rates, and the*

abuses thereof; Brundage, *The making of the New Poor Law*, p. 12; P. Dunkley, 'Whigs and paupers: the reform of the English Poor Laws, 1830–34', *Journal of British Studies*, 20 (1981), 124–49, at 125.

24. Checkland and Checkland (eds), *The Poor Law Report*, pp. 23–6.

25. E. J. Hobsbawm and G. Rudé, *Captain Swing*, London: Lawrence and Wishart, 1969, pp. 125–6; Dunkley, 'Whigs and paupers', pp. 125–6; *ibid.*, *The crisis of the Old Poor Law in England 1795–1834: an interpretative essay*, New York & London: Garland Publishing, Inc., 1982, pp. 95–6; A. Kidd, *State, society and the poor in nineteenth-century England*, Basingstoke: Macmillan (now Palgrave Macmillan), 1999, p. 25.

26. Poynter, *Society and pauperism*, pp. 317–18; Checkland and Checkland (eds), *The Poor Law Report*, p. 29; Brundage, *The making of the New Poor Law*, pp. 15–45.

27. PP 1834 (44) xxvii, 1, *Report from His Majesty's Commissioners for inquiring into the administration and practical operation of the Poor Laws*, pp. 55, 61, 66–84; Checkland and Checkland (eds), *The Poor Law Report*, pp. 181, 191, 203–41.

28. PP 1834 (44) xxvii, 1, *Report from His Majesty's Commissioners for inquiring into the administration and practical operation of the Poor Laws*, pp. 36–55 (see esp. pp. 49, 54); Checkland and Checkland (eds), *The Poor Law Report*, pp. 140–79 (see esp. pp. 167, 177).

29. Webb and Webb, *English Poor Law History*, pp. 84–8.

30. M. Blaug, 'The myth of the Old Poor Law and the making of the New', *Journal of Economic History*, 23 (1963), 151–84; *ibid.*, 'The Poor Law Report reexamined', *Journal of Economic History*, 24 (1964), 229–45; see also D. Baugh, 'The cost of poor relief in south-east England, 1790–1834', *Economic History Review*, 28 (1975), 50–68.

31. J. Huzel, 'The demographic impact of the Old Poor Law: more reflexions on Malthus', *Economic History Review*, 33 (1980), 367–81; see also Malthus, *An essay on the principle of population*, pp. 67–103; PP 1834 (44) xxvii, 1, *Report from His Majesty's Commissioners for inquiring into the administration and practical operation of the Poor Laws*, pp. 49, 130; Checkland and Checkland (eds), *The Poor Law Report*, pp. 167, 341.

32. Boyer, *An economic history of the English Poor Law*, p. 43.

33. PP 1834 (44) xxvii, 1, *Report from His Majesty's Commissioners for inquiring into the administration and practical operation of the Poor Laws*, p. 127; Checkland and Checkland (eds), *The Poor Law Report*, p. 334.

34. PP 1834 (44) xxvii, 1, *Report from His Majesty's Commissioners for inquiring into the administration and practical operation of the Poor Laws*, pp. 127, 147–8; Checkland and Checkland (eds), *The Poor Law Report*, pp. 335, 377–8.

35. A. Brundage, *The English poor laws, 1700–1930*, Basingstoke: Palgrave (now Palgrave Macmillan), 2002, p. 18.

36. PP 1834 (44) xxvii, 1, *Report from His Majesty's Commissioners for inquiring into the administration and practical operation of the Poor Laws*, pp. 167, 176; Checkland and Checkland (eds), *The Poor Law Report*, pp. 418–19, 438–9.

37. S. Finer, *The life and times of Sir Edwin Chadwick*, London: Methuen, 1952, p. 96; Brundage, *The English poor laws*, pp. 67–8.

38. *Parliamentary Debates*, Third series, vol. 22, col. 881; PP 1834 (211) iii, 235, *A Bill for the amendment and better administration of the laws relating to the poor in England and Wales*, Section 46.

39. PP 1834 (0.45) iii, 357, *A Bill for the amendment and better administration of the laws relating to the poor in England and Wales*, Section 48; 4 & 5 William IV C. 76, *An Act for the amendment and better administration of the laws relating to the poor in England and Wales* (1834), Section 52.

40. *Parliamentary Debates*, Third series, Vol. 25, col. 1209; Brundage, *The English poor laws*, p. 68.

41. *Parliamentary Debates*, Third series, Vol. 25, cols. 1207–11.

42. *Parliamentary Debates*, Third series, Vol. 24, cols. 520–41.

43. *Parliamentary Debates*, Third series, Vol. 25, col. 1210; Brundage, *The making of the New Poor Law*, pp. 71–2; *ibid.*, *The English Poor Laws*, pp. 15–16, 69.

44. 4 & 5 William IV C. 76, *An Act for the amendment and better administration of the laws relating to the poor in England and Wales* (1834), Sections 1–2, 7, 15, 23, 26–7, 52; see also Brundage, *The making of the New Poor Law*, p. 69.

45. M. Rose, 'The anti-poor law movement in the north of England', *Northern History*, 1 (1966), 70–91; N. Edsall, *The anti-poor law movement 1834–44*, Manchester: Manchester University Press, 1971; D. Ashforth, 'The urban poor law', in D. Fraser (ed.), *The New Poor Law in the nineteenth century*, London and Basingstoke: Macmillan (now Palgrave Macmillan), 1976, pp. 128–48, at pp. 129–33; D. Fraser, *The evolution of the British welfare state: a history of social policy since the Industrial Revolution*, London and Basingstoke: Macmillan, First edition, 1973, pp. 45–9; Second edition, 1984, pp. 49–53; Third edition, 2003, pp. 52–7; Brundage, *The English Poor Laws*, pp. 71–5.

46. Webb and Webb, *English Poor Law History*, p. 149.

47. Brundage, *The English Poor Laws*, p. 91.

48. U. Henriques, 'How cruel was the Victorian poor law?', *Historical Journal*, 11 (1968), 365–71, at 366.

49. PP 1834 (44) xxvii, 1, *Report from His Majesty's Commissioners for inquiring into the administration and practical operation of the Poor Laws*, p. 172; Checkland and Checkland (eds), *The Poor Law Report*, p. 429; M. A. Crowther, *The workhouse system 1834–1929: the history of an English social institution*, London: Methuen, 1983, pp. 37–8.

50. Finer, *Edwin Chadwick*, p. 93; Crowther, *The workhouse system*, p. 38; Brundage, *The English Poor Laws*, p. 79.

51. D. Roberts, 'How cruel was the Victorian poor law?', *Historical Journal*, 6 (1963), 97–107, at 98, 102–4; Henriques, 'How cruel was the Victorian Poor Law?'; Crowther, *The workhouse system*, pp. 30–53.

52. Brundage, *The English Poor Laws*, pp. 79–81; Crowther, *The workhouse system*, pp. 41, 196–8, 203–4, PP 1834 (44) xxvii, 1, *Report from His Majesty's Commissioners for inquiring into the administration and practical operation of the Poor Laws*, p. 182; Checkland and Checkland (eds), *The Poor Law Report*, p. 450.

53. Brundage, *The English Poor Laws*, pp. 80–1; R. Richardson, *Death, dissection and the destitute*, London: Routledge and Kegan Paul, p. 170.

54. Fraser, *The evolution of the British welfare state*, First edition, p. 48; Second edition, pp. 51–2; Third edition, pp. 55–6.

55. P. Wood, 'Finance and the urban poor law: Sunderland Union 1836–1914', in M. Rose (ed.), *The poor and the city: the English Poor Law in its urban context*, Leicester: Leicester University Press, 1985, pp. 19–56, at p. 33; V. Walsh, 'Old and New Poor Laws in Shropshire 1820–70', *Midland History*, 2 (1974), 225–43; A. Digby, 'The labour market and the continuity of social policy after 1834: the case of the eastern counties', *Economic History Review*, 28 (1975), 69–83; L. H. Lees, *The solidarities of strangers: the English Poor Laws and the people 1700–1948*, Cambridge: Cambridge University Press, 1998, pp. 210–17; M. Rose, 'The allowance system under the New Poor Law', *Economic History Review*, 19 (1966), 607–20; L. Kiesling, 'The long road to recovery: postcrisis coordination of private charity and public relief in Victorian Lancashire', *Social Science History*, 21 (1996), 219–43; G. Boyer, 'Poor relief, informal assistance and short-time during the Lancashire cotton famine', *Explorations in Economic History*, 34 (1997), 56–76.

56. Fraser, *The evolution of the British welfare state*, First edition, p. 46; Second edition, p. 49; Third edition, p. 53.

57. P. Harling, 'The power of persuasion: central authority, local bureaucracy and the New Poor Law', *English Historical Review*, 107 (1992), 30–53.

58. W. Apfel and P. Dunkley, 'English rural society and the New Poor Law: Bedfordshire 1834–47', *Social History*, 10 (1985), 37–68, p. 38.

59. K. Snell, *Annals of the labouring poor: social change and agrarian England 1660–1900*, Cambridge: Cambridge University Press, 1985, pp. 136–7; Apfel and Dunkley, 'English rural society'.

60. N. McCord, 'The implementation of the 1834 Poor Law Amendment Act on Tyneside', *International Review of Social History*, 14 (1969), 90–108, p. 91; H. M. Boot, 'Unemployment and poor relief in Manchester 1845–50', *Social History*, 15 (1990), 217–28, p. 22.

61. P. Searby, 'The relief of the poor in Coventry, 1830–63', *Historical Journal*, 20 (1977), 345–61; Dunkley, 'Whigs and paupers', p. 339; R. Thompson, 'The working of the Poor Law Amendment Act in Cumbria, 1836–71', *Northern History*, 15 (1979), 117–37.

62. Walsh, 'Old and New Poor Laws', 233.

63. K. Williams, *From pauperism to poverty*, London: Routledge and Kegan Paul, 1981, pp. 59–60, 179–95; see also PP 1840 (245) xvii, 397, *6th Annual Report of the Poor Law Commissioners for England and Wales*, p. 5.

64. PP 1860 (2675) xxxvii, 1, *12th Annual Report of the Poor Law Board, 1859–60*, p. 15.

65. Brundage, *The English Poor Laws*, pp. 104–7.

66. T. Mackay, *A history of the English Poor Law*, London: P. S. King & Son, 1899, pp. 485–500; Webb and Webb, *English Poor Law History*, pp. 457–9; M. Rose, *The English Poor Law, 1780–1930*, Newton Abbott: David and Charles, 1971, pp. 222–5; G. Stedman Jones, *Outcast London: a study in the relationship between classes in Victorian London*, Harmondsworth: Penguin, 1984, pp. 241–61; P. Ryan, 'Politics and relief: East London Unions in the late-nineteenth and early-twentieth centuries', in M. Rose (ed.), *The poor and the city: the English Poor Law in its urban context*, Leicester: Leicester University Press, 1985, pp. 133–72, at pp. 142–5; R. H. Crocker, 'The Victorian Poor Law in crisis and change: Southampton 1870–95', *Albion*, 19 (1987), 19–44; M. Mackinnon, 'English Poor Law policy and the crusade against outrelief', *Journal of Economic History*, 47 (1987), 603–25.

67. Wood, 'Finance and the urban poor law', pp. 34–9.

68. P. Thane, 'Women and the Poor Law in Victorian and Edwardian England', *History Workshop*, 6 (1978), 29–51, at 38–40.

69. PP 1872 C. 516 xxviii, 1, *First Report of the Local Government Board 1871–2*, pp. 63–8. According to Thane ('Women and the Poor Law', p. 39), the Guardians 'frequently left the mother with one child to support, without relief, lest she forget her dual role'.

70. Rose, *The English Poor Law*, p. 260.

71. Webb and Webb, *English Poor Law History*, pp. 644–7; J. Harris, *Unemployment and politics: a study in English social policy 1886–1914*, Oxford: Clarendon Press, 1972, pp. 75–7; Rose, *The English Poor Law*, p. 260; Ryan, 'Politics and relief', 151.

72. Thane, 'Women and the Poor Law', 40–1; Ryan, 'Politics and relief', 141–2, 155–66.

73. A. Gillie, 'The origin of the poverty line', *Economic History Review*, 49 (1996), 715–30; B. Harris, 'Educational reform, citizenship and the origins of the school medical service', in M. Gijswijt-Hofstra and H. Marland (eds), *Cultures of Child Health in Britain and the Netherlands in the Twentieth Century*, Wellcome Series in the History of Medicine, Amsterdam and Atlanta, GA: Rodopi, pp. 85–101.

74. J. Macnicol, *The politics of retirement in Britain 1878–1948*, Cambridge: Cambridge University Press, 1998, pp. 60–84; PP 1895 C. 7684 xiv, 1, *Report of the Royal Commission on the Aged Poor*, pp. xii–xiii.

75. B. S. Rowntree, *Poverty: a study of town life*, London: Macmillan and Co. (now Palgrave Macmillan), 1902, p. 120; Macnicol, *The politics of retirement*, pp. 48–59; P. Thane, *Old age in English history: past experiences, present issues*, Oxford: Oxford University Press, 2000, pp. 273–86.

76. PP 1909 Cd. 4499 xxxvii, 1, Report of the Royal Commission on the Poor Laws and the Relief of Distress, p. 12.

77. Rose, *The English Poor Law*, pp. 262–8; M. Rose, *The relief of poverty 1834–1914*, London and Basingstoke: Macmillan (now Palgrave Macmillan), 1986, pp. 41–6; P. Thane, *Foundations of the welfare state*, London: Longman, pp. 81–3.

5 Charity and philanthropy in the nineteenth century

1. G. Finlayson, *Citizen, state and social welfare in Britain 1830–1990*, Oxford: Oxford University Press, 1994, pp. 1, 11, 15; F. Prochaska, *The voluntary impulse: philanthropy in modern Britain*, London: Faber, 1988, p. 88.

2. M. Gorsky, *Patterns of philanthropy: charity and society in nineteenth-century Bristol*, Woodbridge: Royal Historical Society/Boydell Press, 1999, pp. 13–14; O. Checkland, *Philanthropy in Victorian Scotland: social welfare and the voluntary principle*, Edinburgh: John Donald, 1980, p. 2; F. Prochaska, 'Philanthropy', in F. M. L. Thompson (ed.), *The Cambridge social history of Britain 1750–1950, Volume 3*, Cambridge: Cambridge University Press, 1990, pp. 357–94, at p. 360.

3. B. Harrison, 'Philanthropy and the Victorians', *Victorian Studies*, 9 (1966), 353–74, at 359–62; P. Thane, 'Josephine Butler', in P. Barker (ed.), *Founders of the welfare state; a series from New Society*, London: Heinemann, 1984, pp. 17–23, at pp. 18–19.

4. Finlayson, *Citizen, state and social welfare*, p. 52; Harrison, 'Philanthropy', pp. 358–9.

5. Harrison, 'Philanthropy', p. 360; R. J. Morris, 'Voluntary societies and British social elites: an analysis', *Historical Journal*, 26 (1983), 95–118, at 110; Finlayson, *Citizen, state and social welfare*, p. 50; Gorsky, *Patterns of philanthropy*, p. 203.

6. Harrison, 'Philanthropy', p. 360; F. Prochaska, *Women and philanthropy in nineteenth century England*, Oxford: Oxford University Press, 1980, p. 222; see also M. Simey, *Charitable effort in Liverpool in the nineteenth century*, Liverpool: University of Liverpool Press, 1951, pp. 62–80; J. Parker, *Women and welfare: ten Victorian women in public social service*, Basingstoke: Macmillan (now Palgrave Macmillan), 1988; M. Preston, 'Lay women and philanthropy in Dublin 1860–80', *Eire-Ireland*, 28 (1993), 74–85; Gorsky, *Patterns of philanthropy*, pp. 162–77.

7. Harrison, 'Philanthropy', p. 358.

8. D. Fraser, *The evolution of the British welfare state: a history of social policy since the Industrial Revolution*, London and Basingstoke: Macmillan (now Palgrave Macmillan), First edition, 1973, p. 115; Second edition, 1984, p. 124; Third edition, 2003, p. 135.

9. L. Stephen, 'Social equality', in L. Stephen, *Social rights and duties: addresses to Ethical Societies, Volume 1*, London: Swan Sonnenschein, 1896, pp. 175–220, at p. 219; see also N. Annan, *Leslie Stephen: his thought and character in relation to his time*, London: Macgibbon and Kee, 1951, p. 245.

10. PP 1817 (462) vi, 1, *Report from the Select Committee on the Poor Laws*, p. 4; B. Hilton, *The age of atonement: the influence of Evangelicalism on social and economic thought, 1795–1865*, Oxford: Clarendon, 1988, p. 101.

11. S. Low, *The charities of London in 1861, comprising an account of the operations, resources and general condition of the charitable, educational and religious institutions of London*, London: Sampson Low, Son and Co., 1862, p. xiii.

12. G. Stedman Jones, *Outcast London: a study in the relationship between classes in Victorian London*, Harmondsworth: Penguin, p. 252; PP 1817 (462) vi, 1, *Report from the Select Committee on the Poor Laws*, p. 4; B. Hilton, *The age of atonement: the influence of Evangelicalism on social and economic thought, 1795–1865*, Oxford: Clarendon, 1988, p. 101.

13. J. Kay, *The moral and physical condition of the working classes employed in the cotton manufacture in Manchester*, London: Ridgway, 1832, pp. 44, 48.

14. Prochaska, *Women and philanthropy*, p. 52; 'Philanthropy', pp. 370–1.

15. N. McCord, 'The Poor Law and philanthropy', in D. Fraser (ed.), *The New Poor Law in the nineteenth century*, Basingstoke: Macmillan (now Palgrave Macmillan), 1976, pp. 87–110, at p. 106.

16. K. Woodroofe, *From charity to social work in England and the United States*, London: Routledge and Kegan Paul, 1962, p. 43; see also Stedman Jones, *Outcast London*, pp. 239–80.

17. Low, *The charities of London in 1861*, pp. vii–xi; G. Hicks, 'A synopsis of reports of some of the Metropolitan charities', *The Times*, 11 February 1869, pp. 3–5.

18. Harrison, 'Philanthropy', p. 359.

19. D. MacRaild, *Irish migrants in modern Britain, 1750–1922*, Basingstoke: Macmillan (now Palgrave Macmillan), 1999, p. 93; see also R. Samuel, 'The Roman Catholic Church and the Irish poor', in R. Swift and S. Gilley (eds), *The Irish in the Victorian city*, London: Croom Helm, 1985, pp. 267–300; J. Turton, 'Mayhew's Irish: the Irish poor in mid-nineteenth century London', in R. Swift and S. Gilley (eds), *The Irish in Victorian Britain: the local dimension*, Dublin: Four Courts Press, 1999, pp. 122–55.

20. R. Liedtke, *Jewish welfare in Hamburg and Manchester c. 1850–1914*, Oxford: Clarendon Press, 1998, pp. 71–3, 84–7, 121–5, 174–84.

21. L. Magnus, *The Jewish Board of Guardians and the men who made it, 1859–1909: an illustrated record*, London: Jewish Board of Guardians, 1909, p. 11.

22. V. Lipman, *A century of social service 1859–1959: the Jewish Board of Guardians*, London: Routledge and Kegan Paul, 1959, p. 1; L. Gartner, *The Jewish immigrant in England 1870–1914*, London: Simon Publications, 1972, p. 53.

23. D. Fraser, *The evolution of the British welfare state*, First edition, p. 116; Second edition, p. 125; Third edition, p. 136.

24. Prochaska, 'Philanthropy', p. 378; Liedtke, *Jewish welfare*, p. 130.

25. Lipman, *A century of social service*, p. 10; Gartner, *The Jewish immigrant*, pp. 24–56; Liedtke, *Jewish welfare*, p. 102.

26. B. Webb, *My apprenticeship*, London: Longman's, Green, 1926, p. 143.

27. Fraser, *The evolution of the British welfare state*, First edition, p. 118; Second edition, p. 127; Third edition, p. 138; S. Collini, *Public moralists: political thought and intellectual life in Britain 1860–1930*, Oxford: Clarendon Press, 1991, pp. 84–5.

28. L. Stephen, *Hours in a library*, London: Smith, Elder and Co., 1879, p. 221; see also N. Annan, *Leslie Stephen*, pp. 162–95; *ibid., Leslie Stephen: the godless Victorian*, London: Weidenfeld and Nicolson, 1984, pp. 234–66.

29. G. Best, *Mid-Victorian Britain 1851–75*, St Albans: Panther, 1971, pp. 158–60; Checkland, *Philanthropy in Victorian Scotland*, p. 1.

30. Finlayson, *Citizen, state and social welfare*, p. 63; see also D. Owen, *English philanthropy 1660–1960*, Cambridge, MA: Belknap Press, 1964, p. 92.

31. J. Burnett, *Useful toil: autobiographies of working people from the 1820s to the 1920s*, Harmondsworth: Penguin, 1977, p. 55; *ibid., Destiny obscure: autobiographies of childhood, education and family from the 1820s to the 1920s*, London: Allen Lane, 1982, pp. 85, 88, 92.

32. J. Barry, 'The making of the middle class?', *Past and Present*, 145 (1994), 194–208, at 199–200; Morris, 'Voluntary societies', pp. 95–6; M. Roberts, 'Reshaping the gift relationship: the London Mendicity Society and the suppression of begging in England 1818–1869', *International Review of Social History*, 36 (1991), 201–31, at 205; Gorsky, *Patterns of philanthropy*, pp. 137, 139–60.

33. Low, *The charities of London in 1861*, pp. vii–xi; *ibid., Low's one shilling guide to the charities of London, comprising the objects, date, address, income and expenditure, treasurer and secretary of above 700 charities, corrected to April 1863*, London: Sampson Low, Son and Co., 1863; *ibid., A handbook to the charities of London, comprising the objects, date, address, income and expenditure, treasurer and secretary of above 900 charitable institutions and funds, edited and revised to August 1870 by Charles Mackeson*, London: Sampson Low, Son and Marston, 1870; C. Mackeson, *Low's handbook to the charities of London, comprising the objects, date, address,*

income and expenditure, treasurer and secretary of above 900 charitable institutions and funds,
edited and revised to December 31, 1871, by Charles Mackeson, London: Sampson Low, Marston,
Low and Searle, 1872; T. Hawksley, *The charities of London and some errors of their administra-*
tion, with suggestions for an improved system of private and official charitable relief, London:
John Churchill and Sons, 1869, p. 4.

34. S. Low, *The charities of London, comprehending the benevolent, educational and religious insti-*
   tutions, their origins and design, progress and present position, London: Sampson Low, 1850,
   p. 452; *ibid., The charities of London in 1852–3: presenting a report of the operation, resources*
   and general condition of the charities and religious institutions of London, with an introductory
   analysis, London: Sampson Low and Son, 1854, p. vii; *ibid., The charities of London in 1861,*
   pp. vii–xi.

35. Most of the organisations which Hicks identified as 'Book societies' were engaged in the distribution of religious books and Bibles. These organisations accounted for more than 97 per
   cent of the funds disbursed under this heading. The remaining organisations were those concerned with the promotion of book-hawking throughout the country, the promotion and sale
   of a healthy literature as an antidote to the immoral publications of the day, and the preparation and circulation of a superior series of tracts, adapted for the upper classes. For further
   details, see Table 5.3.

36. Hawksley, *The charities of London,* pp. 6–7.

37. Owen, *English philanthropy,* pp. 104–5, 136.

38. D. Fraser, 'Introduction', in D. Fraser (ed.), *The New Poor Law in the nineteenth century,*
   Basingstoke: Macmillan (now Palgrave Macmillan), 1976, pp. 1–24, at p. 11; McCord, 'The
   Poor Law and philanthropy', p. 97.

39. R. Humphreys, *Sin, organised charity and the Poor Law in Victorian England,* Basingstoke:
   Macmillan (now Palgrave Macmillan), 1995, p. 170.

40. Low, *The charities of London in 1861,* pp. vii–xi; Hicks, 'A synopsis'; *ibid.,* 'The Metropolitan
   charities', *The Times,* 11 February 1869, p. 5, cols. a-c.

41. Gorsky, *Patterns of philanthropy,* p. 138; R. Thompson, 'The working of the Poor Law
   Amendment Act in Cumbria, 1836–71', *Northern History,* 15 (1979), 117–37, at 122.

42. W. Jordan, *Philanthropy in England 1480–1660: a study of the changing pattern of English*
   social aspirations, London: George Allen and Unwin, 1959, pp. 109–25; M. Ashby, *Joseph*
   Ashby of Tysoe, 1859–1919: a study of English village life, Cambridge: Cambridge University
   Press, 1961, p. 46; Owen, *English philanthropy,* pp. 69–88; J. Robin, *From childhood to middle*
   age: cohort analysis in Colyton 1851–91, Cambridge: Cambridge Group for the History of
   Population and Social Structure, Working Paper Series, No. 1, n.d., pp. 2–3.

43. P. Searby, 'The relief of the poor in Coventry, 1830–63', *Historical Journal,* 20 (1977),
   345–61, at 338–9.

44. W. Henderson, *The Lancashire cotton famine 1861–65,* Manchester: Manchester University
   Press, 1934, pp. 68–85; L. Kiesling, 'The long road to recovery: postcrisis coordination of private charity and public relief in Victorian Lancashire', *Social Science History,* 21 (1997),
   219–43, at 221–8.

45. Stedman Jones, *Outcast London,* pp. 246, 298.

46. R. Pinker, *English hospital statistics 1861–1938,* London: Heinemann, 1966, pp. 57, 61.

47. Low, *The charities of London in 1861,* pp. vii–xi.

48. Hicks, 'A synopsis'; Hawksley, *The charities of London,* p. 4.

49. Prochaska, *Women and philanthropy,* pp. 132–3; A. S. Wohl, *Endangered lives: public health in*
   Victorian Britain, London: Methuen, pp. 36–8; PP 1904 Cd. 2175 xxxii, 1, Interdepartmental
   Committee on Physical Deterioration, *Report and Appendix,* para. 297.

50. G. Sutherland, 'Education', in F. M. L. Thompson (ed.), *The Cambridge Social History of Britain,*
   Cambridge: Cambridge University Press, 3, 1990, pp. 119–70, at pp. 126–7; T. Laqueur,
   Religion and respectability: Sunday schools and working-class culture 1780–1850, New Haven, CT
   and London: Yale University Press, 1976, p. xi.

51. Fraser, *The evolution of the British welfare state*, First edition, pp. 72–81; Second edition, pp. 78–89; Third edition, pp. 85–97.

52. E. M. Bell, *Octavia Hill*, London: Constable 1942; J. Lewis, *Women and social action in Victorian and Edwardian England*, Aldershot: Edward Elgar, 1991, pp. 51–64.

53. J. N. Tarn, *Five per cent philanthropy: an account of housing in urban areas between 1840 and 1914*, Cambridge: Cambridge University Press, 1973, pp. 15, 22–7, 44–6.

54. Ashby, *Joseph Ashby of Tysoe*, p. 46.

55. B. Harris, 'Responding to adversity: government-charity relations and the relief of unemployment in interwar Britain', *Contemporary Record*, 9 (1995), 529–61, at 542–3.

56. Gorsky, *Patterns of philanthropy*, pp. 192–3.

57. Stedman Jones, *Outcast London*, p. 244.

58. Owen, *English philanthropy*, p. 168.

59. Hicks, 'The Metropolitan charities'.

60. Harrison, 'Philanthropy and the Victorians', 363–4.

61. C. L. Mowat, *The Charity Organisation Society 1869–1913*, London: Methuen, 1961, pp. 1–19.

62. J. Harris, *Private lives, public spirit: Britain 1870–1914*, Harmondsworth: Penguin, 1994, pp. 238–9.

63. Mowat, *The Charity Organisation* Society, p. 38; Stedman Jones, *Outcast London*, p. 257.

64. J. Fido, 'The Charity Organisation Society and social casework in London 1869–1900', in A. P. Donajgrodski (ed.), *Social control in nineteenth century Britain*, London: Croom Helm, 1977, pp. 207–30; J. Lewis, *The voluntary sector, the state and social work in Britain: the Charity Organisation Society/Family Welfare Association since 1869*, Aldershot: Edward Elgar, 1995; *ibid.*, 'The boundary between voluntary and statutory social service in the late-nineteenth and early-twentieth centuries', *Historical Journal*, 39 (1996), 155–77; A. Vincent, 'The Poor Law reports of 1909 and the social theory of the Charity Organisation Society', *Victorian Studies*, 27 (1984), 343–63.

65. J. Harris, *Unemployment and politics: a study in English social policy 1886–1914*, Oxford: Clarendon Press, 1972, pp. 108–9.

66. Mowat, *The Charity Organisation Society*, pp. 21, 92–3; Humphreys, *Sin, organised charity and the Poor Law*, pp. 21–8.

67. Mowat, *The Charity Organisation Society*, pp. 139–42, 159–65.

68. R. H. Crocker, 'The Victorian Poor Law in crisis and change: Southampton 1870–95', *Albion*, 19 (1987), 19–44, at 37–8; Humphreys, *Sin, organised charity and the Poor Law*, pp. 50–174; A. Kidd, 'Charity organisation and the unemployed in Manchester c. 1870–1914', *Social History*, 9 (1980), 45–66, at 57–8.

69. Lewis, *The voluntary sector*, pp. 60–7.

70. M. Moore, 'Social work and social welfare: the organisation of philanthropic resources in Britain 1900–14', *Journal of British Studies*, 16 (1977), 85–104; M. Cahill and T. Jowett, 'The new philanthropy: the emergence of the Bradford City Guild of Help', *Journal of Social Policy*, 9 (1980), 359–82; K. Laybourn, 'The Guild of Help and the changing face of Victorian philanthropy', *Urban History*, 20 (1993), 43–60; *ibid.*, *The Guild of Help and the changing face of Edwardian philanthropy: the Guild of Help, voluntary work and the state, 1904–19*, Lampeter: Edward Mellen Press, 1994; Lewis, *The voluntary sector*, esp. pp. 55–67; *Ibid.*, 'The boundary between voluntary and statutory social service', esp. 162.

71. Prochaska, 'Philanthropy', 362.

6   Welfare from below: self-help and mutual aid

1. F. Engels, *The condition of the working class in England, from personal observations and authentic sources, with an introduction by Eric Hobsbawm*, London: Granada, 1969, p. 154; J. Burnett,

Destiny obscure: autobiographies of childhood, education and family from the 1820s to the 1920s, London: Allen Lane, 1982, p. 157.

2. F. Prochaska, *The voluntary impulse: philanthropy in modern Britain*, London: Faber, 1988, p. 28; *ibid.*, 'Philanthropy', in F. M. L. Thompson (ed.), *The Cambridge social history of Britain 1750–1950, Volume 3*, Cambridge: Cambridge University Press, 1990, pp. 357–94, at p. 365; J. H. Treble, *Urban poverty in Britain 1830–1914*, London: Methuen, 1979, p. 130. Seebohm Rowntree used the term 'primary poverty' to denote the point at which household income fell below the level needed to maintain 'merely physical efficiency'. See B. Harris, 'Seebohm Rowntree and the measurement of poverty, 1899–1951', in J. Bradshaw and R. Sainsbury (eds), *Getting the measure of poverty: the early legacy of Seebohm Rowntree*, Aldershot: Ashgate, 2000, pp. 60–84, at p. 64.

3. See also Prochaska, 'Philanthropy', p. 361.

4. M. Dupree, *Family structure in the Staffordshire Potteries, 1840–80*, Oxford: Oxford University Press., 1995, p. 334.

5. M. Anderson, *Family structure in nineteenth-century Lancashire*, Cambridge: Cambridge University Press, 1971, p. 137.

6. M. Friedman and R. Friedman, *Free to choose: a personal statement*, Harmondsworth: Penguin, 1980, p. 135.

7. Anderson, *Family structure in nineteenth-century Lancashire*, pp. 162–6.

8. Dupree, *Family structure in the Staffordshire Potteries*, p. 350.

9. Anderson, *Family structure in nineteenth-century Lancashire*, pp. 147–8.

10. Dupree, *Family structure in the Staffordshire Potteries*, pp. 278–9.

11. J. Winter, 'Widowed mothers and mutual aid in early-Victorian Britain', *Journal of Social History*, 17 (1983), 115–26, at 118–22.

12. E. Ross, 'Survival networks: women's neighbourhood sharing in London before World War 1', *History Workshop Journal*, 15 (1983), 4–27, at 6–8.

13. P. Johnson, 'Credit and thrift and the British working class', in Jay Winter (ed.), *The working class in modern British history: essays presented to Henry Pelling*, Cambridge: Cambridge University Press, 1983, pp. 147–70, 288–93, at p. 152; *ibid.*, *Saving and spending: the working-class economy in Britain 1870–1939*, Oxford: Oxford University Press, 1985, p. 148.

14. Johnson, 'Credit and thrift', p. 152; *ibid.*, *Saving and spending*, p. 149.

15. H. Bosanquet, *Rich and poor*, London: Macmillan (now Palgrave Macmillan), 1898, p. 99.

16. Johnson, 'Credit and thrift', p. 154; *ibid.*, *Saving and spending*, p. 168–9.

17. R. Roberts, *The classic slum: Salford life in the first quarter of the century*, Harmondsworth: Penguin, 1971, p. 27.

18. Johnson, *Saving and spending*, pp. 188–92.

19. E. Hopkins, *Working-class self-help in nineteenth-century England*, London: UCL Press, 1995, p. 10; M. Gorsky, 'The growth and distribution of English friendly societies in the early nineteenth century', *Economic History Review*, 51 (1998), 489–511, at 507; but see also M. Gorsky, 'Mutual aid and civil society: friendly societies in nineteenth-century Bristol', *Urban History*, 25 (1998), 302–22, at 321.

20. D. Green, *Working class patients and the medical establishment: self-help in Britain from the mid-nineteenth century to 1948*, Aldershot: Gower/Maurice Temple Smith, 1985; J. Riley, *Sick, not dead: the health of British workingmen during the mortality decline*, Baltimore, MD: Johns Hopkins University Press, 1997, pp. 1–123.

21. Quoted in P. Gosden, *Self-help: voluntary associations in nineteenth-century Britain*, London: B. T. Batsford, 1973, p. 104.

22. Hopkins, *Working-class self-help*, pp. 13–15.

23. PP 1874 C. 961 xxiii, 1, *Fourth Report of the Royal Commission on Friendly and Benefit Building Societies*, para. 411; J. Baernreither, *English associations of working men*, London: Swann Sonnenschein, 1889, pp. 171–4, 182–5, 189–98; P. Gosden, *The Friendly Societies in*

England 1815–75, Manchester: Manchester University Press, 1961, pp. 57–61; *ibid.*, *Self-help*, pp. 105–7, 109–10, 115–32; Hopkins, *Working-class self-help*, pp. 21–3, 25, 35–8, 45, 51, 59.

24. C. F. Hanson, 'Welfare before the welfare state', in R. M. Hartwell *et al.*, *The long debate on poverty: eight essays on industrialisation and the 'condition of England'*, London: Institute of Economic Affairs, pp. 111–39, at pp. 120–4; Green, *Working-class patients*, pp. 93–6; PP 1878 (388) lxix, 3, *Reports of the Chief Registrar of Friendly Societies for the year ending 31 December 1876*, p. 46.

25. Gosden, *Self-help*, p. 12; Hopkins, *Working-class self-help*, p. 10.

26. PP 1874 C. 961 xxiii, 1, *Fourth Report of the Royal Commission on Friendly and Benefit Building Societies*, p. 21.

27. PP 1877 lxxviii, 103, *Reports of the Chief Registrar of Friendly Societies for the year ending 31 December 1875*, pp. 9–13; PP 1878 (388) lxix, 3, *Reports of the Chief Registrar of Friendly Societies for the year ending 31 December 1876*, pp. 6–7, 46.

28. PP 1914 (121) lxxvi, 1, *Reports of the Chief Registrar of Friendly Societies for the year ending 31 December 1913*, p. 80; see also Table 6.1.

29. Gosden, *The friendly societies*, pp. 79–82; B. Gilbert, 'The decay of nineteenth-century provident institutions and the coming of old age pensions in Great Britain', *Economic History Review*, 17 (1965), 551–63, at 552; *ibid.*, *The evolution of national insurance in Great Britain: the origins of the welfare state*, London: Michael Joseph, 1966, p. 166; R. Gray, *The labour aristocracy in Victorian Edinburgh*, Oxford: Clarendon Press, 1976, p. 122; G. Crossick, *An artisan élite in Victorian society*, London: Croom Helm, 1978, pp. 181–3, 189–91; Johnson, *Saving and spending*, p. 55; D. Jones, 'Did friendly societies matter? A study of friendly society membership in Glamorgan, 1794–1910', *Welsh Historical Review*, 12 (1985), 324–49; N. Kirk, *The growth of working class reformism in mid-Victorian England*, London: Croom Helm, 1985, pp. 198–9; D. Neave, *Mutual aid in the Victorian countryside: friendly societies in the rural East Riding 1830–1914*, Hull: Hull University Press, 1991, pp. 66–72; F. M. L. Thompson, *The rise of respectable society: a social history of Victorian Britain 1830–1900*, London: Fontana, 1988, p. 202; Hopkins, *Working-class self-help*, pp. 51–2, 60.

30. Gosden, *Friendly societies*, p. 76; Hopkins, *Working-class self-help*, pp. 51–2, 60.

31. Gosden, *Friendly societies*, pp. 80–1; Baernreither, *English associations*, p. 181; Dupree, *Family structure in the Staffordshire Potteries*, p. 181; C. Edwards, M. Gorsky, B. Harris and P. R. A. Hinde, 'Sickness, insurance and health: assessing trends in morbidity through friendly society records', *Annales de Démographie Historique*, 1 (2003), 131–67, at 136.

32. Cf. Hanson, 'Welfare before the welfare state', 138.

33. Hopkins, *Working-class self-help*, pp. 75, 77–8, 146; H. Clegg, A. Fox and A. Thompson, *A history of British trade unions since 1889, Volume 1, 1889–1910*, Oxford: Clarendon Press, 1964, pp. 6–7; Dupree, *Family structure in the Staffordshire Potteries*, p. 307; C. Hanson, 'Craft unions, welfare benefits and the case for trade union law reform, 1867–75', *Economic History Review*, 28 (1975), 243–59, at 248.

34. G. D. H. Cole, *A century of cooperation*, London: George Allen and Unwin for the Cooperative Union Ltd, 1945, p. 26; Gosden, *Self-help*, pp. 180–206; Hopkins, *Working-class self-help*, pp. 185–221.

35. R. Floud, *The people and the British economy 1830–1914*, Oxford: Oxford University Press, 1997, p. 155; Johnson, *Saving and spending*, pp. 126–43.

36. Gosden, *Self-help*, pp. 143–79; A. Power, *Hovels to high rise: state housing in Europe since 1850*, London: Routledge, 1993, p. 235.

37. Gosden, *Self-help*, pp. 207, 213–42; Johnson, *Saving and spending*, p. 89.

38. Gosden, *Self-help*, pp. 246–7; Johnson, *Saving and spending*, pp. 90–4, 116.

39. Gilbert, *The evolution of national insurance*, pp. 318–26; G. Clayton, *British insurance*, London: Elek Books, 1971, pp. 122–8; Gosden, *Self-help*, pp. 129–32; Johnson, *Saving and spending*, pp. 11–47.

40.   J. S. Mill, *Principles of political economy and Chapters on socialism, edited with an Introduction by Jonathan Riley*, Oxford: Oxford University Press, 1994, p. 367; quoted in B. Supple, 'Legislation and virtue: an essay on working-class self-help and the state in the early nineteenth century', in N. McKendrick (ed.), *Historical perspectives: studies in English thought and society in honour of J. H. Plumb*, London: Europa Publications, 1974, pp. 211–54, at p. 211.

41.   S. Yeo, 'Working class association, private capital, welfare and the state in the late-nineteenth and twentieth centuries', in N. Parry, M. Rustin and C. Satyamurti (eds), *Social work, welfare and the state*, London: Edward Arnold, 1979, pp. 48–71, at p. 50.

42.   Hanson, 'Welfare before the welfare state', 138.

7   Medicine and health care in the nineteenth century

1.   V. Berridge, 'Health and medicine', in F. M. L. Thompson (ed.), *The Cambridge Social History of Britain 1750–1950, Volume 3, Social agencies and institutions*, Cambridge: Cambridge University Press, 1990, pp. 171–242; D. Porter, 'The mission of social history of medicine: an historical overview', *Social History of Medicine*, 8 (1995), 345–59.

2.   M. Dobson, *Contours of death and disease in early-modern England*, Cambridge: Cambridge University Press, 1997, pp. 267, 271; J. Lane, 'The medical practitioners of provincial England in 1783', *Medical History*, 28 (1984), 353–71, at 355; R. Porter, 'Before the fringe: "Quackery" and the eighteenth-century medical market', in R. Cooter (ed.), *Studies in the history of alternative medicine*, Basingstoke: Macmillan (now Palgrave Macmillan), 1988, pp. 1–27, at p. 6.

3.   C. Lawrence, *Medicine in the making of modern Britain*, London: Routledge, 1994, pp. 16–20.

4.   I. Loudon, *Medical care and the general practitioner 1750–1850*, Oxford: Clarendon Press, 1986, pp. 48–52, 136; see also *ibid.*, 'Medical practitioners 1750–1850 and the period of medical reform in Britain', in A. Wear (ed.), *Medicine in society: historical essays*, Cambridge: Cambridge University Press, 1992, pp. 219–47, at pp. 230–2.

5.   The Company of Surgeons became the Royal College of Surgeons of London in 1800 and the Royal College of Surgeons of England in 1843. For further information, see Berridge, 'Health and medicine', p. 177; Loudon, *Medical care and the general practitioner*, p. 20; *ibid.*, 'Medical practitioners', *passim*.

6.   C. Newman, *The evolution of medical education in the nineteenth century*, Oxford: Oxford University Press, 1957, p. 77; W. Bishop, 'The evolution of the general practitioner', in E. A. Underwood (ed.), *Science, medicine and history: essays ... written in honour of Charles Singer*, London: Oxford University Press, Vol. 2, 1953, pp. 351–7, at p. 354.

7.   S. Holloway, 'The Apothecaries' Act, 1815: a reinterpretation', *Medical History*, 10 (1966), 107–29, 221–36, at 127, 232.

8.   I. Waddington, *The medical profession in the industrial revolution*, Dublin: Gill and Macmillan Humanities Press, 1984, pp. 126–32, 147–8.

9.   *Ibid.*, p. 126; A. Digby, *Making a medical living: doctors and patients in the English market for medicine 1720–1911*, Cambridge: Cambridge University Press, 1994, pp. 31, 267. The 1886 Act stipulated that three of the representatives on the General Medical Council should be elected by the registered medical practitioners of England, and one each by the registered medical practitioners of Scotland and Ireland. See 49 & 50 Vict. C. 48: section 7, sub-section 1.

10.   H. Marland, *Medicine and society in Wakefield and Huddersfield 1780–1870*, Cambridge: Cambridge University Press, 1987, pp. 101–6, 204, Digby, *Making a medical living*, pp. 240–4; M. Flinn, 'Medical services under the New Poor Law', in D. Fraser (ed.), *The New Poor Law in the nineteenth century*, London and Basingstoke: Macmillan (now Palgrave Macmillan), 1976, pp. 45–66, at p. 49; J. Brand, *Doctors and the State: the British medical profession and Government action in health, 1870–1912*, Baltimore, MD: Johns Hopkins University Press, 1965, p. 109; J. Riley, *Sick, not dead: the health of British workingmen during*

the mortality decline, Baltimore, MD: Johns Hopkins University Press, 1997, pp. 50–1; C. Winegarden and J. Murray, 'The contributions of early health-insurance programs to mortality declines in pre-World War 1 Europe: evidence from fixed-effects models', *Explorations in Economic History*, 35 (1998), 431–46.

11. S. Cherry, *Medical services and the hospitals in Britain 1860–1939*, Cambridge: Cambridge University Press, 1996, p. 29; see also A. Digby, *The evolution of British general practice 1850–1948*, Oxford: Clarendon Press, 1997, p. 27.

12. According to James Riley, the leading causes of sickness-insurance claims among friendly-society members were accidents, influenza and catarrh, bronchitis, rheumatism, lumbago, gastritis, carbuncles, tonsillitis and skin ulcers, together with a range of conditions which were described as being 'poorly identified'. Edwards, Gorsky, Harris and Hinde reported a similar range of findings in their account of the sickness experience of members of the Hampshire Friendly Society between 1875 and 1910. See Riley, *Sick, not dead*, p. 192; C. Edwards, M. Gorsky, B. Harris and P. R. A. Hinde, 'Sickness, insurance and health: assessing trends in morbidity through friendly society records', *Annales de Démographie Historique*, 1 (2003), 131–67, at 150–2.

13. Riley, *Sick, not dead*, p. 197; *ibid.*, 'Reply to Bernard Harris, "Morbidity and mortality during the health transition: a comment on James C. Riley" ', *Social History of Medicine*, 12 (1999), 133–7, at 137. This issue is discussed in more detail in Chapter 8.

14. L. Granshaw, 'Introduction', in L. Granshaw and R. Porter (eds), *The hospital in history*, London: Routledge, 1989, pp. 1–17, at p. 1; see also *ibid.*, 'The rise of the modern hospital in Britain', in A. Wear (ed.), *Medicine in society: historical essays*, Cambridge: Cambridge University Press, 1992, pp. 197–218, at p. 197.

15. M. Fissell, 'The disappearance of the patient's narrative and the invention of hospital medicine', in R. French and A. Wear (eds), *British medicine in an age of reform*, London: Routledge, 1991, pp. 92–109; F. Cartwright, *A social history of medicine*, London: Longman, 1977, pp. 131–50; A. Youngson, *The scientific revolution in Victorian medicine*, London: Croom Helm, 1979; D. Hamilton and M. Lamb, 'Surgeons and surgery', in O. Checkland and M. Lamb (eds), *Health care as social history: the Glasgow case*, Aberdeen: Aberdeen University Press, 1982, pp. 74–85.

16. I. Loudon, 'The origins and growth of dispensary movement in England', *Bulletin of the History of Medicine*, 55 (1981), 322–42, at 322, 324; B. Abel-Smith, *The hospitals 1800–1948: a study in social administration in England and Wales*, London: Heinemann, 1964, pp. 13–15; J. Pickstone, *Medicine and industrial society: a history of hospital development in Manchester and its region 1752–1946*, Manchester: Manchester University Press, 1985, pp. 51–4, 63–77; G. Rivett, *The development of the London hospital system 1823–1982*, London: King Edward's Hospital Fund, 1986, p. 27; Granshaw, 'Introduction', p. 201; *ibid.*, 'The rise of the modern hospital', pp. 205–6; Berridge, 'Health and medicine', p. 206; B. Croxson, 'The public and private faces of eighteenth-century London dispensary charity', *Medical History*, 41 (1997), 127–49.

17. Abel-Smith, *The hospitals*, pp. 16–31; Granshaw, 'Introduction'; Rivett, *The development of the London hospital system*, pp. 43–9; E. Lomax, *Small and special: the development of hospitals for children in Victorian Britain* (*Medical History*, Supplement no. 16), London: Wellcome Institute for the History of Medicine, 1996.

18. S. Cherry, 'The role of a provincial hospital: the Norfolk and Norwich Hospital, 1771–1880', *Population Studies*, 26 (1972), 291–306, at 294; J. Woodward, *To do the sick no harm: a study of the British voluntary hospital system to 1875*, London: Routledge and Kegan Paul, 1974, pp. 1–2, 147–8.

19. A. Berry, 'Community sponsorship and the hospital patient in late-eighteenth century England', in P. Horden and R. Smith (eds), *The locus of care: families, communities, institutions and the provision of welfare since antiquity*, London: Routledge, 1998, pp. 126–50.

20. Abel-Smith, *The hospitals*, pp. 16–19, 41; Berridge, 'Health and medicine', pp. 206–7; Woodward, *To do the sick no harm*, pp. 36–44.

21. Berridge, 'Health and medicine', pp. 206–9.

22. Abel-Smith, *The hospitals*, pp. 32–9, 101–18, 133–51; Rivett, *The development of the London hospital system*, p. 119–23; K. Waddington, 'Unsuitable cases: the debate over outpatient admissions, the medical profession and late-Victorian London hospitals', *Medical History*, 42 (1998), 26–46.

23. Flinn, 'Medical services under the New Poor Law', p. 47, Marland, *Medicine and society in Wakefield and Huddersfield*, p. 71; Digby, *Making a medical living*, 224–33, 244–9, Pickstone, *Medicine and industrial society*, p. 90.

24. R. Hodgkinson, *The origins of the National Health Service: the medical services of the New Poor Law 1834–71*, London: Wellcome Historical Medical Library, 1967; G. M. Ayers, *England's first state hospitals 1867–1930*, London: Wellcome Institute of the History of Medicine, 1971.

25. Abel-Smith, *The hospitals*, pp. 119–33; Pickstone, *Medicine and industrial society*, pp. 214–15.

26. Rivett, *The development of the London hospital system*, pp. 83–5; Pickstone, *Medicine and industrial society*, pp. 156–83; W. M. Frazer, *A history of English public health 1834–1939*, London: Baillière, Tindall and Cox, 1950, pp. 147–54; Abel-Smith, *The hospitals*, pp. 126–8; R. Pinker, *English hospital statistics 1861–1938*, London: Heinemann, 1966, pp. 57–61.

27. T. McKeown and R. G. Brown, 'Medical evidence related to English population changes in the eighteenth century', *Population Studies*, 9 (1955), 119–41, at 120, 125–6; T. McKeown, *The modern rise of population*, London: Edward Arnold, 1976, pp. 147–8, 150–1.

28. Cherry, 'The role of a provincial hospital', pp. 295–6, 302; *ibid.*, 'The hospitals and population growth. Part 1. The voluntary hospitals, mortality and local populations in the English provinces in the eighteenth and nineteenth centuries', *Population Studies*, 34 (1980), 59–75; *ibid.*, 'The hospitals and population growth. The voluntary general hospitals, mortality and local populations in the English provinces in the eighteenth and nineteenth centuries. Part 2', *Population Studies*, 34 (1980), 251–65, at 252; E. Sigsworth, 'Gateways to death? Medicine, hospitals and mortality, 1700–1850', in P. Mathias (ed.), *Science and society 1600–1900*, Cambridge: Cambridge University Press, 1972, pp. 97–110, at pp. 106–8; Woodward, *To do the sick no harm*, p. 144.

29. McKeown and Brown, 'Medical evidence', p. 120; McKeown, *Modern rise*, p. 148; Sigsworth, 'Gateways to death?', p. 105; Cherry, 'The role of a provincial hospital', pp. 301–2, *ibid.*, 'The hospitals and population growth. Part 2', pp. 257, 261.

30. Abel-Smith, *The hospitals*, pp. 50–7; C. Edwards, 'Age-based rationing of medical care in nineteenth-century England', *Continuity and Change*, 14 (1999), 227–65, at 239–42, 248–50, 257.

31. A. Hardy, *The epidemic streets: infectious disease and the rise of preventive medicine 1856–1900*, Oxford: Clarendon Press, 1993, pp. 22–3, 49, 59–64, 188, 208–9, 273, 277–8; B. Luckin, 'Evaluating the sanitary revolution: typhus and typhoid in London, 1851–1900', in R. Woods and J. Woodward (eds), *Urban disease and mortality in nineteenth-century England*, London: Batsford, 1984, pp. 102–19, at p. 117.

32. N. Macfarlane, 'Hospitals, housing and tuberculosis in Glasgow, 1911–51', *Social History of Medicine*, 2 (1989), 59–85, at 85.

33. D. Wright, 'The discharge of pauper lunatics from county asylums in mid-Victorian England: the case of Buckinghamshire, 1853–72', in J. Melling and B. Forsythe (eds), *Insanity, institutions and society, 1800–1914: a social history of madness in comparative perspective*, London: Routledge, 1999, pp. 93–112, at p. 104.

34. A. Scull, *Museums of madness: the social organisation of insanity in nineteenth-century England*, Harmondsworth: Penguin, 1982, pp. 198, 232; *ibid.*, *The most solitary of afflictions: madness and society in Britain 1700–1900*, New Haven, CT and London: Yale University Press, 1993, pp. 281, 343; P. Bartlett and D. Wright, 'Community care and its antecedents', in P. Bartlett

and D. Wright (eds), *Outside the walls of the asylum: the history of care in the community 1750–2000*, London: Athlone Press, 1999, pp. 1–18, at pp. 3, 6.

35. K. Jones, *Lunacy, law and conscience 1744–1845: the social history of the care of the insane*, London: Routledge and Kegan Paul, 1955, p. ix; *ibid., A history of the mental health services*, London: Routledge and Kegan Paul, 1972, p. xii; *ibid., Asylums and after: a revised history of the mental health services: from the early-eighteenth century to the 1990s*, London: Athlone, 1993, pp. 1–4; T. Szasz, *The myth of mental illness: foundations of a theory of personal conduct*, New York: Paul B. Hoeber, Inc., 1959; E. Goffman, *Asylums: essays on the social situation of mental patients and other inmates*, New York: Doubleday, 1961, p. 12.

36. M. Foucault, *Madness and civilisation: a history of insanity in the Age of Reason*, London: Tavistock, 1967; Scull, *Museums of* madness; *ibid.,* 'Rethinking the history of asylumdom', in J. Melling and B. Forsythe (eds), *Insanity, institutions and society, 1800–1914: a social history of madness in comparative perspective*, London: Routledge, 1999, pp. 295–315, at p. 313; S. Payne, 'Outside the walls of the asylum? Psychiatric treatment in the 1980s and 1990s', in P. Bartlett and D. Wright (eds), *Outside the walls of the asylum: the history of care in the community 1750–2000*, London: Athlone, 1999, pp. 244–63.

37. W. Ll. Parry-Jones, *The trade in lunacy: a study of private madhouses in England in the eighteenth and nineteenth centuries*, London: Routledge and Kegan Paul, 1972; R. Porter, *Mindforg'd manacles: a history of madness in England from the Restoration to the Regency*, London: Athlone, 1987, pp. 136–47, 155.

38. Jones, *Lunacy, law and conscience*, pp. 49–57, 74–8, 141–3, 170–95; *ibid., A history of the mental health services*, pp. 40–5, 59–63, 108–9, 132–52, 176–81; *ibid., Asylums and after*, pp. 23–5, 36–8, 78–92, 107–11; Scull, *Museums of madness*, pp. 112–13; *ibid., The most solitary of afflictions*, pp. 267–8; R. Hodgkinson, 'Provision for pauper lunatics 1834–71', *Medical History*, 10 (1966), 138–54.

39. Porter, *Mind-forg'd manacles*, p. 142; Scull, *Museums of madness*, pp. 34–6; *ibid., The most solitary of afflictions*, pp. 33–5; J. Walton, 'Lunacy in the industrial revolution: a study of asylum admissions in Lancashire 1848–50', *Journal of Social History*, 13 (1979), 1–22; *ibid.* 'The treatment of pauper lunatics in Victorian England: the case of Lancaster Asylum, 1816–70', in A. Scull (ed.), *Madhouses, mad-doctors and madmen*, Philadelphia, PA: University of Pennsylvania Press, 1981, pp. 166–97; *ibid.,* 'Casting out and bringing back in Victorian England: pauper lunatics 1840–70', in W. F. Bynum, R. Porter and M. Shepherd (eds), *The anatomy of madness: essays in the history of psychiatry, Volume II, Institutions and society*, London and New York: Tavistock, 1985, pp. 132–46; Jones, *Asylums and after*, pp. 38–9; O. Walsh, ' "The property of the whole community": charity and insanity in urban Scotland: the Dundee Royal Lunatic Asylum, 1805–50', in J. Melling and B. Forsythe (eds), *Insanity, institutions and society, 1800–1914: a social history of madness in comparative perspective*, London: Routledge, 1999, pp. 180–99, at p. 185; D. Wright, 'Getting out of the asylum: understanding the confinement of the insane in the nineteenth century', *Social History of Medicine*, 10 (1997), 137–55; *ibid.,* 'The discharge of pauper lunatics', pp. 95, 104.

40. Scull, *Museums of madness*, pp. 64–100; *ibid., The most solitary of afflictions*, pp. 23–40, 69–77, 96–103; A. Digby, *Madness, morality and medicine: a study of the York retreat, 1796–1914*, Cambridge: Cambridge University Press, 1985, pp. 14–87; Jones, *Lunacy, law and conscience*, pp. 108–32; *ibid., A history of the mental health services*, pp. 64–100; *ibid., Asylums and after*, pp. 23–59; Walton, 'The treatment of pauper lunatics', pp. 191–2; *ibid.,* 'Casting out and bringing back', pp. 141–2; N. Tomes, 'The great restraint controversy: a comparative perspective on Anglo-American psychiatry in the nineteenth century', in W. Bynum, R. Porter and M. Shepherd (eds), *The anatomy of madness: essays in the history of psychiatry, Vol. III, The asylum and its psychiatry*, London and New York, 1988, pp. 190–225; Berridge, 'Health and medicine', pp. 214–5.

41. See also Berridge, 'Health and medicine', p. 215.

42. In his study of the Lancaster Asylum, John Walton remarked that the majority of those who were discharged 'cured' (admittedly, a small proportion of the total admitted) were 'alcoholics who had dried out, exhausted half-starved over-worked women who recovered after a few weeks of limited exertion and reasonable diet, and cases of post-natal depression' (Walton, 'Casting out and bringing back', p. 142). It is difficult to believe that we would use the term 'lunatic' or the term 'insane' to describe such people today.

43. M. Thomson, *The problem of mental deficiency: eugenics, democracy and social policy in Britain c. 1870–1959*, Oxford: Oxford University Press, 1998, p. 10; A. Digby, 'Contexts and perspectives', in D. Wright and A. Digby (eds), *From idiocy to mental deficiency: historical perspectives on people with learning disabilities*, London: Routledge, 1996, pp. 1–21, at p. 2; M. Jackson, *The borderland of imbecility: medicine, society and the fabrication of the feeble mind in late-Victorian and Edwardian England*, Manchester: Manchester University Press, 2000, pp. 1–20.

44. Abel-Smith, *The hospitals*, p. 356; Cherry, *Medical services and the hospitals*, pp. 27–34, 44–8.

45. Jones, *Asylums and after*, pp. 38–40; Walton, 'The treatment of pauper lunatics', pp. 191–2; *ibid.*, 'Casting out and bringing back', p. 143.

8　Public health in the nineteenth century

1. T. McKeown, *The modern rise of population*, London: Edward Arnold, 1976.

2. D. Porter, *Health, civilisation and the state: a history of public health from ancient to modern times*, London: Routledge, 1999, pp. 9–62.

3. P. Razzell, *The conquest of smallpox: the impact of inoculation on smallpox mortality in eighteenth-century Britain*, Sussex: Caliban, 1977, pp. 1–92; J. R. Smith, *The speckled monster: smallpox in England 1670–1970*, Hunstanton, Norfolk: Witley, 1987. The practice of inoculation appears to have taken root much more slowly in Scotland than in England. See D. Brunton, 'Smallpox inoculation and demographic trends in eighteenth-century Scotland', *Medical History*, 36 (1992), 403–29.

4. M. Dobson, *Contours of death and disease in early-modern England*, Cambridge: Cambridge University Press, 1997.

5. J. Riley, *The eighteenth-century campaign to avoid disease*, Basingstoke: Macmillan (now Palgrave Macmillan), 1987, pp. xv–xvi.

6. S. Webb and B. Webb, *English local government from the Revolution to the Municipal Corporations Act: the Manor and the Borough*, London: Longman's, Green and Company, 1908, pp. 26–7; *ibid.*, *English local government: statutory authorities for special purposes*, London, Longman's, Green and Company, 1922, pp. 235–49; C. Hamlin, 'Public sphere to public health: the transformation of "nuisance" ', in S. Sturdy (ed.), *Medicine, health and the public sphere in Britain, 1600–2000*, London: Routledge, 2003, pp. 189–204, at pp. 189–94.

7. E. L. Jones and M. E. Falkus, 'Urban improvement and the English economy in the seventeenth and eighteenth centuries', in P. Borsay (ed.), *The eighteenth century town: a reader in English urban history 1688–1820*, London and New York: Longman, 1990, pp. 116–58; R. Porter, 'Cleaning up the Great Wen: public health in eighteenth-century London', in W. F. Bynum and R. Porter (eds), *Living and dying in London* (Medical History, Supplement no. 11), London: Wellcome Institute for the History of Medicine, 1991, pp. 61–75; J. Landers, *Death and the metropolis: studies in the demographic history of London 1670–1830*, Cambridge: Cambridge University Press, 1993.

8. Webb and Webb, *English local government: statutory authorities for special purposes*, p. 348.

9. E. P. Hennock, 'Urban sanitary reform a generation before Chadwick?', *Economic History Review*, 10 (1957), 113–20, at 117; V. Berridge, 'Health and medicine', in F. M. L. Thompson

(ed.), *The Cambridge Social History of Britain 1750–1950, Volume 3, Social agencies and institutions*, Cambridge: Cambridge University Press, 1990, pp. 171–242, at pp. 192–3.

10. M. W. Flinn (ed.), *Report on the sanitary condition of the labouring population of Great Britain, by Edwin Chadwick, 1842*, Edinburgh: Edinburgh University Press, 1965, pp. 8, 10, 25; R. J. Morris, *Cholera 1832: the social response to an epidemic*, London: Croom Helm, 1976; M. Durey, *The return of the plague: British society and the cholera 1831–2*, Dublin: Gill and Macmillan, 1979.

11. A. S. Wohl, *Endangered lives: public health in Victorian Britain*, London: Methuen, 1984, p. 119.

12. G. Macpherson, *Black's Medical Dictionary*, London: A. & C. Black, 39th edition, 1999, pp. 564–5.

13. Flinn (ed.), *Report on the sanitary condition of the labouring population*, pp. 8–11; Wohl, *Endangered lives*, pp. 125–7.

14. Flinn (ed.), *Report on the sanitary condition of the labouring population*, pp. 18–26, 43–4, 80–99, 219–53.

15. C. Hamlin, 'Predisposing causes and public health in early nineteenth-century medical thought', *Social History of Medicine*, 5 (1992), 43–70, at 65–7, 69–70; *ibid.*, 'Edwin Chadwick, "mutton medicine", and the fever question', *Bulletin of the History of Medicine*, 70 (1996), 233–65, at 237; *ibid.*, *Public health and social justice in the age of Chadwick: Britain 1800–54*, Cambridge: Cambridge University Press, 1997, pp. 90–7, 127, 226; Flinn (ed.), *Report on the sanitary condition of the labouring population*, pp. 63–4; J. Pickstone, 'Dearth, dirt and fever epidemics: rewriting the history of British "public health", 1780–1850', in T. Ranger and P. Slack (eds), *Epidemics and ideas: essays on the historical perception of pestilence*, Cambridge: Cambridge University Press, 1992, pp. 125–48; R. A. Lewis, *Edwin Chadwick and the public health movement, 1832–54*, London: Longman, pp. 62–6.

16. R. A. Cage, *The Scottish Poor Law 1745–1845*, Edinburgh: Scottish Academic Press, 1981, pp. 125–30; B. Hilton, *The age of atonement: the influence of Evangelicalism on social and economic thought, 1795–1865*, Oxford: Clarendon, 1988, pp. 62–3, 108–14, 162; Hamlin, *Public health and social justice*, pp. 132–3; R. Mitchison, *The Old Poor Law in Scotland: the experience of poverty 1574–1845*, Edinburgh: Edinburgh University Press, 2000, pp. 173–80.

17. Lewis, *Edwin Chadwick and the public health movement*, pp. 124–77; S. Finer, *The life and times of Sir Edwin Chadwick*, London: Methuen, 1952, pp. 293–331.

18. Wohl, *Endangered lives*, p. 7; see also Hamlin, *Public health and social justice*, pp. 165–72.

19. Finer, *The life and times of Sir Edwin Chadwick*, pp. 228–9; Lewis, *Edwin Chadwick and the public health movement*, pp. 83–5.

20. PP 1844 (572) xvii, 1, *First report of the Commissioners for enquiring into the state of large towns and populous districts*, pp. vii–xv; PP 1845 (602) xviii, 1, *Second report of the Commissioners for enquiring into the state of large towns and populous districts*, p. 6.

21. Finer, *The life and times of Sir Edwin Chadwick*, pp. 319–22; Lewis, *Edwin Chadwick and the public health movement*, pp. 164–6.

22. Finer, *The life and times of Sir Edwin Chadwick*, pp. 293–331; Lewis, *Edwin Chadwick and the public health movement*, pp. 124–77.

23. PP 1847–8 (83) v, 205. *A Bill for promoting the public health*, section 8; PP 1847–8 (325) v, 341. *A Bill for promoting the public health (as amended by the Committee, and on recommitment)*, Section 7.

24. Finer, *The life and times of Sir Edwin Chadwick*, p. 324.

25. PP 1847–8 (546) v, 497. *Public health bill (as amended by the Lords)*, section 8; *Parliamentary Debates*, Third series, Vol. 100 (1848), col. 1174.

26. Finer, *The life and times of Sir Edwin Chadwick*, p. 325.

27. 11 & 12 Vict. C. 63: sections 1, 4–6, 10–14; see also Flinn (ed.), *Report on the sanitary condition of the labouring population*, p. 71.

28. J. Hanley, 'The public's reaction to public health: petitions submitted to Parliament 1847–1848', *Social History of Medicine*, 15 (2002), 393–411, at 411; J. Simon, *English*

sanitary institutions, reviewed in their course of development, and in some of their political and social relations, London: Cassell & Co., 1890, p. 208; Lewis, *Edwin Chadwick and the public health movement,* p. 279; Wohl, *Endangered lives,* pp. 149–50.

29. PP 1850 (110) xxxiii, 591, *A return of the number, names and population of towns and districts which have asked for inspection under the Public Health Act, and of those which have embraced or are placed under its provisions.*

30. PP 1844 (572) xvii, 505, *Appendix to the first report of the Commissioners for enquiring into the state of large towns and populous districts,* pp. 6–11; PP 1852–3 (704) xcvi, 1. *Return of all places which have petitioned the General Board of Health for the application of the Public Health Act, 1848, with the date when such petitions were received, etc.,* pp. 3–13.

31. *Parliamentary Debates,* Third series, Vol. 135 (1854), col. 235; PP 1854 (1768) xxxv, 1, *Report of the General Board of Health on the administration of the Public Health Act and the Nuisances Removal and Diseases Prevention Acts from 1848 to 1854,* pp. 13–14.

32. E. Royle, *Modern Britain: a social history 1750–1985,* London: Edward Arnold, p. 21.

33. Lewis, *Edwin Chadwick and the public health movement,* p. 351.

34. Finer, *The life and times of Sir Edwin Chadwick,* p. 3; Lewis, *Edwin Chadwick and the public health movement,* p. 353.

35. See also A. Brundage, *England's 'Prussian Minister': Edwin Chadwick and the politics of government growth, 1832–1854,* University Park, PA: Pennsylvania State University Press, 1988, pp. 133–56.

36. R. Lambert, *Sir John Simon, 1816–1904, and English social administration,* London: MacGibbon and Kee, 1963, pp. 35–56, 221–38, 330–71; C. Hamlin, 'State medicine in Great Britain', in D. Porter (ed.), *The history of public health and the modern state,* Amsterdam: Rodopi, 1994, pp. 132–64, at pp. 148–50.

37. Flinn (ed.), *Report on the sanitary condition of the labouring population,* pp. 62–3.

38. Lambert, *Sir John Simon,* pp. 48–55.

39. W. M. Frazer, *A history of English public health 1834–1939,* London: Baillière, Tindall and Cox, pp. 117–25; Lambert, *Sir John Simon,* pp. 514–17.

40. 11 & 12 Vict. C. 63: section 108; Wohl, *Endangered lives,* pp. 112–5, 162–3, 174.

41. R. Lambert, 'A Victorian National Health Service: State vaccination 1855–71', *Historical Journal,* 5 (1962), 1–18; P. Baldwin, *Contagion and the state in Europe 1830–1930,* Cambridge: Cambridge University Press, 1999, pp. 244–354.

42. F. Mort, *Dangerous sexualities: medico-moral politics in England since 1830,* London: Routledge and Kegan Paul, 1987, pp. 65–99.

43. Royle, *Modern Britain,* pp. 197–8.

44. Wohl, *Endangered lives,* pp. 53–4, 110–12, 136–8, 228, 249, 263, 270, 313–5; R. Pinker, *English hospital statistics 1861–1938,* London: Heinemann, 1966, pp. 57–61.

45. Frazer, *A history of English public health,* pp. 250–8; B. Harris, *The health of the schoolchild: a history of the school medical service in England and Wales,* Buckingham: Open University Press, 1995, pp. 6–64; B. Gilbert, *The evolution of national insurance in Great Britain: the origins of the welfare state,* London: Michael Joseph, 1966, pp. 233–399; L. Bryder, *Below the magic mountain: a social history of tuberculosis in twentieth-century Britain,* Oxford: Clarendon Press, 1988, pp. 36–41.

46. McKeown, *The modern rise of population, passim.*

47. A. Hardy, *The epidemic streets: infectious disease and the rise of preventive medicine 1856–1900,* Oxford: Clarendon Press, 1993, pp. 293–4.

48. B. R. Mitchell, *British historical statistics,* Cambridge: Cambridge University Press, 1988, pp. 57–9.

49. P. Razzell, 'Population change in eighteenth-century England: a reinterpretation', *Economic History Review,* 18 (1965), 312–32; *ibid., The conquest of smallpox,* pp. 14–58; A. Mercer, 'Smallpox and epidemiological-demographic change in Europe: the role of vaccination', *Population Studies* (1985), 39, 287–307; *ibid., Disease, mortality and population in*

transition: epidemiological-demographic change in England since the eighteenth century as part of a global phenomenon, Leicester: Leicester University Press, 1990, pp. 46–73.

50. Dobson, *Contours of death, passim*.

51. Jones and Falkus, 'Urban improvement'; Porter, 'Cleaning up the Great Wen'; Landers, *Death and the metropolis*.

52. R. Schofield and D. Reher, 'The decline of mortality in Europe', in R. Schofield, D. Reher and A. Bideau (eds), *The decline of mortality in Europe*, Oxford: Clarendon Press, 1991, pp. 1–17, at p. 5; J. Burnett, 'Housing and the decline of mortality', in R. Schofield, D. Reher and A. Bideau (eds), *The decline of mortality in Europe*, Oxford: Clarendon Press, pp. 158–76, at p. 176; E. A. Wrigley, R. Davies, J. Oeppen and R. Schofield, *English population history from family reconstitution 1580–1837*, Cambridge: Cambridge University Press, 1997, p. 275.

53. M. Livi-Bacci, *Population and nutrition: an essay on European demographic history*, Cambridge: Cambridge University Press, 1991, p. xiv; *ibid.*, *The population of Europe: a history*, Oxford: Blackwell, 2000, pp. 40–60; R. W. Fogel, 'Economic growth, population theory and physiology: the bearing of long-term processes on the making of economic policy', *American Economic Review*, 84 (1994), 369–95, at 371.

54. E. A. Wrigley and R. S. Schofield, *The population history of England 1541–1871: a reconstruction*, Cambridge: Cambridge University Press, 1981, pp. 351–5; Livi-Bacci, *Population and nutrition*, pp. 163–4; Mercer, *Disease, mortality and population in transition*, pp. 30–7; C. H. Feinstein, 'Pessimism perpetuated: real wages and the standard of living in Britain during and after the industrial revolution', *Journal of Economic History*, 58 (1998), 625–58, at 642–4; R. W. Fogel, *The escape from hunger and premature death 1700–2100: Europe, America and the Third World*, Cambridge: Cambridge University Press, 2004.

55. J. Komlos, 'Shrinking in a growing economy? The mystery of physical stature during the industrial revolution', *Journal of Economic History*, 58 (1998), pp. 779–802, at p. 786; M. Haines, 'Shrinking people - growing incomes. Can development be hazardous to your health? Historical evidence for the United States, England and the Netherlands in the nineteenth century', Unpublished conference paper presented to the First International Conference on Economics and Human Biology, University of Tübingen, 11–14 July, 2002, p. 11.

56. S. Horrell, 'Home demand and British industrialisation', *Journal of Economic History*, 56 (1996), 561–604, at 592; Feinstein, 'Pessimism perpetuated', 640, 648, 653.

57. Fogel, *The escape from hunger*; G. Clark, M. Huberman and P. Lindert, 'A British food puzzle, 1770–1850', *Economic History Review*, 48 (1995), 215–37, at 222–3; D. Oddy, 'Food, drink and nutrition', in F. M. L. Thompson (ed.), *The Cambridge social history of Britain 1750–1950, Volume 2, People and their environment*, Cambridge: Cambridge University Press, 1990, pp. 251–78, at pp. 269–74.

58. Wohl, *Endangered lives*, pp. 4–6; F. M. L. Thompson, 'Town and city', in F. M. L. Thompson (ed.), *The Cambridge Social History of Britain, Volume 1, Regions and their communities*, Cambridge: Cambridge University Press, 1990, pp. 1–86, at p. 8.

59. P. Huck, 'Infant mortality and living standards of English workers during the industrial revolution', *Journal of Economic History*, 55 (1995), 528–50, at 534–5.

60. R. Floud, K. Wachter and A. Gregory, *Height, health and history: nutritional status in the United Kingdom 1750–1980*, Cambridge: Cambridge University Press, 1990, pp. 205–6, 326.

61. R. Woods, 'The effects of population redistribution on the level of mortality in nineteenth-century England and Wales', *Journal of Economic History*, 45 (1985), 645–51, at 648, 650; S. Szreter and G. Mooney, 'Urbanisation, mortality and the standard of living debate: new estimates of the expectation of life at birth in nineteenth-century British cities', *Economic History Review*, 51 (1998), 84–112, at 104; R. Woods, *The demography of Victorian England and Wales*, Cambridge: Cambridge University Press, 2000, pp. 362, 369.

62. Floud, Wachter and Gregory, *Height, health and history*, p. 314; B. Harris, ' "The child is father to the man". The relationship between child health and adult mortality in the 19th and 20th centuries', *International Journal of Epidemiology*, 30 (2001), 688–96, at 691.

63. T. McKeown and R. G. Record, 'Reasons for the decline of mortality in England and Wales during the nineteenth century', *Population Studies*, 16 (1962), 94–122, at 109–22; McKeown, *The modern rise of population*, pp. 117–23.

64. McKeown and Record, 'Reasons for the decline of mortality', 117; McKeown, *The modern rise of population*, p. 82; S. Szreter, 'The importance of social intervention in Britain's mortality decline, c. 1850–1914: a reinterpretation of the role of public health', *Social History of Medicine*, 1, 1–37; Hardy, *The epidemic streets*, p. 66; Woods, *The demography of Victorian England and Wales*, p. 323.

65. Szreter, 'The importance of social intervention', 11–17; S. Guha, 'The importance of social intervention in England's mortality decline: the evidence reviewed', *Social History of Medicine*, 7 (1994), 89–113, at 96–100; S. Szreter, 'Mortality in England in the eighteenth and the nineteenth centuries: a reply to Sumit Guha', *Social History of Medicine*, 7 (1994), 269–82, at 274–8.

66. J. Riley, *Sick, not dead: the health of British workingmen during the mortality decline*, Baltimore, MD: Johns Hopkins University Press, 1997, p. 197; *ibid.*, 'Reply to Bernard Harris, "Morbidity and mortality during the health transition: a comment on James C. Riley" ', *Social History of Medicine*, 12 (1999), 133–7, at 137; H. Emery, 'Review of James C. Riley, *Sick, not dead: the health of British workingmen during the mortality decline*'. EH.Net, H-Net Reviews, July 1998. URL: www.h-net.msu.edu/reviews/showrev.cgi?path=17775899999635
C. Edwards, M. Gorsky, B. Harris and P. R. A. Hinde, 'Sickness, insurance and health: assessing trends in morbidity through friendly society records', *Annales de Démographie Historique*, 1 (2003), 131–67.

67. R. Woods and N. Shelton, *An atlas of Victorian mortality*, Liverpool: Liverpool University Press, 1997, pp. 143–4; Woods, *The demography of Victorian England and Wales*, pp. 340, 359; J. Landers, 'Review of Robert Woods and Nicola Shelton, *An atlas of Victorian mortality*', *Continuity and Change*, 15 (2000), 466–8, at 468; S. Szreter, 'Review of Robert Woods, *The demography of Victorian England and Wales*', *Social History of Medicine*, 14 (2001), 562–3, at 563; Livi-Bacci, *The population of Europe*, p. 144.

68. M. E. Pooley and C. G. Pooley, 'Health, society and environment in nineteenth-century Manchester', in R. Woods and J. Woodward (eds), *Urban disease and mortality in nineteenth-century England*, London and New York: Batsford, 1984, pp. 148–75, at pp. 171–2; J. Vögele, *Urban mortality change in England and Germany, 1870–1913*, Liverpool: Liverpool University Press, 1998, p. 145; McKeown, *The modern rise of population*, p. 118; M. Daunton, *House and home in the Victorian city: working class housing 1850–1914*, London: Edward Arnold, 1983, p. 7; *ibid.*, 'Health and Housing in Victorian London', *Medical History*, Supplement no. 11 (1991), 126–44, at 143; G. Cronjé, 'Tuberculosis and mortality decline in England and Wales, 1851–1910', in R. Woods and J. Woodward, (eds), *Urban disease and mortality in nineteenth-century England*, London & New York: Batsford, 1984, pp. 79–101, at p. 99.

69. A. Hardy, *Health and medicine in Britain since 1860*, Basingstoke: Palgrave (now Palgrave Macmillan), 2001, p. 38.

70. J. Burnett, *Plenty and want: a social history of diet in England from 1815 to the present day*, London: Methuen, Third edition, 1989, pp. 108, 176; Oddy, 'Food, drink and nutrition', pp. 267–75; P. Dewey, 'Nutrition and living standards in wartime Britain', in R. Wall and J. Winter (eds), *The upheaval of war: family, work and welfare in Europe 1914–18*, Cambridge: Cambridge University Press, pp. 197–220, at p. 215.

71. S. Preston and E. van de Walle, 'Urban French mortality in the nineteenth century', *Population Studies*, 32 (1978), 275–97, at 280–1.

72. P. Dasgupta and D. Ray, 'Adapting to undernourishment: the biological evidence and its implications', in J. Drèze and A. Sen (eds), *The political economy of hunger, Volume 1, Entitlement and well-being*, Oxford: Clarendon Press, pp. 191–246, at pp. 215–16.

73. McKeown and Record, 'Reasons for the decline of mortality'; McKeown, *The modern rise of population*; Woods, *The demography of Victorian England and Wales*, pp. 355–6.

74. Woods, *The demography of Victorian England and Wales*, pp. 356–8.
75. F. Bell and R. Millward, 'Public health expenditures and mortality in England and Wales 1870–1914', *Continuity and Change*, 13 (1998), 221–49, at 237–42; J. Hassan, 'The growth and impact of the British water industry in the nineteenth century', *Economic History Review*, 38 (1985), 531–47, at 543–4; R. Millward and F. Bell, 'Economic factors in the decline of mortality in nineteenth-century Britain', *European Review of Economic History*, 2 (1998), 263–88.
76. Wohl, *Endangered lives*, pp. 307–8, 327.
77. Flinn (ed.), *The sanitary condition of the labouring population*, p. 87; Daunton, 'Health and housing in Victorian London', p. 137.

9   Housing policy and housing conditions, 1800–1914

1. F. M. Eden, *The state of the poor*, London: B & J. White *et al.*, 1797, Volume 1, p. 554; Volume 3, pp. cccxxxix–cccl; J. Burnett, *A social history of housing 1815–1985*, London: Routledge, 1986, p. 39.
2. Burnett, *A social history of housing*, pp. 34–7; J. Rule, *The labouring classes in early-industrial England 1750–1850*, London: Longman, 1986, pp. 78–81.
3. J. Caird, *English agriculture in 1850–1*, London: Longman, Brown, Green and Longman's, 1852, pp. 474–5; Burnett, *A social history of housing*, p. 40.
4. M. W. Flinn (ed.), *Report on the sanitary condition of the labouring population of Great Britain, by Edwin Chadwick, 1842*, Edinburgh: Edinburgh University Press, 1965, pp. 80–1, 86–7.
5. Burnett, *A social history of housing*, p. 43; PP 1843 (510), xii, 1, *Reports of Special Assistant Poor Law Commissioners on the employment of women and children in agriculture*, p. 20.
6. PP 1865 (3484) xxvi, 1, *Seventh Report of the Medical Officer of the Privy Council, with Appendix, 1864*, pp. 128–9, 143–4.
7. PP 1884–5 C. 4402 xxx, 1, *First Report of Her Majesty's Commissioners for enquiring into the housing of the working classes*, p. 27.
8. E. Gauldie, *Cruel habitations: a history of working class housing 1780–1918*, London: George Allen and Unwin, 1974, p. 21.
9. Rule, *The labouring classes*, pp. 82–7.
10. E. Hopkins, 'Working-class housing in the smaller industrial town of the nineteenth century: Stourbridge – a case study', *Midland History*, 4 (1978), 230–54.
11. K. Sullivan, ' "The biggest room in Merthyr": working-class housing in Dowlais, 1850–1914', *Welsh History Review*, 17 (1994), 155–85.
12. C. Law, 'The growth of urban population in England and Wales, 1801–1911', *Transactions of the Institute of British Geographers*, 41 (1967), 125–43, at 141.
13. M. Daunton, *House and home in the Victorian city: working class housing 1850–1914*, London: Edward Arnold, 1983, p. 12; *ibid.*, 'Housing', in F. M. L. Thompson (ed.), *The Cambridge Social History of Britain 1750–1950, Volume 2, People and their environment*, Cambridge: Cambridge University Press, 1990, pp. 195–250, at p. 202; F. Engels, *The condition of the working class in England, from personal observations and authentic sources, with an introduction by Eric Hobsbawm*, London: Granada, 1969, p. 81.
14. Burnett, *A social history of housing*, p. 62.
15. J. P. Kay, *The moral and physical condition of the working classes employed in the cotton manufacture in Manchester*, London: Ridgway, 1832, p. 3; P. Gaskell, *The manufacturing population of England, its moral, social and physical conditions, and the changes which have arisen from the use of steam machinery, with an examination of infant labour*, London: Baldwin and Cradock, 1833, p. 141.
16. H. Mayhew, *London labour and the London poor: a cyclopædia of the condition and earnings of those that will work, those that cannot work, and those that will not work, Volume 3, The London*

street-folk, London: Frank Cass, 1967, pp. 315–18; *ibid.*, *The Morning Chronicle survey of labour and the poor, Volume 1, The Metropolitan districts*, Sussex: Caliban, 1980, pp. 103–8.

17. A. S. Wohl, *The eternal slum: housing and social policy in Victorian London*, London: Edward Arnold, 1977, p. 74.

18. Flinn (ed.), *The sanitary condition of the labouring population*, pp. 91–2, 105.

19. W. M. Frazer, *Duncan of Liverpool, being an account of the work of Dr W. H. Duncan, Medical Officer of Health of Liverpool 1847–63*, London: Hamish Hamilton, 1947, p. 32; Burnett, *A social history of housing*, pp. 58–61; B. R. Mitchell and P. Deane, *Abstract of British historical statistics*, Cambridge: Cambridge University Press, 1962, p. 24; R. Rodger, *Housing in urban Britain 1780–1914*, Basingstoke: Macmillan (now Palgrave Macmillan), 1989, pp. 31–2.

20. Burnett, *A social history of housing*, pp. 66–7.

21. Kay, *The moral and physical condition*, pp. 36–8.

22. *Parliamentary Debates*, Third series, Vol. 115 (1851), col. 1264; Burnett, *A social history of housing*, p. 66.

23. Gauldie, *Cruel habitations*, pp. 70–1.

24. Flinn (ed.), *The sanitary condition of the labouring population*, pp. 343–4; Burnett, *A social history of housing*, p. 70; but see also E. Hopkins, 'Working-class housing in Birmingham during the industrial revolution', *International Review of Social History*, 31 (1986), 80–94, at 94.

25. M. Beresford, 'The back-to-back house in Leeds, 1787–1937', in S. D. Chapman (ed.), *The history of working class housing: a symposium*, Newton Abbot: David & Charles, 1971, pp. 93–132, at p. 112; PP 1844 (572) xvii, 1, *First report of the Commissioners for enquiring into the state of large towns and populous districts*, QQ. 175–8, 284–6, 660–1, 776–9, 2219.

26. Burnett, *A social history of housing*, pp. 77–9; Rodger, *Housing in urban Britain*, pp. 34–5.

27. Daunton, *House and home in the Victorian city*, pp. 7–8, 38–59, 155, 263–6; *ibid.*, *A property-owning democracy: housing in Britain*, London: Faber, 1987, p. 15.

28. Rodger, *Housing in urban Britain*, pp. 26–7.

29. See also A. S. Wohl, *Endangered lives: public health in Victorian Britain*, London: Methuen, 1984, pp. 149, 180, 308–10; Rodger, *Housing in urban Britain*, p. 27.

30. Gauldie, *Cruel habitations*, p. 243; Wohl, *The eternal slum*, p. 78; *ibid.*, *Endangered lives*, p. 310.

31. PP 1884–5 C. 4402–I xxx, 87, *Minutes of evidence taken before the Royal Commission on the Housing of the Working Classes*, QQ. 4–5, 23–6.

32. J. L. Hammond and B. Hammond, *Lord Shaftesbury*, London: Constable & Company, 1925, p. 164; E. Hodder, *The life and work of the seventh Earl of Shaftesbury*, London: Cassell, 1887, p. 446; Gauldie, *Cruel habitations*, pp. 242–3.

33. Wohl, *The eternal slum*, p. 76.

34. Gauldie, *Cruel habitations*, p. 245; but cf. Rodger, *Housing in urban Britain*, pp. 31, 50.

35. Rodger, *Housing in urban Britain*, pp. 50–1.

36. Daunton, *House and home in the Victorian city*, p. 7.

37. Wohl, *The eternal slum*, pp. 107, 139.

38. A. Mearns, *The bitter cry of outcast London, with leading articles from the Pall Mall Gazette of October 1883 and articles by Lord Salisbury, Joseph Chamberlain and Forster Crozier, edited with an Introduction by Anthony S. Wohl*, Leicester: Leicester University Press, 1970; Wohl, *The eternal slum*, pp. 238–9.

39. PP 1884–5 C. 4402 xxx, 1, *First Report of Her Majesty's Commissioners for enquiring into the housing of the working classes*, pp. 40–4.

40. 48 & 49 Vict. C. 72, section 2.

41. M. Swenarton, *Homes fit for heroes: the politics and architecture of early state housing in Britain*, London: Heinemann, 1981, pp. 28–9; Wohl, *The eternal slum*, pp. 250–84; Daunton, *House and home in the Victorian city*, pp. 18–19; P. Hebbelthwaite, 'The municipal housing programme in Sheffield before 1914', *Architectural History*, 30 (1987), 143–81.

42. Wohl, *The eternal slum*, p. 339.

43. Daunton, *House and home in the Victorian city*, pp. 286–92; *ibid.*, 'Housing', pp. 234–6; Burnett, *A social history of housing*, p. 184; A. Power, *Hovels to high rise: state housing in Europe since 1850*, London: Routledge, 1993, p. 235.

44. R. Whelan, *Octavia Hill and the social housing debate: essays and letters by Octavia Hill*, London: Institute of Economic Affairs, 1998, p. 20; C. Morrell, 'Review of R. Whelan, *Octavia Hill and the social housing debate: essays and letters by Octavia Hill*', *Economic History Review*, 52 (1999), 158.

45. Wohl, *The eternal slum*, pp. 179–200; R. Dennis, 'The geography of Victorian values: philanthropic housing in London, 1840–1900', *Journal of Historical Geography*, 15 (1989), 40–54, at 41; J. Lewis, *Women and social action in Victorian and Edwardian England*, Aldershot: Edward Elgar, 1991, pp. 43–51; PP 1884–5 C. 4402–I xxx, 87, *Minutes of evidence taken before the Royal Commission on the Housing of the Working Classes*, Q. 9119; Whelan, *Octavia Hill*, pp. 11, 16.

46. Dennis, 'The geography of Victorian values', pp. 360–1.

47. J. N. Tarn, *Five per cent philanthropy: an account of housing in urban areas between 1840 and 1914*, Cambridge: Cambridge University Press, 1973, p. 15.

48. J. N. Tarn, 'The Peabody Donation Fund: the role of a housing society in the nineteenth century', *Victorian Studies*, 10 (1966), 7–38; Burnett, *A social history of housing*, p. 177; Whelan, *Octavia Hill*, p. 17.

49. S. Morris, 'Market solutions for social problems: working-class housing in nineteenth-century London', *Economic History Review*, 54 (2001), 525–45, at 531–3.

50. Tarn, 'The Peabody Donation Fund', 15–20; Dennis, 'The geography of Victorian values', 43–52; Burnett, *A social history of housing*, p. 178; P. Malpass, 'The discontinuous history of housing associations in England', *Housing Studies*, 15 (2000), 195–212, at 196–200.

51. M. Daunton, 'Miners' houses: South Wales and the Great Northern coalfield 1880–1914', *International Review of Social History*, 25 (1980), 143–75; J. Melling, 'Employers, industrial housing and the evolution of company welfare policies in Britain's heavy industry: West Scotland, 1870–1920', *International Review of Social History*, 26 (1981), 255–301; Burnett, *A social history of housing*, pp. 82–4.

52. Burnett, *A social history of housing*, pp. 180–1.

53. W. Ashworth, *The genesis of modern British town planning: a study in economic and social history of the nineteenth and twentieth centuries*, London: Routledge and Kegan Paul, 1954, pp. 118–46, 160–4, 179; Burnett, *A social history of housing*, pp. 181–3; see also D. Jeremy, 'The enlightened paternalist in action: William Hesketh Lever at Port Sunlight before 1914', *Business History*, 33 (1991), 58–81.

54. Burnett, *A social history of housing*, pp. 144–5; Wohl, *Endangered lives*, pp. 305, 408.

55. A. Offer, *Property and politics 1870–1914*, Cambridge: Cambridge University Press, 1981, pp. 254–313; D. Englander, *Landlord and tenant in urban Britain 1888–1918*, Oxford: Clarendon Press, 1983, pp. xvii–xviii; R. Rodger, 'Political economy, ideology and persistence of working-class housing problems in Britain, 1850–1914', *International Review of Social History*, 32 (1987), 109–43, at 13–39; *ibid.*, *Housing in urban Britain*, pp. 52–62.

56. F. M. L. Thompson, 'How they lived then', *Times Literary Supplement*, No. 3,778 (2 August 1974), 823; Daunton, *House and home in the Victorian city*, pp. 2–3, 286–307; *ibid.*, *A property-owning democracy*, pp. 13–39; *ibid.*, 'Housing', pp. 223–34.

10   Education and schooling, 1800–1914

1. A. M. Rees, *T. H. Marshall's Social Policy*, London: Hutchinson, 1985, p. 12; D. Fraser, *The evolution of the British welfare state: a history of social policy since the Industrial Revolution*, London and Basingstoke: Macmillan (now Palgrave Macmillan), First edition, 1973; Second

edition, 1984; Third edition, 2003; P. Thane, *The foundations of the welfare state*, London: Longman's, First edition, 1982; Second edition, 1996; D. Gladstone, *The twentieth-century welfare state*, Basingstoke: Macmillan, 1999; H. Glennerster, *British social policy since 1945*, Oxford: Basil Blackwell, First edition, 1995; Second edition, 2000; R. Lowe, *The welfare state in Britain since 1945*, London & Basingstoke: Macmillan, First edition, 1993; Second edition, 1999.

2. H. Hendrick, *Child welfare: England 1872–1989*, London: Routledge, 1994, p. xii.

3. T. H. Marshall, 'Citizenship and social class', in T. H. Marshall, *Sociology at the crossroads and other essays*, London: Heinemann, 1963, pp. 84–6, 111–15.

4. *Parliamentary Debates*, Third series, Vol. 199 (1870), cols. 465–6.

5. L. Stone, 'Literacy and education in England, 1640–1900', *Past and Present*, 42 (1969), 69–139, at 104–5; M. Sanderson, 'Literacy and social mobility in the industrial revolution in England', *Past and Present*, 56 (1972), 75–104; *ibid.*, *Education, economic change and society in England 1780–1870*, Basingstoke: Macmillan (now Palgrave Macmillan), 1991, pp. 11–13.

6. R. Schofield, 'Dimensions of illiteracy', *Explorations in Economic History*, 10 (1973), 437–54, at 445–6, 451–3.

7. H. Kiesling, 'Nineteenth-century education according to West: a comment', *Economic History Review*, 36 (1983), 416–25, at 423–4.

8. G. Sutherland, 'Education', in F. M. L. Thompson (ed.), *The Cambridge Social History of Britain, Volume 3, Social agencies and institutions*, Cambridge: Cambridge University Press, 1990, pp. 119–70, at p. 120.

9. E. G. West, 'Resource allocation and growth in early-nineteenth-century British education', *Economic History Review*, 23 (1970), 68–95, at 77.

10. *Parliamentary Debates*, First series (1807), Vol. 9, col. 798.

11. P. McCann, 'Popular education, socialisation and social control: Spitalfields 1812–1824', in P. McCann (ed.), *Popular education and socialisation in the nineteenth century*, London: Methuen, 1977, pp. 1–40, at p. 1; *Parliamentary Debates*, Third series, Vol. 20 (1833), cols. 145–6.

12. Fraser, *The evolution of the British welfare state*, Second edition, p. 79; Third edition, p. 86.

13. W. B. Stephens, *Education in Britain 1750–1914*, Basingstoke: Macmillan (now Palgrave Macmillan), 1998, pp. 1–2; see also A. F. Roberts, 'A new view of the infant school movement', *British Journal of Educational Studies*, 20 (1972), 154–64; J. Higginson, 'Dame schools', *British Journal of Educational Studies*, 22 (1974), 166–81; D. P. Leinster-Mackay, 'Dame schools: a need for review', *British Journal of Educational Studies*, 24 (1976), 33–48; P. Gardner, *The lost elementary schools of Victorian England: the people's education*, London: Croom Helm, 1984, pp. 15–44.

14. Stephens, *Education in Britain*, p. 2; see also M. G. Jones, *The charity school movement: a study of eighteenth-century Puritanism in action*, Cambridge: Cambridge University Press, 1938.

15. T. Laqueur, *Religion and respectability: Sunday schools and working-class culture 1780–1850*, New Haven, CT and London: Yale University Press, 1976; M. Dick, 'The myth of the working-class Sunday school', *History of Education*, 9 (1980), 27–41.

16. Sanderson, *Education, economic change and society*, p. 13.

17. Laqueur, *Religion and respectability*, p. 44.

18. PP 1861 (2794) xxi (Part I), 1, *Report of the Commissioners appointed to enquire into the state of popular education in England*, p. 82.

19. R. Johnson, 'Educational policy and social control in early-Victorian England', *Past and Present*, 49 (1970), 96–119; McCann, 'Popular education, socialisation and social control', p. 1; J. Burnett, *Destiny obscure: autobiographies of childhood, education and family from the 1820s to the 1920s*, London: Routledge, 1994, pp. 144, 172–3.

20. G. F. Bartle, 'The role of the British and Foreign Schools Society in the education of poor children of the Metropolis during the first half of the nineteenth century', *Journal of Educational Administration and History*, 24, No. 1 (1992), 74–90; *ibid.*, 'The impact of the

British and Foreign Schools Society on elementary education in the main textile areas of the industrial north', *History of Education*, 22 (1993), 33–48; Stephens, *Education in Britain*, pp. 5–6.

21. PP 1861 (2794) xxi (Part I), 1, *Report of the Commissioners appointed to enquire into the state of popular education in England*, pp. 79–83.

22. *Ibid.*, pp. 84–5, 170–4, 648–9, 653, 655; Stephens, *Education in Britain*, p. 83.

23. J. Murphy, *Church, state and schools in Britain 1800–1970*, London: Routledge and Kegan Paul, 1971, pp. 10–48; Fraser, *The evolution of the British welfare state*, First edition, pp. 74–5; Second edition, pp. 81–2; Third edition, pp. 87–8.

24. Murphy, *Church, state and schools*, pp. 16–17.

25. Sanderson, *Education, economic change and society*, pp. 21–2; see also Table 10.2.

26. *Parliamentary Debates*, Third series, Vol. 148 (1858), cols. 1184–248.

27. K. Evans, *The development and structure of the English educational system*, London: University of London Press, 1975, p. 23.

28. PP 1861 (2794) xxi (Part I), 1, *Report of the Commissioners appointed to enquire into the state of popular education in England*, p. 544.

29. See for example *The Times*, 1 April 1861, p. 6, cols. e–f; *ibid.*, 3 April 1861, p. 8, col. f– p. 9, col. a.

30. *Parliamentary Debates*, Third series, Vol. 165 (1862), cols. 229–30.

31. G. Sutherland, *Policy-making in elementary education 1870–1895*, Oxford: Oxford University Press, 1973, p. 9; M. Sanderson, *Education and economic decline in Britain, 1870s to the 1990s*, Cambridge: Cambridge University Press, 1999, p. 5. Payment by results did not become fully established in England and Wales before 1 July 1863, and in Scotland until 1 April 1864. See PP 1862 (3007) xlii, 1, *Report of the Committee on Council on Education, with Appendix, 1861–2*, pp. vii–ix; PP 1864 (3349) xlv, 1, *Report of the Committee of Council on Education, with Appendix, 1863–4*, p. vii.

32. *Parliamentary Debates*, Third series, Vol. 165 (1862), col. 230.

33. See also D. Sylvester, *Robert Lowe and education*, Cambridge: Cambridge University Press, 1974, pp. 80–115.

34. Sanderson, *Education, economic change and society*, pp. 9–27; Stephens, *Education in Britain*, pp. 21–39.

35. B. Simon, *Studies in the history of education 1780–1870*, London: Lawrence and Wishart, 1960, pp. 350–67.

36. Fraser, *The evolution of the British welfare state*, First edition, p. 79; Second edition, p. 86; Third edition, p. 93.

37. A. J. Marcham, 'The myth of Benthamism, the Second Reform Act and the extension of popular education', *Journal of Educational Administration and History*, 2, No. 2 (1970), 20–29, at 23.

38. J. S. Hurt, *Elementary schooling and the working classes 1860–1918*, London: Routledge and Kegan Paul, 1979, pp. 3–24.

39. *Parliamentary Debates*, Third series, Vol. 199 (1870), cols. 438, 465–6.

40. See also G. Baker, 'The romantic and radical nature of the 1870 Education Act', *History of Education*, 30 (2001), 211–32.

41. Marcham, 'The myth of Benthamism', 26; see also T. Taylor, ' "A flame more bright than lasting?" The Tory party, political reform and educational change, 1865–70', *Journal of Educational Administration and History*, 23, No. 2 (1991), 62–73, at 73; Stephens, *Education in Britain*, p. 81.

42. *Parliamentary Debates*, Third series, Vol. 199 (1870), cols. 442–63.

43. A. Davin, ' "Mind that you do as you are told": reading books for Board school girls, 1870–1902', *Feminist Review*, 3 (1979), 89–98, at 89; M. Gomersall, 'Ideals and realities: the education of working-class girls 1800–70', *History of Education*, 17 (1988), 37–53, at 42; *ibid.*, *Working-class girls in nineteenth-century England: life, work and schooling*, Basingstoke: Macmillan (now Palgrave Macmillan), 1997, pp. 91–2.

44. Davin, ' "Mind that you do as you are told" '; C. Dyhouse, *Girls growing up in late-Victorian and Edwardian England*, London: Routledge and Kegan Paul, 1981, pp. 79–114; A. Turnbull, 'Learning her womanly work: the elementary school curriculum 1870–1914', in F. Hunt (ed.), Lessons for life: the schooling of girls and women 1850–1950, Oxford: Basil Blackwell, pp. 83–100; P. Horn, 'The education and employment of working-class girls 1870–1914', *History of Education*, 17 (1988), 71–82, at 73.

45. Davin, ' "Mind that you do as you are told" ', pp. 97–8; *ibid.*, *Growing up poor: home, school and street in London 1870–1914*, London: Rivers Oram Press, pp. 102–11; Dyhouse, *Girls growing up in late-Victorian and Edwardian England*, p. 102; Gomersall, *Working-class girls*, p. 113.

46. West, 'Resource allocation and growth; *ibid.*, 'The interpretation of early-nineteenth-century education statistics', *Economic History Review*, 24 (1971), 633–42; *ibid.*, *Education and the industrial revolution*, London: Batsford, 1975; *ibid.*, 'Literacy and the industrial revolution', *Economic History Review*, 31 (1978), 369–83; *ibid.*, 'Nineteenth-century educational history: the Kiesling critique', *Economic History Review*, 36 (1983), 426–34; *ibid.*, *Education and the state: a study in political economy*, Indianapolis, IN: Liberty Fund, 1994. See also J. Hurt, 'Professor West on early-nineteenth-century education', *Economic History Review*, 24 (1971), 624–32; Kiesling, 'Nineteenth-century education according to West'.

47. Gardner, *The lost elementary schools of Victorian England*; K. Stannard, 'Ideology, education and social structure: elementary schooling in mid-Victorian England', *History of Education*, 19 (1990), 105–22.

48. See for example J. Rose, 'Willingly to school: the working class response to elementary education in Britain, 1875–1918', *Journal of British Studies*, 32 (1993), 114–38.

49. Stephens, *Education in Britain*, pp. 81–90.

50. *Parliamentary Debates*, Third series, Vol. 199 (1870), col. 444.

51. G. Sutherland, *Elementary education in the nineteenth century*, London: Historical Association, 1971, pp. 29–30; *ibid.*, *Policy-making in elementary education*, pp. 110–12, 350–1, 356–60.

52. *Parliamentary Debates*, Third series, Vol. 199 (1870), col. 462; 33 & 34 Vict. C. 75: section 74 [1].

53. *Parliamentary Debates*, Third series, Vol. 199 (1870), cols. 454–5.

54. B. Simon, *Education and the labour movement 1870–1920*, London: Lawrence and Wishart, 1965, pp. 126–33; Sutherland, *Policy-making in elementary education*, pp. 163–90, 283–309; Hurt, *Elementary schooling and the working classes*, pp. 157–61.

55. *Parliamentary Debates*, Third series, Vol. 354 (1891), col. 1239.

56. E. Eaglesham, *From school board to local authority*, London: Routledge and Kegan Paul, 1956, pp. 7, 29–142; Simon, *Education and the labour movement*, pp. 176–86, 191–6.

57. Simon, *Education and the labour movement*, pp. 186–91; Murphy, *Church, state and schools*, pp. 76–95.

58. *Parliamentary Debates*, Fourth series, Vol. 105, cols. 848–9.

59. Simon, *Education and the labour movement*, pp. 203–7; G. Searle, *The quest for national efficiency: a study in British politics and political thought, 1899–1914*, Oxford: Basil Blackwell, 1971, pp. 1–33, 54–106, 207–16.

60. Simon, *Education and the labour movement*, pp. 208–46.

61. Stephens, *Education in Britain*, p. 103.

62. Sanderson, *Education and economic decline*, pp. 10–11; D. Reeder, 'The reconstruction of secondary education in England 1869–1920', in D. Muller, F. Ringer and B. Simon (eds), *The rise of the modern educational system 1870–1920*, Cambridge: Cambridge University Press, 1987, pp. 135–50, at pp. 148–9.

63. H. Cunningham, *Children and childhood in western society since 1500*, London: Longman, 1995, pp. 161–2.

11   The Liberal welfare reforms, 1906–14

1. A. V. Dicey, *Lectures on the relation between law and public opinion in England during the nineteenth century*, London: Macmillan (now Palgrave Macmillan), 1962, p. liii.

2. B. R. Mitchell, *British historical statistics*, Cambridge: Cambridge University Press, 1988, pp. 15, 42–3, 57–8; M. Anderson, 'The social implications of demographic change', in F. M. L. Thompson (ed.), *The Cambridge Social History of Britain, Vol. 2, People and their environment*, Cambridge: Cambridge University Press, 1990, pp. 1–70, at pp. 38–9, 47; R. Floud and B. Harris, 'Health, height and welfare: Britain 1700–1980', in R. Steckel and R. Floud (eds), *Health and welfare since industrialisation*, Chicago: Chicago University Press, 1997, pp. 91–126, at p. 116.

3. P. Joyce, 'Work', in F. M. L. Thompson (ed.), *The Cambridge Social History of Britain, Vol. 2, People and their environment*, Cambridge: Cambridge University Press, 1990, pp. 131–94, at pp. 132–7; R. Floud, 'Britain, 1860–1914: a survey', in R. Floud and D. McCloskey (eds), *The economic history of Britain since 1700, Vol. 2, 1860–1939*, Cambridge: Cambridge University Press, 1993, pp. 1–28, at p. 18.

4. D. Baines, 'Population, migration and regional development, 1870–1939', in R. Floud and D. McCloskey (eds), *The economic history of Britain since 1700, Vol. 2, 1860–1939*, Cambridge: Cambridge University Press, 1993, pp. 29–61, at pp. 51–5; J. Davis, *A history of Britain, 1885–1939*, Basingstoke: Macmillan (now Palgrave Macmillan), 1999, pp. 15–16.

5. P. Waller, *Town, city and nation: England 1850–1914*, Oxford: Oxford University Press, 1983, p. 8; F. M. L. Thompson, 'Town and city', in F. M. L. Thompson (ed.), *The Cambridge Social History of Britain, Volume 1, Regions and communities*, Cambridge: Cambridge University Press, 1990, pp. 1–86, at p. 8.

6. Mitchell, *British historical statistics*, pp. 26–9.

7. C. Ó Gráda, 'British agriculture, 1860–1914', in R. Floud and D. McCloskey (eds), *The economic history of Britain since 1700, Vol. 2, 1860–1939*, Cambridge: Cambridge University Press, 1993, pp. 145–72, at pp. 146–9; Davis, *A history of Britain*, p. 16.

8. C. H. Feinstein, 'Changes in nominal wages, the cost of living and real wages in the United Kingdom over two centuries, 1780–1990', in P. Scholliers and V. Zamagni (eds), *Labour's reward: real wages and economic change in 19th- and 20th-century Europe*, Aldershot: Edward Elgar, 1995, pp. 3–36, 258–66, at pp. 31, 264–5.

9. A. Gillie, 'The origin of the poverty line', *Economic History Review*, 49 (1996), 715–30; PP 1895 C. 7684 xiv, 1, *Report of the Royal Commission on the Aged Poor*, pp. xi–xiii.

10. G. Stedman Jones, *Outcast London: a study in the relationship between classes in Victorian London*, Harmondsworth: Penguin, 1984, pp. 298–300; Mitchell, *British historical statistics*, p. 124.

11. G. Peden, *British economic and social policy: Lloyd George to Margaret Thatcher*, Hemel Hempstead: Philip Allan, 1991, p. 8.

12. C. Booth, *Life and labour of the people in London*, London: Macmillan and Co. (now Palgrave Macmillan), 1902, Vol. 1, pp. 131, 147, 154; Vol. 2, pp. 20–2; Vol. 17, pp. 9, 208–10; PP 1904 Cd. 2210 xxxii, 145, Interdepartmental Committee on Physical Deterioration, *List of witnesses and evidence*, pp. 47–8.

13. For contemporary criticisms of Booth's work, see the discussion in C. Booth, 'The inhabitants of Tower Hamlets (School Board division), their condition and occupations', *Journal of the Royal Statistical Society*, 50 (1887), 326–401, at 394–400; and H. Bosanquet, *Rich and poor*, London: Macmillan (now Palgrave Macmillan), 1898, p. 79.

14. See also G. Himmelfarb, *Poverty and compassion: the moral imagination of the late Victorians*, New York: Vintage, 1991, pp. 77–178.

15. See also F. Maurice, 'National health: a soldier's study', *Contemporary Review*, 83 (1903), 41–56. Maurice wrote that 'the ditch, with falling into which we are ... threatened by Rowntree, is a very deep one. On the other hand, I do not think that anyone who has studied Mr Booth's book can doubt that what he presents to us is a hopeful and encouraging picture of our modern life' (p. 49).

16. B. S. Rowntree, *Poverty: a study of town life*, London: Macmillan and Co. (now Palgrave Macmillan), 1902, pp. viii–x, 297–8; *ibid.*, 'Poverty: the York enquiry', *Times*, 1 January 1902, p. 13, col. b.

17. Rowntree, *Poverty: a study of town life*, p. 145.

18. P. Townsend, 'The meaning of poverty', *British Journal of Sociology*, 18 (1962), 210–27, at 215; J. Veit-Wilson, 'Paradigms of poverty: a rehabilitation of B. S. Rowntree', *Journal of Social Policy*, 15 (1986), 69–99.

19. B. Harris, 'Seebohm Rowntree and the measurement of poverty, 1899–1951', in J. Bradshaw and R. Sainsbury (eds), *Getting the measure of poverty: the early legacy of Seebohm Rowntree*, Aldershot: Ashgate, pp. 60–84, at p. 67.

20. M. Bentley, *Politics without democracy, 185–1914: perception and preoccupation in British government*, London: Fontana, 1984, pp. 182–94, 250–1, 254–5; N. Blewett, 'The franchise in the United Kingdom, 1885–1918', *Past and Present*, 32 (1965), 27–56, at 31; Davis, *A history of Britain*, pp. 21–4; H. Pelling, *A history of British trade unionism*, London and Basingstoke: Macmillan (now Palgrave Macmillan), 1968, p. 10; K. Burgess, *The challenge of labour: shaping British society, 1850–1930*, London: Croom Helm, 1982, p. 99.

21. *Parliamentary Debates*, Third series, Vol. 354 (1891), cols. 1100–01; Dicey, *Lectures on the relation between law and public opinion*, pp. lii–lxx, 211–58.

22. H. Pelling, 'The working class and the origins of the welfare state', in H. Pelling, *Popular politics and society in late-Victorian Britain*, London and Basingstoke: Macmillan (now Palgrave Macmillan), 1968, pp. 1–18.

23. B. Simon, *Education and the labour movement 1870–1920*, London: Lawrence and Wishart, 1965, pp. 133–7, 278–89; J. H. Treble, 'The attitudes of friendly societies towards the movement in Great Britain for state pensions 1878–1908', *International Review of Social History*, 15 (1970), 266–99; P. Thane, 'Non-contributory versus insurance pensions 1878–1908', in P. Thane (ed.), *The origins of British social policy*, London: Croom Helm, pp. 84–106, at pp. 91–6; *ibid.*, 'The working class and state "welfare" in Britain 1880–1914', *Historical Journal*, 27 (1984), 877–900, at 879, 882–92; J. R. Hay, *The origins of the Liberal welfare reforms*, Basingstoke: Macmillan (now Palgrave Macmillan), 1983, pp. 27–8; S. Blackburn, 'Working-class attitudes to social reform: Black Country chainmakers and anti-sweating legislation 1880–1930', *International Review of Social History*, 33 (1988), 42–69; J. Stewart, 'Ramsay MacDonald, the Labour Party and child welfare, 1900–14', *Twentieth century British History*, 4 (1993), 105–25.

24. Thane, 'The working class and state "welfare" ', 896; see also Blackburn, 'Working-class attitudes to social reform', 64–9.

25. Thane, 'The working class and state "welfare" ', 881; D. Fraser, *The evolution of the British welfare state: a history of social policy since the Industrial Revolution*, London and Basingstoke: Macmillan (now Palgrave Macmillan), First edition, p. 129; Second edition, p. 139; Third edition, p. 152.

26. Quoted in J. Harris, *Unemployment and politics: a study in English social policy 1886–1914*, Oxford: Clarendon Press, 1972, pp. 365–6; see also M. Langan, 'Reorganising the labour market: unemployment, the state and the labour movement, 1880–1914', in M. Langan and B. Schwarz (eds), *Crises in the British state 1880–1930*, London: Hutchinson, 1985, pp. 104–25, at p. 112.

27. S. Blackburn, 'Employers and social policy: Black County chain-masters, the minimum wage campaign and the Cradley Heath strike of 1910', *Midland History*, 12 (1987), 85–102.

28. J. R. Hay, 'Employers and social policy in Britain: the evolution of welfare legislation, 1905–14', *Social History*, 4 (1977), 435–55.

29. J. Melling, 'Welfare capitalism and the origins of welfare states: British industry, workplace welfare and social reform, c. 1870–1914', *Social History*, 17 (1992), 453–78, at 467–78.

30. J. Cantlie, *Degeneration amongst Londoners: the Parkes Museum of Hygiene Lecture for 1885*, London: Field and Tuer, 1885; J. P. Williams-Freeman, *The effect of town-life on the general health, with especial reference to London*, London: W. H. Allen & Co., 1890.

31. B. Harris, *The health of the schoolchild: a history of the school medical service in England and Wales*, Buckingham: Open University Press, 1995, pp. 9, 22–3.

32. G. Searle, *The quest for national efficiency: a study in British politics and political thought, 1899–1914*, Oxford: Basil Blackwell, 1971, pp. 33–9.

33. *Ibid.*, pp. 54–60.

34. M. Bentley, *The climax of liberal politics: British liberalism in theory and practice 1868–1918*, London: Edward Arnold, 1987, pp. 76–83; M. Freeden, *The new liberalism: an ideology of social reform*, Oxford: Clarendon, 1978, pp. 1–116; *ibid.*, *Ideologies and political theory: a conceptual approach*, Oxford: Clarendon Press, 1996, pp. 178–200.

35. W. S. Churchill, 'Liberalism and socialism', in W. S. Churchill, *Liberalism and the social problem*, London: Hodder and Stoughton, Second edition, 1909, pp. 67–84, at p. 79; Freeden, *The new liberalism*, p. 161.

36. See also Fraser, *The evolution of the British welfare state*, First edition, pp. 144–50; Second edition, pp. 155–62; Third edition, pp. 168–76.

37. *Parliamentary Debates*, Fourth series, Vol. 189 (1908), col. 875.

38. Churchill, 'Liberalism and socialism', pp. 82–3; see also Freeden, *The new liberalism*, p. 161; M. Daunton, *Trusting Leviathan: the politics of taxation in Britain 1799–1914*, Cambridge: Cambridge University Press, p. 363.

39. *Parliamentary Debates*, Fourth series, Vol. 145 (1905), cols. 531–71; B. Gilbert, *The evolution of national insurance in Great Britain: the origins of the welfare state*, London: Michael Joseph, 1966, p. 108.

40. PP 1905 (132) i, 485, *A Bill to amend the Education Act, 1902*; PP 1905 (196) i, 489, *A Bill to amend the Education Act, 1902*; PP 1905 (126) ii, 211, *A Bill to make provision for the feeding of children in public elementary schools*.

41. PP 1906 (10) i, 1109, *A Bill to amend the Education Acts, 1902 and 1903; Parliamentary Debates*, Fourth series, Vol. 152 (1906), cols. 1390–1448; Gilbert, *The evolution of national insurance*, p. 111.

42. Simon, *Education and the labour movement*, pp. 282–3; Gilbert, *The evolution of national insurance*, p. 111; J. Burnett, 'The rise and decline of school meals in Britain 1860–1990', in J. Burnett and D. Oddy (eds), *The origins and development of food policies in Europe*, Leicester: Leicester University Press, 1994, 55–69, p. 63.

43. PP 1906 (10) i, 1109, *A Bill to amend the Education Acts, 1902 and 1903*; PP 1906 (331), i, 1113, *A Bill (as amended by the Select Committee) to make provision for meals for children attending public elementary schools in England, Wales and Scotland*; PP 1906 (367) i, 1117, *A Bill (as amended by the Select Committee and in Committee) to make provision for meals for children attending public elementary schools in England, Wales and Scotland*; PP 1906 (383) i, 1121, *Lords' amendments to the Education (Provision of Meals) Bill*.

44. Dicey, *Lectures on the relation between law and public opinion*, p. l; Gilbert, *The evolution of national insurance*, p. 113.

45. Harris, *The health of the schoolchild*, pp. 2, 43–7.

46. H. Hendrick, *Child welfare: England 1872–1989*, London: Routledge, 1994, p. 122; *Parliamentary Debates*, Fourth series, Vol. 183 (1908), cols. 1432–8, 1251–300; H. Cunningham, *Children and childhood in western society since 1500*, London: Longman, 1995, pp. 159–62.

47. *Parliamentary Debates*, Fourth series, Vol. 152 (1906), col. 1398.

48. Hendrick, *Child welfare*, pp. 82–5.

49. J. Macnicol, *The politics of retirement in Britain 1878–1948*, Cambridge: Cambridge University Press, 1998, pp. 60–84; Thane, 'Non-contributory versus insurance pensions', pp. 84–91.

50. *Parliamentary Debates*, Fourth series, Vol. 190 (1908), cols. 567–71, 578–80, 825–30; see also 8 Edw. 7 C. 40: sections 2–3.

51. P. Thane, *The foundations of the welfare state*, London: Longman's, First edition, 1982, p. 83; Second edition, 1996, p. 77.

52. *Parliamentary Debates*, Fourth series, Vol. 190 (1908), cols. 572, 575, 672, 828–9; Macnicol, *The politics of retirement*, pp. 153–63, P. Thane, *The foundations of the welfare state*, First edition, p. 84; Second edition, p. 77; *ibid.*, *Old age in English history: past experiences, present issues*, Oxford: Oxford University Press, 2000, pp. 223–8.

53. Harris, *Unemployment and politics*, pp. 278–89.

54. *Ibid.*, pp. 334–46.

55. D. Bythell, *The sweated trades: outwork in nineteenth-century Britain*, London: Batsford, 1978.

56. See also E. P. Hennock, 'Poverty and social reforms', in P. Johnson (ed.), *Twentieth century Britain: economic, social and cultural change*, London: Longman, 1994, pp. 79–93, at pp. 89–90.

57. W. Ashworth, *The genesis of modern British town planning: a study in economic and social history of the nineteenth and twentieth centuries*, London: Routledge and Kegan Paul, 1954, pp. 167–90; G. Cherry, *The evolution of British town planning: a history of town planning in the United Kingdom during the 20th century and of the Royal Town Planning Institute, 1914–74*, Leighton Buzzard: Leonard Hill Books, 1974, pp. 63–7; E. S. Morris, *British town planning and urban design: principles and policies*, London: Longman, 1997, p. 75; PP 1904 Cd. 2175 xxxii, 1, Interdepartmental Committee on Physical Deterioration, *Report and Appendix*, paras. 94–9, 423/6.

58. See esp. Sections 1, 54–6, 68.

59. M. Daunton, 'Payment and participation: welfare and state formation in Britain 1900–51', *Past and Present*, 150 (1996), 169–216; *ibid.*, *Trusting Leviathan*, pp. 303–29.

60. B. K. Murray, *The People's Budget 1909/10: Lloyd George and Liberal politics*, Oxford: Clarendon Press, 1980, pp. 1–208; Peden, *British economic and social policy*, pp. 25–6; Daunton, *Trusting Leviathan*, pp. 321–65.

61. Murray, *The People's Budget*, pp. 288–91; Peden, *British economic and social policy*, p. 26; Daunton, *Trusting Leviathan*, pp. 365–6.

62. Gilbert, *The evolution of national insurance*, pp. 289–353; Harris, *Unemployment and politics*, pp. 295–328.

63. 1 & 2 Geo. V C. 55, sections 1, 3. Although the majority of workers were liable for flat-rate contributions, employees earning less than nine shillings a week were not required to pay contributions, and workers receiving between nine and 15 shillings a week paid a reduced rate. See *ibid.*, Schedule 2.

64. 1 & 2 Geo. V C. 55, sections 8, 17; Gilbert, *The evolution of national insurance*, pp. 353–99.

65. 1 & 2 Geo. V C. 55, section 85 and Eighth Schedule.

66. Harris, *Unemployment and politics*, pp. 295–334. The original scheme covered workers employed in the following industries: building, construction, shipbuilding, mechanical engineering, iron-founding, vehicle construction, and sawmilling. See 1 & 2 Geo. V C. 55: Sixth Schedule.

67. P. Johnson, 'Risk, redistribution and social welfare in Britain from the Poor Law to Beveridge', in M. Daunton (ed.), *Charity, self-interest and welfare in the English past*, London: UCL Press, 1996, pp. 225–48, at pp. 245–6; Thane, 'The working class and state "welfare"', 898–9; E. Roberts, 'The recipients' view of welfare', in J. Bornat, R. Perks, P. Thompson and J. Walmsley (eds), *Oral history, health and welfare*, London: Routledge, 2000, pp. 203–26, at p. 215.

68. *House of Commons Debates*, Fifth series, Vol. 26 (1911), col. 721.

69. Harris, *Unemployment and politics*, p. 310.

70. Freeden, *The new liberalism*, pp. 190–3.

71. M. Jackson, *The borderland of imbecility: medicine, society and the fabrication of the feeble mind in late-Victorian and Edwardian England*, Manchester: Manchester University Press, 2000; see also K. Jones, *A history of the mental health services*, London: Routledge and Kegan Paul, 1972, pp. 182–215; H. G. Simmons, 'Explaining social policy: the English Mental Deficiency

Act of 1913', *Journal of Social History*, 11 (1978), 387–403; C. Unsworth, *The politics of mental health legislation*, Oxford: Clarendon Press, 1987, pp. 151–61; M. Thomson, *The problem of mental deficiency: eugenics, democracy and social policy in Britain c. 1870–1959*, Oxford: Oxford University Press, 1998, pp. 36–51.

72. PP 1912–13 (213) iii, 993, *A Bill to make further and better provision with respect to feeble-minded and other mentally defective persons*, sections 2, 17.

73. *House of Commons Debates*, Fifth series, Vol. 53 (1913), col. 221.

74. *Ibid.*, cols. 243–4.

75. A. Briggs, 'The welfare state in historical perspective', *Archives Européenes du Sociologie*, 2, 221–58, at 228; Hay, *The origins of the Liberal welfare reforms*, p. 12.

12 The First World War and social policy

1. J. Winter, *The Great War and the British people*, Basingstoke: Macmillan (now Palgrave Macmillan), 1986, pp. 72–3; D. Thom, 'Women and work in wartime Britain', in R. Wall and J. Winter (eds), *The upheaval of war: family, work and welfare in Europe 1914–18*, Cambridge: Cambridge University Press, pp. 297–326, at pp. 318–23.

2. E. Hobsbawm, *Age of extremes: the short twentieth century, 1914–91*, London: Michael Joseph, 1994.

3. A. Marwick, *The deluge: British society and the First World War*, Basingstoke: Macmillan (now Palgrave Macmillan), 1991, p. 350; P. Abrams, 'The failure of social reform 1918–20', *Past and Present*, 24 (1963), 43–64; R. Lowe, 'The erosion of state intervention in Britain 1917–24', *Economic History Review*, 31, 270–86; *ibid.*, *Adjusting to democracy: the role of the Ministry of Labour in British politics 1916–39*, Oxford: Clarendon Press, 1986; M. A. Crowther, *British social policy 1914–39*, Basingstoke: Macmillan, 1988, p. 39; W. G. Runciman, 'Has British capitalism changed since the First World War?', *British Journal of Sociology*, 44 (1993), 53–67, at 56–7; *ibid.*, 'Why social inequalities are generated by social rights', in M. Bulmer and A. M. Rees (eds), *Citizenship today: the contemporary relevance of T. H. Marshall*, London: UCL Press, 1996, pp. 49–64, at p. 51.

4. R. Roberts, *The classic slum: Salford life in the first quarter of the century*, Harmondsworth: Penguin, 1971, pp. 199–203.

5. Winter, *The Great War and the British people*, pp. 233–4; C. H. Feinstein, 'Changes in nominal wages, the cost of living and real wages in the United Kingdom over two centuries, 1780–1990', in P. Scholliers and V. Zamagni (eds), *Labour's reward: real wages and economic change in 19th- and 20th-century Europe*, Aldershot: Edward Elgar, 1995, pp. 3–36, 258–66, at p. 265.

6. J. Macnicol, *The politics of retirement in Britain 1878–1948*, Cambridge: Cambridge University Press, 1998, p. 168; P. Thane, *Old age in English history: past experiences, present issues*, Oxford: Oxford University Press, 2000, pp. 308–11.

7. B. Waites, *A class society at war, 1914–18*, Leamington Spa: Berg, 1987, p. 163; R. Wall, 'English and German families in the First World War, 1914–18', in R. Wall and J. Winter (eds), *The upheaval of war: family, work and welfare in Europe 1914–18*, Cambridge: Cambridge University Press, 1988, pp. 43–106, at pp. 47–50; B. Harris, *The health of the schoolchild: a history of the school medical service in England and Wales*, Buckingham: Open University Press, 1995, p. 84; 'Effects of unemployment and rationing of provision of meals on health of public elementary school children. Extracts from replies received from certain School Medical Officers in response to Dr Eichholz' enquiry of 6 April 1923', Public Record Office ED50/34.

8. B. Harris, 'The demographic impact of the First World War: an anthropometric perspective', *Social History of Medicine*, 6 (1993), 343–66; *ibid.*, *The health of the schoolchild*, pp. 85–9.

9. Winter, *The Great War and the British people*, pp. 107, 112, 142; *ibid.*, 'Some paradoxes of the First World War', in R. Wall and J. Winter (eds), *The upheaval of war: family, work and welfare*

in Europe 1914–18, Cambridge: Cambridge University Press, 1988, pp. 9–42, at pp. 12–16; Harris, 'The demographic impact of the First World War', 345–51.

10. Winter, *The Great War and the British people*, pp. 138–9; L. Bryder, 'The First World War: healthy or hungry?', *History Workshop Journal*, 24 (1987), 141–57, 145–60; J. Winter, 'Public health and the political economy of war: Reply to Linda Bryder', *History Workshop Journal*, 26 (1988), 143–52, 168; *ibid.*, 'Surviving the war: life expectation, illness and mortality rates in Paris, London and Berlin, 1914–19', in J. Winter and J.-L. Robert, *Capital cities at war: Paris, London, Berlin 1914–19*, Cambridge: Cambridge University Press, 1997, pp. 487–523, at pp. 520–2; C. Rollet, 'The "other war" II. Setbacks in public health', in Winter and Robert, *Capital cities at war*, pp. 456–86, at pp. 467–80; A. Hardy, *Health and medicine in Britain since 1860*, Basingstoke: Palgrave (now Palgrave Macmillan), 2001, p. 54; Thane, *Old age in English history*, p. 309.

11. S. Andrzejewski, *Military organisation and society*, London: Routledge and Kegan Paul, 1954, pp. 71, 124; R. Titmuss, 'War and social policy', in B. Abel-Smith and K. Titmuss (eds), *The philosophy of welfare: selected writings of Richard M. Titmuss*, London: Allen and Unwin, 1987, pp. 102–12, at p. 106; Abrams, 'The failure of social reform'; A. Marwick, *Britain in the century of total war: war, peace and social change 1900–67*, Penguin: Harmondsworth, 1970, p. 14; *ibid.*, *War and social change in the twentieth century; a comparative study of Britain, France, Germany, Russia and the United States*, Basingstoke: Macmillan (now Palgrave Macmillan), 1974, p. 223; *ibid.*, 'Introduction', in A. Marwick (ed.), *Total war and social change*, Basingstoke: Macmillan, 1988, pp. x–xxi, at p. xvi; *ibid.*, *The deluge*, p. 20.

12. A. Peacock and J. Wiseman, *The growth of public expenditure in the United Kingdom*, Princeton, NJ: Princeton University Press, 1961, p. xxiv.

13. J. Cronin, *The politics of state expansion: war, state and society in twentieth-century Britain*, London: Routledge, 1991, pp. 65, 76; J. Stevenson, *British society 1914–45*, Harmondsworth: Penguin, 1984, pp. 60, 92; R. Whiting, 'Taxation and the working class, 1915–24', *Historical Journal*, 33 (1990), 895–916; M. Daunton, 'How to pay for the war: state, society and taxation in Britain 1917–24', *English Historical Review*, 111 (1996), 882–919, at 889; *ibid.*, *Just taxes: the politics of taxation in Britain, 1914–79*, Cambridge: Cambridge University Press, 2002, pp. 38–47, 55–7; S. Pollard, *The development of the British economy, 1914–80*, London: Edward Arnold, 1983, p. 32; K. Burgess, *The challenge of labour: shaping British society, 1850–1930*, London: Croom Helm, 1982, p. 156; P. Dewey, 'The new warfare and economic mobilisation', in J. Turner (ed.), *Britain and the First World War*, London: Unwin Hyman, pp. 70–84, at pp. 80–3.

14. Stevenson, *British society*, pp. 62–74.

15. T. Wilson, *The myriad faces of war: Britain and the Great War 1914–18*, Cambridge: Polity Press, 1986, pp. 533–6.

16. 'D. P.', 'Scientific agriculture and the nation's food', *The Times*, 19 July 1916, cols. 6d-f. See also D. Fraser, *The evolution of the British welfare state: a history of social policy since the Industrial Revolution*, London and Basingstoke: Macmillan (now Palgrave Macmillan), First edition, 1973, p. 165; Second edition, 1984, p. 178; Third edition, 2003, p. 194.

17. K. Middlemas, *Politics in industrial society: the experience of the British system since 1911*, London: André Deutsch, 1979, pp. 73–7; Burgess, *The challenge of labour*, pp. 154, 159–64.

18. J. Melling, 'Clydeside housing and the evolution of state rent control 1900–39', in J. Melling (ed.), *Housing, social policy and the state*, London: Croom Helm, 1980, pp. 139–67, at pp. 139–51.

19. Burgess, *The challenge of labour*, pp. 165–83; Stevenson, *British society*, pp. 85–6.

20. Harris, *The health of the schoolchild*, p. 71.

21. 'Lord Milner and the future', *The Times*, 1 July 1916, p. 10, col. b; Fraser, *The evolution of the British welfare state*, First edition, p. 166; Second edition, p. 179; Third edition, p. 195.

22. P. Johnson, *Land fit for heroes: the planning of British reconstruction 1916–19*, Chicago: University of Chicago Press, 1968, p. 222.

23. 'George Newman to President, 4 August 1914', Public Record Office ED24/1371, para. 2; J. Welshman, 'School meals and milk in England and Wales 1906–45', *Medical History*, 41 (1997), 6–29, at 10–11; Harris, *The health of the schoolchild*, pp. 77÷8.

24. Wilson, *The myriad faces of war*, p. 610.

25. B. R. Mitchell and P. Deane, *Abstract of British historical statistics*, Cambridge: Cambridge University Press, 1962, p. 398; S. Pedersen, 'Gender, welfare and citizenship in Britain during the Great War', *American Historical Review*, 95 (1990), 983–1006, at 985–91; P. Thane, *The foundations of the welfare state*, London: Longman's, First edition, 1982, pp. 127–8; Second edition, 1996, pp. 120–1.

26. PP 1916 Cd. 8320 xxiii, 367, *Administration concessions made to old age pensioners.*

27. PP 1916 Cd. 8373 xxiii, 369, *Copy of Treasury scheme for the award of additional allowances to old age pensioners suffering special hardship owing to the war*, para. 1; Macnicol, *The politics of retirement*, pp. 168–9.

28. J. Burnett, *Plenty and want: a social history of diet in England from 1815 to the present day*, London: Methuen, 1983, pp. 271–82; P. Dewey, 'Nutrition and living standards in wartime Britain', in R. Wall and J. Winter (eds), *The upheaval of war: family, work and welfare in Europe 1914–18*, Cambridge: Cambridge University Press, 1988, pp. 197–220, at pp. 201–10; D. F. Smith, 'Nutrition science and the two world wars', in D. F. Smith (ed.), *Nutrition in Britain: science, scientists and politics in the twentieth century*, London: Routledge, pp. 142–65, at pp. 142–9.

29. PP 1920 Cmd. 722 xv, 45, *Report of the Board of Education to the King's Most Excellent Majesty in Council for the year 1918–19*, pp. 17–18, 39.

30. Marwick, *The deluge*, pp. 156–8, 282–6; PP 1916 Cd. 8274 viii, 39, *Report of the Board of Education to the King's Most Excellent Majesty in Council for the year 1914–15*, pp. 1–49; PP 1920 Cmd. 722 xv, 45, *Report of the Board of Education to the King's Most Excellent Majesty in Council for the year 1918–19*, pp. 42–3.

31. B. Abel-Smith, *The hospitals 1800–1948: a study in social administration in England and Wales*, London: Heinemann, 1964, pp. 252–83; N. R. Eder, *National health insurance and the medical profession in Britain 1913–39*, New York and London: Garland, 1982, pp. 90–2.

32. Harris, *The health of the schoolchild*, pp. 73–5.

33. Abel-Smith, *The hospitals*, pp. 279–83; L. Bryder, *Below the magic mountain: a social history of tuberculosis in twentieth-century Britain*, Oxford: Clarendon Press, 1988, pp. 43–5; Thane, *The foundations of the welfare state*, First edition, pp. 133–4; Second edition, pp. 125–6.

34. N. Whiteside, 'Industrial welfare and labour regulation in Britain at the time of the First World War', *International Review of Social History*, 25 (1980), 307–31; G. Braybon, *Women workers in the First World War*, London: Routledge, 1989, pp. 131–49.

35. Melling, 'Clydeside housing', pp. 139–52; M. Daunton, *A property-owning democracy: housing in Britain*, London: Faber, 1987, p. 91; Thane, *The foundations of the welfare state*, First edition, pp. 131–3; Second edition, pp. 124–5.

36. D. Dwork, *War is good for babies and other young children: a history of the infant and child welfare movement in England 1898–1918*, London: Tavistock, 1987, pp. 124–66, 208–20; Harris, *The health of the schoolchild*, pp. 77–8; Thane, *The foundations of the welfare state*, First edition, pp. 134–6; Second edition, pp. 126–8.

37. PP 1918 Cd. 9231 xiii, 27, Ministry of Reconstruction, *Report on the work of the Ministry for the period ending 31 December 1918*; Johnson, *Land fit for heroes, passim.*

38. C. Booth, *Life and labour of the people in London*, London: Macmillan and Co. (now Palgrave Macmillan), 1902, Vol. 1, p. 147; B. S. Rowntree, *Poverty: a study of town life*, London: Macmillan and Co., 1902, pp. 119–21; A. L. Bowley and A. R. Burnett-Hurst, *Livelihood and poverty: a study of economic conditions in working-class households in Northampton, Warrington, Stanley and Reading*, London: G. Bell and Sons, 1915, pp. 40–2; E. P. Hennock, 'Poverty and social reforms', in P. Johnson (ed.), *Twentieth century Britain: economic, social and cultural change*, London: Longman, 1994, pp. 79–93, at pp. 89–90.

39. C. L. Mowat, *Britain between the wars 1918–40*, London: Methuen, 1968, pp. 37, 125–6; Lowe, *Adjusting to democracy*, pp. 92–5, 99–105; W. R. Garside, *British unemployment 1919–39: a study in public policy*, Cambridge: Cambridge University Press, 1990, p. 287; Thane, *The foundations of the welfare state*, First edition, pp. 148–51; Second edition, pp. 139–41.

40. Rowntree, *Poverty*, pp. 119–21; Bowley and Burnett-Hurst, *Livelihood and poverty*, p. 41; *House of Commons Debates*, Fifth series, Vol. 26 (1911), cols. 493–510.

41. N. Whiteside, 'Welfare legislation and the unions during the First World War', *Historical Journal*, 23 (1980), 857–84, at 857–66.

42. Thane, *The foundations of the welfare state*, First edition, pp. 140–1; Second edition, pp. 131–2.

43. PP 1919 Cmd. 410 xxvii, 279, *Report of the Departmental Committee on Old Age Pensions*, pp. 8–12.

44. Thane, *The foundations of the welfare state*, First edition, pp. 142–3; Second edition, pp. 133–4; Macnicol, *The politics of retirement*, pp. 167–80.

45. PP 1917–18 Cd. 8917 xviii, 529, Ministry of Reconstruction, Local Government Committee, *Report on transfer of functions of Poor Law Authorities in England and Wales*, pp. 11, 24–6; Thane, *The foundations of the welfare state*, First edition, pp. 140–1; Second edition, pp. 131–2.

46. 8 & 9 Geo. V C. 29; Thane, *The foundations of the welfare state*, Second edition, p. 134.

47. Abel-Smith, *The hospitals*, pp. 276–7; see also D. Evans, 'Tackling the "hideous scourge": the creation of the venereal disease treatment centres in early-twentieth-century Britain', *Social History of Medicine*, 5 (1992), 413–34.

48. B. Gilbert, *British social policy 1914–39*, London: Batsford, 1970, pp. 98–137; F. Honigsbaum, *The struggle for the Ministry of Health*, London: G. Bell and Sons, 1972; Thane, *The foundations of the welfare state*, First edition, pp. 137–8; Second edition, pp. 129–30.

49. B. Simon, *Education and the labour movement 1870–1920*, London: Lawrence and Wishart, 1965, pp. 342–64; *ibid.*, *The politics of educational reform 1920–40*, London: Lawrence and Wishart, 1974, pp. 33–4; Harris, *The health of the schoolchild*, p. 5, note 2.

50. M. Swenarton, 'An "insurance against revolution": ideological objectives of the provision and design of public housing in Britain after the First World War', *Bulletin of the Institute of Historical Research*, 54 (1980), 86–101; *ibid.*, *Homes fit for heroes: the politics and architecture of early state housing in Britain*, London: Heinemann, 1981.

51. Mowat, *Britain between the wars*, p. 44; K. O. Morgan, *Consensus and disunity: the Lloyd George Coalition Government 1918–22*, Oxford: Clarendon Press, 1979, pp. 88–106.

52. Harris, *The health of the schoolchild*, pp. 77–82; Thane, *The foundations of the welfare state*, First edition, pp. 137–42; Second edition, pp. 129–32; Abel-Smith, *The hospitals*, pp. 293–4; F. Honigsbaum, *The division in British medicine: a history of the separation of general practice from hospital care 1911–68*, London: Kogan Page, 1979, pp. 45–133.

53. Abrams, 'The failure of social reform', 50; Johnson, *Land fit for heroes*, p. 489; Gilbert, *British social policy*, pp. 7–8.

54. Lowe, 'The erosion of state intervention'; *ibid.*, 'Bureaucracy triumphant or denied?; *ibid.*, The expansion of the British civil service 1919–39', *Public Administration*, 62 (1984), 291–310; *ibid.*, *Adjusting to democracy*.

55. R. Davidson and R. Lowe, 'Bureaucracy and innovation in British welfare policy 1870–1945', in W. J. Mommsen and W. Mock (eds), *The emergence of the welfare state in Britain and Germany 1850–1950*, London: Croom Helm, pp. 263–95, at pp. 280–5; K. Burk, 'The Treasury: from impotence to power', in K. Burk (ed.), *War and the state: the transformation of British government 1914–19*, London: Allen and Unwin, pp. 84–107.

56. H. Samuel, 'The taxation of the various classes of the people', *Journal of the Royal Statistical Society* (1919), 82, 143–82, at 176–81; Whiting, 'Taxation and the working class', pp. 896, 908; Daunton, 'How to pay for the war', pp. 883, 888–90, 893, 896–903; *ibid.*, *Just taxes*, pp. 60–102; Pollard, *The development of the British economy*, p. 31; R. Middleton, *Government*

versus the market: the growth of the public sector, economic management and British economic performance, c. 1890–1979, Cheltenham: Edward Elgar, 1996, p. 118.

57. Daunton, 'How to pay for the war', pp. 889–90.

58. Morgan, *Consensus and disunity*, pp. 80–108.

59. R. H. Tawney, 'The abolition of economic controls 1918–21', *Economic History Review*, 13 (1941), 1–30; *ibid.*, 'The abolition of economic controls 1918–21', in J. Winter (ed.), *History and society: essays by R. H. Tawney*, London: Routledge and Kegan Paul, pp. 129–86; G. Peden, *British economic and social policy: Lloyd George to Margaret Thatcher*, Hemel Hempstead: Philip Allan, 1991, pp. 49–51.

60. W. R. Garside, *British unemployment 1919–39: a study in public policy*, Cambridge: Cambridge University Press, 1990, pp. 31–43.

61. S. Marriner, 'Cash and concrete: liquidity problems in the mass-production of "homes for heroes" ', *Business History*, 16 (1976), 152–89; Morgan, *Consensus and disunity*, pp. 91–2; J. Burnett, *A social history of housing 1815–1985*, London: Routledge, 1986, p. 227.

62. Swenarton, 'An "insurance against revolution" ', pp. 96–101; *ibid.*, *Homes fit for heroes*, p. 161.

63. Crowther, *British social policy*, pp. 36–7.

64. Morgan, *Consensus and disunity*, pp. 96–103; Daunton, *A property-owning democracy*, pp. 56–7, 63, 91–2.

65. G. DeGroot, *Blighty: British society in the era of the Great War*, London: Longman, 1996, pp. 257–61; PP 1929–30 (175) xvi, 947, *Thirteenth Annual Report of the Minister of Pensions from 1 April 1929 to 31 March 1930*, p. 8.

66. J. Short, *Housing in Britain: the postwar experience*, London: Methuen, 1982, p. 30; A. Holmans, 'Housing', in A. H. Halsey and J. Webb (eds), *Twentieth century British social trends*, Basingstoke: Macmillan (now Palgrave Macmillan), 2000, pp. 469–510, at p. 487.

67. H. R. Williams, *Report on the administration of out-relief in the following unions: Bridgend and Cowbridge, Pontypridd, Bedwellty and Merthyr Tydfil*, Public Record Office MH57/106, 12 July 1919, p. 2.

13   Voluntary action and the 'new philanthropy', 1914–39

1. G. Finlayson, 'A moving frontier: voluntarism and the state in British social welfare 1911–49', *Twentieth Century British History*, 1 (1990), 183–206, at 185–6.

2. F. Prochaska, *The voluntary impulse: philanthropy in modern Britain*, London: Faber, 1988, pp. 74–6; S. Cherry, 'Before the National Health Service: financing the voluntary hospitals, 1900–39', *Economic History Review*, 50 (1997), 305–26, at 313; T. Wilson, *The myriad faces of war: Britain and the Great War 1914–18*, Cambridge: Polity Press, 1986, pp. 159, 775; G. Finlayson, *Citizen, state and social welfare in Britain 1830–1990*, Oxford: Oxford University Press, 1994, p. 205.

3. J. Davis Smith, 'The voluntary tradition: philanthropy and self-help in Britain 1500–1945', in J. Davis Smith, C. Rochester and R. Hedley (eds), *An introduction to the voluntary sector*, London and New York: Routledge, 1995, pp. 9–39, at p. 25.

4. S. Pedersen, 'Gender, welfare and citizenship in Britain during the Great War', *American Historical Review*, 95 (1990), 983–1006, at 992; Finlayson, *Citizen, state and social welfare*, p. 218.

5. Wilson, *The myriad faces of war*, p. 775.

6. B. Abel-Smith, *A history of the nursing profession*, London: Heinemann, 1960, pp. 85–6.

7. Wilson, *The myriad faces of war*, p. 775.

8. Finlayson, *Citizen, state and social welfare*, pp. 218–20; see also Wilson, *The myriad faces of war*, pp. 233–4; PP 1919 Cmd. 82 xi, 49, *66th Report of the Charity Commissioners for England and Wales*, p. 5.

9. Finlayson, *Citizen, state and social welfare*, p. 265.

10. Finlayson, *Citizen, state and social welfare*, p. 239; J. Lewis, *The voluntary sector, the state and social work in Britain: the Charity Organisation Society/Family Welfare Association since 1869*, Aldershot: Edward Elgar, 1995, p. 82.

11. Pedersen, 'Gender, welfare and citizenship', p. 992; PP 1914–16 Cd. 7835 xi, 605, *62nd Report of the Charity Commissioners for England and Wales*, pp. 29–44; Prochaska, *The voluntary impulse*, p. 76.

12. B. Abel-Smith, *The hospitals 1800–1948: a study in social administration in England and Wales*, London: Heinemann, 1964, pp. 252–3.

13. *Ibid.*, p. 282.

14. Finlayson, *Citizen, state and social welfare*, pp. 236–7.

15. Cherry, 'Before the National Health Service', p. 313.

16. Prochaska, *The voluntary impulse*, pp. 80–1; *ibid.*, 'Philanthropy', in F. M. L. Thompson (ed.), *The Cambridge Social History of Britain 1750–1950, Volume 3, Social agencies and institutions*, Cambridge: Cambridge University Press, 1990, pp. 357–94, at pp. 389–90.

17. Finlayson, *Citizen, state and social welfare*, pp. 221–3; E. Macadam, *The new philanthropy: a study of the relations between the statutory and voluntary social services*, London: George Allen and Unwin, 1934, pp. 270, 277.

18. Finlayson, *Citizen, state and social welfare*, pp. 145–6, 152, 216, 234–5; V. Lipman, *A century of social service 1859–1959: the Jewish Board of Guardians*, London: Routledge and Kegan Paul, 1959, pp. 155–6; Political and Economic Planning, *Report on the British social services: a survey of the existing public social services in Great Britain with proposals for future development*, London: Political and Economic Planning, 1937, p. 174.

19. Finlayson, *Citizen, state and social welfare*, pp. 239–40.

20. M. Brasnett, *Voluntary social action: a history of the National Council of Social Service*, London: National Council of Social Service, 1969, pp. 1–35.

21. B. Harris, 'Responding to adversity: government–charity relations and the relief of unemployment in interwar Britain', *Contemporary Record*, 9 (1995), 529–61, at 536.

22. Finlayson, *Citizen, state and social welfare*, pp. 216, 234–48.

23. Macadam, *The new philanthropy*, pp. 129–30; C. Braithwaite, *The voluntary citizen: an enquiry into the place of philanthropy in the community*, London: Methuen, 1938, pp. 98–9, 120–2, 175; *ibid.*, 'Statistics of finance', in H. A. Mess *et al.*, *Voluntary social services since 1918*, London: Kegan Paul, Trench, Trubner and Co., 1948, 195–203, at pp. 198–201; Political and Economic Planning, *Report on the British social services*, p. 233.

24. G. D. H. Cole, 'A retrospect of the history of voluntary social service', in A. F. C. Bourdillon (ed.), *Voluntary social services: their place in the modern state*, London: Methuen and Co., 1945, pp. 11–30, at p. 24.

25. Macadam, *The new philanthropy*, pp. 18, 287.

26. See for example National Council of Social Service, *New housing estates and their social problems*, London: National Council of Social Service, 1938, p. 4.

27. A. Olechnowicz, *Working-class housing in England between the Wars: the Becontree estate*, Oxford: Oxford University Press, 1997, pp. 137–79; see also Brasnett, *Voluntary social action*, pp. 62–5.

28. B. Harris, 'Voluntary action and unemployment: charity in the south Wales coalfield between the wars', in E. Aerts and B. Eichengreen (eds), *Unemployment and underemployment in historical perspective*, Leuven: Leuven University Press, 1990, pp. 101–10; *ibid.*, 'Government and charity in the distressed mining areas of England and Wales, 1928–30', in J. Barry and C. Jones (eds), *Medicine and charity in western Europe before the welfare state*, London: Routledge, 1991, pp. 207–24; *ibid.*, 'Responding to adversity'.

29. Harris, 'Voluntary action and unemployment', pp. 104–6; *ibid.*, 'Responding to adversity', pp. 546–8.

30. G. Orwell, *The road to Wigan Pier*, Harmondsworth: Penguin, 1962, p. 74; W. Hannington, *The problem of the distressed areas*, London: Gollancz, 1937, p. 197.

31. A. D. Lindsay, 'Unemployment: the "meanwhile" problem', *Contemporary Review*, 143 (1933), 687–95, at 687.

32. P. Johnson, *Saving and spending: the working-class economy in Britain 1870–1939*, Oxford: Oxford University Press, 1985.

33. E. Roberts, *A woman's place: an oral history of working-class women 1890–1940*, Oxford: Blackwell, 1984, pp. 183, 187; *ibid.*, 'The working-class extended family: functions and attitudes 1890–1940', *Oral History*, 12 (1984), 48–55, at 54.

34. A. McInnes, 'Surviving the slump: an oral history of Stoke-on-Trent between the wars', *Midland History*, 18, 121–40, at 126–7; K. Nicholas, *The social effects of unemployment in Teeside*, Manchester: Manchester University Press, 1986, p. 191.

35. Harris, 'Responding to adversity', p. 546.

36. W. Greenwood, *Love on the dole*, Penguin: Harmondsworth, 1969, p. 32.

37. Quoted in D. Vincent, *Poor citizens: the state and the poor in twentieth-century Britain*, London: Longman, 1991, p. 92.

38. M. Tebbutt, *Making ends meet: pawnbroking and working class credit*, London: Methuen, 1983, pp. 137–204; Johnson, *Saving and spending*, pp. 165–88.

39. Tebbutt, *Making ends meet*, pp. 146, 155, 157; see also Women's Group on Public Welfare, *Our towns: a close-up: a study made during 1939–42*, London: Oxford University Press, 1943, p. 21.

40. Tebbutt, *Making ends meet*, pp. 130–1, 139, 200.

41. Women's Group on Public Welfare, *Our towns*, p. 18.

42. Tebbutt, *Making ends meet*, p. 169.

43. Johnson, *Saving and spending*, pp. 157–8; Vincent, *Poor citizens*, p. 93.

44. B. Gilbert, *British social policy 1914–39*, London: Batsford, 1970, pp. 264–5; Finlayson, *Citizen, state and social welfare*, pp. 207–8.

45. Johnson, *Saving and spending*, pp. 205–7.

46. W. Beveridge, *Voluntary action: a report on methods of social advance*, London: George Allen and Unwin, 1948, pp. 78–9.

47. Johnson, *Saving and spending*, p. 67; W. Beveridge and A. F. Wells, *The evidence for voluntary action, being memoranda by organisations and individuals and other material relevant to voluntary action*, London: George Allen and Unwin, 1949, p. 20.

48. See also Beveridge, *Voluntary action*, pp. 30, 88.

49. Johnson, *Saving and spending*, pp. 16–19, 41–2, 205.

50. Abel-Smith, *The hospitals*, pp. 135–7, 315–17; S. Cherry, 'Beyond National Health Insurance: the voluntary hospitals and hospital contributory schemes: a regional study', *Social History of Medicine*, 5 (1992), 455–82, at 462, 467; *ibid.*, 'Accountability, entitlement and control issues and voluntary hospital funding *c.* 1860–1939', *Social History of Medicine*, 9 (1996), 215–33, at 219–21; *ibid.*, 'Before the National Health Service', pp. 317–18; Political and Economic Planning, *Report on the British health services: a survey of the existing health services in Great Britain with proposals for future development*, London: Political and Economic Planning, 1937, pp. 234–5.

51. Beveridge, *Voluntary action*, p. 116; J. Pickstone, *Medicine and industrial society: a history of hospital development in Manchester and its region 1752–1946*, Manchester: Manchester University Press, 1985, p. 252; Cherry, 'Accountability, entitlement and control issues', 221; *ibid.*, 'Before the National Health Service', 324–5.

52. Beveridge, *Voluntary action*, p. 99; L. Hannah, *Inventing retirement: the development of occupational pensions in Britain*, Cambridge: Cambridge University Press, 1986, pp. 31–45.

53. See for example J. Short, *Housing in Britain: the postwar experience*, London: Methuen, 1982, p. 149.

54. J. Parker and C. Mirrlees, 'Welfare', in A. H. Halsey (ed.), *British social trends since 1900: a guide to the changing social structure of Britain*, Basingstoke: Macmillan (now Palgrave Macmillan), 1988, pp. 357–97, at p. 395.

55. Macadam, *The new philanthropy*, pp. 29, 287.

56. Braithwaite, *The voluntary citizen*, p. 25.

57. Johnson, *Saving and spending*, pp. 193–216.

14 Unemployment and poverty between the wars

1. B. Harris, 'Unemployment, insurance and health in interwar Britain', in B. Eichengreen and T. Hatton (eds), *Interwar unemployment in international perspective*, Dordrecht: Kluwer Academic Publishers, 1988, pp. 149–83, at p. 149.

2. A. L. Bowley and M. H. Hogg, *Has poverty diminished?* London: P. S. King, 1925, p. 18; H. Llewellyn Smith, *New survey of London life and labour, Vol. 3, Survey of social conditions, (1) The eastern area*, London: P. S. King, 1932, p. 116; B. S. Rowntree, *Poverty and progress: a second social survey of York*, London: Longman, 1941, pp. 29–30; H. Tout, *The standard of living in Bristol: a preliminary report of the University of Bristol social survey*, Bristol: Arrowsmith, 1938, pp. 25–6.

3. Harris, 'Unemployment, insurance and health', p. 156; *ibid.*, 'Seebohm Rowntree and the measurement of poverty, 1889–1951', in J. Bradshaw and R. Sainsbury (eds), *Getting the measure of poverty: the early legacy of Seebohm Rowntree*, Aldershot: Ashgate, pp. 60–84, at pp. 73–4, 76, 78–80.

4. Bowley and Hogg, *Has poverty diminished?*, pp. 78, 104, 128, 158, 197; Smith, *New survey of London life and labour*, pp. 12, 156.

5. Harris, 'Unemployment, insurance and health', pp. 155–9.

6. J. Harris, *Unemployment and politics: a study in English social policy 1886–1914*, Oxford: Clarendon Press, 1972, p. 2; J. Garraty, *Unemployment in history: economic thought and public policy*, New York: Harper Colophon, 1978, p. 4; B. Eichengreen and T. Hatton, 'Interwar unemployment in international perspective: an overview', in B. Eichengreen and T. Hatton (eds), *Interwar unemployment in international perspective*, Dordrecht: Kluwer Academic Publishers, 1988, pp. 1–59, at p. 3.

7. M. Thomas, 'Unemployment in interwar Britain', in B. Eichengreen and T. Hatton (eds), *Interwar unemployment in international perspective*, Dordrecht: Kluwer Academic Publishers, pp. 97–148, at pp. 115–25; N. Crafts, 'Long-term unemployment in Britain in the 1930s', *Economic History Review*, 40 (1987), 417–31, at 420; W. R. Garside, *British unemployment 1919–39: a study in public policy*, Cambridge: Cambridge University Press, 1990, pp. 10–13.

8. Pilgrim Trust, *Men without work*, Cambridge: Cambridge University Press, 1938, p. 16.

9. E. Cannan, 'The problem of unemployment', *Economic Journal*, 40 (1930), 45–55; D. Benjamin and L. Kochin, 'Searching for an explanation of unemployment in interwar Britain', *Journal of Political Economy*, 87 (1979), 441–78, at 474; see also *ibid.*, 'Unemployment and unemployment benefits in twentieth-century Britain: a reply to our critics', *Journal of Political Economy*, 90 (1982), 410–36.

10. Garside, *British unemployment*, pp. 20–8.

11. PP 1928–9 Cmd. 3272 viii, 689, *Report on investigation in the coalfields of South Wales and Monmouth*, p. 9; PP 1934–5 Cmd. 4886 ix, 627, *Report on the effect of existing economic circumstances on the health of the community in the county borough of Sunderland and certain districts of Durham*, p. 27.

12. J. L. Halliday, 'Psychoneurosis as a cause of incapacity among insured persons', *Supplement to the British Medical Journal*, 1 (1935), 85–8, 99–102, at 100.

13. E. W. Bakke, *The unemployed man*, London: Nisbet, 1933, pp. 63–4, 71–4; H. Jennings, *Brynmawr: a study of a distressed area*, London: Allenson and Co., 1934, p. 140; P. Eisenberg and P. Lazarsfeld, 'The psychological effects of unemployment', *Psychological Bulletin*, 35 (1938), 358–90; Pilgrim Trust, *Men without work*, p. 150; Harris, 'Unemployment, insurance and health', pp. 161–4.

14. R. McKibbin, 'The social psychology of unemployment in interwar Britain', in R. McKibbin, *The ideologies of class: social relations in Britain 1880–1950*, Oxford: Oxford University Press, 1990, pp. 228–58, at p. 258; see also B. Harris, 'Unemployment and the dole in interwar Britain', in P. Johnson (ed.), *Twentieth-century Britain: economic, social and cultural change*, London: Longman, 1994, pp. 203–20, at pp. 217–18.

15. PP 1928–9 Cmd. 3272 viii, 689, *Report on investigation in the coalfields of South Wales and Monmouth*, p. 6; 'Unemployment and the young', *Medical Officer*, 50 (1933), 12; W. Hannington, *The problem of the distressed areas*, London: Gollancz, 1937, p. 62.

16. Ministry of Health, *On the state of the public health. Annual Report of the Chief Medical Officer of the Ministry of Health for the year 1932*, London: HMSO, 1933, p. 41; *ibid.*, *On the state of the public health. Annual Report of the Chief Medical Officer of the Ministry of Health for the year 1933*, London: HMSO, 1934, p. 220.

17. J. Winter, 'Infant mortality, maternal mortality and public health in Britain in the 1930s', *Journal of European Economic History*, 8 (1979), 439–62, at 443; M. Mitchell, 'The effects of unemployment on the social condition of women and children in the 1930s', *History Workshop Journal*, 19 (1985), 105–27, at 107; A. Hardy, *Health and medicine in Britain since 1860*, Basingstoke: Palgrave (now Palgrave Macmillan), 2001, p. 95.

18. C. Webster, 'Healthy or hungry 'thirties?', *History Workshop Journal*, 13 (1982), 110–29; J. Winter, 'Unemployment, nutrition and infant mortality in Britain, 1920–50', in Jay Winter (ed.), *The working class in modern British history: essays in honour of Henry Pelling*, Cambridge: Cambridge University Press, 1983, pp. 232–56, 303–5, at pp. 252–5.

19. Harris, 'Unemployment, insurance and health', pp. 170–7; *ibid.*, 'The height of schoolchildren in Britain, 1900–50', in J. Komlos (ed.), *Stature, living standards and economic development: essays in anthropometric history*, Chicago: University of Chicago Press, pp. 25–38, at pp. 36–8; *ibid.*, *The health of the schoolchild: a history of the school medical service in England and Wales*, Buckingham: Open University Press, 1995, pp. 136–42.

20. See also L. H. Lees, *The solidarities of strangers: the English Poor Laws and the people 1700–1948*, Cambridge: Cambridge University Press, 1998, pp. 310–42.

21. S. Webb and B. Webb, *English Poor Law History, Part II, The last hundred years* (first edition 1929), London: Frank Cass, 1963, pp. 814–20; A. J. Vinson, 'Poor relief, public assistance and the maintenance of the unemployed in Southampton between the Wars', *Southern History*, 2 (1980), 179–225, at 179, 206.

22. M. A. Crowther, *The workhouse system 1834–1929: the history of an English social institution*, London: Methuen, 1983, pp. 95–6.

23. Webb and Webb, *English Poor Law History*, pp. 896–945.

24. B. Gilbert, *British social policy 1914–39*, London: Batsford, 1970, pp. 214–19; P. Thane, *The foundations of the welfare state*, London: Longman's, First edition, 1982, pp. 185–8; Second edition, 1996, pp. 173–6; Lees, *The solidarities of strangers*, pp. 327–33.

25. Gilbert, *British social policy*, pp. 219–35; D. Dilks, *Neville Chamberlain, Vol. 1, Pioneering and reform, 1869–1929*, Cambridge: Cambridge University Press, 1984, pp. 571–8; M. A. Crowther, *British social policy 1914–39*, Basingstoke: Macmillan (now Palgrave Macmillan), 1988, pp. 46–50; Thane, *The foundations of the welfare state*, First edition, pp. 188–9; Second edition, pp. 176–7.

26. PP 1930–1 (137) xxv, 947, *Return showing the number of persons in receipt of poor relief in England and Wales on the night of 1st January 1931*, p. 8; PP 1934–5 (96) xvii, 817, *Return showing the number of persons in receipt of poor relief in England and Wales on the night of 1st January 1935*, p. 8.

27. E. M. Burns, *British unemployment programs, 1920–38*, Washington: Social Science Research Council, 1941, pp. 111–13, 149–60; Garside, *British unemployment*, pp. 66–81.

28. Political and Economic Planning, *Report on the British social services: a survey of the existing public social services in Great Britain with proposals for future development*, London: Political and Economic Planning, 1937, p. 145; PP 1938–9 (135) xxi, 385, *Return showing the number of persons in receipt of poor relief in England and Wales on the night of 1st day of January 1939*, pp. 20–2.

29. Gilbert, *British social policy*, pp. 54–61; A. Deacon, *In search of the scrounger: unemployment insurance in Britain 1920–31* (Occasional Papers in Social Administration, No. 60), London: G. Bell and Sons, 1976, pp. 12–13; Garside, *British unemployment*, pp. 34–5.

30. Gilbert, *British social policy*, pp. 61–74; Deacon, *In search of the scrounger*, pp. 13–15; Garside, *British unemployment*, pp. 37–8.

31. Gilbert, *British social policy*, pp. 75–86; Deacon, *In search of the scrounger*, pp. 15–18; Garside, *British unemployment*, pp. 38–43.

32. D. Fraser, *The evolution of the British welfare state: a history of social policy since the Industrial Revolution*, London and Basingstoke: Macmillan (now Palgrave Macmillan), First edition, 1973, p. 160; Second edition, 1984, p. 172; Third edition, 2003, p. 187.

33. Deacon, *In search of the scrounger*, pp. 21–39; 98–102; Garside, *British unemployment*, pp. 43–6.

34. Deacon, *In search of the scrounger*, pp. 41–53; Garside, *British unemployment*, pp. 46–7.

35. Deacon, *In search of the scrounger*, pp. 69–86; Garside, *British unemployment*, pp. 49–65.

36. R. Lowe, *Adjusting to democracy: the role of the Ministry of Labour in British politics 1916–39*, Oxford: Clarendon Press, 1986, pp. 139–40.

37. Garside, *British unemployment*, pp. 66–7.

38. Hannington, *The problem of the distressed areas*, pp. 43–55.

39. Harris, 'Unemployment and the dole in interwar Britain', pp. 213, 219.

40. Burns, *British unemployment programs*, p. 141; see F. M. Miller, 'The British unemployment assistance crisis of 1935', *Journal of Contemporary History*, 14 (1979), 329–52, at 332; Garside, *British unemployment*, pp. 67–70.

41. Miller, 'The British unemployment assistance crisis'; Burns, *British unemployment programs*, pp. 149–50; Garside, *British unemployment*, pp. 80–1.

42. K. J. Hancock, 'The reduction of unemployment as a problem of public policy, 1920–29', *Economic History Review*, 15 (1962), 328–43, at 328.

43. *Ibid.*, 334–5.

44. Ministry of Labour, *Report of the Unemployment Insurance Committee, Vol. 1*, London: HMSO, 1927, p. 26.

45. PP 1928 Cmd. 3156 x, 783, Industrial Transference Board, *Report*, p. 16.

46. Hancock, 'The reduction of unemployment', 341. Of course, the figure of 280,000 transferees does not include workers who migrated without the assistance of the industrial-transference scheme.

47. A. D. K. Owen, 'The social consequences of industrial transference', *Sociological Review*, 29 (1937), 331–54, at 338, 343; Garside, *British unemployment*, pp. 269–70. The Ministry of Labour estimated that 27 per cent of adults and 35 per cent of juveniles returned to their original areas, implying that the total number of transferees who did not return was $(0.7092 \times 285,058) = 202,173$. If one local job was lost for each transferee who failed to return, the net reduction in unemployment would be equal to $(0.8 \times 202,173) = 161,739$. For further information, see D. R. Pitfield, 'Labour migration and the regional problem in Britain, 1920–39', University of Stirling PhD thesis, 1973, Table 34.

48. Owen, 'The social consequences of industrial transference', 331, 339–54.

49. Garside, *British unemployment*, pp. 251–6.

50. Garside, *British unemployment*, pp. 256–8; B. Harris, 'Responding to adversity: government–charity relations and the relief of unemployment in interwar Britain', *Contemporary Record*, 9, 529–61, at 535.

51. See for example N. Whiteside, 'Counting the cost: sickness and disability among working people in an era of industrial recession', *Economic History Review*, 40 (1987), 228–46; *ibid*. 'The social consequences of interwar unemployment', in S. Glynn and A. Booth (eds), *The road to full employment*, London: Allen and Unwin, 1987, 17–30.

52. H. Levy, *National health insurance: a critical study*, Cambridge: Cambridge University Press, 1944, pp. 38, 61–9; Gilbert, *British social policy*, pp. 261–70, 284–300; N. Whiteside, 'Private agencies for public purposes: some new perspectives on policy making in health insurance between the wars', *Journal of Social Policy*, 12 (1983), 165–93, at 181–2.

53. PP 1938–39 Cmd. 6089 xi, 325, *Twentieth Annual Report of the Ministry of Health 1938–39*, pp. 148–9, 210–11; PP 1938–9 Cmd. 5969 xi, 651, *Tenth Annual Report of the Department of Health for Scotland 1938*, p. 238; PP 1938–9 Cmd. 5969 xi, 651, *Tenth Annual Report of the Department of Health for Scotland 1938*, pp. 82–3.

54. Political and Economic Planning, *Report on the British health services: a survey of the existing health services in Great Britain with proposals for future development*, London: Political and Economic Planning, 1937, pp. 204–5; PP 1936–7 Cmd. 5516 x, 693, *Eighteenth Annual Report of the Ministry of Health 1936–7*, p. 195; Levy, *National health insurance*, pp. 74–5.

55. Levy, *National health insurance*, pp. 63–4.

56. Gilbert, *British social policy*, p. 297.

57. British Medical Association, 'Report of the Committee on Nutrition', *Supplement to the British Medical Journal*, 25 November 1933; C. Webster, 'Health, welfare and unemployment during the depression', *Past and Present*, 109, 204–30, at 211; Levy, *National health insurance*, p. 78.

58. Gilbert, *British social policy*, pp. 300–4.

59. Whiteside, 'Private agencies for public purposes'; see also F. Honigsbaum, 'The interwar health insurance scheme: a rejoinder', *Journal of Social Policy*, 12 (1983), 515–23; N. Whiteside and M. Krafchik, 'Interwar health insurance revisited: a reply to Frank Honigsbaum', *Journal of Social Policy*, 12 (1983), 525–9.

60. Webster, 'Health, welfare and unemployment', pp. 204, 229; see also J. Lewis, *The politics of motherhood: child and maternal welfare in England, 1900–39*, London: Croom Helm, 1980, pp. 165–95; J. Hurt, 'Feeding the hungry schoolchild in the first half of the twentieth century', in D. J. Oddy and D. S. Miller (eds), *Diet and health in modern Britain*, London: Croom Helm, 1985, 178–206, pp. 183–97; A. J. Welshman, 'School meals and milk in England and Wales 1906–45', *Medical History*, 41 (1997), 6–29, pp. 11–25.

61. Webster, 'Health, welfare and unemployment', 213–29; R. Lee, 'Uneven zenith: towards a geography of the high period of municipal medicine in England and Wales', *Journal of Historical Geography*, 14 (1988), 260–80; M. A. Powell, 'Did politics matter? Municipal public health expenditure in the 1930s', *Urban History*, 22 (1995), 360–79; Harris, *The health of the schoolchild*, pp. 112–15.

62. 'The need for increased financial assistance to the Special Areas in aid of expenditure on the special services', Public Record Office ED50/181, p. 12.

63. Webster, 'Health, welfare and unemployment', 222–3.

64. Harris, *The health of the schoolchild*, pp. 120–4.

65. *Ibid.*, pp. 122–6; P. Atkins, 'The pasteurisation of England: the science, culture and health implications of milk processing, 1900–50', in D. Smith and J. Phillips (eds), *Food, science, policy and regulation in the twentieth century: international and comparative perspectives*, London: Routledge, 2000, pp. 37–51, at p. 44.

66. J. Macnicol, *The politics of retirement in Britain 1878–1948*, Cambridge: Cambridge University Press, 1998, pp. 216–24; see also Gilbert, *British social policy*, pp. 235–51.

67. Gilbert, *British social policy*, pp. 244–53; Macnicol, *The politics of retirement*, pp. 213–16; Thane, *The foundations of the welfare state*, First edition, pp. 198–9; Second edition, p. 186.

68. Gilbert, *British social policy*, p. 246; Macnicol, *The politics of retirement*, pp. 216–21.

69. Political and Economic Planning, *Report on the British social services: a survey of the existing public social services in Great Britain with proposals for future development*, London: Political and Economic Planning, 1937, p. 129; Gilbert, *British social policy*, pp. 253–4; Macnicol, *The politics of retirement*, pp. 220–21, 265–84; S. Pedersen, *Family, dependence and the origins of the welfare state: Britain and France 1914–45*, Cambridge: Cambridge University Press, 1993, pp. 167–77.

70. Webster, 'Health, welfare and unemployment', 229.

71. Crowther, *British social policy*, p. 73; Thane, *The foundations of the welfare state*, Second edition, p. 203.

72. J. Stevenson and C. Cook, *Britain in the Depression: society and politics 1929–39*, London: Longman, 1994, p. 37.

73. Political and Economic Planning, *Report on the British social services*, p. 145.

74. *Ibid.*, p. 131.

75. P. Ford, 'The coordination of means tests', *Public Administration*, 25 (1937), 385–92; *ibid.*, 'Family incomes and personal incentives', *Economica*, 5 (1938), 72–83; *ibid.*, *Incomes, means tests and personal responsibility*, London: P. S. King and Son, 1939, pp. 14–23.

76. Thane, *The foundations of the welfare state*, Second edition, p. 205; Webster, 'Health, welfare and unemployment', 228.

77. A. Deacon, 'Systems of interwar unemployment relief', in S. Glynn and A. Booth (eds), *The road to full employment*, London: Allen and Unwin, 1987, pp. 30–42, at p. 34.

78. Political and Economic Planning, *Report on the British social services*, p. 28; Levy, *National health insurance*, pp. 63–6.

79. B. Abel-Smith, 'Whose welfare state?', in N. Mackenzie (ed), *Conviction*, London: MacGibbon and Kee, 1958, pp. 55–73, at p. 57; Thane, *The foundations of the welfare state*, Second edition, p. 203.

80. Thane, *The foundations of the welfare state*, First edition, pp. 190–1, 199; Second edition, pp. 178–9, 186; R. Goodin and J. Le Grand, 'Not only the poor', in R. Goodin and J. le Grand (eds), *Not only the poor: the middle classes and the welfare state*, London: Unwin Hyman, 1987, pp. 203–27.

15 Health and medical care, 1918–39

1. U. Tröhler, 'Surgery (modern)', in W. F. Bynum and R. Porter (eds), *Companion encyclopaedia of the history of medicine*, London: Routledge, 1993, pp. 984–1028, at p. 999; R. Cooter, 'War and modern medicine', in W. F. Bynum and R. Porter (eds), *Companion encyclopaedia of the history of medicine*, London: Routledge, 1993, pp. 1536–73, at p. 1544; A. Hardy, *Health and medicine in Britain since 1860*, Basingstoke: Palgrave (now Palgrave Macmillan), 2001, pp. 63–8.

2. J. Lewis, 'The prevention of diphtheria in Canada and Britain 1914–45', *Journal of Social History*, 20 (1986), 163–76; Hardy, *Health and medicine*, pp. 100–01.

3. P. Weindling, 'The immunological tradition', in W. F. Bynum and R. Porter (eds), *Companion encyclopaedia of the history of medicine*, London: Routledge, 1993, pp. 192–204, at p. 199; R. Porter, *The greatest benefit to mankind: a medical history of humanity from antiquity to the present*, London: Harper Collins, 1997, p. 442. These fears were not entirely unfounded. In 1930, 73 infants had died after being injected with a contaminated supply of the vaccine in Lübeck, leading to widespread concern not only in England, but also in France and Germany (see Hardy, *Health and medicine*, p. 101).

4. Porter, *The greatest benefit to mankind*, pp. 557–8, 567; Hardy, *Health and medicine*, pp. 101–3.

5. R. Cooter, *Surgery and society in peace and war: orthopaedics and the organisation of modern medicine, 1880–1948*, Basingstoke: Macmillan (now Palgrave Macmillan), 1993, pp. 199–217.

6. B. Harris, *The health of the schoolchild: a history of the school medical service in England and Wales*, Buckingham: Open University Press, 1995, pp. 109–11; Porter, *The greatest benefit to mankind*, p. 608.

7. Hardy, *Health and medicine*, p. 104; Porter, *The greatest benefit to mankind*, p. 608.

8. I. Loudon, 'Puerperal fever, the streptococcus, and the sulphonamides, 1911–45', *British Medical Journal*, 295 (1987), 485–90; *ibid.*, *Death in childbirth: an international study of maternal care and maternal mortality 1800–1950*, Oxford: Clarendon Press, 1992, pp. 258–61; *ibid.*, 'Childbirth', in W. F. Bynum and R. Porter (eds), *Companion encyclopaedia of the history of medicine*, London: Routledge, 1050–71, at p. 1066; see also Hardy, *Health and medicine*, pp. 104–5.

9. B. Harris, 'The height of schoolchildren in Britain, 1900–50', in J. Komlos (ed), *Stature, living standards and economic development: essays in anthropometric history*, Chicago: University of Chicago Press, 1994, pp. 25–38, at pp. 32–5; R. Floud and B. Harris, 'Health, height and welfare: Britain 1700–1980', in R. Steckel and R. Floud, eds., *Health and welfare since industrialisation*, Chicago: Chicago University Press, 1997, pp. 91–126, at p. 107; R. Fitzpatrick and T. Chandola, 'Health', in A. H. Halsey and J. Webb (eds), *Twentieth-century British social trends*, Basingstoke: Macmillan (now Palgrave Macmillan), 2000, pp. 94–127, at pp. 95, 101–2.

10. D. Coleman, 'Population and family', in A. H. Halsey and J. Webb (eds), *Twentieth-century British social trends*, Basingstoke: Macmillan (now Palgrave Macmillan), 2000, pp. 27–93, at pp. 71–5.

11. W. P. D. Logan, 'Mortality in England and Wales from 1848 to 1947: a survey of the changing causes of death during the past hundred years', *Population Studies*, 4 (1950), 132–78, at 138–9.

12. K. Carpenter, 'Nutritional diseases', in W. F. Bynum and R. Porter (eds), *Companion encyclopaedia of the history of medicine*, London: Routledge,1993, pp. 464–83, at p. 475; Porter, *The greatest benefit to mankind*, pp. 551–60.

13. F. C. Kelly, 'Fifty years of nutritional science', *Medical Officer*, 53 (1935), 65–6.

14. Political and Economic Planning, *Report on the British health services: a survey of the existing health services in Great Britain with proposals for future development*, London: Political and Economic Planning, 1937, p. 394.

15. Hardy, *Health and medicine*, pp. 15–18; J. Riley, *Sick, not dead: the health of British workingmen during the mortality decline*, Baltimore, MD: Johns Hopkins University Press, 1997, p. 49.

16. 'Medicine as a career', *Medical Officer*, 1 (1909), 745; S. Cherry, *Medical services and the hospitals in Britain 1860–1939*, Cambridge: Cambridge University Press, 1996, p. 29; A. Digby and N. Bosanquet, 'Doctors and patients in an era of national health insurance and private practice, 1913–38', *Economic History Review*, 41 (1988), 74–94; A. Digby, *The evolution of British general practice 1850–1948*, Oxford: Clarendon Press, 1999, pp. 27, 67, 99, 149.

17. H. Levy, *National health insurance: a critical study*, Cambridge: Cambridge University Press, 1944, pp. 33–7.

18. Digby and Bosanquet, 'Doctors and patients', 90–1; Digby, *The evolution of British general practice*, pp. 200, 318.

19. C. Webster, *The health services since the War, Vol. 1, Problems of health care: the National Health Service before 1957*, London: HMSO, 1988, p. 11; Political and Economic Planning, *Report on the British health services*, p. 205; Levy, *National health insurance*, p. 75.

20. Political and Economic Planning, *Report on the British health* services, p. 207; Levy, *National health insurance*, p. 254.

21. Digby, *The evolution of British general practice*, p. 317; L. Oren, 'The welfare of women in labouring families in England, 1860–1950', in L. Banner and M. Hartman (eds), *Clio's consciousness raised: new perspectives on the history of women*, New York: Harper and Row, 1974, pp. 226–44, at pp. 234–5.

22. Political and Economic Planning, *Report on the British health services*, pp. 153–4; J. L. Nicholson, 'Variations in working-class family expenditure', *Journal of the Royal Statistical Society*, Series A, 112 (1949), 359–418, at 391–5. Nicholson examined the average

weekly expenditures of 704 families in Great Britain (excluding London) on the eve of the Second World War, using data from the 1937–8 working-class family budget survey. The proportion of average expenditure devoted to medical care ranged from 1.06 per cent, in families whose total expenditure fell between 30 and 40 shillings, to 3.46 per cent among families whose total expenditure exceeded 100 shillings. P. Massey ('The expenditure of 1360 British middle-class households in 1938–39', *Journal of the Royal Statistical Society*, 105 (1942), 159–96, pp. 181–5) found that middle-class households devoted an average of 3.92 per cent of their normal weekly expenditure to health care.

23. Digby and Bosanquet, 'Doctors and patients', 89; Digby, *The evolution of British general practice*, p. 242.

24. B. Moore and C. Parker, 'The case for a state medical service re-stated', *Lancet*, 2 (1918), 85–7; PP 1920 Cmd. 693 xvii, 1001, Consultative Council on Medical and Allied Services, *Interim report on the future provision of medical and allied services*.

25. C. Webster, 'Conflict and consensus: explaining the British health service', *Twentieth Century British History*, 1 (1990), 115–51, at 121–33.

26. PP 1926 Cmd. 2596 xiv, 311, *Report of the Royal Commission on National Health Insurance*, pp. 280–1, 299, 301–2, 312–18.

27. Levy, *National health insurance*, p. 35; B. Gilbert, *British social policy 1914–39*, London: Batsford, 1970, pp. 282–3.

28. British Medical Association, 'The British Medical Association's proposals for a general medical service for the nation', *Supplement to the British Medical Journal*, 26 April 1930, 165–82; *ibid.*, 'A general medical service for the nation', *Supplement to the British Medical Journal*, 30 April 1938, 253–66.

29. C. Webster, 'Labour and the origins of the National Health Service', in N. Rupke (ed.), *Science, politics and the public good: essays in honour of Margaret Gowing*, Basingstoke: Macmillan (now Palgrave Macmillan), pp. 184–202; J. Stewart, 'Socialist proposals for health reform in interwar Britain: the case of Somerville Hastings', *Medical History*, 39 (1995), 338–57; *ibid.*, *'The battle for health'. A political history of the Socialist Medical Association, 1930–51*, Aldershot: Ashgate, 1999, pp. 37–84.

30. B. Abel-Smith, *The hospitals 1800–1948: a study in social administration in England and Wales*, London: Heinemann, 1964, pp. 295, 303; G. Rivett, *The development of the London hospital system 1823–1982*, London: King Edward's Hospital Fund, 1986, p. 186; G. Finlayson, *Citizen, state and social welfare in Britain 1830–1990*, Oxford: Oxford University Press, 1994, pp. 236–7; S. Tomkins, 'The failure of expertise: public health policy in Britain during the 1918–19 influenza epidemic', *Social History of Medicine*, 5 (1992), 435–54, at 435, 441; N. P. A. S. Johnson, 'The overshadowed killer: influenza in Britain in 1918–19', in H. Phillips and D. Killingray (eds), *The Spanish influenza pandemic of 1918–19: new perspectives*, London: Routledge, 2003, 132–55, at p. 132.

31. Abel-Smith, *The hospitals*, pp. 282–302; F. Honigsbaum, *The division in British medicine: a history of the separation of general practice from hospital care 1911–68*, London: Kogan Page, 1979, pp. 64–89.

32. PP 1921 Cmd. 1335 xiii, 813, Voluntary Hospitals Committee, *Final Report*; Abel-Smith, *The hospitals*, pp. 307–9.

33. Voluntary Hospitals Commission, *Second Interim Report*, London: HMSO, 1924, pp. 6–7; see also 'The recovery of the voluntary hospitals', *Lancet*, 2 (1924), 615–16.

34. C. Braithwaite, *The voluntary citizen: an enquiry into the place of philanthropy in the community*, London: Methuen, 1938, pp. 139–40, 144–5; *ibid.*, 'Statistics of finance', in H. A. Mess *et al.*, *Voluntary social services since 1918*, London: Kegan Paul, Trench, Trubner and Co., 1948, pp. 195–203, at pp. 196–9; Political and Economic Planning, *Report on the British health services*, p. 233; S. Cherry, 'Accountability, entitlement and control issues and voluntary hospital funding *c.* 1860–1939', *Social History of Medicine*, 9 (1996), 215–33; *ibid.*, 'Before the

National Health Service: financing the voluntary hospitals, 1900–39', *Economic History Review*, 50 (1997), 305–26.

35. Abel-Smith, *The hospitals*, p. 322; Political and Economic Planning, *Report on the British health services*, p. 231.

36. H. Joules, 'Partnership of voluntary hospitals', *Supplement to the British Medical Journal*, 29 July 1944, 24.

37. Political and Economic Planning, *Report on the British health services*, p. 231.

38. J. Mohan and M. Gorsky *Don't look back? Voluntary and charitable finance of hospitals in Britain, past and present*, London: Office of Health Economics and Association of Chartered Certified Accountants, 2001, pp. 79–84; M. Gorsky, M. Powell and J. Mohan, 'British voluntary hospitals and the public sphere: contribution and participation before the National Health Service', in S. Sturdy (ed.), *Medicine and the public sphere*, London: Routledge (2002), pp. 123–44, at pp. 138–9; see also Cherry, 'Accountability, entitlement and control issues'.

39. Political and Economic Planning, *Report on the British health services*, 1937, pp. 232, 249, 400; M. Gorsky and J. Mohan, 'London's voluntary hospitals in the interwar period: growth, transformation or crisis?', *Nonprofit and Voluntary Sector Quarterly*, 30 (2001), 247–75.

40. Abel-Smith, *The hospitals*, p. 408; M. Powell, 'Hospital provision before the NHS: territorial justice or inverse care law?', *Journal of Social Policy*, 21 (1992), 145–63, at 145, 159.

41. Political and Economic Planning, *Report on the British health services*, p. 262; Abel-Smith, *The hospitals*, pp. 405–23; S. Cherry, 'Change and continuity in the cottage hospitals *c*. 1859–1948: the experience in East Anglia', *Medical History*, 36 (1992), 271–89, at 282–6.

42. Political and Economic Planning, *Report on the British health services*, pp. 263–5; see also British Medical Association, 'A general medical service for the nation'; D. Fox, 'The National Health Service and the Second World War: the elaboration of consensus', in H. L. Smith (ed.), *War and social change: British society in the Second World War*, Manchester: Manchester University Press, pp. 32–57; *ibid.*, *Health policies, health politics: the British and American experience 1911–65*, Princeton, NJ: Princeton University Press, 1986, pp. 63–9.

43. M. Powell, 'An expanding service: municipal acute medicine in the 1930s', *Twentieth Century British History*, 8 (1997), 334–57, at 344–5.

44. Abel-Smith, *The hospitals*, pp. 352–3; L. Bryder, *Below the magic mountain: a social history of tuberculosis in twentieth-century Britain*, Oxford: Clarendon Press, 1988, pp. 75–87.

45. J. Lewis, *The politics of motherhood: child and maternal welfare in England, 1900–39*, London: Croom Helm, 1980, pp. 117–39; General Register Office, *The Registrar-General's Statistical Review of England and Wales for the year 1937 (New Annual Series, No. 17). Text.*, London: HMSO, 1940, p. 217; Joint Committee of the Royal College of Obstetricians and Gynaecologists and the Population Investigation Committee, *Maternity in Great Britain: a survey of social and economic aspects of pregnancy and childbirth undertaken by a Joint Committee of the Royal College of Obstetricians and Gynaecologists and the Population Investigation Committee*, London: Oxford University Press, 1948, pp. 48–9.

46. Abel-Smith, *The hospitals*, pp. 353, 355–7; M. A. Crowther, *The workhouse system 1834–1929: the history of an English social institution*, London: Methuen, 1983, pp. 182, 186.

47. Abel-Smith, *The hospitals*, pp. 356–7, 360–7, 369; Political and Economic Planning, *Report on the British health services*, p. 255.

48. Powell, 'An expanding service', pp. 341, 345, 348; J. R. Hicks and U. K. Hicks, *Standards of local expenditure: a problem of the inequality of incomes*, Cambridge: Cambridge University Press (National Institute of Economic and Social Research, Occasional Papers, No. 3), 1943, p. 37; R. M. Titmuss, *Problems of social policy*, London: HMSO, 1950, p. 69.

49. Abel-Smith, *The hospitals*, p. 383; Titmuss, *Problems of social policy*, pp. 69–70.

50. Quoted in Powell, 'An expanding service', p. 338.

51. R. Klein, *The new politics of the NHS*, London: Longman, 1995, pp. 16–18; Webster, *The health services since the War*, pp. 12–25.

52. K. Jones, *A history of the mental health services*, London: Routledge and Kegan Paul, 1972, pp. 226–61; C. Unsworth, *The politics of mental health legislation*, Oxford: Clarendon Press, 1987, pp. 112–229.

53. J. Walmsley, D. Atkinson and S. Rolph, 'Community care and mental deficiency 1913 to 1945', in P. Bartlett and D. Wright (eds), *Outside the walls of the asylum: the history of care in the community 1750–2000*, London: Athlone Press, 1999, pp. 181–203, at pp. 185–6.

54. M. Thomson, *The problem of mental deficiency: eugenics, democracy and social policy in Britain c. 1870–1959*, Oxford: Oxford University Press, 1998, pp. 149–79.

55. Harris, *The health of the schoolchild*, pp. 77–8.

56. 5 & 6 Geo. V C. 64: section 3.

57. 8 & 9 Geo. V C. 29: Sections 1–2; see also P. Thane, 'Visions of gender in the making of the British welfare state: the case of women in the British Labour Party and social policy, 1906–45', in G. Bock and P. Thane (eds), *Maternity and gender policies: women and the rise of the European welfare states 1880s-1950s*, London: Routledge, 1991, pp. 93–118, at pp. 105–6.

58. Hicks and Hicks, *Standards of local expenditure*, p. 9; G. C. Baugh, 'Government grants in aid of the rates in England and Wales 1889–1990', *Historical Research*, 65 (1992), 215–37, at 215–20.

59. C. Webster, 'Health, welfare and unemployment during the depression', *Past and Present*, 109 (1985), 204–30, at 222.

60. L. Marks, *Metropolitan maternity: maternal and infant welfare services in early-twentieth century London*, Amsterdam: Rodopi, 1996, p. 133; Webster, 'Health, welfare and unemployment', pp. 222–5.

61. E. Peretz, 'A maternity service for England and Wales: local authority maternity care in the interwar period in Oxfordshire and Tottenham', in J. Garcia, R. Kilpatrick and M. Richards (eds), *The politics of maternity care: services for childbearing women in twentieth-century Britain*, Oxford: Clarendon Press, 1990, pp. 30–46, at p. 37.

62. Political and Economic Planning, *Report on the British health services*, pp. 96–9, 106–7.

63. Lewis, *The politics of motherhood*, pp. 108, 165–96.

64. G. F. McCleary, *The maternity and child welfare movement*, London: P. S. King and Son, Ltd., 1933, p. 121; see also Political and Economic Planning, *Report on the British health services*, p. 115.

65. Harris, *The health of the schoolchild*, pp. 98–104.

66. *Ibid.*, pp. 104–11.

67. *Ibid.*, pp. 111–15.

68. J. Lewis, *What price community medicine? The philosophy, practice and politics of public health since 1919*, Brighton: Harvester, 1986, pp. 1–56.

69. Harris, *The health of the schoolchild*, pp. 6–47.

70. See for example C. Webster, *The National Health Service: a political history*, Oxford: Oxford University Press, 1998, p. 4.

71. Digby and Bosanquet, 'Doctors and patients', 87; Digby, *The evolution of British general practice*, pp. 149–50.

16 Housing policy between the wars

1. J. Melling, 'Clydeside housing and the evolution of state rent control 1900–39', in J. Melling (ed.), *Housing, social policy and the state*, London: Croom Helm, 1980, pp. 139–67, at pp. 139–51.

2. M. Daunton, 'Introduction', in M. Daunton (ed.), *Councillors and tenants: local authority housing in English cities, 1919–39*, Leicester: Leicester University Press, pp. 1–38, 1984, at p. 9.

3. *Ibid.*

4. *Ibid.*, p. 12.

5. PP 1930–31 Cmd. 3911 xvii, 281, *Report of the Interdepartmental Committee on the Rent Restriction Acts*, p. 23; P. Thane, *The foundations of the welfare state*, London: Longman's, First edition, 1982, p. 207; Second edition, 1996, p. 194.

6. M. Bowley, *Housing and the state 1919–44*, London: George Allen and Unwin, 1945, p. 86; A. Holmans, *Housing policy in Britain: a history*, London: Croom Helm, 1987, p. 7; A. Power, *Hovels to high rise: state housing in Europe since 1850*, London: Routledge, 1993, pp. 179–80.

7. C. G. Pooley, 'England and Wales', in C. G. Pooley (ed.), *Housing strategies in Europe 1880–1930*, Leicester: Leicester University Press, 1992, pp. 73–104, at p. 81.

8. PP 1918 Cd. 9235 xiii, 73, *Report of the Committee on the Increase of Rent and Mortgage Interest (War Restrictions) Acts*, pp. 5–6; PP 1923 Cmd. 1803 xii, Part II, 557, *Final Reports of the Departmental Committee on the Increase of Rent and Mortgage Interest (Restrictions) Act, 1920*, pp. 6–7.

9. PP 1923 Cmd. 1803 xii, Part II, 557, *Final Reports of the Departmental Committee on the Increase of Rent and Mortgage Interest (Restrictions) Act, 1920*, p. 7; H. Richardson and D. Aldcroft, *Building in the British economy between the wars*, London: George Allen and Unwin, 1968, p. 226; S. Merrett, *State housing in Britain*, London: Routledge and Kegan Paul, 1979, p. 52; J. Humphries, 'Interwar house building, cheap money and building societies: the housing boom revisited', *Business History*, 29 (1987), 325–45, at 337.

10. Bowley, *Housing and the state*, pp. 86–7; *ibid.*, *The British building industry: four studies in response and resistance to change*, Cambridge: Cambridge University Press, 1966, p. 363; Richardson and Aldcroft, *Building in the British economy*, pp. 192–5; Merrett, *State housing in Britain*, pp. 52–3.

11. PP 1930–31 Cmd. 3911 xvii, 281, *Report of the Interdepartmental Committee on the Rent Restriction Acts*, pp. 25–7.

12. Daunton, 'Introduction', p 15.

13. PP 1937–8 Cmd. 5621 xv, 217, *Reports of the Interdepartmental Committee on the Rent Restriction Acts*, pp. 13–16.

14. M. Daunton, *A property-owning democracy: housing in Britain*, London: Faber, 1987, pp. 3–4; *ibid.*, 'Housing', in F. M. L. Thompson (ed.), *The Cambridge Social History of Britain 1750–1950, Vol. 2, People and their environment*, Cambridge: Cambridge University Press, 1990, pp. 195–250, at p. 218; Power, *Hovels to high rise*, p. 235.

15. 9 & 10 Geo. V. C. 35: sections 1, 7.

16. J. Burnett, *A social history of housing 1815–1985*, London: Routledge, 1986, p. 234.

17. M. Swenarton, *Homes fit for heroes: the politics and architecture of early state housing in Britain*, London: Heinemann, 1981, pp. 116, 120, 123.

18. PP 1920 Cmd. 917 xvii, 227, *First Annual Report of the Ministry of Health 1919–20, Part II, Housing and Town Planning*, pp. 33–4; F. Berry, *Housing: the great British failure*, London: Charles Knight, 1974, p. 35; Daunton, 'Introduction', p. 33.

19. Daunton, 'Introduction', p. 8; *ibid.*, *A property-owning democracy*, p. 92; *ibid.*, 'Housing', pp 237–8, 247–8; D. Englander, *Landlord and tenant in urban Britain 1888–1918*, Oxford: Clarendon Press, pp. 191–317; Swenarton, *Homes fit for heroes*, p. 86.

20. Burnett, *A social history of housing*, p. 227.

21. J. Short, *Housing in Britain: the postwar experience*, London: Methuen, 1982, p. 33.

22. Bowley, *Housing and the state*, pp. 36–41; Burnett, *A social history of housing*, pp. 231–2.

23. Bowley, *Housing and the state*, pp. 39, 271.

24. PP 1930–31 Cmd. 3937 xiv, 1, *Twelfth Annual Report of the Ministry of Health 1930–1*, p. 114; R. L. Reiss, *Municipal and private enterprise housing*, London & Letchworth: J. M. Dent & Sons (for the Cooperative Building Society), 1945, p. 34.

25. Richardson and Aldcroft, *Building in the British economy*, p. 174.

26. M. McKenna, 'The suburbanisation of the working-class population of Liverpool between the Wars', *Social History*, 16 (1991), 173–89, at 175.

27. P. Dickens and P. Gilbert, 'Interwar housing policy: a study of Brighton', *Southern History*, 3 (1981), 201–31, at 217–8; R. Finnigan, 'Council housing in Leeds 1919–39: social policy and urban change', in M. Daunton (ed.), *Councillors and tenants: local authority housing in English cities, 1919–39*, Leicester: Leicester University Press, 1984, pp. 101–53, at pp. 115–16; M. Dresser, 'Housing policy in Bristol, 1919–30', in M. Daunton (ed.), *Councillors and tenants*, pp. 155–216, at pp. 197–202; Burnett, *A social history of housing*, pp. 238–9; A. Olechnowicz, *Working-class housing in England between the Wars: the Becontree estate*, Oxford: Oxford University Press, 1997, pp. 31–71.

28. D. Caradog Jones (ed.), *The social survey of Merseyside, Volume 1*, London: Hodder and Stoughton, 1934, pp. 271–7, 282–3; R. Durant, *Watling: a survey of social life on a new housing estate*, London: P. S. King and Son, 1939, pp. 3–8; T. Young, *Becontree and Dagenham: a report made for the Pilgrim Trust*, London: Becontree Social Service Committee, 1934, pp. 112–13; Finnigan, 'Council housing in Leeds', pp. 115–16; Dickens and Gilbert, 'Interwar housing policy: a study of Brighton', pp. 217–18; Olechnowicz, *Working-class housing*, pp. 32–4, 49–55; National Council of Social Service, *New housing estates and their social problems*, London: National Council of Social Service, 1938, p. 7; Mass Observation, *An enquiry into people's homes. A report prepared by Mass Observation for the Advertising Service Guild*, London: John Murray, 1943, pp. 35–46; R. Jevons and J. Madge, *Housing estates: a study of Bristol Corporation policy and practice between the wars*, Bristol: Arrowsmith, 1946, pp. 35–45; McKenna, 'The suburbanisation of the working-class population of Liverpool', p. 179.

29. Young, *Becontree and Dagenham*, p. 217; Dickens and Gilbert, 'Interwar housing policy: a study of Brighton', p. 224; see also McKenna, 'The suburbanisation of the working-class population of Liverpool', pp. 183–4.

30. J. Yelling, *Slums and redevelopment: policy and practice in England 1918–45, with particular reference to London*, London: UCL Press, 1992, pp. 23–4.

31. PP 1937–38 Cmd. 5621 xv, 217, *Reports of the Interdepartmental Committee on the Rent Restrictions Acts*, pp. 13–16; Bowley, *Housing and the state*, p. 53. The proportion of new homes built for working-class use in Scotland was significantly higher. In the period between 1919 and 1931, local authorities and private builders constructed 137,000 new homes, of which 92,000 (67.15 per cent) had a rateable value of £26 5s or under (PP 1937–38 Cmd. 5621 xv, 217, *Reports of the Interdepartmental Committee on the Rent Restrictions Acts*, pp. 12–13; see also Richardson and Aldcroft, *Building in the British economy*, p. 173).

32. Bowley, *Housing and the state*, p. 271; Holmans, *Housing policy in Britain*, pp. 64–7; ibid., 'Housing', in A. H. Halsey and J. Webb (eds), *Twentieth century British social trends*, Basingstoke: Macmillan (now Palgrave Macmillan), 2000, pp. 469–510, at pp. 470–5.

33. PP 1930–31 Cmd. 3937 xiv, 1, *Twelfth Annual Report of the Ministry of Health 1930–1*, p. 115; Yelling, *Slums and redevelopment*, pp. 38, 43–7.

34. Bowley, *Housing and the state*, pp. 135–6.

35. *Ibid.*, note 1.

36. Finnigan, 'Council housing in Leeds', p. 109.

37. PP 1933–34 Cmd. 4535 xxi, 543, *Housing Act, 1930. Particulars of slum clearance programmes furnished by local authorities*, p. 2; Bowley, *Housing and the state*, pp. 147–8, 271.

38. PP 1932–33 Cmd. 4200 xiv, 1, *Report of the Committee on Local Expenditure (England and Wales)*, pp. 53, 57–8, 68.

39. Bowley, *Housing and the state*, p. 138; Finnigan, 'Council housing in Leeds', p. 114.

40. PP 1933–34 Cmd. 4535 xxi, 543, *Housing Act, 1930. Particulars of slum clearance programmes furnished by local authorities*, pp. 2, 4; Bowley, *Housing and the state*, p. 140.

41. J. L. Marshall, 'The pattern of housebuilding in the interwar period in England and Wales', *Scottish Journal of Political Economy*, 15 (1968), 184–205, at 191–5, 201–3; Richardson and Aldcroft, *Building in the British economy*, pp. 182–3; Yelling, *Slums and redevelopment*, p. 110.

42. See for example B. Lund, *Housing problems and housing policy*, London: Longman, 1996, p. 115.

43. 25 & 26 Geo. V C. 40: Section 2.

44. Ministry of Health, *Housing Act, 1935. Report on the Overcrowding Survey in England and Wales, 1936*, London: HMSO, 1936, pp. xii–xvi; Bowley, *Housing and the state*, p. 144.

45. Bowley, *Housing and the state*, pp. 152–3, 160–1.

46. See also Burnett, *A social history of housing*, p. 244.

47. See also Melling, 'Clydeside housing and the evolution of state rent control'.

48. Bowley, *Housing and the state*, pp. 113–31, 161–8; R. Finnigan, 'Housing policy in Leeds between the wars', in J. Melling (ed.), *Housing, social policy and the state*, London: Croom Helm, 1980, pp. 113–38; *ibid.*, 'Council housing in Leeds'; Burnett, *A social history of housing*, p. 240.

49. Burnett, *A social history of housing*, pp. 245–7.

50. A. Ravetz, 'From working-class tenement to modern flat: local authorities and multi-storey housing between the wars', in A. Sutcliffe (ed.), *Multi-storey living: the British working-class experience*, London: Croom Helm, 1974, pp. 122–50; Burnett, *A social history of housing*, pp. 247–8.

51. Ministry of Health, *Report to the Minister of Health by the Departmental Committee on Valuation for Rates, 1939*, London: HMSO, 1944, p. 7; M. Swenarton and S. Taylor, 'The scale and nature of the growth of owner-occupation in Britain between the wars', *Economic History Review*, 38 (1985), 373–92, at 376–8.

52. Swenarton and Taylor, 'The scale and nature of the growth of owner–occupation', pp. 382–3; Daunton, *A property-owning democracy*, p. 72; *ibid.*, 'Housing', pp. 218–19, 234, 242–3; Holmans, 'Housing', pp. 487–8; Pooley, 'England and Wales', p. 84.

53. Burnett, *A social history of housing*, pp. 250–1; D. Gallie, 'The labour force', in A. H. Halsey and J. Webb (eds), *Twentieth century British social trends*, Basingstoke: Macmillan (now Palgrave Macmillan), 2000, pp. 281–323, at p. 288.

54. Daunton, *A property-owning democracy*, pp. 31, 73–5; *ibid.*, 'Housing', p. 244; Finnigan, 'Housing policy in Leeds, p. 116; *ibid.*, 'Council housing in Leeds', p. 109.

55. H. Bellman, *The silent revolution: the influence of building societies on the modern housing problem*, London: Methuen & Co., 1928, p. 14; Daunton, *A property-owning democracy*, p. 70.

56. H. Bellman, *The thrifty three millions: a study of the building society movement and the story of the Abbey Road Society*, London: Abbey Road Society, 1935, p. 220.

57. Merrett, *State housing in Britain*, p. 53.

58. Short, *Housing in Britain*, p. 40; Daunton, *A property-owning democracy*, pp. 75–6.

59. Holmans, *Housing policy in Britain*, pp. 82–3.

60. A. Nevitt, *Housing, taxation and subsidies: a study of housing in the United Kingdom*, London: Thomas Nelson, 1966, pp. 43–7; Daunton, *A property-owning democracy*, pp. 76–7; *ibid.*, 'Housing', p. 245.

61. PP 1930–31 Cmd. 3911 xvii, 281, *Report of the Interdepartmental Committee on the Rent Restriction Acts*, p. 15; PP 1932–3 Cmd. 4208 xxi, 705, *Statistics of Houses: Memorandum by the Minister of Health and the Secretary of State for Scotland*, p. 4. For 1937 figures, see Table 16.1.

62. Daunton, *A property-owing democracy*, p. 77; see also *ibid.*, 'Housing', p. 246.

63. PP 1930–31 Cmd. 3937 xiv, 1, *Twelfth Annual Report of the Ministry of Health 1930–1*, p. 114; C. L. Mowat, *Britain between the wars 1918–40*, London: Methuen, 1968, p. 165; Pooley, 'England and Wales', p. 84.

64. Richardson and Aldcroft, *Building in the British economy*, pp. 227–36.

65. *Ibid.*, p. 75; S. Merrett, *Owner–occupation in Britain* (with Fred Gray), London: Routledge and Kegan Paul, 1982, p. 9; Holmans, *Housing policy in Britain*, p. 69.

66. S. Pollard, *The development of the British economy, 1914–80*, London: Edward Arnold, 1983, pp. 134–45; G. Peden, *British economic and social policy: Lloyd George to Margaret Thatcher*, Hemel Hempstead: Philip Allan, 1991, pp. 57–95.

67. Humphries, 'Interwar house building', pp. 325–9, 337; see also Richardson and Aldcroft, *Building in the British economy*, p. 74.

68. P. Craig, 'The house that Jerry built? Building societies, the state and the politics of owner-occupation', *Housing Studies*, 1 (1981), 87–108, at 92–7; Humphries, 'Interwar house building', p. 341.

69. Burnett, *A social history of housing*, pp. 254–7.

70. W. Ashworth, *The genesis of modern British town planning: a study in economic and social history of the nineteenth and twentieth centuries*, London: Routledge and Kegan Paul, 1954, p. 224; J. B. Cullingworth, *Town and country planning in England and Wales: an introduction*, London: George Allen and Unwin, 1972, pp. 28–31; G. Cherry, *The evolution of British town planning: a history of town planning in the United Kingdom during the 20th century and of the Royal Town Planning Institute, 1914–74*, Leighton Buzzard: Leonard Hill Books, 1974, pp. 79–138.

71. Holmans, 'Housing', pp. 473–7.

72. Burnett, *A social history of housing*, p. 249; J. Stevenson, *British society 1914–45*, Harmondsworth: Penguin, 1984, p. 221.

73. PP 1938–39 Cmd. 6089 xi, 325, *Twentieth Annual Report of the Ministry of Health 1938–39*, p. 85.

74. Mass Observation, *An enquiry into people's homes*, p. 35.

75. L. Mumford, *The city in history*, Harmondsworth: Penguin, 1966, p. 553; see also Burnett, *A social history of housing*, p. 256.

17   Educational provision between the wars

1. T. H. Marshall, *Social policy*, London: Hutchinson University Library, 1967, p. 7.

2. B. Gilbert, *British social policy 1914–39*, London: Batsford, 1970, p. viii.

3. B. Simon, *The politics of educational reform 1920–40*, London: Lawrence and Wishart, 1974, p. 9.

4. PP 1920 Cmd. 968 xv, 385, *Report of the Departmental Committee on Scholarships and Free Places*, p. 3; B. Simon, *Education and the labour movement 1870–1920*, London: Lawrence and Wishart, 1965, p. 270.

5. Simon, *Education and the labour movement*, pp. 349–50; G. DeGroot, *Blighty: British society in the era of the Great War*, London: Longman, 1996, p. 219.

6. 'A Bradford scheme', *Times Educational Supplement*, 19 October 1916, 180; see also J. R. Brooks, 'Labour and educational reconstruction, 1916–26: a case study in the evolution of policy', *History of Education*, 20 (1991), 245–59, at 245–55.

7. 'Labour and education', *The Times Educational Supplement*, 26 October 1916, 185; *House of Commons Debates*, Fifth series, Vol. 92 (1917), cols. 1912–14; *ibid.*, Vol. 97 (1917), cols. 806–11.

8. 'A Bradford scheme'.

9. *House of Commons Debates*, Fifth series, Vol. 97 (1917), cols. 796–8.

10. See for example 'Second thoughts', *Times Educational Supplement*, 17 January 1918, 27; H. A. L. Fisher, *An unfinished autobiography*, London: Oxford University Press, 1940, p. 106; B. Doherty, 'Compulsory day continuation education: an examination of the 1918 experiment', *The Vocational Aspect*, Vol. 18, No. 39 (1966), 41–56, at 44–5; D. W. Thoms, 'The emergence and failure of the day continuation school experiment', *History of Education*, 4 (1975), 36–50, at 36.

11. 'The two Bills: an official comparison', *The Times Educational Supplement*, 24 January 1918, 37.

12. 8 & 9 Geo. V C. 39: Sections 2–3, 7–8, 10, 18–19, 26, 44.

13. B. Harris, *The health of the schoolchild: a history of the school medical service in England and Wales*, Buckingham: Open University Press, 1995, p. 5; Simon, *Education and the labour movement*, pp. 342–64; *ibid.*, *The politics of educational reform*, pp. 33–4.

14. *House of Commons Debates*, Fifth series, Vol. 92 (1917), col. 1898.

15. 8 & 9 Geo. V C. 39: Sections 2, 44; Fisher, *An unfinished autobiography*, p. 104.

16. D. W. Thoms, 'The Education Act and the development of central government control of education', *Journal of Educational Administration and History*, Vol. 6, No. 2 (1974), 26–30, at 29; see also J. Vaizey and J. Sheehan, *Resources for education: an economic study of education in the United Kingdom, 1920–65*, London: George Allen & Unwin, 1968, p. 37.

17. Fisher, *An unfinished autobiography*, pp. 110–11; Simon, *Education and the labour movement*, pp. 353–7; *ibid., The politics of educational reform*, pp. 21–8; D. Dean, 'H. A. L. Fisher, reconstruction and the development of the 1918 Education Act', *British Journal of Educational Studies*, 18 (1970), 259–76, at 266–8; R. Barker, *Education and politics 1900–51: a study of the Labour party*, Oxford: Clarendon Press, 1972, pp. 28–33; G. Sherington, *English education, social change and war, 1911–20*, Manchester: Manchester University Press, 1981, pp. 101–7, 118–20; Brooks, 'Labour and educational reconstruction, pp. 255–9

18. PP 1897 C. 8447 xxv, 1, *Special Reports on Educational Subjects 1896–7*, p. 51; Board of Education, *Report of the Consultative Committee on infant and nursery schools*, London: HMSO, 1933, p. 29; N. Whitbread, *The evolution of the nursery-infant school: a history of nursery and infant education in Britain, 1800–1970*, London: Routledge and Kegan Paul, 1972, pp. 43–4, 63–6.

19. Board of Education, *Infant and nursery schools*, p. 29; Whitbread, *The evolution of the nursery-infant school*, pp. 24–5, 57–60.

20. Board of Education, *Infant and nursery schools*, pp. 36–7; Whitbread, *The evolution of the nursery-infant school*, pp. 65–7.

21. For Fisher's comments on nursery education, see House of Commons Debates, Fifth series, Vol. 92 (1917), cols. 1911–12; *ibid.*, Vol. 97 (1917), cols. 803–4.

22. 8 & 9 Geo. V C. 39: Section 19.

23. Board of Education, *Infant and nursery schools*, pp. 43, 46; Whitbread, *The evolution of the nursery-infant school*, pp. 67, 79.

24. Board of Education, *Infant and nursery schools*, p. 45; Whitbread, *The evolution of the nursery-infant school*, pp. 79, 87–99.

25. Simon, *The politics of educational reform*, pp. 14–40; Thoms, 'The emergence and failure of the day continuation school experiment', 44.

26. PP 1922 Cmd. 1581 ix, 1, *First Interim Report of Committee on National Expenditure*, p. 2.

27. Simon, *The politics of educational reform*, pp. 33–6.

28. PP 1922 Cmd. 1581 ix, 1, *First Interim Report of Committee on National Expenditure*, pp. 1–6–26; Simon, *The politics of educational reform*, pp. 37–40.

29. Harris, *The health of the schoolchild*, pp. 32–6.

30. PP 1924–25 Cmd. 2443 xii, 37, *Report of the Board of Education for the year 1923/24*, p. 53; PP 1935–36 Cmd. 5290 ix, 735, *Education in 1935, being the Report of the Board of Education and the Statistics of Public Education for England and Wales*, p. 5; G. A. N. Lowndes, *The silent social revolution: an account of the expansion of public education in England and Wales 1895–1965*, Oxford: Oxford University Press, 1969, p. 24.

31. PP 1935–36 Cmd. 5290 ix, 735, *Education in 1935, being the Report of the Board of Education and the Statistics of Public Education for England and Wales*, p. 6. Although many of the new schools were built to replace existing schools, others were constructed to meet the needs of the new suburbs (see R. Moore, 'Hadow reorganisation in a community setting: A. H. Whipple and the William Crane School in Nottingham 1931–8', *History of Education*, 30 (2001), 379–400).

32. PP 1926 Cmd. 2695 x, 33, *Report of the Board of Education for the year 1924/25*, p. 32; PP 1938–39 Cmd. 6013 x, 661, *Education in 1938, being the Report of the Board of Education and the Statistics of Public Education for England and Wales*, pp. 6–7, 110; B. Simon, *Education and the social order 1940–90*, London: Lawrence and Wishart, 1991, p. 576.

33. R. Selleck, *English primary education and the progressives, 1914–39*, London: Routledge and Kegan Paul, 1972.

34. Board of Education, *Report of the Consultative Committee on the primary school*, London: HMSO, 1931, pp. 116–17.

35. PP 1935–36 Cmd. 5290 ix, 735, *Education in 1935, being the Report of the Board of Education and the Statistics of Public Education for England and Wales*, p. 6.

36. Selleck, *English primary education*, pp. vi, 152.

37. Board of Education, *Report on … the primary school*, pp. 138–9.

38. B. Swinnerton, 'The 1931 Report of the Consultative Committee on the Primary School: tensions and contradictions', *History of Education*, 25 (1996), 73–90, at 79–90.

39. B. Allen, 'Continuation schools, evening institutes and works schools', *Journal of Education and School World*, 58 (1926), 579–81, at 580.

40. Doherty, 'Compulsory day continuation education'; G. Bernbaum, *Social change and the schools 1918–44*, London: Routledge and Kegan Paul, 1967, pp. 30–2; Thoms, 'The emergence and failure of the day continuation school experiment'; H. Hendrick, ' "A race of intelligent unskilled labourers": the adolescent worker and the debate on compulsory part-time day continuation schools, 1900–22', *History of Education*, 9 (1990), 159–73.

41. R. H. Tawney (ed.), *Secondary education for all: a policy for Labour*, London: George Allen & Unwin and the Labour Party, 1922, pp. 7, 16.

42. Moore, 'Hadow reorganisation in a community setting', pp. 381–2.

43. Board of Education, *The education of the adolescent: Report of the Consultative Committee*, London: HMSO, 1927, p. iv; emphasis added.

44. PP 1927 Cmd. 2866 viii, 653, *Report of the Board of Education for the year 1925/26*, p. 85.

45. Board of Education, *The new prospect in education (Educational pamphlets, no. 60)*, London: HMSO, 1928, p. 1.

46. Board of Education, *The education of the adolescent*, pp. 145–6, 178.

47. R. McKibbin, *Classes and cultures: England 1918–51*, Oxford: Oxford University Press, 1998, p. 212; Board of Education, *The education of the adolescent*, pp. 174–5.

48. Board of Education, *The new prospect in education*, p. 1.

49. PP 1934–35 Cmd. 4968 viii, 237, *Education in 1934, being the Report of the Board of Education and the Statistics of Public Education for England and Wales*, pp. 6–8.

50. PP 1938–39 Cmd. 6013 x, 661, *Education in 1938, being the Report of the Board of Education and the Statistics of Public Education for England and Wales*, pp. 6–7. This reflected the reduction in the school-building programme following the collapse of the second Labour government and the implementation of public spending cuts during the early-1930s (see Simon, *The politics of educational reform*, p. 370).

51. Simon, *The politics of educational reform*, pp. 125–32.

52. Moore, 'Hadow reorganisation in a community setting', p. 399.

53. D. Parker, ' "Not worth spending money on": The demand for variety and parity in post-primary educational provision: the Hertfordshire experience', *Journal of Educational Administration and History*, Vol. 32, No. 2 (2000), 19–45, at 19, 40–1.

54. D. Dean, 'The difficulties of a Labour educational policy: the failure of the Trevelyan Bill, 1929–31', *British Journal of Educational Studies*, 17 (1969), 286–300, at 288; Simon, *The politics of educational reform*, pp. 132–5.

55. McKibbin, *Classes and cultures*, pp. 213–14.

56. *House of Commons Debates*, Fifth series, Vol. 244 (1930), cols. 1146, 1186; Dean, 'The difficulties of a Labour educational policy', 290–3; Simon, *The politics of educational reform*, pp. 161–7.

57. 'The Education Bill', *The Times*, 12 February 1936, p. 15, cols. b–c; *House of Commons Debates*, Fifth series, Vol. 308 (1936), cols. 1188–91.

58. Simon, *The politics of educational reform*, pp. 217–24; McKibbin, *Classes and cultures*, p. 213.

59. Simon, *Education and the labour movement*, pp. 176–246, 270–3.

60. PP 1920 Cmd. 968 xv, 385, *Report of the Departmental Committee on Scholarships and Free Places*, pp. 1, 9–10, 34.

61. Simon, *The politics of educational reform*, pp. 50, 56, 366.

62. J. Floud, 'The educational experience of the adult population of England and Wales as at July 1949', in D. V. Glass (ed.), *Social mobility in Britain*, London: Routledge and Kegan Paul, 1954, pp. 98–140, at pp. 106, 110–11, 116–17, 129; A. Heath and P. Clifford, 'Class inequalities in education in the twentieth century', *Journal of the Royal Statistical Society*, Series A, 153 (1990), Part I, 1–16, at 4–5, 15.

63. Quoted in G. Sutherland, *Ability, merit and measurement: mental testing and English education 1880–1940*, Oxford: Clarendon Press, 1984, p. 276.

64. See for example Simon, *The politics of educational reform*, pp. 225–50; Sutherland, *Ability, merit and measurement*, pp. 191–269.

65. M. Sanderson, *Education and economic decline in Britain, 1870s to the 1990s*, Cambridge: Cambridge University Press, 1999, p. 61.

66. Board of Education, *A review of junior technical schools in England (Educational pamphlets, No. 111)*, London: HMSO, 1937, pp. 6–7.

67. PP 1938–39 Cmd. 6013 x, 661, *Education in 1938, being the Report of the Board of Education and the Statistics of Public Education for England and Wales*, p. 91.

68. B. Bailey, 'Technical education and secondary schooling, 1905–45', in P. Summerfield and E. Evans (eds), *Technical education and the state since 1850: historical and contemporary perspectives*, Manchester: Manchester University Press, 1990, pp. 97–119; Sanderson, *Education and economic decline*, pp. 58–60.

69. B. Bailey, 'The development of technical education, 1934–9', *History of Education*, 16 (1987), 49–65, (see esp. 61–2); Board of Education, *Report of the Consultative Committee on secondary education, with special reference to grammar schools and technical high schools*, London: HMSO, 1938, pp. 371–2.

70. See R. Anderson, *Universities and élites in Britain since 1800*, Basingstoke: Macmillan (now Palgrave Macmillan), 1992, p. 12.

71. See for example M. Sanderson, *The Universities and British industry, 1850–1970*, London: Routledge and Kegan Paul, 1972, p. 247; McKibbin, *Classes and cultures*, p. 249.

72. PP 1938–39 Cmd. 6013 x, 661, *Education in 1938, being the Report of the Board of Education and the Statistics of Public Education for England and Wales*, pp. 56–8; G. Leybourne and K. White, *Education and the birth-rate: a social dilemma*, London: Jonathan Cape, 1940, pp. 252–7. Leybourne and White believed that the higher cost of living at Oxford and Cambridge tended to exclude students who did not have access to additional sources of income from attending these universities (see p. 254).

73. Floud, 'The educational experience of the adult population', pp. 112–16, 136–9.

74. Sanderson, *The Universities and British industry*, pp. 263–75.

75. The Technical and Extension College in Exeter, which had been founded in 1894, became a University College in 1922 (see V. H. H. Green, *The Universities*, Harmondsworth: Penguin, 1969, p. 143; McKibbin, *Classes and cultures*, p. 252).

76. W. H. Armytage, *Civic universities: aspects of a British tradition*, London: Ernest Benn, 1955, pp. 256–8, 265; Green, *The Universities*, pp. 129–34, 143; McKibbin, *Classes and cultures*, p. 250.

77. Armytage, *Civic universities*, p. 276.

78. Sanderson, *The Universities and British industry*, pp. 214–42, 250–63; *ibid.*, *Education and economic decline*, pp. 68–9; Armytage, *Civic universities*, p. 251–5, 272.

79. Lowndes, *The silent social revolution*, p. 180.

80. Sanderson, *Education and economic decline*, pp. 55–73; see also McKibbin, *Classes and cultures*, p. 269.

81. P. Gordon, R. Aldrich and D. Dean, *Education and policy in England in the twentieth century*, London: Woburn, 1990, pp. 59–60.

82. Lowndes, *The silent social revolution*, p. 185.

18 The Second World War and after

1. J. Stevenson and C. Cook, *Britain in the Depression: society and politics 1929–39*, London: Longman, p. 83.

2. R. M. Titmuss, *Problems of social policy*, London: HMSO, 1950, pp. 4–11.

3. *Ibid.*, pp. 45–53, 251–68; J. Hinton, 'Voluntarism and the welfare/warfare state: women's voluntary services in the 1940s', *Twentieth Century British History*, 9 (1998), 274–305, at 284–91.

4. Unfortunately, the official figures do not distinguish between individuals who were rendered homeless on one occasion and those who were rendered homeless on more than one occasion, so the actual number of individuals who experienced a period of homelessness was probably less than the figures quoted in this chapter. For further details, see Titmuss, *Problems of social policy*, pp. 273, 301.

5. Titmuss, *Problems of social policy*, pp. 272–303.

6. *Ibid.*, p. 515; S. Ferguson and H. Fitzgerald, *Studies in the social services*, London: HMSO, 1954, pp. 9–10; A. Deacon and J. Bradshaw, *Reserved for the poor: the means test in British social policy*, Oxford: Martin Robertson, 1983, pp. 36–42; D. Fraser, *The evolution of the British welfare state: a history of social policy since the Industrial Revolution*, London and Basingstoke: Macmillan (now Palgrave Macmillan), First edition, 1973, pp. 193–7; Second edition, 1984, pp. 208–13; Third edition, 2003, pp. 228–33.

7. Titmuss, *Problems of social policy*, pp. 23–34.

8. Titmuss, *Problems of social policy*, pp. 101–9, 355–69, 424–30, 562–4. For more detailed accounts, see also A. Calder, *The people's war: Britain 1939–45*, London: Jonathan Cape, 1969, pp. 35–50, 128–9; J. Macnicol, 'The effect of the evacuation of schoolchildren on official attitudes to state intervention', in H. L. Smith (ed.), *War and social change: British society in the Second World War*, Manchester: Manchester University Press, 1986, pp. 3–31; T. Crosby, *The impact of civilian evacuation in the Second World War*, London: Croom Helm, 1986; A. J. Welshman, 'Evacuation and social policy during the Second World War: myth and reality', *Twentieth Century British History*, 9 (1997), 28–53; A. Howkins 'A country at war: Mass-Observation and rural England, 1939–45', *Rural History*, 9 (1998), 75–97.

9. Titmuss, *Problems of social policy*, pp. 110–36, 507–8; Macnicol, 'The effect of the evacuation of schoolchildren', pp. 25–8.

10. See for example H. Jones, *Health and society in twentieth-century Britain*, London: Longman, 1994, p. 94.

11. B. Harris, *The health of the schoolchild: a history of the school medical service in England and Wales*, Buckingham: Open University Press, 1995, pp. 144–51; Welshman, 'Evacuation and social policy', pp. 33–40.

12. 'LCC Record of Evacuation. Chapter 21: Conclusion', Public Record Office ED138/49. In 'Evacuation and social policy' (p. 53), John Welshman attributed these comments to members of the Board of Education, but they were actually written by staff of the London County Council in a report included in the Board's own papers.

13. Titmuss, *Problems of social policy*, pp. 63–4; B. Abel-Smith, *A history of the nursing profession*, London: Heinemann, 1960, pp. 161–2; *ibid.*, The hospitals 1800–1948: a study in social administration in England and Wales, London: Heinemann, 1964, pp. 425–7.

14. Titmuss, *Problems of social policy*, pp. 188, 447, 492–3.

15. Abel-Smith, *The hospitals*, p. 435.

16. Titmuss, *Problems of social policy*, pp. 64–5; Abel-Smith, *The hospitals*, p. 436.

17. Titmuss, *Problems of social policy*, pp. 457, 469–72, 500–01; Abel-Smith, *The hospitals*, pp. 436–9; C. Webster, *The health services since the War, Vol. 1, Problems of health care: the National Health Service before 1957*, London: HMSO, 1988, pp. 28–34; A. Hardy, *Health and medicine in Britain since 1860*, Basingstoke: Palgrave (now Palgrave Macmillan), 2001, pp. 126–32.

18. I. Zweiniger-Bargielowska, *Austerity in Britain: rationing, controls and consumption, 1939–45*, Oxford: Oxford University Press, 2000, pp. 13–14.

19. In July 1942 the government decided to amend the regulations so that children became eligible for the full meat ration on reaching the age of five (R. J. Hammond, *Food, Volume 2, Studies in administration and control*, London: HMSO, 1956, pp. 452–5, 651–2; Zweiniger-Bargielowska, *Austerity in Britain*, p. 18).

20. R. J. Hammond, *Food, Volume 1, The growth of policy*, London: HMSO, 1951, pp. 111–96; Zweiniger-Bargielowska, *Austerity in Britain*, pp. 15–22.

21. Zweiniger-Bargielowska, *Austerity in Britain*, p. 33.

22. Harris, *The health of the schoolchild*, pp. 155–60.

23. A. Sen, 'Economic progress and health', in D. Leon and G. Walt (eds), *Poverty, inequality and health: an international perspective*, Oxford: Oxford University Press, 2001, pp. 333–45, at p. 341; J. Drèze and A. Sen, *Hunger and public action*, Oxford, Clarendon Press, 1989, pp. 105, 181–2; B. Harris, 'Poverty, inequality and health in international perspective', *Contemporary British History*, 16 (2002), 221–8, at 227.

24. M. Nelson, 'Social class trends in British diet 1860–1980', in C. Geissler and D. Oddy (eds), *Food, diet and economic change past and present*, Leicester: Leicester University Press, 1993, pp. 101–20, at pp. 106–9; Harris, *The health of the schoolchild*, pp. 165–71; Jones, *Health and society*, p. 112; I. Zweiniger-Bargielowska, 'Rationing, austerity and the Conservative party recovery after 1945', *Historical Journal*, 37 (1994), 173–97; *ibid.*, *Austerity in Britain*, pp. 31–45, 128–40, 203–42.

25. R. S. Wood, 'Policy and planning for postwar reconstruction', 17 January 1941, Public Record Office ED136/212, para. 3.

26. PP 1946–7 Cmd. 7067 xii, 361, *Eighty-ninth report of the Commissioners of His Majesty's Inland Revenue for the year ended 31st March 1946*, pp. 45–68; M. Daunton, *Just taxes: the politics of taxation in Britain, 1914–79*, Cambridge: Cambridge University Press, 2002, pp. 176–93.

27. J. Harris, *William Beveridge: a biography*, Oxford: Clarendon Press, 1977, pp. 362–77; P. Addison, *The road to 1945: British politics and the Second World War*, London: Jonathan Cape, 1975, pp. 164–7; K. Williams and J. Williams, *A Beveridge reader*, London: Allen and Unwin, 1987, p. 3; P. Thane, *The foundations of the welfare state*, London: Longman's, First edition, 1982, pp. 223–5; Second edition, 1996, pp. 211–13.

28. Harris, *William Beveridge*, pp. 378–418; V. George and P. Wilding, *Ideology and social welfare*, London: Routledge and Kegan Paul, 1985, pp. 44–68; T. Cutler, K. Williams and J. Williams, *Keynes, Beveridge and beyond*, London: Routledge and Kegan Paul, 1986, pp. 6–36; Williams and Williams, *A Beveridge reader*, pp. 1–11; R. Silburn, 'Beveridge', in V. George and R. Page (eds), *Modern thinkers on welfare*, Hemel Hempstead: Prentice Hall/Harvester Wheatsheaf, 1995, pp. 84–101, at pp. 92–3.

29. PP 1942–3 Cmd. 6404 vi, 119, *Report by Sir William Beveridge on Social Insurance and Allied Services*, pp. 9–17, 167 (see esp. paras. 19–20, 25–7).

30. *Ibid.*, pp. 141–5; W. Beveridge, *Voluntary action: a report on methods of social advance*, London: George Allen and Unwin, 1948.

31. PP 1942–3 Cmd. 6404 vi, 119, *Report by Sir William Beveridge on Social Insurance and Allied Services*, pp. 120, 154–65. It is important to note that Beveridge's definition of the 'working' population was a largely male one. As many writers have pointed out, Beveridge's plan for full employment was a plan for full male employment. He believed that the majority of married women would make 'marriage their main occupation', and that their principal task was to 'ensur[e] the adequate continuance of the British race and of British ideals in the world' (*Social Insurance and Allied Services*, pp. 49–53; see also G. Pascall, *Social policy: a feminist analysis*, London: Tavistock, 1986, pp. 7–8). For further information about Beveridge's views on full employment, see W. Beveridge, *Full employment in a free society*, London: George Allen and Unwin, 1944.

32. PP 1942–3 Cmd. 6404 vi, 119, *Report by Sir William Beveridge on Social Insurance and Allied Services*, p. 6.

33. Quoted in K. Jefferys, 'British politics and social policy during the Second World War', *Historical Journal*, 30 (1987), 123–44, at 131.

34. Harris, *William Beveridge*, p. 428; Thane, *The foundations of the welfare state*, First edition, pp. 252–3; Second edition, pp. 236–7.

35. PP 1943–4 Cmd. 6550 viii, 463, *Social insurance, Part I, Government proposals for social insurance generally and for family allowances*, pp. 5–7; Harris, *William Beveridge*, p. 428; Deacon and Bradshaw, *Reserved for the poor*, pp. 42–6; P. Alcock, *Poverty and state support*, London: Longman, 1987, pp. 56–8.

36. Harris, *William Beveridge*, pp. 434–41.

37. PP 1943–4 Cmd. 6527 viii, 119, *Employment policy*, p. 3.

38. P. Gosden, *Education in the Second World War: a study in policy and administration*, London: Methuen, 1976, pp. 309–31, 367–87.

39. *Ibid.*, pp. 309–31; Jefferys, 'British politics and social policy', 140; *ibid.*, *The Churchill Coalition and wartime politics, 1940–45*, Manchester: Manchester University Press, pp. 125–9. The school-leaving age was finally raised to 16 in 1972 (see B. Simon, *Education and the social order 1940–90*, London: Lawrence and Wishart, 1991, pp. 422–3).

40. Gosden, *Education in the Second World War*, pp. 411–17, 420–2; W. H. Armytage, *Civic Universities: aspects of a British tradition*, London: Ernest Benn, 1955, p. 286.

41. Armytage, *Civic Universities*, pp. 283–6; Gosden, *Education in the Second World War*, pp. 417–20, 422–30; R. Lowe, *Education in the postwar years: a social history*, London: Routledge, 1988, pp. 56–69; W. A. C. Stewart, *Higher education in postwar Britain*, Basingstoke: Macmillan (now Palgrave Macmillan), 1989, pp. 36–8, 78–85, 270–1.

42. Webster, *Problems of health care*, pp. 17–43.

43. *Ibid.*, p. 44; *ibid.*, 'Doctors, public service and profit: general practitioners and the National Health Service', *Transactions of the Royal Historical Society*, Fifth series, 40, 197–216.

44. British Medical Association, 'The British Medical Association's proposals for a general medical service for the nation', *Supplement to the British Medical Journal*, 26 April 1930, 165–82; *ibid.*, 'A general medical service for the nation', *Supplement to the British Medical Journal*, 30 April 1938, 253–66.

45. Medical Planning Commission, 'Draft Interim Report', *British Medical Journal*, 20 June 1942, 743–53; PP 1942–3 Cmd. 6404 vi, 119, *Report by Sir William Beveridge on Social Insurance and Allied Services*, p. 160.

46. PP 1942–3 Cmd. 6404 vi, 119, *Report by Sir William Beveridge on Social Insurance and Allied Services*, pp. 158–63; Webster, *Problems of health care*, p. 40.

47. British Institute of Public Opinion, 'The White Paper and the Questionary', *Supplement to the British Medical Journal*, 5 August 1944, 25–9, at 25–6; 'Heard at Headquarters', *Supplement to the British Medical Journal*, 7 April 1945, 51.

48. British Medical Association, 'Proceedings of Council', *Supplement to the British Medical Journal*, 13 February 1943, 23–5, at 24; G. Anderson, 'Evolution, not revolution', *Supplement to the British Medical Journal*, 4 September 1943, 29–34, at 30–1.

49. British Medical Association, 'Proceedings of Council', *Supplement to the British Medical Journal*, 5 August 1944, 29–32, at 30; 'Annual panel conference: debate on future of medical services', *Supplement to the British Medical Journal*, 11 November 1944, 103–10, at 104.

50. British Medical Association, 'Proceedings of Council', *Supplement to the British Medical Journal*, 13 February 1943, 23–5.

51. PP 1920 Cmd. 693 xvii, 1001, *Consultative Council on Medical and Allied Services, Interim report on the future provision of medical and allied services* [the Dawson Report]; Webster, *Problems of health care*, p. 37.

52. British Medical Association, 'Annual Representative Meeting', *Supplement to the British Medical Journal*, 26 September 1942, 33–6, at 35; *ibid.*, 'Annual Representative Meeting,

London, 1943', *Supplement to the British Medical Journal*, 2 October 1943, 51–6, at 55–6; British Institute of Public Opinion, 'The White Paper and the Questionary', p. 28; 'Gallup poll on White Paper: Comparison with Council's report', *Supplement to the British Medical Journal*, 16 September 1944, 57–9, at 58; Webster, *Problems of health care*, pp. 88–120.

53. 'The White Paper: mass meeting of London practitioners', *Supplement to the British Medical Journal*, 11 March 1944, 41–3, at 41.

54. 'The White Paper: an analysis', *Supplement to the British Medical Journal*, 18 March 1944, 47–53, at 52.

55. PP 1943–4 Cmd. 6502 viii, 315, Ministry of Health/Department of Health for Scotland, *A national health service*, p. 23.

56. 'Administrative aspects of the White Paper: Dr Hill's address at Bristol', *Supplement to the British Medical Journal*, 25 March 1944, 59–60, at 60; 'A National Health Service: Report of the Council of the BMA to the representative body', *British Medical Journal*, 13 May 1944, 643–52, at 645.

57. PP 1943–4 Cmd. 6502 viii, 315, Ministry of Health/Department of Health for Scotland, *A national health service*, pp. 14–26; 'The White Paper: mass meeting of London practitioners', *Supplement to the British Medical Journal*, 11 March 1944, 41–3, at 42; 'Voluntary hospitals in National Health Service', *Supplement to the British Medical Journal*, 10 June 1944, 139–40, at 139.

58. 'A National Health Service: Report of the Council of the BMA to the representative body', pp. 646–7; 'The Government's health service proposals', *Supplement to the British Medical Journal*, 17 June 1944, 145–7, at 145.

59. C. Webster, 'Labour and the origins of the National Health Service', in N. Rupke (ed.), *Science, politics and the public good: essays in honour of Margaret Gowing*, Basingstoke: Macmillan (now Palgrave Macmillan), pp. 184–202; J. Stewart, *'The battle for health': a political history of the Socialist Medical Association, 1930–51*, Aldershot: Ashgate, 1999, pp. 1–84.

60. Jefferys, 'British politics and social policy', pp. 133–7; *ibid.*, *The Churchill Coalition*, pp. 129–32.

61. A. J. Willcocks, *The creation of the National Health Service: a study of pressure groups and a major social policy decision*, London: Routledge and Kegan Paul, 1967, pp. 67–8; J. Pater, *The making of the National Health Service*, London: King Edward's Hospital Fund for London, 1981, pp. 102–4.

62. Webster, *Problems of health care*, p. 82.

63. R. Levitt, *The reorganised National Health Service*, London: Croom Helm, 1979, pp. 19–21; C. Ham, *Health policy in Britain: the politics and organisation of the National Health Service*, Basingstoke: Macmillan (now Palgrave Macmillan), 1992, pp. 15–17; R. Klein, *The new politics of the NHS*, London: Longman, 1995, pp. 82–90; C. Webster, *The health services since the War, Volume II, Government and health care, The National Health Service 1958–79*, London: HMSO, 1996, pp. 322–31.

64. PP 1938–9 Cmd. 6016 xii, 79, Ministry of Labour, *Annual Report for the year 1938*, p. 6.

65. J. B. Cullingworth, *Town and country planning in England and Wales: an introduction*, London: George Allen and Unwin, 1964, pp. 23–5.

66. A. Meynell, 'Location of industry', *Public Administration*, 37 (1959), 9–20, at 14–15.

67. W. Ashworth, *The genesis of modern British town planning: a study in economic and social history of the nineteenth and twentieth centuries*, London: Routledge and Kegan Paul, 1954, pp. 226–7; Cullingworth, *Town and country planning*, pp. 27–8.

68. Ashworth, *The genesis of modern British town planning*, pp. 228–9; see also J. Stevenson, 'Planners' moon? The Second World War and the planning movement', in H. L. Smith (ed.), *War and social change: British society in the Second World War*, Manchester: Manchester University Press, 1986, pp. 58–77, at pp. 69–70.

69. Ashworth, *The genesis of modern British town planning*, p. 231.

70. PP 1941–2 Cmd. 6386 iv, 15, *Final Report of the Expert Committee on Compensation and Betterment*, pp. 1, 141, 157–66.

71. Addison, *The road to 1945*, pp. 252–3.

72. PP 1943–4 Cmd. 6537 viii, 273, *The control of land use*, pp. 7–9; Addison, *The road to 1945*, pp. 252–3; Jefferys, 'British politics and social policy', 140–1; *ibid.*, *The Churchill Coalition*, pp. 177–8, 212.

73. J. Burnett, *A social history of housing 1815–1985*, London: Routledge, 1986, pp. 285–6.

74. Addison, *The road to 1945*, pp. 247, 267.

75. G. Peden, *British economic and social policy: Lloyd George to Margaret Thatcher*, Hemel Hempstead: Philip Allan, 1991, pp. 149–50; K. Morgan, *Labour in power 1945–51*, Oxford: Oxford University Press, 1984, pp. 170, 485.

76. Daunton, *Just taxes*, pp. 217–21, 311, 335–7.

77. J. Macnicol, *The politics of retirement in Britain 1878–1948*, Cambridge: Cambridge University Press, 1998, p. 398; Deacon and Bradshaw, *Reserved for the poor*, pp. 44–6; Alcock, *Poverty and state support*, pp. 83–4.

78. B. S. Rowntree and G. R. Lavers, *Poverty and the welfare state: a third social survey of York dealing only with economic questions*, London: Longman's, Green and Co., 1951, pp. 26–45; B. Abel-Smith and P. Townsend, *The poor and the poorest*, London: G. Bell & Sons, 1965, p. 9.

79. K. Banting, *Poverty, politics and policy: Britain in the 1960s*, Basingstoke: Macmillan (now Palgrave Macmillan), 1979, pp. 66–108.

80. R. Lowe, *The welfare state in Britain since 1945*, Basingstoke: Macmillan (now Palgrave Macmillan), 1999, pp. 179–81; J. Allsop, *Health policy and the NHS: Towards 2000*, London: Longman, 2000, pp. 292–3.

81. Webster, *Problems of health care*, pp. 177–96; Klein, *The new politics of the NHS*, pp. 60–1, 82–90; Ham, *Health policy in Britain*, pp. 24–30.

82. J. Short, *Housing in Britain: the postwar experience*, London: Methuen, 1982, pp. 47–9, 55.

83. Lowe, *Education in the postwar years*, pp. 37–55; Simon, *Education and the social order*, pp. 102–10.

84. M. Sanderson, *Educational opportunity and social change in England*, London: Faber and Faber, 1987, pp. 45–63; Simon, *Education and the social order*, pp. 406–20, 586–8; Lowe, *The welfare state in Britain since 1945*, p. 213.

85. T. Hatton and K. A. Chrystal, 'The Budget and fiscal policy', in N. Crafts and N. Woodward (eds), *The British economy since 1945*, Oxford: Oxford University Press, 1991, pp. 52–88, at p. 71.

86. J. Le Grand, 'The state of welfare', in J. Hills (ed.), *The state of welfare: the welfare state in Britain since 1974*, Oxford: Clarendon, 1990, pp. 338–61, at p. 361; P Johnson, 'The welfare state', in R. Floud and D. McCloskey (eds), *The economic history of Britain since 1700, Vol. 3, 1939–92*, Cambridge: Cambridge University Press, 1994, pp. 284–317, at p. 298.

87. Lowe, *The welfare state in Britain since 1945*, pp. 356–7.

88. C. Hamnett, 'A stroke of the Chancellor's pen: the social and regional impact of the Conservatives' 1988 higher rate tax cuts', *Environment and Planning* A, 29 (1997), 129–47, at 132–3; Inland Revenue, *Inland Revenue statistics 2000*, London: The Stationery Office, 2000, pp. 177–8.

89. Lowe, *The welfare state in Britain since 1945*, p. 323.

90. A. Holmans, 'Housing', in A. H. Halsey and J. Webb (eds), *Twentieth century British social trends*, Basingstoke: Macmillan (now Palgrave Macmillan), 2000, pp. 469–510, at p. 487.

91. M. McVicar, 'Education policy: education as a business?', in S. Savage and L. Robins (eds), *Public policy under Thatcher*, Basingstoke: Macmillan (now Palgrave Macmillan), 1990, pp. 131–44, at pp. 137–40; H. Glennerster, *British social policy since 1945*, Oxford: Basil Blackwell, First edition, 1995, pp. 198–201; Lowe, *The welfare state in Britain since 1945*, pp. 333–7. In 1996/97, the total number of appeals lodged by parents against the non-admission of their children to the school of their choice was 72,664, out of a total number of pupil admissions of 1,175,140, but only 27.3 per cent of these appeals were resolved in the parents' favour (Department for Education and Skills, *Statistics of education: Schools in England, 2002 edition*, London: The Stationery Office, 2002, p. 84).

92. Glennerster, *British social policy since 1945*, First edition, p. 207; C. Webster, *The National Health Service: a political history*, Oxford: Oxford University Press, 1998, pp. 199–204.

93. A. Giddens, *The third way: the renewal of social democracy*, Cambridge: Polity Press, 1998; *ibid.*, The third way and its critics, Cambridge: Polity Press, 2002.

94. M. Powell and M. Hewitt, *Welfare state and welfare change*, Buckingham: Open University Press, 2002, p. 61.

95. Inland Revenue, *Report of the Commissioners of Her Majesty's Inland Revenue for the year ending 31 March 1998, One hundred and fortieth report*, London: HMSO (Cm. 4079), 1998, pp. 61–2; *ibid., Inland Revenue Annual Report. Report of the Commissioners for her Majesty's Inland Revenue for the year ending 31 March 1999. One hundred and forty-first report*, London: HMSO (Cm. 4477), 1999, pp. 80–1; H. Glennerster, *British social policy since 1945*, Oxford: Basil Blackwell, Second edition, 2000, p. 214; M. Powell, 'Conclusion', in M. Powell (ed.), *Evaluating New Labour's welfare reforms*, Bristol: Policy Press, 2002, pp. 231–49, at p. 242; D. Fraser, *The evolution of the British welfare state*, Third edition, p. 291; HM Treasury, *Public expenditure: statistical analyses 2002–03*, London: The Stationery Office (Cm. 5401), 2002, p. 44.

96. Fraser, *The evolution of the British welfare state*, Third edition, pp. 290–1.

97. M. Hewitt, 'New Labour and the redefinition of social security', in M. Powell (ed.), *Evaluating New Labour's welfare reforms*, Bristol: Policy Press, 2002, pp. 189–210, at p. 192.

98. *Ibid.*, pp. 196–8.

99. Department for Work and Pensions, *Simplicity, security and choice: working and saving for retirement*, London: HMSO (Cm. 5677), 2002, pp. 3, 19.

100. Powell and Hewitt, *Welfare state and welfare change*, p. 66; Office of the Deputy Prime Minister, 'Table 641. Social housing: sale and transfer of local authority and RSL dwellings, United Kingdom, from 1990/91', 2002. URL: http://www.housing.odpm.gov.uk/statistics/live/socialhousing/shst1-uk.xls

101. Glennerster, *British social policy since 1945*, Second edition, pp. 220–2; R. Naidoo and Y. Muschamp, 'A decent education for all?', in M. Powell (ed.), *Evaluating New Labour's welfare reforms*, Bristol: Policy Press, 2002, pp. 145–66; Department for Education and Skills, *The future of higher education*, London: HMSO (Cm. 5735), 2003, pp. 5, 76.

102. Glennerster, *British social policy since 1945*, Second edition, p. 217. Glennerster argued that the demise of fundholding in Scotland was largely unlamented, but 'it would be replaced by something that looked very like it in England where it had mostly taken root'.

103. A. Milburn, 'Foundation hospitals', *The Source Public Management Journal*, 5 June 2002. URL: www.sourceuk.net/indexf.html?02546; F. Dobson, 'Labour and the new élite', *Observer*, 3 November 2002. URL: www.observer.co.uk/comment/story/0,6903,824934,00.html

104. Glennerster, *British social policy since 1945*, Second edition, pp. 226–30; Fraser, *The evolution of the British welfare state*, Third edition, pp. 294–5.

105. T. Blair, 'My vision for Britain', *Observer*, 10 November 2002, 26. URL: http://www.observer.co.uk/comment/story/0,6903,837002,00.html

Select bibliography

The following list provides a starting-point for those readers who wish to delve more deeply into individual aspects of the history of British welfare policy. Full details of all the works cited in the text can be found in the notes which accompany each chapter.

1 General histories of social policy

M. A. Crowther, *British social policy 1914–39*, Basingstoke: Macmillan (now Palgrave Macmillan), 1988.

A. Digby, *British welfare policy: workhouse to workfare*, London: Faber, 1989.

D. Fraser, *The evolution of the British welfare state: a history of social policy since the Industrial Revolution*, London and Basingstoke: Macmillan (now Palgrave Macmillan), First edition, 1973; Second edition, 1984; Third edition, 2003.

D. Gladstone, *The twentieth-century welfare state*, Basingstoke: Macmillan (now Palgrave Macmillan), 1999.

D. Gladstone (ed.), *British social welfare: past, present and future*, London: UCL Press, 1995.

H. Glennerster, *British social policy since 1945*, Oxford: Basil Blackwell, First edition, 1995; Second edition, 2000.

J. R. Hay, *The origins of the Liberal welfare reforms*, Basingstoke: Macmillan (now Palgrave Macmillan), First edition, 1975; Second edition, 1983.

H. Hendrick, *Child welfare: England 1872–1989*, London: Routledge, 1994.

U. Henriques, *Before the welfare state: social administration in early industrial Britain*, London: Longman, 1979.

K. Jones, *The making of social policy in Britain: from the Poor Law to New Labour*, London: Athlone, 2000.

K. Laybourn (1995), *The evolution of British social policy and the welfare state*, Keele: Keele University Press, 1995.

R. Lowe, *The welfare state in Britain since 1945*, London and Basingstoke: Macmillan (now Palgrave Macmillan), First edition, 1993; Second edition, 1999.

R. M. Page and R. Silburn (eds), *British social welfare in the twentieth century*, Basingstoke: Palgrave (now Palgrave Macmillan), 1999.

G. Peden, *British economic and social policy: Lloyd George to Margaret Thatcher*, Oxford: Phillip Allan, First edition, 1985; Hemel Hempstead: Philip Allan, Second edition, 1991.

A. M. Rees, *T. H. Marshall's Social Policy*, London: Hutchinson, 1985.

P. Thane, *The foundations of the welfare state*, London: Longman's, First edition, 1982; Second edition, 1996.

N. Timmins, *The five giants: a biography of the welfare state*, London: Harper Collins, First edition, 1995; Second edition, 2001.

2 British history since 1800

J. Davis, *A history of Britain, 1885–1939*, Basingstoke: Macmillan (now Palgrave Macmillan), 1999.

R. Floud, *The people and the British economy 1830–1914*, Oxford: Oxford University Press, 1997.

R. Floud and D. McCloskey (eds), *The economic history of Britain since 1700*, Cambridge: Cambridge University Press, First edition, 1981; Second edition, 1994.

J. Harris, *Private lives, public spirit: Britain 1870–1914*, Harmondsworth: Penguin, 1994.

P. Johnson (ed.), *Twentieth century Britain: economic, social and cultural change*, London: Longman, 1994.

C. Lee, *The British economy since 1700: a macroeconomic perspective*, Cambridge: Cambridge University Press, 1986.

R. McKibbin, *Classes and cultures: England 1918–51*, Oxford: Oxford University Press, 1998.

C. L. Mowat, *Britain between the wars 1918–40*, London: Methuen, First edition, 1955; Second edition, 1968.

S. Pollard, *The development of the British economy, 1914–90*, London: Edward Arnold, 1992.

M. Pugh, *Britain since 1789: a concise history*, Basingstoke: Macmillan (now Palgrave Macmillan), 1999.

E. Royle, *Modern Britain: a social history 1750–1985*, London: Edward Arnold, 1987.

J. Rule, *The labouring classes in early-industrial England 1750–1850*, London: Longman, 1986.

J. Stevenson, *British society 1914–45*, Harmondsworth: Penguin, 1984.

P. Thane, *Old age in English history: past experiences, present issues*, Oxford: Oxford University Press, 2000.

F. M. L. Thompson (ed.), *The Cambridge social history of Britain*, Cambridge: Cambridge University Press, 1990.

F. M. L. Thompson, *The rise of respectable society: a social history of Victorian Britain 1830–1900*, London: Fontana, 1988.

3 Self-help, charity and mutual aid

G. Finlayson, *Citizen, state and social welfare in Britain 1830–1990*, Oxford: Oxford University Press, 1994.

P. Gosden, *Self-help: voluntary associations in nineteenth-century Britain*, London: B. T. Batsford, 1973.

P. Gosden, *The Friendly Societies in England 1815–75*, Manchester: Manchester University Press, 1961.

M. Gorsky, *Patterns of philanthropy: charity and society in nineteenth-century Bristol*, Woodbridge: Royal Historical Society/Boydell Press, 1999.

E. Hopkins, *Working-class self-help in nineteenth-century England*, London: UCL Press, 1995.

R. Humphreys, *Sin, organised charity and the Poor Law in Victorian England*, Basingstoke: Macmillan (now Palgrave Macmillan), 1995.

P. Johnson, *Saving and spending: the working-class economy in Britain 1870–1939*, Oxford: Oxford University Press, 1985.

K. Laybourn, *The Guild of Help and the changing face of Edwardian philanthropy: the Guild of Help, voluntary work and the state, 1904–19*, Lampeter: Edward Mellen Press, 1994.

J. Lewis, *The voluntary sector, the state and social work in Britain: the Charity Organisation Society/Family Welfare Association since 1869*, Aldershot: Edward Elgar, 1995.

J. Lewis, *Women and social action in Victorian and Edwardian England*, Aldershot: Edward Elgar, 1991.

D. Owen, *English philanthropy 1660–1960*, Cambridge, MA: Belknap Press, 1965.

J. Parker, *Women and welfare: ten Victorian women in public social service*, Basingstoke: Macmillan (now Palgrave Macmillan), 1988.

F. Prochaska, *The voluntary impulse: philanthropy in modern Britain*, London: Faber, 1988.

F. Prochaska, *Women and philanthropy in nineteenth century England*, Oxford: Oxford University Press, 1980.

M. Tebbutt, *Making ends meet: pawnbroking and working class credit*, London: Methuen, 1983.

K. Woodroofe, *From charity to social work in England and the United States*, London: Routledge & Kegan Paul, 1962.

4   Poverty

A. Brundage, *The English poor laws, 1700–1930*, Basingstoke: Palgrave (now Palgrave Macmillan), 2002.

J. Burnett, *Destiny obscure: autobiographies of childhood, education and family from the 1820s to the 1920s*, London: Allen Lane, 1982.

J. Burnett, *Useful toil: autobiographies of working people from the 1820s to the 1920s*, Harmondsworth: Penguin, 1977.

M. A. Crowther, *The workhouse system 1834–1929: the history of an English social institution*, London: Methuen, 1983.

I. Gazeley, *Poverty in Britain, 1900–1965*, Basingstoke: Palgrave (now Palgrave Macmillan), 2003.

J. Harris, *Unemployment and politics: a study in English social policy 1886–1914*, Oxford: Clarendon Press, 1972.

G. Himmelfarb, *The idea of poverty: England in the early-industrial age*, London: Faber and Faber, 1984.

A. Kidd, *State, society and the poor in nineteenth-century England*, Basingstoke: Macmillan (now Palgrave Macmillan), 1999.

L. H. Lees, *The solidarities of strangers: the English Poor Laws and the people 1700–1948*, Cambridge: Cambridge University Press, 1998.

J. Macnicol, *The politics of retirement in Britain 1878–1948*, Cambridge: Cambridge University Press, 1998.

R. Roberts, *The classic slum: Salford life in the first quarter of the century*, Harmondsworth: Penguin, 1971.

M. Rose, *The relief of poverty 1834–1914*, London and Basingstoke: Macmillan (now Palgrave Macmillan), 1982.

E. Ross, *Love and toil: motherhood in outcast London 1870–1918*, New York: Oxford University Press, 1993.

P. Slack, *From Reformation to improvement: public welfare in early-modern England*, Oxford: Clarendon Press, 1999.

P. Slack, *The English Poor Law 1531–1782*, Cambridge: Cambridge University Press, 1995.

K. Snell, *Annals of the labouring poor: social change and agrarian England 1660–1900*, Cambridge: Cambridge University Press, 1985.

G. Stedman Jones, *Outcast London: a study in the relationship between classes in Victorian London*, Harmondsworth: Penguin, 1984.

J. H. Treble, *Urban poverty in Britain 1830–1914*, London: Methuen, 1979.

D. Vincent, *Poor citizens: the state and the poor in twentieth-century Britain*, London: Longman, 1991.

K. Williams, *From pauperism to poverty*, London: Routledge & Kegan Paul, 1981.

5   Health and medicine

B. Abel-Smith, *The hospitals 1800–1948: a study in social administration in England and Wales*, London: Heinemann, 1964.

A. Digby, *The evolution of British general practice 1850–1948*, Oxford: Clarendon Press, 1999.

A. Digby, *Making a medical living: doctors and patients in the English market for medicine 1720–1911*, Cambridge: Cambridge University Press, 1994.

S. E. Finer, *The life and times of Sir Edwin Chadwick*, London: Methuen, 1952.

R. Floud, K. Wachter and A. Gregory, *Height, health and history: nutritional status in the United Kingdom 1750–1980*, Cambridge: Cambridge University Press, 1990.

C. Hamlin, *Public health and social justice in the age of Chadwick: Britain 1800–54*, Cambridge: Cambridge University Press, 1997.

A. Hardy, *Health and medicine in Britain since 1860*, Basingstoke: Palgrave (now Palgrave Macmillan), 2001.

B. Harris, *The health of the schoolchild: a history of the school medical service in England and Wales*, Buckingham: Open University Press, 1995.

H. Jones, *Health and society in twentieth-century Britain*, London: Longman, 1994.

K. Jones, *Asylums and after: a revised history of the mental health services: from the early-eighteenth century to the 1990s*, London: Athlone, 1993.

R. Klein, *The new politics of the NHS*, London: Longman, 1995.

R. Lambert, *Sir John Simon, 1816–1904, and English social administration*, London: MacGibbon and Kee, 1963.

C. Lawrence, *Medicine in the making of modern Britain*, London: Routledge, 1994.

J. Lewis, *The politics of motherhood: child and maternal welfare in England, 1900–39*, London: Croom Helm, 1980.

I. Loudon, *Medical care and the general practitioner 1750–1850*, Oxford: Clarendon Press, 1986.

J. Pickstone, *Medicine and industrial society: a history of hospital development in Manchester and its region 1752–1946*, Manchester: Manchester University Press, 1985.

J. Riley, *Sick, not dead: the health of British workingmen during the mortality decline*, Baltimore: Johns Hopkins University Press, 1997.

J. Riley, *The eighteenth-century campaign to avoid disease*, Basingstoke: Macmillan (now Palgrave Macmillan), 1987.

A. Scull, *The most solitary of afflictions: madness and society in Britain 1700–1900*, New Haven, CT and London: Yale University Press, 1993.

M. Thomson, *The problem of mental deficiency: eugenics, democracy and social policy in Britain c. 1870–1959*, Oxford: Oxford University Press, 1998.

C. Webster, *The National Health Service: a political history*, Oxford: Oxford University Press, First edition, 1998; Second edition, 2002.

A. Wohl, *Endangered lives: public health in Victorian Britain*, London: Methuen, 1984.

6 Housing

M. Bowley, *Housing and the state 1919–44*, London: George Allen and Unwin, 1945.

J. Burnett, *A social history of housing 1815–1985*, London: Routledge, 1986.

M. Daunton, *A property-owning democracy: housing in Britain*, London: Faber, 1987.

M. Daunton (ed.), *Councillors and tenants: local authority housing in English cities, 1919–39*, Leicester: Leicester University Press, 1984.

M. Daunton, *House and home in the Victorian city: working class housing 1850–1914*, London: Edward Arnold, 1983.

E. Gauldie, *Cruel habitations: a history of working class housing 1780–1918*, London: George Allen and Unwin, 1974.

A. Olechnowicz, *Working-class housing in England between the Wars: the Becontree estate*, Oxford: Oxford University Press, 1997.

A. Power, *Hovels to high rise: state housing in Europe since 1850*, London: Routledge, 1993.

R. Rodger, *Housing in urban Britain 1780–1914*, Basingstoke: Macmillan (now Palgrave Macmillan), 1989.

J. Short, *Housing in Britain: the postwar experience*, London: Methuen, 1982.

M. Swenarton, *Homes fit for heroes: the politics and architecture of early state housing in Britain*, London: Heinemann, 1981.

J. N. Tarn, *Five per cent philanthropy: an account of housing in urban areas between 1840 and 1914*, Cambridge: Cambridge University Press, 1973.

A. Wohl, *The eternal slum: housing and social policy in Victorian London*, London: Edward Arnold, 1977.

J. Yelling, *Slums and redevelopment: policy and practice in England 1918–45, with particular reference to London*, London: UCL Press, 1992.

7 Education

J. Hurt, *Elementary schooling and the working classes 1860–1918*, London: Routledge & Kegan Paul, 1979.

T. Laqueur, *Religion and respectability: Sunday schools and working-class culture 1780–1850*, New Haven, CT and London: Yale University Press, 1976.

R. Lowe, *Education in the postwar years: a social history*, London: Routledge, 1988.

P. McCann (ed.), *Popular education and socialisation in the nineteenth century*, London: Methuen, 1977.

J. Murphy, *Church, state and schools in Britain 1800–1970*, London: Routledge & Kegan Paul, 1971.

M. Sanderson, *Education and economic decline in Britain, 1870s to the 1990s*, Cambridge: Cambridge University Press, 1999.

M. Sanderson, *Education, economic change and society in England 1780–1870*, Basingstoke: Macmillan (now Palgrave Macmillan), First edition, 1983; Second edition, 1991.

M. Sanderson, *Educational opportunity and social change in England*, London: Faber and Faber, 1987.

M. Sanderson, *The Universities and British industry, 1850–1970*, London: Routledge & Kegan Paul, 1972.

R. Selleck, *English primary education and the progressives, 1914–39*, London: Routledge & Kegan Paul, 1972.

W. B. Stephens, *Education in Britain 1750–1914*, Basingstoke: Macmillan (now Palgrave Macmillan), 1998.

G. Sutherland, *Ability, merit and measurement: mental testing and English education 1880–1940*, Oxford: Clarendon Press, 1984.

N. Whitbread, *The evolution of the nursery-infant school: a history of nursery and infant education in Britain, 1800–1970*, London: Routledge & Kegan Paul, 1972.

8 Theoretical and comparative surveys

D. Ashford, *The emergence of the welfare states*, Oxford: Basil Blackwell, 1986.

P. Baldwin, *The politics of social solidarity: class bases of the European welfare state*, Cambridge: Cambridge University Press, 1990.

G. Bock and P. Thane (eds), *Maternity and gender policies: women and the rise of the European welfare states 1880s–1950s*, London: Routledge, 1991.

A. Briggs, 'The welfare state in historical perspective', *Archives Européenes du Sociologie*, 2 (1961), 221–58.

F. G. Castles (ed.), *The comparative history of public policy*, Oxford and Cambridge: Polity Press, 1989.

A. De Swaan, *In care of the state: health care, education and welfare in Europe and the USA in the modern era*, Oxford and Cambridge: Basil Blackwell and Polity Press, 1988.

P. Dunleavy and B. O'Leary, *Theories of the state: the politics of liberal democracy*, Basingstoke: Macmillan (now Palgrave Macmillan), 1987.

G. Esping-Andersen, *The three worlds of welfare capitalism*, Oxford and Cambridge: Basil Blackwell and Polity Press, 1990.

P. Flora and A. Heidenheimer (eds), *The development of welfare states in Europe and America*, New Brunswick, NJ and London: Transaction Publishers, 1981.

V. George and R. Page (eds), *Modern thinkers on welfare*, London: Prentice-Hall, 1995.

V. George and P. Wilding, *Welfare and ideology*, New York and London: Harvester Wheatsheaf, 1994.

V. George and P. Wilding, *Ideology and social welfare*, London: Routledge & Kegan Paul, 1985.

I. Gough, *The political economy of the welfare state*, London and Basingstoke: Macmillan (now Palgrave Macmillan), 1979.

E. P. Hennock, *British social reform and German precedents: the case of social insurance 1880–1914*, Oxford: Clarendon Press, 1987.

D. King, *The New Right: politics, markets and citizenship*, London and Basingstoke: Macmillan (now Palgrave Macmillan), 1987.

S. Koven and S. Michel (eds), *Mothers of a new world: maternalist politics and the origins of welfare states*, London: Routledge, 1993.

T. H. Marshall, 'Citizenship and social class', in T. H. Marshall, *Sociology at the crossroads and other essays*, London: Heinemann, 1963, pp. 67–127.

R. Mishra, *Society and social policy: theories and practice of welfare*, London and Basingstoke: Macmillan (now Palgrave Macmillan), 1981.

A. Peacock and J. Wiseman, *The growth of public expenditure in the United Kingdom*, Princeton, NJ: Princeton University Press, 1961.

S. Pedersen, *Family, dependence and the origins of the welfare state: Britain and France 1914–45*, Cambridge: Cambridge University Press, 1993.

C. Pierson, *Beyond the welfare state? The new political economy of welfare*, Oxford and Cambridge: Basil Blackwell and Polity Press, First edition, 1991; Second edition, 1998.

9 Documentary sources

R. C. Birch (ed.), *The shaping of the welfare state*, London: Longman, 1974.

M. Bruce (ed.), *The rise of the welfare state: English social policy, 1601–1971*, London: Weidenfeld & Nicolson, 1973.

L. Butler and H. Jones (eds), *Britain in the twentieth century: a documentary reader*, Oxford: Heinemann, 1995.

G. Davey Smith, D. Dorling and M. Shaw (eds), *Poverty, inequality and health in Britain 1800–2000: a reader*, Bristol: Policy Press, 2001.

E. Evans (ed.), *Social policy 1830–1914*, London: Routledge & Kegan Paul, 1978.

J. R. Hay (ed.), *The development of the welfare state 1880–1975*, London: Edward Arnold, 1978.

P. Keating (ed.), *Into unknown England: selections from the social explorers*, London: Fontana, 1976.

J. S. Maclure (ed.), *Educational documents: England and Wales, 1816 to the present day*, London: Methuen, 1985.

R. Pope, A. Pratt and B. Hoyle (eds), *Social welfare in Britain 1885–1985*, London: Croom Helm, 1986.

J. Stevenson (ed.), *Social conditions in Britain between the wars*, Harmondsworth: Penguin, 1977.

A. Thorpe (ed.), *The Longman companion to Britain in the era of the two World Wars, 1914–45*, London: Longman, 1994.

B. Watkin (ed.), *Documents on health and social services: 1834 to the present day*, London: Methuen, 1975.

10 Statistical sources

C. H. Feinstein, *National income, expenditure and output of the United Kingdom, 1855–1965*, Cambridge: Cambridge University Press, 1972.

P. Flora (ed.), *State, economy and society in western Europe 1815–1975: a data handbook, Vol. 1, The growth of mass democracies and welfare states*, London: Macmillan (now Palgrave Macmillan), 1983.

A. H. Halsey (ed.), *British social trends since 1900: a guide to the changing social structure of Britain*, London & Basingstoke: Macmillan (now Palgrave Macmillan), 1988.

A. H. Halsey (ed.), *Trends in British society since 1900: a guide to the changing social structure of Britain*, London & Basingstoke: Macmillan (now Palgrave Macmillan), 1972.

A. H. Halsey and J. Webb (eds), *Twentieth century British social trends*, Basingstoke: Macmillan (now Palgrave Macmillan), 2000.

B. R. Mitchell, *British historical statistics*, Cambridge: Cambridge University Press, 1988.

B. R. Mitchell, *European Historical Statistics 1750–1980*, London and Basingstoke: Macmillan (now Palgrave Macmillan), 1978.

Index